Methods and Materials for Teaching the Gifted

2nd edition

Methods

and Materials

for **Teaching**

the **Gifted**

2nd edition

edited
by

Frances A. Karnes

and

Suzanne M. Bean

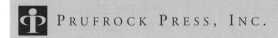 PRUFROCK PRESS, INC.

Library of Congress Cataloging-in-Publication Data

Methods and materials for teaching the gifted / edited by Frances A. Karnes and Suzanne
M. Bean.—2nd ed.
    p. cm.
    Includes bibliographical references.
    ISBN 1-59363-022-0
    1. Gifted children—Education. 2. Gifted children—Identification. I. Karnes, Frances
A. II. Bean, Suzanne M., 1957-

    LC3993.M48 2005
    371.95—dc22

                                                                    2004018969

Cover and layout design by James Kendrick

Printed in the United States of America.

At the time of this book's publication, all facts and figures cited are the most current available. All telephone numbers, addresses, and Web site URLs are accurate and active. All publications, organizations, Web sites, and other resources exist as described in the book, and all
have been verified. The authors and Prufrock Press, Inc., make no warranty or guarantee concerning the information and materials given out by organizations or content found at Web
sites, and we are not responsible for any changes that occur after this book's publication. If
you find an error, please contact Prufrock Press, Inc.

Prufrock Press, Inc.
P.O. Box 8813
Waco, Texas 76714-8813
(800) 998-2208
Fax (800) 240-0333
http://www.prufrock.com

We dedicate this book to our families:

Ray, John, Leighanne, Mary Ryan, Mo, and Emma, Mark,
Meriweather, and Hudson for their love and support
and to Christopher Karnes, for his special love and guidance.

This book is also dedicated to all gifted learners
who need differentiated instruction to reach their potential
and to their specialized teachers.

Contents

Introduction to the Second Edition   xv
Acknowledgements   xvii

Section I: Characteristics and Needs of Gifted Learners

1. The Varied and Unique Characteristics Exhibited   3
   by Diverse Gifted and Talented Learners
   by Sally M. Reis and Melissa A. Small

   Giftedness and Talent: An Introduction   5
   Characteristics of Individuals With High Intellectual Ability or Creative Potential   8
   Characteristics of Individuals With High Creative Ability or Potential   13
   Developmental Considerations in Recognizing Traits of Talented Students   15
   Diverse Characteristics of Special Populations of Gifted and Talented Learners   17
   Understanding the Diverse Ways in Which Talents and Gifts Emerge and Develop   27
   Teacher Statement   30
   Discussion Questions   31
   References   32

2. Planning the Learning Environment   37
   by Barbara G. Hunt and Robert W. Seney

   The Modifications   38
   The Responsive Learning Environment   39
   Understanding Giftedness   43
   Assessment of Gifted Students   44
   The Teacher of the Gifted   54
   Counseling Needs of the Gifted Learner   57
   Behavior and Classroom Management   59
   Summary   63
   Teacher Statement   64
   Discussion Questions   65
   Teacher Resources   66
   References   70

Section II: Instructional Planning and Evaluation

3. An Analysis of Gifted Education Curricular Models   75
    by Joyce Van Tassel-Baska and Elissa F. Brown

    History of Curricular Models   75
    Definition of a Curricular Model: Subjects for Analysis   76
    Methodology   78
    The Curricular Models   79
    Key Findings   91
    Conclusions   92
    Teacher Statement   94
    Discussion Questions   95
    Teacher Resources   96
    References   101

4. Layering Differentiated Curricula for the Gifted and Talented   107
    by Sandra N. Kaplan

    A History of Differentiated Curricula: A Perspective   108
    The Layered Approach to Differentiating the Core Curriculum   113
    Implementing the Layered Curriculum   126
    Conclusion   128
    Teacher Statement   129
    Discussion Questions   130
    References   131

5. Process Skills and the Gifted Learner   133
    by Robert W. Seney

    Process Modifications   135
    Critical Thinking   137
    The Constructivist Perspective   138
    Process Skills   139
    Summary   146
    Teacher Statement   147
    Discussion Questions   147
    Teacher Resources   148
    References   149

6. Product Development for Gifted Students   151
    by Kristen R. Stephens and Frances A. Karnes

    What is a Product?   152
    The Importance of Product Development in Gifted Education   152
    Types of Products   153

Design and Product Development 155
Stages of Product Development 157
Communication Through Products 165
How to Foster Product Development in the Classroom 171
Summary 174
Teacher Statement 175
Discussion Questions 175
Teacher Resources 176
References 178

7. Writing Units That Remove the Learning Ceiling 179
   by Julia Link Roberts and Richard A. Roberts

Planning the Unit 181
Model of the Relationship of Unit Components 182
Steps in Planning a Unit 183
The Learning Experiences: Building Blocks of the Unit 189
Teacher Statement 205
Discussion Questions 206
Teacher Resources 207
References 209

8. Making the Grade or Achieving the Goal? Evaluating 211
   Learner and Program Outcomes in Gifted Education
   by Carolyn M. Callahan

The Importance of Careful Assessment of Learning Outcomes 212
Planning for Good Classroom Evaluation 214
The Cognitive Dimension: Content, Process, and Product Outcomes 217
Creating or Selecting the Tools to Use in Classroom Assessment 225
The Importance of Evaluating Programs for Gifted Students 231
Assessment of Other Program Components 235
The Instructional Circle 241
Teacher Statement 242
Discussion Questions 243
References 244

Section III: Strategies for Best Practices

9. Teaching Analytical and Critical Thinking Skills in Gifted Education 249
   by Sandra Parks

Analytical and Critical Thinking Instruction for Gifted Students 250
Approaches to Teaching Analytical and Critical Thinking 256
Assessing Analytical and Critical Thinking 275

Teacher Statement   279
Discussion Questions   280
Teacher Resources   281
References   283

10. Adapting Problem-Based Learning for Gifted Students   285
by Shelagh A. Gallagher

Matching Curriculum and Characteristics: Gifted Students and Problem Solving   285
Problem-Based Learning: A Promising Road to Expertise   289
Adapting PBL for Gifted Students: New Applications of Familiar Recommendations   292
Where and When to Use PBL   299
Teacher Statement   303
Discussion Questions   305
Teacher Resources   306
References   310

11. Developing Creative Thinking   313
by Bonnie Cramond

Who is Creative?   317
Enhancing Creativity Through the Environment   318
Strategies for Promoting Creativity in the Classroom   321
Competitions   338
The Incubation Model   340
Summary   343
Conclusion   344
Teacher Statement   345
Discussion Questions   346
Teacher Resources   347
References   349

12. Developing Research Skills in Gifted Students   353
by Barbara Moore

Historical Perspective   356
Program Models   358
The Research Process   359
Steps in the Research Process   360
Evaluating Student Researchers   369
Research and Gifted Students With Learning Disabilities   370
Conclusions   371
Teacher Statement   372
Discussion Questions   373
Teacher Resources   374
References   376

13. Teaching Gifted Students Through Independent Study   379
         by Susan K. Johnsen and Krystal K. Goree

    Independent Study Models   380
    Guidelines for Independent Study   387
    Steps in Independent Study   389
    Conclusion   397
    Teacher Statement   398
    Discussion Questions   400
    Teacher Resources   401
    References   407

14. Affective Education: Addressing the Social and Emotional   409
    Needs of Gifted Students in the Classroom
         by Stephanie A. Nugent

    What Is Affective Education?   409
    Why Include Affective Education in the Curriculum?   417
    How Can the Affective Domain Be Addressed in the Classroom? 418
    Closing Thoughts   426
    Teacher Statement   428
    Discussion Questions   428
    Teacher Resources   429
    References   436

15. Developing the Leadership Potential of Gifted Students   439
         by Suzanne M. Bean and Frances A. Karnes

    Definitions of Leadership   440
    Theories of Leadership   441
    Changing Generations and Paradigms   442
    Current Research on Leadership and Youth   444
    Leadership and Giftedness   445
    Screening and Identification of Gifted Leaders   446
    Instructional Programs and Materials for Leadership   452
    Incorporating Leadership Into the Curriculum for Gifted Students 456
    Summary   460
    Teacher Statement   461
    Discussion Questions   462
    Teacher Resources   463
    References   467

16. Extending Learning Through Mentorships   473
         by Del Siegle and D. Betsy McCoach

    Definition of a Mentorship   475
    The Effectiveness of Mentorships   476

Benefits to Mentors   477
Mentoring at Different Ages   478
Mentoring Underserved Populations   479
Telementoring   482
Establishing a Mentorship Program   484
An Example of a Secondary Level Mentoring Program Design   507
Conclusion   509
Mentorship in Action   511
Discussion Questions   512
Teacher Resources   513
References   515

17. Cooperative Learning and Gifted Learners   519
    by Mary Ruth Coleman

Cooperative Learning Models   520
Cooperative Learning With Gifted Students   521
Special Factors to Consider   522
Strategies for Cooperative Learning With Gifted Students   525
Sample CL Activities for Different Grades and Settings   527
Role of the Teacher   534
Conclusion   534
Teacher Statement   535
Discussion Questions   536
Teacher Resources   537
References   540

18. Teaching the Gifted Through Simulation   543
    by Dorothy Sisk

Background and Definitions   543
Why is Simulation Effective for Gifted Students?   547
Major Benefits for Gifted Students Derived From Simulation Games   550
Examples of Simulation Games   553
A Comparison of Elements of Simulations Games   556
Using Simulation Effectively   557
Designing a Simulation Game   558
Situations in Which Simulation Games Are Useful   562
Benefits and Outcomes From Using Simulation Games   563
Comparison With Other Teaching Methods   563
Conclusion   564
Teacher Statement   566
Discussion Questions   567
Teacher Resources   568
References   573

19. Teaching Gifted and Talented Students in Regular Classrooms   577
      by Tracy L. Riley

    Not Just Gifted on Wednesdays   578
    Qualitative Differentiation   580
    Getting to Know Gifted and Talented Students   582
    Putting the Theory Into Practice   586
    Other Issues in Educating Gifted and Talented Students in the Regular Classroom   607
    Conclusion   609
    Discussion Questions and Activities   610
    Teacher Resources   611
    References   613

20. Public Relations and Advocacy for the Gifted   615
      by Joan D. Lewis and Frances A. Karnes

    Definition of Terms   616
    Rationale for Public Relations in Gifted Education   616
    Targeting Your Audience   618
    Public Relations Strategies   620
    Basic Planning for Effective Public Relations   627
    The Message   630
    Talent Identification   631
    Involving Others   638
    Use of Organizers   640
    Involving Other Constituencies   642
    Summary   649
    Teacher Statement   650
    Discussion Questions   651
    Teacher Resources   652
    References   655

21. Teaching on a Shoestring: Materials   657
      for Teaching Gifted and Talented Students
      by Tracy L. Riley

    Differentiated Materials   658
    Materials and Criteria for their Selection   659
    The Search for Materials   666
    Free and Inexpensive Materials   675
    The Search for Free and Inexpensive Materials   678
    Tips for Teachers and Their Students   680
    A Sampling of Free (or Almost Free) Ideas   682
    Tying It All Together   685

Teacher Statements   687
Discussion Questions and Activities   688
Teacher Resources   689
References   699

22. Getting What You Need: Locating and Obtaining   701
    Money and Other Resources
        by Kristen R. Stephens and Frances A. Karnes

Status of Federal Funding For Gifted Education   701
Types of Funding   703
Developing an Idea   704
Locating a Funding Source   704
Analyzing Sources   707
Major Components of a Grant Proposal   708
Sources of Funding in Your Community   710
Creative Fundraising   710
Old Strategies/New Practices   712
Conclusion   713
Teacher Statement   714
Discussion Questions   715
Teacher Resources   716
References   720

About the Authors   721

Index   729

Introduction
to the Second Edition

he first edition of *Methods and Materials for Teaching the Gifted*, published 5 years ago, was extremely well received by teachers, administrators, state consultants, colleges and university professors and their students, and others interested in differentiated and quality education for gifted children and youth. With the overwhelming response to the first edition and the rapid growth of knowledge in the field of gifted education, the second edition became an immediate priority.

The purpose of this revised edition of *Methods and Materials for Teaching the Gifted* is to give updated strategies and resources for differentiating the instruction of gifted learners. Although there is general agreement in the field of gifted education as to the need to modify regular instruction to address the unique characteristics and behaviors of gifted learners more appropriately, the original edition of this book was one of the first to focus on specific ways differentiation can be accomplished. Methods were given for developing appropriate learning environments, blending advanced content with instructional processes, and selecting products that match the needs of this population of students.

The revised text continues to give an array of current books, teaching materials, Web sites, and other resources for teaching gifted students. In addition to the updated and expanded information, teacher statements on each topic and discussion questions have been added to each chapter, and a comprehensive index has been included.

After determining the chapters to be included in the revised edition, the editors selected contributors from across the nation who have specific expertise in the areas defined and are recognized leaders in the field of gifted education. The goal continues to be to provide readers with current information about best practices for gifted learners from experts who have developed and tested these strategies.

This book begins by revisiting the characteristics and needs of gifted learners, for these understandings have a critical role in determining appropriate learning environments, content, processes, products, and resources for this population. While the introductory chapter gives an excellent summary of the nature and needs of gifted learners, the editors believe that more information may be necessary as a prerequisite to this text in order to give educators the essential understandings about gifted learners they need to work with them effectively. Therefore, this text would best be used following a text/course about the general characteristics and needs of gifted learners.

The first section of the book offers chapters that address the unique needs of gifted learners and how to plan appropriate learning environments for them. The second section features chapters focusing on instructional planning, including content, process, and product differentiation for gifted learners. Also included is a chapter on writing units that are appropriate for gifted learners. The culmination of this section is a chapter on evaluating learner and program outcomes. The third section of the text provides chapters on specific strategies for best practices with gifted learners. From critical and creative thinking to strategies for research, independent study, and mentorships, rich and substantive ideas are highlighted. Also included in this section are chapters on affective education, leadership development, and cooperative learning for gifted learners. The fourth section presents often-neglected areas of importance in supporting and enhancing programs for gifted learners: public relations and advocacy, locating funding sources, finding appropriate resources and materials, teaching on a shoestring, and teaching the gifted in the regular classroom. Though these areas may not be considered critical to the daily work of teachers, they are critical to the overall success and defensibility of strong gifted programs and services.

Educators in all areas can benefit from this book. Certainly, preservice and in-service teachers in elementary and secondary schools who are training to work with gifted learners in specialized programs could use it for instructional planning. Many sections of the text might also be used by coordinators of gifted programs as they conduct staff-development programs to address the needs of various groups. General classroom teachers may also find it helpful as they prepare to individualize their instruction to meet the needs of gifted learners. Other school personnel, such as administrators, counselors, and school psychologists, could use the book to increase their understanding about gifted students and to develop strong programs for them. Parents of gifted students may use it to assist them in their own home instruction or to compare these best practices with what is offered for their children in specialized programs for the gifted.

Acknowledgements

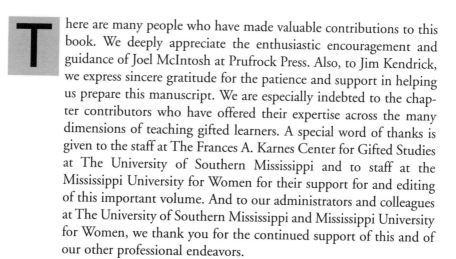

There are many people who have made valuable contributions to this book. We deeply appreciate the enthusiastic encouragement and guidance of Joel McIntosh at Prufrock Press. Also, to Jim Kendrick, we express sincere gratitude for the patience and support in helping us prepare this manuscript. We are especially indebted to the chapter contributors who have offered their expertise across the many dimensions of teaching gifted learners. A special word of thanks is given to the staff at The Frances A. Karnes Center for Gifted Studies at The University of Southern Mississippi and to staff at the Mississippi University for Women for their support for and editing of this important volume. And to our administrators and colleagues at The University of Southern Mississippi and Mississippi University for Women, we thank you for the continued support of this and of our other professional endeavors.

Characteristics and Needs of Gifted Learners

The Varied and Unique Characteristics Exhibited by Diverse Gifted and Talented Learners

by **Sally M. Reis** and **Melissa A. Small**

o gifted and talented learners exhibit similar types of characteristics, or do they display a wide variety? Do students from different cultural groups and socioeconomic backgrounds display their abilities in a similar way? An awareness of the characteristics of advanced learners is essential in any discussion of methods, materials, and resources appropriate for developing their potential. However, as the title of this chapter implies, gifted and talented learners are not homogeneous; to the contrary, they are varied and unique.

Despite this diversity, some common characteristics can be found in many in this population. As Passow (1981) wrote, "Despite the tremendous variation which exists among a group of gifted and talented children, they do have many characteristics which differentiate them from other learners" (p. 3). In this chapter, some of the general characteristics of gifted and talented learners identified in the research literature are discussed, but the objective is not to provide a checklist by which students may be classified or identified as "gifted and talented." Rather, our intent is to provide educators with an overview of some of the characteristics that may be present in some high-ability students, with a clear understanding that these characteristics may vary by gender or sociocultural group, or they may manifest differently among gifted children with disabilities, with different linguistic backgrounds, or high-potential students who underachieve in school. A better understanding of some generally recognized attributes of gifted and talented learners may help educators better provide appropriate opportunities for them to develop their gifts and talents. Understanding the ways in which gifts and talents may be manifested in diverse students can help educators to look beyond the stereotypical notion of gifted students. Consider, for example, the following case studies:

Julia is a smart, confident 6th grader who consistently achieves top grades in all subjects on her report card. Teachers frequently comment on her aptitude, as well as her achievement. She has many friends, and her teachers are proud of her promising academic and leadership abilities. Though very task-committed about her homework, she has a tendency to procrastinate on longer projects; but, when she demonstrates an interest in something, she can work with eagerness and vigor. Her finished products, especially those that are computer-related, are exceptional for her grade level, and her achievement and aptitude test scores are extremely high.

Justin, a 10th grader, is less than interested in school, although he was a stellar student in elementary school who excelled in everything. Though achievement test scores have indicated he is well above grade level, especially in verbal areas, his grades in high school have been B's and C's. He recently designed the logo and painted the entranceway sign for a local business (a project few teachers at his school knew about), which drew many positive comments and praise from community members. Justin has many friends, but he also enjoys time by himself, which he often spends producing graphic design work for his high school's yearbook, pen and ink sketches for his parents' holiday cards, and paintings for his art portfolio.

Nakesha lives in a large urban city, is in 1st grade, and reads at a 4th-grade level, often finishing a 50-page paperback book in the hour she reads to herself before she falls asleep each night. The next day in school, she is bored and sleepy; on several occasions, she has begged her parents to let her stay home and read. Only one other student in her classroom can read. While her peers learn beginning sounds, Nakesha finishes her assigned work in a fraction of the time it takes other students to finish their work and is left on her own. No mandate exists to provide services to gifted students in the state in which Nakesha lives. Her parents watch as their child, who was excited about learning and motivated when she began 1st grade, gradually begins to dislike school and cry each morning as she gets ready to leave their apartment.

Mark's work in school had frustrated his parents for years. Always a child of remarkably high potential with an IQ over 150, Mark's grades had fluctuated in elementary school and in junior and senior high school. He took advanced math classes in school and achieved a near perfect score on the math section of the SAT in his junior year of high school. However, he was labeled an "underachiever" because of his variable attitudes toward school. He always did well on his exams, even when he had done none of the assigned work in class. He simply lost credit for every bit of homework and classwork that he did not do. Mark was not lazy. In fact, his parents had to plead with him to go to bed in the evening because he was reading books about artificial intelligence or pursuing his own interests, which happened to be designing software and building computers from discarded materials. In his senior year, Mark received recruitment letters from the best colleges in the country because of his SAT scores, but, unfortunately, he did not graduate from high school, failing both English and history. He did not like his teachers, and the work was too easy in the lower track classes to which he had been assigned because of his lack of effort in earlier years and his variable performance in his classes. Not graduating from high school was for Mark the lesser of two fates. The worse fate, in his opinion, was pretending to be interested in boring, uninspiring classes taught by teachers he believed did not care about him.

Based on these brief case studies, it is interesting to consider which characteristics might lead some of these students to be identified as gifted and talented, while others are not.

Giftedness and Talent: An Introduction

For many years, researchers and psychologists, following in the footsteps of Lewis Terman, have equated giftedness with high IQ. This "legacy" survives to the present day, as giftedness and high IQ are often still equated in the ways that some researchers, educators, and parents regard giftedness. Since Terman's time, however, other researchers have argued that intellect cannot be expressed in a unitary manner and have suggested more multifaceted approaches to intelligence (Wallace & Pierce, 1992). Research conducted in the last two decades has supported multiple components of intelligence. This is particularly evident in the reexamination of giftedness in Sternberg and Davidson's (1986) *Conceptions of Giftedness*, in which giftedness is regarded as multiple qualities, not all of which are intellectual, and IQ scores are often viewed as inadequate measures of giftedness. Motivation, high self-concept, and creativity are key qualities in many of these broadened conceptions of giftedness (Siegler & Kotovsky, 1986).

Gardner's (1983) theory of multiple intelligences (MI) and Renzulli's (1978) three-ring definition of gifted behaviors serve as good examples of multifaceted and well-researched conceptualizations of intelligence and giftedness. Gardner's definition of intelligence is the ability to solve problems or create products that are valued within one or more cultural settings. In his MI theory, he articulates eight specific intelligences: linguistic, musical, logical-mathematical, spatial, bodily-kinesthetic, naturalistic, interpersonal, and intrapersonal. Gardner believes that people are much more comfortable using the term *talents* and that *intelligence* is generally reserved for describing linguistic or logical "smartness." However, he does not believe that certain human abilities should arbitrarily qualify as "intelligence" over others (e.g., language as an intelligence vs. dance as a talent; Gardner, 1993).

Renzulli's (1978) definition, which defines gifted behaviors, rather than gifted individuals, is composed of three components as follows:

> Gifted behavior consists of behaviors that reflect an interaction among three basic clusters of human traits—above-average ability, high levels of task commitment, and high levels of creativity. Individuals capable of developing gifted behavior are those possessing or capable of developing this composite set of traits and applying them to any potentially valuable area of human performance. Persons who manifest or are capable of developing an interaction among the three clusters require a wide variety of educational opportunities and services that are not ordinarily provided through regular instructional programs. (Renzulli & Reis, 1997, p. 8)

Characteristics that may be manifested in Renzulli's three clusters are presented in Table 1.

The United States government's most recent federal definition, which was discussed in a national report on the state of gifted and talented education (U.S. Department of Education, 1993), defined gifted and talented children as:

> Children and youth with outstanding talent perform or show the potential for performing at remarkably high levels of accomplishment when compared with others of their age, experience, or environment. These children and youth exhibit high performance capability in intellectual, creative, and/or artistic areas, possess an unusual leadership capacity, or excel in specific academic fields. They require services or activities not ordinarily provided by the schools. Outstanding talents are present in children and youth from all cultural groups, across all economic strata, and in all areas of human endeavor. (p. 26)

Though many school districts adopt this or other broad definitions as their philosophy, others still only pay attention to "high intellectual" ability when both identifying and serving students. And, even though we have more diverse definitions of giftedness and intelligence today, many students with gifts and talents are still unrecognized and underserved (Hishinuma & Tadaki, 1996; Kloosterman, 1997), perhaps due to the differing characteristics found in intellectually gifted, creatively gifted, and diverse gifted learners. During the past four decades, educators have recognized the need to reform and enhance the education of culturally and linguistically diverse students in U.S. schools (Castellano & Diaz, 2002). Even with this consideration, diverse students continue to be overidentified for remedial classes and underrepresented in gifted and talented (GT) programs and services (National Academy of Sciences, 2002). Few doubts exist regarding the reasons that economically disadvantaged and culturally, linguistically, and ethnically diverse student groups are underrepresented in gifted programs. Frasier and Passow (1994) found that many current identification and selection procedures may be ineffective and

Table I

Taxonomy of Behavioral Manifestations of Giftedness According to Renzulli's "Three-Ring" Definition of Gifted Behaviors

Above-Average Ability (general)

- high levels of abstract thought
- adaptation to novel situations
- rapid and accurate retrieval of information

Above-Average Ability (specific)

- applications of general abilities to a specific area of knowledge
- capacity to sort out relevant from irrelevant information
- capacity to acquire and use advanced knowledge and strategies while pursuing a problem

Task Commitment

- capacity for high levels of interest, enthusiasm
- hard work and determination in a particular area
- self-confidence and drive to achieve
- ability to identify significant problems within an area of study
- setting high standards for one's work

Creativity

- fluency, flexibility, and originality of thought
- open to new experiences and ideas
- curious
- willing to take risks
- sensitive to aesthetic characteristics

Note. Adapted from *The Schoolwide Enrichment Model: A How-to Guide for Educational Excellence*, 2nd ed. (p. 9), by J. S. Renzulli and S. M. Reis, 1997, Mansfield Center, CT: Creative Learning Press. Copyright ©1997 by Creative Learning Press. Adapted with permission.

inappropriate for the identification of these young people and that limited referrals and nominations of culturally and linguistically diverse students affect their eventual placement in programs. An examination of the constructs of giftedness and subsequent identification practices in varied cultural and environmental contexts suggests the need to recognize talents with an understanding of how differences in learning styles and expressions may affect their manifestation in children from various cultural and economic groups (Frasier, García, & Passow, 1995).

Educational research has suggested that certain factors may affect the identification of gifted students and their placement in gifted programs, including test bias (Ford & Harris, 1999), cultural awareness training in teacher education programs (Rios & Montecinos, 1999), and alternative characteristics that indicate giftedness (Maker & Schiever, 1989). While some literature has identified problems and recommended potential changes in culturally and linguistically diverse students' access to gifted programs and services, these changes have not yet occurred. A recent report from the National Academy of Sciences (2002) recommended additional research in this area to develop a broader knowledge base on early identification and intervention with advanced learners. It also cautioned about using checklists of gifted characteristics in the majority population to identify giftedness in students who are from diverse or underrepresented backgrounds.

Characteristics of Individuals With High Intellectual Ability or Creative Potential

Characteristics of high intellectual ability or potential and high creative ability or potential must be considered separately because existing research and discussion has identified two broad categories, which Renzulli (1986) referred to as "schoolhouse giftedness" and "creative/productive giftedness." Schoolhouse giftedness refers to test taking, lesson learning, or academic giftedness often manifested by students who score well on more traditional intellectual or cognitive assessments and have the capacity to perform well in school. Creative/productive giftedness, on the other hand, is reflected in individuals who tend to be producers (rather than consumers) of original knowledge, materials, or products and who employ thought processes that are more inductive, integrated, and problem-oriented. Recent longitudinal research supports Renzulli's distinction between schoolhouse giftedness and creative/productive giftedness (Delcourt, 1993; Hébert, 1993; Perleth, Sierwald, & Heller, 1993). Renzulli believes that both types of giftedness should be developed and that an interaction exists between them (Renzulli & Reis, 1985). The interaction between aptitude and creativity leads to interesting discussions of the ways in which talents and gifts are manifested, as discussed later in this chapter.

Cognitive and Affective Characteristics

Many different researchers and textbook writers have summarized the characteristics of gifted students, and the most extensive is Clark's (1988) list of characteristics summarized in Table 2. Again, this list cannot be considered an exclusive

Table 2

Clark's Differentiating Characteristics of Gifted Students

Cognitive (Thinking) Characteristics

- retention of large quantities of information
- advanced comprehension
- varied interests and high curiosity
- high level of language development and verbal ability
- unusual capacity for processing information
- flexible thought processes
- accelerated pace of thought processes
- comprehensive synthesis of ideas
- early ability to delay closure
- ability to see unusual relationships
- ability to generate original ideas and solutions
- capacity to integrate ideas and disciplines
- early differential patterns for thought processing
- early ability to use and form conceptual frameworks
- evaluative approach towards self and others
- unusual intensity
- persistent and goal-directed behavior

Affective (Feeling) Characteristics

- large accumulation of information about emotions
- unusual sensitivity to the feelings of others
- keen sense of humor
- heightened self-awareness, feelings of being different
- idealism and sense of justice

- inner locus of control
- unusual emotional depth and intensity
- high expectations of self/others
- perfectionism
- strong need for consistency between values/actions
- advanced levels of moral judgment

Physical (Sensation) Characteristics

- heightened sensory awareness
- unusual discrepancy between physical and intellectual development
- low tolerance for lag between their standards and their athletic skills

Intuitive Characteristics

- early involvement and concern for intuitive knowing
- open to intuitive experiences
- creativity apparent in all areas of endeavor
- ability to predict
- interest in future

Societal Characteristics

- strongly motivated by self-actualization needs
- advanced capacity for conceptualizing and solving societal problems
- leadership
- involvement with the meta-needs of society (i.e., justice, truth, beauty)

Note. From *Growing Up Gifted*, 3rd ed. (pp. 126–132), by B. Clark, 1988, Columbus, OH: Merrill. Copyright ©1988 by Prentice-Hall. Adapted with permission of Prentice-Hall, Inc., Upper Saddle River, NJ.

Table 3

Common Characteristics of Intellectually Gifted Students

- have the ability to learn more rapidly than average students
- display the ability to understand complex and abstract concepts
- move ahead of agemates in basic skills
- demonstrate advanced verbal ability
- use advanced thinking skills, processing skills, and problem-solving skills
- demonstrate a focus or intensity in either interests and/or academic work

---

checklist for the identification of talented and gifted students, as any individual student cannot and will not exhibit all of these characteristics. For example, one characteristic of many gifted students is their focus on one area (e.g., technology or dinosaurs or castles) as opposed to their varied interests. Some very high-potential students have early verbal abilities and language, while others develop these abilities with age and opportunities. Perhaps the best use of such lists is to provide information about students who may be in need of special services or modifications in their academic, counseling, or extracurricular programs.

Other researchers have also discussed characteristics of intellectually gifted learners. A consensus from the work of scholars such as Feldhusen (1989), Renzulli (1986), Clark (1988), and Reis (1989) is that gifted and talented students have some common characteristics as described in Table 3.

In addition to these general characteristics, in research about gifted students from multicultural and diverse backgrounds, Frasier and Passow (1994) referred to "general/common attributes of giftedness": traits, aptitudes, and behaviors they have found to be consistently identified by researchers as common to gifted students. They noted that these basic elements of giftedness are similar across cultures, though each is not displayed by every student (see Table 4). Each of these characteristics may be manifested in different ways by students from different cultural groups, and educators must be especially careful in attempting to identify these characteristics in students from diverse backgrounds, as specific behavioral manifestations of the characteristics may vary with context (Frasier & Passow). The most comprehensive, well-researched compilation of characteristics of talented students across numerous content areas and areas of strengths is the Scales for Rating the Behavioral Characteristics of Superior Students (SRBCSS; Renzulli, Smith, White, Callahan, & Hartman, 1976; Renzulli, Smith, White, Callahan, Hartman, & Westberg, 2002). The SRBCSS (2002) were recently expanded to include scales in reading, math, and technology, in addition to the original scales in the areas of learning, motivation, creativity, leadership, artistic, musical, dramatic, communication, and planning.

Table 4

Common Attributes of Giftedness

- motivation
- communication skills
- well-developed memory
- insight
- imagination/creativity
- advanced ability to deal with symbol systems

- advanced interests
- problem-solving ability
- inquiry
- reasoning
- sense of humor

Note. From *Towards a New Paradigm for Identifying Talent Potential* (pp. 49–51), by M. M. Frasier and A. H. Passow, 1994, Storrs, CT: The National Research Center on the Gifted and Talented, University of Connecticut. Copyright ©1994 by National Research Center on the Gifted and Talented. Adapted with permission.

Characteristics of talented students can also be manifested within content areas such as reading, and identifying the characteristics of talented readers has been the focus of a recent research study by researchers at the National Research Center on the Gifted and Talented at the University of Connecticut (Reis et al., 2003). Research indicates that not all gifted students are talented readers and not all talented readers are academically gifted, but many demonstrate some or most of the characteristics summarized in Table 5.

Social and Emotional Traits

Whether or not gifted and talented learners have unique affective, social, and emotional characteristics has been an area of debate and discussion for decades. Recently, a comprehensive review of research was conducted by a task force of researchers, psychologists, and educators from the National Association for Gifted Children (Neihart, Reis, Robinson, & Moon, 2002). Although this task force found only a limited research base on which to draw conclusions about the important question of whether or not gifted and talented learners have unique social and emotional characteristics, it did reach several consistent findings. The most important is that there is no evidence that gifted children or youth—as a group—are inherently any more vulnerable or flawed in adjustment than any other group. The task force failed to discover evidence of social or emotional vulnerabilities or flaws unique to intellectually gifted learners or those with high creative potential. With the exception of mood disorders in creative writers and artists, indices of serious maladjustment, such as suicide, delinquency, and severe behavior disorders, appear no more (or less) frequently in this group than in the general population. Rather, many gifted young people possess assets that, when

Table 5

Characteristics of Talented Readers

Enjoyment in the reading process	• read avidly and with enjoyment • use reading differently for different reading purposes • demonstrate thirst for insight and knowledge satisfied through reading • pursue varied interests in and curiosity about texts • view books and reading as a way to explore the richness of life • seek and enjoy depth and complexity in reading • develop a deeper understanding of particular topics through reading • demonstrate preferences for non-fiction • pursue interest-based reading opportunities
Read early and above level	• read at least two grade levels above chronological grade placement • begin reading early and may be self-taught
Advanced processing	• retain a large quantity of information for retrieval • automatically integrate prior knowledge and experience in reading • utilize higher-order thinking skills such as analysis and synthesis • process information and thoughts at an accelerated pace • synthesize ideas in a comprehensive way • perceive unusual relationships and integrate ideas • grasp complex ideas and nuances
Advanced language skills	• enjoy the subtleties and complexities of language • demonstrate advanced understanding of language • use expansive vocabulary • use reading to acquire a large repertoire of language skills • use language for humor • display verbal ability in self-expression • use colorful and descriptive phrasing • demonstrate ease in use of language

supported, may enhance their resilience to highly negative life events and enable them to utilize their talents to achieve productive and satisfying lives.

When troubling social and emotional traits are present in this population, they most frequently reflect the interaction of an ill-fitting environment with an individual's personal characteristics. Gifted students require special educational experiences that are seldom forthcoming in regular classrooms (U.S. Department of Education, 1993), and too much of their school days are spent relearning material they have already mastered or could master in a fraction of the time that it takes their chronological peers. Many, therefore, never have the opportunity to learn strategies of problem solving to cope with the challenges related to effort and perseverance that other children encounter throughout their childhood. In addition, the maturity of their personal outlook, which is in many ways similar to that of older students, may result in a mismatch not only with the curriculum, but also with the maturity of their classmates. They may encounter a variety of intellectual and social issues, in addition to the developmental tasks usually encountered by persons of their age. They may have difficulty finding friends who share their understandings, and far too they often endure not only the burden of loneliness, but also enormous peer pressure to "be like everyone else." Far from finding that "gifted children are all alike," this task force found marked differences among this group, which is at least as varied as any other highly diverse group. This recent research (Neihart, Reis, Robinson & Moon, 2002) also highlights the need to respect the unique and varied characteristics of the diverse range of gifts and talents exhibited by students.

Characteristics of Individuals
With High Creative Ability or Potential

The ways in which academically gifted and creatively gifted students vary have been discussed by many researchers and educators, most of whom would probably agree with Sternberg and Lubart's (1993) assertion that the "academically successful children of today are not necessarily the creatively gifted adults of tomorrow" (p. 12). Individuals with high intelligence may or may not have high creative ability or potential, as well (Davis & Rimm, 1998; Renzulli & Reis, 1985). Some evidence suggests the existence of a "threshold concept," discussed by MacKinnon (1965), in which a base level IQ of about 120 is believed to be necessary for creative productivity. This theory indicates that, beyond that threshold, there is no relationship between creativity and intelligence as measured by IQ tests (Davis & Rimm; Sternberg & Lubart).

What are the traits that help to define an individual with high creative ability or potential? Gardner's (1993) conception of a creative individual is one who "regularly solves problems or fashions products in a domain, and whose work is considered both novel and acceptable by knowledgeable members of a field" (p. xvii). Gardner argued that creativity should not be regarded as a construct in the mind or personality of an individual; rather, it is something that emerges from the interactions of intelligence (personal profile of competencies), domain (disciplines or crafts within a culture), and field (people and institutions that judge quality within a domain).

Sternberg and Lubart (1993) viewed creativity as a type of giftedness in itself, rather than as one dimension of intelligence. They proposed that a person's "resources" for creativity allow a process of creative production to occur. Because they believe that six separate resources have to combine interactively to yield creativity, they find creative giftedness to be a rare occurrence. Sternberg and Lubart's five "resources" describe many traits of creative individuals:

1. *Intellectual processes.* Creatively gifted people excel in problem defining, using insight (selective encoding, selective comparison, and selective combination) to solve problems, and using divergent thought as a problem-solving strategy. These intellectual processes of creatively gifted learners are all immeasurable by traditional IQ tests.
2. *Knowledge.* Knowledge of the domain allows for one to identify areas where new and novel work is needed and, to some extent, may serve as a hindrance to creativity, as too much knowledge can limit the ability to have fresh ideas.
3. *Intellectual (cognitive) styles.* Creatively gifted people tend to prefer a legislative style (creating, formulating, and planning) and a global mode of processing information (thinking abstractly, generalizing, and extrapolating), which can be encouraged through approaches such as the Schoolwide Enrichment Model (Renzulli & Reis, 1985, 1997).
4. *Personality.* Five key personality attributes are important to creative giftedness: tolerance of ambiguity, moderate risk taking, willingness to surmount obstacles and persevere, willingness to grow, and belief in self and ideas.
5. *Motivation.* A task-focused orientation (drive or goal that leads a person to work on a task), as opposed to a goal-focused orientation (extrinsic motivators, rewards, or recognition that lead a person to see a task as a means to an end), often exists in creatively gifted individuals (see also Renzulli, 1978).

After reviewing many lists of personality characteristics compiled by researchers, Davis (1992) summarized a list of characteristics of individuals with high creative ability or potential, some of which may be considered "negative" (see Table 6). These "negative" traits may tend to upset the parents and educators, as well as some of the peers, of creative children, since they may lead to behaviors considered inappropriate in some traditional classrooms. A challenge exists for educators and parents to identify these characteristics of creativity in children and to channel their creative energy into constructive outlets (Davis & Rimm, 1998) by encouraging playfulness, flexibility, and the production of wild and unusual ideas (Torrance, 1962).

Table 6

Positive and Negative Characteristics of Creativity

Positive Characteristics	Negative Characteristics
• aware of their own creativeness	• questioning rules and authority
• independent	• indifference to common conventions
• energetic	• low interest in details
• keen sense of humor	• forgetfulness
• artistic	• carelessness and disorganization
• stubbornness	with unimportant matters
• original	• tendency to be emotional
• willing to take risks	• absentmindedness
• curious	• rebelliousness
• attracted to complexity and novelty	
• open-minded	
• perceptive	

Note. From *Creativity is Forever*, 3rd ed. (pp. 68–80), by G. A. Davis, 1992, Dubuque, IA: Kendall/Hunt. Copyright ©1992 by Kendall/Hunt. Adapted with permission.

In summary, some creatively gifted and talented children may exhibit different characteristics than some academically gifted and talented children. Those with high academic abilities have the potential to develop creative gifts and talents, yet many creatively gifted students do not necessarily display high academic performance in school.

Developmental Considerations in Recognizing Traits of Talented Students

Developmental issues are important to consider in the recognition of the diverse characteristics of talented and gifted individuals. Traits and behaviors unique to learners of varying age levels may provide clues regarding the manifestations of talent at different ages.

The Young Gifted Child

Early signs of precocity exist in some children (Baum, Reis, & Maxfield, 1998). Parents are quite capable of describing their child's early behaviors, though they may not necessarily identify the behaviors as precocious. Because of this, parents should be viewed by educators as important sources of information about children's talents (Robinson, 1987). Early language development, advanced gross motor competence, and early reading are precocious behaviors easily identified and assessed in young children. In general, though, assessing advanced abilities and talents in young children proves quite difficult and unreliable, especially when using traditional intelligence tests. According to Robinson, several researchers have found that strength in very early novelty preferences, visual attention, and visual recognition memory during infancy can be somewhat effective predictors of intelligence in childhood. Because little research exists in this area (as compared to research on older gifted students), parents and teachers should keep their "views broad and flexible if we are to identify reliable and significant indices of precocious development" (Robinson, p. 162). Feldman's (1993) research on child prodigies, defined as children (usually younger than 10 years old) who are performing at the levels of highly skilled adults, suggests that prodigies have highly focused talent, extreme motivation to develop the talent, and unusual self-confidence in their ability to do so. Psychometric intelligence plays a role in a prodigy's development, but not a central one (Feldman).

The Gifted Adolescent

Along with the multitude of issues faced by any adolescent, particular social and career choice issues may present unique challenges to gifted and talented teenagers. And, as any parent knows, characteristics of many adolescents can change dramatically in a short period of time, and talented adolescents have certain qualities that other teenagers do not. Csikszentmihalyi, Rathunde, and Whalen (1993) conducted an in-depth longitudinal study of 200 talented teenagers. They identified a strong core of personal attributes that distinguished the talented teenagers in their study from their average-ability counterparts: intellectual curiosity, active reception of information from the world, strong desire to achieve, perseverance to attain their goals, preference for leading and controlling, desire to display accomplishments and gain other's attention, and little questioning of their own worth. Some personality attributes were displayed by only one gender. For example, talented male teens, in comparison to average male teens, valued stability and predictability more, preferred to avoid physical risks, enjoyed arguments more, and had an unusual need for social recognition. The talented female teens, when compared to their average counterparts, were less inclined to identify with values often seen as "feminine" (e.g., orderliness, neatness, and predictability). Overall, the researchers found that the cluster of attributes that described the talented teens suggested an "autotelic" (self-directed or self-rewarding) personality. The teens in this study "entered adolescence with personality attributes well suited to the difficult struggle of establishing their mastery over a domain: a desire to achieve, persistence, and a curiosity and openness to experience" (Csikszentmihalyi et al., p. 82).

Karnes and McGinnis (1996) also found support for differences between academically talented and average adolescents. Their study showed that a sample of academically talented adolescents indicated a more internal locus of control than average students. Locus of control is the extent to which individuals believe that their behavior causes subsequent reinforcement; individuals who perceive reinforcement as contingent upon behavior or characteristics usually have an internal locus of control.

Diverse Characteristics of Special Populations of Gifted and Talented Learners

The last two decades have been marked by an increasing interest in the atypical gifted who are generally described as consisting of ethnic, racial, and linguistic minorities; the economically disadvantaged; gifted females; gifted underachievers; gifted students who are gay, lesbian, or bisexual; and the gifted/disabled. In these populations, the identification of giftedness may be masked by other characteristics and prejudices (Bireley, Languis, & Williamson, 1992). During the last two decades, researchers in the field of gifted education have increasingly turned their attention to the underrepresentation of these populations in gifted programs. Ethnic, racial, and linguistic minorities have also been targeted by federal and state policies.

The pervasive disparity in the proportion of culturally and linguistically diverse (e.g., limited English proficient [LEP], bilingual, English as a second language) students identified and served in programs for the gifted is a major concern of many researchers and educators in gifted education (Maker, 1983; Mitchell, 1988). The primary reason cited for this underrepresentation is the absence of adequate assessment procedures and programming efforts (Frasier, García, & Passow, 1995; Frasier & Passow, 1994; Kitano & Espinosa, 1995). In the U.S. Department of Education report, *National Excellence: A Case for Developing America's Talent* (1993), it was acknowledged that "special efforts are required to overcome the barriers to achievement that many economically disadvantaged and minority students face" (p. 28). This report also addressed the need to identify talents in youngsters of different socioeconomic and cultural background. In this regard, although efforts have been made in the last decade to overcome these limitations, school districts and individuals still find themselves lacking systematic research support to design and implement a more equitable system of identifying these students. However, careful attention needs to be devoted to the relevance of the current checklists of characteristics leading to the identification of advanced students. For instance, teacher judgment poses difficulties in referring and identifying culturally and linguistically diverse students due to negative teacher attitudes, resistance, or unsatisfactory knowledge of the manifestations of giftedness in these students. It is crucial that educators hold positive and high expectations for their bilingual/LEP and culturally diverse students and become aware of the family culture, which may differ greatly from majority families. It is also critical that unique characteristics of each population be included as a part of the identification process.

Recognizing the need to acknowledge characteristics of different cultures in the identification of talent among diverse groups, Maker and Schiever (1989) identified common attributes of giftedness, cultural values specific to certain racial or ethnic groups, and the behavioral manifestations of giftedness one might observe in a student from a particular group. The characteristics they identified of gifted students of Hispanic, Native American Indian, Asian American, and low socioeconomic status background are summarized in Table 7.

Researchers at the National Research Center on the Gifted and Talented at the University of Connecticut completed a 3-year study of 35 economically disadvantaged, ethnically diverse, talented high school students who either achieved or underachieved in their urban high school (Reis, Hébert, Díaz, Ratley, & Maxfield, 1995). A number of common personal characteristics were found to be exhibited by the participants, including motivation and inner will, positive use of problem solving, independence, realistic aspirations, heightened sensitivity to each other and the world around them, and appreciation of cultural diversity. A determination to succeed was consistently echoed by most of the high-achieving participants, despite what could be considered prejudice leveled against them. Rosa, one of the participants in the study, said that she had experienced various types of prejudice in her community and occasionally in academic experiences, which she attributed to the fact that she was both intelligent and Puerto Rican. This prejudice occurred in school from both teachers and students, and in the summer programs she participated in for high-achieving students, which were held at some of the most prestigious private schools in the state. She explained, "I know that people will occasionally look at me and say, when they find out that I'm smart, 'How can that be? She's Puerto Rican.'"

Each of the high-achieving participants in this study referred to an internal motivation that kept him or her driven to succeed in an urban environment. One participant referred to this drive as an "inner will" that contributed to the strong belief in self that was observed in the participants. Resilience was also exhibited by many of the participants, as the majority came from homes that had been affected by periodic or regular unemployment of one or more parents; poverty; family turmoil caused by issues such as alcohol, drugs, and mental illness; and other problems. All participants also lived in a city plagued by violence, drugs, poverty, and crime. Their school district had often been called one of the worst in the country, and it had the dubious distinction of having the state eliminate the local board of education and take over the schools. Despite these challenges, the majority of the high-achieving participants in this study developed the resilience necessary to overcome problems associated with their families, their school, and their environment by accepting their circumstances and accepting the opportunities given to them.

These culturally diverse gifted students and those who are acquiring English as a second language represent a heterogeneous group. According to Kitano and

Table 7

Characteristics of Giftedness and Cultural Values of Minorities and Possible Behavioral Manifestations of Giftedness Resulting From Their Interaction

Absolute Aspects of Giftedness	Characteristic Cultural Values	Behavioral Differences
Hispanics		
Leadership	Collaborative, rather than competitive dynamic	Accomplishes more, works better in small groups than individually
Emotional depth and intensity	"Abrazo," a physical or spiritual index of personal support	Requires touching, eye contact, feeling of support to achieve maximum productivity
Native American Indians		
Unusual sensitivity to expectations and feelings of others	Collective self—the Tribe	Is a good mediator
Creativity in endeavors	Traditions, heritage, beliefs	Makes up stories or poems
Asian Americans		
High expectations of self	Confucianist ethic—people can be improved by proper effort and instruction	Academic orientation and achievement
Perfectionism	Conformity, correctness, respect for and obedience to authority	Patience and willingness for drill and rote exercises; decreased risk taking and creative expression
Low Socioeconomic Status		
Persistent, goal-directed behavior	Survival in circumstances	"Streetwiseness,"community-based entrepreneurship
Accelerated pace of thought processes	Physical punishment, blunt orders rather than discussion	Manipulative behavior, scapegoating

Note. From *Critical Issues in Gifted Education: Defensible Programs for Cultural and Ethnic Minorities*, Vol. II (p. 4, 78, 152, 211), by C. J. Maker and S. W. Schiever, 1989, Austin, TX: PRO-ED. Copyright ©1989 by PRO-ED. Adapted with permission.

Espinosa (1995), "Their diversity suggests a need for a broad range of programs that provide options for different levels of primary and English language proficiency, different subject-matter interests, and talent areas" (p. 237). These authors called for new strategies for identifying diverse gifted students, including developmental curricula and enriched programs that "evoke" a gifted student's potential, broader conceptions of intelligence, alternative definitions and characteristics of giftedness, and assessment models developed for specific populations.

Gifted Females

What factors cause some smart young girls with hopes and dreams to become self-fulfilled talented women in their later lives? For the last two decades, educators have speculated on the answers to this question, and, while some research has addressed the issue, much more is needed. In this section, characteristics of some gifted and talented girls are discussed (Reis, 1998).

Some gifted females begin to lose self-confidence in elementary school, and this continues through college and graduate school. They may increasingly doubt their intellectual competence, perceive themselves as less capable than they actually are, or believe that they must work hard while boys can rely on innate ability. Talented girls in school may choose more often to work in groups, and they may appear more concerned about teacher reactions, more likely to adapt to adult expectations, and less likely than boys to describe themselves or to be described as autonomous and independent. Some bright girls also use affiliations and their relationships to assess their level of ability and to achieve at higher levels, and they often believe that their grades will be higher if their teachers like them. Some bright young women deliberately understate their abilities; they try to appear to be like everyone else and work to get good, but not outstanding, grades. Displaying academic talents may also be problematic for females because of adverse social consequences. Some adolescent females believe that it is a social disadvantage to be smart because of the potential negative reactions this may generate from others.

Reis (1998) recently completed a comprehensive analysis of research related to gifted females, summarizing research on talented girls' social and emotional development through elementary and secondary school. She concluded that girls achieve well in school, but that self-confidence and self-perceived abilities decrease and that professional and work-related achievement in life is generally lower than males of comparable ability. Some gifted females value their own personal achievements less as they get older, indicating that the aging process has a negative impact on both their achievement and the self-confidence. However, Reis also found that, as gifted females approach middle to later age, many of the emotional conflicts they faced as young women decrease and they are consequently able to excel.

Recent research indicates that, in some situations, high-ability females exhibit more positive characteristics regarding their achievement and talents. In one study by Ford (1992), African American talented males and females in an urban school district expressed great support for the achievement ideology, and gifted females believed they had the highest teacher feedback on their efforts. Similar findings emerged in research conducted by Reis, Hébert, et al. (1995) with talented female adolescents in an urban environment. Spielhagen (1994) found that 45 young talented females who participated in programs for talented youth were clearly aware of their abilities and did not deny or hide their potential. They also demonstrated a more balanced view of female achievement, understanding that achievement in school and life does not always take the same form. Again, the same theme emerges: Characteristics of gifted and talented girls vary by age, cultural group, and circumstance, and it is not possible to generalize from one population to another or to use one characteristic of one gifted girl to describe another. Too many intervening variables affect the complex reasons that one girl grows up to be self-confident and able to achieve, while another of similar ability, but different personality and environment, does not.

Gifted Students Who Are Gay, Lesbian, or Bisexual (GLB)

Students who are both gifted and gay may feel marginalized, both externally and internally. Cohn (2002) has pointed out that

> Instead of being in the top 3% of their age group in intellectual potential, they fall within the 3–10% (depending upon one's source for an estimate of gays, lesbians, and bisexuals [GLB] in the population at large) of that top 3%, dropping from a statistical probability of 3 in 100 to 1–3 in 1,000. (p. 146)

He further pointed out that, in a large urban high school of 3,000 or so students, one might expect to find only 3 to 9 students who are both gifted and gay. Spread across four grade levels, the likelihood of such individuals finding one another or even feeling safe seeking out others like themselves is miniscule. Little research exists on this population, but Cohn believes that the feelings of alienation and isolation in this group of adolescents may cause them to hide who they really are. It is difficult to summarize research about characteristics when only a handful of studies have examined the topic.

Gifted Students With Disabilities

The potential frustrations experienced by students with both high potential and learning disabilities may place them at risk for social and emotional problems. The balancing act required for these students to find suitable opportunities that both nurture their abilities and concurrently accommodate their impediments may contribute to a number of difficulties. Current research has indicated that the co-occurrence of high ability and disabilities is confusing for children and young adults and can create affective difficulties for students as they seek to understand fully why they can do some things so well, yet struggle so much with others.

Identifying the characteristics of gifted and talented students with disabilities is complicated by the fact that their abilities often mask their disabilities, and, in turn, their disabilities may disguise their giftedness. As a result, students who are gifted and also have disabilities are at risk of being underidentified (Baum, Owen, & Dixon, 1991; Olenchak, 1994; Reis, Neu, & McGuire, 1995) or excluded from both programs for students with learning disabilities and those for gifted and talented students. This is also true of gifted students with other exceptionalities such as attention-deficit/hyperactivity disorder (AD/HD; Moon, 2002) and Asperger's syndrome (Neihart, 2000). Research about characteristics of various populations is ongoing and will be briefly discussed by specific exceptionality.

Hearing-disabled gifted students. Children with hearing impairments were judged by teachers to exhibit similar characteristics of giftedness to hearing peers, except for academic achievement, which may be delayed by 4 or 5 years. Yewchuk and Bibby (1989) concluded that "giftedness in both hearing and hearing impaired populations is manifested in similar ways" (p. 48), that is, in eagerness to learn, visual skills, superior recall, quick understanding, superior reasoning ability, and expressive language.

Gifted students with cerebral palsy. Willard-Holt (1994) explored the experiences of two talented students with cerebral palsy who were not able to communicate with speech. Using qualitative cross-case methodology, she found that these students demonstrated the following characteristics of giftedness: advanced academic abilities (especially math and verbal skills), broad knowledge base, quickness of learning and recall, sense of humor, curiosity, insight, desire for independence, use of intellectual skills to cope with disability, and maturity (shown in high motivation, goal orientation, determination, patience, and recognition of their own limitations). Several educational factors contributed to the development of these characteristics in these students, such as willingness of the teachers to accommodate for the disabilities, mainstreaming with nondisabled students, individualization and opportunities for student choice, and hands-on experiences.

Gifted students with learning disabilities. During the last two decades, increasing attention has been given to the perplexing problem of high-ability/talented students who also have learning disabilities. The specific research concerning this population began following the passage of PL 94-142, when the expanded emphasis on the education of students with disabilities created an interest in students who were both gifted and learning disabled. Although the literature has addressed this topic, problems still exist regarding the identification and provision of support services and programs for this population. Research on high-ability students with learning disabilities continues to be difficult because of problems in defining and describing each population (Boodoo, Bradley, Frontera, Pitts, & Wright, 1989; Renzulli, 1978; Taylor, 1989; Ysseldyke & Algozzine, 1983).

Baum and Owen (1988), in a study of 112 high-ability/LD students in grades 4–6, found that the major characteristic distinguishing high-ability/LD students from both LD/average and high-ability/non-LD groups was a heightened sense of inefficacy in school. The high-ability/LD students also displayed high levels of creative potential, along with a tendency to behave disruptively and to achieve low levels of academic success. Also, 36% of the students in their study who had been identified as having a learning disability simultaneously demonstrated behaviors associated with giftedness. Baum (1990) later identified four recommendations for working with gifted students with learning disabilities: (1) encourage compensation strategies, (2) encourage awareness of strengths and weaknesses, (3) focus on developing the child's gift, and (4) provide an environment that values individual differences.

Gifted students with learning disabilities may demonstrate some of the following affective characteristics: strong, personal need for excellence in performance and in outcomes that approaches or embodies unhealthy perfectionism; intensity of emotions; oversensitivity as described by Dabrowski (1938); unrealistic expectations of self; a tendency toward intense frustration with difficult tasks that often produces a general lack of motivation, as well as disruptive or withdrawn behavior; and feelings of learned helplessness and low self-esteem (Baum & Owen, 1988; Baum, Owen, & Dixon, 1991; Reis, Neu, & McGuire, 1995).

After a thorough review of the literature on gifted/LD students, Reis, Neu, and McGuire (1995) compiled a list of their characteristics that may hamper their being identified as gifted. These characteristics are the result of the interaction of their high abilities and their learning disabilities, and many display more negative than positive characteristics (see Table 8). In addition, Reis, Neu, and McGuire found that almost half of the postsecondary gifted students with learning disabilities they studied had sought counseling for social and emotional problems, ranging from mild depression to contemplation of suicide.

Students who exhibit characteristics of both the gifted and learning-disabled populations pose challenges for educators. The misconceptions, definitions, and expected outcomes for these students further complicate appropriate programming for them (Baum, Owen, & Dixon, 1991; Whitmore, 1986). Gifted/LD students require unique educational programs and services for both their academic and affective development. By studying eminent adults with learning disabilities, Gerber and Ginsberg (1990) concluded that certain behaviors contributing to success can be cultivated and shaped, and their conclusions about successful adults with learning disabilities can be reasonably applied to the education of gifted/LD students. Educators are more likely to succeed with gifted/LD students when they nurture self-control and empowerment, increase a desire to succeed, and set an orientation toward establishing and attaining reason-

Table 8

Characteristics of Gifted Students With Learning Disabilities

Characteristics That Hamper Identification as Gifted

- frustration with inability to master certain academic skills
- learned helplessness
- general lack of motivation
- disruptive classroom behavior
- perfectionism
- supersensitivity
- failure to complete assignments
- lack of organizational skills
- demonstration of poor listening and concentration skills
- deficiency in tasks emphasizing memory and perceptual abilities
- low self-esteem
- unrealistic self-expectations
- absence of social skills with some peers

Characteristic Strengths

- advanced vocabulary use
- exceptional analytic abilities
- high levels of creativity
- advanced problem-solving skills
- ability to think of divergent ideas and solutions
- specific aptitude (artistic, musical, or mechanical)
- wide variety of interests
- good memory
- task commitment
- spatial abilities

Social and Emotional Characteristics of Gifted/LD Students

- exhibit feelings of inferiority
- show an inability to persevere in the accomplishment of goals
- demonstrate a general lack of self-confidence
- exhibit confusion as they struggle to understand why they can know an answer, but are not able to say it or write it correctly
- have their abilities mask their disabilities
- have their disabilities mask their giftedness
- demonstrate a strong, personal need for excellence in performance and in outcomes that nears and often embodies unhealthy perfectionism
- exhibit an intensity of emotions
- have unrealistic expectations of self
- also have a tendency to experience intense frustration with difficult tasks that often produces a general lack of motivation
- experience feelings of learned helplessness
- exhibit low self-esteem

Note. From *Talent in Two Places: Case Studies of High Ability Students with Learning Disabilities Who Have Achieved* (pp. 16–17), by S. M. Reis, T. W. Neu, and J. M. McGuire, 1995, Storrs, CT: The National Research Center on the Gifted and Talented, University of Connecticut. Copyright ©1995 by NRC/GT. Adapted with permission.

able goals. Further, when schools reframe the learning disability as a personal attribute for which compensatory strategies can be learned and exercised, increase individual persistence, emphasize student abilities, and deemphasize the disabilities, gifted/LD students have more opportunities to be successful.

Gifted students with AD/HD. Children with attention-deficit/hyperactivity disorder (AD/HD) and gifted children may exhibit similar behaviors (e.g., inattention, high energy level, impulsivity), and mounting evidence suggests that many children being identified as having AD/HD are also very bright and creative (Cramond, 1995; Moon, 2002; Webb & Latimer, 1993) Similar evidence suggests that many gifted children exhibit symptoms similar to those demonstrated by students with AD/HD when they are bored or unchallenged. Bright students may be inattentive when they are not appropriately challenged, while also demonstrating a high energy level in areas of intense interest.

Although similarities exist between the behaviors of gifted students and those with AD/HD, some of the defining features of AD/HD are not usually associated with giftedness. Children with AD/HD usually show variability in the quality of their performance on specific tasks, whereas gifted students are usually more consistent with their level of effort and performance, especially when they are interested and challenged. For example, a defining feature of AD/HD is that a child has difficulty sustaining attention in most tasks or play activities, and they struggle to complete tasks (American Psychiatric Association, 1994). In contrast, gifted students may tire easily of boring, repetitive, unchallenging activities; however, they can usually sustain focused attention when they are working on tasks of their own choosing. In addition, to be diagnosed as AD/HD, the impulsive, hyperactive, or inattentive behaviors must occur in at least two or more settings (e.g., home and school). Usually, parents of gifted students without AD/HD report that their children can concentrate, sustain attention, and behave appropriately for long periods of time at home or during extracurricular activities. To distinguish whether a gifted student may also have AD/HD, the school and home situation and settings must be closely monitored because gifted children typically will not display similar behaviors in all settings (i.e., home, school, music lessons, etc.), whereas AD/HD children will exhibit disordered behavior in most or all environments.

Giftedness and AD/HD can exist in the same child (Moon, 2002). A careful professional evaluation is needed to make this diagnosis, followed by appropriate medical, psychological, and curricular and instructional modifications (Webb & Latimer, 1993). Of course, the behavioral characteristics associated with giftedness should be considered when determining whether behavior patterns stem from AD/HD. The presence of AD/HD in addition to a learning disability would make many of the interventions for school more difficult for students to implement, slowing progress and requiring additional understanding and patience from educators. This is yet another reason why it is important to assess whether AD/HD is present in addition to LD.

Baum, Owen, and Dixon (1991) found that, when schools implement comprehensive programs that identify and develop individual gifts and talents, gifted/LD pupils begin to behave socially, emotionally, and academically more like gifted students without disabilities than like nongifted students with learning disabilities. These findings, later corroborated by Bender and Wall (1994) and Olenchak (1994), indicate that, as educators diminish the attention to and importance of the disability and concentrate instead on the gifts, gifted/LD students become creatively productive. Reis, Neu, and McGuire (1997) also found evidence of the need to focus on gifts and talents in successful university students with learning disabilities.

Gifted students with behavioral problems. Gifted students with emotional and behavioral problems are often not referred for gifted programs or they are terminated from gifted programs because of their behavior, and they often experience periods of underachievement (Reid & McGuire, 1995).

Neu (1993) studied talented students with these types of problems and found a variety of issues that characterize their experiences. Most of the participants in Neu's study were underchallenged in school, thus escalating their emotional and behavioral problems. Many of these students had the most difficulty during classroom "dead time," when they waited for instruction that would challenge them while their chronological peers finished their work. In a review of the sparse research on this population, Reid and McGuire (1995) found that many talented students drop out of high school, experience behavior problems, and are not recommended for gifted programs. As a result of their emotional and behavioral disorders, "students often unpredictably engage and disengage in learning opportunities, resulting in inconsistencies in academic skills and knowledge foundations" (p. 16). Well-designed and careful research on the characteristics and needs of this population is necessary.

Gifted students with psychological issues and problems. Contrary to myth and popular opinion, the prevalence of psychological disorders is similar within gifted and nongifted populations. Students who are experiencing acute psychological distress may experience sudden, severe underachievement. Students who have a psychological condition may become chronic underachievers. Many serious psychological illnesses, such as schizophrenia and bipolar disorder, begin in early to late adolescence (American Psychiatric Association, 1994), and it is important for educators to be aware of signs of psychological distress, notify parents immediately, and refer the student to the school counselor or the school psychologist.

Underachieving gifted students. Student performance that falls noticeably short of potential, especially for young people with high ability, is bewildering and perhaps the most frustrating of all challenges both teachers and parents face (Reis & McCoach, 2000). According to a 1990 national needs assessment survey, most educators of the gifted identified the problem of underachievement as their number one concern (Renzulli, Reid, & Gubbins, 1991). Too often, students who show great academic potential fail to perform at a level commensurate with their abilities.

Gifted students who underachieve do so for different reasons: Some have not learned to work, while others may have poor self-regulation skills, low self-confidence, or low self-efficacy. Other low achievers may suffer from either obvious or hidden disabilities, and still others may underachieve in response to inappropriate educational conditions. Some students underachieve or fail in school for obvious reasons: excessive absences from school, poor performance, disruptive behavior, low self-esteem, family problems, and poverty. In addition to the risk factors that clearly predict why most students fail, another longstanding problem that causes underachievement in gifted or high-potential students is the totally inappropriate curriculum and content some of them encounter on a daily basis. The hundreds of hours spent each month in classrooms in which students rarely encounter new or challenging curricula, the boredom of being assigned routine tasks mastered long ago, the low levels of discussion, and the mismatch of content to students' abilities lead to frustration in many of our brightest students. In fact, dropping out of school is the only way that some students believe they can address these issues honestly. The characteristics most often associated with high-potential students who underachieve as summarized by Reis and McCoach (2000) are listed in Table 9.

Understanding the Diverse Ways
in Which Talents and Gifts Emerge and Develop

In the past, the general approach to the study of the gifted could easily lead the casual reader to believe that giftedness is an absolute condition that is magically bestowed upon someone in much the same way that nature endows us with blue eyes, red hair, or a dark complexion (Renzulli, 1980). This position is not supported by the current research cited in this chapter. Multiple lists of characteristics exist—some for girls and some for boys, some for students from the majority culture, others for students from diverse cultural backgrounds. For too many years, we have pretended that we can identify *the* traits of gifted children in an absolute and unequivocal fashion. Many people have been led to believe that certain individuals have been endowed with a golden chromosome that makes him or her "a gifted person." This belief has further led to the mistaken idea that all we need to do is find the right combination of traits that prove the existence of this "gift." The further use of phrases such as "the truly gifted," "the highly gifted," the "moderately gifted," and the "borderline gifted" has only served to confound the issue. The misuse of the concept of giftedness has given rise to both criticism and confusion about both identification and programming, and the result has been mixed messages sent to educators and the public at large.

Most of the confusion and controversy surrounding characteristics of giftedness can be placed into proper perspective if we examine a few key questions. Do

Table 9

Characteristics of Gifted Underachievers

Personality Characteristics

- low self-esteem, low self-concept, low self-efficacy
- feelings of pessimism, distrust
- anxious, impulsive, inattentive
- aggressive, hostile
- depressed
- dependent
- socially immature

Internal Mediators

- fear of failure
- fear of success
- negative attitude toward school
- antisocial, rebellious
- self-critical or perfectionistic

Maladaptive Strategies

- lack goal-directed behavior
- poor coping skills
- poor self-regulation strategies
- use defense mechanisms

Positive Attributes

- creative
- intense outside interests
- demonstrate honesty and integrity when rejecting inappropriate schoolwork

we use specific characteristics of one group of people to identify another group? Are the characteristics of giftedness reflected in high-ability Puerto Rican students in Connecticut the same characteristics of giftedness as those demonstrated by above-average Mexican students in Texas? Are there characteristics common to each group? If so, how are they exhibited? What happens to a child who consistently manifests these characteristics when he or she is in the primary grades, but who learns to underachieve in school because of an unchallenging curriculum? What about a gifted child with a learning disability whose disability masks the talents? Are characteristics of giftedness static (i.e., you have them or you don't have them) or are they dynamic (i.e., they vary within people and among learning/performance situations)?

These questions have led us to advocate a fundamental change in the ways in which the characteristics of giftedness should be viewed in the future. The characteristics of any advanced learner should be identified within various population groups. That is, we should attempt to identify the characteristics of talented students within each educational context and population. This information should be used to help us differentiate between all students and those who need different levels of service or a continuum of services (Renzulli & Reis, 1997) in school to realize their potential. This shift might appear insignificant, but we believe that it has implications for how we think about the characteristics of giftedness and how we should structure our identification and programming endeavors. This change may also provide the flexibility in both identification and programming endeavors that will encourage the inclusion of diverse students in our programs. A shift in our beliefs about how we can move from identifying characteristics associated with the remediation of weaknesses to the development of characteristics associated with interests and strengths will also benefit talented students.

Defining and understanding the types of characteristics that suggest talents and gifts in diverse populations will help us to identify and then decide which services are offered to all students and what is qualitatively necessary for gifted students based on the traits of the population. This, in turn, will help us develop programs that are internally consistent. At the very minimum, we must understand that giftedness is manifested by different traits in different populations, and we must develop programs that both celebrate and reflect the diversity of talents and gifts displayed by the many different types of students who live and go to school in our society.

Teacher Statement

For the secondary school gifted course that I developed and teach, "Enrichment and Independent Study" (EIS), a single list of characteristics would not be adequate or appropriate to select students. Any identification practices should match the goals of a program. The goals of EIS are to provide multidisciplinary, stimulating, and challenging activities; build research and critical thinking skills; foster positive social and emotional development; and guide students through a long-term, in-depth study in their own interest area. The selection committee is composed of an administrator and the EIS teacher, as well as a content expert in the student's primary interest area. The committee considers multiple criteria, looking for an interaction among high ability, dedication to task/work ethic, and creative productivity or creative potential. It is easy for us to spot intellectual giftedness in the academic setting, but EIS is designed to serve all types of gifts and talents, so we look beyond subject grades (we do not use IQ or other standardized test scores) and pay equal attention to students' extracurricular and community involvement; portfolios; and teacher, parent, and self-nominations. The EIS curriculum is very student-centered, built around students' interests and talent areas, and it also offers many general enrichment and skill-building opportunities.

Because EIS is an elective class, it is important that students are internally motivated, can work independently, and are intellectually curious, but it is not necessary for them to be accomplished when they enter the class. EIS is meant to develop many kinds of gifts and talents, rather than just spotlighting existing talents. Furthermore, adolescents are in a constant state of developmental flux, and their interests and abilities change with age and experience. Cultural and gender differences, personality attributes, learning styles, ability, and aptitude—all these factors and more have to be considered for the purpose of inclusion to EIS, rather than exclusion from it. I choose not to reduce the complexity of teaching and learning to a simplistic "one-list-fits-all" mentality so that there is diversity in the EIS class and, thus, different points of view. This chapter effectively conveys the diverse characteristics and traits that so many different gifted and talented students demonstrate.

—Meredith Greene

Discussion Questions

1. Why would it be potentially discriminatory to use a list of characteristics to identify *the* gifted and talented students in a large school district?

2. Does any consensus exist among scholars and researchers in the field of gifted education about some common characteristics of talented and gifted students that can be used to help in identification and programming?

3. How should lists of gifted and talented students' characteristics be used in establishing gifted programs?

4. What are some examples of how characteristics of high-potential students vary among cultural groups?

5. In what ways may having a disability mask characteristics of giftedness?

6. How can parents be involved in helping to use characteristics of high ability or talent in identification and programming for gifted and talented students?

7. What would be the most appropriate way for classroom and gifted education teachers to use known and emerging characteristics of high-potential students in school?

References

American Psychiatric Association. (1994). *Diagnostic and statistical manual of mental disorders* (4th edition). Washington, DC: Author.

Baum, S. (1990). *Gifted but learning disabled: A puzzling paradox* (ERIC Digest #E479). Reston, VA: Council for Exceptional Children.

Baum, S., & Owen, S. V. (1988). High ability/learning disabled students: How are they different? *Gifted Child Quarterly, 32,* 321–325.

Baum, S., Owen, S. V., & Dixon, J. (1991*). To be gifted and learning disabled: From definitions to practical intervention strategies.* Mansfield Center, CT: Creative Learning Press.

Baum, S., Reis, S. M., & Maxfield, L. R. (Eds.). (1998). *Nurturing the gifts and talents of primary grade students.* Mansfield Center, CT: Creative Learning Press.

Bender, W. N., & Wall, M. E. (1994). Social-emotional development of students with learning disabilities. *Learning Disabilities Quarterly, 17,* 323–341.

Bireley, M., Languis, M., & Williamson, T. (1992). Physiological uniqueness: A new perspective on the learning disabled/gifted child. *Roeper Review, 15,* 101–107.

Boodoo, G. M., Bradley, C. L., Frontera, R. L., Pitts, J. R., & Wright, L. P. (1989). A survey of procedures used for identifying gifted learning disabled children. *Gifted Child Quarterly, 33,* 110–114.

Castellano, J. A., & Diaz, E. I. (2002). *Reaching new horizons: Gifted and talented education for culturally and linguistically diverse students.* Boston: Allyn and Bacon.

Clark, B. (1988). *Growing up gifted* (3rd ed.). Columbus, OH: Merrill.

Clark, B. (2002). *Growing up gifted* (6th ed.). Upper Saddle River, NJ: Merrill/Prentice-Hall.

Cohn, S. J. (2002). Gifted students who are gay, lesbian, or bisexual. In M. Neihart, S. M. Reis, N. M. Robinson, & S. M. Moon (Eds.), *The social and emotional development of gifted children: What do we know?* (pp. 145–154). Waco, TX: Prufrock Press.

Cramond, B. (1995). *The coincidence of attention deficit hyperactivity disorder and creativity.* Storrs: The National Research Center on the Gifted and Talented, University of Connecticut.

Csikszentmihalyi, M., Rathunde, K., & Whalen, S. (1993). *Talented teenagers: The roots of success and failure.* Cambridge, England: Cambridge University Press.

Dabrowski, K. (1938). Typy wzmozonej pobudliwosci psychicznej (Types of increased psychic excitability). *Biul. Inst. Hig. Psychicznej, 1*(3/4), 3–26.

Davis, G. A. (1992). *Creativity is forever* (3rd ed.). Dubuque, IA: Kendall/Hunt.

Davis, G. A., & Rimm, S. B. (1998). *Education of the gifted and talented* (4th ed.). Boston: Allyn and Bacon.

Delcourt, M. A. B. (1993). Creative productivity among secondary school students: Combining energy, interest, and imagination. *Gifted Child Quarterly, 37,* 23–31.

Feldhusen, J. F. (1989). Why the public schools will continue to neglect the gifted. *Gifted Child Today, 12*(2), 56–59.

Feldman, D. H. (1993). Child prodigies: A distinctive form of giftedness. *Gifted Child Quarterly, 37,* 188–193.

Ford, D. Y. (1992). Determinants of underachievement as perceived by gifted, above-average, and average Black students. *Roeper Review, 14,* 130–136.

Ford, D. Y., & Harris, J. J., III. (1999). *Multicultural gifted education.* New York: Teachers College Press.

Frasier, M. M., García, J. H., & Passow, A. H. (1995). *A review of assessment issues in gifted education and their implications for identifying gifted minority students.* Storrs:

The National Research Center on the Gifted and Talented, University of Connecticut.

Frasier, M. M., & Passow, A. H. (1994*). Towards a new paradigm for identifying talent potential.* Storrs: The National Research Center on the Gifted and Talented, University of Connecticut.

Gardner, H. (1983). *Frames of mind: The theory of multiple intelligences.* New York: BasicBooks.

Gardner, H. (1993). *Frames of mind: The theory of multiple intelligences* (10th anniversary ed.). New York: BasicBooks.

Gerber, P. J., & Ginsberg, R. J. (1990). *Identifying alterable patterns of success in highly successful adults with learning disabilities: Executive summary.* Washington, DC: U.S. Department of Education, Educational Information Center. (ERIC Document No. ED342168)

Hébert, T. P. (1993). Reflections at graduation: The long-term impact of elementary school experiences in creative productivity. *Roeper Review, 16,* 22–28.

Hishinuma, E., & Tadaki, S. (1996). Addressing diversity of the gifted/at risk: Characteristics for identification. *Gifted Child Today, 19*(5), 20–25, 28–29, 45, 50.

Karnes, F. A., & McGinnis, J. C. (1996). Self-actualization and locus of control with academically talented adolescents. *Journal of Secondary Gifted Education, 7,* 369–372.

Kitano, M. K., & Espinosa, R. (1995). Language diversity and giftedness: Working with gifted English language learners. *Journal for the Education of the Gifted, 18,* 234–254.

Kloosterman, V. (1997). *Talent identification and development in high ability, Hispanic, bilingual students in an urban elementary school.* Unpublished doctoral dissertation, University of Connecticut, Storrs.

MacKinnon, D. W. (1965). Personality and the realization of creative potential. *American Psychologist, 20,* 273–281.

Maker, C. J. (1983). Quality education for gifted minority students. *Journal for the Education for the Gifted, 6,* 140–153.

Maker, C. J., & Schiever, S. W. (1989). *Critical issues in gifted education: Defensible programs for cultural and ethnic minorities* (Vol. II). Austin, TX: PRO-ED.

Mitchell, B. M. (1988). The last national assessment of gifted education. *Roeper Review, 10,* 239–240.

Moon, S. M. (2002). Gifted children with attention-deficit/hyperactivity disorder. In M. Neihart, S. M. Reis, N. M. Robinson, & S. M. Moon (Eds.), *The social and emotional development of gifted children: What do we know?* (pp. 193–204). Waco, TX: Prufrock Press.

Neihart, M. (2000). Gifted children with Asperger's syndrome. *Gifted Child Quarterly, 44,* 222–230.

Neihart, M., Reis, S. M., Robinson, N. M., & Moon, S. M. (Eds.). (2002). *The social and emotional development of gifted children: What do we know?* Waco, TX: Prufrock Press.

National Academy of Sciences. (2002). *Minority children in gifted and special education.* Washington, DC: The National Academies Press.

Neu, T. W. (1993). *Case studies of gifted students with emotional or behavioral disorders.* Unpublished doctoral dissertation, University of Connecticut, Storrs.

Olenchak, F. R. (1994). Talent development: Accommodating the social and emotional needs of secondary gifted/learning disabled students. *Journal of Secondary Gifted Education, 5*(3), 40–52.

Passow, A. H. (1981). The four curricula of the gifted and talented: Toward a total learning environment. *Gifted Child Today, 4*(5), 2–7.

Perleth, C., Sierwald, W., & Heller, K. A. (1993). Selected results of the Munich longitudinal study of giftedness: The multidimensional/typological giftedness model. *Roeper Review, 15*, 149–155.

Reid, B. D., & McGuire, M. D. (1995*). Square pegs in round holes—these kids don't fit: High ability students with behavioral problems.* Storrs: The National Research Center on the Gifted and Talented, University of Connecticut.

Reis, S. M. (1989). Reflections on policy affecting the education of gifted and talented students: Past and future perspectives. *American Psychologist, 44*, 399–408.

Reis, S. M. (1998). *Work left undone: Choices and compromises of talented females.* Mansfield Center, CT: Creative Learning Press.

Reis, S.M., Gubbins, E. J., Renzulli, J. S., Briggs, C., Schreiber, F. Richards, S., Jacobs, J., & Eckert, R. D. (2003). *Reading instruction for talented readers.* Manuscript submitted for publication.

Reis, S. M., Hébert, T. P., Díaz, E. I., Maxfield, L. R., & Ratley, M. E. (1995*). Case studies of talented students who achieve and underachieve in an urban high school.* Storrs: The National Research Center on the Gifted and Talented, University of Connecticut.

Reis, S. M., & McCoach, D. B. (2000). The underachievement of gifted students: What do we know and where do we go? *Gifted Child Quarterly, 44,* 152–170.

Reis, S. M., Neu, T. W., & McGuire, J. M. (1995). *Talent in two places: Case studies of high ability students with learning disabilities who have achieved.* Storrs: The National Research Center on the Gifted and Talented, University of Connecticut.

Renzulli, J. S. (1978). What makes giftedness?: Reexamining a definition. *Phi Delta Kappan, 60*, 180–184.

Renzulli, J. S. (1980). Will the gifted child movement be alive and well in 1990? *Gifted Child Quarterly, 24,* 3–9.

Renzulli, J. S. (1986). The three-ring conception of giftedness: A developmental model for creative productivity. In R. J. Sternberg & J. E. Davidson (Eds.), *Conceptions of giftedness* (pp. 53–92). Cambridge, England: Cambridge University Press.

Renzulli, J. S., Reid, B. D., & Gubbins, E. J. (1991*). Setting an agenda: Research priorities for the gifted and talented through the year 2000.* Storrs: The National Research Center on the Gifted and Talented, University of Connecticut.

Renzulli, J. S., & Reis, S. M. (1985). *The schoolwide enrichment model: A comprehensive plan for educational excellence.* Mansfield Center, CT: Creative Learning Press.

Renzulli, J. S., & Reis, S. M. (1997). *The schoolwide enrichment model: A how-to guide for educational excellence* (2nd ed.). Mansfield Center, CT: Creative Learning Press.

Renzulli, J. S., Smith, L. H., White, A. J., Callahan, C. M., & Hartman, R. K. (1976). *Scales for rating the behavioral characteristics of superior students.* Mansfield Center, CT: Creative Learning Press.

Renzulli, J. S., Smith, L. H., White, A. J., Callahan, C. M., Hartman, R. K., & Westberg, K. L. (2002). *Scales for rating the behavioral characteristics of superior students* (Rev. ed.). Mansfield Center, CT: Creative Learning Press.

Rios, F., & Montecinos, C. (1999). Advocating social justice and cultural affirmation: Ethnically diverse pre-service teachers' perspectives on multicultural education. *Equity and Excellence in Education, 32*(3), 66–75.

Robinson, N. M. (1987). The early development of precocity. *Gifted Child Quarterly, 31,* 161–164.

Siegler, R. S., & Kotovsky, K. (1986). Two levels of giftedness: Shall ever the twain meet? In R. J. Sternberg & J. E. Davidson (Eds.), *Conceptions of giftedness* (pp. 417–435). Cambridge, England: Cambridge University Press.

Spielhagen, F. R. (1994). Perceptions of achievement among high-potential females between 9 and 26 years of age. In K. D. Arnold, K. D. Noble, & R. F. Subotnik (Eds.), *Remarkable women: Perspectives on female talent development* (pp. 193–208). Cresskill, NJ: Hampton Press.

Sternberg, R. J., & Davidson, J. E. (1986). *Conceptions of giftedness.* Cambridge, England: Cambridge University Press.

Sternberg, R. J., & Lubart, T. I. (1993). Creative giftedness: A multivariate investment approach. *Gifted Child Quarterly, 37*, 7–15.

Taylor, H. G. (1989). Learning disabilities. In E. J. Mash & R. Barkley (Eds.), *Treatment of childhood disorders* (pp. 347–380). New York: Guilford Press.

Torrance, E. P. (1962). *Guiding creative talent.* Huntington, NY: Krieger.

U.S. Department of Education, Office of Educational Research and Improvement. (1993). *National excellence: A case for developing America's talent.* Washington, DC: U.S. Government Printing Office.

Wallace, B., & Pierce, J. (1992). The changing nature of giftedness: An examination of various strategies for provision. *Gifted Education International, 8*, 4–9.

Webb, J. T., & Latimer, D. (1993). ADHD and children who are gifted. *Exceptional Children, 60*, 183–184.

Whitmore, J. (1986). Conceptualizing the issue of underserved populations of gifted students. *Journal for the Education of the Gifted, 10*, 141–153.

Willard-Holt, C. (1994). *Recognizing talent: Cross-case study of two high potential students with cerebral palsy.* Storrs: The National Research Center on the Gifted and Talented, University of Connecticut.

Yewchuk, C. R., & Bibby, M. A. (1989). Identification of giftedness in severely and profoundly hearing impaired students. *Roeper Review, 12*, 42–48.

Ysseldyke, J. E., & Algozzine, B. (1983). LD or not LD: That's not the question. *Journal of Learning Disabilities, 16*(1), 29–31.

Chapter 2

Planning the Learning Environment

by **Barbara G. Hunt** and **Robert W. Seney**

If teachers are to play the lead role in effectively helping students become self-directed learners, they must first embrace learning as their primary function: they must learn how they themselves learn and how they in turn can create learning environments.
—Susan J. Poulsen (1997, p. 7)

In this chapter, the elements of creating an effective learning environment will be investigated. While process, product, and content are often intentionally modified, the importance of modifying the environment for students is often overlooked. At the same time, it is readily acknowledged that the environment affects students' learning. The way classrooms are structured reflects the teacher's thoughts and philosophies on how students learn and how the students, in turn, will perform. For example, if learning by investigation is the goal in the classroom, then the learning environment should be structured for exploration by providing many resources, opportunities for movement, and provisions for more interaction between students. If the purpose is to invite students to raise questions, to experiment, and to work cooperatively with others, then an environment that will enhance and facilitate these interactions should be designed. Carefully planned and differentiated activities may fall short of the teacher's goals and expectations if the students' learning environment is not also modified.

This chapter addresses the question, "Now that the students have been identified, how should the learning environment be modified to reflect the unique needs of gifted and high-potential learners?"

The Modifications

Without needed modifications to the environment, opportunities are restricted and gifted students cannot develop their abilities effectively.
—C. June Maker and Aleene B. Nielson (1996, p. 23)

In their text, *Curriculum Development and Teaching Strategies for Gifted Learners* (2nd ed., 1996), Maker and Nielson have provided guidelines to help the teacher make learning experiences appropriate for gifted learners. Basing their precepts on the "acid test" of relating curriculum and teaching strategies to the characteristics that make students different, they have provided an important guide. These guidelines are built upon the touchstones of modification: process, product, content, and environment.

While modifications in all four of these areas are important, an emphasis is placed upon modifying the environment:

Learning environment modifications are prerequisites for making modifications in content, process, and product. The learning context shapes input, processing, and output. The environment affords certain kinds of learning experiences; when the environment is properly modified, great opportunities are afforded to its inhabitants. Without needed modifications to the environment, opportunities are restricted and gifted students cannot develop their abilities effectively. (Maker & Nielson, 1996, p. 23)

With this in mind, Maker and Nielson offered a set of principles to guide in modifying learning environments for gifted learners.

The environment should

1. be learner-centered, rather than teacher- or content-centered;
2. focus on independence, rather than emphasizing dependence;
3. be open, rather than closed, to new ideas, innovations, and exploration;
4. promote acceptance, rather than judgment;
5. focus on complexity, rather than simplicity;
6. provide for a variety of group options, rather than one grouping as a general organization;
7. be flexible, rather than having a rigid structure or chaotic lack of structure; and
8. provide for high mobility, rather than low mobility (p. 31).

These principles of the classroom are discussed in terms of a continuum, with the most appropriate environment for gifted learners occurring near the extreme. By using these as guidelines, environments are created that provide the comfort, autonomy, and opportunities gifted learners need for optimum growth and development.

Modifying the Environment

Modifying the environment will facilitate necessary changes in the three other areas: content, process, and products. For appropriate modifications to be made, the focus must be on gifted learners and the many differences that exist among them. Learning styles, interests, learning needs, and characteristics must be taken into account when planning for gifted learners. Determining their learning styles and learning preferences are of primary importance. This issue is discussed later in this chapter.

Different Environmental Needs

In working with gifted learners, awareness of the diversity, even within a single classroom, becomes obvious. While these learners share many characteristics, there is a great deal of variety and diversity. *Uniqueness* becomes the key term. When dealing with special populations of gifted learners, there is almost a quantum leap in diversity. It is important to be aware of cultural differences, cultural values, the concept of giftedness within the context of specific cultures, and the behavioral differences exhibited and expected in other cultures.

It is also important for educators to identify their own attitudes and belief systems about minorities, socioeconomic status, and other cultures. Diversity must be valued, and potential contributions to the gifted classroom must be identified. In addition, cultural bridges have to be built within the classroom setting. These elements must be considered and must become key ingredients in the design of learning environments for gifted learners.

The Responsive Learning Environment

In an environment where each student is considered a unique individual, a positive self-concept can be developed naturally. Students can learn responsibility and an inner sense of control when expectations and opportunities for choice, sharing responsibility, and self-evaluation are a planned part of their day.

—Barbara Clark (2002, p. 384)

Clark's work in the responsive learning environment (RLE) identifies key ingredients for designing appropriate settings. The RLE is approached from the point of view of optimizing learning. The seven areas of the teaching process that must be developed to optimize learning are

1. create a responsive learning environment;
2. integrate the intellectual processes during instruction;
3. differentiate the content;
4. assess the learner's knowledge, understanding, and interests;
5. individualize the instruction;
6. evaluate learning and teaching; and
7. reflect on the entire process and reform the learning plan to incorporate all new insights gained (Clark, 2002, p. 378).

The first step in providing optimal learning for all students, and especially for meeting the unique needs of gifted learners, is to create a responsive learning environment. It can be defined as a flexible environment that allows learners to pursue educational requirements and interests in depth and with a minimum of time limitations. Learners either have the opportunity to move at their own pace and work individually or they are grouped with other students as learning needs require (Clark, 2002).

In order to evaluate a learning environment, Clark (2002) has developed a Responsive Learning Environment Checklist (see Figure 1). She has also provided guidelines for developing both the physical learning environment and the social/emotional learning environment.

The Physical Learning Environment

Clark's (2002) basic premise is to create "people space." This involves space that is inviting, flexible, and large enough to allow students to be engaged in a variety of instructional groupings at the same time. In short, the goal should be to "create a laboratory for learning" (p. 382). Suggestions for creating usable physical space in the classroom are

1. remove furniture;
2. carpet areas of the room;
3. use floors, walls, window, closets, and drawers;
4. bring in comfortable, movable furniture;
5. use color to support learning;
6. order materials at many levels in smaller numbers; and
7. provide areas for designated activities (p. 383).

Clark (2002) also provided suggestions for developing a safe and caring social/emotional setting, one in which students are free to be themselves and where it is safe to be smart. Gifted learners often have much more in common with their intellectual peers than they do with their chronological peers, who

You will know that the physical environment is responsive when

1. There is space for students to simultaneously participate in a variety of activities.
2. Students have access to materials with a range of levels and topics.
3. There is space for the students to engage in a variety of instructional groupings, and flexible grouping is used.
4. There are areas supportive of student self-management.
5. Desks are not individually owned.
6. The classroom has a comfortable, inviting ambiance supportive of exploration, application, and personal construction of knowledge.

You will know that the social/emotional environment is responsive when

1. The emotional climate is warm and accepting.
2. The class operates with clear guidelines decided upon cooperatively.
3. Instruction is based on each individual student's needs and interests as assessed by the teacher from the student's interaction with the materials and the concepts.
4. Student activities, products, and ideas are reflected around the classroom.
5. Student choice is evident in planning, instruction, and products of evaluation.
6. Building and practicing affective skills are a consistent and valued part of the curriculum and of each teaching day.
7. Students and teachers show evidence of shared responsibility for learning.
8. Empowering language is evident between teacher and students and among students.
9. Students show evidence of becoming independent learners with skills of inquiry and self-evaluation.

Figure 1. A responsive learning environment checklist

Note. From *Growing Up Gifted*, 6th ed. (p. 381), by B. Clark, 2002, Upper Saddle River, NJ: Merrill. Copyright ©2002 by Merrill. Reprinted with permission.

often tease them. Therefore, a supportive environment must be created where gifted learners can express their thoughts and pursue their interests without distracting interference. In addition, this climate must be conducive to risk taking, exploration, and growth. In this supportive environment, students will be able to build trust in others and themselves, build self-confidence, address issues of giftedness, and know that the teacher is aware of their counseling needs.

The Psychological and Social/Emotional Environment

The goodness of fit, the appropriate coincidence of individual characteristics and needs with an understanding and supportive environment, is crucial for proper development.
    —Franz J. Mönks (Mönks & Peters, 1992, p. 191)

In order to create an environment for optimal adjustment, Leta Hollingworth recommended grouping gifted students together for compacting the curriculum and for enrichment. This allows for lively discussions and happier, more well-adjusted human beings through meeting not only students' cognitive needs, but also their equally important social and emotional needs (Silverman, 1990). In order for the teacher of the gifted to create an optimal learning environment, he or she must collect enough information through cumulative records and different assessment instruments to answer clearly the question, "Who are these gifted individuals?"

I made most of my friends in the advanced classes at school. Their goals were compatible with mine and that's what made me feel so comfortable around them.
    —Boy, 16 (Galbraith & Delisle, 1996, p. 212)

I have a lot of trouble relating to kids my age. It's as though we're on a totally different wavelength. I prefer adult company over kid company because I can contribute in their conversations without being thought of as strange for knowing what's going on.
    —Billy, 14 (Galbraith & Delisle, 1996, p. 213)

In an environmental support system, the internal world of the individual must be considered, and peer relationships are a vital element. Because of the gifted child's asynchronous development, an 8-year-old can find peers among early adolescents. The teacher of the gifted can help gifted learners with peer and social relationships through

1. providing more flexibility in schools to foster peer relationships (multi-age groups, adoption programs in which an older gifted child works with a younger gifted child, or small groups formed where personality and learning styles are considered);
2. promoting acceleration for some gifted learners (offer "survival courses" for grade-level changes);
3. providing an effective counseling/advisement program (develop peer counseling);
4. incorporating self-esteem development into the curriculum;
5. incorporating leadership and social skills into the curriculum;

6. developing programs that are sensitive to diversity (forming peer groups that are from diverse populations); and

7. understanding the special problems involved in peer relationships for adolescent gifted girls (utilize female role models and mentors; Silverman, 1993, pp. 169–170, 271–274, 309–316).

In promoting positive social development, Roedell (1985) found that gifted children develop social skills more easily when they interact with their true peers. When gifted learners are grouped together in special classes, in summer programs (e.g., governor schools, programs for gifted), or in special schools (e.g., high schools for mathematics and science, International Baccalaureate), some teenagers report that, for the first time in years, they are able to meet, enjoy, and interact deeply with peers.

Understanding Giftedness

Galbraith (1985) found that, of the "eight great gripes of gifted children," the most often rated one was that no one explains what being gifted is all about. Kunkel, Chapa, Patterson, and Walling (1992) found the same complaint. If gifted children do not understand what giftedness is, how can we as teachers create an optimal learning environment? A student's confusion about giftedness and its implications for his or her life was an abiding and overriding theme. Their ambivalence about giftedness manifested itself largely as an apparent eagerness to diminish their own uniqueness, enforce equality (e.g., "Everybody's gifted in his or her own way"), and broaden the definition of giftedness to include all variation in human ability. For adolescents in whom the most powerful social imperative is conformity, denial of giftedness may serve an important psychosocial function. The conflict, whether mild or intense, must be resolved by gaining ownership and responsibility for the recognized talent (p. 13).

Teachers of the gifted can encourage the emergence of self through self-acceptance. It may be helpful to incorporate a unit on being gifted, study eminent gifted people, teach leadership skills, use self-assessment tools, incorporate counseling strategies, study brain research, incorporate role-playing and problem solving directly related to giftedness, and introduce mentors to these students.

Risk Taking

Life is either a daring adventure, or nothing.
—Helen Keller

Many young gifted learners are willing to be risk takers, but gifted adolescents seem more cautious, while other adolescents become less cautious. This may be because gifted adolescents are more aware of consequences or more skilled at judging the advantages and disadvantages of the situation (Galbraith & Delisle, 1996).

In a responsive social/emotional environment, the gifted learner is more likely to take risks. Teaching these students how to accept mistakes and treat them as learning experiences can help them see the benefits of risk taking. Teaching gifted learners to be risk takers means letting them be open to criticism, give input, work in unstructured situations, and defend their ideas. Williams' (1982) Model for Implementing Cognitive-Affective Behaviorism in the Classroom includes the element of risk taking. Some other strategies to implement risk taking into the curriculum are creative problem solving, synectics, SCAMPER, role-playing, and debate (Mississippi State Department of Education, 1995).

Assessment of Gifted Students

In designing an appropriate learning environment, the teacher needs assessment data to plan and differentiate a student's program of study. In order to select academic options for gifted students, careful assessment of individual student ability, aptitude, interests, and personal values is essential. Collecting profile data on each gifted student and then translating the data into a workable format for planning can prove helpful. Data from a student's cumulative records, screening and identification information, intelligence tests, portfolios, and affective instruments (e.g., learning styles, personality types) all combine to give the teacher a profile of the student. The counselor and teacher can work together to develop a plan, based on assessment information, that meets both the academic and the social/emotional needs of the gifted student. This plan needs to address the following critical issues:

1. *Academic planning provides a blueprint for gifted students in negotiating a program of study that truly reflects their abilities and interests.* In that sense, it offers an opportunity for students to assess their academic profiles at key stages. They are then able to build on their strengths and weaknesses in such a way that they can see progress and make changes or corrections in the planning process as needed based on good information.

2. *Academic planning is the vehicle through which comprehensive curricula and services can be made available to students and parents.* Many times, schools offer a wide variety of opportunities, but these options are never fully explained and presented so that gifted students can see their importance to their course of study. Assessing a student's test results (e.g., Torrance Tests of Creative Thinking) may open the door for participation in the arts as a cocurricular area of study. For instance, a student who demonstrated spatial abilities on an IQ test might find stimulation in a chess club, or a student who showed strong verbal and problem-solving skills might join the debate team.

3. *Academic planning influences the extent of articulation in programming for gifted students.* Without it, it would not be unusual to find a patchwork quilt model of program delivery. With effective planning, students may put together an appropriate scope and sequence of offerings, thus eliminating the kind of fragmentation that is often typical of the larger secondary school environment.

4. *Academic planning provides a way to enhance personalized education for gifted students.* This is particularly the case for students from special populations (e.g., minority, low-income, highly gifted, and twice-exceptional students) whose discrepant profiles and extraordinary needs may dictate annual review of an individualized program of study in all major areas.

5. *Early academic planning prevents the narrowing of options for gifted learners at important transition points in their program.* In the secondary curriculum there are several classes that serve to separate students in courses of study at essential stages in their academic development; the most notable are algebra and calculus in mathematics, physics in science, and foreign languages. If gifted students do not take these academic options at some point in their secondary experience, they could be penalized at the college level when attempting to enter into areas of mathematics, science, and foreign language at advanced levels. Absence of these courses can also narrow career options (Silverman, 1993, pp. 203–204). Another option can be the International Baccalaureate's Diploma Program, a demanding preuniversity course of study designed for highly motivated students aged 16 to 19. The IB balances transdisciplinary programs of inquiry and traditional disciplines. It meets the academic and social/emotional needs of the gifted through its goals, which encourage students to be active, compassionate, and lifelong learners (International Baccalaureate Organization, n.d.).

Teachers must become more flexible when assessing students. More trust should be put in students' abilities to set goals and evaluate their own learning in order to meet their cognitive and affective needs.

Learning Styles

Gifted students need to understand their own learning styles, as well as their strengths and weaknesses. Griggs and Dunn (1984) found a positive relationship between improvement in academic achievement, attitudes, and behaviors and accommodation of the student's learning style preferences in the classroom. Gifted students appear to show evidence of preferring certain cognitive learning styles. Gifted elementary and middle school students show similar patterns for high tactile and kinesthetic and low auditory preferences. Most gifted students prefer little structure, less supervision, more independence, flexibility in learning, and real-life experiences to lectures, discussions, and more small-group or individual self-designed instructional opportunities (Clark, 2002).

Creative or divergent thinkers have unique learning styles. They are immersion learners who want to find out everything about one subject at once. These thinkers are holistic and sometimes find the artificial boundaries around school subjects annoying. The ability to make something happen or the novelty of an idea is more often rewarding than the extrinsic reward system in our schools (Silverman, 1993).

Silverman (2002) stated that there are two major ways of learning: auditory-sequential and visual-spatial. Auditory-sequential learners are good listeners, learn well in a step-by-step process, process information rapidly, and express themselves verbally. On the other hand, visual-spatial learners are excellent observers, comprehend holistically, think in images, struggle with word retrieval, and intertwine their emotions with their thinking. Silverman's book *Upside-Down Brilliance: The Visual-Spatial Learner* gives voice to this much neglected group of gifted learners.

Teachers need to use learning style instruments to get a clearer picture of the gifted students they teach. Silverman (1989) found that children who exhibit visual-spatial learning styles appear to have difficulties with risk taking and accepting failure, spatial learners can become panic-stricken if they do not know the answer, and introverts and visual-spatial learners find the computer an invaluable asset to learning. Instruments to aid the teacher in assessing students' learning style preferences are found in the Teacher Resources section at the end of this chapter.

Personality/Psychological Types

Personality (like biology) is not destiny. Talented students, in fact all students, need to recognize the shortcomings of their natural dispositions and to value as acquired skills specific techniques to help them become balanced adults. (Gallagher, 1990, p. 12)

Myers and McCaulley (1985, cited in Gallagher, 1990) used the Myers-Briggs Type Indicator (MBTI) to study the personality types of high school gifted students across the country. A total of 1,725 gifted learners' preferences was compared to a sample of adolescents' preferences in the general population. Several strong patterns were found:

1. Almost 50% of the talented students were extroverts, and 50% introverts, while 63% of the general population were extroverts.
2. More than 75% of the talented sample preferred intuition to sensing, while only 32% of the general population preferred intuition.
3. Talented high school males equally preferred thinking (64%) with their nontalented male counterparts (61%), while 55% of the talented females

preferred feeling; 66% of the nontalented high school females preferred feeling.

4. Talented students were more likely to prefer perceiving (61%) over judging, while 46% of the high school students preferred perceiving (Gallagher, p. 12).

Again, the importance of uncovering these basic dispositions creates a new level of understanding of giftedness. Also, it gives the teacher of the gifted learner another tool for knowing their uniqueness in order to create a responsive environment.

Individual Education Plans (IEPs)

A planning document that makes the most of the student's aptitudes and abilities is the Individual Educational Plan (IEP). IEPs have traditionally been used in developing an academic plan for students with disabilities, but now they are being utilized in several states for gifted students (Clark, 2002). An IEP is developed based on the assessment of a student's profile. In addition to the profile data, objectives must be identified that will reflect the needs shown by the profile; activities must be planned to meet them; a timeline must be developed for implementation; and an evaluation must be conducted of the student's progress toward these objectives. Since an IEP is written in collaboration with the parents, the regular education teachers, the gifted specialist, and other appropriate school personnel, a cooperative spirit is created that brings positive outcomes to all concerned (Clark, 2002). References for commercial IEP instruments can be found in the Teacher Resources section at the end of this chapter. Several commercial IEP instruments can be used, or one can create his or her own tool. An example of an IEP is included in Figures 2 and 3 (Renzulli & Smith, 1978a, 1978b, pp. 77–78; Reis, Burns, & Renzulli, 1992).

Portfolios

Like the particular qualities associated with a testing culture, authentic assessment doesn't automatically happen in the classroom . . . an assessment culture means that teachers and students are continually asking themselves, How can I make use of this knowledge and feedback?
—Howard Gardner (Hart, 1994, p. 12)

The portfolio is a powerful tool for authentic assessment. Assessment is authentic when it involves students in tasks that are worthwhile, significant, and meaningful and when students are actively involved in evaluating their own work. Authentic assessments are standard-setting, rather than standardized, assessment tools (Hart, 1994). Paulson, Paulson, and Meyer (1991) formulated this definition:

INDIVIDUAL EDUCATIONAL PROGRAMMING GUIDE

Strength - A - Lyzer

Prepared by: Joseph S. Renzulli
Linda H. Smith

NAME _____

SCHOOL _____

AGE _____ TEACHER(S) _____

GRADE _____ PARENT(S) _____

Individual Conference Dates And Persons Participating In Planning Of IEP

ABILITIES

INTELLIGENCE - APTITUDE - CREATIVITY

In the spaces below, enter the results of standardized test scores and circle all scores above the _____ percentile.

Test	Area	Date	Raw Score	Grade Equiv.	% ile

TEACHER RATINGS

In the spaces below, enter the scores from the Scale for Rating Behavioral Characteristics of Superior Students. Circle unusually high scores.

Scale	Score Mean	Scale	Group Score Mean
Learning		Musical	
Motivation		Dramatic	
Creativity		Comm.: Precision	
Leadership		Comm.: Expressive	
Artistic		Planning	

END OF YEAR GRADES

Enter final grades for the past two years.

Reading		Art	
Mathematics		Foreign Language	
Language Arts		Other	
Social Studies		Other	
Science			
Music			

☐ Check here if additional assessment information is recorded on the reverse side.

INTERESTS

As a result of student responses to the Interest-A-Lyzer or other interest assessment procedures, indicate the general area(s) in which levels of interest seem to be High, Average and Low.

	H	A	L		H	A	L
Fine Arts/Crafts				Managerial			
Scientific/Technical				Business			
Literary/Writing				Historical			
Political/Judicial				Performing Arts			
Mathematical				Other			
Athletic							

SPECIFIC AREAS OF INTEREST

As a result of individual discussions with the student, indicate particular topics, issues, or areas of study in which the student would like to do advanced level work.

LEARNING STYLES

Enter the scores from the Learning Styles Inventory in the spaces below. Circle the highest area(s).

Learning Style	Score	Learning Style	Score
Projects		Teaching Games	
Simulation		Independent Study	
Drill and Recitation		Programmed Instruction	
Peer Teaching		Lecture	
Discussion			

Comments regarding informal observations about Learning Styles and relationships between areas of interest and learning styles.

SUMMARY AND RECOMMENDED ACTION BASED ON ASSESSMENT INFORMATION

In the space below summarize (1) strengths, interests, and learning styles, (2) areas in which remedial work or additional skill building appears to be warranted, and (3) specific higher mental processes and advanced skills that should be developed.

Copyright © 1978 by Creative Learning Press, Inc. PO Box 320 Mansfield Center, Ct. 06250. All rights reserved.

Figure 2. Example of an IEP: The Strength-a-Lyzer

Note. From *Strength-a-Lyzer* (pp. 77–78), by J. S. Renzulli and L. H. Smith, 1978b, Mansfield Center, CT: Creative Learning Press. Copyright ©1978 by Creative Learning Press. Reprinted with permission.

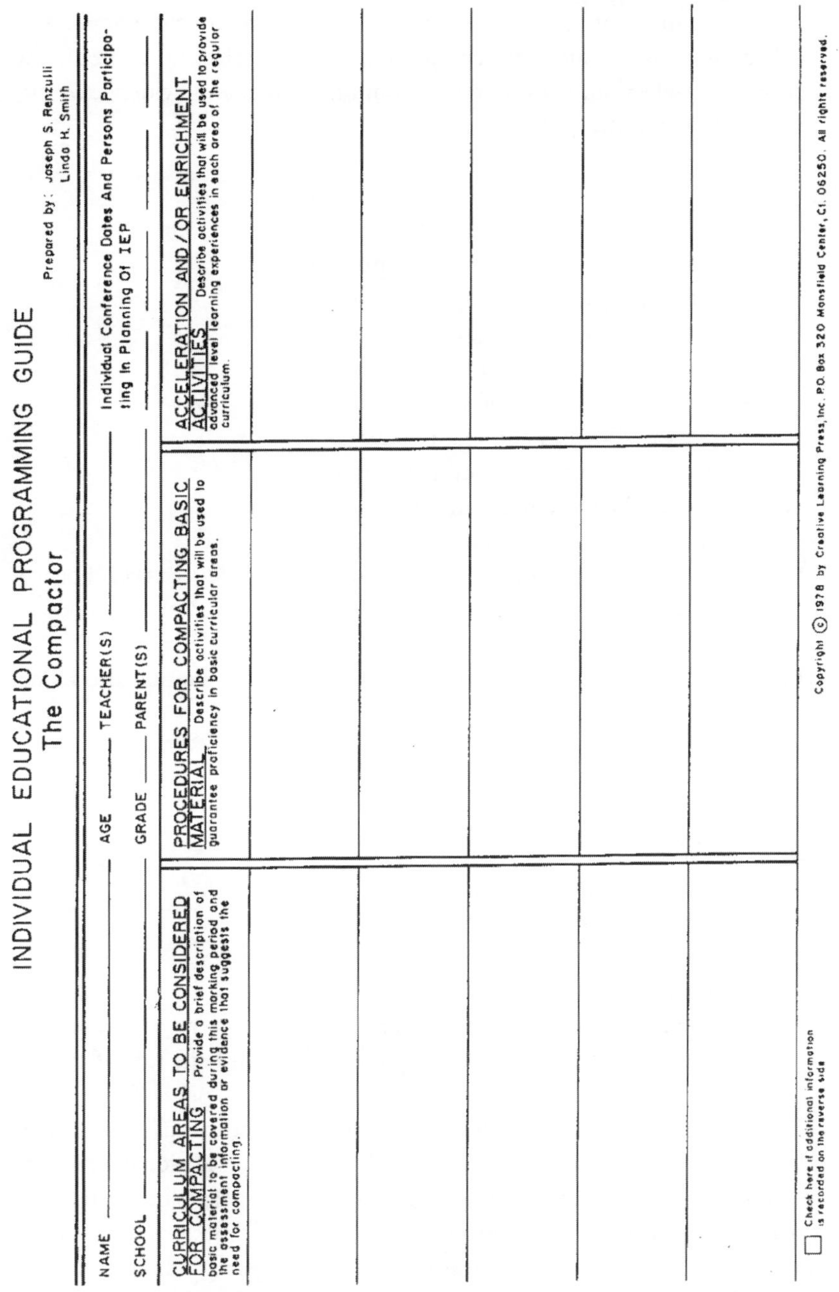

Figure 3. Example of an IEP: The Compactor

Note. From *The Compactor* (pp. 77–78), by J. S. Renzulli and L. H. Smith, 1978a, Mansfield Center, CT: Creative Learning Press. Copyright ©1978 by Creative Learning Press. Reprinted with permission.

A portfolio is a purposeful collection of student work that exhibits the student's efforts, progress, and achievements in one or more areas. The collection must include student participation in selecting content, the criteria for selection, the criteria for judging merits, and evidence of student self-reflection. (p. 60)

The portfolio process will

1. project the purposes and types of portfolios;
2. collect and organize artifacts over time;
3. select key artifacts based on criteria;
4. interject personality through signature pieces;
5. reflect metacognitively on each item;
6. inspect to self-assess and align goals;
7. perfect and evaluate . . . and grade if you must;
8. connect and conference with others;
9. inject and eject artifacts continually to update; and
10. respect accomplishments and show with pride (Burke, Fogarty, & Belgrad, 1994).

Important elements of portfolio assessment are self-evaluation and reflection, which are particularly necessary for the gifted learner.

Student Self-Evaluation

Being gifted is like
. . . being a leader and a follower all at the same time.
having the world to yourself.
sticking out like a sore thumb.
being a Ruffles in a bag of Fritos.
opening the doors that others cannot.
—6th-Grade Gifted Students (Hunt, 1984)

Gifted students need to reflect on who they are academically and personally. Academic self-assessing can be done through portfolios, individual learning contracts, rubrics, checklists, learning logs, journals, and conferences between both peers and teachers. Individually and personally, gifted students need to assess their own learning style, personality type, and learning preferences (e.g., multiple intelligences).

The gifted student must understand his or her own giftedness. A student questionnaire (see Figure 4) lets the gifted student assess him- or herself personally (Schmitz & Galbraith, 1985). The Piers-Harris Children's Self-Concept Scale (Piers, 1984) can be another way that the gifted student can reflect on him- or herself. Teachers of the gifted are responsible for guiding these students in self-assessment and helping them find resources.

Dear Students,

This questionnaire is about you—and I'd like you to fill it out so I can be a better teacher for this class. There are no "right" or "wrong" answers. The most important thing is to think honestly about the questions. You may remain anonymous if you wish and choose to skip some of the questions. But, try answering them all—you'll get more out of the exercise if you do. All answers will be kept strictly confidential, although we'll be talking about some of these questions later on as a group.

A. Demographics

- your age _____   • your gender _____

- number of years in a gifted program or class
  (please circle one) 0   1   2   3   4   5   6   more

B. Questions You May Already Be Asking Yourself

1. What does gifted mean to you? _____

2. How do you feel about the label? _____

3. How were you selected for this class or program? _____

4. How do you feel about the selection process? _____

5. What do you think the purpose of this class/program is?

_____ I don't know	_____	Learn something new
_____ Harder work than other classes	_____	Be stimulated to try new things
_____ More work than other classes	_____	Nothing different
_____ More challenging or interesting work		from other classes
_____ Friendships with people like me	_____	Other (write it down)
_____ Place to have fun		_____
_____ Place where I'm not considered weird		_____

C. Feelings About Yourself

6. In what ways are you the same as most other kids your age? What things do you have in common? _____

   _____

7. In what ways are you different from most other kids your age? What makes you unique?

   _____

   _____

8. In terms of popularity . . . (check one)

   _____   I have no close friends
   _____   I have one or two close friends
   _____   I have several (four or five) close friends
   _____   I have lots of close friends
   _____   I have tons of close friends and am liked by most everybody

   continued on the next page

9. In terms of how you feel about yourself . . . (check one)

_____ I hate myself
_____ I don't like myself much
_____ I like parts of myself, but dislike other parts
_____ I feel okay about myself
_____ Most of the time, I like myself a lot
_____ I've always liked myself a whole lot

10. If there's one thing you'd like to change about yourself, it would be: _____

_____

11. The best thing about you, as far as you're concerned, is: _____

_____

D. Conflicts

12. Indicate how often you experience the following feelings or problems by circling 1, 2, 3, 4, or 5, based on this scale: 1 = not at all; 2 = hardly ever; 3 = sometimes; 4 = a lot; 5 = all the time

Feeling or Problem   How Frequently Felt?

   a. I wonder what gifted means.   1 2 3 4 5
   b. I wonder why they say I'm gifted, and what is expected of me.   1 2 3 4 5
   c. School is too easy, boring.   1 2 3 4 5
   d. Parents, teachers, and friends expect me to be perfect all the time. 1 2 3 4 5
   e. Friends who really understand me are hard to find.   1 2 3 4 5
   f. Kids often tease me about being smart (or for being
       interested in certain things, getting high grades, etc.).   1 2 3 4 5
   g. I feel overwhelmed by the number of things
       I can understand or do.   1 2 3 4 5
   h. I feel different, alienated, alone.   1 2 3 4 5
   i. I worry about world problems, or problems in my family,
       and feel helpless to do anything about these problems.   1 2 3 4 5

13. What's your biggest problem or difficulty in life right now? _____

_____

14. Generally, how do you feel about your life? (Make a slash somewhere along the continuum.)

|—————————————————————————————————|

Feel extremely bad, upset,   Feel really great,
worried; think about dying.   confident, happy.

E. Support Systems

15. Who do you share your feelings or problems with when you're wondering what life is all about or who you are? Who do you go to—or like to be around—when things aren't so great? (Check all that apply.)

_____	friend	_____	school counselor
_____	mother	_____	camp counselor
_____	father	_____	official Big Brother or Big Sister
_____	sister	_____	other grown-up (neighbor)
_____	brother	_____	teacher
_____	other relative	_____	I prefer being alone
_____	pet (dog, cat)	_____	I don't think about that kind
_____	coach		of stuff
_____	clergy		

16. What do you do to feel good about yourself?

_____	think or study hard	_____	earn some extra money
_____	get some exercise (get on my bike, go for a run, head for the gym, dance)	_____	get outdoors and go somewhere (shopping, park)
		_____	watch TV
_____	call up a friend on the phone	_____	talk to my parents
_____	write in a journal	_____	talk to my teacher
_____	paint or do other artwork or crafts	_____	listen to music
		_____	eat
_____	play an instrument	_____	use relaxation techniques
_____	work on a project (club, play, newspaper)		(yoga, meditation)
		_____	other (please write it down)
_____	play harder in sports	_____	

17. And, finally, if you could get this class/program to do or provide **one thing** for you, it would be: _____

_____

• name (optional): _____

Figure 4. Example of a student questionnaire

Note. From _Managing the Social and Emotional Needs of the Gifted_ (p. 47), by C. Schmitz and J. Galbraith, 1985, Minneapolis, MN: Free Spirit. Copyright ©1985 by Free Spirit. Reprinted with permission.

Galbraith and Delisle (1996) found that gifted students can take charge of their education, are responsible for their own performance, and are competent and capable of assessing their educational options. Teachers may pose the following questions to gifted students:

1. Is the work in most of your classes too easy for you?
2. Is one specific subject too easy?
3. Do you have a special interest that isn't taught by any teachers: Astronomy? Paleontology? Chinese? Computer networks?
4. Have you taken most of the courses required for graduation and you're only a sophomore?

5. Are you planning on going to college? Do you want a head start?
6. Do you find you need more uninterrupted work time for projects that interest you?
7. Do you wish there were more gifted students in your classes?
8. Do you want to work independently more often?
9. Is there someone in your community you'd like to spend time with and learn from? (p. 158)

The teacher of the gifted and the student need to work together to find coursework, program options, and resources to answer these questions. Many schools offer a variety of possibilities to make school more meaningful and enjoyable for the gifted student. Some options to consider are shown in Figure 5.

It has finally dawned on me that if the system won't change, it's up to me to make my classes more interesting. Now, as a result of learning to do things differently, I can honestly say school is really looking up! All the action feels good—I'm having fun. I've realized I have more opportunities and choices available to me than most kids, all I have to do is go get them.
—Janice, 15 (Galbraith & Delisle, 1996, p. 148)

The Teacher of the Gifted

To meet gifted students' psychological and social/emotional needs successfully, the teacher must develop a nurturing and positive environment. He or she is the key to establishing a supportive atmosphere where self-esteem can grow. A supportive environment is characterized by a general air of acceptance, confidence, mutual support, respect for effort, and reduction of tension and anxiety in the learning interaction. The effective teacher is involved with the dissemination of knowledge and becomes the facilitator in enhancing the students' self-esteem. Building a nonthreatening environment includes a harmonious relationship among the students where all feel accepted and are encouraged to work together, help one another, and learn from each other. "Gifted students strengthen the inner locus of control by continuous encounters with the intrinsic values in learning from their own interests or from real need" (Clark, 2002, p. 413). The gifted classroom needs to be a safe haven, a place where students can express their fears and dreams. The teacher must create an environment where gifted students learn to be considerate of others and accept their own social responsibilities in order to release their potential for self-fulfillment.

Characteristics and Competencies of Teachers of the Gifted

As an educator of gifted students, it is the teacher's obligation to meet not only the cognitive needs of these children, but their affective needs, as well.

Enrichment in the classroom	A differentiated program of study is provided by the classroom teacher within the regular classroom without assistance from an outside resource or consultant.
Consultant-teacher program	Differentiated instruction is provided within the classroom by the classroom teacher with the assistance of a specially trained consultant teacher who provides extra materials and teaches small groups of children in the regular classroom.
Resource room/ pull-out	Gifted students leave the classroom on a regular basis for differentiated instruction provided by a specially trained teacher.
Interest classes	Students volunteer for challenging classes on topics beyond or outside the regular curriculum.
Community mentor program	Gifted students interact on an individual basis with selected members of the community for an extended time period on a topic of special interest to the student.
Independent study program	Differentiated instruction consists of independent study projects supervised by a qualified teacher or mentor.
Special class	Gifted students are grouped together for most of the day and receive instruction from a specially trained teacher.
Special school	Gifted students receive differentiated instruction in a specialized school established for that purpose.
Magnet school	A school is established that focuses on specific areas. Students with interest in a particular area are encouraged to volunteer for these programs even if they are outside the students' own neighborhood school.
Summer program	Enrichment or fast paced summer programs that attract gifted students in art, mathematics, or general programs.
Acceleration	Allows you to move to a higher level of class work, skip a class, or entire grades.
Advanced Placement	AP classes are college-level courses taught in high schools by trained high school teachers. Provides a greater challenge and college credit.
Early college entrance	Entrance into college, usually at end of the junior year, because of high grades and ACT/SAT scores.
Dual enrollment	Students take college courses while they are enrolled in high school. This is sometimes available in special summer programs.

Figure 5. Program options

From *Teaching the Gifted Child* (p. 89), by J. Gallagher and S. Gallagher, 1994, Boston: Allyn and Bacon. Copyright ©1994 by Allyn and Bacon. Adapted with permission. *Gifted Kid's Survival Guide: A Teen Handbook.* (pp. 158–166), by J. Galbraith and J. R. Delisle, 1996, Minneapolis, MN: Free Spirit. Copyright ©1996 by Free Spirit. Adapted with permission.

Programs for the gifted cannot achieve excellence without teachers who possess personal characteristics and competencies to meet those needs. The characteristics, behaviors, and attitudes of effective teachers of the gifted shape the learning environment. Roeper (1997) called upon educators of the gifted to "create an environment which allows the blossoming of the *Self*" (p. 1).

Research by Hansen and Feldhusen (1994) has suggested that teachers who are trained in gifted education will develop skills deemed necessary by experts to teach gifted students effectively. When compared to teachers not educated in gifted education, trained teachers showed an appreciation for giftedness, were flexible and highly intelligent, and showed the capacity to meet gifted students' personal and social needs.

Johnsen (1991, pp. 7–12) listed a set of 11 competencies that support the various roles a teacher of the gifted might assume, 4 of which directly pertain to developing the psychological and social/emotional environment:

1. understands the characteristics of gifted students and the influence of these characteristics on their educational, psychological, and sociological development;
2. understands strategies for modifying or designing learning experiences for gifted/talented students appropriate for nurturing creative and critical thinking;
3. understands the effect of the interaction of various environmental and personality characteristics on the social/emotional development of gifted students and strategies for addressing these effects; and
4. understands program models and how these models adapt for gifted students.

Gifted students know what characteristics they want in a teacher of the gifted. According to Galbraith (1983), gifted students want teachers who are flexible, have a good sense of humor, do not expect perfection, are willing to help, make learning fun and use resources other than the textbook, understand the pluses and minuses of giftedness, are inspiring, and do not pretend to know everything.

The Role of the Teacher of the Gifted

Once in the classroom, the role of the teacher is one of providing differentiation to meet the cognitive and affective needs of gifted students. Silverman (1993) referred to the unique role of the teacher of the gifted as one that meets the psychological counseling needs of these students. Trained counselors with in-depth knowledge of gifted children's needs are in short supply; therefore, it is imperative that teachers of the gifted have special training to meet the affective development of these students (p. 181). Teachers of the gifted, in their role as teacher/counselor, need the following strengths:

1. awareness of the unique social and emotional needs of the gifted;
2. training in effective intervention techniques with gifted students;
3. sensitivity to affective issues;
4. availability to handle psychological issues daily in the classroom;
5. training to translate assessment information into program options; and
6. familiarity with gifted individuals who could serve as role models.

The teacher of the gifted has a wide spectrum of responsibilities to enhance the psychological and social/emotional environment of the classroom. He or she is a facilitator of learning, a model, a mentor, a collaborator, and a lifelong learner. To create a secure and positive environment for the gifted learner, the educator must collaborate with and gain the support of regular classroom teachers, counselors, administrators, parents, and the community. Only after these individuals are educated about gifted learners can a substantive and well-coordinated environment be established.

Counseling Needs of the Gifted Learner

The emotional aspects of giftedness lead to concerns about meeting the gifted learners' psychological and social/emotional needs. Silverman (1993) stated that "giftedness has an emotional as well as cognitive substructure: cognitive complexity gives rise to emotional depth" (p. 3). Not only do gifted learners think differently, but they also feel differently. Silverman has defined giftedness in a way that highlights the gifted student's internal experience:

> Giftedness is asynchronous development in which advanced cognitive abilities and heightened intensity combine to create inner experiences and awareness that are qualitatively different from the norm. This asynchrony increases with higher intellectual capacity. The uniqueness of the gifted renders them particularly vulnerable and requires modifications in parenting, teaching, and counseling in order for them to develop optimally. (p. 3)

While the gifted child's intellectual or academic achievements may be more like those of older children or adults, his or her physical, psychomotor, and emotional development may be age-appropriate. This lack of synchronicity creates greater inner tension and may affect children by making them feel "out of sync" (feeling that they are different or that they do not, should not, or cannot fit in) or "out of phase" (alienated and distant from a peer group with which to interact; Silverman, 1993). The unique role of the teacher of the gifted is to meet some of the psychosocial counseling needs of these students. When the teacher acts as a teacher/counselor, there are multiple advantages to the student:

1. The gifted student can receive counseling assistance in the context of the regular classroom or specialized gifted setting, rather than being "taken out" for one or more type of activity.
2. The gifted student can begin to perceive his or her program as holistic, not segmented by concerns for affective issues separate from cognitive ones.
3. The gifted student can discuss common interests and problems in a small group of gifted peers with an adult who knows the student in another context.
4. The gifted student can receive reinforcement and encouragement on an ongoing basis, rather than postponing it until a special appointment has been made (Silverman, p. 182).

Some counseling needs can be met by the teacher of the gifted who is aware of the special affective needs of the gifted learner:

1. understanding one's differences, yet recognizing one's similarities to others;
2. understanding how to accept and give criticism;
3. being tolerant of oneself and others;
4. developing an understanding of one's strengths and weaknesses; and
5. developing skills in areas that will nurture both cognitive and affective development (Silverman, 1993, p. 182).

Strategies that teachers may use to address the social and emotional needs of the gifted learner include role-playing, tutorials, mentorships, internships, bibliotherapy, discussion groups, special projects, simulation, gaming, special interest clubs, skill development seminars, and career exploration (Silverman, 1993). These strategies can be used for preventive counseling.

However, a cautionary note needs to be addressed. Teachers of the gifted who do not have training in counseling should be instructed in counselor/client ethics, particularly in regard to confidentiality. Teachers should be aware of all district policies related to counseling students. Noncounselor educators without training in counseling should seek advice from counselors, take coursework in counseling, and attend conferences in order to gain knowledge about appropriate strategies and techniques. Teachers must realize their limitations in this important domain and be ready to recommend professional counseling for students with serious emotional problems.

Until trained professionals are available, though, teachers of the gifted are responsible for meeting their students' emotional needs; therefore, it is important to know the essential elements of good counseling. Effective counselors ask pertinent questions, listen well, give honest feedback, sincerely respect the client and his or her problems, and enable the client to share deep feelings by providing a safe, confidential, nonjudgmental atmosphere (Silverman, 1993). Because teachers of the gifted understand the special needs of the gifted and have established a trust relationship, gifted students may be willing to participate openly. One student put it this way:

> It is nothing more than having a person here to talk with who has dealt exclusively with people who are similar to you—not with the whole student body. That seems to be the key to having enough trust to let down the guard and be real. (Silverman, p. 126)

Behavior and Classroom Management

Even though we're gifted, we still are human. We can make mistakes. No matter how smart we are supposed to be, inside we are just like everyone else.
—Matt, 12 (Schmitz & Galbraith, 1985, p. 21)

Behavior

The teacher of the gifted needs to know characteristics of gifted students, understand behavior, become proactive, set goals for positive behavior, build feelings of self-worth in students, use effective listening skills, and create an environment where the teacher and students can express ideas and feelings openly. Again, a responsive social/emotional environment eliminates many behavioral problems through determining rules and guidelines together, basing instruction on individual's needs and interests, giving students choices, sharing responsibility, being flexible, encouraging independence, and showing acceptance for differences.

Probably the most helpful advice when dealing with behavior management is to know the characteristics of gifted students. Lovecky (1992) described five social/emotional traits common to gifted students: divergent thinking ability, excitability, sensitivity, perceptiveness, and entelechy. Each one of these traits brings with it some behavior problems that need to be addressed by the teacher of the gifted.

Divergent thinkers prefer the unusual, original, and creative aspects of any topic. These students ask a lot of questions and march to a different drummer. Negative behaviors can be expressed through rebellion, inattentiveness, disorganization, refusal to participate in group work, and social ineptness. The teacher can use positive techniques to let them see the value in their uniqueness: give them creative outlets in their work, help them find someone who shares their ideas, and teach them organization and social skills.

The trait of excitability is expressed through high levels of energy, long concentration spans on topics of interest, powerful emotions, and the desire to take risks. Behavioral problems include inattentiveness to routine tasks, silliness, disruptive behavior (class clown), and extreme competitiveness. In this case, the teacher can use stress reduction, self-control, and self-pacing techniques. Creative problem solving through group dynamics is also valuable.

Sensitivity is a trait that is expressed through great passion (depth of feelings that color life experiences) and compassion (sense of caring for others, intense commitment to others). Problems arise for the teacher when the student withdraws from situations and people. The teacher can help the student understand the difference between empathy and sympathy and the difference between selfishness and asserting one's self.

The awareness of fairness, truth, and justice are traits of perceptiveness. Gifted students have clear values; they see truth as more important than feelings, and they are puzzled by those who do not understand. Negative behaviors result in intolerance of others, expectations of adults to practice what they preach, and fear of making wrong choices. The teacher can help gifted students see the limits of people and problems through teaching coping, compromise, and negotiation strategies. Empathy can be taught through studying the viewpoints of others.

Entelechy is expressed through traits of self-motivation, self-determination, high goal structure, and personal courage. The problems that arise with this trait are unwillingness to compromise, single-mindedness, and rebelliousness. Again, the teacher of these students can help by finding an adult mentor or a true friend, showing students how to use their strengths in positive ways, and letting them see both sides of an issue (Lovecky, 1992). Being aware of the traits and other characteristics of gifted students will make behavior management more viable for the teacher of the gifted.

Classroom Management

Classroom management is discussed in terms of two elements: the management of the "business" of the classroom and classroom discipline. Both of these elements are extremely important in a responsive learning environment. The management of learning must be designed with clear objectives in mind. Generally accepted objectives for gifted learners are

1. students will be able to learn at their own level;
2. students will be able to learn at their own pace; and
3. students will be able to assume responsibility for their own learning.

For these objectives to be achieved, a management plan for instruction and a plan for the physical layout of the classroom must be designed. These objectives provide the guidelines teachers need to plan the physical environment. By using strategies such as independent study projects, contracts, group investigations, and research projects, students can work with self-selected material at their own ability levels and be able to move at their own pace. As they plan their projects, they take on the responsibility for their own learning. The teacher, as facilitator, must provide the tools for recordkeeping, progress reports, and deadlines. Teachers can purchase preexisting commercial management plans, such as the Management Plan for Individual and Small Group Investigations (Renzulli & Reis, 1997), or they can easily design their own. Items should include steps in the investigation, resources needed, ideas for a final product, and potential audiences. Other items that are appropriate for the project or are needed to meet the teacher's goals can be added.

In the classroom, resources should be readily available and clearly labeled. Office letter boxes and trays provide both accessibility and organization. Art supplies and activities should be located in an area where they can be stored and used. Study carrels and small-group study areas should be provided. Reference materials should be easily accessible and located. In and out boxes for assignments, questions, or requests should be provided. The overall layout of the room should be planned carefully for traffic flow to avoid distraction. In short, the room should be designed as a learning laboratory. It should be designed for the accomplishment of learning tasks and for student comfort.

The second element of classroom management is classroom discipline. Problems in classroom discipline will be minimized if appropriate, challenging learning activities are provided for gifted learners. However, it is important to delineate clear expectations for students, which become the basis of classroom management. Charles (1996) suggested that a helpful way to view discipline is to see it as having three faces: (1) preventive, (2) supportive, and (3) corrective. If a careful program of preventive discipline has been designed, then the needs for both supportive and corrective discipline are diminished. Charles offered the following suggestions for preventive discipline:

1. make the curriculum as worthwhile and enjoyable as possible;
2. remain the ultimate authority in the classroom;
3. with the students, create good rules for class conduct; and
4. continually emphasize good manners and abidance by the Golden Rule (p. 226).

Suggestions for supportive discipline include

1. use signals directed to a student needing support;
2. use physical proximity when signals are ineffective;
3. restructure difficult work or provide help;
4. inject humor into lessons that have become tiring;
5. remove seductive objects;
6. acknowledge good behavior in appropriate ways at appropriate times; and
7. request good behavior (p. 227).

Suggestions for corrective discipline are

1. stop the misbehavior;
2. invoke a consequence appropriate to the misbehavior;

3. follow through consistently;
4. redirect misbehavior in positive directions; and
5. be ready to invoke an insubordination rule (p. 228).

Each teacher must ultimately design his or her own personalized system of discipline. There is little need for corrective discipline when gifted learners are challenged, engaged in appropriate learning activities, allowed to assume responsibility for their own learning, and have the freedom to follow their own academic interests.

Grouping Strategies

> *I like working with bunches of brains.*
> —6th-Grade Girl (Hunt, 1994, p. 150)

Ability grouping or homogeneous grouping has positive academic and social effects for the gifted, according to extensive research by Rogers (1991). In homogeneous classes, the gifted student faces mutual reinforcement of enthusiasm for academics or areas of interest. Kulik and Kulik (1982, 1987) found homogeneously grouped high-ability students, when compared to heterogeneously grouped high-ability students, did better academically and had a better attitude toward the subject. Hunt (1994), in a study of gifted 6th-grade mathematics students, found that the gifted in homogeneous groups had higher postachievement than gifted students in heterogeneous groups, completed more differentiated activities, and preferred working alone or in homogeneous groups in mathematics. VanTassel-Baska (1992) stated, "The greater the commitment to serving gifted students, the greater the acceptance of advancing and grouping them appropriately" (p. 68).

Flexible grouping where gifted students are separated for part of the day or for particular classes is probably more acceptable and more effective overall. Flexible, homogeneous grouping provides peer stimulation, supports skill development, and meets specific cognitive and affective needs. Heterogeneous grouping develops social skills, introduces new experiences of information needed by the whole class, and builds a community of learners (Clark, 2002).

> Among our goals must be providing experiences for individuals to continue their own educational progress and to learn from others, to meet their personal needs and to understand the needs of others, to learn to be independent and self-reliant and to have the skills of working with others. (Clark, pp. 271)

There are key characteristics when forming groups: composition, size, cohesion, and level of structure (Silverman, 1993). When working with groups of students (especially adolescents), the composition is important for success. By using interest inventories, learning style inventories, and test results, the teacher can blend personalities from knowledge of individual strengths and weaknesses (see Teachers Resources).

It is important not to form groups of only highly aggressive, uncommunicative, or creatively gifted students. The size of the group is also important, usually three to five students per group (decision making is more effective when there are odd numbers). The togetherness or cohesion of the group is the "psychological glue" (Blocher, 1987, cited in Silverman, 1993). The use of activities that enhance self-disclosure among members leads to successful groups. Letting students select a group name gives another level of mutual bonding. The feeling of solidarity creates an ambiance to the social/emotional and physical environment. Finally, the flexible structure approach to grouping allows different groups to be formed. Highly structured groups might be created for academics, while natural-forming groups are created for discussions and problems dealing with the students' social/emotional needs. Remember, groups are not successful unless social skills are modeled and taught by the teacher.

Summary

Leta Hollingworth believed that life was very precious, talent was a blessing to be nurtured and shared for the good of others, and that people were to be cherished and helped.

—M. C. T. Overton (Silverman, 1990, p. 172)

In this chapter, the most appropriate learning environment for gifted students has been defined as a flexible environment that allows learners to pursue educational requirements and interests in-depth and with a minimum of time limitation. The importance of recognizing the diversity among gifted learners and modifying for their various needs has been discussed in terms of both the physical and social/emotional environments. It has been noted that modifications of the environment facilitate the curricular modifications that make learning appropriately differentiated for gifted students. Each aspect of the environment has been discussed in terms of the contributions of both gifted learners and teachers of the gifted. This chapter has also emphasized the key role of the teacher in designing and maintaining a safe and nurturing environment for gifted learners. Various guidelines, models, strategies, and resources have been suggested to guide the teacher in designing the appropriate learning and social/emotional environment for gifted students. Hollingworth articulated an important attitude in establishing the learning environment for gifted learners by emphasizing that we cherish these individuals and support them in their journeys to realize their full potential and to discover their true and unique selves.

Teacher Statement

As a teacher of the gifted, I have become a CEO or a "coordinator of educational opportunities." The majority of my work is done outside of class in the preparation of materials and resources with the correlation of learning styles to process skills and content areas. Actual class time is spent directing and monitoring students in the expansion of their interest areas.

The gifted classroom is a protective environment where students feel a definite ownership and a sense of belonging. Problems can be addressed in a round-table discussion where constructive criticism is accepted and resolutions of conflict are practiced. With the use of various activities, students develop social skills and emotional maturity. In this classroom, students gain a better understanding of their giftedness and style of learning, which prepares them to handle the expectations of themselves and others.

Educational challenges in the gifted classroom must exceed those of the regular classroom with the provision of various audiences, guidelines, and evaluations. Here, students expand their areas of interests and engage in problem-solving activities while refining skills en route to the completion of a product. The knowledge that I have gained through this textbook and this chapter has added to my expertise as a teacher of the gifted.

—Melinda Brown

Discussion Questions

1. In what ways will modifying the learning environment meet the cognitive, psychological, and social/emotional needs of the gifted learner?

2. How does Clark's Responsive Learning Environment Checklist optimize learning for gifted learners?

3. How do the characteristics and social/emotional traits of gifted learners affect classroom management both positively and negatively?

4. As a teacher of the gifted, what elements of academic planning will you implement in order to create the optimal learning environment?

5. What program options for gifted learners are most adaptable to your school environment? Explain your choice(s).

6. Explain how understanding one's own giftedness is tied to self-evaluation.

7. How can you as a teacher of the gifted learner encourage risk-taking? Why is this so important?

8. How are peers like life preservers in the asynchronous development of the gifted child?

Teacher Resources

Publications

American Association for Gifted Children. (1978). *On being gifted.* Reston, VA: Author.

Bennis, W., & Nanus, B. (1985). *Leaders: The strategies for taking charge.* New York: Harper & Row.

Brophy, J. E. (1979). Teacher behavior and student learning. *Educational Leadership, 37,* 33–38.

Brown, B. (1990). Peer group and peer cultures. In S. Shirley Feldman & G. R. Elliott (Eds.), *At the threshold: The developing adolescent* (pp. 171–197). Cambridge, MA: Harvard University Press.

Burke, K., Fogarty, R., & Belgard, S. (1994). *The portfolio connection.* Palatine, IL: Skylight.

Butler, K. A. (1987). *Learning and teaching style in theory and practice.* Columbia, CT: The Learner's Dimension.

Butler, K. A. (1988). *It's all in your mind.* Columbia, CT: The Learner's Dimension.

Butterfield, S. M., Kaplan, S. N., Meeker, M., Renzulli, J. S., Smith, L. S., & Treffinger, D. (1979). *Developing IEP's for the gifted/talented.* Ventura, CA: Office of Ventura County Superintendent of Schools.

Charles, C. (1996). *Building classroom discipline.* White Plains, NY: Longman.

Coleman, J. (1980). Friendship and peer group in adolescence. In J. Adelson (Ed.), *Handbook of adolescent psychology* (pp. 408–431). New York: Wiley.

Corey, G. (1990). *Theory and practice of group counseling* (3rd ed.). Pacific Grove, CA: Brooks/Cole.

Covey, S. R. (1989). *The seven habits of highly effective people.* New York: Simon & Schuster.

Crosby, N., & Marten, E. (1981). *Discovering psychology.* Buffalo, NY: D.O.K.

Curwin, R. L., & Mendler, A. N. (1988). *Discipline with dignity.* Rochester, NY: Association for Supervision and Curriculum Development.

Delisle, J. R. (1987). *Gifted kids speak out: Hundreds of kids ages 6–13 talk about school, friends, their families, and future.* Minneapolis, MN: Free Spirit.

Delisle, J., & Galbraith, J. (1987). *The gifted kids survival guide II: A special to the original gifted kids survival guide (for ages 11–18).* Minneapolis, MN: Free Spirit.

Dunn, R., Dunn, K., & Price, G. E. (1985). *Learning style inventory.* Lawrence, KS: Price Systems.

Farris, D. (1991). *Type tales.* Palo Alto, CA: Consulting Psychologists Press.

Galbraith, J. (1983). *The gifted kids survival guide (for ages 11–18).* Minneapolis, MN: Free Spirit.

Galbraith, J., & Delisle, J. (1996). *The gifted kids' survival guide: A teen handbook* (Rev. ed.). Minneapolis, MN: Free Spirit.

Gazda, G. M. (1989). *Group counseling: A developmental approach* (3rd ed.). Needham Heights, MA: Allyn and Bacon.

Gregorc, A. (1979). Learning/teaching styles: Their nature and effects. *Educational Leadership 36,* 234–237.

Halsted, J. (1988*). Guiding gifted readers from pre-school to high school: A handbook for parents, teachers, counselors, and librarians.* Columbus: Ohio Psychology Press.

Hart, D. (1994). *Authentic assessment.* Menlo Park, CA: Addison-Wesley.

Hooker, D., & Gallagher, R. (1984). *I am gifted, creative, & talented.* New York: Educational Design.

Jensen, E. (2000). *Brain-based learning.* San Diego, CA: The Brain Store.

Johnson, D. W., & Johnson, F. P. (1987). *Joining together: Group theory and group skills* (3rd ed.). Englewood Cliffs, NJ: Prentice Hall.

Karnes, F. A., & Bean, S. M. (2004). *Process skills rating scales–Revised.* Waco, TX: Prufrock Press.

Karnes, F. A., & Bean, S. M. (1993). *Girls and young women leading the way: 20 true stories about leadership.* Minneapolis, MN: Free Spirit.

Karnes, F. A., & Bean, S. M. (1995). *Leadership for students: A practical guide for ages 8–18.* Waco, TX: Prufrock Press.

Keirsey D., & Bates, M. (1978). *Please understand me: Character and temperament types.* Del Mar, CA: Prometheus Nemesis.

Kerr, B. A. (1994). *Smart girls* (Rev. ed.). Scottsdale, AZ: Gifted Psychology Press.

Kincher, J. (1995). *Psychology for kids II: 40 fun experiments that help you learn about others.* Minneapolis, MN: Free Spirit.

Kulik, J. A. (1991). Findings on grouping are often distorted. *Educational Leadership, 46*(6), 67.

Lawrence, G. (1982*). People types and tiger stripes: A practical guide to learning styles* (2nd ed.). Gainesville, FL: Center for Applications of Psychological Type.

McCarthy, B. (1981). *The 4 MAT System: Teaching to learning styles with right/left mode techniques.* Barrington, IL: Excel.

Madigan, M. M. (1977). *Philosophers: A source guide for self-directed units.* Tucson, AZ: Zephyr Press.

Maker, J., & Neilson, A. (1996). *Curriculum development and teaching strategies for gifted learners* (2nd ed.). Austin, TX: PRO-ED.

Meisgeier, C., & Murphy, E. (1987). *Murphy-Meisgeier type indicator for children.* Palo Alto, CA: Consulting Psychologists Press.

Myers, I. B., & Myers, P. B. (1980). *Gifts differing: Understanding personality type.* Palo Alto, CA: Davies-Black.

Pedersen, P. (1988). *A handbook for developing multicultural awareness.* Alexandria, VA: America Counseling Association.

Porter, A., & Brophy, J. (1988). Synthesis of research on good teaching. *Educational Leadership, 45*(8), 74–85.

Purkey, W. W., & Novak, J. (1984). *Inviting school success: A self-concept approach to teaching and learning* (2nd ed.). Belmont, CA: Wadsworth.

Purkey, W. W., & Schmidt, J. J. (1987). *The inviting relationship: An expanded perspective for professional counseling.* Englewood Cliffs, NJ: Prentice Hall.

Purkey, W. W., & Stanley, P. H. (1991). *Invitational teaching, learning, and living.* Washington, DC: National Education Association.

Reis, S. M., Burns, D. E., & Renzulli, J. S. (1992). *Curriculum compacting: The complete guide to modifying the regular curriculum for high ability students.* Mansfield Center, CT: Creative Learning Press.

Renzulli, J., & Smith, L. H. (1978). *Learning styles inventory.* Mansfield Center, CT: Creative Learning Press.

Rogers, K. (1991). *The relationship of grouping practices to the education of the gifted and talented learner.* Report to National Research Center on the Gifted and Talented, University of Connecticut, Storrs.

Rogers, K. (2002). *Re-forming gifted education: How parents and teachers can match the program to the child.* Scottsdale, AZ: Great Potential Press.

Sattler, J. M. (1988). *Assessment of children's intelligence and special abilities* (3rd ed.). San Diego, CA: Sattler.

Schmitz, C. C., & Galbraith, J. (1985). *Managing the social and emotional needs of the gifted: A teacher's survival guide.* Minneapolis, MN: Free Spirit.

Scott, G. G. (1990). *Resolving conflicts with others and with yourself.* Oakland, CA: New Harbringer.

Seeley, A. E. (1994). *Portfolio assessment.* Westminster, CA: Teacher Created Materials.

Torrance, P., McCarthy, B., & Kolesinski, M. (1988*). Style of learning and thinking (SOLAT).* Bensenville, IL: Scholastic Testing Services.

Webb, J. T., & Meckstroth, J. T. (1982*). Guiding the gifted child.* Scottsdale, AZ: Gifted Psychology Press.

Wilt, J. (1980). *A kid's guide to making friends.* Waco, TX: Educational Product Division, Word.

Yalom, I. D. (1985). *The theory and practice of group psychotherapy* (3rd ed.). New York: Basic Books.

Addresses

Myers-Briggs Type Indicator
Consulting Psychologists Press, Inc.
3803 E. Bayshore Rd.
Palo Alto, CA 94303

Web Sites

America's Promise—http://www.americaspromise.org
The Alliance for Youth ensures access to the five fundamental resources necessary to enable young people to maximize their potential, live the American dream, and give back to society.

Amnesty International—http://www.amnesty.org
This site contains news, information, campaigns, library, and links.

Center for World Dialogue—http://www.worlddialogue.org
This site initiates dialogue on political, social, economic, and religious issues of global and regional concern.

Creativity & Spirit Chronicles–http://www.hopeandhealing.com
This site addresses the need to be aware of creativity in fostering a positive learning environment and celebrating the spirit.

Fund for Peace—http://www.fundforpeace.org
This site promotes education and research on global problems that threaten human survival and proposes practical solutions.

International Baccalaureate Organization—http://www.ibo.org
This site gives the history of the program, samples of curricula, a profile of the student, and opportunities for the program nationally and internationally.

Institute for Global Communications—http://www.igc.org/igc
IGC's five online communities of activists and organizations are gateways to articles, headlines, features, and Web links on progressive issues.

International Peace Bureau—http://www.ipb.org
This is the world's oldest international peace federation.

New Horizon for Learning–http://www.newhorizons.org
This site is a leading resource for educational change through research from advisory boards, neuroscience, cognitive sciences, human development, and learning.

Search for Common Ground—http://www.sfcg.org
This site seeks workable solutions to divisive national and international conflicts.

References

Blocher, D. H. (1987). *The professional counselor.* New York: Macmillan.

Burke, K., Fogarty, R., & Belgrad, S. (1994). *The mindful school: The portfolio connection.* Palatine, IL: IRI/Skylight.

Charles, C. (1996). *Building classroom discipline.* White Plains, NY: Longman.

Clark, B. (2002). *Growing up gifted* (6th ed.). Upper Saddle River, NJ: Merrill/Prentice Hall.

Galbraith, J. (1983). *The gifted kids survival guide (for ages 11–18).* Minneapolis, MN: Free Spirit.

Galbraith, J. (1985). The eight great gripes of gifted kids: Responding to special needs. *Roeper Review, 8,* 15–18

Galbraith, J., & Delisle, J. R. (1996*). The gifted kid's survival guide: A teen handbook.* Minneapolis, MN: Free Spirit.

Gallagher, J., & Gallagher, S. (1994). *Teaching the gifted child.* Boston: Allyn and Bacon.

Gallagher, S. (1990). Personality patterns of the gifted. *Understanding Our Gifted, 3*(1), 1–13.

Griggs, S., & Dunn, R. (1984). Selected case studies of the learning style preferences of gifted students. *Gifted Child Quarterly, 28,* 115–119.

Hansen, J., & Feldhusen, J. (1994). Comparison of trained and untrained teachers of gifted students. *Gifted Child Quarterly, 38,* 115–121.

Hart, D. (1994). *Authentic assessment: A handbook for educators.* Menlo Park, CA: Addison-Wesley.

Hunt, B. (1984). Analogies of being gifted. *Chart Your Course, 3*(1), 19.

Hunt, B. (1994). The effect of homogeneous and heterogeneous grouping of gifted sixth-grade students on mathematics achievement and attitude (Doctoral dissertation, University of Houston, 1994). *Dissertation Abstracts International,* 9516742.

International Baccalaureate Organization. (n.d.). *International Baccalaureate Organization.* Retrieved January 12, 2004, from http://www.ibo.org

Johnsen, S. (1991, Fall). Excellence in the education of teachers of the gifted and talented. *TAGT Tempo, 9*(4), 6–12.

Kulik, C., & Kulik, J. (1982). Research synthesis on ability grouping. *Educational Research, 39,* 619–621.

Kulik, J., & Kulik, C. (1987). Mastery testing and student learning: A meta-analysis. *Journal of Educational Technology Systems, 15,* 325–345.

Kunkel, M., Chapa, B., Patterson, G., & Walling, D. (1992). Experiences of giftedness: "Eight great gripes" six years later. *Roeper Review, 15,* 10–13.

Lovecky, D. (1992). Exploring social and emotional aspects of giftedness in children. *Roeper Review, 15,* 18–25.

Maker, C., & Nielson, A. (1996). *Curriculum development and teaching strategies for gifted learners* (2nd ed.). Austin, TX: PRO-ED.

Mississippi State Department of Education. (1995*). Suggested teaching strategies for teachers of the intellectually gifted.* Jackson: Office of Gifted Education Programs.

Mönks, F., & Peters, W. (1992). *Talent for the future: Social and personality development of gifted children. Proceedings of the Ninth World Conference on Gifted and Talented Children.* Assen/Maastricht, The Netherlands: Van Gorcum.

Myers, I. B., & McCaulley, M. H. (1985*). Manual: A guide to the development and use of the Myers-Briggs Type Indicator.* Palo Alto, CA: Consulting Psychologists Press.

Paulson, F., Paulson, P., & Meyer, C. (1991, February). What makes a portfolio a portfolio? *Educational Leadership*, 60–63.

Piers, E. V. (1984). *The Piers-Harris children's self-concept scale*. Los Angeles: Western Psychological Services.

Poulsen, S. (1997). What if . . . teachers are also learners? *Wingspread Journal, 19*(3) 7–8.

Reis, S. M., Burns, D. E., & Renzulli, J. S. (1992). *Curriculum compacting: The complete guide to modifying the regular curriculum for high ability students*. Mansfield Center, CT: Creative Learning Press.

Renzulli, J. S., & Reis, S. M. (1997). *The schoolwide enrichment model: A how-to guide guide for education excellence* (2nd ed.). Mansfield Center, CT: Creative Learning Press.

Renzulli, J. S., & Smith, L. H. (1978a). *The compactor.* Mansfield Center, CT: Creative Learning Press.

Renzulli, J. S., & Smith, L. H. (1978b). *Strength-a-lyzer.* Mansfield Center, CT: Creative Learning Press.

Roedell, W. (1985). Developing social competence in gifted preschool children. *Remedial and Special Education, 6*(4), 6–11.

Roeper, A. (1997). My hopes and my mission. *NAGC Counseling and Guidance Division Newsletter,* 1–3.

Rogers, K. (1991). *The relationship of grouping practices to the education of gifted and talented learner.* Report to the National Research Center on the Gifted and Talented, University of Connecticut, Storrs.

Schmitz, C., & Galbraith, J. (1985). *Managing the social and emotional needs of the gifted.* Minneapolis, MN: Free Spirit.

Silverman, L. (1989). The visual-spatial learner. *Preventing School Failure, 34*(1), 15–20.

Silverman, L. (1990). Social and emotional education of the gifted: The discoveries of Leta Hollingworth. *Roeper Review, 12,* 171–177.

Silverman, L. (1993). *Counseling the gifted and talented.* Denver: Love.

Silverman, L. K. (2002). *Upside-down brilliance: The visual-spatial learner.* Glendale, CO: DeLeon.

Williams, F. (1982). *Classroom ideas book* (Vol. 2). Buffalo, NY: D.O.K.

VanTassel-Baska, J. (1992). Educational decision making on acceleration and grouping. *Gifted Child Quarterly, 36,* 68–72.

Instructional Planning and Evaluation

An Analysis of Gifted Education Curricular Models

by **Joyce VanTassel-Baska** and **Elissa F. Brown**

uch of gifted education as a field rests on the approaches that are used to serve gifted students in schools and other contexts. Consequently, the importance of programmatic and curricular models cannot be overestimated. The purpose of this chapter is to review systematically existing program/curricular models in the field and to determine the evidence for their use and their effectiveness with gifted populations.

History of Curricular Models

The history of curriculum development for the gifted has been fraught with problems, similar to the general history of curriculum development in this country. Some of the most successful curricular models for gifted learners have been developed based on acceleration principles for advanced secondary students (VanTassel-Baska, 1998, pp. 232–236). Many educators worldwide perceive the International Baccalaureate program and the College Board Advanced Placement program as representing the highest levels of academic attainment available. These programs are thought to provide important stepping stones to successful college work since they constitute the beginning entry levels of such work. Thus, one approach to curriculum development for the gifted may be seen as a "design down" model, where all K–12 curricula are organized to promote readiness for college and the process is both accelerated and shortened along the way for the most apt.

Alternatives to this viewpoint abound, however, and tend to focus on learning beyond or in lieu of traditional academics. Most of the curricular models cited in this chapter ascribe to an enriched view of curriculum development for the gifted, one that addresses a broader conception of giftedness by taking into account principles of creativity, motivation, and independence as crucial constructs to the development of high ability. These enrichment views also tend to see process skills, such as critical thinking and creative problem solving, as central to the learning enterprise, with content choices being more incidental. Evidence of student work through high-quality products and performances is also typically highly valued in these models.

Most of the enrichment-oriented approaches to curriculum development for the gifted emanated from the early work of Leta Hollingworth and her curricular template for New York City self-contained classes. Strongly influenced by Deweyian progressivism, she organized curricular units that allowed students to discover connections about how the world worked and the role of creative people in societal progress by having them study biographies and promoting the role of group learning through discussion about ideas (Hollingworth, 1926). In some respects, contemporary curricular development efforts fall short of Hollingworth's early work in scope, purpose, and delivery.

Accelerative approaches to learning owe much to the work of Terman and Oden (1947), Pressey (1949), and early developers of rapid learning classes that enabled bright students to progress at their own rates. Early educational examples of autodidacticism and tutorials also encouraged a view of learning that promoted independent interest and a self-modulated pace (VanTassel-Baska, 1995). Thus, current curricular models are grounded in a history of research, development, and implementation of both accelerative and enrichment approaches, typically used in self-contained classes since the level of content instruction could be modified based on the group. Chief differentiation approaches, early in the history of this field, incorporated attention to differences between gifted and nongifted populations. One might argue that today's views of differentiation tend to center far more on individual differences among the gifted than on the group difference paradigm for curricula employed both in and out of school.

Definition of a Curricular Model: Subjects for Analysis

One of the issues in the field of gifted education rests with the differences between a program model and a curricular model. Several of the models that were researched in this study could be said to cut both ways: They meet the criteria for a curricular model, but they also work as a broad program framework. Others were clearly developed with curriculum as the organizing principle. The operational definition of a curricular model used was one that had the following components:

- *A framework for curriculum design and development.* The model had to provide a system for developing and designing an appropriate curriculum for the target population. As such, it had to identify elements of such a design and show how these elements interacted in a curricular product.
- *Transferable and usable in all content areas.* The model had to be utilitarian in that it was easily applied to all major areas of school-based learning.
- *K–12 applicability.* The model had to be flexible in respect to the age groups to which it would be applied. The central elements would have to work for kindergarten-age gifted children, as well as high school students.
- *Applicable across schools and grouping settings.* The model had to have relevance in multiple locations and learning settings. It would need to work in tutorials, as well as large classes.
- *Incorporates differentiated features for gifted/talented learners.* The model had to spell out the ways in which it responded to the particular needs of the gifted for curriculum and instruction.

If models met this definition, they were included in this chapter. Obviously, some well-known curricula, such as Man: A Course of Study (MACOS; Bruner, 1970), were excluded because they were not developed with the target population in mind. Other curricular models were excluded because they were focused in only one subject area, such as Philosophy in the Classroom (Lipman, Sharp, & Oscanyan, 1980) or Junior Great Books. Still others were excluded because they were limited to particular grade levels, such as Advanced Placement (AP) or International Baccalaureate (IB). Originally, 20 models were identified and then sifted according to the definitional structure, yielding 11 models for continued analysis.

Criteria Used to Assess Model Effectiveness

At a second stage of the process, we were interested in comparing the selected curricular models according to criteria found in the literature to be important indicators of effectiveness. These criteria, taken together, constituted the basis for yielding the overall effectiveness of the model. The criteria employed were the following:

- *Research evidence to support use (student learning impact).* Studies have been conducted to document the effectiveness of the curriculum with target populations.

- *Application to actual curriculum (products in use).* The model has been translated into teaching segments.
- *Quality of curricular products based on the model.* The curricular products based on the model have been evaluated by appropriate audiences and show evidence of curriculum design features (goals, objectives, activities, assessment, resources).
- *Teacher receptivity.* Teachers have commented positively on the curriculum in implementation.
- *Teacher training component for use of the model.* The model has a defined training package so that practitioners can learn how to implement it.
- *Ease of implementation.* The model shows evidence of feasible implementation.
- *Evidence of application of the model in practice.* The model can be seen employed in various schools.
- *Sustainability.* The model has been in operation in schools for at least 3 years.
- *Systemic (operational in respect to elements, input, output, interactions, and boundaries).* The model is definable as a system.
- *Alignment or relationship to national standards.* The model has a defined relationship to the national content standards (e.g., American Association for the Advancement of Science, 1989, 1993; National Council of Teachers of English & International Reading Association, 1996; National Research Council, 1996).
- *Relationship to school-based core curricula.* The model has a defined relationship to other curricular emphases in schools.
- *Comprehensiveness.* The model applies broadly to all areas and domains of curricula and to all types of gifted learners at all stages of development.
- *Evidence of scope and sequence considerations.* The model has been applied using a progressive development of skills and concepts approach.
- *Longitudinal evidence of effectiveness with gifted students.* The model has evidence of effectiveness over at least 3 years with a given student cohort.
- *Evidence of use in teacher-developed curricula (planning and organizing on paper).* The model shows evidence of being used to organize a new curriculum that is teacher-developed.

Methodology

The approach employed to carry out the study of these curricular models was organized around four phases. Phase I constituted the search for models that fit the definition described. Several comprehensive texts were reviewed for potential models. Moreover, additional searches were made in the broader literature. Once models were selected, Phase II constituted a review of both ERIC and Psychology Abstracts for research and program data about the models published from 1990 onward. It was determined that the models had to be contemporary and currently in use in order to be judged effective. Therefore, models written in roughly the last 10 years would be found in this limited year search. After such material was located for each model, we decided to contact each model's developer to ensure that no research or technical data that were available had been overlooked. This phase of the study took 5 months, utilizing a written query followed by a telephone call to nonrespondents. All developers were asked to corroborate our findings using the same checklist of criteria described earlier. Three of the developers did not respond directly about their work. Several of the developers sent additional data and suggested changes in the rating of their work based on this new information. The original developers' interpretations of the criteria for judgment of the work has been acknowledged in the text by the incorporation of key ideas and studies.

Limitations of the Study

While the study used established research procedures for investigation, there are clear limitations to the findings generated. No attempt was made to judge the technical adequacy of the various studies reported except where sample size or lack of comparison group was a clear problem. Consequently, metaanalytic techniques to arrive at effect sizes were not done, rendering the findings cautionary. A follow-up study should be conducted on the seven models that have yielded research evidence to ascertain the integrity of the research designs and the power of the findings.

The Curricular Models

Each of the models is discussed in the following section according to the criteria used to assess effectiveness. The two megamodels are described first, those of Julian Stanley and Joseph Renzulli, because both have defined the major curricular efforts of the gifted education field since the mid-1970s and both also represent well the persistent programmatic division in the field between accelerative and enrichment approaches. Moreover, each of these models has more than a decade of research, development, and implementation behind it. None of the other models described in the study enjoy such longevity, widespread use, or research attention.

The Stanley Model of Talent Identification and Development

The overall purpose of the Stanley model is to educate for individual development over the lifespan. Major principles of the model include (1) the use of a secure and difficult testing instrument that taps into high-level verbal and mathematical reasoning to identify students; (2) a diagnostic testing–prescriptive instructional approach (DT-PI) in teaching gifted students through special classes, allowing for appropriate-level challenge in instruction; (3) the use of subject matter acceleration and fast-paced classes in core academic areas, as well as advocacy for various other forms of acceleration; and (4) curricular flexibility in all schooling. The model has been developed at key university sites across the country with some adoptions by local school districts that have established fast-paced classes.

The Study of Mathematically Precocious Youth (SMPY) officially started in September of 1971 at Johns Hopkins University (JHU) and has been continued, since 1986, at Iowa State University. From 1972 through 1979, SMPY pioneered the concept of searching for youth who reason exceptionally well mathematically (i.e., a talent search). In 1980, the talent search was extended to verbally gifted youth by others at JHU. For the students identified by the talent searchers, SMPY provided educational facilitation by utilizing acceleration or curricular flexibility and by developing fast-paced academic programs. Gifted students in 7th and 8th grade can participate in these talent searches by taking the College Board's Scholastic Aptitude Test (SAT) or the ACT. Almost 150,000 gifted students do so every year. These centers and other universities and organizations also offer residential and commuter academic programs in several disciplines to qualified students.

The research work of SMPY has been strong over the past 27 years, with more than 300 published articles, chapters, and books about the model. Findings of these studies have consistently focused on the benefits of acceleration for continued advanced work in an area by precocious students (Stanley, Keating, & Fox, 1974), a clear rationale for the use of acceleration in intellectual development (Keating, 1976), and the long-term positive repeated impacts of accelerative opportunities (Benbow & Arjmand, 1990). Case study research also has been undertaken to demonstrate how these processes affect individual students (Brody & Stanley, 1991). Other studies have focused more specifically on student gains from fast-paced classes (Lynch, 1992). The use of the model has been extensive across all of the United States and in selected foreign countries. Curricular materials have been developed by talent search staff at various sites and by individual teachers in the summer and academic year programs. Especially noteworthy are the curricular guides for teaching Advanced Placement courses developed at the Talent Identification Program (TIP) at Duke University. Strong use of articulated course materials are employed toward AP coursework and testing in mathematics, science, and the verbal areas, including foreign language. These materials have been reviewed by practicing professionals and content specialists.

Over its 33 years of operation, the Stanley model has been well received by parents and students who constitute the major client groups. Schools have been less receptive based on their conservative attitudes toward accelerative practices and the model's emphasis on highly gifted students in subject areas.

The Stanley model does not have a formal training component, although selection of teachers is a rigorous process carried out carefully in each university and school setting. Content expertise and work with highly gifted secondary students are primary considerations for selection. The model is easy to understand, but difficult to implement in schools based on prevailing philosophies. The application of the model that has been most successful is in afterschool and summer settings where students complete the equivalent of high school honors classes in 3 weeks.

The SMPY model has proven to be highly sustainable, exhibiting strong replication capacity. Even where countries do not conduct talent searches, students from those countries routinely attend summer programs at talent search universities.

Because the model is content-based, it aligns well with the national content standards, although some of the enrichment emphasis of the standards would be overlooked in implementation. SMPY represents core curricula on an accelerated and streamlined level. The model is not totally comprehensive in that it addresses students in grades 3–12 who reason exceptionally well mathematically and verbally. Some studies on spatially gifted students at those levels have also been conducted. Curricular areas are comprehensive, including all of the 26 Advanced Placement course strands. Scope and sequence work has been articulated for grades 7–12 in some areas of learning. Northwestern University has developed a guide for educational options for grades 5–12.

Longitudinal data, collected over 20 years on 300 highly gifted students, have demonstrated the viability of the Stanley model with respect to the benefits of accelerative study, early identification of a strong talent area, and the need for assistance in educational decision making (Lubinski & Benbow, 1994). A 50-year follow-up study (1972–2022) is in progress at Iowa State University with 6,000 students in the sample. This study already rivals Terman's longitudinal study in respect to its longevity and exceeds it in regard to its understanding of the talent development process at work. A recent review of longitudinal studies on acceleration continues to demonstrate the positive results of accelerative practices and the lack of negative consequences such as knowledge gaps or loss of interest (Swiatek, 2000).

The Renzulli Schoolwide Enrichment Model (SEM)

The Schoolwide Enrichment Model (SEM) evolved after 15 years of research and field testing by both educators and researchers (Renzulli, 1988). It combined the previously developed Enrichment Triad Model (Renzulli, 1977) with a more flexible approach to identifying high-potential students, the Revolving Door Identification Model (Renzulli, Reis, & Smith, 1981). This combination of services was initially field tested in 11 school districts of various types (rural, suburban, and urban) and sizes. The field tests resulted in the development of the SEM (Renzulli & Reis, 1985), which has been widely adopted throughout the country.

In the SEM, a talent pool of 15–20% of above-average-ability/high-potential students is identified through a variety of measures, including achievement tests, teacher nominations, and assessment of potential for creativity and task commitment, as well as alternative pathways of entrance, such as self-nomination and parent nomination. High achievement test and IQ scores automatically include a student in the talent pool, enabling those who are underachieving in their academic schoolwork to be considered.

Once students are identified for the talent pool, they are eligible for several kinds of services. First, interest and learning style assessments are used with talent pool students. Second, curriculum compacting is provided to all eligible students; that is, the regular curriculum is modified by eliminating portions of previously mastered content, and alternative work is substituted. Third, the Enrichment Triad Model offers three types of enrichment experiences: Type I, II, and III. Type III enrichment is usually more appropriate for students with higher levels of ability, interest, and task commitment.

Type I enrichment consists of general exploratory experiences such as guest speakers, field trips, demonstrations, interest centers, and the use of audiovisual materials designed to expose students to new and exciting topics, ideas, and fields of knowledge not ordinarily covered in the regular curriculum. Type II enrichment includes instructional methods and materials purposefully designed to promote the development of thinking, feeling, research, communication, and methodological processes. Type III enrichment, the most advanced level of the model, is defined as investigative activities and artistic productions in which the learner assumes the role of a firsthand inquirer: thinking, feeling, and acting like a practicing professional, with involvement pursued at a level as advanced or professional as possible, given the student's level of development and age.

One comparative case study (Heal, 1989) compared the effects of SEM to other enrichment models or strategies on students' perceptions of labeling. Other studies have reported results using within-model comparisons (Delisle, 1981; Reis, 1981) or the SEM program as compared to no intervention (Karafelis, 1986; Starko, 1986). Because control or comparison groups of students participating in alternate or comparison models were not used, it is difficult to attribute various results to participation in the SEM. Evaluation studies have been conducted in 29 school districts on the perceptions of the model with parents, teachers, and administrators. Researchers documented positive change in teacher attitudes toward student work.

Delcourt (1988) investigated characteristics related to creative/productive behavior in 18 high school students who consistently engaged in firsthand research on self-selected topics within or outside school. Starko (1986) also examined the effects of the Schoolwide Enrichment Model on student creative productivity. Results indicated that students who became involved in independent study projects in the SEM more often initiated their own creative products both *in and outside school* than did students in the comparison group. In addition, multiple creative products were linked to self-efficacy.

Several studies have examined the use of the model with underserved populations. Emerick (1988) investigated underachievement patterns of high-potential students. Baum (1985, 1988) examined highly able students with learning disabilities, identifying both characteristics and programmatic needs. Findings suggested positive effects of the model with these populations. Two authors (Ford, 1999; Johnson, 2000) have theorized about the use of the model with minority underachieving learners, suggesting its emphasis on creative thinking as an antidote to underachieving behavior.

Compacting studies have sought to document the fact that gifted students are capable of rapidly progressing through the regular school curriculum in order to spend time on Type III project work. Results have demonstrated knowledge scores that were high or higher on in-grade standardized tests than noncompacted peers (Reis & Purcell, 1993). Another study demonstrated that students (N = 336) utilizing curriculum compacting strategies resulted in no decline in achievement test scores (Reis, Westberg, Kulikowich, & Purcell, 1998).

Two SEM longitudinal studies have been conducted with 18 and 9 students, respectively. These studies showed that students in the sample maintained similar or identical career goals from their plans in high school, remained in major fields of study in college, and were satisfied in current project work. Moreover, the Type III process appeared to serve as important training for later productivity.

The SEM is widely used in some form in schools nationally and internationally. Summer training on the model is available at the University of Connecticut, reportedly training more than 600 educators annually. Renzulli perceives that the model is closely linked to core curricula, offers a scope and sequence within Type II activities, and has the potential to be aligned with national content standards. Both teachers and selected students are especially enthusiastic about the model. A special volume of the *Journal for the Education of the Gifted* (Coleman, 1999) was devoted to Renzulli's work, including the SEM.

The Betts Autonomous Learner Model

The Autonomous Learner Model for the Gifted and Talented was developed to meet the diverse cognitive, emotional, and social needs of gifted and talented students in grades K–12 (Betts & Knapp, 1980). The model proposes that, as their needs are met, gifted students will develop into autonomous learners who are responsible for the development, implementation, and evaluation of their own learning. The model is divided into five major dimensions: (1) orientation, (2) individual development, (3) enrichment activities, (4) seminars, and (5) in-depth study.

One of the criteria used for assessing the appropriateness of a curricular model is the evidence of research to support its use with gifted and talented learners. To date, no research evidence of effectiveness has been shown with regard to this model's student learning impact or longitudinal effectiveness with gifted learners. However, several curricular units and guides have been produced as a result of the dissemination of its ideas. One article reviewed and described the model by presenting guidelines for developing a process-based scope and sequence, as well as independent study programs for gifted learners (Betts &

Neihart, 1986). Recently, the model has been included in a volume on work with twice-exceptional gifted learners as a strong framework for programming for this population (Kiesa, 2000).

Regardless of the paucity of research on this model, it is one of the most widely recognized and used in the United States (Betts, 1986). It has been employed at selected sites in the United States and in other countries, and teachers have commented positively on its implementation. Formal teacher training occurs in 3- and 5-day segments annually. Its design suggests a 3-year timeline for model implementation. It does contain a degree of comprehensiveness in that the model applies broadly to all curricular domains and ages of learners. However, it does not incorporate any features of accelerated learning, thereby limiting one aspect of its comprehensiveness.

Gardner's Multiple Intelligences (MI)

Multiple intelligences (MI) as a curricular approach was built on a multidimensional concept of intelligence (Gardner, 1983). Seven areas of intelligence were defined in the original published work in 1983, with an eighth intelligence added by Gardner in 1995. They are (1) verbal/linguistic, (2) logical/mathematical, (3) visual/spatial, (4) musical/rhythmic, (5) bodily/kinesthetic, (6) interpersonal, (7) intrapersonal, and (8) naturalistic.

Evidence of research based on multiple intelligences translated into practice has been recently documented (Latham, 1997; Smith, Odhiambo, & El Khateeb, 2000; Strahan, Summey, & Banks, 1996). Most of the research, however, lacks control groups; therefore, generalizations about the model are difficult to infer (Latham). Longitudinal evidence of effectiveness with gifted students over at least 3 years has not been documented, although some research has been conducted on incorporating multiple intelligences with other forms of curricular models (Maker, Nielson, & Rogers, 1994).

The multiple intelligences approach has been used in the formation of new schools, in identifying individual differences, for curricular planning and development, and as a way to assess instructional strategies. A plethora of curricular materials has been produced and marketed based upon MI theory. This approach holds widespread appeal for many educators because it can be adapted for any learner, subject domain, or grade level. The model is not easy to implement and does require teacher training, financial resources, and time. Best-known project sites for the model are the Key School in Indianapolis, IN, and the Atlas Project in New York City. While the model has been readily adapted to curricula, it remains primarily a conception of intelligence applied broadly to school settings as a way to promote talent development for all learners.

Developer concerns about application fidelity of the ideas and variability in implementation quality are strong, which has led to a new project specifically designed to monitor implementation of MI in classrooms nationally where positive impacts have been reported (Gardner, 1999).

The Purdue Three-Stage Enrichment Model for Elementary Gifted Learners (PACE) and The Purdue Secondary Model for Gifted and Talented Youth

The concept of a three-stage model, initiated by Feldhusen and his graduate students, was first introduced as a course design for university students in 1973. It evolved into the Three-Stage Model by 1979. It is primarily an ordered enrichment model that moves students from simple thinking experiences to complex independent activities (Feldhusen & Kolloff, 1986):

- Stage I focuses on the development of divergent and convergent thinking skills;
- Stage II provides development in creative problem solving; and
- Stage III allows students to apply research skills in the development of independent study skills.

The Purdue Secondary Model is a comprehensive structure for programming services at the secondary level. It has 11 components supporting enrichment and acceleration options, with each component designed to act as a guide for organizing opportunities for secondary gifted students. They are (1) counseling services, (2) seminars, (3) Advanced Placement courses, (4) honors classes, (5) math/science acceleration, (6) foreign languages, (7) arts, (8) cultural experiences, (9) career education, (10) vocational programs, and (11) extraschool instruction (Feldhusen & Robinson-Wyman, 1986).

Research has documented gains with regard to enhancement of creative thinking and self-concept using the Three-Stage Enrichment Model for Elementary Gifted Students (Kolloff & Feldhusen, 1984), and one study documented limited long-term gains of the elementary program PACE (Moon & Feldhusen, 1994; Moon, Feldhusen, & Dillon, 1994).

The application and implementation of either the elementary or secondary models are not conclusive, yet they appear to be sustainable (Moon & Feldhusen, 1994). Teacher training has accompanied the site implementation of both the elementary and secondary models; however, it is difficult to ascertain the degree of widespread application beyond Indiana. Neither model utilizes a scope and sequence, and neither may be viewed as a comprehensive model in terms of applying broadly to all areas of the curriculum, all types of gifted learners, or all stages of development.

The Kaplan Grid

The Kaplan Grid was a model designed to facilitate the curriculum developer's task of deciding what constitutes a differentiated curriculum and how one can be constructed. The model uses the components of process, content, and product organized around a theme. Content is defined as "the relationship between economic, social, personal, and environmental displays of power, and the needs and the interests of individuals, groups, and societies (interdisciplinary)" (Kaplan, 1986, p. 184, 187). The process component utilizes productive thinking, research skills, and basic skills. The product component culminates the learning into a mode of communication.

Research evidence could not be found to support the effectiveness of this model with a target population. The quality of the curricular products that have been produced based upon this model has not been reported in the literature. However, there has been extensive implementation of the approach at both state and local levels.

Teacher training has been conducted throughout the United States, initially through the National/State Leadership Training Institute and now independently by the developer so that practitioners can learn how to implement it. Thousands of teachers have developed their own curricula based upon the model. The Grid is intended as a developmental framework for curricular planning for gifted learners, but it does not contain a scope and sequence. Additionally, within the model itself, no provisions are explicitly made for accelerated learning.

The Maker Matrix

The Maker Matrix, developed to categorize content, process, environmental, and product dimensions of an appropriate curriculum for the gifted, represents a set of descriptive criteria that may be used to develop classroom-based curricula (Maker, 1982). Recent work on the model represents primarily an enhancement of its problem-solving component. The Discover project is a process for assessing problem solving in multiple intelligences. The problem-solving matrix incorporates a continuum of five problem types for use within each of the intelligences:

- Type I and II problems require convergent thinking;
- Type III problems are structured, but allow for a range of methods to solve them and have a range of acceptable answers;
- Type IV problems are defined, but the learner selects a method for solving and establishing evaluation criteria for the solution; and
- Type V problems are ill-structured and the learner must define the problem, discover the method for solving, and establish criteria for creating a solution (Maker, Nielson, & Rogers, 1994).

The project is typically used by teachers for curriculum planning and assessing learner problem-solving abilities.

Research on problem types is currently underway involving 12 classrooms in a variety of settings. However, to date, the results have not been published. A pilot study has shown that use of the matrix enhances the process of problem solving (Maker, Rogers, Nielson, & Bauerle, 1996). Studies to evaluate the long-term validity of the process are in progress.

School systems in several states have applied the matrix as a framework for organizing and developing classroom-level curricula. There is evidence of an individual teacher-developed curriculum, and teachers have been receptive to its use. Some training exists for its application. The sustainability of the Maker Matrix for at least 3 years is not known. It is not comprehensive in nature, yet it does have a strong emphasis in its relationship to core subject domains.

The Meeker Structure of Intellect (SOI) Model

The Structure of Intellect (SOI) model for gifted education was based upon a theory of human intelligence called the Structure of Intellect (SI) developed by J. P. Guilford (1967). The SI model of human intelligence describes 90 kinds of cognitive functions organized into content, operation, and product abilities. The SOI system applies Guilford's theory into the areas of assessment and training. The model is definable as a system and applies broadly to all types of gifted learners at varying developmental stages; but, due to its comprehensiveness and emphasis on cognition, only a few sites have actually implemented it. Those sites have used it for identifying students or for training teachers to view intelligence as a nonfixed entity.

Studies of the model do not include effectiveness data (Meeker, 1976); rather, they primarily focus on findings for its use as identification criteria, as a means for organizing information about a gifted child, or as a means for overall program design. SOI has been successfully used in selected sites for identification with culturally diverse (Hengen, 1983) and preschool screening for multiethnic disadvantaged gifted students (Bonne, 1985).

Although now somewhat dated, SOI offered a means of understanding students by delineating profiles of their intellectual abilities. It contained a teacher-training component that used teacher modules designed to train one SOI ability at a time. Training materials included mini-lesson plans for group teaching and self-help modules for individualized instruction with selected students (Meeker, 1969).

The Parallel Curriculum Model

The Parallel Curriculum Model (PCM) is a model for curricular planning based upon the composite work of Tomlinson, Kaplan, Renzulli, Purcell, Leppien, and Burns (2002). This heuristic model employs four dimensions, or parallels, that can be used singly or in combination: the core curriculum, the curriculum of connections, the curriculum of practice, and the curriculum of identity.

The PCM assumes that the core curriculum is the basis for all other curricula and that it should be combined with any or all of the three other parallels. It is the foundational curriculum that is defined by a given discipline. National, state, and/or local school district standards should be reflected in this dimension. It establishes the basis of understanding within relevant subjects and grade levels. The second parallel, the curriculum of connections, supports students in discovering the interconnectedness among and between disciplines of knowledge. It builds from the core curriculum and has students exploring those connections for both intra- and interdisciplinary studies. The third parallel, the curriculum of practice, also derives from the core curriculum. Its purpose is to extend students' understandings and skills in a discipline through application. The curriculum of practice promotes student expertise as a practitioner of a given discipline. The last parallel, the curriculum of identity, helps students think about themselves within the context of a particular discipline—to see how a particular discipline relates to their own lives. The curriculum of identity uses the curriculum as a catalyst for self-definition and self-understanding. The authors suggest that the level of intellectual demand in employing the elements of the Parallel Curriculum Model should be matched to student needs.

To date, no research-based evidence of effectiveness has been shown with regard to this model's use with gifted or nongifted learners. However, several curricular units and guides have been produced as a result of a wide dissemination effort by the National Association for Gifted Children (NAGC). Additionally, curricular units are currently being created by practitioners at various levels guided by the model's authors. The model holds appeal for many educators because it can be adapted for any learner, subject domain, or grade level. While flexible, it is not easy to implement and does require a degree of teacher training. Professional development on the implementation of the PCM typically requires two days and may be adjusted depending on the needs of the employing school district. Implementation sessions have been offered for both regular classroom use and as a series of "trainer of trainer" offerings sponsored by NAGC.

The Schlichter Models for Talents Unlimited and Talents Unlimited to the Secondary Power (TU²)

Talents Unlimited was based upon Guilford's (1967) research on the nature of intelligence. Taylor, Ghiselin, Wolfer, Loy, & Bourne (1964), also influenced by Guilford, authored the multiple talent theory, which precipitated the development of a model to be employed in helping teachers identify and nurture students' multiple talents. Talents Unlimited features four major components:

- a description of specific skill abilities, or talents, in addition to academic ability that include productive thinking, communication, forecasting, decision making, and planning;
- model instructional materials;
- an in-service training program for teachers; and
- an evaluation system for assessing students' thinking skills development (Schlichter, 1986).

Talents Unlimited is the K–6 model, and Talents Unlimited to the Secondary Power is a model for grades 7–12.

Research has documented gains using the model in developing students' creative and critical thinking (Schlichter & Palmer, 1993). Rodd (1999) used action research to demonstrate the model's effectiveness in an English setting with young children. Additionally, there is evidence that the use of the model enhances academic skill development on standardized achievement tests (McLean & Chisson, 1980). However, no longitudinal studies have been conducted.

Staff development and teacher training constitute a strong component of the model. Teachers may become certified as Talents Unlimited trainers. Due to the strong emphasis on teacher training, Talents Unlimited has widespread applicable student use across the United States and worldwide. Part of its implementation success came as a result of funding and membership in the U.S. Department of Education's National Diffusion Network.

The model has been used most effectively as a classroom-based approach with all learners, thus rendering it less differentiated for the gifted in practice than some of the other models.

Sternberg's Triarchic Componential Model

Sternberg's Triarchic Componential Model is based upon an information processing theory of intelligence (Sternberg, 1981). In the model, three components represent the mental processes used in thinking. The executive process component is used in planning, decision making, and monitoring performance. The performance component processes are used in executing the executive problem-solving strategies within domains. The knowledge-acquisition component is used in acquiring, retaining, and transferring new information. The interaction and feedback between the individual and his or her environment within any given context allows cognitive development to occur.

An initial study has shown the effectiveness of the triarchic model with students learning psychology in a summer program (Sternberg & Clinkenbeard, 1995). More recent work has been conducted in studies using psychology as the curricular base with larger samples of students. Students continue to show growth patterns when assessment protocols are linked to measuring ability profiles (Sternberg, Ferrari, Clinkenbeard, & Grigorenko, 1996). Primary to these studies is the validation of the Sternberg Triarchic Abilities Test (STAT) and its utility for finding students strong on specific triarchic components. Other recent studies (Sternberg, Torff, & Grigorenko, 1998a, 1998b) have focused on the use of triarchic instructional processes in classrooms at the elementary and middle school levels. Results suggest slightly stronger effects for triarchic instruction over traditional and critical thinking approaches. Descriptions of teacher-created curricula and instructional instrumentation processes were limited, but were clearly organized along discipline-specific lines of inquiry. Sustainability of the curricular model beyond summer program implementation and pilot settings is not known.

There is not a packaged teacher-training or staff-development component, partially because the model is based upon a theory of intelligence, rather than a deliberate curricular framework. It is a systemic, but not a comprehensive, model with some applications in selected classrooms.

VanTassel-Baska's Integrated Curriculum Model (ICM)

The VanTassel-Baska (1986) Integrated Curriculum Model (ICM) was specifically developed for high-ability learners. It has three dimensions: (1) advanced content, (2) high-level process and product work, and (3) intra- and interdisciplinary concept development and understanding. VanTassel-Baska, with funding from the Jacob Javits Program, used the ICM to develop specific curricular frameworks and underlying units in language arts and science.

Research has been conducted to support the effectiveness of these curricular units with gifted populations within a variety of educational settings. Specifically, significant growth gains in literary analysis and interpretation, persuasive writing, and linguistic competency in language arts have been demonstrated for experimental gifted classes using the developed curricular units in comparison to gifted groups not using them (VanTassel-Baska, Johnson, Hughes, & Boyce, 1996; VanTassel-Baska, Zuo, Avery, & Little, 2002). Other studies have shown that using the problem-based science units embedded in an exemplary science curriculum significantly enhances the capacity for integrating higher order process skills in science (VanTassel-Baska, Bass, Reis, Poland, & Avery, 1998) regardless of the grouping approach employed. Further, research has documented positive change in teacher attitude, student motivational response, and school and district change (VanTassel-Baska, Avery, Little & Hughes, 2000) as a result of using the ICM curriculum over 3 years. A subanalysis of the language arts data across settings suggested that it is successful with low-income students, can be used in all grouping paradigms, and that learning increases with multiple units employed (VanTassel-Baska, Zuo, Avery, & Little, 2002). Recent research using comparison groups suggests that use of the social studies units significantly impacts critical thinking and content mastery (Little, Feng, VanTassel-Baska, Rogers, & Avery, 2002).

Teacher training is an integral component of the ICM model. Training workshops have been conducted in 30 states, and the College of William and Mary offers training annually. There is a strong relationship to core subject domains, as well as national standards alignment. The curriculum, based on the model, was developed using the national standards work as a template. Alignment charts have been completed for national and state standards work in both language arts and science.

The ICM units are moderately comprehensive in that they span grades 2–10 in language arts and 2–8 in science. New social studies units are now available for grades 2–8, as well. The ICM model has been used for specific district curriculum development and planning in Australia and Canada, as well as selected districts in the United States.

There is evidence of broad-based application, but some questions remain regarding the ease of implementation of the teaching units and the fidelity of implementation by teachers (Burruss, 1997). Some districts use the units as models for developing their own curricula. The developer reported that 100 school districts are part of a National Curriculum Network using both the science and language arts units. Data on student impact have been collected from over 120 classrooms nationally. A new Javits grant will assess the effectiveness of the language arts units with low-income learners in Title I schools using critical thinking as the outcome variable of interest.

Studies of effectiveness are ongoing in classrooms nationally. The curriculum is reported to be used in all 50 states. Internationally, the model is being used in 18 countries.

Key Findings

An important part of the curricular model analysis was also to compare the models to one another using the same criteria as the basis for comparison. Some models were more organizational than curricular in nature, which helps teachers get started on differentiation in their classroom; others were more programmatic in nature and were intended as a defining framework in schools. Examples of the former were the Kaplan Grid and the Maker Matrix, both of which are heavily used by practitioners as designs for teacher-made materials. No studies of effectiveness have been conducted to date, however, to show the benefits of such models in practice with gifted learners. The Purdue Secondary Model exemplifies the programmatic framework model as a supraorganizer at the school level, rather than at the level of curricular units. The application and implementation of the Purdue Secondary Model is not conclusive, yet appears to be sustainable (Moon & Feldhusen, 1994).

Only seven models showed evidence of having been the focus of research studies. Of those, only five of the models employed comparison groups where treatment might be attributed to the curricular approach employed. The Stanley, Renzulli, Feldhusen, VanTassel-Baska, and Schlichter models all have some evidence of effectiveness with gifted populations in comparison to other treatments or no treatments. While the Talents Unlimited Model has some evidence of effectiveness, much of the research base is on nongifted populations.

Evidence for the translation of these curricular models into effective practice varies considerably. Seven models have training packages that provide staff development for implementation, while only four models explicitly consider scope and sequence issues. Betts and Renzulli consider scope and sequence within their models. For Betts, it is in the movement from one stage to another; for Renzulli, it occurs within Type II activities. Stanley and VanTassel-Baska have both developed scope-and-sequence models linked to Advanced Placement work.

Data on curricular and instructional practices with the gifted clearly favor advanced work in the subject areas of language arts, science, and mathematics, although the approach to content acceleration may vary. While both the Stanley and VanTassel-Baska models have elements of acceleration within them, only the Stanley model has empirically demonstrated its clear impact on learning over time.

Curricula organized around higher order processes and independent study have yielded few studies of student impacts, nor are the findings across studies consistent. Even longitudinal studies, such as those of Feldhusen and Renzulli, have produced limited evidence of outcomes relevant to clear student gains. Limited sample size and other confounding variables, such as lack of comparison groups, also render these studies less credible.

Conclusions

A strong body of research evidence exists supporting the use of advanced curricula in core areas of learning at an accelerated rate for high-ability learners. Some evidence also exists that more enrichment-oriented models are effective. This conclusion has not changed much in the past 20 years (Daurio, 1979). Moreover, recent metaanalytic studies continue to confirm the superior learning effects of acceleration over enrichment in tandem with grouping the gifted (Kulik & Kulik, 1993). In comparison to other strategies (e.g., independent study, various modes of grouping, and problem solving), acceleration not only shows performance gains, but also has a powerful treatment effect, meaning that the gains are educationally, as well as statistically, significant (Walberg, 1991). Despite the lack of convincing research to support their use, several of the enrichment models enjoy widespread popularity and are used extensively in schools.

General Implications

Several implications might be drawn from these findings, related to both research and practice in gifted education. Too frequently, it is assumed that, if a model is written about and used enthusiastically, such popularity is sufficient for proclaiming its effectiveness. Nothing could be further from the truth. Research-based practice is critical to defensible gifted programs. Therefore, practitioners must proceed carefully in deciding on curricula for use in gifted programs. The evidence strongly suggests that content-based accelerative approaches should be employed in any curriculum used in school-based programs for the gifted and that schools need to apply curricular models faithfully and thoroughly in order to realize their potential impacts over time.

In the area of research, it is clear that there is a limited base of coherent studies that can make claims about the efficacy of enriched approaches to curricula for the gifted. Thus, an important direction for future research would be to conduct curricular intervention studies testing these models, as well as to replicate existing studies to build a base of deeper understanding about what works well with gifted students in school programs. More research on differential student learning outcomes in gifted programs using different curricular approaches clearly needs to be undertaken.

Implications for Schools

Decisions about curricular approaches and their implications for classrooms need to be made with a sense of what works for our best learners in schools. This chapter has delineated a set of criteria for considering the state of the art in curricular interventions for gifted learners. These criteria are important considerations for schools in making curricular decisions. The fundamental questions upon which schools need to focus are the following:

- Do gifted students show evidence of learning as a result of the curricular approach? What is the nature and extent of the evidence and how credible is it?
- Is the curricular approach currently being used in schools where we can talk to teachers and observe it in practice?
- Are classroom materials available to use in implementation?
- Is training available for school staff?

These questions are crucial to ask before schools decide what curriculum to employ for gifted populations. From a process perspective, school administrators of gifted programs might wish to do the following:

1. Review each curricular model with their staff, noting the advantages and disadvantages of each in a particular school context.
2. Visit schools using the most appropriate models.
3. Review existing curricular materials for the selected models with an eye to implementation issues.
4. Consider staffing match-ups. Who could teach each of the models based on background and experience?
5. Select one of the models for piloting in the school district for 1 year.
6. Secure appropriate training for teachers.
7. Provide additional planning time for implementation issues.
8. Provide follow-up classroom monitoring through visitation, videotaping, or peer/mentor coaching strategies.
9. Assess the effectiveness of the pilot based on student learning data and student and teacher feedback.

By following these processes in using research-based curricular approaches, the level of curricular services to gifted learners may become elevated over current practice.

Teacher Statement

I first read this chapter during a time when I was both working with elementary gifted and talented students and pursuing a master's degree in education with a specialization in gifted and talented education. This chapter was one of many assigned from the Karnes and Bean text for a graduate course that covered various instructional strategies and models implemented in gifted education programs.

I found this chapter to be helpful because it provided a clear and concise overview of the most widely used program and curricular models in the field of gifted education. Specifically, it emphasized the research evidence for each of the models discussed and their effectiveness with gifted students. The evidence presented in this chapter contributed positively to my instructional decision-making process by influencing me to incorporate more accelerative curricular and instructional strategies related to student ability and interests.

This chapter also emphasized the caution with which educators should embrace new models and theories. After reading this chapter, I became more aware of and interested in the research behind the instructional strategies and curricular materials I incorporate into teaching. It encouraged me to ask for more evidence of the materials' and strategies' effectiveness with gifted students and appropriateness for meeting their needs.

I recommend this chapter to all educators in the field of gifted education, as well as parents and others interested in the program and curricular models used in a community's gifted education program. The authors provide useful information about prominent models used in the field of gifted education, as well as guidelines and procedures for evaluating other programs and curricular models that might be implemented with gifted students.

—Bess B. Worley II

Discussion Questions

1. Based on research evidence, what models appear to be most successful?

2. What models appear to work with special populations? Why?

3. What models lack research studies of effectiveness?

4. Why do you think the research base is so limited on curricular interventions with gifted students?

5. What features across models are critical to employ in a curriculum, according to your understanding of their characteristics and needs?

6. How can professional development in the field become more influential in helping curricular models become institutionalized?

Teacher Resources

Publications and Web Sites

Schoolwide Enrichment Model—http://www.gifted.uconn.edu

Integrated Curriculum Model (ICM)—http://www.cfge.wm.edu

Language Arts Publications

Libraries Link Learning: Program and Curriculum Resource Manual for Use With At-Risk Gifted Children
Change Through Choices (grades 10–12)
William and Mary *Navigators* (novel study guides): *Charlotte's Web* by E. B. White (grades 3–4), *The Dark is Rising* by Susan Cooper (grades 6–7), *The Egypt Game* by Zilpha Keatley Snyder (grades 4–5), *Everything on a Waffle* by Polly Horvath (grades 4–5), *Number the Stars* by Lois Lowry (grades 4–6), *Sarah Bishop* by Scott O'Dell (grades 5–6), *Sarah, Plain and Tall* by Patricia MacLachlan (grades 3–4), *Snow Treasure* by Marie McSwigan (grades 4–5), *Tuck Everlasting* by Natalie Babbitt (grades 5–7), *Walk Two Moons* by Sharon Creech (grades 5–7)

Social Studies Publications

Defining Nations: Cultural Identity and Political Tension (grades 9–10)
Primary Sources and Historical Analysis (grades 9–10)
Post-Colonialism in the 20th Century: Perspectives on Tradition and Change (grades 9–10)
Renaissance and Reformation in Europe (grades 9–10)

Science and Mathematics Publications

Curriculum Assessment Guide to Science Materials
Resource Guide to Mathematics Curriculum Materials for High-Ability Learners (grades K–8)
Notes From a Scientist: Activities and Resources for Gifted Children
Guide to Key Science Concepts
Models: A Study of Animal Populations (grades 7–8)

Additional Curricular Publications

A Guide to Teaching Research Skills and Strategies for Grades 4–12
The Practitioner's Guide to Exemplary School Change

Kendall/Hunt Publications—http://www.kendallhunt.com

Language Arts Publications

Guide to Teaching a Language Arts Curriculum for High-Ability Learners
Journeys & Destinations (grades 2–3)
Literary Reflections (grades 4–5)
Autobiographies (grades 5–6)
Persuasion (grades 5–7)
The 1940s: A Decade of Change (grades 6–10)
Threads of Change in 19th Century American Literature (grades 7–11)

Science Publications

A Guide to Teaching a Problem-Based Science Curriculum
Dust Bowl (grades 1–3)
What A Find! (grades 2–4)
Acid, Acid Everywhere (grades 4–6)
Electricity City (grades 4–6)
Hot Rods (grades 6–8)
No Quick Fix (grades 6–8)
The Chesapeake Bay (grades 6–8)

Social Studies Publications

Ancient Egypt: Gift of the Nile (grades 2–3)
Ancient China: The Middle Kingdom (grades 2–3)
Building a New System: Colonial America 1607–1763 (grades 4–5)
The World Turned Upside Down: The American Revolution (grades 4–5)
A House Divided? The Civil War: Its Causes and Effects (grades 5–6)
The 1920s in America: A Decade of Tensions (grades 6–7)
The 1930s in America: Facing Depression (grades 6–7)
The Road to the White House: Electing the American President (grades
    6–8)

Addresses

American Association for the Advancement of Science
1200 New York Ave., NW
Washington, DC 20005
(202) 326–6400
http://www.aaas.org

Advanced Placement Program Manuals
Duke University TIP
1121 W. Main St., Ste. 100
Durham, NC 27701
(919) 668-9100
http://www.tip.duke.edu

Each manual in the series contains suggestions for discussions, homework assignments, projects, reference materials, and test items that are appropriate for bright,
capable students across all academic tracks. The manuals range from 275–475
pages in length and provide comprehensive course material for each subject area.
TIP's AP manuals were designed and written by teachers with extensive experience in Advanced Placement and honors courses.

Betts' Formal Teacher Training
Division of Special Education
University of Northern Colorado
McKee Hall
Room 29, Box 141
Greeley, CO 80639
(970) 351-2691

Education Development Center
55 Chapel St.
Newton, MA 02458–1060
(800) 225-4276
http://main.edc.org

Gardner's Multiple Intelligence Teacher Training
The Project Zero Classroom
Harvard Graduate School Education
124 Mount Auburn St.
Fifth Floor
Cambridge, MA 02138
(617) 496-7097
http://www.pzweb.harvard.edu

The Great Books Foundation
35 E. Wacker Dr., Ste. 2300
Chicago, IL 60601-2298
(800) 222-5870
http://www.greatbooks.org

Integrated Curriculum Model Training Workshops and Summer Institute in Curriculum Development
Center for Gifted Education
The College of William and Mary
P.O. Box 8795
Williamsburg, VA 23187–8795
http://www.cfge.wm.edu

Kaplan Grid Teacher Training
Dr. Sandra N. Kaplan
10231–6 White Oak Ave.
Northridge, CA 91324
(213) 740-3291

Maker's Matrix Training
Special Education and Rehabilitation
College of Education
P.O. Box 210069
Tucson, AZ 85721–0069
(520) 621-8832

Meeker's Structure of Intellect Model Teacher Training
SOI Systems
45755 Goodpasture Rd.
Box D
Vida, OR 97488
(541) 896-3936

National Council of Teachers of English
1111 W. Kenyon Rd.
Urbana, IL 61801–1096
(877) 369-6283
http://www.ncte.org

The National Academies Press
500 Fifth St., NW
Lockbox 285
Washington, DC 20055
(888) 624-8373
(202) 334-3313
http://www.nap.edu

Northwestern University
Center for Talent Development
School of Education and Social Policy
617 Dartmouth Pl.
Evanston, IL 60208-4175
(847) 491-3782
fax (847) 467-4283
http://www.ctd.northwestern.edu

Purdue Three-Stage Enrichment Model for Elementary Gifted Learners
and the Purdue Secondary Model for Gifted and Talented Youth Teacher Training
Gifted Education Resource Institute
Purdue University
Beering Hall, Rm. 5113
100 N. University St.
West Lafayette, IN 47907-2098
(765) 494-7243
http://www.geri.soe.purdue.edu

Renzulli's Summer Training
Neag Center for Education and Talent Development
3 Summers Program
2131 Hillside Road, Unit 3007
Storrs, CT 06269-3007
(860) 486-6013
fax (860) 486-2900
http://www.gifted.uconn.edu

Talents Unlimited and Talents Unlimited
to the Secondary Power Teacher Training
Talents Unlimited Inc.
Mobile County Public Schools
109 S. Cedar St.
Mobile, AL 36602
(334) 690-8060
http://www.sharingsuccess.org/code/eptw/profiles/68.html

Temple University Press
1601 N. Broad St.
USB Route 306
Philadelphia, PA 19122–6099
(800) 621-2736
http://www.temple.edu/tempress

References

American Association for the Advancement of Science. (1989). *Science for all Americans.* New York: Oxford University Press.

American Association for the Advancement of Science. (1993). *Benchmarks for science literacy.* New York: Oxford University Press.

Baum, S. (1985). *Learning disabled students with superior cognitive abilities: A validation study of descriptive behaviors.* Unpublished doctoral dissertation, University of Connecticut, Storrs.

Baum, S. (1988). An enrichment program for gifted learning disabled students. *Gifted Child Quarterly, 32,* 226–230.

Benbow, C. P., & Arjmand, O. (1990). Predictors of high academic achievement in mathematics and science by mathematically talented students: A longitudinal study. *Journal of Educational Psychology, 82,* 430–431.

Betts, G. T. (1986). The autonomous learner model for the gifted and talented. In J. S. Renzulli (Ed.), *Systems and models for developing programs for the gifted and talented* (pp. 27–56). Mansfield Center, CT: Creative Learning Press.

Betts, G., & Knapp, J. (1980). Autonomous learning and the gifted: A secondary model. In A. Arnold (Ed.), *Secondary programs for the gifted* (pp. 29–36). Ventura, CA: Office of Ventura County Superintendent of Schools.

Betts, G. T., & Neihart, M. (1986). Implementing self-directed learning models for the gifted and talented. *Gifted Child Quarterly, 30,* 174–177.

Bonne, R. (1985). *Identifying multi-ethnic disadvantaged gifted.* Brooklyn, NY: Community School District #19.

Brody, L. E., & Stanley, J. C. (1991). Young college students: Assessing factors that contribute to success. In W. T. Southern & E. D. Jones (Eds.), *Academic acceleration of gifted children* (pp. 102–132). New York: Teachers College Press.

Bruner, J. (Ed.). (1970). *Man: A course of study.* Newton, MA: Education Development Center.

Burruss, J. D. (1997). *Walking the talk: Implementation decisions made by teachers.* Chicago: American Educational Research Association.

Coleman, L. J. (1999). Renzulli: Retrospective and prospective [Special issue]. *Journal for the Education of the Gifted, 23*(1).

Daurio, S. P. (1979). Education enrichment versus acceleration: A review of the literature. In W. C. Gregory, S. J. Cohn, & J. C. Stanley (Eds.), *Educating the gifted: Acceleration and enrichment* (pp. 13–63). Baltimore: Johns Hopkins University Press.

Delcourt, M. A. B. (1988). *Characteristics related to high levels of creative/productive behavior in secondary school students: A multi-case study.* Unpublished doctoral dissertation, University of Connecticut, Storrs.

Delisle, J. R. (1981). *The revolving door identification model: Correlates of creative production.* Unpublished doctoral dissertation, University of Connecticut, Storrs.

Emerick, L. (1988). *Academic underachievement among the gifted: Students' perceptions of factors relating to the reversal of the academic underachievement pattern.* Unpublished doctoral dissertation, University of Connecticut, Storrs.

Feldhusen, J. F., & Kolloff, M. B. (1986). The Purdue three-stage model for gifted education. In J. S. Renzulli (Ed.), *Systems and models for developing programs for the gifted and talented* (pp. 126–152). Mansfield Center, CT: Creative Learning Press.

Feldhusen, J. F., & Robinson-Wyman, A. (1986). The Purdue secondary model for gifted education. In J. S. Renzulli (Ed.), *Systems and models for developing programs for the gifted and talented* (pp. 153–179). Mansfield Center, CT: Creative Learning Press.

Ford, D. Y. (1999). Renzulli's philosophy and program: Opening doors and nurturing potential. *Journal for the Education of the Gifted, 23*, 117–124.

Gardner, H. (1983). *Frames of mind: The theory of multiple intelligences.* New York: BasicBooks.

Gardner, H. (1999). *Intelligence reframed: Multiple intelligences for the 21st century.* New York: BasicBooks.

Guilford, J. P. (1967). *The nature of human intelligence.* New York: McGraw-Hill.

Heal, M. M. (1989). *Student perceptions of labeling the gifted: A comparative case study analysis.* Unpublished doctoral dissertation, University of Connecticut, Storrs.

Hengen, T. (1983). *Identification and enhancement of giftedness in Canadian Indians.* Paper presented at the annual meeting of the National Association for Gifted Children, New Orleans.

Hollingworth, L. (1926). *Gifted children: Their nature and nurture.* New York: World Book.

Johnson, G. M. (2000). Schoolwide enrichment: Improving the education of students (at risk) at promise. *Teacher Education Quarterly, 27*(4), 45–61.

Kaplan, S. (1986). The Kaplan Grid. In J. S. Renzulli (Ed.), *Systems and models for developing programs for the gifted and talented* (pp. 56–68). Mansfield Center, CT: Creative Learning Press.

Karafelis, P. (1986). *The effects of the tri-art drama curriculum on the reading comprehension of students with varying levels of cognitive ability.* Unpublished doctoral dissertation, University of Connecticut, Storrs.

Keating, D. P. (Ed.). (1976). *Intellectual talent: Research and development.* Baltimore: Johns Hopkins University Press.

Kiesa, K. (2000). *Uniquely gifted: Identifying and meeting the needs of twice-exceptional students.* Gilsum, NH: Avocus.

Kolloff, M. B., & Feldhusen, J. F. (1984). The effects of enrichment on self-concept and creative thinking. *Gifted Child Quarterly, 28*, 53–57.

Kulik, J., & Kulik, C.-L. (1993). Meta-analytic findings on grouping programs. *Gifted Child Quarterly, 36*, 73–77.

Latham, A. S. (1997). Quantifying MI's gains. *Educational Leadership, 55*(1), 84–85.

Lipman, M., Sharp, A. M., & Oscanyan, F. F. (1980). *Philosophy in the classroom.* Philadelphia, PA: Temple University Press.

Little, C. A., Feng, A. X., VanTassel-Baska, J., Rogers, K. B., & Avery, L. D. (2002*). Final report on social studies curriculum effectiveness study.* Williamsburg, VA: Center for Gifted Education, The College of William and Mary.

Lubinski, D., & Benbow, C. P. (1994). The Study of Mathematically Precocious Youth: The first three decades of a planned 50-year study of intellectual talent. In R. Subotnik & K. D. Arnold (Eds.), *Beyond Terman: Contemporary longitudinal studies of giftedness and talent* (pp. 375–400). Norwood, NJ: Ablex.

Lynch, S. J. (1992). Fast-paced high school science for the academically talented: A six-year perspective. *Gifted Child Quarterly, 36*, 147–154.

Maker, C. J. (1982). *Curriculum development for the gifted.* Rockville, MD: Aspen.

Maker, C. J., Nielson, A. B., & Rogers, J. A. (1994). Multiple intelligences: Giftedness, diversity, and problem solving. *Teaching Exceptional Children, 27*(1), 4–19.

Maker, C. J., Rogers, J. A., Nielson, A. B., & Bauerle, P. R. (1996). Multiple intelligences, problem solving, and diversity in the general classroom. *Journal for the Education of the Gifted, 19,* 437–460.

McLean, J. E., & Chisson, B. S. (1980). *Talents unlimited program: Summary of research findings for 1979–80.* Mobile, AL: Mobile County Public Schools.

Meeker, M. (1969). *The structure of intellect: Its interpretation and uses.* Columbus, OH: Merrill.

Meeker, M. (1976). *A paradigm for special education diagnostics: The cognitive area* (Report No. EC082519). Paper presented at the annual meeting of the American Educational Research Association, San Francisco. (ERIC Document Reproduction Service No. ED 121 010)

Moon, S., & Feldhusen, J. F. (1994). The program for academic and creative enrichment (PACE): A follow-up study 10 years later. In R. Subotnik & K. D. Arnold (Eds.) *Beyond Terman: Contemporary longitudinal studies of giftedness and talent* (pp. 375–400). Norwood, NJ: Ablex.

Moon, S. M., Feldhusen, J. F., & Dillon, D. R. (1994). Long-term effects of an enrichment program based on the Purdue Three-Stage Model. *Gifted Child Quarterly, 38,* 38–48.

National Council of Teachers of English & International Reading Association. (1996). *Standards for the English language arts.* Urbana, IL: Author.

National Research Council. (1996). *National science education standards.* Washington, DC: National Academy Press.

Pressey, S. L. (1949). *Educational acceleration: Appraisal and basic problems.* Columbus: Ohio State University Press.

Reis, S. M. (1981). *An analysis of the productivity of gifted students participating in programs using the Revolving Door Identification Model.* Unpublished doctoral dissertation, University of Connecticut, Storrs.

Reis, S. M., & Purcell, J. H. (1993). An analysis of content elimination and strategies used by elementary classroom teachers in the curriculum compacting process. *Journal for the Education of the Gifted, 16,* 147–170.

Reis, S. M., Westberg, K. L, Kulikowich, J. M., & Purcell, J. H. (1998). Curriculum compacting and achievement test scores: What does the research say? *Gifted Child Quarterly, 42,* 123–129.

Renzulli, J. S. (1977). *The enrichment triad model: A guide for developing defensible programs for the gifted and talented.* Mansfield Center, CT: Creative Learning Press.

Renzulli, J. S. (Ed.). (1988). *Technical report of research studies related to the Revolving Door Identification model.* Storrs, CT: Bureau of Educational Research, University of Connecticut.

Renzulli, J. S., & Reis, S. M. (1985). *The schoolwide enrichment model: A comprehensive plan for educational excellence.* Mansfield Center, CT: Creative Learning Press.

Renzulli, J. S., Reis, S. M., & Smith, L. (1981). The revolving-door model: A new way of identifying the gifted. *Phi Delta Kappan, 62,* 648–649.

Rodd, J. (1999). Encouraging young children's critical and creative thinking skills: An approach in one English elementary school. *Childhood Education, 75,* 350–354.

Schlichter, C. (1986). Talents Unlimited: Applying the multiple talent approach in mainstream and gifted programs. In J. S. Renzulli (Ed.), *Systems and models for developing programs for the gifted and talented* (pp. 352–390). Mansfield Center, CT: Creative Learning Press.

Schlichter, C. L., & Palmer, W. R. (Eds.). (1993). *Thinking smart: A premiere of the Talents Unlimited model*. Mansfield Center, CT: Creative Learning Press.

Smith, W., Odhiambo, E., & El Khateeb, H. (2000, November). *The typologies of successful and unsuccessful students in the core subjects of language arts, mathematics, science, and social studies using the theory of multiple intelligences in a high school environment in Tennessee.* Paper presented at the annual meeting of the Mid-South Educational Research Association, Bowling Green, KY.

Stanley, J. C., Keating, D., & Fox, L. (Eds.). (1974). *Mathematical talent: Discovery, description, and development.* Baltimore: Johns Hopkins University Press.

Starko, A. J. (1986). *The effects of the Revolving Door Identification model on creative productivity and self-efficacy.* Unpublished doctoral dissertation, University of Connecticut, Storrs.

Sternberg, R. (1981). A componential theory of intellectual giftedness. *Gifted Child Quarterly, 25,* 86–93.

Sternberg, R., & Clinkenbeard, P. R. (1995). The triadic model applied to identify, teach, and assess gifted children. *Roeper Review, 17,* 255–260.

Sternberg, R. J., Ferrari, M., Clinkenbeard, P., & Grigorenko, E. L. (1996). Identification, instruction, and assessment of gifted children: A construct validation of a triarchic model. *Gifted Child Quarterly, 40,* 129–137.

Sternberg, R. J., Torff, B., & Grigorenko, E. L. (1998a). Teaching for successful intelligence raises school achievement. *Phi Delta Kappan, 79,* 667–699.

Sternberg, R. J., Torff, B., & Grigorenko, E. L. (1998b). Teaching triarchically improves school achievement. *Journal of Educational Psychology, 90,* 374–384.

Strahan, D., Summey, H., & Banks, N. (1996). Teaching to diversity through multiple intelligences: Student and teacher responses to instructional improvement. *Research in Middle Level Education Quarterly, 19*(2), 43–65.

Swiatek, M. A. (2000). A decade of longitudinal research on academic acceleration through the study of mathematically precocious youth. *Roeper Review, 24,* 141–144.

Taylor, C. W., Ghiselin, B., Wolfer, J., Loy, L., & Bourne, L. E., Jr. (1964). *Development of a theory of education from psychology and other basic research findings* (Final Report, USOE Cooperative Research Project, No. 621). Salt Lake City: University of Utah.

Terman, L. M., & Oden, M. H. (1947). *The gifted child grows up: Twenty-five years' follow-up of a superior group* (*Genetic studies of genius,* Vol. 4). Stanford, CA: Stanford University Press.

Tomlinson, C. A., Kaplan, S. N., Renzulli, J. S., Purcell, J., Leppien, J., & Burn, D. (2002). *The parallel curriculum: A design to develop high potential and challenge high-ability learners.* Thousand Oaks, CA: Corwin Press.

VanTassel-Baska, J. (1986). Effective curriculum and instruction models for talented students. *Gifted Child Quarterly, 30,* 164–169.

VanTassel-Baska, J. (1995). A study of life themes in Charlotte Brönte and Virginia Woolf. *Roeper Review, 18,* 14–19.

VanTassel-Baska, J. (1998). *Excellence in educating the gifted.* Denver: Love.

VanTassel-Baska, J., Avery, L. D., Little, C. A., & Hughes, C. E. (2000). An evaluation of the implementation: The impact of the William and Mary units on schools. *Journal for the Education of the Gifted, 23,* 244–272.

VanTassel-Baska, J., Bass, G. M., Ries, R. R., Poland, D. L., & Avery, L. D. (1998). A national study of science curriculum effectiveness with high-ability students. *Gifted Child Quarterly, 42,* 200–211.

VanTassel-Baska, J., Johnson, D. T., Hughes, C. E., & Boyce, L. N. (1996). A study of the language arts curriculum effectiveness with gifted learners. *Journal for the Education of the Gifted, 19*, 461–480.

VanTassel-Baska, J., Zuo, L., Avery, L. D., & Little, C. A. (2002). A curriculum study of gifted student learning in the language arts. *Gifted Child Quarterly, 46*, 30–44.

Walberg, H. (1991). Productive teaching and instruction: Assessing the knowledge base. In H. C. Waxman & H. J. Walberg (Eds.), *Effective teaching: Current research* (pp. 33–62). Berkeley, CA: McCutchan.

Chapter 4

Layering Differentiated Curricula for the Gifted and Talented

by **Sandra N. Kaplan**

t has been said by many educators of the gifted that it is easier to define what differentiation of the curriculum is not than it is to define what differentiation of the curriculum is. Over the years, the concept of differentiating the curriculum for gifted students has changed commensurate to the changes in the definition of giftedness, the contemporary emphasis in general education, and the political and parental responses to general and gifted education. The many definitions of differentiation have resulted in the term becoming a referent for any learning experience that attends to individual differences. In reality, differentiation can be defined by the *who*—the learner and his or her needs, interest, and abilities; the *what*—the content and skills of the subject matter to be taught; the *how*—the pedagogy to be used to teach the content, skills, or both; and the *where*—the setting, grouping, or both needed to implement effectively the curriculum (the what) to the learner (the who).

The original need to differentiate the curriculum for gifted students was based on the recognized strengths of these learners and the acknowledged inadequacy of the regular or core curriculum to meet these needs. The discrepancy theory assesses the core curriculum against the traits of gifted students in order to determine the missing curricular elements that would be responsive to the needs of students. This comparative analysis between the needs, interests, and abilities of gifted students and the content, processes, and product components of the core curriculum traditionally justified the purpose for a differentiated curriculum. To the degree that the core curriculum correlates with the defined attributes of gifted students, it is perceived as either appropriately or inappropriately differentiated.

A History of Differentiated Curricula: A Perspective

The development of differentiated curricula follows the definition and redefinition of the basic elements that comprise all curricula: content, process, and product. The development of all curricula is dependent on the same elements and answers to these questions: (1) What content do you want the students to know? (2) What skills or processes should the students master? (3) How should the students demonstrate understanding of the content and mastery of the skills through the products they create? Decisions to modify one, some, or all of these elements ultimately determine the differentiated nature of the core curriculum. The history of differentiated curricula can be reconstructed from the decisions made to adjust the content, process, and product elements of the core curriculum. An examination of the interaction among the content, process, and product elements that form a learning experience provides the basis for telling the history of differentiation (see Table 1).

The first real modification of basic learning experiences seemed to have paralleled the definition of taxonomies and strategies to develop higher level thinking skills. The rationale for pursuing critical, creative, and problem-solving skills was responsive to the theoretical emphasis to develop gifted students as complex thinkers and the correlation between the traits of gifted students to be productive thinkers and the nature and scope of higher level thinking skills. Thus, the primary change in the content, process, and product curricular equation was to redefine and replace the process element, namely thinking skills. Originally, thinking skills in most of the core curricula were identified as basic or lower level thinking skills. This change enabled teachers responsible for the education of the gifted to pinpoint where in the teaching and learning of the core curriculum the needs of gifted students could be met. More importantly, the identification of thinking skills in the definition of the curricular learning experience or objective provided substantive distinction of the curriculum as one that differed from the type of learning experiences constructed and presented to all students (see Table 2).

The next significant change in the equation to design differentiated curricula was also a process modification: the modification of the resources or research skills necessary for the input of content students would be pondering. This modification was a natural consequence of replacing lower order with higher order thinking skills. For example, higher order thinking skills demanded more and varied resources to build a richer background of information or content. It became apparent that students could not apply creative, critical, and problem-

Table 1

Basic Elements Defining the Core Curriculum

Process: Thinking Skills	Content	Process: Research Skills	Product
Thinking Skill	Subject Matter	Research Skills and/or Resources	Culmination or Exhibition
List	The causes and effects of the Industrial Revolution	After reading the text, pages 42–49.	Write a paragraph to share the information.

Table 2

**Differentiating the Core:
Modifying the Process Element—Thinking Skills**

Process: Thinking Skills	Content	Process: Research Skills	Product
~~List~~ Judge with criteria	The causes and effects of the Industrial Revolution	After reading the text, pages 42–49.	Write a paragraph to share the information.

solving skills to simplistic content if these skills were to be practiced with efficacy. The use of more advanced and sophisticated resources was praised by both parents and students. Adjustments in the resources and research skills were tangible evidence that the gifted learner was being accelerated and enriched (see Table 3).

Modifying the product element in the curriculum equation was easy to accomplish because it provided teachers and students with opportunities to exemplify gifted students' productivity. Modifications in the product element

Table 3

Differentiating the Core:
Modifying the Process Element—Research Skills

Process: Thinking Skills	Content	Process: Research Skills	Product
Judge with criteria	The causes and effects of the Industrial Revolution	~~After reading the text, pages 42–49.~~	Write a paragraph to share the information.
		Interview an American history professor at the university; use the Internet; and read the text, Chapter IV.	

became the visible indicators of the effort and concern directed toward the gifted. In many instances, the flamboyancy of the product was believed to be equal to the quality of the gifted program and the recognition of the traits of giftedness. Long and exotic lists of unusual products were provided to teachers of the gifted as references to select products for gifted students to do beyond those traditionally completed by students at the grade or age level to demonstrate their content understanding and skill mastery. For many gifted students, the modifications of products signified the grandiosity of their abilities. For many parents, the modifications of the product became synonymous with gifted education. And, for many teachers, the modification of the product was the clearest means by which to justify their responsiveness to the needs of the gifted (see Table 4).

The nature of the times, the maturity of gifted education, and the infusion of new theories and ideas about curriculum development all lent support to the idea that the modifications in what we wanted students to know and understand—the content areas—were imperative. The controversy centered on what significant modifications were to be made in the content element. Some educators of the gifted advocated the need to rethink the value of the core curriculum and replace it entirely. Others advocated on behalf of enriching the core curriculum by identifying more challenging content that could be distinctive from, yet aligned to, the core. Many educators of the gifted advocated the need to main-

Table 4

Differentiating the Core: Modifying the Content Element

Process: Thinking Skills	Content	Process: Research Skills	Product
Judge with criteria	The causes and effects of the Industrial Revolution	Interview an American history professor at the university; use the Internet; and read the text, Chapter IV.	~~Write a paragraph to share the information.~~ Write an editorial and debate the positive and negative consequences of the Industrial Revolution.

tain the core curriculum and modify the approach to learning it by emphasizing aspects of the discipline in which the core content was embedded so it correlated more directly with the needs, interests, and abilities of gifted students. Currently, the modification of the core content still represents the area of greatest attention and concern in curriculum development for gifted learners.

One attempt to distinguish the appropriate means by which to modify the core curriculum was defined as a consequence of the Javits Grant-funded collaborative work conducted by the California Department of Education and the California Association for the Gifted (1994). An outcome of this work was the articulation of *depth* and *complexity* as two means by which the content element in the learning experience equation could be modified (see Figures 1 and 2). Each dimension of depth and complexity provides a prompt to probe or investigate the content (see Table 5).

Altering the content, process, or product elements of the curriculum equation provides opportunities to differentiate the core curriculum for gifted students. Recognizing those elements that are appropriate to differentiate the curriculum for gifted learners, the teacher as curriculum designer can modify one, some, or all elements of the core curriculum. A basic skill for a higher level critical thinking skill, a simple and concrete concept for a complex or universal con-

Table 5

Differentiating the Core:
Modifying the Content Element

Process: Thinking Skills	Content	Process: Research Skills	Product
Judge with criteria	~~The causes and effects of the Industrial Revolution~~ The patterns in the behaviors and trends of consumers and producers who contributed to the causes and subsequent effects of the Industrial Revolution.	Interview an American history professor at the university; use the Internet; and read the text, Chapter IV.	Write an editorial and debate the positive and negative consequences of the Industrial Revolution.

cept, and an authentic product of a discipline such as a report based on the development of a questionnaire used to conduct a survey represent the types of modifications teachers can make. The altering of one or more elements in the curriculum equation not only demands an understanding of why these modifications are needed, but it also presents a delineation of the scope of options most appropriate to satisfying the needs of gifted students. Altering the content, process, and product elements in the core curriculum is a means of attaining the clearly defined goals of learning for gifted students.

Modifications of each of the content, process, and product elements in the curriculum equation have significantly affected the definition of differentiating the core curriculum. The content, process, and product elements of the curriculum equation have allowed educators to address inquiries about the nature and structure of a differentiated curriculum. It has enabled gifted students to participate in learning experiences without being penalized by both the differentiated and core curricula. However, the definition of differentiation is constantly evolving. New demands in general education, analysis of the achievements of gifted students, and concerns for validation that a differentiated curriculum is responsive to the emerging definitions of intelligence and giftedness all pressure educators to reconsider consistently the meaning of differentiated curricula and how they are constructed.

The Layered Approach to Differentiating the Core Curriculum

The conception of a layered approach to differentiating the core curriculum for the gifted was derived from many factors. First, it came from the awareness of the ever-changing and increasing demands placed on teachers of the gifted. Second, it is a consequence of recognizing that gifted education needs to be more inclusive of many theories, rather than a single curriculum theory. Last, it is related to the significant works of educators in the field of gifted education.

More specifically, the concept of a layered approach to differentiating the curriculum for gifted students emerged from these concerns:

1. Gifted students should not be exonerated from the basic, regular, or core curriculum. While there was a time when the core curriculum was dismissed and devalued as an appropriate curriculum for gifted students, the articulation of national, state, and even local content and performance standards has shown the merit of the core curriculum. Data regarding the academic achievements of gifted students measured against their learning of core content indicates the need to reinforce, rather than abolish, the importance of this curriculum.
2. A single curricular design cannot attend to the diverse needs of gifted students. Therefore, there was a need to develop and implement a differentiated curriculum that included many facets responsive to the heterogeneity among gifted learners.
3. An emphasis on simple linear progress has been found to inhibit the quality of the curriculum. A curriculum that emphasizes a linear progression of learning experiences can deter the gifted student from becoming an expert in particular areas of need or interest. Thus, a curriculum that provides alternative pathways for learning seems to have greater flexibility for the teacher and learner. Alternative pathways can be those that foster breadth, as well as depth.
4. Educators need a curricular structure that defines a field of curricular options and enables them to be responsive to groups, as well as to individual gifted students.

The layered curriculum approach emphasizes the acquisition of content. It is content dependent. The initial decisions made by curriculum developers revolve around the need to articulate the content. Decisions about the inclusion of creative, critical, or problem-solving skills are made only after the content has been defined. Similarly, decisions about the nature of products are deferred until the content has been defined. Processes and products do not lead content selection;

5	Theme	
6	Generalization	
1	Core	
2	Differentiated	
3	Classical	
4	Individualized	

Figure 1. Design for the layered curriculum

rather, content selection determines the processes and products identified for the curriculum. Simply, there is enough evidence to warrant a more judicious concern for content that is appropriate for gifted students and to relinquish the decisions regarding product and higher level thinking skills until the content has been determined. Thus, the plan to format a layered curriculum is a first step, and the consequence of following this format is the development of a content map that leads to other curriculum development decisions. The construction of learning experiences or objectives is dependent on the content map. Lessons are created from these learning experiences, resources are allocated, and assessment procedures and tools are decided. Both learning experiences (objectives) and lessons follow the development of the layers in the content map. The format for developing the layered curriculum content map is numbered to aid the curriculum developer in following a step-by-step process. This numbered system defines the how-to of curriculum development. When the layered curriculum content map is complete, it is read from top to bottom without regard for the numbering system. In other words, the procedure used to develop the curriculum is not commensurate to the method used to read and subsequently implement or instruct the curriculum (see Figure 1).

The Core Curriculum Layer

The first layer is the core curriculum, defined as the basic, rudimentary, or regular curriculum. This curriculum forms the basis of the layered curriculum

5	Theme	
6	Generalization	
1	Core	Students will explain the importance of the Industrial Revolution and its political, social, and economic impact on the nation.
2	Differentiated	
3	Classical	
4	Individualized	

Figure 2. Layer 1: The core curriculum content

design. Derived from an accepted set of standards, the core curriculum outlines the fundamental expectations for gifted learners and does not exonerate them from basic learning because they are gifted or evidence readiness beyond grade-level expectations. The stress to differentiate the core curriculum has sometimes resulted in the absence of the basic curriculum in order to ensure time and learning space, so to speak, for the more enriched or accelerated learning opportunities for the gifted students. The curriculum decision maker must make sure that the concepts, principles, or theories of the core curriculum are aligned to the demands of the needs, interests, and abilities of gifted students. This task is not only crucial to determining the appropriateness of this layer of the curriculum for these learners, but it also serves as the foundation for decisions regarding all other layers of the curriculum.

While the content standard is the foundation on which decisions about the suitability of the core content is made for gifted students, adjustments to the core curriculum must parallel both the needs of the gifted and the philosophy of the gifted program. Many gifted programs exist without a specific definition of differentiation and without a specific definition of expectations or exit criteria distinguishing the anticipated academic accomplishments derived from participation in the gifted program. The interaction of the needs of the gifted, the definition of differentiation, and the philosophy of the gifted program are the factors that ultimately shape the response to the standard and, subsequently, the core curriculum placed into the first layer of the layered curriculum (see Figure 2).

The Differentiated Curriculum Layer

The dimensions of depth and complexity facilitate the differentiation of the core curriculum. The dimensions of depth have been named to focus the teacher's and student's attention on increasingly more difficult, divergent, and abstract qualities of knowing a discipline or area of study. These can be introduced in descending order from simple to difficult, concrete to abstract, specific to general. They do not have to be included in every lesson or unit of study, nor do they necessarily need to be taught in the order in which they were originally introduced to the students. They are guides to developing questions and tasks that outline the essential understandings of subject matter. The dimensions of depth are not to be confused with the various levels of Bloom's (1956) Taxonomy of Educational Objectives in the cognitive domain. The dimensions of depth define what students are to know; the levels of Bloom's taxonomy define the cognitive operations students are to employ with content. The definitions and icons illustrating the dimensions of depth are illustrated in Figure 3.

Complexity can be defined as the means by which knowledge is extended or broadened. The dimensions of complexity afford the teacher and the student with opportunities to identify the associations: connections, relationships, and links exist within, between, and among areas or disciplines of study. It is these interactions that enable learners to broaden their understanding of the knowledge. The icons that symbolize the dimensions of complexity and their definitions are shown in Figure 4.

The current value placed on content assimilation is validated by the importance of national and state discipline-related standards and state and district accountability instruments and procedures. The effort to facilitate gifted students' ability to delve into content to increase their understanding led to the development of the content imperatives. These content imperatives have been introduced as key words to prompt more advanced and sophisticated comprehension of content or the subject matter under study. These key words have been identified as those most representative of what experts might know and understand in their respective disciplines. Following are the definitions and nonlinguistic representations of the content imperatives (see Figure 5). The use of the content imperatives is supported by these factors: (1) the demand for gifted students to recognize a set of universal and common concepts that facilitate study in the disciplines, (2) the concern for providing gifted students with sophisticated key concepts to specify their inquiry into content, and (3) the realization that self-directed learners need the requisite tools to probe content without adult intervention.

The content imperatives provide greater specificity and directionality to the dimensions of depth and complexity and are used in conjunction with the dimensions of depth and complexity (see Figure 6). For example, the coupling of *origins* with *patterns* requires learners to define the point of initiation or beginning of the pattern, or establishing the relationship between *contributions*

 **Language** of the disciplines refers to learning the specific specialized and technological terms associated with a specific area of study or discipline.

 Details refer to the learning of the specific attributes, traits, and characteristics that describe a concept, theory, principle, and even a fact.

 Patterns refer to recurring events represented by details.

 Trends refer to the factors that influence events.

 Unanswered questions refer to the ambiguities and gaps of information recognized within an area or discipline under study.

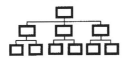 **Rules** refer to the natural or human-made structure or order of things that explain the phenomena within an area of study.

 Ethics refer to the dilemmas or controversial issues that plague an area of study or discipline.

 Big ideas refer to the generalizations, principles, and theories that distinguish themselves from the facts and concepts of the area or discipline under study.

Figure 3. Dimensions of depth

Note. Definitions from *Differentiating the Core Curriculum and Instruction to Provide Advanced Learning Opportunities*, by S. Kaplan (California Department of Education and California Association for the Gifted), 1994, University of Southern California. Copyright ©1994 by Sandra Kaplan. Icons from S. Kaplan, 1994, University of Southern California. Copyright ©1994 by Sandra Kaplan. Reprinted with permission.

relate over time

Over time refers to the understanding of time as an agent of change and recognition that the passage of time changes our knowledge of things.

view from different perspectives

Points of view refer to the concept that there are different perspectives and that these perspectives alter the way ideas and objects are viewed and valued.

across disciplines

Disciplinary connections refer to both integrated and interdisciplinary links in the curriculum. Disciplinary connections can be made within, between, and among various areas of study or disciplines.

Figure 4. Dimensions of complexity

Note. Definitions from *Differentiating the Core Curriculum and Instruction to Provide Advanced Learning Opportunities*, by S. Kaplan (California Department of Education and California Association for the Gifted), 1994, University of Southern California. Copyright ©1994 by Sandra Kaplan. Icons from S. Kaplan, 1994, University of Southern California. Copyright ©1994 by Sandra Kaplan. Reprinted with permission.

and *rules* requires the learner to describe the value rendered from the establishment or implementation of the rules. The use of the content imperatives in conjunction with the dimensions of depth and complexity does not add another layer to the curriculum, but refines the differentiated curriculum layer (see Figure 7).

The core and the differentiated layers are symbiotically related and are taught in tandem. While the core layer usually precedes the differentiated layer in the curriculum design, it is possible that the dimensions of depth and complexity can preface the core curriculum in the implementation or pedagogical practice. How the layers are written in the curriculum format does not imply that they must be taught in the same way. In fact, teachers need to understand that writing a curriculum in accord with a given format is intended to guide the development process and tell them what to think about as they construct the curriculum; it is not intended to tell them how to teach the curriculum they are generating. Rather, the instructional plan for teaching the curriculum is described in activities and lessons derived from the curricular format and should be seen as a separate section that follows the design outlining the layers of the curriculum (see Figure 8).

Origin

The catalyst, roots, cause, or beginning of something

Contribution

The achievements, consequences, effects of something

Parallel

The comparable, similar, analogous relationship of something

Paradox

The fallacy or incongruities of something

Convergence

The meeting points of ideas or events of something

Figure 5. Content imperatives

Origin

Patterns

The origin of patterns

Contribution

Rules

The contribution of rules

Figure 6. Content imperatives and depth and complexity

Differentiated	Defining the origin of the rules affecting employers and employees, men and women, and children and adults in the workplace during and after the Industrial Revolution.

Figure 7. Redefining the differentiated curriculum layer

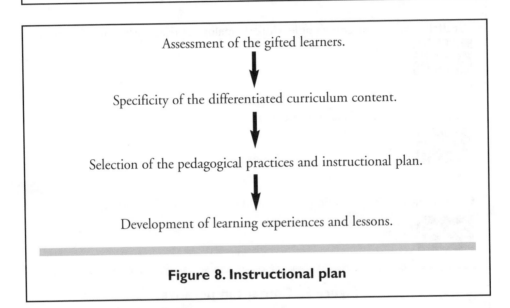

Assessment of the gifted learners.

Specificity of the differentiated curriculum content.

Selection of the pedagogical practices and instructional plan.

Development of learning experiences and lessons.

Figure 8. Instructional plan

The Classical Curriculum Layer

This is perhaps the most controversial of the curriculum layers (see Figure 9). In the context of this curriculum, the classical layer is based on a humanities approach to teaching the gifted. It is intended to present the teacher and the students with an orientation to subject areas that are often deferred due to the age of the student; the time involved in teaching these subjects; and, most importantly, the prevailing beliefs about who gifted students are and what they can learn or are supposed to learn at school. Another controversial aspect of this layer is that it is fraught with issues about what is considered to be a classic. Arguments emerge regarding the inclusion of eastern versus western classics, old world versus contemporary classics, cultural representation in the selection and presentation of the classics, and the developmental appropriateness of the classics. Of course, there is always the argument about the justification of the classics in an already full curriculum that is hurrying to prepare students in prerequisites necessary for tests to enter specialized programs and colleges.

5	**Theme**	
6	**Generalization**	
1	**Core**	Students will explain the importance of the Industrial Revolution and its political, social, and economic impact on the nation.
2	**Differentiated**	Define the origin of the parallel affecting the relationships between employers and employees, men and women, and children and adults in the workplace during and after the Industrial Revolution.
3	**Classical**	
4	**Individualized**	

Figure 9. Layer 2: Differentiating the core curriculum content

The major objective of this layer is not to expect mastery of classical ideas of philosophy, psychology, and the arts, but rather to expose learners to them. Much has been written about the need to expose gifted students to a variety of experiences (e.g., Renzulli, 1977). The obligation of a curriculum to provide a sampling of nontraditional areas and disciplines of study is crucial if the concept of developing gifted students into lifelong learners is more than simply rhetoric. It is important to note that issues of both the quality and quantity of general versus specific studies for gifted students have never really reached consensus in the field. Many educators of the gifted will support the need for gifted students to specialize early in their academic careers, while others will fight for the gifted students' right to be introduced to the many and varied areas that are available for more intense study at a later time in their educational careers. Too often, gifted students are hampered in their academic choices because they were not given the chance to see the broad range of subject areas and disciplines from which they can choose. This classic layer is dedicated to introducing the structure of the disciplines and reinforcing the dimensions of depth and complexity to investigate the common features of any discipline: language, rules, big ideas, and perspectives.

The selection of the classical area of a discipline to include in the curriculum is dependent on both the core and differentiated curriculum layers. There must be a natural, rather than contrived, alignment of these layers. The curriculum developer must perceive this layer as an interdependent and individualistic member of the total curriculum. The entries on this layer should not have meaning as separate areas or disciplines of study; rather, they have meaning

5	Theme	
6	Generalization	
1	Core	Students will explain the importance of the Industrial Revolution and its political, social, and economic impact on the nation.
2	Differentiated	Define the origin of the parallel affecting the relationships between employers and employees, men and women, and children and adults in the workplace during and after the Industrial Revolution.
3	Classical	Investigate Kurt Lenin's psychological study describing the distribution of power in groups.

Relate Plato's concept of differential roles in society (philosophers, kings, artisans, warriors, etc.) to the needs and interests of people in the industrialization of a society. Explore the parallel ideas of artists in illustrating "industry" or "revolution." |
| 4 | Individualized | |

Figure 10. Layer 3: Classical learning

only as they augment the understanding and stimulate investigations to enhance the core and differentiated layers. This layer is dependent on many and varied resources. Technology can be the tool that bridges the study of an area in a discipline with the real world by including contemporary resources as important reference materials. The inclusion of this layer in the curriculum is to ensure that gifted students understand the relationship between past learning and current happenings. This layer forces the connection between today's world and any subject or topic the gifted students are studying in the curriculum designed for them (see Figure 10).

The Individualized Curriculum Layer

This layer is the formalized opportunity for gifted students to study further a teacher-selected defined topic within the core and differentiated curriculum layers or a topic that is student-selected and is an extension of the core curriculum. An important factor of this particular layer is that it affords gifted students the time to conduct an independent study that introduces learning-to-learning skills while simultaneously affording the student the time to delve more independently and individualistically into a topic of choice. This layer provides the prime opportunity for students to integrate into the independent study the dimensions of depth and complexity as prompts to form questions they want to

5	Theme	
6	Generalization	
1	Core	Students will explain the importance of the Industrial Revolution and its political, social, and economic impact on the nation.
2	Differentiated	Define the origin of the parallel affecting the relationships between employers and employees, men and women, and children and adults in the workplace during and after the Industrial Revolution.
3	Classical	Investigate Kurt Lenin's psychological study describing the distribution of power in groups. Relate Plato's concept of differential roles in society (philosophers, kings, artisans, warriors, etc.) to the needs and interests of people in the industrialization of a society. Explore the parallel ideas of artists in illustrating "industry" or "revolution."
4	Individualized	Select a specific topic of interest to investigate from among these areas: Inventions Standardizations Immigrants Unionism Supply and Demand Workers' Rights Form factual, analytic, and evaluative questions to organize and conduct a historical case study or descriptive type of study.

Figure 11. Layer 4: Individualized learning

pursue. Unfortunately, this layer is a part and not the entire focus of the curriculum, so it is necessary to schedule time for the implementation of this layer without diminishing the other layers or demanding too little or too much from the students.

Self-discovery should be one of the outcomes derived from learning at this layer of the curriculum. The discovery of their preferred learning style, interests and abilities, as well as academic strengths and weaknesses represent the types of accomplishments students should acquire as they work at this layer. In addition to these discoveries, gifted students should be aided in learning about how they allocate their study time, what types of intrinsic and extrinsic rewards are most conducive to sustained motivation and effort, and what types of activities seem to require independent versus dependent behaviors (see Figure 11).

The Organizing Element or Theme and Generalization Curriculum Layer

This last layer (see Figure 12) represents the organizing element for the curriculum or the theme and its corresponding generalization. Its purpose is to excite the ability to connect information, debate ideas, and discuss the implica-

5	**Theme**	Systems
6	**Generalization**	Systems are made of parts and work together to accomplish a purpose. Systems follow rules and procedures.
1	**Core**	Students will explain the importance of the Industrial Revolution and its political, social, and economic impact on the nation.
2	**Differentiated**	Define the origin of the parallel affecting the relationships between employers and employees, men and women, and children and adults in the workplace during and after the Industrial Revolution.
3	**Classical**	Investigate Kurt Lenin's psychological study describing the distribution of power in groups. Relate Plato's concept of differential roles in society (philosophers, kings, artisans, warriors, etc.) to the needs and interests of people in the industrialization of a society. Explore the parallel ideas of artists in illustrating "industry" or "revolution."
4	**Individualized**	Sam will study inventions. Melinda will study the effects of child labor.

Figure 12. Layers 5 and 6: Theme and generalization

tions of the content as it relates to the designated theme and generalization. In other words, the generalization serves as the purpose for investigating, comprehending, and summarizing all the layers of content: core, differentiated, classical, and individualized.

Following is a list of themes with some accompanying generalizations that have been used by teachers of the gifted in various programs throughout the country. These themes represent a set of universal concepts suggested by educators throughout the years. The generalizations are defined by scholars in the disciplines. The conventional wisdom derived from the usage of those themes and generalizations dictates the need to select a theme in accordance with age appropriateness, to develop a sequence of these themes so they are not repeated yearly and become redundant to students, and to understand as educators that there is no mastery of these themes because understanding them is a lifelong pursuit.

Patterns
  Generalizations:
  - Patterns can be predictors.
  - Some patterns are determined by nature; some patterns are human-made.
  - Patterns reveal the parts of the whole.

Change

Generalizations:

- Change can be planned or spontaneous, evolutionary or revolutionary.
- Change has a ripple effect—one change stimulates another.
- Change can create dissonance.

Systems

Generalizations:

- Systems are made of parts that work together to perform a function.
- Systems interact, and these interactions are positive or negative.
- Systems change over time in form and function.

Conflict

Generalizations:

- Conflict is inevitable.
- Conflict can lead to growth and can be generative.
- Conflict is a consequence of change.

Structure

Generalizations:

- Structure can follow function.
- Structures can be formed within structures.
- Structure is inherent in everything.

Power

Generalizations:

- Power can be destructive or constructive.
- Power can influence.
- Power can be natural or developed.

Relationships

Generalizations:

- Relationships are formed for many and varied purposes.
- Some relationships endure longer than others.
- Everything is related in some way.

Adaptation

Generalizations:

- Adaptation is necessary for survival.
- Adaptation is a consequence of many factors that are biotic or abiotic.
- Adaptation is facilitated by diffusion.

Experiential Readiness of Gifted Learners and the Layered Curriculum

The discrepancy between the recognized potential and performance of gifted students has always presented educators of the gifted with a dilemma. The economic, geographic, linguistic, and cultural diversity among gifted students contributes to gifted students' readiness and the quality of their participation in a differentiated curriculum. Often, identification of students as gifted underachievers or "not really gifted" is a consequence of a lack of preparation to engage in a differentiated curriculum. The expectations in the differentiated curriculum and the varied readiness levels among gifted students also have caused an achievement gap within the gifted student population.

The lack of prerequisite experiences attributed to this achievement gap can be ameliorated by a layered curriculum design that exposes students to a range of advanced and sophisticated understandings. Each layer of the curriculum can serve as a prerequisite and transition from one set of performance expectations to another. Success with the core layer provides the readiness for the differentiated layer; success with the differentiated layer provides the readiness for the classical layer. Each layer of the curriculum provides an apprenticeship for the movement to a more intellectually challenging layer. The layered curriculum design has also been used as a scope and sequence to assess the readiness needs of diverse gifted learners to participate successfully in the gifted program and to target appropriate intervention for these learners. All these practices are aimed at reducing the designation of the label of underachiever to these students and the attrition of such students from the gifted program.

A 3rd-grade teacher in a large urban school district whose population is 90% Latino has employed the layered curriculum with her entire class. While the pacing of the lessons, resources used to augment the lessons, and amount of assistance to learners varies with respect to individual and group needs, the teacher is making the differentiated curriculum for gifted students available to all learners. Challenged by colleagues who state that the curriculum is too hard for all except the gifted students, the teacher explains how she uses Sheltered English techniques such as nonlinguistic representations (the icons of depth and complexity and content imperatives) and artifacts to make abstract content concrete. Most significantly, the implementation of the layered curriculum in this teacher's classroom has provided the curricular catalyst needed to identify more students as gifted. The layered curriculum can become the arena for developing and recognizing giftedness.

Implementing the Layered Curriculum

Many factors ultimately determine the effectiveness of the curriculum developed for gifted students. Some of these factors have less to do with the curriculum's structure and the scope and more to do with the milieu in which it is taught.

1. The curriculum for gifted students must be consonant with the purpose, philosophy, and structure of the gifted program. The implementation of a layered curriculum in a pull-out program has a very different effect and requires a different timeline than that same curriculum in a regular classroom with a cluster grouping of gifted students.

2. The curriculum should not have to compete with other types of curricula or programs developed or purchased to respond to the needs of the gifted. The implementation of a layered curriculum that has to compete with other programs is doomed to failure. Teachers who have to divide their loyalty between curricula that have incompatible philosophies opt to ignore the curricula given to them. Of concern is how the various layers can support teacher-designed and commercial curricular experiences.

3. The curriculum for gifted students must be used as a whole with integrated and mutually reinforcing features or elements. The implementation of a layered curriculum in a situation where teachers are led to believe they can mix and match the elements to create their own eclectic curriculum is not appropriate. A disjointed selection or the incremental implementation of a layered curriculum abuses the integrity of the curriculum. It also makes the curriculum less appropriate to the needs of gifted students and the comprehensive plan to educate them. The lack of a comprehensive curricular approach has been more injurious than helpful to the gifted.

4. The curriculum for gifted students must be accompanied by the resources that augment it. The implementation of a layered curriculum demands attention to surveying and gathering resources that are comprehensible, yet challenging, and clearly extend beyond textbooks and other traditionally available resources. Teachers and students must understand that the layered curriculum requires materials that extend beyond the textbook, yet are parallel to the textbook's core content used by all learners.

5. The curriculum for gifted students must be introduced with clarity within professional staff development activities. However, just providing staff development is insufficient to successful implementation of a curriculum for the gifted. The implementation of a layered curriculum requires a targeted set of staff development sessions within the context of a plan of action. This means that staff development sessions must be clearly defined and scheduled over a given time period. There needs to be some type of accountability that travels with the educator from the in-service venue to the classroom to ensure that what was presented in staff development sessions is practiced in the classroom. It has been noted that the failure of the curriculum is not always a consequence of the in-service; rather, it is a consequence of the lack of follow-up. On-site, in-classroom observations of the curriculum are crucial if it is to be practiced with efficacy.

6. The curriculum for the gifted needs to be understood for what it provides, as well as for what it does not provide. Many times, the curriculum for the gifted is blamed for academic weaknesses of the gifted student and the inadequacies of the gifted program. The implementation of the layered curriculum cannot guarantee high SAT scores, motivated gifted students, or students being accepted to universities of their choice. The implementation of the layered curriculum can provide only what it has been designed to accomplish:

- develop the core curriculum;
- provide for greater depth and complexity of the core curricular content;
- introduce classical ideas and correlate the past with the present;
- allow opportunities to study independently; and
- make connections within, between, and among areas and disciplines of study using a global theme and related generalizations.

Conclusion

The layered approach to differentiate the curriculum for gifted students is only one of many ways suggested to provide appropriate curricula for the gifted. There are many other models that can be used to develop or design differentiated curricula. Sometimes educators are confused when confronted by all the different models, theories, and philosophies available to differentiate the core curriculum for the gifted, and they ask for assistance in identifying the "best" from among these models. There are criteria that can be used to help teachers of the gifted, curriculum developers, and administrators select the model, theory, or philosophy to be used to define differentiated curriculum for the gifted. A design to differentiate the curriculum for the gifted should

- match the needs assessment data that answers the questions about the nature and needs of these students;
- match the program prototype selected to administer or implement the gifted program;
- match the competencies and the knowledge of the teachers of the gifted responsible for implementing the curriculum;
- match the expectations for both the general and gifted educational programs and reinforce rather than isolate gifted students from the basic educational program;
- match the understandings and interests of the parents of the gifted; and
- match the gifted students' expectations for their current and future educational aspirations.

Teacher Statement

When creating my learning environment, which is a standards-based hetero-geneous classroom setting, I modify the curriculum to make an appropriate match between the grade-level curriculum and the interests, needs, and abilities of the students. I believe a differentiated curriculum is the key to maximizing the effectiveness of learning successfully. With this in mind, a standards-based curriculum becomes most powerful when I have combined it with depth and complexity, the content imperatives, and the strategy of thinking like a disciplinarian.

I layer the curriculum to best meet the needs of students relative to the standard being addressed. Making the match between the elements of depth and complexity and the standards provides my students with a clearly defined tool to solidify their learning of the content or skill. For example, when I address the concept of multiplication in the 3rd grade, the concept becomes much clearer through the study of the depth dimensions of patterns and rules. Suddenly, the rote skill of multiplying becomes an understood concept, which then supports further study in division and decimals. Utilizing the dimensions of depth and complexity provides tacit ways of differentiating the prescribed curriculum for my students. While studying fairy tales in literature, the depth dimension of details relates to identifying the beginning, middle, and end of the story. Learners can look for the dimensions of patterns within fairy tales and then discuss the literary elements of characters, setting, or events more easily. Standards-based research skills can also be guided by the study of one or more dimensions of depth and complexity.

Similar to the use of depth and complexity, the content imperatives of origin, parallel, paradox, contribution, and convergence can be aligned to the curriculum and add to student understanding. While learning about culture in the study of social science, I think it is important that students recognize that culture began somewhere (origin). Making connections between different areas of grade-level content helps students understand big ideas. Within the standards, the content imperatives appear and need to be recognized. When they are identified, students are able to learn the subject area "one step further." Again, like most anything, the use of the content imperatives can range in difficulty. A lesson focused on the content imperative of origin is then an appropriate match to help solidify student understanding for novices. Content imperatives provide an immediate path to help students understand the effects of subjects such as culture. Within that subject, parallels can be identified between other cultures, as well as differences that can also be known as paradoxes. Concepts that sometimes appear too sophisticated for my students become clearer with the use of the content imperatives.

Finally, I add another layer to the standards-based curriculum. This layer is the study of grade-level curricula as seen through the eyes of a disciplinarian. This enables students to apply the learned content in an even more sophisticated manner. Allowing students to identify the relationship between content and the study of disciplinarians not only provides them the opportunity to recognize the effects of one thing to another, but it also facilitates thinking that requires a more thorough and reflective understanding of the material being discussed or researched. Looking at something from a different perspective truly broadens a student's understanding of the content. Although not all students need to speak from the perspective of another, learning to think as a disciplinarian develops a student's vocabulary, thinking skills, and comprehension. Used alone or together, depth and complexity, the content imperatives, and thinking like a disciplinarian not only facilitate effective use of the curriculum, but, more importantly, they evoke meaningful student learning.

—Kimberly Dodds

Discussion Questions

1. What rationale can be used to support the need to develop a differentiated curriculum for gifted students?

2. What factors need to be considered by curriculum designers to construct a differentiated curriculum for gifted students?

3. What contemporary educational issues affect the development and implementation of a differentiated curriculum for gifted students?

4. How can a differentiated curriculum become a tool to advocate for the educational needs of gifted students?

5. Why is it important to distinguish between differentiation of curriculum, instruction, and program services?

References

Bloom, B. (Ed.). (1956). *Taxonomy of educational objectives: The classification of educational goals. Handbook I: Cognitive domain.* New York: Longman Green.

California Department of Education & California Association for the Gifted. (1994). *Differentiating the core curriculum and instruction to provide advanced learning opportunities.* Sacramento: California Department of Education.

Renzulli, J. S. (1977). *The enrichment triad model: A guide for developing defensible programs for the gifted and talent.* Mansfield Center, CT: Creative Learning Press.

References

Chapter 5

Process Skills and the Gifted Learner

by **Robert W. Seney**

key position in curriculum design for gifted learners is that modifications must be made in content, process, product, and environment to differentiate appropriately for these students. The area of process skills has become most commonly associated with gifted learning and curricula. Indeed, they have sometimes been popularly designated as "the curriculum for the gifted." In the big picture, this is unfortunate, but it is easy to see how this concept has developed. A major emphasis in learning programs for gifted learners is that these students should learn to manipulate or use knowledge instead of concentrating on the acquisition of knowledge. The phrase "producer of knowledge and not just a user" typifies this appropriate attitude.

In order to become a producer, educators believed it was necessary to teach skills of processing. For students to manipulate knowledge, solve problems, and think critically and creatively, the focus highlighted process strategies, eventually becoming the educational center of the curriculum in many gifted programs. While important and the subject of this chapter, it is necessary to acknowledge at the onset that teaching process skills in isolation, instead of in the context of high-level or abstract content (either teacher-designated or student-selected), is inappropriate for gifted learners. Athletic skills or performance skills are not taught separately; as soon as possible, the skills are put into the game or the performance. This is just as true for the gifted learner and process skills. Simply put, process skills are taught in order for students to handle advanced content—the focus of their studies—more appropriately.

However, process skills need to be investigated, and their importance for gifted learners should be emphasized. It must be noted that, in using the various skills, the procedures and models of these strategies must be taught. The phases, processes, and vocabulary of each of these approaches must be understood by the learner in order for these tools to be used effectively with advanced content. This progression of learning the skills and then applying them is readily seen in Betts' Autonomous Learner Model (Betts & Kercher, 1999). Dimension Two of this model is Individual Development, which is divided into six basic areas: (1) inter/intrapersonal, (2) learning skills, (3) technology, (4) college and career involvement, (5) organizational skills, and (6) productivity. In learning skills, Betts (1985) listed 12 skill areas that should be taught for later use in becoming a self-directed learner. These identified skills are (1) problem-solving skills, (2) organizational skills, (3) creativity skills, (4) thinking skills, (5) writing skills, (6) decision-making skills, (7) goal-setting skills, (8) photographic skills, (9) research skills, (10) computer skills, (11) study skills, and (12) additional skills designed by the teacher/facilitator and the students.

Obviously, other program models depend heavily upon process skills (these models are discussed in more detail in Chapter 3, "An Analysis of Gifted Education Curricular Models"). In Renzulli and Reis' (1985) Schoolwide Enrichment Model (formerly called the Enrichment Triad/Revolving Door Model), Type II activities are primarily process skills. Feldhusen's (1980) Purdue Three-Stage Model, in particular, relies heavily on process skills in both Stage 1 and Stage 2, and the application of process skills is found in Stage 3. Treffinger's Effective Independent Learner Model (1985) lists process development as one of its four major components. The Multiple Talent Approach and Talents Unlimited (Schlichter, 1985) is itself not only a program model based on process skills, but also a model for developing thinking skills. Other program models rely heavily upon process skills, as well (see Renzulli, 1986).

An emphasis on higher level thinking skills has long been an accepted hallmark in designing appropriate curricula for gifted learners. It was in the gifted classroom that Bloom's (1956) Taxonomy of Educational Objectives became popular. This taxonomy, which has now trickled down into objectives and activities in the regular classroom, classifies thinking processes into six levels, each of which depends on the levels below it: (1) knowledge or recall, (2) comprehension, (3) application, (4) analysis, (5) synthesis, and (6) evaluation. In learning activities for the gifted, the focus of learning and curricula has been on analysis, synthesis, and evaluation—the higher level thinking skills. While all learners need exposure to all levels of thinking, gifted learners flourish and thrive on higher level thinking skills and are often frustrated when instruction focuses primarily at the knowledge and comprehension levels. A good description of strategies for using Bloom's taxonomy in the classroom can be found in Winebrenner (1992). While

Bloom's taxonomy can still be considered a primer for gifted education, in order to ensure that the curriculum is truly differentiated for gifted learners, it is important to look for more sophisticated and advanced strategies.

The purpose of this focus on higher level thinking skills is to guide students into thinking independently and to help them "transfer these skills from one curriculum area to another and from one dimension (such as academic) to another dimension (such as their personal lives)" (VanTassel-Baska, 1994, p. 56). VanTassel-Baska suggested the following organization to ensure maximum internalization and transfer effect. The process skills must be (1) well-defined; (2) consistently addressed over time; (3) taught within basic content domains, as well as with intensity as a separate instructional set; (4) organized by scope and sequence from K–12; (5) modeled by the teacher in the classroom; and (6) employed as questioning techniques by the teacher (pp. 56–57).

Maker and Nielson's (1996) use of eight modifications is recommended. They suggested a process modification that emphasizes higher levels of thinking, open-endedness, discovery learning, evidence of reasoning, freedom of choice, group interaction, pacing, and variety of processes. A synopsis of each process modification follows.

Process Modifications

Higher Levels of Thinking

As we move the instructional emphasis from the lower levels of thinking (memory or recall) to the higher levels of thinking (application, analysis, synthesis, and evaluation), we take an important step in building greater student involvement in learning. The emphasis becomes one of using information, rather than focusing on the acquisition of facts and skills (Maker & Neilson, 1996).

Open-Endedness

This concept is different from the convergent-divergent emphasis found in much of the literature. Open-endedness requires a teacher attitude that is reflected in questioning techniques and the content of the questions. It also impacts the design of learning activities, materials, and the approach to evaluating student responses to questions. Maker and Nielson (1996) listed these advantages to open-ended questions:

> They (a) encourage many students to give responses; (b) encourage student–to-student rather than teacher-to-student interaction patterns; (c) elicit more complete and more complex responses; (d) allow students to give knowledgeable answers; (e) encourage students to question them-

selves, their classmates, and their teachers; and (f) stimulate further thought and exploration of a topic. (p. 107)

Discovery Learning

The importance of discovery learning is that it helps students learn and "acquire knowledge that is uniquely their own because they discover it themselves" (Carin & Sund, 1980, p. 100). This process requires the use of information as tools for inductive thinking. Students must find the meaning, structure, and organization of ideas. The primary mental processes of observing, classifying, labeling, describing, and inferring must be used as they draw conclusions and form generalizations. "Through doing, rather than listening, students learn to think inductively; to see a pattern among items, events, or phenomena that are presented (or observed); and to discern reasons why a particular pattern occurs" (Maker & Nielson, 1996, p. 110).

Evidence of Reasoning

It is important for gifted students to be able to explain the reasoning process or analysis that produced an answer. Three reasons are listed for this importance: (1) learners benefit from hearing or seeing how others analyze a problem; (2) it provides an opportunity to evaluate the processes, as well as the products, of their thinking; and (3) it is important for students to be aware of their own mental processes in order to control and refine them (Maker & Nielson, 1996).

Freedom of Choice

"Gifted students need freedom to choose topics to study, methods to use in the process of manipulating and transforming information, the type of products to create, and the context of the learning environment in which to purse their studies" (Maker & Nielson, 1996, p.120). As freedom is provided for students, keep in mind the degree and kind of freedom allowed, plus the ability of the student to manage or profit from the freedom. The teacher must also be able to surrender some control of part of the student's learning. While maximum freedom is seen in independent study, teachers can also use the element of choice in teacher-directed activities, as well (Maker & Nielson).

Group Interaction

"Group process and group interaction activities should be an integral part of curricula for gifted students" (Maker & Nielson, 1996 p. 126). These activities provide the opportunity to build group effectiveness and to assist individuals in developing skills in relating to others. Betts (1985) has suggested that group-building activities are an essential element in gifted programming. These activities provide the setting for learning important social and leadership skills (Maker & Nielson).

Pacing

Maker and Nielson (1996) consider pacing as one of the most important process modifications for gifted students. "Pace of instruction" refers to how quickly or slowly the information is presented in learning situations. "Accelerated pacing" refers to introducing new material, skills, or both in instruction and moving through the curriculum at a faster pace. In addition, it is generally recognized that gifted students do not need as much time to assimilate and process information. Modification of pacing should not be seen as cutting short student thinking time. In fact, rapid movement through standard or required curricula can provide more time for thinking and analysis (Maker & Nielson, 1996).

Variety of Processes

"Variety of process" refers to the number and types of learning procedures used. Teachers should use many different presentation strategies: Film, lectures, television, demonstrations, field trips, computer-based instruction, and learning centers are only a few ways in which information can be presented. Students should be encouraged to participate in discussions, learning games, independent research, and small-group activities. The key to this modification is to discard the erroneous belief that all students must do the same thing at the same time (Maker & Nielson, 1996).

Maker and Nielson's (1996) treatment of these process skills, as summarized above, provides important lessons in differentiating learning for gifted students. Maker and Nielson see these processes as "crucial methodologies for manipulating content information and transforming it into personal knowledge" (p. 134). Some may not see "variety of processes" as a process skill as such, but it has been included in this synopsis of Maker and Nielson's work to emphasize that a variety of process skills and activities may be at work in the classroom at any given moment.

Critical Thinking

The interactions between critical thinking and process skills are important. Many of these skills are, in fact, models of critical thinking. The Creative Problem Solving Model (CPS; Parnes, 1967) is a prime example. This model, with its unique combination of divergent and convergent thinking, demonstrates the interaction of critical thinking and processing. Models discussed later in other chapters project this same interaction. Other thinking models with this interaction are de Bono's (1986) Six Thinking Hats, Harnadek's (1981a, 1981b) Critical Thinking and Mind Bender programs, and Eberle and Stanish's (1995) CPS for Kids, to mention only a few. As various models are investigated, the importance of integrating critical thinking, learning processes, and significant content becomes obvious.

With this interaction of critical thinking and decision making, the work of Ennis (1964) provides some important guidelines. He suggested that students develop critical thinking skills by judging whether a statement follows from the premises, something is an assumption, an observation statement is reliable, a simple generalization is warranted, a hypothesis is warranted, a theory is warranted, an argument depends on ambiguity, a statement is over vague or over specific, and an alleged authority is reliable (pp. 600–610). As students master these "judging" skills, they become adept in critical thinking, and these skills provide a taxonomy that moves them beyond Bloom.

If a program or teacher is thinking of designing and implementing a critical thinking program, the extensive works of Beyer (1987, 1988, 1997, 1999) may be helpful.

The Constructivist Perspective

Constructivism is a theory about knowledge and learning that requires "a dramatic change in the focus of teaching by putting the students' own efforts to understand at the center of the educational enterprise" (Prawat, 1992, p. 357). This requires a learning setting in which "the traditional telling-listening relationship between teacher and student is replaced by one that is more complex and interactive" (p. 357). In the summary of Maker and Nielson's comments on discovery learning earlier in this chapter, the reader may well have been reminded of the theory of constructivism. This approach lends itself extremely well to education of gifted learners because it embodies many of the concepts that have been listed as important in learning activities for gifted learners. Brooks and Brooks (1993) suggested five principles of a constructivist pedagogy:

- posing problems of emerging relevance to students;
- structuring learning around primary concepts (the quest for essence);
- seeking and valuing students' points of view;
- adapting the curriculum to address students' suppositions; and
- assessing student learning in the context of teaching (p. 33).

In this approach to learning, the teacher begins with a large question (the "umbrella" question) that prompts students to share their points of view. The teacher then encourages students to construct new understandings through probing questions and encouraging elaboration. Key words in this approach are *classifying*, *analyzing*, and *predicting*. With the focus on the learner, it is readily seen how appropriate this approach could be with gifted learners.

Process Skills

This section will focus on those skills that develop a student's ability to think, reason, search for knowledge, communicate, and interact effectively with others. For the purpose of this discussion, the Process Skills Rating Scales–Revised (PSRS-R) developed by Karnes and Bean (2004) will be used as a guide. The PSRS-R, as seen in Table 1, obtain a rating of students' use of process skills. The scales can be used with elementary and secondary students, and they focus on those areas that will enhance students' abilities to function well both in school and in the adult world.

Verbal Communication Skills

It is important for gifted learners to realize that the greatest ideas and solutions in the world are not worth anything unless they can be communicated effectively. The primary means of communicating those ideas is often through oral communication skills—the "ubiquitous" skills. These skills pervade every aspect of our lives. Oral communication is the primary form of communication. Even students who do not like to read or write find pleasure in talking in both informal and formal learning situations (Tchudi & Mitchell, 1999).

The importance of oral communication in the classroom and in the learning process cannot be ignored. Teacher talk is often seen as the most important talk in the classroom, but oral interaction between and among students may be more important, especially for gifted learners. Through oral communication, students assimilate new knowledge, make sense of it, and integrate it. By talking, students show us they can think and solve problems.

Talking is not only a medium for thinking, but also an important means by which people learn how to think. From a Vygotskian perspective, thinking is an internal dialogue, an internalization of dialogues with others. The ability to think depends upon the many previous dialogues, that is, people learn to think by participating in dialogue (Dudley-Marling & Sarle, 1991). Tchudi and Mitchell (1999) suggested a five-phase process to use oral communication as a learning tool:

1. *Involving and engaging.* Teachers engage students in considering new material. Students use brainstorming or discuss what they know about a topic. The purpose is to give all students a chance to be heard and to get them to "buy into" the topic.
2. *Exploring.* Students in small groups begin to make sense of the information by sharing questions about the topic and discussing areas of interest.
3. *Transforming.* Students begin to focus their thinking and make decisions as they seek new understanding about the topic.
4. *Presenting.* Students make formal presentations before the larger group. The purpose is not only to inform, but to allow the larger

Table I

Process Skills Rating Scales–Revised

Skills	Descriptor
Verbal communication skills (speech)	A continuum of skills including the ability to express ideas in conversation and group discussion; to develop logically the points of a speech; to develop and deliver various types of speeches; and to obtain appropriate feedback.
Verbal communication skills (group discussion)	A continuum of skills including the ability to apply proper techniques for leading a group discussion; to keep the group focused on a topic; and to facilitate the contributions of the group members.
Verbal communication skills (interviewing)	A continuum of skills including the ability to construct appropriate interview questions; to develop a positive relationship with the respondent; and to analyze the information received.
Verbal communication skills (debate)	A continuum of skills including the ability to know various styles of debate; to identify appropriate materials for a debate; and to formulate and analyze rebuttals.
Written communication skills	A continuum of skills including the ability to write sentences and paragraphs; to evaluate writing; and to proofread and edit.
Receptive/nonverbal communication skills	A continuum of skills including the ability to listen with a purpose; to recognize nonverbal techniques to influence thinking; and to translate ideas from one verbal form to another.
Critical thinking and reasoning skills	A continuum of skills including the ability to solve problems independently; to identify cause-and-effect relationships; and to verify assumptions by using deductive reasoning.

Creative thinking skills	A continuum of skills including the ability to develop a flow of ideas; to combine unlike materials or ideas in unusual ways; and to plan for implementation of alternative solutions.
Personal growth and human relations skills	A continuum of skills including the ability to recognize a different point of view; to admit a mistake or failure; to evaluate the effects of personal decision on others.
Library research skills	A continuum of skills including the ability to compile a bibliography of books on a given subject; to locate and use periodicals; and to understand copyright laws.
Scientific research skills	A continuum of skills including the ability to develop inferences from observation and to synthesize collected data.
Independent study skills	A continuum of skills including the ability to identify a topic; to establish a sequential work schedule; and to determine the appropriate format for the presentation of the independent study.
Technology skills	A continuum of skills including the ability to use a computer for a variety of purposes.

Note. From *Process Skills Rating Scales–Revised* (pp. 4–5), by F. A. Karnes and S. Bean, 2004, Waco, TX: Prufrock Press. Copyright ©2004 by Frances Karnes and Suzanne Bean. Reprinted with permission.

group to react to their thinking. It is at this phase that the formal presentation skills are important.

5. *Reflecting.* Students move back to their small groups and talk about what they have learned, how their learning was affected by interaction with other people, and the impact of the presentation on their thinking. (Tchudi & Mitchell, 1999, pp. 316–317)

Tchudi and Mitchell (1999) summarized their position on the importance of oral communication in learning by citing the work of the National Oracy Project (National Curriculum Council, 1991):

- We talk to make sense of the world and to try to exert some control over it.
- We talk in order to find out what others know and to share what we know.
- We talk in order to develop our thinking.
- We use talk to entertain, to tell stories or recite poetry, to create new roles and imaginative worlds.
- We use talk to evaluate our work, achievements, and learning.
- We use talk to demonstrate and to describe what we know or have found out. (Tchudi & Mitchell, 1999, p. 323)

The PSRS-R lists four areas of verbal communication: speech, group discussion, interviewing, and debate. These skills represent the basic presentation skills (some appropriate resources for each of these areas are listed at the end of this chapter). It is important to note that, as we address these skills, oral communication involves both the speaker and the listener. It is the interaction of these two parties that is, in fact, communication. Galvin's model (Galvin & Book, 1990; see Table 2) includes three elements: the speaker, the message, and the listener. The speaker and listener are affected by images, attitudes, and verbal or nonverbal delivery. Each of these elements can affect communication.

Interviewing

The skills of interviewing are important for gifted learners. Human resources are a significant element in primary research; other people are valuable sources of information. Therefore, it is important that students know how to talk and listen to individuals in order to obtain and record this firsthand data. Sebranek, Meyer, and Kemper (1990) provided some helpful tips for better interviewing. They provided guidelines (see Figure 1) for the student before the interview, during the interview, and after the interview.

These tips should make the interview more comfortable and successful. Students will not only have discovered a great primary resource for their research, but will have had the opportunity to expand their interpersonal skills.

Debate

Debate is important for gifted learners because this skill provides the opportunity to research, define, and defend both sides of any given argument or issue. If the learner thinks of debate as arguing, he or she misses the point of this important strategy. Therefore, it is necessary to teach the accepted terminology and procedures for formal debate. In this process, many skills are brought together. The student must be able to research, distinguish between vital and unimportant information, support statements with valid evidence and sound reasoning, work cooperatively with other students, and present ideas in a clear and effective man-

Table 2

The Galvin Model

Speaker	The sender controls the message's content and organization. Physical and social image, attitudes toward the message and the receiver, and verbal and nonverbal delivery affect the way the speaker presents himself or herself. The sender is also affected by his or her level of creativity. (See Cramond's chapter on creativity for more information on the importance of creativity for the speaker and the listener.)
Listener	Each listener has his or her own attitudes when receiving information. They can be indifferent, interested, or uninterested toward the message and can be neutral, friendly, or hostile to sender. The listener can receive information in a positive or negative way. (Parks' chapter on thinking provides some important elements in how listeners process the sender's message.)
Message	The message is the link between the speaker and the listener, and the components of the message are occasion, content, and organization. Occasion includes reason, time, and place. Content encompasses the topic and materials, and organization includes ideas and words. Effective communicators use messages to draw the listener into an interactive process. Messages are constructed in order to inform, persuade, entertain, inspire, or exercise the vocal cords. (Moore's chapter further explains the research skills that are important in developing the message.)
Interference	External and internal interference can cause breakdowns between the speaker and the listener.
Feedback	Communication is a two-way street between the speaker and listener linked through the message. A continuous exchange of feedback takes place between the two.

Note. From *Person to Person*, by K. Galvin and C. Book, 1990, Lincolnwood, IL: National Textbook Company, as cited in *Suggested Teaching Strategies for Teachers of the Intellectually Gifted* (Speaking Skills, Section XXXII, p. 1), by Mississippi State Department of Education, 1994, Jackson, MS: Office of Gifted Education. Copyright ©1994 by Office of Gifted Education. Reprinted with permission.

Before the Interview

- Carefully select the person who has the special knowledge in the area that is being researched.
- Write out all the questions that are to be asked.
- Make an appointment for a time and place that is convenient for the person to be interviewed.
- Inform the individual beforehand of the nature of your project.
- Study your topic beforehand so you will not be overwhelmed by new information and you will be an informed listener.
- Practice with your tape recorder so you know how to operate it and how to quickly and unobtrusively change tapes and batteries.
- Practice asking questions and writing down responses.

During the Interview

- Begin by introducing yourself, thanking your subject for the interview, and asking if it is all right to take notes or use a tape recorder.
- Ask a good first question and listen carefully.
- Keep eye contact with the subject and note the subject's facial expressions and gestures.
- Show that you are actively involved and interested in the topic by active listening.
- Do not interrupt your subject unless necessary.
- Before the interview is finished, review your notes for any clarification or follow-up questions.

After the Interview

- Thank the subject for the interview and offer to share a copy of the finished product.
- As soon as possible, write down everything you remember. Later, write a transcript of the interview from the tape.
- Double check any questionable facts or information with the subject or another authority before including it in the final product.
- Be sure that the subject gets a copy of the final work if requested.

Figure 1. Tips for interviewing

Note. From *Write Source 2000* (pp. 405–407) by P. Sebranek, V. Meyer, and D. Kemper, 1990, Burlington, WS: Write Source Education. Copyright ©1990 by D. C. Heath Company, a division of Houghton Mifflin. Reprinted with permission of Great Source Education Group, Inc. All rights reserved.

I. Preparation for the debate
    A. Analyze the proposition.
    B. Determine position.
        1. Affirmative
        2. Negative
    C. Assign responsibilities within the team.
    D. Build a case.
    E. Support the case.
        1. Research for evidence/proof
        2. Use logical reasoning
    F. Develop strategies.
        1. Affirmative
        2. Negative

II. Participation in the debate contest.
    A. Select format.
        1. Standard format
        2. Cross-examination format
        3. Lincoln-Douglas format
    B. Present speeches.
        1. Constructive speeches
        2. Cross-examinations
        3. Rebuttals
    C. Judge effectiveness.

Figure 2. Tips for debate

Note. From *Suggested Teaching Strategies for Teachers of Intellectually Gifted* (section VII, p. 1), Mississippi State Department of Education, 1994, Jackson, MS: Office of Gifted Education. Copyright ©1994 by the Office of Gifted Education. Reprinted with permission.

ner (Summers, Whan, & Rousee, 1963). In many ways, debate may be one of the richest opportunities for training in leadership.

In formal debate, the preparation phase is considered to be as important (maybe more so) than the formal debate itself. The O'Connor (1988) format is particularly helpful to novice debaters (see Figure 2). This clear and concise approach to debate brings this important skill into the reach of any gifted learner. Debate stimulates student interest in current issues, develops critical thinking abilities, sharpens communication skills, and improves research abilities while demonstrating to students a method by which thoughtful, positive, and orderly change may be made in a democratic society (O'Connor, 1988). The importance of debate for gifted learners cannot be overemphasized. In this process skill, there is a celebration of the other process skills and an opportunity to provide a truly appropriate challenge for gifted learners.

Summary

In this chapter, the importance of process skills in the education of the gifted has been discussed with the emphasis that they are tools to assist gifted learners in handling advanced content. These skills may be introduced in isolation, but they should be applied to advanced content as quickly as possible. Betts' Autonomous Learner Model (Betts & Kercher, 1999) is a good example of this progression. Bloom's taxonomy (1956) is a basic tool in educating the gifted, but in order to ensure appropriate differentiation, other models should be identified.

The process modifications (Maker & Nielson, 1996) suggested the close connections between critical thinking and various process skills. The Ennis model (1964) is an appropriate model for critical thinking and decision making. The constructivist perspective is highly appropriate for gifted learners. Additional definitions of the process skills (Karnes & Bean, 2004) and notes on oral communication skills are supported in the work by Tchudi and Mitchell (1999), the Galvin Model (1990), and the Mississippi State Department of Education's *Suggested Teaching Strategies for Teachers of the Gifted* (1994). Tips for interviewing (Sebranek, Meyer, & Kemper, 1990) and the O'Connor model for debate (1988) contribute to the importance and pervasiveness of oral communication skills.

The use of process skills in differentiating for gifted learners should continue to play a major role in the education of gifted learners. While these skills are central to curricula for the gifted, gifted students are shortchanged if these skills become "the curricula for the gifted." If these students are to become "producers of knowledge and not just users," then process skills must be taught to empower them to handle advanced content.

Teacher Statement

The chapter on process skills was an important reminder to me that the process skills, while important, need to be integrated into the study of content. This chapter, however, was not just a reminder, but it also provided a quick and ready reference to various process skills and strategies. I found the Process Skills Rating Scales–Revised very helpful. It can serve as a "scope and sequence" for teaching various process skills in the classroom.

—Mark Mishou

Discussion Questions

1. Discuss the role of modifications in content, process, product, and environment in differentiating curricula for gifted students. Give examples of modifications in each area.

2. What is the appropriate role of process skills in curricula for gifted learners? Defend your position.

3. What is meant by the phrase "producer of knowledge, not just user"?

4. How can we best move beyond Bloom's taxonomy in learning for gifted students?

5. Give specific examples of how Maker's process skills could be applied to a specific curricular unit.

6. How does the constructivist theory relate to gifted students' learning?

7. Describe how the use of the Process Skills Rating Scales–Revised could be used in developing curricula for gifted learners.

Teacher Resources

Benjamin, S. (1996). *The public speaking handbook*. Reading, MA: Addison-Wesley.

Berry, M. (1990). *Stepping into research*. Old Tappan, NJ: Prentice Hall.

Cray-Andrews, M., & Baum, S. (1992). *Creativity 1, 2, 3*. Unionville, NY: Royal Fireworks Press.

Delisle, D., & Delisle, J. (1996). *Growing good kids*. Minneapolis, MN: Free Spirit.

Goodnight, L. (1987). *Getting started in debate*. Lincoln, IL: National Textbook.

Kincher, J. (1995). *Psychology for kids*. Minneapolis, MN: Free Spirit.

McCutcheon, R. (1991). *Can you find it?* Minneapolis, MN: Free Spirit.

McIntosh, J., & Meacham, A. (1992). *Creative problem solving in the classroom*. Waco, TX: Prufrock Press.

Otfinoski, S. (1997). *Speaking up, speaking out*. Brookfield, CT: Millbrook Press.

Romain, T. (1997). *How to do homework without throwing up*. Minneapolis, MN: Free Spirit.

Seymour, D., & Beardslee, E. (1990). *Critical thinking activities in patterns, imagery, logic*. White Plains, NY: Dale Seymour.

Standley, K. (1987). *How to study*. White Plains, NY: Dale Seymour.

Stanish, B. (1999). *The giving book*. Waco, TX: Prufrock Press.

Stay, B. (1996*). A guide to argumentative writing*. San Diego, CA: Greenhaven Press.

Stone, F. (1998). *Write makes might*. Waco, TX: Prufrock Press.

References

Betts, G. (1985). *Autonomous learner model for the gifted and talented learner.* Greeley, CO: ALPS.

Betts, G. T., & Kercher, J. K. (1999). *Autonomous learner model: Optimizing ability.* Greeley, CO: ALPS.

Beyer, B. (1987). *Practical strategies for the teaching of thinking.* Boston: Allyn and Bacon.

Beyer, B. (1988). *Developing a thinking skills program.* Boston: Allyn and Bacon.

Beyer, B. (1997). *Improving student thinking: A comprehensive approach.* Boston: Allyn and Bacon.

Beyer, B. (1999). *Teaching thinking skills: A handbook for elementary school teachers.* Boston: Allyn and Bacon.

Bloom, B. (Ed.). (1956). *Taxonomy of educational objectives: The classification of educational goals. Handbook I: Cognitive domain.* New York: Longman.

Brooks, J., & Brooks, M. (1993). *The case for constructivist classrooms.* Alexandria, VA: Association for Supervision and Curriculum Development.

Carin, A., & Sund, R. (1980). *Teaching science through discovery* (4th ed.). Columbus, OH: Merrill.

de Bono, E. (1986). *CoRT thinking program.* New York: Pergamon Press.

Dudley-Marling, C., & Sarle, D. (1991). *When students have time to talk.* Portsmouth, NH: Heinemann.

Eberle, B., & Stanish, B. (1995). *CPS for kids.* Waco, TX: Prufrock Press.

Ennis, R. (1964). A definition of critical thinking. *The Reading Teacher, 18,* 599–612.

Feldhusen, J. (1980). *The three-stage model of course design.* Englewood Cliffs, NJ: Educational Technology.

Galvin, K., & Book, C. (1990). *Person to person.* Lincolnwood, IL: National Textbook.

Harnadek, A. (1981a). *Critical thinking: Books one and two.* Pacific Grove, CA: Critical Thinking Books & Software.

Harnadek, A. (1981b). *Mind bender: Books A, B, and C.* Pacific Grove, CA: Critical Thinking Books & Software.

Karnes, F. A., & Bean, S. M. (2004). *Process skills rating scales–Revised.* Waco, TX: Prufrock Press.

Maker, C. J., & Nielson, A. (1996). *Curriculum development and teaching strategies for gifted learners* (2nd ed). Austin, TX: PRO-ED.

Mississippi State Department of Education. (1994). *Suggested teaching strategies for teachers of the intellectually gifted.* Jackson, MS: Office of Gifted Education Programs.

National Curriculum Council. (1991). *National oracy project: Teaching talking and learning.* York, United Kingdom: Author.

O'Connor, J. (1988). *Speech: Exploring communication.* Englewood Cliffs, NJ: Prentice-Hall.

Parnes, S. (1967). *Creative behavior guidebook.* New York: Charles Scribner's Sons.

Prawat, R. (1992). Teachers' beliefs about teaching and learning: A constructivist perspective. *American Journal of Education, 110,* 354–395.

Renzulli, J. S. (Ed.). (1986). *Systems and models for developing programs for the gifted and talented.* Mansfield Center, CT: Creative Learning Press.

Renzulli, J. S., & Reis, S. J. (1985). *The schoolwide enrichment model: A comprehensive plan for educational excellence.* Mansfield Center, CT: Creative Learning Press.

Schlichter, C. (1985). Talents unlimited: Applying the multiple talent approach in mainstream and gifted programs. In J. S. Renzulli (Ed.), *Systems and models for developing programs for the gifted and talented* (pp. 352–389). Mansfield Center, CT: Creative Learning Press.

Sebranek, P., Meyer, V., & Kemper, D. (1990). *Write source 2000*. Burlington, WS: Write Source Education.

Summers, H., Whan, F., & Rousee, T. (1963). *How to debate*. New York: H.W. Wilson.

Tchudi, S., & Mitchell, D. (1999). *Exploring and teaching the English language arts* (4th ed.). New York: Addison-Wesley.

Treffinger, D. (1985). Fostering effective, independent learning through individualized programming. In J. S. Renzulli (Ed.), *Systems and models for developing programs for the gifted and talented* (pp. 429–460). Mansfield Center, CT: Creative Learning Press.

VanTassel-Baska, J. (1994). *Comprehensive curriculum for gifted learners*. Boston: Allyn and Bacon.

Winebrenner, S. (1992). *Teaching gifted kids in the regular classroom*. Minneapolis, MN: Free Spirit.

Chapter 6

Product Development for Gifted Students

by **Kristen R. Stephens** and **Frances A. Karnes**

---

ulie, a 2nd-grade girl, proudly wears the T-shirt she designed to reflect the knowledge gained through the various units she explored during the school year. John, a 7th-grade boy, writes a script, designs a costume, and creates a set for a performance to depict the life, accomplishments, and impact of Abraham Lincoln on America. These are both examples of positive student products.

Meanwhile, David, an 8th-grade boy, writes his 10th book report this year. He has not been exposed to the variety of other products that could possibly be used to display his knowledge. Sarah, a 4th-grade girl, creates yet another unsuccessful poster. She has never been taught the elements of design that are necessary for the creation of a successful product.

Creative products are essential to curricula for the gifted. They allow students to express themselves and convey their ideas and knowledge in unique and complex ways. Product development also serves to motivate students, and it provides practical contexts in which they can develop knowledge and skills. This chapter provides teachers with the information necessary to assist students through the various stages of product development.

What is a Product?

Maker and Nielson (1996) defined a product as "The tangible evidence of student learning" (p. 186). The transformation of knowledge into creative products is a critical goal for gifted students (Feldhusen & Kolloff, 1988; Renzulli, 1977). The types of products expected from students should be highly creative and perhaps abstract. In other words, products created by gifted students should be comparable to those made by professionals in the designated field. Furthermore, the products of gifted students should represent an application, analysis, and synthesis of knowledge acquired from their research.

The Importance of Product Development in Gifted Education

The act of product development is multifaceted in scope and sequence, and, through the production process, gifted students can develop, enhance, and evaluate a wide spectrum of content and process skills, thus adding to the advancement of self-esteem, self-analysis, and self-actualization. The content or knowledge displayed through products can encompass all areas of human endeavor and provide an integration of the arts, humanities, mathematics, science, literature, religion, and other subject matter. In addition, the process skills of creativity and creative problem solving, higher level and critical thinking, oral and written communication, scientific and library research, and social and personal development will be refined with each new product created. Furthermore, the organizational skills of planning, time management, record keeping, and delegating will be enhanced, as they play a crucial role in the process of achieving the intended goal.

Through product design, gifted youth become responsible for their own learning, thus fostering independence and accountability. Moreover, product development allows learners to explore, investigate, design, and formulate their own ideas, feelings, and thoughts, which encourages risk taking and stimulates creativity. Students are allowed to proceed at their own established pace through selected activities that accommodate their individually diverse learning styles. Finally, through research of a selected problem, presentation of solutions, and self-evaluation to assess demonstrated outcomes, students are exposed to authentic learning experiences.

Diverse Learners

Product development is an ideal way for diverse gifted students to express what they have learned. Oftentimes, students with learning disabilities are unable to demonstrate adequately their mastery of new material through traditional methods (e.g., essay, oral report, test, etc.). Product development allows such students to capitalize on their strengths and reveal what they have learned through different media. Providing such successful learning experiences to these students helps create an environment where stress and anxiety are reduced, thus allowing students to maintain their motivation to learn and participate. Product development also allows for mobility and fosters kinesthetic activities that may be of benefit to students with diagnosed attention-deficit disorders, as they are afforded the flexibility they need in order to be successful. In addition, product development helps to individualize learning experiences so students can express themselves in ways that are most relevant to their own style of information processing.

Types of Products

Products have long been used to assess student progress. Unfortunately, many classrooms are still limited to products such as written reports and posters. However, the variety of products that students can create is abundant. Figure 1 lists an assortment of products that students can produce to display knowledge from their research (Karnes & Stephens, 2000). The list of products in Figure 1 can be divided into several categories: written, visual, performance, oral, and multi-categorical products. Several examples of each type of product are displayed below.

Written: letter of inquiry, persuasive essay, poem, research paper, friendly letter, newspaper story, report, business letter, description, explanation, story, advertisement, book report, classified advertisement, creative writing, critique, diary, dictionary, editorial, essay, checklist, script, glossary, journal, magazine article, musical composition, play, puppet show, questionnaire, test, worksheet, book, biography, song

Visual: book jacket, drawing, poster, story map, bar graph, concept cube, timeline, pie chart, tree chart, web, collage, flowchart, Venn diagram, advertisement, blueprint, brochure, bulletin board, bullet chart, multimedia project, cross-section, film, graph, illustration, map, mobile, mural, cartoon, storyboard, carving, costume, diorama, photograph, quilt, sculpture

Performance: dance, monologue, puppet show, demonstration, skit, dramatization, simulation, comedy sketch, experiment, musical performance, play

Oral: debate, oral report, persuasive speech, roundtable discussion, class discussion, mock interview, newscast, oral book report, informative speech, panel discussion, description/show and tell, "how to" talk, reading to the class, audiotape, conference presentation, documentary, group discussion, lecture, commentary, seminar, speech, trial

Multicategorical (products that require the use of two or more of the above product types): exhibit, game, invention, multimedia slide show, oral history, television show, video, Web site, broadcast, computer program, museum, time capsule

Abstract	Button	Costume	Fact file	Hologram	List	Musical composition	Photo album	Quilt	Shadow play	Time capsule
Acronym	Campaign	Crest	Fairy tale	How-to book	Literary analysis	Musical instrument	Photo essay	Quotations	Short story	Timeline
Activity sheet	Cartoon	Critique	Family tree	Hypermedia	Log	Musical performance	Photograph	Radio show	Sign	Toy
Advertisement	Carving	Cross section	Field	Hypothesis	Logo	Mystery	Photo journalism	Rap	Silk screening	Trademark
Alphabet book	Catalog	Crossword puzzle	Experience	Illuminated manuscript	Logic puzzle	Narrative	Pictograph	Rebus story	Simulation	Travelogue
Animation	Celebration	Dance	Film	Illusion	Machine	Needlecraft	Pictorial essay	Recipe	Sketch	Triptych
Annotated bibliography	Chart	Database	Flag	Illustrated story	Magazine	Newsletter	Picture dictionary	Recitation	Skit	Venn diagram
Aquarium	Club	Debate	Flannel board Story	Illustration	Magazine article	Newspaper	Picture story	Reenactment	Slide show	Video
Archive	Coat of arms	Demonstration	Flip book	Index cards	Magic show	Novel	Pie chart	Relief map	Sociogram	Video game
Art gallery	Collage	Design	Flow chart	Instructions	Manual	Origami	Plan	Report	Song	Virtual field trip
Autobiography	Collection	Diagram	Flyer	Internet search	Manuscript	Oral report	Plaque	Riddle	Speech	Vocabulary list
Banner	Coloring book	Dialogue	Folder game	Interview	Map with key	Organization	Play	Role-play	Spreadsheet	Wall hanging
Bibliography	Comedy skit	Diary	Fractal	Invention	Mask	Ornament	Poem	Routine	Stage setting	Watercolor
Biography	Comic strip	Dictionary	Game	Investigation	Matrix	Outline	Pointillism	Rubber stamp	Stained glass	Weaving
Big book	Commemorative stamp	Diorama	Game show	Itinerary	Menu	Overhead transparency	Political cartoon	Rubbing	Stencil	Webbing
Blueprint	Commentary	Display	Geodesics	Jewelry	Metaphor	Packet	Pop-up book	Rubric	Stitchery	Web page
Board game	Commercial	Document	Geometric model	Jigsaw puzzle	Mini-center	Painting	Portfolio	Samples	Story	Woodworking
Book	Competition	Documentary	Glossary	Jingle	Mobile	Pamphlet	Portrait	Sand casting	Storyboard	Word puzzle
Book jacket	Computer document	Doll	Graph	Journal	Mock trial	Panel discussion	Position paper	Scavenger hunt	Summary	Written paper
Bookmark	Computer program	Dramatization	Graphic	Kit	Model	Pantomime	Poster	Scenario	Survey	
Book review	Conference presentation	Drawing	Graphic organizer	Laser show	Monologue	Papier mâché	Prediction	Science fiction story	Table	
Broadcast	Construction	Editorial	Greeting card	Law	Monument	Pattern	Presentation	Scrapbook	Tape recording	
Brochure	Cookbook	Equation	Guest speaker	Learning center	Montage	Performance	Program	Script	Television show	
Budget	Cooked concoction	Essay	Guide	Lecture	Mosaic	Personal experience	Project cube	Sculpture	Terrarium	
Bulletin board		Etching	Handbook	Lesson	Motto	Petition	Prototype	Self-portrait	Tessellation	
Bumper sticker		Evaluation checklist	Hidden picture	Letter	Multimedia presentation		Puppet	Seminar	Test	
Business plan		Event	Histogram	Limerick	Mural		Puppet show	Service project	Textbook	
		Exhibit			Museum		Questionnaire	Shadow box	Theory	
		Experiment							3-D model	

Figure 1. Product ideas

Note. From *The Ultimate Guide for Student Product Development and Evaluation* (p. 2), by F. A. Karnes and K. R. Stephens, 2000, Waco, TX: Prufrock Press. Copyright ©2000 by Prufrock Press. Reprinted with permission.

Students' learning styles may influence which types of product they prefer to create. For example, a student who excels in writing might select a product from the written category, while one who enjoys hands-on activities would probably favor those products in the performance or multicategorical areas.

To determine the type of product a student prefers, Kettle, Renzulli, and Rizza (1998) devised My Way . . . An Expression Style Inventory, an instrument used to gather information on the types of products students are interested in creating. Students are asked to rate their interests in various activities on a Likert-type scale. The Expression Style Inventory divides products into 10 different categories: written, oral, artistic, computer, audio-visual, commercial, service, dramatization, manipulative, and musical. Students determine which type of product they would most likely be interested in developing by adding up the total of their responses to the 50 items on the inventory.

Although information relating to the type of product a student would like to create is important, other circumstances must also be considered before selecting one. For example, with what audiences will this product be shared? What subject matter is the product attempting to display? While a puppet show might be appropriate to teach young children about the importance of recycling, it might not be suitable to convince community leaders about the necessity of a detailed plan to improve inner-city environments.

Furthermore, it is important for teachers to encourage students to try creating a variety of products. Even though a student who is an outstanding artist prefers to engage in products involving drawing and painting, it is also important that he or she be assisted in developing his or her skills in other areas through the creation of an assortment of products. For example, he or she might include illustrations with a written story or design a set for a performance. Assisting gifted students in applying their strengths to a variety of areas encourages them to see connections and expand their developing concepts. Also, by encouraging students to develop a type of product that may be out of their "comfort zone," they become engaged in healthy risk taking. Neihart (1999) suggested that such intellectual risk taking helps to "increase self-esteem, confidence, and courage in gifted youth" (p. 289). Challenging students' limitations is necessary to foster high levels of achievement and leadership (Neihart).

Design and Product Development

Burnette, Norman, and Browning (1997) described design as "a way of thinking and doing that is both creative and practical . . . and [is] the key to innovative thinking and invention" (p. 11). Before students begin their product endeavors, it is necessary that they have a preliminary knowledge of the processes, principles, and elements of design. Oftentimes, it is assumed that students already possess most skills necessary for product design. However, they need prior instruction and guidance in such skills, from the basic uses of stencils, rulers, compasses, and protractors, to the selection of appropriate colors, sizes, and shapes, to the recognition of other aesthetic elements such as the more complex skills of superimposed imaging, voice synthesizing, and computer-generated graphics.

An introduction to the design process will assist students in planning for future product development. Davis, Hawley, McMullan, and Spilka (1997) described the following steps in the design process:

1. identifying and defining the problem;
2. gathering and analyzing information;
3. determining performance criteria for successful solutions;
4. generating alternative solutions and building prototypes;
5. evaluating and selecting appropriate solutions;
6. implementing choices; and
7. evaluating outcomes.

Another model depicting the design process is the I/DEPPE/I model (Burnette, Norman, & Browning, 1997). This model is an acronym for the following dimensions:

- Intending—committing to a goal;
- Defining—identifying the problem;
- Exploring—generating possible solutions;
- Planning—making and communicating decisions;
- Producing—doing and making what is required;
- Evaluating—assessing the product and determining if you attained the goal; and
- Integrating—accommodating what was learned from the entire experience with previous knowledge.

Both of the above models almost mirror the stages involved in product development and creative problem solving. Keep in mind that design is not restricted to any one discipline. It can be applied to anything where problems are solved. Designing is something that everyone does and can learn to do more effectively.

In addition to an introduction to the design process, students should become familiar with the elements and principles of design. Elements such as color, line, value, shape, form, balance, and texture must be explored, as well as the principles of repetition, unity, emphasis, economy, proportion, and variety.

Instructional materials and other resources that assist in teaching the process, principles, and elements of design are listed at the end of this chapter. Consult with the arts or technology instructor or department for additional resources and information at your school.

Stages of Product Development

There are several stages a student goes through when creating a product (Karnes & Stephens, 2000). Each step assists students in developing and practicing numerous skills. These stages are as follows:

1. formulation of a topic;
2. organization of production aspects;
3. transformation of content;
4. communication through products;
5. evaluation;
6. celebration; and
7. reflection.

Formulation of a Topic

The first stage in developing a product is selecting a topic to investigate. It may be selected through brainstorming or creating a web. It can be content-specific, such as pirates, Egypt, wolves, or architecture, or it may be concept-related, such as freedom, leadership, change, or cultures.

Narrow it down. It is important for students to narrow the topic from broad to specific. For example, the topic of astronomy might be focused to the Big Dipper or black holes. This will assist students in focusing research questions to the selected topic.

Build new knowledge. Students must be encouraged to select a topic from which they can learn new knowledge. One who has read every book about tornadoes and has already developed several products pertaining to tornadoes should select a different topic from which new knowledge can be gained.

Select an area of interest. Students should choose topics in which they have a genuine interest. This will serve as a motivator for the student to carry out product development to completion. Those who have been interested in tornadoes, for example, might find the topic of hurricanes fascinating, as well.

Make sure resources are available. A topic should be selected that requires utilizing more than a single source of information during the research process. In other words, students must select a topic using a variety of sources, including books, encyclopedias, the Internet, films, interviews, newspapers, authentic documents, atlases, experiments, and so forth.

Organization of Production Aspects

The second phase, the organization stage, runs the length of the product-producing experience. Several organizational techniques can be utilized to help keep students focused and provide structure to daily activities relating to product development. For example, Figure 2 illustrates how students might document their production plan. Keep in mind that a well-developed organizational plan teaches students the necessity of setting and achieving both short- and long-term goals. Never assume that students have already acquired methods for organizing their work. Organizational skills need to be taught and can benefit students in a variety of academic endeavors. The following are examples of some organizational techniques that can be applied by students.

Timelines. Before getting too deep into a project, it is important to generate a timeline with a reasonable date for project completion. For example, daily activities may be placed on a calendar to build time-management skills. This will assist students in staying on task and will further allow them to visualize an end to their means. Furthermore, they should reflect on their accomplishments at the end of each day and evaluate their progress toward meeting established goals. By staying organized and working toward a projected date, students demonstrate the ability to be responsible for their own learning.

Logs. Students can record daily progress toward completion of goals and plan activities for the next day in a project log. This will encourage them to think in advance about what materials they will need to bring to the subsequent class session in order to complete the next planned stage of product development. Logs can be kept in a spiral notebook or on a product log form, which can be designed by the teacher or student. Such forms may require students to answer questions pertaining to current progress and future agendas. Sample questions on a product log form might include the following: What did I accomplish today? What do I plan to do next class session? What materials will I need to bring? By answering these questions, students will further enhance their organizational and planning skills.

Research readiness. "Research readiness" refers to the organizational activities that precede the research process. Research readiness can include generating a list of questions pertaining to the topic, which will help guide research. The development of a KWL chart (What I *Know*? What I *Want* to Know? What I *Learned*?) may be beneficial at this stage. Furthermore, students may want to produce a list of resources in which they might possibly locate the answers to formulated questions.

Students may actually be engaged in more than one research endeavor at a time. It is essential for them not only to conduct research about the topic they are investigating, but also to conduct research regarding the development of their product. For example, a student researching the roles of women in ancient Egypt

Let's Get Organized!

Name: _____   Date: _____

Topic: _____   Product: _____

Description and components of proposed product	
Resources and contact people	
Criteria to meet: What are my goals?	
Materials I will need and where I might obtain them	

Possible audiences	<u>Within school</u>	<u>Outside school</u>

Figure 2. Product planner

will obviously be reading books and surfing the Internet for information regarding Egyptian women during this period. If the student has selected to design a costume that is representative of what Egyptian women wore, then he or she may also be reading books and interviewing costume designers to gather information about fabrics, patterns, sewing techniques, and so forth. Essentially, two different types of research are going on simultaneously: research to gather content knowledge and research to gather product knowledge.

Determining audiences. Before students decide what type of product will best convey their new knowledge, it is essential that they create a list of possible audiences with whom to share their creations. Consider possible audiences both inside and outside of school. The characteristics of the audience, along with the information to be conveyed, will greatly influence the type and complexity of the product selected. Possible audiences might include peers, community leaders, younger students, retirement communities, the school board, clubs, and so forth.

Product selection. Once the audience and presentation content have been selected, students can determine which type of product will be most suitable. Media are the mode through which ideas are communicated. Selecting appropriate forms of media may be a complicated step for some students. They often tend to select media that reflect their particular learning style. For example, authors will write and artists will illustrate.

Atwood (1974) described the three levels of media forms as demonstrative, representational, and symbolic. Demonstrative media, the most literal form of communication, might include displays, step-by-step procedures, and experiments. Representational media, which are used to represent reality when it is not easily displayed, might include sculptures, photographs, models, plays, and drawings. Symbolic media, which are considered translations of reality, might include speeches, advertisements, dances, graphs, maps, and computer programs.

Depending on the content of the project and the audience, gifted students must decide what form of media is most suited to communicating learned ideas accurately. Sometimes, the medium that will best demonstrate, represent, or symbolize an idea may not be the one the student would have normally selected. Keeping a list of possible products, as found in Figure 1, may help students choose varied media that will communicate their thoughts most effectively.

Material gathering. Once the product type has been selected, students should generate a list of materials needed to complete the proposed products. Students may need to make accommodations for certain materials due to expense and availability. These accommodations allow them to utilize their creative problem-solving abilities in authentic situations. Furthermore, materials that students first thought were appropriate may not work as planned. Through substitution and experimentation with alternate materials, they will enhance their problem-solving abilities.

Evaluation criteria. Before creating their product, they should develop criteria with which to evaluate the finished work. By establishing product criteria for evaluation early on, students are made aware of the standards set for themselves. Since product types vary, different criteria will need to be established for each type.

Students may consult with an expert in the topic field in order to develop a list of components and exemplary characteristics for the proposed product. For example, a cartographer or geography professor may be an excellent resource for a student who desires to create a map; a genealogist would provide information relating to the components and characteristics of an ideal family tree; and a local reporter may offer advice on how to conduct a professional quality interview. Baker and Schacter (1996) suggested using adult expert performance as a benchmark for assessment. The Center for Research on Evaluation, Standards, and Student Testing (CRESST) employed expert models to assess student performance in a variety of content areas. In addition, Wiggins (1996) suggested that teachers look for "exemplars" or "anchors," which are examples of a particular product that demonstrate an exceptional standard. These exemplars can serve as a basis for setting performance standards for students. The following is a suggested list of specific products with the experts that may be consulted when developing evaluation criteria:

- blueprint → architect
- brochure → marketing consultant
- debate → speech-debate teacher
- exhibit → museum curator
- experiment → scientist
- family tree → genealogist
- magazine → editor
- map → cartographer or geographer
- musical composition → music professor
- photograph → photographer
- play → actor or professor of theater
- sculpture → local artist
- Web page → computer expert

Experts are everywhere. Many can be found in your local community through the following sources:

- colleges and universities;
- businesses;
- clubs and organizations;
- friends;
- craft guilds;
- local media;
- the Internet;
- the telephone directory; and
- the library.

The Internet provides a valuable source of experts if they cannot be found within your community. For instance, students can send questions related to a specific discipline to experts in that field. Additional "Ask an Expert" sites can be found by discipline at http://www.askanexpert.com. Here are just a few examples:

- Ask a Geologist (http://walrus.wr.usgs.gov/ask-a-geologist);
- Ask a Physics Question (http://www.physlink.com/Education/AskExperts);
- Ask a NASA Scientist (http://imagine.gsfc.nasa.gov/docs/ask_astro/ask_an_astronomer.html);
- Ask Dr. Math (http://mathforum.org/dr.math);
- Ask a Historian or an Archeologist (http://www.cr.nps.gov/history/askhist.htm);
- Ask the Oracle (http://vrd.org/locator/sites/oracle.shtml);
- Ask an Architect (http://infopoint.theriver.com/aiasac/ask_welc.htm);
- Ask Dr. Econ (http://www.frbsf.org/education/activities/drecon/askecon.cfm);
- Ask a Mayo Clinic Physician (http://www.mayoclinic.com/findinformation/answers/index.cfm?);
- Ask Dr. Internet (http://promo.net/drnet);
- Ask a Biologist (http://askabiologist.asu.edu);
- Ask Shamu (http://www.seaworld.org/ask-shamu/index.htm);
- Ask a Paleontologist (http://www.isgs.uiuc.edu/dinos/rjjinput_form.html);
- Ask a Hurricane Hunter (http://www.hurricanehunters.com/askus.htm);
- Ask a Weather Expert (http://www.usatoday.com/weather/weatherfront.aspx);
- Ask a Construction Expert (http://www.siue.edu/ENGINEER/CONSTRUCT/ask.htm);
- Ask a Linguist (http://linguist.emich.edu/~ask-ling);
- Ask the Word Wizard (http://wordwizard.com);
- Ask an Astronaut (http://www.ari.net/nss/askastro);
- Ask a Zoo Keeper (http://www.niabizoo.com/Askazookeeperpage.html);
- Ask an Ecologist (http://www.nceas.ucsb.edu/nceas-web/kids/ecology/index.htm);
- Ask an Entomologist (http://www.ent.iastate.edu/mailinglist/bugnet/question.html);
- Ask Dr. Universe (http://www.wsu.edu/DrUniverse);
- Ask Jeeves for Kids (http://www.ajkids.com); and
- How Stuff Works (http://people.howstuffworks.com).

Transformation of Content

Since the attainment of higher level thinking skills is an essential focus in gifted programs, the type of products expected from students should be highly creative and perhaps abstract. Products should represent more than the mere acquisition of new knowledge. They should convey a genuine application of synthesis and analysis. This process of transformation allows the student to turn new knowledge into something more meaningful. Maker and Nielson (1996) outlined several elements of transformation: viewing from a different perspective, reinterpreting, elaborating, extending, and combining simultaneously. When evaluating a product, it is important to look for some of these elements in students' work. Students should turn learned content into their own creation instead of repeating or summarizing general information. Forster (1990) described the process of project development as "the act of surprising oneself with new ideas" (p. 40). The ultimate goal of product development is to transform student research into new thoughts, ideas, and perspectives.

Transformation involves many steps and processes. Students should be taught these steps and the types of activities in which they need to be engaged as they move through the process. The steps include:

1. Research: The student locates, comprehends, and classifies information in order to gain knowledge.
2. Information filtration: The student processes, interprets, refines, and extrapolates the knowledge and ideas gained from research.
3. Idea generation: From the selected information, the student emphasizes and analyzes various elements, concepts, and ideas of interest.
4. Centralization: The student selects, decides, and focuses on a specific element or idea.
5. Reflection: The student considers, ponders, and judges the selected idea.
6. Manipulation: The student tests and experiments with the idea and changes, improves, and adapts it as necessary.
7. Execution: The student decides, organizes, prepares, and produces a product to display the idea.
8. Communication: The student shares, performs, displays, or disseminates the product to an authentic audience.

A model of the above transformation process appears in Figure 3.

It is important to note the percentage of time students are spending in each phase of the transformation model. Typically, students spend little time planning and dive headfirst into the actual creation of their product. How often have students been observed with a fresh piece of poster board and a box of markers getting to work immediately without planning, sketching a draft, or constructing a prototype? How would the quality of what they are able to produce be impacted if more time and consideration were devoted to these initial steps? The steps in the transformation model should be taught to students, and each phase should receive ample time and consideration. Perhaps one of the first goals in fostering successful product development in students is teaching them how to slow down and think and plan prior to acting. When introducing

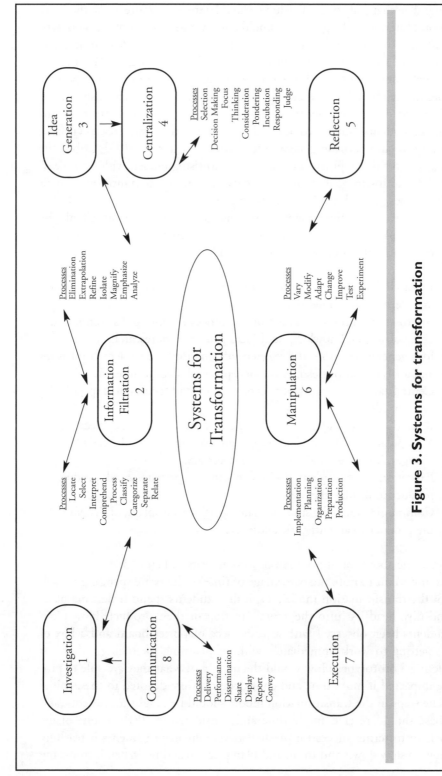

Figure 3. Systems for transformation

Note. From *The Ultimate Guide for Student Product Development and Evaluation* (p. 12), by F. A. Karnes and K. R. Stephens, 2000, Waco, TX: Prufrock Press. Copyright ©2000 by Prufrock Press. Reprinted with permission.

the model, it is suggested that the teacher initially designate an amount of time to be spent by students at each step (e.g., three class periods for investigation, two class periods for information filtration, etc.). However, keep in mind that, depending on the complexity and depth of the topic being researched, time periods for each step may vary. Spending a thorough amount of time researching and reflecting on the topic will help students generate novel ideas. Otherwise, they will likely resort to a mere regurgitation of what they read from a book—which is not *transformation*.

The Transformation Model can easily be adapted for use with younger students. Teachers can rename each step and provide further elaboration so that younger students have a better understanding of the type of activities that need to be occurring along the way. For example:

- explore the topic in depth (investigation);
- determine what is important (information filtration);
- record your thoughts and ideas (idea generation);
- decide which idea you like best (centralization);
- think about your idea overnight (reflection);
- develop a draft or prototype (manipulation);
- design your product (execution); and
- share the results (communication).

Communication Through Products

During the communication stage, students share their ideas and products with a selected audience. Sharing the final product with an audience gives added purpose to the product. Instead of being stored in the back of a closet to collect dust, student products can provide valuable learning opportunities for many types of audiences.

Speaking Skills

Speaking skills will be enhanced through the continued exposure to a wide variety of audiences. Eye contact, clear speech, and confidence are a few components of an effective presentation. Students should become more comfortable with practice and experience in presenting their products and ideas. Never assume that a student who is unable to give an effective presentation has not synthesized and analyzed information from his or her study. Presenting the product in class should be the first step, followed by audiences within the school and community. Younger students will need time to feel comfortable expressing themselves in front of others. It is advisable to keep audiences small and familiar for younger students until they build confidence presenting to larger, more unfamiliar groups.

Authentic Audiences

It is important for students to share their products and ideas with authentic audiences. These may vary from product to product and student to student. Potential audiences may be peers, teachers, family members, topic experts, clubs, the school board, retirement community, or councilmen, to name a few. Students should be involved in selecting the audience.

Other Sharing Showcases

Products can also be attractively displayed in many areas throughout the community. This gives a sense of pride and importance to the student while serving as a great public relations tool by introducing to the rest of the world the excitement and learning that is being generated in the gifted classroom. Some places that student products may be displayed in your community are

- bank lobbies
- public and school libraries
- shopping malls
- airports
- restaurants
- stores
- newsletters
- real estate offices
- hospitals
- fairs or festivals
- PTA meetings
- post offices
- colleges and universities
- governmental offices
- clubs and organizations
- train and bus stations
- school administrative offices
- magazines
- newspapers
- retirement communities
- preschools
- town halls
- school board meetings
- business offices

Students may also choose to enter their products in various competitions. Information related to specific academic areas, as well as fine and performing arts, leadership, and service learning, can be found in the book *Competitions: Maximizing Your Abilities* (Karnes & Riley, 1996). The possibilities of potential audiences and display areas are abundant.

Evaluation

Evaluation of student products should be multidimensional so that students can receive helpful and extensive feedback from a wide array of sources. Assessment may be determined by the teacher using preselected criteria, self-evaluation by the students, and feedback from an audience. Forster (1990) suggested that projects should have self-regulatory and constant evaluation methods so that students can stay on course throughout the duration of the project. Students may wish to develop questionnaires to determine their audiences' perceptions of their products and presentations. Before beginning their projects, it is also advisable that students choose a support person with whom they can conference periodically to share progress and receive feedback. Gibbons (1991) suggested that this support person be an expert in the particular topic, if possible.

Establishing Criteria

Students should be involved in establishing the criteria for product evaluation. If students are familiar with the criteria prior to beginning work on the projects, they will be more apt to produce successful products. Establishing criteria for evaluating products that are complex in nature can be difficult. Byrnes and others (1982) developed an easy-to-use scale for creative products such as drama, poetry, music, and dance. The scales contain glossaries of the important components of these unique products, making them easy for students and teachers to use effectively. Topic experts can also be asked to assist in developing criteria for certain products. Renzulli, Reis, and Smith (1981) developed the Student Product Assessment Form, which rates eight factors in product developing: purpose; problem focusing; level of resources; diversity of resources; appropriateness of resources; logic, sequence, and transition; action orientation; and audience.

When each student in a class is engaged in developing a different product, the task of evaluating each one can overwhelm teachers. How does one evaluate a diorama, a skit, or an illustration objectively? Therefore, getting students involved in the process of developing an effective evaluation instrument is crucial. It not only assists them in developing goals and criteria for the anticipated outcome, but it also holds them accountable in working toward and meeting these goals. Rubrics can be designed for every type of product. You can practice creating rubrics as a class and then have students develop their own rubrics for their products.

Creating Rubrics

A rubric is a framework for evaluating products on an established scale. The first step in constructing a rubric is to list all the components of the proposed product. For example, if the product is a poster, the basic components might include title, labels, graphics, and layout.

Components will vary according to the expected complexity of the product and the abilities of the student. For example, older students may wish to add additional components beyond the basic ones. Students may need to conduct research relating to their proposed product in order to determine the components. It is important that students learn and use the terminology associated with their product so they acquire the same vocabulary of a professional who might design this same type of product. For example, *legend, topography, scale, orientation, neatline,* and *cartographer* are terms that might be associated with a map.

After a list of components has been generated, exemplary characteristics of each component should be listed. For example:

Title
- legible, neat
- prominent, visible
- representative of topic, appropriate
- correct spelling/grammar

Labels
- legible, neat
- appropriate placement
- correct spelling/grammar

Graphics
- clear, visible
- appropriate to theme
- securely attached

Layout
- balanced
- noncluttered
- interesting
- appropriate emphasis

Students may want to examine good examples of a particular product to determine the exemplary characteristics of each component. It may be helpful for students to find out who is considered to be exemplary producers of this particular product. For example, students might investigate the work of Frank Lloyd Wright for an architectural product or the poetry of Phillis Wheatley if they choose to write a poem.

Once the exemplary characteristics of each component have been listed, a scale for each characteristic must be set. It is recommended that a four- or six-point scale be used, rather than one that is odd-numbered. With odd-numbered scales there is a tendency for the rater to select the middle value. In addition, if using a numbered scale, each value should be clearly defined. For example, a "1" may be designated as "Poor" or "Incomplete," while a "4" may designate "Superior" production (Karnes & Stephens, 2000).

Figure 4 is an example of a completed rubric that was created using the above procedure. Many ready-made rubrics can be found in books and on the Internet. *The Ultimate Guide for Student Product Development and Evaluation* (Karnes & Stephens, 2000) contains ready-made rubrics for more than 40 unique products, each of which can be modified and enhanced as needed. A great Web site that can assist in rubric development is Rubistar (http://rubistar.4teachers.org), which is free to use and supported by the U.S. Department of Education. You can customize the rubrics generated by the site to meet your specific purposes. In addition, resource books related to specific products are

Components	Characteristics	Ratings
Title	• legible; neat	1 2 3 4 5 6
	• prominent; visible	1 2 3 4 5 6
	• representative of topic; appropriate	1 2 3 4 5 6
	• correct spelling/grammar	1 2 3 4 5 6
Labels	• legible; neat	1 2 3 4 5 6
	• appropriate placement	1 2 3 4 5 6
	• correct spelling/grammar	1 2 3 4 5 6
Graphics	• clear; visible	1 2 3 4 5 6
	• appropriate to theme	1 2 3 4 5 6
	• securely attached	1 2 3 4 5 6
Layout	• balanced	1 2 3 4 5 6
	• not cluttered	1 2 3 4 5 6
	• interesting	1 2 3 4 5 6
	• appropriate emphasis	1 2 3 4 5 6

1 = Incomplete; 2 = Needs Improvement; 3 = Fair;
4 = Emerging; 5 = Good; 6 = Superior

Figure 4. Completed rubric

Note. From *The Ultimate Guide for Student Product Development and Evaluation* (p. 17), by F. A. Karnes and K. R. Stephens, 2000, Waco, TX: Prufrock Press. Copyright ©2000 by Prufrock Press. Reprinted with permission.

helpful in determining the components of, and terminology associated with, particular products. Several product-related books are included at the end of this chapter.

Teachers can create separate rubrics to evaluate content knowledge and process skills demonstrated during the research and product development phase, or they can incorporate all items related to content, process, and product into one rubric.

Evaluators

As mentioned earlier, evaluation of student products should be multidimensional, which can be achieved by having a variety of evaluators. These might include peers, audience members, teachers, the student, topic experts, or school administrators.

Celebration

What better motivator to work diligently and produce a high-quality product than to have the chance to celebrate and reflect upon your accomplishments? Gibbons (1991) suggested that students have a pizza party and share their products with one another informally, which allows them to see the wide variety of products they are capable of producing. Students can share the thought processes that went into designing their products and perhaps even have the opportunity to explore the topic further, as more questions are generated when minds meet.

Product Fair

Celebration is an important component of product development. It allows students to build confidence and feel good about their achievements. A product fair can provide students with the opportunity to share their products in a completely different type of stress-free setting. Renzulli and Reis (1991) suggested an end-of-year product fair, which includes coverage by local newspapers and television and radio stations. Such coverage would expand the students' audience and provide excellent public relations for the gifted program. Through such an event they can also share the stages in the development, implementation, and evaluation of their products.

Reflection

As students pack up their products on the bus and depart for home, the time for reflection begins. They should be encouraged to reflect on the entire process of creating their product from beginning to end. Is there anything else about the topic that needs further research? What could have been done differently? What really worked? These reflections will be a valuable contribution toward improvement as students begin a new journey into another product frontier. They will learn from both their successes and failures. In a sense, they will learn a great deal about themselves and others. Often, people reflect on things without even realizing it; but, by purposely doing so, a great deal can be learned that will be of value in the future.

Product Journals

One method students can use to reflect on their product-producing experience is keeping a detailed journal. This will help them keep track of the steps of product development and will also serve as a way for them to remember and reflect on the entire process. Students will have gained an abundance of new knowledge through their research, planning, and creative problem-solving experiences.

Student: _____

Date	Type of Product	Academic Subject	Grade Level/Teacher

Figure 5. Student product inventory

How to Foster Product Development in the Classroom

There are many ways teachers can encourage and promote creative product development within their classrooms. By providing the necessary resources, creative ideas are more likely to be generated.

Posting a Product List

A simple way to encourage product development is by merely posting a list of products as seen in Figure 1 on the wall in the classroom. When students need an idea for a product, they can go to this list and select something that is appropriate to their topic and audience. By displaying the list, students are motivated to try their hand at a variety of different products, beyond the report and poster.

Product Portfolios and Inventories

Teachers can keep product portfolios and inventories on each student. This will allow teachers across grade levels to see what types of products a particular student has made during his or her school career. Visually, product portfolios provide an excellent way for students to see their growth and progress over the years. Figure 5 displays a technique that can be used to keep track of the various products a student develops.

Don't Throw It Away

Teachers throughout the school can send a notice home asking parents to donate a variety of items to the school or classroom that inspire creative product development. A designated corner in the classroom or closet within the school can house these materials. By having them available, students will be encouraged to use their creative abilities. Requested materials might include:

- egg and milk cartons
- aluminum foil
- buttons
- boxes (shoe, jewelry, etc.)
- yogurt cups
- ribbon
- toilet paper tubes
- wire coat hangers
- nuts, bolts, screws
- greeting cards
- newspapers
- clothespins
- broken costume jewelry

- cans (coffee, soup, etc.)
- fabric scraps
- plastic berry baskets
- microwave meal trays
- butter tubs
- wrapping paper
- paper towel tubes
- packaging popcorn
- colored paper scraps
- old magazines
- old keys
- yarn/string
- beads

Product Resource Files

When students complete a product, they can take a photograph of it and write on a special form the directions and materials necessary for creating it (see Figure 6). This form and photograph can be stored in a product resource file to be used by other students to obtain ideas for new products. Students should be encouraged not merely to copy someone else's idea, but to expand on it. How might they make that particular product better? How might they display information relating to the topic using a similar product?

Many of the products on the list may be unfamiliar to students, like a geodesic or triptych. Having a photograph and generic directions on how to create these unfamiliar products may assist students in better understanding what they are and how they are created.

"How To" Library

Having a library of books that describe how to create various products may further inspire students. Books designed for both students and professionals can be used to provide an abundance of information. A bibliography of several "how to" books is provided at the end of this chapter.

Name: _____

Product: _____

Subject: _____

Materials: What You Need, and Where to Get it!

What   Where

1.
2.
3.
4.
5.
6.

The Process: Procedures for Production

1.
2.
3.
4.
5.
6.
7.
8.
9.
10.

Comments:

Pros:

Cons:

Advice:

* Attach a photo of product to this form *

Figure 6. Product description

Internet Resources

There are many Web sites that can assist students in developing products. Internet searches can be conducted to obtain information related to research and specific products. Some examples of specific topic-related Web sites include:

- holography (http://holo.com/holo/book/book1.html);
- family tree (http://www.genhomepage.com);
- Web design (http://www.worldkids.net/kotw/ownpage.htm); and
- animation (http://www.sci.fi/~animato).

Such sites can provide an array of information with links to more resources that may not be found elsewhere. Students should perform Internet searches on the topics and product types as a means of accumulating additional information for their endeavors.

Computer Software

There is also an abundance of computer software that can assist students in the development of products. Software to make family trees, design multimedia presentations, learn origami, compose music, discover animation, and much more is available. Some suggested design software to have in the classroom that can be used in creating a variety of products are:

- Kids Pix Deluxe, by Broderbund (ages 3–12);
- Crayola Make a Masterpiece, by IBM (ages 5 and up);
- Disney Magic Artist Studio, by Disney Interactive (ages 4 and up); and
- Flying Colors 2, by Magic Mouse Productions (ages 8 and up).

Check your local computer supply store or favorite software catalog for the latest programs.

Summary

Product development is an excellent way to encourage both creative and independent learning. Students can create original products to extend an idea or thought pertaining to a particular topic of interest and, in the process, learn the value of flexibility when meeting time and material restraints during product construction. They engage in creative problem solving as they overcome obstacles during the process, and they learn that careful planning and organization can assist in making the product-producing experience a positive one. Product development is an essential component in any gifted education program that meets the complex and advanced needs of gifted students as they become tomorrow's creative problem solvers and thinkers (Stephens, 1996).

Teacher Statement

Products students have created in my class contain meaningful work in the subject areas. The rubrics for evaluation are in place and are solid ones. Many students have told me they enjoyed the assignments and learned lots from them. So why am I not satisfied with the results? Why haven't I encouraged an even higher quality product from my students? Up until now, it was because I didn't know where to start, where to look for information, how to structure a more meaningful assignment, or how to get started on my own.

Information from this chapter has given me a solid framework and direction to make the changes that give my students opportunities for additional growth, creativity, and learning with ownership. I must understand that I do not have to start from scratch in revising what I do. There is no failure in using the good, well-researched information given within this chapter to help lighten my load and produce better outcomes. Change is difficult. I expect my students to push their comfort levels in order to grow. I plan to start with one product opportunity and build from there. I think the framework set forth in this chapter just might work for me as I set the stage for new learning opportunities for my students. Ready, set, I'll grow right along with my students—together we'll learn a lot!

—Eloise Williamson

Discussion Questions

1. What strategies can be used to foster *transformation* of content into creative products and avoid mere repetition of what students have read pertaining to their topic?

2. Discuss the variety of process skills that are developed and enhanced through creative product development.

3. In what ways does the knowledge of design elements and principles enhance student products?

4. Think about your classroom and the units of study you currently teach. How can the incorporation of creative product development enhance your students' learning experiences?

5. How does creative product development help to differentiate learning experiences for gifted students?

6. What strategies can be implemented by teachers to assist them in evaluating the variety of products generated by students?

Teacher Resources

Publications

Bauer, M. D. (1992). *What's your story?: A young person's guide to writing fiction.* New York: Houghton Mifflin.

Benjamin, S. (1996). *The public speaking handbook: Grades 8–12.* Glenview, IL: Goodyear Books.

Bentley, N., & Guthrie, D. (1996). *Putting on a play: The young playwright's guide to scripting, directing, and performing.* Brookfield, CT: Millbrook Press.

Chapman, G., & Robson, P. (1991). *Making books: A step-by-step guide to your own publishing.* Brookfield, CT: Millbrook Press.

Craig, D. (1993). *Making models.* Brookfield, CT: Millbrook Press.

Dearing, S. (1992). *Elegantly frugal costumes.* Colorado Springs, CO: Meriwether.

Draze, D., & Palouda, A. (1992). *Design studio.* San Luis Obispo, CA: Dandy Lion.

Everett, F., & Garbera, C. (1987). *Make your own jewelry.* London: Usbourne.

Gamble, K. (1994). *You can draw anything.* St. Leonards, Australia: Allen & Unwin.

Gibbons, G. (1997). *Click: A book about cameras and taking pictures.* Boston: Little, Brown.

Gibson, R. (1993). *Masks.* London: Usbourne.

Gibson, R. (1995). *Papier mache.* London: Usbourne.

Gibson, R. (1995). *Stencil fun.* London: Usbourne.

Gibson, R. (1996). *Printing.* London: Usbourne.

Guthrie, D., Bentley, N., & Arnsteen, K. K. (1994). *The young author's do-it-yourself book.* Brookfield, CT: Millbrook Press.

Irvine, J. (1987). *How to make pop-ups.* New York: Beechtree Books.

Irvine, J. (1990). *Homemade holograms* . New York: TAB Books.

Karetnikova, I. (1990). *How scripts are made.* Carbondale: Southern Illinois University Press.

Kronenwetter, M. (1995). *How to write a news article.* New York: Franklin Watts.

Lade, R. (1996). *The most excellent book of how to be a puppeteer.* Brookfield, CT: Millbrook Press.

Lightfoot, M. (1993). *Cartooning for kids.* Buffalo, NY: Firefly Books.

Needham, K. (1995). *Collecting things.* London: Usbourne.

Pearson, C. (1982). *Make your own games workshop.* Carthage, IL: Fearon Teacher Aids.

Pederson, T., & Moss, F. (1995). *Internet for kids: A beginner's guide to surfing the net.* Los Angeles: Price Stern Sloan.

Phillips, K. (1995). *How to write a story.* New York: Franklin Watts.

Potter, T,. & Peach, S. (1987). *Graphic design.* London: Usbourne.

Provenzo, E. F., Provenzo, A. B., & Zorn, P. (1984). *Pursuing the past.* Menlo Park, CA: Addison-Wesley.

Ryan, M. (1994). *How to give a speech*. New York: Franklin Watts.

Slafer, A., & Cahill, K. (1995). *Why design? Activities and projects from the national building museum*. Chicago: Chicago Review Press.

Wingate, P. (1996). *Projects for windows*. London: Usbourne.

Woods, H., Verboys, J., & Evans, G. (1990). *Lasers: Activities for the classroom*. Albany, NY: Delmar.

Addresses

The Center for Research on Evaluation, Standards,
and Student Testing (CRESST/UCLA)
301 GSE&IS
Mailbox 951522
300 Charles E. Young Dr. North
Los Angeles, CA 90095–1522
http://cresst96.cse.ucla.edu/index5.htm

References

Atwood, B. (1974). *Building independent learning skills*. Palo Alto, CA: Learning Handbooks.

Baker, E. L., & Schacter J. (1996). Expert benchmarks for student academic performance: The case for gifted children. *Gifted Child Quarterly, 40*, 61–65.

Burnette, C., Norman, J. T., & Browning, K. (1997). *D-K12 designs for thinking*. Philadelphia: The University of the Arts.

Byrnes, P. A., & others. (1982, April). *Creative products scales—Detroit public schools*. Paper presented at the annual meeting of the Council for Exceptional Children, Houston, TX. (ERIC Document Reproduction No. ED218903)

Davis, M., Hawley, P., McMullan, B., & Spilka, G. (1997). *Design as a catalyst for learning*. Alexandria, VA: Association for Supervision and Curriculum Development.

Feldhusen, J., & Kolloff, M. (1988). A three-stage model for gifted education. *Gifted Child Today, 11*(1), 53–58.

Forster, B. R. (1990). Let's build a sailboat: A differentiated gifted education project. *Teaching Exceptional Children, 22*(4), 40–42.

Gibbons, M. (1991). *How to become an expert: Discover, research, and build a project in your chosen field*. Tucson, AZ: Zephyr Press.

Karnes, F. A., & Riley, T. L. (1996). *Competitions: Maximizing your abilities*. Waco, TX: Prufrock Press.

Karnes, F. A., & Stephens, K. R. (2000). *The ultimate guide to student product development and evaluation*. Waco, TX: Prufrock Press.

Kettle, K. E., Renzulli, J. S., & Rizza, M. G. (1998). Products of mind: Exploring student preferences for product development using My Way . . . an expression style inventory. *Gifted Child Quarterly, 42*, 49–60.

Maker, J. C., & Nielson, A. B. (1996). *Curriculum development and teaching strategies for gifted learners* (2nd ed.). Austin, TX: PRO-ED.

Neihart, M. (1999). Systematic risk-taking. *Roeper Review, 21*, 289–293.

Renzulli, J. S. (1977). *The enrichment triad model: A guide for development defensible programs for the gifted and talented*. Mansfield Center, CT: Creative Learning Press.

Renzulli, J. S., & Reis, S. M. (1991). Building advocacy through program design, student productivity, and public relations. *Gifted Child Quarterly, 35*, 182–187.

Renzulli, J. S., Reis, S. M., & Smith, L. H. (1981). *The revolving door identification model*. Mansfield Center, CT: Creative Learning Press.

Stephens, K. R. (1996). Product development for gifted students: Formulation to reflection. *Gifted Child Today, 19*(6), 18–21.

Wiggins, G. (1996). Anchoring assessment with exemplars: Why students and teachers need models. *Gifted Child Quarterly, 40*, 66–69.

Chapter 7

Writing Units That Remove the Learning Ceiling

by **Julia Link Roberts** and **Richard A. Roberts**

Many children who are gifted and talented spend most of their time learning in classrooms with children who have varying levels of ability, multiple interests, and a range of readiness. This chapter presents a model for writing units that provides a starting point for teachers who have primarily been using the same learning experiences for the whole class. The model is a framework for teachers to embark on differentiation in their classrooms.

All children and youth benefit when the learning ceiling is removed, as each can become the best learner he or she can be. All children and youth must master basic skills and core content; yet, as they reach mastery, they need and deserve opportunities to continue learning at challenging levels. Educators must design learning experiences with accommodations for each child to make continuous progress because no one can learn what he or she already knows. Yes, a teacher can teach what the child already knows, but a child cannot learn it if he or she already knows it. For all children to make continuous progress, learning experiences must be differentiated to lift the learning ceiling. Differentiation allows each student who is ready to learn at a more complex level and at a faster pace to continue learning each day.

All K–12 teachers have the responsibility to write and implement units of study. Hopefully, all teachers are striving to promote learning for all students, including those who are gifted and talented.

Educators who plan units that allow for continuous progress expect all students to perform academically at the highest level possible by providing opportunities for those who demonstrate readiness for advanced learning. They recognize that fairness is matching learning experiences to student need, rather than providing the same instruction for all. The title of Julian Stanley's (2000) article "Helping Students Learn Only What They Don't Already Know" truly sums up the goal of education: continuous progress.

Support for differentiating instruction comes from many sources. In 1989 at the Education Summit, the governors and the president established six National Education Goals, which they later expanded to eight. Goal 3 in the National Education Goals specifies the following:

> By 2000, American students will leave grades 4, 8, and 12 having demonstrated competency in challenging subject matter—including English, mathematics, science, foreign languages, civics and government, economics, arts, history, and geography; and every school in America will ensure that all students learn to use their minds well so they may be prepared for responsible citizenship, further learning, and productive employment in our nation's modern economy. (U.S. Department of Education, 1991, p. 19)

Although the year 2000 has come and gone without achieving them, these goals remain important. What constitutes challenging subject matter will differ from student to student depending on what he or she already knows and is able to do.

> These words are about excellence. Meeting them [the goals] will require that the performance of our highest achievers be boosted to levels that equal or exceed the performance of the best students anywhere. (U.S. Department of Education, 1991, p. 60)

Providing challenging subject matter requires differentiating so that the content and process match the varying levels of readiness among children who are in the same age bracket. All children are not ready to achieve at the same high level and on the same time schedule any more than they are ready to wear the same size shoes when they reach a certain age. Teachers must address the needs of all children, including those who are gifted and talented in a specific academic content area or in all content areas. Learning to use their minds well speaks to providing challenging levels of thinking and problem solving, as well as challenging content.

The No Child Left Behind legislation has led to heightened interest in reducing achievement gaps. Emphasis is being placed on teaching children to achieve at grade level. Of course, grade-level achievement is important for children who are not there yet; however, if children are to learn to their potential, any child who enters a grade already achieving above grade level needs to have higher goals to make continuous progress. A gap between achievement and potential is unacceptable, and this can be addressed by using units that remove the learning ceiling, which allows teachers to plan so each child can learn at the highest level possible.

Prisoners of Time, the report released by the National Education Commission on Time and Learning in 1994, stated:

> The strongest message this commission can send to the American people is that education must become a new national obsession as powerful as sports and entertainment if we are to avoid a spiral of economic and social decline. (p. 10)

This vivid and ominous statement is worthy of reflection in this time of educational reform. If the focus of schooling is on learning and student achievement, educators must build flexibility into planning and implementing instruction to accommodate children who require less time to learn and who need more challenging content if they are to reach their potential for high-level learning, as well as those children who need more time to learn. All children benefit when a teacher implements a differentiated unit of study.

National Excellence: A Case for Developing America's Talent (U.S. Department of Education, 1993), the second national report on gifted and talented children and youth, emphasizes the need for a rigorous curriculum. Highlighting the importance of working hard on challenging tasks, Winebrenner (2001) stated:

> When gifted students discover during elementary school that they can get high praise for tasks or projects they complete with little or no effort, they may conclude that being smart means doing things easily. The longer they are allowed to believe this, the harder it is to rise to the challenge when they finally encounter one. (p. 1)

Winebrenner (1999) also emphasized the critical need to challenge advanced learners because "self-esteem actually is enhanced when success is attained at a task that has been perceived as difficult or challenging" (p. 13). Differentiating the curriculum for students who already have mastered much of the content of a unit prior to its implementation allows them to work hard at challenging academic tasks and to enhance their self-esteem as capable learners.

Planning the Unit

Planning offers the key to effective differentiation. A unit that is planned on a day-to-day basis will lack the necessary components to preassess the students' knowledge and skills in relation to the unit's goals and objectives. Just being different or offering choices to students does not make a differentiated unit. A differentiated curriculum is well planned; otherwise, it would be impossible to match learning experiences to the students' needs, interests, and abilities. Good planning is essential when preparing a unit that is differentiated to address the wide range of learner needs in a classroom.

If children and young people are to study rigorous curricula and reach high state and national standards, units of instruction must provide continuous progress for all students so that learning becomes a way of life, not an end product. The teacher's focus for each unit must be on what students should know and be able to do, taking into account what students already know and are able to do prior to implementing the unit. What individual students know and are able to do in relation to the topic and content selected for the unit will guide the teacher in determining challenging learning experiences for individuals, clusters of students, or both. Teachers must be knowledgeable of the content and be student-centered in order to plan and implement units that will challenge each student appropriately.

Before a school year begins, teachers need to have an overview of the curriculum for the year, even though they will often design specific learning opportunities unit by unit. Each unit must fit into the alignment of content for the academic year. A unit does not imply a specific amount of time that will be needed, as some units may be planned for 2 weeks, while others will need more time to optimize learning. Within a unit, the time individual students need to master the objectives will also differ. Therefore, in planning the unit, the teacher must include options that allow all students to be challenged to work at high levels.

Planning must precede differentiation. Good planning is essential for appropriate differentiation just as it is for effective teaching. In fact, differentiation is a necessary component of effective teaching. Unless planning is done well, there is no basis for differentiating learning experiences. Good planning makes it possible to preassess student learning, which provides the basis for differentiating learning experiences in such a way that it can be documented and explained to parents or educators. Without such documentation, differentiating learning experiences may be perceived as whimsical; and, in fact, such decisions are often made in ways that cannot be supported.

Model of the Relationship of Unit Components

The Model of the Relationship of Unit Components provides the broad overview for planning (see Figure 1). The model highlights the importance of the universal theme and generalizations that form the outer ring of the model, the unbroken ring encircling all other components. The theme and related generalizations provide the framework needed to develop a variety of topics within or across content areas. A theme and related generalizations encompass the topic and related content, the preassessment and postassessment, as well as all of the learning experiences. All of the components must relate to each other if the learning experiences are to be meaningful and appropriately challenging to the learners. If learning is

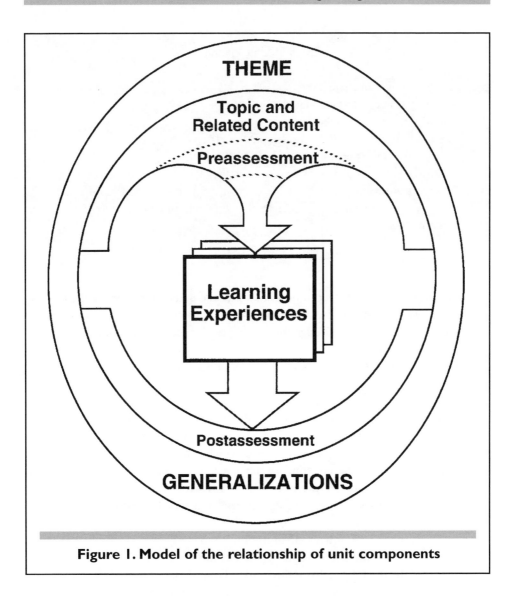

Figure 1. Model of the relationship of unit components

to be maximized, unit planning must be focused on the components, since a unit is much more than a loosely connected set of learning experiences.

Steps in Planning a Unit

Selecting the universal theme or identifying the topic provides the starting place to begin the planning process of a differentiated unit of study. Once the topic is chosen, it is important to identify the universal theme and develop the related generalizations. Both steps must be planned early in the unit-writing process to ensure that the unit maximizes opportunities for learning. The topic and the universal theme

Steps in Unit Planning

1. Select a universal theme.
2. Develop generalizations related to the theme.
3. Identify the topic of study.
4. Identify core content and complex content related to the topic.
5. Design the postassessment or culminating activity.
6. Plan/identify preassessment strategies.
7. Design learning experiences incorporating content (core and complex content), process (basic and higher-level processes), and product (a variety of products).

work together to add power to units and offer the potential to remove the learning ceiling. Together, the topic and the universal theme provide the focus for the teacher to use when selecting and designing learning experiences for the unit.

The Universal Theme and Related Generalizations

A universal or broad-based theme maximizes learning potential because it can be used in various content areas to allow students to see how and where their learning in one content area applies to other content areas or situations. They can see how learning inside school connects to what they learn outside school and vice versa. Universal themes enhance the power of learning and help children and youth become lifelong learners. Kaplan (1993) wrote that the following criteria can be used to assess a theme for its universal and broad-based nature:

1. Is the theme "universal" in its application?
2. Is the theme "timeless" in its application?
3. Is the theme equally usable across disciplines?
4. Is the theme appropriate for students across age groups?
5. Is the theme capable of "carrying" important information?
6. Is the theme useful in making connections between and among disciplines?
7. Are there generalizations (or big ideas) that can be used with the theme?

Universal themes add breadth and depth to learning. Figure 2 illustrates the need for balance among the unit components and balance among content areas related to the universal theme.

Examining a few of the criteria for a universal or broad-based theme will demonstrate issues involved in the selection of a theme. First, the theme must be applicable for the past, present, and future—not being bound by time or space. For example, "The Roaring '20s" and "The Age of Dinosaurs" are topics, not uni-

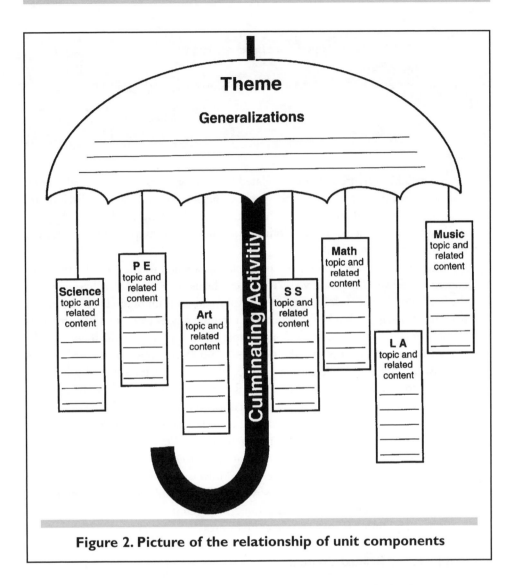

Figure 2. Picture of the relationship of unit components

versal themes because they are limited by time and space. Second, the theme must be equally usable by teachers of all content areas, including mathematics, physical education, and the visual arts, without manufacturing content to "fit" into the theme. Requiring all teachers to base instruction on a topic (often mistakenly called a theme) instead of a broad-based or universal theme often results in one or more teachers being forced to generate contrived learning experiences. For example, a physical education or mathematics teacher has a difficult time developing meaningful learning activities on "Bears" or "Holidays Around the World." A universal theme promotes interdisciplinary learning, and it establishes an optimum situation for differentiating learning opportunities. Finally, the universal theme is capable of carrying important information; generalizations can be developed that link major concepts to important statements about the universal theme.

Examples of Universal Themes

Change   Patterns   Structures   Adaptation

Systems   Exploration   Power

Generalizations are statements related to the broad-based or universal themes that will hold true across time and space. Generalizations allow interdisciplinary connections to be discovered by students or modeled by teachers as they are applied to content across the disciplines, and they can be amplified as the student matures in his or her thinking.

Themes and generalizations empower learners when teachers use them across content areas over time. A universal theme can be used by a single teacher; however, the impact of the theme is greater when employed by a team of teachers—by all the teachers at one grade level, all teachers on a middle school team, or all the teachers in the school rotated by the year. For example, "Change" may be the theme for the first school year, "Patterns" for the next year, and "Structures" for the 3rd year. A schoolwide universal theme can be a powerful mechanism for enhancing interdisciplinary connection making. A theme and related generalizations can be used for an entire year, but they also may be planned for shorter periods of time.

Some themes, while not universal, allow for the use of generalizations that are appropriate for a limited number of content areas. "Revolutions," "Expression," and "Culture" are examples of themes that apply to one or a few, rather than to all, content areas. These themes differ from universal themes in that they are not equally applicable in all content areas, yet they are capable of carrying important information through their generalizations. These content-specific themes can be useful in providing a focus in some content areas.

The Topic and Related Content

The topic describes the content of the unit in more specific terms. Examples of topics that are appropriate for various content areas at the elementary level include "Simple Machines," "Folk Tales and Legends," "Rhythm and Pitch," "Weather," and "Multiplication." Sample middle school topics include "Ecosystems," "State Government," "Perspective," and "Probability." "Social Issues," "Chemical Reactions," "Medical Technology," and "Mathematical Notation" are topics taught during high school. High school topics are often the same topics that were taught during earlier school years, but at a higher that presupposes previous mastery. At all levels, topics are related to major concepts in specific disciplines. The power of topics to enhance student learning at all levels increases when they are linked to universal themes, thus facilitating the making of connections across disciplines.

Example of a Universal Theme and Related Generalizations

Change ⟶
1. Change brings about change.
2. Change can have positive and negative results.
3. Change is universal.

There is no set number of generalizations. Teachers should develop generalizations that provide a broad view of the content for their students.

Sources of Content

1. Local curriculum guidelines
2. State curriculum frameworks or guidelines
3. National curriculum standards

Selecting the core and complex content follows the identification of the topic. Core content is the content that every student in the class is expected to master. Complex content relates to the core content, but goes beyond. It is more abstract and often relates to issues and problems tied to the core content. In a differentiated unit, all children are learning about the same topic, but some are learning core content while others who have demonstrated that they already know the core content are learning complex content. However, as all children share their learning experiences with the class, they are all tied to the same topic, concepts, and generalizations, which enhances learning for all.

The topic and the content of the unit come from three major sources: local curriculum guides, state curricular frameworks or guidelines, and the national curriculum standards. Local and state curricular documents are enhanced when used in conjunction with the national curriculum standards:

- Principles and Standards for School Mathematics (National Council of Teachers of Mathematics, 2000)
- National Standards for Civics and Government (Center for Civic Education, 1994)
- National Standards for American History (National Council for History Standards, 1994a; 1994b)
- National Standards for World History (National Council for History Standards, 1994c)
- National Geography Standards (Geography Education Standards Project, 1994)
- National Standards for Arts Education (Consortium of National Arts Education, 1994)

- National Science Education Standards (National Research Council, 1996)
- National Standards in Foreign Language Learning (National Standards in Foreign Language Education Project, 1996)
- Standards for the English Language Arts (National Council of Teachers of English & International Reading Association, 1996).

Local, state, and national standards combine to provide the content to be considered when identifying topics and selecting the key content that will provide the focus of the unit.

Various content-based professional organizations have responded to the call for high standards by developing and issuing curriculum standards that spell out high-level content, including concepts and skills, to guide curriculum development. The national standards in the various content areas establish the benchmarks for which educators must plan. For all children, they set high standards that will require quality teaching if they are to be met.

National standards provide the minimal standards for children who are gifted and talented. These standards should be in hand when planning curricula, as they provide the bottom line for the level of content and process that must be mastered by gifted and talented students who can learn at complex levels and at rapid paces. In line with the model presented in this chapter, preassessment for new units of instruction (related to the standards) will provide the important information needed to match differentiated learning experiences to student needs so that students can make continuous progress.

Postassessment

Also encompassed by the universal theme and generalizations in Figure 1 is the postassessment, which may be a culminating activity or an exit exhibition. The postassessment should be planned after the topic and related content have been specified, and it should provide the opportunity for students to demonstrate the breadth of their learning during the unit in a context typical of real-life situations. The postassessment should be planned before designing learning experiences because these experiences can be selected or developed to build skills and incorporate knowledge needed to complete the culminating or exit activity successfully. As a child learns to play a sport, he or she learns requisite skills one by one; however, the integration of knowledge and skills is necessary to play the sport well. The culminating activity requires a similar integration of what the student has learned and is able to do as a result of the learning experiences in the unit.

The postassessment or culminating activity is to the unit what a product is to the learning experience. In each case, the culminating activity and the product in the learning experience are the demonstration of what the student knows and is able to do. However, the postassessment encompasses what the student knows and is able to do at the conclusion of the unit, rather than being the result of a single learning experience. The postassessment may be designed by the teacher or by the

Example of a Culminating Activity

A student or group of students writes a play/short story that ties together what they have learned about the culture, politics, and history of ancient Rome.

student(s). The activity may be a problem-solving task that requires integrating knowledge (content) and skill (process) into a demonstration of what a student or students working together in a cluster know and are able to do to solve the problem. A well-constructed essay exam can also be an appropriate postassessment. A student or a cluster of students can design the culminating activity, a unique opportunity for students for whom the learning experiences have been differentiated in response to evidence that they already can meet the expectations of the core curriculum. Whether the teacher or the student(s) plans the postassessment, it is important to have a scoring guide or rubric that will set the standards for excellence.

Preassessment

Once the goals and objectives for the unit have been established and the postassessment has been planned, the next step is to assess who already knows and can do what the unit is planned to teach. Assessment is the key to knowing for whom and when differentiated learning experiences are appropriate and necessary. Prior to teaching a unit, teachers must assess the children to find out who has already mastered the objectives or is close to doing so. Otherwise, teachers may not know how much their students already know about the topic and therefore may assume that the assessment at the end of the unit revealed how much the students learned as the unit was taught. Preassessment provides necessary information for teachers to plan challenging learning opportunities for all children who can demonstrate that they already know the core content and are ready to move on to more challenging learning experiences. Of course, assessment at the conclusion of the unit allows for the teacher to have additional information to inform planning for the next unit of instruction.

The Learning Experiences: Building Blocks of the Unit

Designing Learning Experiences

After the theme has been chosen, the generalizations have been identified, the topic and related content have been specified, the postassessment or culminating activity has been planned, and students have completed a preassessment, the next level of unit planning is the development of learning experiences. Learning expe-

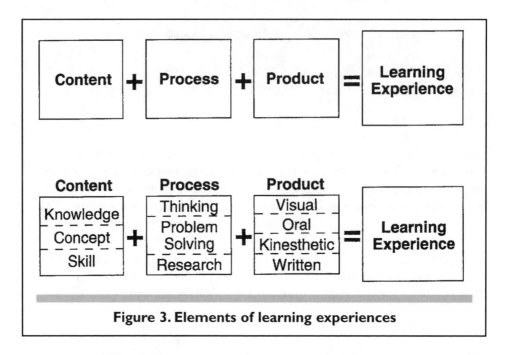

Figure 3. Elements of learning experiences

riences are the building blocks of units. Units contain numerous learning experiences, each of which is designed to teach important content, processes, and products. The Elements of Learning Experiences, as shown in Figure 3, illustrate how a learning experience is built by combining content, process, and product.

The content is what the teacher wants the students to know at the end of the unit. Related content includes the concepts and knowledge to be learned to reach unit learning goals. Content has been specified earlier in the unit-planning process; each learning experience focuses on a concept or knowledge to be learned as the unit is implemented. If the concept to be taught is "the cell," then the cell becomes the content of the learning experience. In addition, teaching students how to produce a new or untried product can become the content for a learning experience. If the students have never produced a Venn diagram, it would be the content of the learning experience. If a new process skill is being introduced, that skill can become the content for that learning experience.

The process is what the students are to be able to do cognitively with the content. The process includes thinking, problem solving, and research skills. The national curriculum standards include process, as well as content, within their standards. Although Bloom's (1956) Taxonomy of Educational Objectives in the cognitive domain represents only one way of developing process skills, it is used within this model because it is well known and a good starting point for teachers who are new to differentiation. Bloom's taxonomy provides a known system for writing learning experiences at various levels of thinking. For example, on the level of knowledge/comprehension, the desired outcome of a learning experience could be to explain the functions of the various parts of the cell.

Elements of a Learning Experience

Content: Plant and Animal Cells
Process: Analysis
Product: Venn Diagram (visual/written)

Objective of the learning experience: The student will compare and contrast the structure of plant and animal cells producing a Venn diagram.

At the analysis level, the student could compare and contrast the structure of plant and animal cells. At the evaluation level, the student could justify a position about continuing stem cell research. Another more comprehensive approach to process skills can be found in the Process Skills Rating Scales–Revised (Karnes & Bean, 2004).

The product is the means used to demonstrate what one has learned. In other words, the product is how the teacher wants students to show what they know and are able to do as the result of being involved in the learning experience. Karnes and Stephens (2000) described products as visual, oral, performance, written, or multicategorical. Samara and Curry (1994) categorized products as visual, oral, kinesthetic, or written. Providing a balance in the types of products allows students the opportunity to show what they have learned in a preferred way or with a learning style that is one of their strengths. Products that have been the traditional mainstays of the curriculum are papers (written), reports (oral or written), posters (visual), illustrations (visual), and laboratory experiments (kinesthetic). However, the possibilities for products are much broader than those most frequently used. In fact, a wide array of products can motivate students by tapping into their learning interests and preferences.

Using different combinations of content, processes, and products allows teachers to create learning experiences in which different student needs, abilities, and interests can be addressed. It is important to remember that many gifted students' needs are based on strengths, rather than weaknesses or deficiencies. A learning environment in which students have an element of choice and can engage in learning experiences that are matched to their needs and interests is a positive one for teacher and students.

Differentiating Learning Experiences

In order to differentiate the content of learning experiences, the following three curricular components must be in place:

1. The core content must be specified so that students know what they all should know and be able to do by the completion of the unit.

2. Strategies for ongoing assessment are planned in order to provide a solid rationale for compacting the curriculum and differentiating learning experiences.
3. Core and complex content, basic and higher order processes, and a variety of products must be identified/developed in order to plan differentiated learning experiences to match students' needs and prior knowledge/experiences.

Because of their importance, each of these components will be discussed in more detail.

1. Identifying the core content in the unit planning sequence is necessary before proceeding with planning to differentiate learning experiences. It is impossible to plan to differentiate appropriately without specifying what all children in a particular grade and content area are expected to know and be able to do with the topic and related content by the conclusion of the unit of study. The core content must be specified so that both teacher and students understand what all students should know and be able to do by the completion of the unit. Planning the topic and related content at the core content level is a prerequisite for differentiation. Without this preplanning, there is no point of reference for compacting and differentiating the curriculum. Likewise, it is difficult to know if the teacher and students reach the unit goals if they are not stated in advance.

Topics are usually large enough that teachers could go in numerous directions, and it is not possible to teach all content that could be tied to the topic. For example, a unit on the Civil War could be taught chronologically or it could focus on battles, political events, or cultural history. Since it is possible to study the Civil War at the graduate level, it is impossible for students to master all of the content on a meaningful level during a 2- or 3-week unit. Narrowing the topic and focusing the related content will provide the rationale for selecting/developing some learning experiences over others. Likewise, the universal theme and generalizations will facilitate making interdisciplinary connections and provide criteria for designing learning experiences.

For example, if the universal theme of "Change" is used and generalizations include "Change can be either good or bad" and "Change brings about change," a learning activity that examines the Civil War in light of the generalizations could ask students to compare and contrast life on a plantation in a Southern state before, during, and after the Civil War with a focus on evaluating whether these changes were good or bad and providing the rationale for the decisions. Product choices could include a written diary or a series of illustrations. Thus, the learning experience is tied to the topic and core content, yet it also relates to the universal theme and generalizations. Learning is more powerful and long-lasting if it is consciously tied to a universal theme and related generalizations.

2. Strategies for ongoing assessment must be planned in order to provide a solid rationale for compacting the curriculum and differentiating learning expe-

Examples of Preassessment Strategies

- Pretest
- Five Most Difficult Questions
- Mind Map
- Individual KW Chart

riences. Without evidence from assessment, differentiating learning experiences for students will appear capricious, and the teacher will be subject to criticism. The purpose of differentiation is to match a learning experience to the need(s) of a student or a cluster of students for whom the learning experience is appropriately challenging. If everyone can complete the learning experiences planned for differentiation, then the learning experiences are not really appropriate for only some of the students, nor do they provide appropriately differentiated experiences. When assessment strategies demonstrate that the student already knows the content and is able to do what is expected at the conclusion of the unit, the rationale is provided for differentiating. Ongoing assessment can make it possible for all students to make continuous progress.

Preassessment is a critical element in unit planning. Different strategies for preassessment can provide variety and bring in information on students' prior knowledge and interests relative to the content. Various assessment measures can be used to document what students know and what they might need for differentiation. Following are four examples.

1. *Using a pretest, which may be the end-of-the-unit assessment given prior to teaching the unit.* The pretest will reveal what students already know about the topic and provide the documentation of the need for differentiated learning experience. Since the postassessment is already planned, it is easy to use as a preassessment.

2. *Asking the five most difficult questions to be learned before beginning the unit.* A student who can answer the five most difficult questions that the unit is planned to teach prior to the unit being taught deserves to have alternate learning experiences (Winebrenner, 2001, p. 35).

3. *Giving students the opportunity to design a mind map.* A mind map (Buzan, 1983) provides the opportunity for students to map out visually what they know about the topic or focal subject matter of the unit, making connections between the major ideas or concepts. A mind map has some of the characteristics of webbing; however, the strategy depends upon using key words to detail what students already know about the topic. The mind map allows students who know a great deal about a topic to share the information, as well as experiences they have had that

Planning for Differentiated Learning Experiences

- Identify/select the core content.
- Assess student knowledge of core content.
- Identify/plan core and complex content, basic and higher level processes, and a variety of products.

relate to the topic or concept that will be studied. A mind map also allows students to show the relationships among concepts that they understand about the topic.

4. *Providing the opportunity for students to tell/write what they already know about a topic and what they would like to know through a KW assessment or chart.* Another assessment measure that will show the need for differentiation is an individual KW chart on which the student details what he or she knows (K) and wants to find out (W). Having the student provide questions concerning what he or she wants to learn can provide the direction for differentiated learning opportunities.

With each of these four methods of preassessment, students bring what they have learned about a topic in school and outside school to the forefront so the knowledge and skills can be taken into account when matching learning experiences to students. The value of the preassessment depends on how the teacher uses the information to allow individual students or clusters of students to learn more complex content and to have differentiated learning experiences based on what they already know and are able to do.

3. Learning experiences are designed by combining content, process, and product. During planning, core and complex content, basic and higher order processes, and a variety of products must be identified and developed in order to provide differentiated learning experiences. Learning experiences can be differentiated on one, two, or all three dimensions—content, process, and product. Complex content includes abstract concepts, issues and problems, and advanced knowledge related to the core content, universal themes, and related generalizations. Complex/abstract content related to the core content allows students to continue learning about the same topic or universal theme with the rest of the class; however, it elevates the level of the content to match the students' advanced knowledge of the content and readiness to process the information at higher levels.

Differentiated learning experiences must be appropriately matched to the students' readiness to learn more complex content, use higher level processes to demonstrate what they have learned, and develop a wide range of products. The same students may not always need differentiation in all subjects or in all topics within a content area. If preassessment confirms that the core content is known

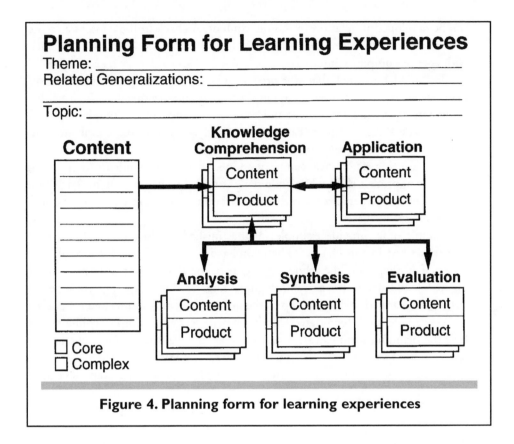

Planning Form for Learning Experiences

Theme: _____

Related Generalizations: _____

Topic: _____

Figure 4. Planning form for learning experiences

at the 80% level or above, the content needs to be compacted to include differentiated learning experiences with a focus on complex content.

More and more states (for example, Kentucky) are specifying core content that requires thinking and problem solving for all children. Goals 2000, as mentioned previously, states that all children will learn to use their minds well. The national curriculum standards include content and process standards that all children and youth should reach before exiting grades 4, 8, and 12. Since thinking and problem solving are expectations for all children, more complex and challenging experiences must be available for children who have mastered these process skills. The content for those gifted students who are ready for differentiated learning experiences must be complex, providing for continuous progress and the development of their academic capabilities. A variety of products can be used to demonstrate mastery of complex content.

To facilitate the planning process, the Planning Form for Learning Experiences was developed (see Figure 4). This form can be used to plan differentiated learning experiences with both core and complex content. The planning form allows the planner to see the theme and related generalizations, as well as the topic and related content, as he or she designs learning activities. The layering of the learning experiences boxes suggests that numerous learning experiences can be developed in relationship to the content. A check in the content area box allows for using the same planning form for differentiated learning experiences with core or complex content.

It should be noted that the process skills of knowledge, comprehension, application, analysis, synthesis, and evaluation are not arranged in the usual linear hierarchy. Instead, knowledge and comprehension form the foundation for all other process skills. A student cannot apply, analyze, synthesize, or evaluate using criteria without knowledge of the topic. Starting with knowledge and comprehension, learning experiences can be developed that require students to utilize the full range of process skills while addressing core and complex content. Each time the student applies, analyzes, synthesizes, or evaluates the content, he or she adds to the knowledge base.

Sample units provide examples of the finished product resulting from the steps described in this chapter. The completed planning forms for topical units on Ancient Egypt (middle school) in Figure 5, the Rain Forest (intermediate) in Figure 6, and Patterns (primary) in Figure 7 illustrate how the core learning experiences are planned in relationship to the universal themes and related generalizations. Examples of differentiated learning experiences with complex content show how the planning form can be used to remove the learning ceiling. The layered boxes on the form indicate that there can be several learning experiences at each level with the same content, but with a variety of products. The examples can be expanded to provide more student choice and to take the learning into greater depth.

The sample units illustrate how differentiation can be planned for individual students or clusters of students based on information from the preassessment. They also show how learning experiences can be matched to needs, interests, and abilities. Not all children need to complete all learning experiences; rather, the match is the key to removing the learning ceiling. All children, including those who are gifted and talented, need challenging learning experiences in all content areas on an ongoing basis. They need to have the floor to learning raised and the ceiling removed.

Planning Form for Learning Experiences

Theme: _____Adaptations_____

Related Generalizations: (1) Cultures adapt to their environment. (2) Cultures adapt their environment to fit their needs. (3) Adaptation is necessary for progress.

Topic: Ancient Egypt

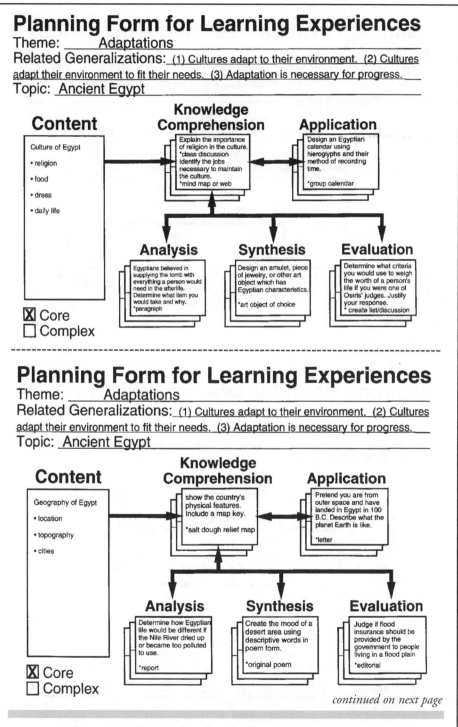

Content

Culture of Egypt

• religion

• food

• dress

• daily life

☒ Core
☐ Complex

Knowledge Comprehension

Explain the importance of religion in the culture. *class discussion Identify the jobs necessary to maintain the culture. *mind map or web

Application

Design an Egyptian calendar using hieroglyphs and their method of recording time.

*group calendar

Analysis

Egyptians believed in supplying the tomb with everything a person would need in the afterlife. Determine what item you would take and why. *paragraph

Synthesis

Design an amulet, piece of jewelry, or other art object which has Egyptian characteristics.

*art object of choice

Evaluation

Determine what criteria you would use to weigh the worth of a person's life if you were one of Osiris' judges. Justify your response. * create list/discussion

---

Planning Form for Learning Experiences

Theme: _____Adaptations_____

Related Generalizations: (1) Cultures adapt to their environment. (2) Cultures adapt their environment to fit their needs. (3) Adaptation is necessary for progress.

Topic: Ancient Egypt

Content

Geography of Egypt

• location

• topography

• cities

☒ Core
☐ Complex

Knowledge Comprehension

show the country's physical features. Include a map key.

*salt dough relief map

Application

Pretend you are from outer space and have landed in Egypt in 100 B.C. Describe what the planet Earth is like.

*letter

Analysis

Determine how Egyptian life would be different if the Nile River dried up or became too polluted to use.

*report

Synthesis

Create the mood of a desert area using descriptive words in poem form.

*original poem

Evaluation

Judge if flood insurance should be provided by the government to people living in a flood plain

*editorial

continued on next page

Figure 5. Example of completed planning form for learning experiences

Planning Form for Learning Experiences

Theme: ___Adaptations___

Related Generalizations: (1) Cultures adapt to their environment. (2) Cultures adapt their environment to fit their needs. (3) Adaptation is necessary for progress.

Topic: _Ancient Egypt_

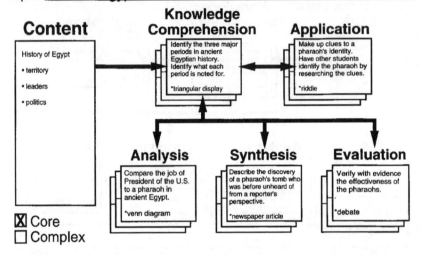

Content

History of Egypt
- territory
- leaders
- politics

☒ Core
☐ Complex

Knowledge Comprehension

Identify the three major periods in ancient Egyptian history. Identify what each period is noted for.

*triangular display

Application

Make up clues to a pharaoh's identity. Have other students identify the pharaoh by researching the clues.

*riddle

Analysis

Compare the job of President of the U.S. to a pharaoh in ancient Egypt.

*venn diagram

Synthesis

Describe the discovery of a pharaoh's tomb who was before unheard of from a reporter's perspective.

*newspaper article

Evaluation

Verify with evidence the effectiveness of the pharaohs.

*debate

Planning Form for Learning Experiences

Theme: ___Adaptations___

Related Generalizations: (1) Cultures adapt to their environment. (2) Cultures adapt their environment to fit their needs. (3) Adaptation is necessary for progress.

Topic: _Ancient Egypt_

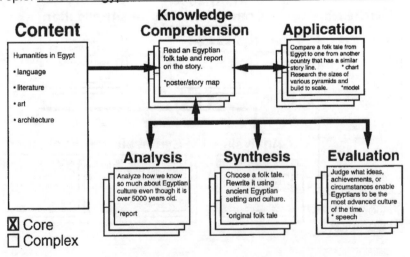

Content

Humanities in Egypt
- language
- literature
- art
- architecture

☒ Core
☐ Complex

Knowledge Comprehension

Read an Egyptian folk tale and report on the story.

*poster/story map

Application

Compare a folk tale from Egypt to one from another country that has a similar story line.   * chart
Research the sizes of various pyramids and build to scale.   *model

Analysis

Analyze how we know so much about Egyptian culture even though it is over 5000 years old.

*report

Synthesis

Choose a folk tale. Rewrite it using ancient Egyptian setting and culture.

*original folk tale

Evaluation

Judge what ideas, achievements, or circumstances enable Egyptians to be the most advanced culture of the time.
* speech

Figure 5 continued

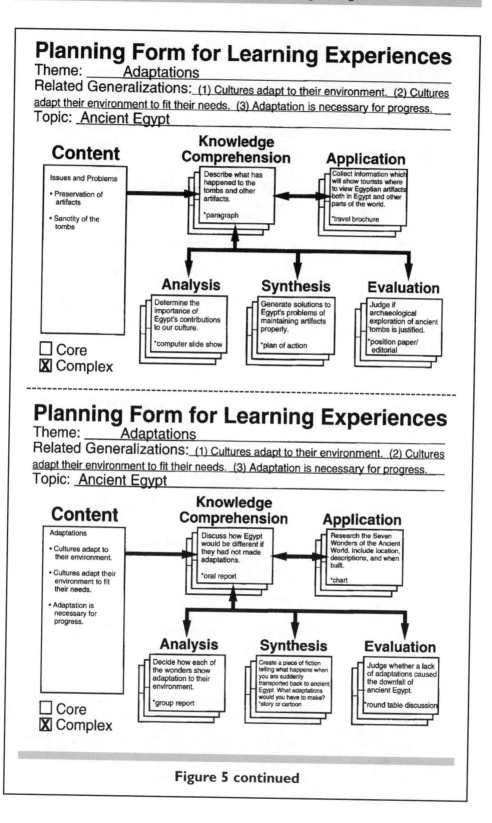

Planning Form for Learning Experiences

Theme: _____ Adaptations

Related Generalizations: (1) Cultures adapt to their environment. (2) Cultures adapt their environment to fit their needs. (3) Adaptation is necessary for progress.

Topic: Ancient Egypt

Content

Issues and Problems

• Preservation of artifacts

• Sanctity of the tombs

☐ Core
☒ Complex

Knowledge Comprehension

Describe what has happened to the tombs and other artifacts.

*paragraph

Application

Collect information which will show tourists where to view Egyptian artifacts both in Egypt and other parts of the world.

*travel brochure

Analysis

Determine the importance of Egypt's contributions to our culture.

*computer slide show

Synthesis

Generate solutions to Egypt's problems of maintaining artifacts properly.

*plan of action

Evaluation

Judge if archaeological exploration of ancient tombs is justified.

*position paper/editorial

Planning Form for Learning Experiences

Theme: _____ Adaptations

Related Generalizations: (1) Cultures adapt to their environment. (2) Cultures adapt their environment to fit their needs. (3) Adaptation is necessary for progress.

Topic: Ancient Egypt

Content

Adaptations

• Cultures adapt to their environment.

• Cultures adapt their environment to fit their needs.

• Adaptation is necessary for progress.

☐ Core
☒ Complex

Knowledge Comprehension

Discuss how Egypt would be different if they had not made adaptations.

*oral report

Application

Research the Seven Wonders of the Ancient World. Include location, descriptions, and when built.

*chart

Analysis

Decide how each of the wonders show adaptation to their environment.

*group report

Synthesis

Create a piece of fiction telling what happens when you are suddenly transported back to ancient Egypt. What adaptations would you have to make?

*story or cartoon

Evaluation

Judge whether a lack of adaptations caused the downfall of ancient Egypt.

*round table discussion

Figure 5 continued

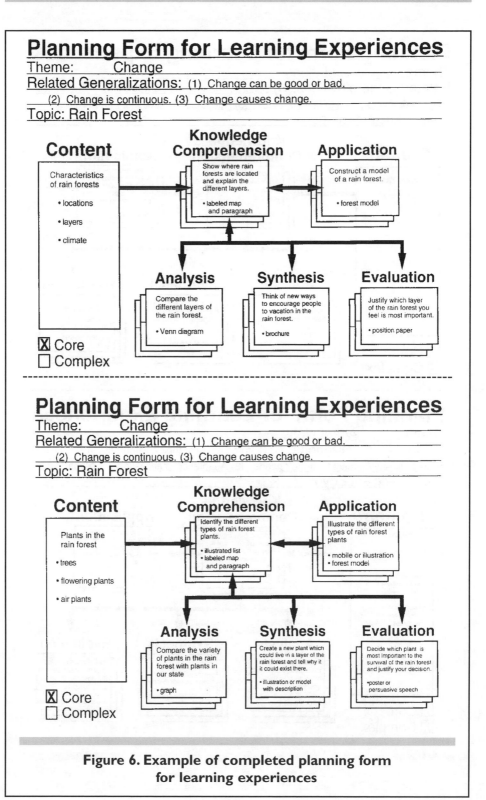

Planning Form for Learning Experiences
Theme: Change
Related Generalizations: (1) Change can be good or bad.
(2) Change is continuous. (3) Change causes change.
Topic: Rain Forest

Content

Characteristics of rain forests

- locations
- layers
- climate

☒ Core
☐ Complex

Knowledge Comprehension

Show where rain forests are located and explain the different layers.

- labeled map and paragraph

Application

Construct a model of a rain forest.

- forest model

Analysis

Compare the different layers of the rain forest.

- Venn diagram

Synthesis

Think of new ways to encourage people to vacation in the rain forest.

- brochure

Evaluation

Justify which layer of the rain forest you feel is most important.

- position paper

Planning Form for Learning Experiences
Theme: Change
Related Generalizations: (1) Change can be good or bad.
(2) Change is continuous. (3) Change causes change.
Topic: Rain Forest

Content

Plants in the rain forest

- trees
- flowering plants
- air plants

☒ Core
☐ Complex

Knowledge Comprehension

Identify the different types of rain forest plants.

- illustrated list
- labeled map and paragraph

Application

Illustrate the different types of rain forest plants

- mobile or illustration
- forest model

Analysis

Compare the variety of plants in the rain forest with plants in our state

- graph

Synthesis

Create a new plant which could live in a layer of the rain forest and tell why it could exist there.

- illustration or model with description

Evaluation

Decide which plant is most important to the survival of the rain forest and justify your decision.

- poster or persuasive speech

Figure 6. Example of completed planning form for learning experiences

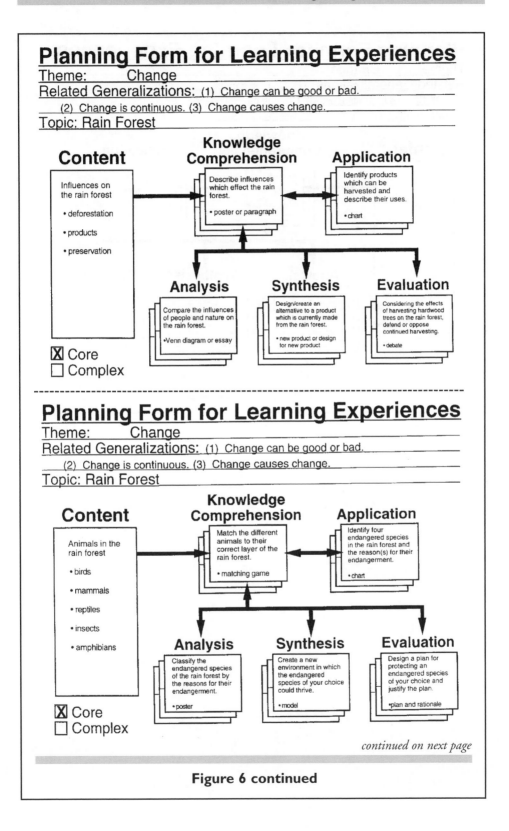

Planning Form for Learning Experiences

Theme: Change

Related Generalizations: (1) Change can be good or bad.

   (2) Change is continuous. (3) Change causes change.

Topic: Rain Forest

Content

Influences on the rain forest

• deforestation

• products

• preservation

Knowledge Comprehension

Describe influences which effect the rain forest.

• poster or paragraph

Application

Identify products which can be harvested and describe their uses.

• chart

Analysis

Compare the influences of people and nature on the rain forest.

•Venn diagram or essay

Synthesis

Design/create an alternative to a product which is currently made from the rain forest.

• new product or design for new product

Evaluation

Considering the effects of harvesting hardwood trees on the rain forest, defend or oppose continued harvesting.

• debate

☒ Core
☐ Complex

Planning Form for Learning Experiences

Theme: Change

Related Generalizations: (1) Change can be good or bad.

   (2) Change is continuous. (3) Change causes change.

Topic: Rain Forest

Content

Animals in the rain forest

• birds

• mammals

• reptiles

• insects

• amphibians

Knowledge Comprehension

Match the different animals to their correct layer of the rain forest.

• matching game

Application

Identify four endangered species in the rain forest and the reason(s) for their endangerment.

• chart

Analysis

Classify the endangered species of the rain forest by the reasons for their endangerment.

• poster

Synthesis

Create a new environment in which the endangered species of your choice could thrive.

• model

Evaluation

Design a plan for protecting an endangered species of your choice and justify the plan.

•plan and rationale

☒ Core
☐ Complex

continued on next page

Figure 6 continued

Planning Form for Learning Experiences

Theme: Change

Related Generalizations: (1) Change can be good or bad.

(2) Change is continuous. (3) Change causes change.

Topic: Rain Forest

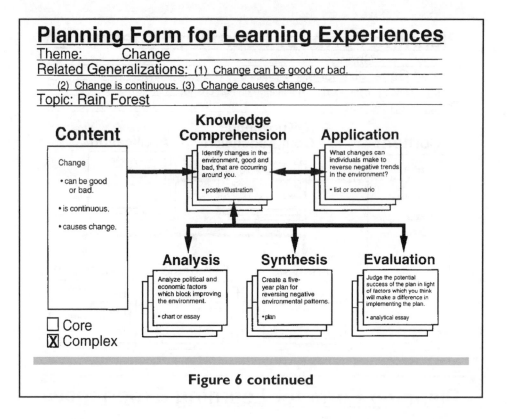

Figure 6 continued

Planning Form for Learning Experiences

Theme: Patterns

Related Generalizations: (1) Patterns repeat. (2) Patterns maintain order.
(3) Patterns are found everywhere. (4) Patterns predict.

Topic: Patterns in Seasons

Content

Patterns in seasons

· Sequence of seasons

· Characteristics
  of each season

· Each season's
  influence on life
  (clothing, food,
  holidays)

Knowledge Comprehension

Illustrate the order of
the seasons.

*picture or cartoon

Application

Plan field trips that you
would enjoy in each
season and explain
your choices.

*paragraphs or
brochures

Analysis

Compare two seasons,
including clothing, food,
and holidays.

*chart or Venn diagram

Synthesis

Change a summer holiday
into one in another season.
Describe the changes and
the reasons for changes.

*paragraph or poem

Evaluation

Justify a move to
another part of the
country or world based
on family needs and
preferences.

*speech or diary

☒ Core
☐ Complex

Planning Form for Learning Experiences

Theme: Patterns

Related Generalizations: (1) Patterns repeat. (2) Patterns maintain order.
(3) Patterns are found everywhere. (4) Patterns predict.

Topic: Patterns in Math

Content

Patterns in math

· Counting

· Calendar

· Time

Knowledge Comprehension

Describe patterns
you can use in
counting to 100.

*poster

Application

Find patterns in telling
time and share them
with a small group.

*display or illustration

Analysis

Look at the calendar for
June and December.
Show ways these
months are alike and
different.

*chart

Synthesis

Create an ab, an abc, and
an aba math pattern with
numbers or shapes.
Then make up a math
pattern all your own.

*display or demonstration

Evaluation

Justify the importance of
the math pattern that you
found most useful and
explain your rationale.

*paragraph
(illustration optional)

☒ Core
☐ Complex

continued on next page

**Figure 7. Example of completed planning form
for learning experiences**

Planning Form for Learning Experiences

Theme: Patterns

Related Generalizations: (1) Patterns repeat. (2) Patterns maintain order. (3) Patterns are found everywhere. (4) Patterns predict.

Topic: Patterns in Families

Content

Patterns in families

- Holidays
- Food
- Pastimes
- Customs
- Stories

Knowledge Comprehension

Relate a family story.

*written or audio taped story

Application

Survey the class about family pastimes, food, and holidays and show the results.

*graph

Analysis

Compare a custom from your grandparent's childhood with a custom from your childhood.

*audio taped story with illustration

Synthesis

Create a new custom for your family and describe how to get everyone involved.

· illustration or paragraph

Evaluation

Justify a change in your neighborhood that would improve life for families and create a new pattern in your area.

*Letter to editor

☒ Core
☐ Complex

Planning Form for Learning Experiences

Theme: Patterns

Related Generalizations: (1) Patterns repeat. (2) Patterns maintain order. (3) Patterns are found everywhere. (4) Patterns predict.

Topic: Patterns

Content

Patterns

- Patterns repeat.
- Patterns maintain order.
- Patterns are found everywhere.
- Patterns predict.

Knowledge Comprehension

Illustrate a pattern that keeps order.

*poster

Application

Find three patterns in nature to see that patterns are everywhere.

*objects or illustrations

Analysis

Describe two patterns that predict and compare them.

* chart or paragraph

Synthesis

Create a patterns in art, music, or movement and illustrate, sing/play, or dance the pattern.

*performing the pattern

Evaluation

Observe and record patterns for a week. Justify the importance of patterns in understanding our bodies, our days, etc.

*paper or illustration

☐ Core
☒ Complex

Figure 7 continued

Teacher Statement

Julia Roberts and Dick Roberts have developed a very teacher-friendly model for designing units; but, most importantly, their model benefits kids by requiring them to perform at the higher levels of Bloom's taxonomy.

I became familiar with this unit design during Julia Roberts' class. I used the model to plan a United States government unit for my 5th-grade gifted students. Since that class, I have used the model or graphic organizer to plan a multicultural unit, and I am currently developing an arts and humanities unit. The success I have experienced with the government unit convinced me to continue using this model.

When teachers use this model to plan, the unit covers the core content and provides complex activities that require higher order thinking skills. The unit can remain a work in progress because it is easy to move, add, or delete items. It is often difficult to teach the core content while offering challenging and enriching activities; however, by organizing units into subtopics and writing activities at Bloom's different levels of thinking, this model allows students to learn the content while using critical and creative thinking skills.

Students are *required* to cover the same content, but teachers must allow for all students to experience continuous progress within that content. The Roberts and Roberts model for planning units allows this to happen without seeming like an impossible task. This is a win-win situation for teachers and students.

—Kimberly K. Wolfram

Discussion Questions

1. What factors in a classroom or school create a learning ceiling?

2. What can a teacher do to remove the learning ceiling for a student or for a cluster of students?

3. What are the benefits of removing the learning ceiling? You may want to interview a couple of gifted students and their parents while considering the benefits.

4. Julian Stanley wrote an article entitled "Helping Students Learn Only What They Don't Already Know." Would teachers in your school agree or disagree with that idea? Why or why not?

5. What methods have you used to assess your students' knowledge and skills prior to teaching a unit, and how did you use that information to ensure continuous progress for each student in your class? How could you use that preassessment information to guide future instruction?

6. If you were observing in a classroom in which the teacher was differentiating the curriculum, what teacher behaviors could you observe?

7. If you were observing in a classroom in which the curriculum was being differentiated, what could you observe students doing?

8. Various professional organizations stress the importance of providing a rigorous curriculum to students. Think about the students you teach. What does providing a rigorous curriculum mean to each student in your class? Does the meaning of what a rigorous curriculum is differ from one student to another?

Teacher Resources

Publications

Center for Gifted Studies. (1996). *Incorporating broad-based thematic units into the curriculum*. [Videotape]. Bowling Green: Western Kentucky University.

Center for Gifted Studies. (1996). *Opening up the curriculum: Getting rid of the ceiling*. [Videotape]. Bowling Green: Western Kentucky University.

Clarke, C. L., & Agne, R. M. (1997). *Interdisciplinary high school teaching: Strategies for integrated learning*. Needham Heights, MA: Allyn and Bacon.

Kaplan, S. N. (1993). *Developing thematic interdisciplinary curriculum for middle schools*. Bowling Green: Western Kentucky University.

Karnes, F. A., & Stephens, K. R. (2000). *The ultimate guide for student product development and evaluation*. Waco, TX: Prufrock Press.

Samara, J., & Curry, J. (1994). *Developing units for primary students*. Bowling Green: Kentucky Association for Gifted Education.

Samara, J., & Curry, J. (1995). *Product guides*. Austin, TX: The Curriculum Project.

Web Sites

American Association for the Advancement of Science: Benchmarks for Science Literacy—http://www.project2061.org/tools/benchol/bolintro.htm

American Council on the Teaching of Foreign Languages: Standards for Foreign Language Learning—http://www.actfl.org/index.cfm?weburl=/public/articles/details.cfm?id=33

Center for Civic Education: National Standards for Civics and Government—http://www.civiced.org/stds.html

Center for Civic Education: CIVITAS: A Framework for Civic Education Executive Summary—http://www.civiced.org/civitasexec.html

Center for Civic Education Curricular Materials—http://www.civiced.org/curriculum.html

National Center for History in the Schools: National Standards for History for Grades K–12—http://www.sscnet.ucla.edu/nchs/standards

National Center for History in the Schools: National Standards for World History Grades 5–12—http://www.sscnet.ucla.edu/nchs/standards/worldera1.html

National Council for the Social Studies: Curriculum Standards for Social Studies—http://www.socialstudies.org/standards

*National Council of Teachers of English: Standards for the English Language Arts—*http://www.ncte.org/standards/standards.shtml

*National Council of Teachers of Mathematics: Principles and Standards for School Mathematics—*http://standards.nctm.org/document/index.htm

*National Geographic Society: Geography Standards 1994—*http://www.radford.edu/~geog-web/standard.html

*National Council for Geographic Education: The Eighteen National Geography Standards—*http://www.ncge.org/publications/tutorial/standards

*National Research Council: National Science Education Standards—*http://www.nap.edu/books/0309053269/html/index.html

*National Standards for Arts Education—*http://artsedge.kennedy-center.org/teach/standards.cfm

References

Bloom, B. S. (Ed.). (1956). *Taxonomy of educational objectives: The classification of educational goals. Handbook I: Cognitive domain.* New York: Longman.

Buzan, T. (1983). *Use both sides of your brain.* New York: Dutton.

Consortium of National Arts Education Associations. (1994). *National standards for arts education: What every young American should know and be able to do in the arts.* Reston, VA: Music Educators National Conference.

Center for Civic Education. (1994). *National standards for civics and government.* Calabasas, CA: Author.

Geography Education Standards Project. (1994). *National geography standards: Geography for life.* Washington, DC: National Geographic Society.

Kaplan, S. N. (1993). *Developing thematic interdisciplinary curriculum for middle schools.* Bowling Green: Western Kentucky University.

Karnes, F. A., & Bean, S. M. (2004). *Process skills rating scales–Revised.* Waco, TX: Prufrock Press.

Karnes, F. A., & Stephens, K. R. (2000). *The ultimate guide for student product development and evaluation.* Waco, TX: Prufrock Press.

National Council for History Standards. (1994a). *National standards for United States history: Expanding children's world in time and space, grades K–4.* Los Angeles: National Center for History in the Schools.

National Council for History Standards. (1994b). *National standards for United States history: Exploring the American experience, grades 5–12.* Los Angeles: National Center for History in the Schools.

National Council for History Standards. (1994c). *National standards for world history: Exploring paths to the present, grades 5–12.* Los Angeles: National Center for History in the Schools.

National Council of Teachers of English & International Reading Associates. (1996). *Standards for the English language arts.* Urbana, IL: National Council of Teachers of English.

National Council of Teachers of Mathematics. (2000). *Principles and standards for school mathematics.* Reston, VA: Author.

National Education Commission on Time and Learning. (1994). *Prisoners of time.* Washington, DC: Author.

National Research Council. (1996). *National science education standards.* Washington, DC: National Academy Press.

National Standards in Foreign Language Education Project. (1996). *Standards for foreign language learning: Preparing for the 21st century.* Yonkers, NY: Author.

Samara, J., & Curry, J. (1994). *Developing units for primary students.* Bowling Green: Kentucky Association for Gifted Children.

Stanley, J. C. (2000). Helping students learn only what they don't already know. *Psychology, Public Policy, and Law, 47,* 216–222.

U.S. Department of Education. (1991). *America 2000: An education strategy.* Washington, DC: Author.

U.S. Department of Education, Office of Educational Research and Improvement. (1993). *National excellence: A case for developing America's talent.* Washington, DC: U.S. Government Printing Office.

Winebrenner, S. (1999). Shortchanging the gifted. *The School Administrator, 56*(9), 12–16.

Winebrenner, S. (2001). *Teaching gifted kids in the regular classroom.* Minneapolis, MN: Free Spirit Press.

Chapter 8

Making the Grade
or Achieving the Goal?

Evaluating Learner and Program Outcomes in Gifted Education

by **Carolyn M. Callahan**

oo often in planning curricula and instruction for gifted students, we neglect some of the fundamentally important questions—those revolving around the degree to which students are achieving the outcomes we expect from our instructional efforts. Are students learning what we expect them to learn? Are they achieving goals and objectives they would not otherwise achieve if not for this instruction? Are student achievements new achievements? Is instruction leading to high-level student performance?

Good decision making by teachers in the classroom is based on the collection of reliable and valid data about how curricular choices, instructional planning, and delivery of instruction changes students' knowledge and understanding of the disciplines and the development of their skills in a variety of tasks. And, of course, teachers cannot neglect assessment of the ways in which such variables as attitudes, sense of self, and other affective domains are influenced by instruction.

We also may fail to examine the ways in which the design of programs and services contributes to the ultimate goal of gifted student growth and development. To ensure full and complete attention to quality educational services for gifted students, teachers and administrators must assume responsibility for evaluating all components of the services offered to gifted students. And, most importantly, they must collect sound information about both the immediate outcomes of ongoing instruction and the long-term goals and objectives of the program. Administrators can only make good program decisions when they collect appropriate information and correctly interpret data about various components of service delivery modes, particularly those features of the program that positively influence the accomplishments of students and those that detract from maximum achievement. Hence, administrators are responsible for ensuring the clear delineation of long-term goals, assessing the degree to which those goals are achieved, and modifying the program to enhance the probability for success.

The evaluation of learner outcomes is, therefore, a vital activity in the instructional process and also an integrated part of the overall process of program evaluation. This chapter focuses on the assessment of both student change and the program components that contribute to or detract from student learning.

The Importance of Careful Assessment of Learning Outcomes

The collection of valid and reliable student data is critical at two points in the instructional process: (1) during preassessment prior to planning instruction and (2) when conducting outcome assessment to determine the success of our teaching.

Preassessment

Theorists and researchers have demonstrated that the most effective instruction and the greatest learning will occur when learning activities are designed so that the tasks presented are not already within the repertoire of the learner. After all, students are not learning if they are just doing what they already know how to do. Yet, the learning activity must not be so difficult that the learner perceives the task to be so far beyond reach that any efforts would be fruitless. Learning is maximized when successful performance of a task is just within reach, giving students an opportunity to develop new knowledge, skills, or understandings built on existing frameworks (content and skill knowledge already mastered). The "newness" in a learning task may include the requirement of attainment of new ideas, concepts, principles, or generalizations. Or, newness may be derived from structuring a task based on the student's current levels of discipline mastery that requires him or her to use more advanced skills in applying that knowledge to a problem, consideration of an issue, or production of a product. Or, the task may press the student to probe for deeper and more complex understanding of familiar concepts, principles, or generalizations from the discipline.

The difference between what a child can do on his or her own and what can be accomplished with a little assistance and processing is called "the zone of proximal development" (Vygotsky, 1934/1986). Vygotsky believed instruction should be aimed slightly beyond what a learner currently knows and can do. Hence, in order to fashion appropriate curricula for any group of children, teachers must gather information about the current state of the learners' expertise, that is, pre-assessment. For gifted students, this process is critical because their current levels of knowledge and skills are likely to be out of the normative range of their age or grade peers. That is, teachers cannot rely on traditional assumptions about the developmental accomplishments or curricular achievements of the average 4th grader as a guide to the appropriate instructional level for a gifted 4th grader. Similarly, teachers cannot make the mistake of assuming that all gifted students of the same age level are alike or that a particular gifted student is equally advanced across all disciplines or potential talent domains. A child with very advanced skills in reading may have achieved mastery of mathematics concepts and skills at a level that is average for his or her age. In preparing instructional activities for gifted students, teachers must recognize the great variability in achievement and aptitude across gifted students and within the individual gifted child. Hence, data from one unit of instruction about attained level of knowledge, skill, and understanding is critical to informing the next stage of instruction.

A teacher also cannot assume that an instructional activity or a series of activities that make up an instructional unit will be equally successful with all gifted students. Making accurate judgments about what students have learned in response to any curricular segment provides essential information about the success of individual students and also about the instruction. Assessment may also yield data about unintended outcomes, as well. Thus, evaluation information provides critical data about what to teach next to an individual gifted child and to groups of gifted children.

Outcome Assessment

The second important reason for collecting evaluative information is the obligation to provide students (and their parents) with feedback about their growth and achievements in response to the learning activities and in relation to expected outcomes and levels of performance. Carefully developed and clear procedures for evaluating students provide them with information about what they have achieved, their areas of strengths and weaknesses, and how their performance relates to standards of excellence. Informing students of standards of performance, rewarding efforts to achieve, and providing guidance in the next steps in further growth and development toward expertise are very important to ensuring that students get the most of their learning experiences.

Thus, the evaluation of learner outcomes serves many purposes. It provides students and their parents with information about the quantity and quality of student learning and performance. It serves as a basis for assessing the effectiveness of instruction, is one variable to consider in future instructional planning, and is a critical cornerstone of good program evaluation.

Planning for Good Classroom Evaluation

In order for the learner outcomes to be meaningfully assessed, educators must carefully plan the evaluation process beginning with clearly articulated goals and objectives at the program, curricular, and daily lesson level. Of course, there are often unintended outcomes (positive and negative) that cannot be anticipated, but evaluation must begin with a clear sense of expectations for learning.

One of the most difficult tasks for educators in the field of gifted education is the specification of the expected outcomes of instruction. However, to assess the degree to which an instructional activity or a curricular unit has been successful, educators must be able to specify the ways in which they expect the learner to be different as a result of the teaching/learning process. The level of specificity of outcomes ranges from broad, general, and long-term statements of expectations as goals, to specific activity-guiding objectives for the teachers to use on a daily basis. Teachers must be able to specify what students will be expected to know, understand, and do as a result of the experiences provided by the instructional program.

Sources of Program Goal Statements Relating to Learner Outcomes: Program and Curricular Models

Many of the models proposed for developing programs or curricula for gifted students have explicitly stated goals, while many others imply goals. For example, a program basing its instruction on the Schoolwide Enrichment Model (Renzulli & Reis, 1997) would be expected to have learner outcomes such as:

- applying interests, knowledge, creative ideas, and task commitment to a self-selected problem or area of study;
- acquiring advanced level understanding of the knowledge (content) and methodology (process) that are used within specific disciplines, artistic areas of expression, and interdisciplinary studies;
- developing authentic products that are primarily directed toward bringing about a desired impact on a specified audience;
- developing self-directed learning skills in the areas of planning, organization, resource utilization, time management, decision making, and self-evaluation; and
- developing task commitment, self-confidence, and feelings of creative accomplishment (p. 15).

Programs based on the Autonomous Learner Model (Betts, 1986) would include objectives such as:

- students will comprehend the dynamics of the group process; and
- students will be able to apply the dynamics of group process to their environment (p. 39).

Kaplan's (1986) curricular model, derived from the Principles of Differentiated Curriculum for the Gifted and Talented, implies that students will develop

- an in-depth learning of a self-selected study topic within an area of study;
- productive, complex, abstract, and/or higher level thinking skills;
- research skills and methods; and
- products that will challenge existing ideas and produce "new" ideas.

Specific curricular units developed using models such as these should reflect the overall goals of the model or program, but should also indicate more specific objectives. Specificity may come from fitting the goal into more narrowly defined parameters, specifying a level or achievement, or defining the discipline within which a process will be applied. For example, a unit based on Kaplan's model includes the following specific objective:

Students will define, explain, and exemplify the statement that systems follow rules, procedures, and an order by studying the communications system of writing, the ecological system of the rain forest, the governmental system of how a bill becomes a law, and the mathematical system of measurement. (California Department of Education, 1996, pp. 1–2)

A program focusing on Renzulli's (1977) Enrichment Triad Model might elect to specify certain Type II outcomes (process skill development) during a given time period. For example, the teachers might focus on objectives such as making sure that students are able to

- generate clear, researchable, correctly worded hypotheses;
- discriminate between primary and secondary sources; and
- evaluate the relative reliability and validity of historical documents.

Programs not based on specific models must generate their own goals and objectives. One program might operate from a set of outcomes such as ensuring that students

- exhibit improved critical thinking and problem solving skills;
- demonstrate greater independent learning;
- produce products that represent excellence and creative productivity;
- demonstrate greater self-esteem;
- demonstrate positive attitudes toward school and excellence in learning; and
- demonstrate in-depth understanding of the epistemology of at least one discipline (Callahan & Caldwell, 1993).

These goals need to be translated into specific objectives that are clearly delineated and evaluated in the classroom for each unit of instruction. For example, Burns (1993) has broken critical thinking skills into specific objectives: Students will

- recognize statements within an argument that reflect appraisals of worth that cannot be documented through objective means;
- recognize the various individuals or groups that may have differing sets of observations or priorities that influence their perspectives on a given argument;
- recognize information within an argument that is value laden or stereotypical; and
- distinguish between statements in an argument that can be proven and those statements that reflect personal beliefs or judgments (p. 10).

Sources of Program Goal Statements Relating to Learner Outcomes: National and State Standards

Two current trends in education have implications for the instruction and assessment of gifted students. First, many schools are implementing service delivery models for gifted students based on differentiation within the regular classroom. Second, current emphasis on national and state standards and accountability has impacted instruction at all levels.

The challenge to the classroom teacher is to find ways to differentiate the instruction in ways that will challenge all learners while addressing the standards *and* to create measures of achievement that reflect the students' level of learning. In these cases, teachers need to adapt their instruction to ensure student mastery of the basic skills while modifying tasks and assessment to reflect multiple levels of sophistication of mastering the more complex objectives. For example, because all students would be likely to master objectives such as "use centimeters, meters, liters, degrees Celsius, grams, kilograms in measurement" (Virginia Department of Education, 2001, p. 1), the teacher would likely use common paper-and-pencil or simple performance assessments that would be the same for all students. On the other hand, if the objective is to "conduct simple experiments, make predictions, gather data from those experiments, repeat observations to improve accuracy, and draw conclusions" (Virginia Department of Education, p. 1), assessments would likely be more complex and differentiated for different levels of expected sophistication in the design of experiments, complexity and subtlety of predictions, and depth of conclusions that could be drawn from more complex data and findings.

However, whether the program is directed by goals specified by models in gifted education, by goals and objectives that emanate from the administrators or teachers, or by state and national standards, the outcomes specified for learners should come from both the cognitive and affective domains and sometimes from the psychomotor domain.

The Cognitive Dimension:
Content, Process, and Product Outcomes

Content Assessment

The first of the three dimensions critical in the evaluation of student cognitive outcomes for gifted students is the content dimension. While the dimensions of process, product, and content should be integrated in the instructional plan and can often be most efficiently and effectively evaluated in a single product or performance task, they are separated here for ease of discussion. There are also occasions when it is appropriate to assess the dimensions separately. These occasions would include attempts to assess the ways in which particular aspects of the instructional process have been effective in achieving particular goals in one of the domains. When measuring low-level content outcomes, particularly those at the basic knowledge and comprehension level, or basic skills (e.g., the measurement skills noted earlier), then one dimension only is typically assessed. However, it is usually more efficient to measure the content, process, and product in some combination in more sophisticated assessment tasks because high levels of cognition normally require an integration of these domains in the thinking and production process.

Outcome evaluation will be more valid if the teacher is able to specify the aspects of content, process, and product that will be evaluated. The examples that have been given thus far have suggested specific content. Within the example from the Kaplan model, the content to be assessed would come from the area of mathematics, ecology, government, and communication. The teacher would identify the specific concepts, principles, and generalizations to be taught and assessed.

Content objectives that can form the basis of instruction and assessment from the specific disciplines are available from compendia developed as part of the national standards projects in mathematics (National Council of Teachers of Mathematics, 1993), science (American Association for the Advancement of Science, 1993; National Research Council, 1995), social studies (National Council for History in the Schools, 1995), and the arts (Consortium of National Arts Education Associations, 1994) or by state standards as illustrated earlier. The highest levels of learning described by the documents reflect the discipline outcomes appropriate for gifted learners. Gifted programs based on both enrichment and acceleration models can easily find specific outcomes statements to serve as standards for assessing learner performance. These references also indicate the ways in which content should be acted upon by learners to help them effectively incorporate the content into their cognitive structures, make meaning of the learning, apply the content to meaningful situations, and create new ideas and products. This leads to the second domain of cognitive assessment: process assessment.

Process Assessment

Within the process dimension, developers of curricula for gifted learners should consider the domains of accomplishment relating to the application of critical thinking, creative thinking, and problem-solving skills. Educators need to determine the accomplishments of students in the realm of using, making sense of, and evaluating the new knowledge they encounter. They also need to evaluate the ways in which students use the new information to create new solutions, products, and ideas. Some of the outcomes specified in prior sections, such as the ability to generate clearly stated and researchable hypotheses, to discriminate between primary and secondary sources, and to evaluate the relative reliability and validity of secondary sources, represent objectives in the process domain. While the dimensions of process, product, and content are addressed independently in some assessments to be discussed in this chapter, it is nearly impossible to separate process from content. Students think about *something*; they create products in some *domain;* and they critically examine evidence and ideas about some *content*. Therefore, in classrooms, process skills are generally measured within a content domain. For example, the items in Figure 1, adapted from the National Council for the Social Studies (Morse, McCune, Brown, & Cook, 1971), illustrate how some of the process objectives mentioned above might be assessed within the social studies domain.

One excellent source of process skill objectives relating to the development of critical thinking skills is the work of Robert Ennis (1985, 1993). Ennis and his colleagues have created a comprehensive list of skills in the critical thinking domain and developed tests that measure those skills. Burns and Reis (1991) have created a scope and sequence of process skills specific to instruction for gifted learners. A useful assessment of process skills is the Process Skills Rating Scales–Revised (Karnes & Bean, 2004).

Product Assessment

Some designs for gifted programs explicitly call for product outcomes. For example, the Enrichment Triad Model (Renzulli, 1977) and the Schoolwide Enrichment Model (Renzulli & Reis, 1997) call for Type III activities as hallmarks of appropriate curricular activities for the gifted. These activities are characterized as individual or small-group "real-life" investigations on a real problem with a real audience in mind. The definition of the expected product in the Schoolwide Enrichment Model provides an outline of the expectations for evaluation. Similarly, Kaplan's (1986) framework for curriculum development includes a component calling for products that serve as both tools of learning and verification of learning. Because the models of gifted education and the goals for their achievement are so often tied to sophisticated performance and products, educators have been urged to use authentic assessments to evaluate and provide feedback to gifted students (Reis, 1984).

1. Some of the sentences in the list below are statements of fact, and others are statements of opinion. Indicate in which class you think a statement belongs by placing an **F** on the line next to the statement if you think the statement is a **fact**. Place an **O** on the line if you think the sentence is a statement of **opinion**.

    _____ The Democratic Party has done more for this country than the Republican Party.

    _____ In 1939, there were two World's Fairs held in the United States.

    _____ Alaska is northwest of Oregon.

    _____ No war has ever accomplished any good for the world.

2. Next to each item described below, write the letter **P** beside those items you believe should be classified as **primary sources** and an **S** beside those items you think should be classified as **secondary sources**.

    _____ The Treaty of Versailles

    _____ A newspaper editorial concerning the Munich Pact of 1938

    _____ *Napoleon*, a biography written by Emil Ludwig.

Figure 1: Sample items to measure process skills in social studies

Note. From *Selected Items for the Testing of Study Skills and Critical Thinking*, by H. T. Morse, G. H. McCune, L. P. Brown, & E. Cook, 1971, Washington, DC: National Council for the Social Studies. Copyright ©1971 by the National Council for the Social Studies.

The keys to making the use of product assessments meaningful in gifted programs are twofold. First, creators of the assessment tools must find ways to set appropriate benchmarks for gifted learners. As Baker and Schacter (1996) have suggested, the process of setting standards may require several stages, including:

- finding ways to set the high standards to be attained by looking for good descriptions of expert performance,
- describing that performance level in terms understood by both the teachers and their students, and
- translating the performance standards into scoring rubrics that are valid reflections of the standards.

Standards of excellence for gifted students have too often been set as "better than others of the same age," rather than as the level of performance of those who

	Rework	Near Completion	Publishable	Classic
Sound: Music in the words (i.e., rhythm, speed of lines, alliteration, repetition, consonance, assonance)	Words and lines do not follow the principles of rhythm and rhyme. The sound of the poem does not enhance its meaning.	Most words and lines follow the principles of rhythm and rhyme. The sound of the poem supports its meaning.	Words and lines follow the principles of rhythm and rhyme. The sound of the poem supports its meaning.	*I never saw a moor,* *I never saw the sea;* *Yet I know how the heather looks And what a wave must be.* —Emily Dickinson
Imagery: Words that hint at the magic of the world (i.e., metaphor, simile, symbols, pictures for the senses)	The imagery is confused, cliched, or ineffective.	The imagery is effective in places, ineffective in others.	The imagery is effective and successfully extends the meaning of the poem.	*My bull is like the silver fish in the river white like the simmering crane bird on the river bank White like fresh milk* —Dinka Tribe

Figure 2: Rubric exemplifying professional standards of performance

Note. From *Rubric for Scoring a Poetry Unit,* by M. Libernetz, unpublished manuscript, National Research Center on the Gifted and Talented, University of Virginia, Charlottesville.

are accomplished. As Wiggins (1993) has pointed out, it is critical to set high standards representing professional levels of performance even though, at a given grade level, the teacher may not have expectations that all students, or even *any* students, at a given age level will attain the standard. He noted the important distinction between expectations and standards: Standards are set representing the highest level of performance, while expectations represent how far a teacher might presume a given student will move toward achieving the standard at a particular point in time. Interestingly, children with talent in athletics and the arts learn at a very young age to look to models of adult accomplishment as their standard. They watch and seek to emulate Michael Jordan or Jean-Pierre Rampal.

	John	Carol	Javier	Jacob
Attends to the comments and suggestions of others				
Offers suggestion to others to help solve problems				
Responds appropriately to the ideas of others				
Accepts suggestions and help from others graciously				
Willingly shares materials and resources				
Offers encouragement to others				
Willingly shares ideas				

Figure 3: Checklist for rating collaborative group behavior

Not only do students need to know the standard, but, to make performance assessment meaningful, they must come to know and understand the steps necessary to achieve that standard. Only looking at professional work without a sense of the progressive growth and development necessary to achieve the standard may frustrate both student and teacher. Well-developed rubrics will reflect stages of development toward the highest standards. An example of a rubric used to score poetry exemplifies how a standard can be translated for students so they can see the progression toward professional excellence and the way it is manifested (see Figure 2).

Affective Outcomes

The goals of services to gifted students are often drawn from the affective domain, as well as the cognitive domain. They may include outcomes relating to

	Master	Apprentice	Novice	Dependent
Planning Skills	Student creates reasonable timeline, can work backward from due date to create specific task deadlines and plan of action. All goals reflected.	Student creates timeline and sees sequence appropriately, but timeline does not reflect all important goals.	Student creates unreasonable timelines with few checkpoints; can see a progression of tasks is necessary, but misses critical steps; needs considerable help in creating plan.	Student doesn't know where to begin task plan; must have deadlines created by others to complete the task.
Meeting deadlines	Student meets all deadlines or can present "mitigating circumstances."	Student fails to meet 1–2 deadlines; progress is consistent.	Student fails to meet 1–2 deadlines; progress is inconsistent.	Student fails to meet 3 or more deadlines; fails to make progress toward the goal.
Uses class time wisely	Student consistently and independently uses class time toward completion of assignment; can adapt when obstacles occur.	Student consistently uses class time wisely; stymied when obstacles arise.	Student uses class time wisely only when directed to do so.	Student fails to use time wisely even when directed by teacher.

Figure 4. Student independence

students' social behaviors, emotional adjustments, or both. Group process goals, such as were illustrated by the outcome expectations stated earlier from the Autonomous Learner Model, would fall in this category. These goals might also reflect expectations that students will learn social skills, such as the ability to offer and accept constructive criticism, accept the role of leader and follower in a group as appropriate, and respect the ideas of others, (see Figure 3) or that students will be able to adapt emotionally to their world.

Also within the realm of goals in this area are self-concept, self-esteem, and self-efficacy goals. Educators might also wish to assess the degree to which students' attitudes toward school and learning (in general or in specific academic areas) are influenced by the services offered. After all, of what value is helping students achieve high levels of performance in a given domain if the students simultaneously develop a dislike for and aversion to ever studying this content again?

Another group of outcomes that is not easily categorized as cognitive or affective is the set of behaviors that includes accepting responsibility for one's own learning; becoming an independent learner, as in Treffinger's model (1986) for self-directed learning; or becoming autonomous learners (Betts, 1986). See Figure 4 for an illustration of several items on a rubric relating to this type of outcome.

Also within the scope of expected outcome behaviors for gifted students are those that are categorized as habits of mind, including openness to considering new evidence, willingness to consider varying viewpoints, looking for connections and relationships, disposition to consider or speculate on possibilities, and assessing the value both socially and personally.

Psychomotor Outcomes

Within the academic domain, we often require students to create products and perform tasks that require the use of psychomotor skills, but neglect to evaluate achievement of those skills (e.g., use of laboratory equipment such as microscopes). In the arts areas, many skills are reflected in production or performance (consider, for example, dramatic performance and musical performance). Sample items from a drama rating scale are presented in Figure 5.

Individual vs. Group Outcomes

In many curricular frameworks designed for gifted learners and in many instructional strategies used in gifted classrooms, there are specific opportunities for the students to work in groups either by direction of the teacher or by choice. The task itself may require group participation for successful completion. For example, the Lunchroom Waste unit (Dow, 1978), based on the Enrichment Triad Model, could be completed individually, but the unit as presented requires group effort and would be evaluated as a group investigation. Sharan and Sharan's (1992) Group Investigation Model and Elizabeth Cohen's model for cooperative learning (Cohen, Lotan, Whitcomb, Balderrama, Cossey, & Swanson, 1994),

Demonstrates or Projects Sensory Awareness

0: The child does not use any indicators of sensory awareness.
1: The child uses his or her body and facial features in the most basic way to indicate the sense, but is somewhat exaggerated. For example, the child's eyes are squinted to show difficulty in seeing, moves head from side to side or up and down to show looking behavior, cocks head to show listening behavior, chewing behavior for eating.
2: The child uses slightly more sophisticated facial and bodily indicators—more in proportion to the dramatic event—and exhibits the secondary characteristics of the sense. For example, facial expressions indicate sweetness, sourness, goodness, or unpleasantness of taste; eyes move to follow an object or look intently at an object; or the child is very still with appropriate facial expression to show listening intentions.
3: The child exhibits sophisticated indicators of sensory awareness. For taste, the child can show stickiness or other texture of food; for sight, there is appropriate reaction to what is seen (laugher, fear, etc.); for sound, there is a reaction to what is being heard (e.g., rhythmic reaction to music).

Emotional Responsiveness

0: The child is wooden and deadpan or maintains an unchanging facial expression with no change in emotion throughout
1: The child changes only facial expression using only the common and broad expression associated with simple emotions (e.g., smiling or frowning) with some exaggeration
2: The child uses facial expression and some part of the body in expressing the emotion (e.g., shrugging shoulders for indifference), but still seems somewhat forced.
3: The emotion is expressed more subtly and appears to emanate naturally from within the child.

Figure 5: Sample item for scoring children's dramatic performance

however, are specifically structured so that the students are *required* to do tasks that reflect individual strengths and individual contributions are combined for the greatest success in completion of the task.

One of the critical issues for assessment of cooperative learning is the clear specification of how the individual student will be evaluated in these settings. Slavin (1994) recommended that there be a clear individual accountability and assessment, as well as group assessments. The students should be clearly informed regarding the ways in which they will be evaluated, both individually and collectively. Further, if the group process is to be evaluated along with the group product, the teacher needs to be clear from the start about the criteria and expectations for good group work.

One of the critical steps in the assessment process is being sure that the level of specificity and definition of expected outcomes will lead to using a valid assessment tool. For example, to say that one wishes to measure creativity is too broad and nebulous. Is the intent to measure the student's creative productivity? What will be the specific characteristics of that productivity? To what degree are novelty, appropriateness of solution to the problem, technical quality of the product, and so forth important in assessing the product? To what degree is it appropriate to include the process that the student uses in creating the product? What about attitudes and dispositions? Before selecting or constructing an instrument to assess student growth and achievement in any of the areas discussed thus far, it is critical to specify exactly what will be assessed with clear meanings for the terms used.

Creating or Selecting the Tools to Use in Classroom Assessment

The process of selecting or constructing the appropriate tools for assessing student progress toward achieving specified goals and objectives must be based on two critical judgments. First, the instrument or tool must be valid. That is, it is important to ensure that there is evidence that the selected instrument, procedures, or both truly measure the specified objectives. Second, it is important to pay close attention to ensuring that any tool we select or construct it is reliable. That is, the score or rating given on one day should not be overly affected by how the student felt on that day, the scorer's mood on that day, error from confusion regarding directions, and so forth. The measure should yield consistent scores regardless of who administers or scores the test, performance, or product.

Types of Instruments

In the assessment process, the teacher will have to choose between formal or informal instruments and procedures; a standardized or nonstandardized instrument; self-report, peer evaluation, or teacher report; and paper-and-pencil or performance or observational tools. However, these categories are not always mutually exclusive.

For example, a formal assessment is one that is planned with specific guidelines for gathering information, while informal assessments are done in the course of everyday classroom activities. An observation, therefore, may be formal or informal. Teachers always informally observe learners throughout the course of the day, but at times they may observe for specific behaviors and record their observations using a formal rating scale or checklist to ensure that particular behaviors are (or are not) exhibited and to provide systematically collected data for reporting or planning purposes. For example, a teacher might use the checklist that was illustrated earlier in Figure 3 in observing students working in a group.

Standardized instruments are those that are developed to be administered and scored according to specific guidelines, including the manner in which directions are given and the timing of the test. Most published achievement, personality, and aptitude tests are considered formal and standardized. A teacher's classroom test is usually formal, but not standardized. The reliability and validity, as well as the advantages and disadvantages, of each approach depend to some degree on the outcomes to be measured, the purpose for which data are being collected, the audience for the evaluation information collected, and the time available to construct and use the instrument or procedures.

Use of Tests to Assess Learner Outcomes

Up until the last several years, paper-and-pencil tests dominated classroom assessment. These instruments included true/false, multiple-choice, matching, fill-in-the blank, and short and extended essay questions. The advantage of using multiple choice, such as the social studies process items illustrated earlier, or other objective formats in assessment are threefold: (1) The range of topics or behaviors that can be assessed in a short period of time is very large, (2) the instruments can be administered to large groups and scored relatively quickly, and (3) they are very reliable. The disadvantages of such assessments, particularly in measuring many of the goals and objectives of gifted programs, are the limited range of outcomes measured and the mismatch between the goals of a gifted program and the types of outcomes that can be measured by such tests.

Performance and Product Assessments

Many of the goals and objectives characterizing gifted programs cannot be assessed by traditional paper-and-pencil tests. Any goals that suggest creative productivity, the investigation of authentic problems, the use of alternative means of expression, or performance that emulates or represents the performance of professionals must be assessed using performance and product assessments. These products or performances may be stimulated or elicited by specific task descriptions that reflect extensions (in-depth, complexity, abstractness, etc.) or enrichment of the traditional curriculum. They allow for all students to engage in the activity with clear standards representing appropriate expectations for gifted students and ways of dealing with advanced content, sophisticated process, and authentic products. An example of a structured prompt for such an assessment is presented in Figure 6.

Other products or performances to be evaluated may result from long-term assignments or projects such as those described earlier as part of the Schoolwide Enrichment Model. An example of one item on a rating scale to evaluate prod-

The Best of Times

Throughout history, progress (social, technological, artistic, etc.) has led people to believe that the time in which they are living is, in many ways, the "best of times."

Travel back in time to [the teacher would fill in the appropriate year here depending on the unit of study]. Develop a role for yourself. Are you male or female? How old are you? What race are you? What are your ethnic origins? Where do you live? How long has your family lived in this region? Are you employed? What is your occupation? If you are a kid, what are your aspirations? What do you want to do when you grow up?

Think about ways your life is better than it was for people in years past.

From the perspective of your role, write an essay or develop a monologue to be presented in class that will convince others that, for you, these are the best of times. In doing this, describe your life relative to *at least three* of the following areas:

- Art
- Civil Rights Movements/Social Movements
- Economic Circumstances
- Military Conflicts
- New Inventions/Technology
- Politics

In collecting information for this task, you may use any electronic or print material you like, but you are to go beyond the information provided in your textbook. Please prepare a written reference list detailing your sources of information and how you located them.

Evaluation Criteria

Your project will be evaluated using the following criteria:

- Historical accuracy (How accurate are your facts?)
- Perspective/Point of view (How true are you to your role? Do the opinions you present correspond to the life and circumstances of the individual you are portraying?)
- Persuasiveness (How convincing are you? Does the reader/listener believe you are from this time period?)
- Thoroughness (To what extent did you use a variety of information-gathering techniques? Do you rely primarily on primary resources?)
- Referencing skills (Do you report your references in a standardized format?)

Figure 6: A sample performance assessment task

Note. From *The Best of Times*, by E. Coyne, n.d., unpublished manuscript, The National Research Center on the Gifted and Talented, University of Virginia, Charlottesville.

In this rating scale, an example of performance is given that would represent the highest level of expectation.

Level of Resources
Is there evidence that the student used resources, materials, or equipment that are more advanced, technical, or complex than materials ordinarily used by students at this age/grade level?

For example, a 6th-grade student utilizes a nearby university library to locate information about the history of clowns from the 12th through the 16th century in major European countries.

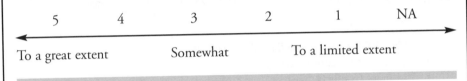

| 5 | 4 | 3 | 2 | 1 | NA |

To a great extent   Somewhat   To a limited extent

Figure 7. One dimension of a rating scale to evaluate Type III products

Note. From *The Schoolwide Enrichment Model: A Comprehensive Plan for Educational Excellence* (pp. 474–476), by J. S. Renzulli and S. M. Reis, 1985, Mansfield Center, CT: Creative Learning Press. Copyright ©1985 by Creative Learning Press. Adapted with permission.

ucts produced by students completing a Type III activity enrolled in a program based on the Schoolwide Enrichment Model is provided in Figure 7.

It is not sufficient to create the task and leave the definition of expectations and standards to chance or to comparative evaluation. As noted earlier, it is critical that teachers explore what is considered the highest level of performance in the domain. Once appropriate standards of excellence or expert performance have been identified, educators must ensure that the rubrics (scoring guidelines) used to evaluate the student clearly describe for the learner the progression of development from novice-level performance to expert performance. Schack (1994) has effectively outlined such a rubric for adolescent research projects. The dimensions along which research projects should be evaluated include (1) formulating the research question, (2) generating hypotheses, (3) determining sample selections, (4) selecting and implementing data-gathering techniques, (5) representing and analyzing data, (6) drawing conclusions, and (7) reporting findings. Figure 8 illustrates the levels of performance that can be used to evaluate the degree to which students are learning the skills of reporting in a secondary-level research project.

Wiggins (1996) has provided generic, initial dimensions or criteria for scoring the products of gifted students. He suggested considering *impact* by evaluat-

Novice

Findings not presented or presentation is inaccurate or unclear; surface feature errors (technical details like spelling or punctuation or clarity of drawings) seriously interfere with comprehension.

Apprentice

Findings communicated with some clarity, but surface feature errors distract the reader.

Proficient

Findings communicated clearly and accurately; appropriate format for audience; some surface feature errors, but are not distracting.

Distinguished

Creative format or content; multiple ways of reporting (graphic, written, kinesthetic); few or no errors in surface features.

Figure 8. Levels of performance for reporting data as an aspect of secondary research projects

Note. From "Authentic Assessment Procedures for Secondary Students' Original Research," by G. D. Schack, 1994, *Journal of Secondary Gifted Education, 6.* Copyright ©1994 by Prufrock Press. Adapted with permission.

ing the degree of effectiveness, the level of quality of the product, and the process of creating the product:

- Does the product created solve the problem? Does it persuade an audience? (Degree of effectiveness)
- Is the product outstanding in its class? Is it novel? Is it ethical? (Level of quality)
- Is the process of creation purposeful? Was the process efficient? Was it adaptive? Was the creator self-critical? (Process)
- Is the process of creation thoughtful? Does it reflect consideration (considerate, responsive, inquisitive, etc.)?
- And, finally, does the student use the appropriate skills? These skills would be those linked to the task and product and would be situation-specific for each product.

Wiggins also suggested that the *form* of the product be rated. He recommended looking to see if the product is well designed by asking questions such as: Does form follow function? Is the product authentic? Is it elegant? Is it clever? To determine whether a product is well crafted, he provided guidelines for considering organization, the price, clarity, and mechanical soundness. Another dimension he listed as important is *style*. He recommended considering the voice on such aspects as authenticity and grace. And, of course, Wiggins would consider the *content* to be important. He included accuracy (correctness, validity), sophistication (depth, insightfulness, power, expertise), and aptness (focus) within this category.

Wiggins (1996) has also provided examples of ways in which exemplary models have been collected for setting the highest level of performance we might require for gifted students. He suggested looking at the products of older students to identify models for younger students and examining the models of experts for the more advanced students. Others have suggested that students also identify accomplished works and derive the criteria from their own understanding of excellence. Marzano, Pickering, and McTighe (1993) have outlined other generic rubrics for performance-based assessment.

Specific learner outcomes should be reflected in the tasks developed by the teacher and the rubrics used to assess them. A rubric designed to evaluate the task illustrated previously in Figure 6 and structured to address the range of perform-ance possible in a heterogeneous classroom that includes highly able learners is presented in Figure 9.

Sometimes, teachers wish to use a common rubric across many products over the course of a year's instruction to be able to show student growth in particular areas. Several items from one teacher's rubric for scoring creative writing products illustrate this principle (see Figure 10). The scoring rubrics in these examples are particularly exemplary in that they describe the levels of expected performance at the top, middle, and bottom of the scale.

While all of these scales were designed for teacher assessment of student progress, students should be encouraged to use them to evaluate their own work and that of their peers. These skills in self-evaluation provide a base for students to develop intrinsic standards of performance. Using the scales to evaluate others can also be valuable in helping students understand the standards by seeing mod-els of each level and discussing the meaning of the levels of performance.

Observations

Certainly, the observation of musical, artistic, and other performances that may represent a student product will use carefully developed rubrics such as those described as performance assessment. However, as mentioned earlier, teachers may do more informal assessments of student behaviors relevant to the goals of instruc-tion. In particular, outcomes that are in the affective realm are often assessed using more informal observational strategies. Checklists or rating scales are often used to accomplish this assessment in a systematic fashion. An example of a teacher check-list used to evaluate social outcomes, particularly in group work, was provided in Figure 6. Figure 11 provides an example of a rating scale that might be used by students to evaluate themselves on their social behavior in class.

	Exceeds Expectations	Meets Expectations	Below Expectations
Perspective/ Point of View	Views and opinions expressed consistently reflect both the time period and the character's circumstances.	Views and opinions are mostly appropriate to the time period and the character's circumstances. Minor inconsistencies do not detract from the overall effect.	There are many or major inconsistencies between the views expressed and the character's time period, circumstances, or both.
Persuasiveness	Multiple methods (vocabulary, tone, costume, etc.) are effectively used to convince the reader/audience of the character's authenticity. You make us feel we know the person.	You use more than one method (vocabulary, tone, costume, etc.) to persuade the reader/listener that the individual is from the target period, but you have not completely gotten into character.	Little or no effort is made to convince the reader/audience that the character is from the time period portrayed that go beyond the historical facts presented.

Figure 9. Sample dimensions of the rubric for scoring the "The Best of Times" task

Note. From *The Best of Times*, by E. Coyne, n.d., unpublished manuscript, The National Research Center on the Gifted and Talented, University of Virginia, Charlottesville.

The Importance of Evaluating Programs for Gifted Students

The evaluation of learning outcomes is also a critical component of program evaluation. The major stakeholders in education programs for gifted students (the identified gifted students, their parents, the funding agencies, the teachers and administrators) are all interested in the degree to which program expenditures (including student time, teacher effort, and money) result in student learning and achievement that would not be possible without the program.

Standardized tests are often considered first in deciding how to measure the outcomes of gifted programming efforts. The major shortcomings of these tests are twofold. First, very few standardized tests measure the intended outcomes of gifted

The full rating scale is divided into two sections. The first is substance and includes clarity of ideas, fluency, description, and overall effectiveness. The second section is grammar and includes sentence structure, spelling, and neatness. The first two items illustrated in this figure are from the substance section; the third is from the grammar section.

Fluency

4 = The writing is very fluent and melodic. The writer uses language very effectively to create flow. Choice of words is often unusual and imaginative, but appropriate. The composition is not filled with clichés. The writer is not afraid to experiment with words or sentence structure and does so effectively.

3 = For the most part, the choice of words and sentence structure is successful. A few mistakes do not distract from the overall beauty and flow of the language of the piece.

2 = The writer uses clichés. The piece does not surprise the reader with its choice of words. The composition flows smoothly and is technically fluent, but it is not powerful because the language and wording is conventional. The writer uses no particularly descriptive or unusual words or seems to have used a thesaurus inappropriately.

1 = The writer uses words very poorly. There is no regard at all for whether the choice of words is suitable. The writing is disjointed and inappropriately short. Words are inappropriately simple or common.

Description

4 = The writer uses descriptive language well. Imagery is creative, imaginative, unusual, and clearly conveys a sense of that which is described. The reader can see or feel or taste that which is described. The setting for the theme is well developed. You are there. A clear mood is set. The characters and setting are vivid and three-dimensional.

3 = The writer provides a setting, describes character, and uses imagery, but the descriptions are sometimes flat. The choice of descriptive words sometimes brings a vivid image to mind, but sometimes common.

2 = The writer provides a setting, describes character, and attempts imagery, but the descriptions are flat. The choice of words does not pull the reader into the setting or give the character life. The settings, characters, and scenes are not fully developed. You have an idea of where the writer wants you to be, but you are not there. The description lacks imagination.

1 = There is neither setting nor imagery. Characters are identified in the most mechanical terms. The writer makes no effort to set a scene or provide descriptive language.

Sentence Structure

4 = There are no major errors and only one or two minor errors in sentence structure (such as split infinitives). The sentence structure is correct regardless of the complexity of the sentence.

3 = There are very few major or minor errors in sentence structure; they occur in very complex sentences.

2 = There are a few serious errors in sentence structure and many minor errors, but the meaning remains clear. Errors occur in very complex and simpler sentences.

1 = The sentence structure is so full of errors that the meaning of the text is often obscured.

Figure 10. Selected items from a rating scale to score creative writing compositions

Note. Adapted from *Creative Writing Compositions*, by A. Moss, 1977, unpublished manuscript.

Getting Along With Others and Contributing to the Group

Directions: Think about the ways in which you participate in our classroom. Then check the box that best describes how you think you respond to others.

	Always or nearly always	Usually	Sometimes	Never
I willingly participate in class activities.				
I pay attention to my classmates' ideas.				
I offer to help others.				
I try to be a cooperative group member.				
I respect others' opinions.				
I stay with my assigned task in a group until I am finished.				
I wait until others finish speaking before I begin.				
I try not to dominate discussions and decisions in my group.				

Figure 11. Student self-assessment rating scale

programs. Second, ceiling effects may hamper assessment. A ceiling effect occurs when a test is unable to measure accurately the full extent of growth in gifted students. This is because gifted students score at the very top of an instrument on the pretest, leaving very few items for them to answer correctly on the posttest (sometimes all items are answered correctly on the pretest). Ceiling effects may also occur because the instrument does not sufficiently measure a broad enough range of content or process or contain enough difficult items to tap the full extent of student growth on a posttest. In most cases, standardized achievement tests measure the traditional curriculum, with most items focusing on knowledge or low-level understandings and processes. Gifted students often demonstrate mastery of grade-level expectations before instruction, so a standardized, on-grade-level test will not measure the impact of instruction. In some cases where acceleration is the service offered to gifted students, out-of-level testing may be used to demonstrate mastery of more advanced levels of learning within the traditional curriculum.

There are a limited number of tests of process skills that claim to be discipline independent, and nearly all of those depend on reading and fluency with language. The most widely used are the Ross Test of Higher Cognitive Processes (Ross & Ross, 1976), the Torrance Tests of Creative Thinking (Torrance & Ball, 1984), the New Jersey Test of Reasoning Skills (Shipman, 1983), the Watson-Glaser Critical Reasoning Appraisal (Watson & Glaser, 1980), the Cornell Critical Reasoning Test (Ennis, Gardiner, Guzzeta, Morrow, Paulus, & Ringel, 1964), and the Cornell Critical Thinking Test (Ennis, Millman, & Tomko 1985). Other sources of instruments that measure process skills used within specific disciplines are available through professional organizations such as the National Council for the Social Studies, which published Selected Items for the Testing of Study Skills and Critical Thinking (Morse, McCune, Brown, & Cook, 1971). The Process Skills Rating Scales–Revised (Karnes & Bean, 2004) can be used to assess process skills in a variety of areas. Teachers may, of course, construct their own classroom tests to assess the success of gifted children in achieving instructional goals and objectives. These are not considered standardized tests.

In the domain of affective outcomes, there are a variety of instruments that have been used to assess changes in students as part of program evaluation. Self-concept has been measured by such instruments as the Piers-Harris Children's Self-Concept Scale (Piers, 1984), the Perceived Confidence Scale for Children (Harter, 1982) and the Self-Description Questionnaire (Marsh & O'Neil, 1984). One cautionary note in using these scales and expecting to document improved self-concept: Because gifted children generally exhibit relatively more positive self-concepts than average peers (Hoge & Renzulli, 1991; Robinson, 2002), expectations for growth may be unrealistic. However, educators should monitor programming efforts to ensure that they do not have detrimental effects on students.

One affective area of concern that is often identified by parents, teachers, and counselors who work with gifted children is the stress and burnout a child might face in a gifted program. Instruments that have been used to monitor such effects are the Student Stress Inventory and the Maslach Burnout Inventory (Fimian, Fastenau, Tashner, & Cross, 1989). Social adjustments can be assessed through the use of sociograms.

Learner outcomes are important, but they represent only a narrow perspective when evaluating programs or services for the gifted. Program excellence can only be verified through the collection of data demonstrating that the many goals and objectives of the program, including learner outcomes, have been achieved. We cannot expect to achieve high levels of student achievement if other components of the program do not work as expected. So, questions that address the related functions or the prerequisite accomplishments must be asked. For example, have regular classroom teachers developed the skills that allow for development of full potential and demonstration of a wide range of talents? Are goals and objectives for gifted programs clearly specified at the district and classroom level? Achievement of unknown or vague goals is highly unlikely. Are teachers well prepared to meet the needs of gifted students? Does the curriculum represent the most current theory and research about appropriate differentiation for the gifted? To what degree is the instructional program successful in helping gifted students achieve program goals and objectives? Answers to these questions and others relating to the quality of all dimensions of gifted services are critical in ensuring that educators are making the best use of resources.

The process of program evaluation can be used to answer these questions accurately and makes it possible to validate those components of a program that are working and to modify those that are not. That is, a carefully planned program evaluation will help administrators and teachers plan and modify services most likely to lead to expected outcomes.

Unfortunately, in the process of developing or modifying programs for gifted students and in the development of curricular frameworks and instructional practice, the process of planning for evaluation is often an afterthought or is not given serious and concentrated attention. If administrators fail to collect the kinds of evidence necessary to provide students with complete and accurate pictures of their accomplishments, if educators fail to examine the degree to which their instructional efforts have been successful, and if they hesitate in documenting the outcomes of programmatic efforts, then they will fail to provide the highest quality programs to gifted students. Neglecting to plan for accurate data gathering at the time program frameworks, curricula, and instructional strategies are developed may result in the failure to collect the most complete, necessary, significant, and meaningful information.

Assessment of Other Program Components

While learner outcomes are one critical set of goals for gifted programs, there are many other important aspects of a gifted program that also must be evaluated. These commonly fall in the categories of identification and selection of students to be served, the adequacy of a definition of giftedness and philosophy of gifted education, teacher selection and training, curriculum development and implementation of instructional strategies, management of the program, and communication. While each program will have different specific goals, examples of general evaluation concerns and questions that fall into each of these categories are given below.

- *Definition and philosophy*: Do the definition of giftedness and the philosophy of gifted education reflect current theory, research, and practice in the field? Are they defensible? Are they well articulated to administrators, teachers, parents, students, and the community?
- *Identification and placement of students*: Is the identification process effective and efficient in identifying students who reflect the stated definition of giftedness?

- *Teacher selection and training*: Does the staff development program provide teachers with the will and skills to develop and implement an instructional program appropriate for gifted students?
- *Curriculum development*: Does the curriculum meet the could, would, and should test of Harry Passow? Is this a curriculum in which only gifted students could, should, and would be successful? Does the curriculum and instructional practice reflect sound principles of differentiation? Is the curriculum implemented as developed? Are the components of a differentiated curriculum being implemented in the classroom?
- *Management*: Are there adequate resources and facilities to implement this program?
- *Communication*: Does the plan for communication provide parents with sufficient information about their children's experiences, expectations, and the evaluation of student achievements?

Determining Areas of Concern and Evaluation Questions

The principle guides used in selecting priority areas for program evaluation are:

- Does this area of concern or question reflect an important outcome of the program?
- Will the information collected about this area of concern or question be of use to the key decision makers?
- Is this an area of concern or question of critical concern to the stakeholders in the program (those most affected by program decisions)?
- Can studying this area of concern help improve services to the students? To decide which questions fit these criteria, it is very useful to establish an advisory committee made up of representatives of key decision makers and stakeholder groups.

In formulating the key evaluation questions, it is also critical to consider formative or in-process questions such as, "Is the program being implemented as described and intended?" Outcome or summative questions are, of course, also important. An example of an outcome question asked about implementation of the Enrichment Triad Model might be, "Did the students in this program use the tools of the discipline to produce creative, authentic products that addressed a real problem and were presented to a real audience?" For an in-depth discussion regarding the selection of evaluation concerns and questions, see Callahan and Caldwell (1993).

Sources of Information

The next stage in program evaluation is identifying sources that will provide valid and reliable information. Several sources of data regarding student outcomes have been discussed in detail in the earlier section of this chapter, including tests, performance and product rating scales, and observations. Student performance on both formal and informal assessments can become part of the program evaluation process. It is also possible to use other data such as the results of Advanced Placement (AP) or International Baccalaureate (IB) exams; performance in competitions; awards and special recognition; and surveys and interviews of students, parents, and teachers regarding student performance.

Parents are particularly good sources of information about the program's communication, the degree of challenge provided by the curriculum, and their children's reactions to program components. Teachers (both gifted specialists and regular classroom teachers) are also good sources of information about areas of concern regarding communication, as well as program management and the identification process.

Program documents could be reviewed by experts to determine whether the definition, philosophy, identification process, and curriculum meet the standard of reflecting best practice in the field. Of course, it is also critical to determine whether the documents reflect practice; therefore, in most cases, observation of classrooms will be necessary. An example of a document review form is found in Figure 12.

Data Collection

One of the primary issues in program evaluation is the question of who evaluates the program. Is it best to have an external evaluator, someone outside of the program or district? Or, should school staff do the evaluation? The answer to this question depends on the purposes to be served, the demands of the audiences, and the expertise of staff.

In high-stakes situations, if the program staff is presumed to be biased, then it is wise to consider bringing in an outside evaluator to construct and administer surveys and interviews, observe classes, analyze data, and make reports. Similarly, if the staff does not have expertise in the field of evaluation, survey construction, interviewing, and data analysis, then outside expertise should be sought. Teachers are in the best position to administer surveys to their students; they are also the most appropriate people to administer tests because of student comfort with a familiar person. However, it may be necessary to have scoring done by people considered less biased in those cases where subjectivity of scoring is an issue. One final consideration is staff time. If the evaluation will be done hurriedly with little attention to detail and accuracy, then the results will be useless at best and damaging if bad decisions are made based on unreliable or invalid assessments or interpretations.

Quantitative and qualitative data. Quantifiable data are the data derived from test scores, scores on performance assessment scales, frequency counts of responses on surveys or questionnaires, and responses on observational scales.

	Novice	Apprentice Level I	Apprentice Level II	Master
Evidence of preassessment of student readiness	No evidence of preassessment.	Some nonsystematic assessment.	Assessment data collected systematically, but not used to assign tasks.	Systematic data collection and clear match of readiness to task difficulty.
Uses a variety of materials other than standard text	No suggestion of alternative resources or materials.	One or two alternatives, but with no range of challenge or interest. All in same medium (e.g., all printed material).	Multiple alternatives, but with limited range of challenge, reflecting limited interests, or a limited range of media.	Many options with appropriate variability in challenge, types of resources, and match to interests.

Figure 12. Sample items from a document review form

Qualitative data are derived from interviews, observations, analyses of program documents, and open-ended questions on surveys. When analyzing qualitative data, evaluators are looking for common themes and deeper insights into the perceptions, understandings, and explanations surrounding the program.

Surveys. Surveys are the most common source of quantitative data in gifted program evaluations. A survey to one sample of constituents may be used to address many evaluation questions, or it may focus on one topic.

Rating scales. Experts may use a rating scale to evaluate the quality of the curriculum that has been developed for use with a gifted population. Figure 13 is an example of an instrument designed for such use.

Other objective assessment strategies. A useful strategy for assessing social adjustment, an affective outcome, is the sociogram. If there is concern that the way in which services are provided to gifted students is creating problems of isolation, a simple technique is to administer three questions: Who would you most

In evaluating this curriculum document, please indicate the degree to which the framework addresses each principle. 1 = no attention to this principle, 2 = minimal attention to this principle (surface features only), 3 = some attention to the principle with good likelihood of substantial effectiveness, 4 = substantial and effective attention to the principle, NA = not applicable

1. The framework suggests an appropriate level of involvement of the gifted learner in decisions concerning choice of educational experience   1   2   3   4   NA
2. Individual responsibility for learning is promoted.   1   2   3   4   NA
3. The teaching strategies selected and recommended replace the traditional superior/authority/dispenser of knowledge role of the teacher with the knowledgeable facilitator role.   1   2   3   4   NA
4. There is appropriate integration of content, process, and product goals.   1   2   3   4   NA
5. Included instructional strategies use hypothesizing, collecting and verifying data, predicting, and synthesizing at the level of sophistication appropriate for gifted children of this age.   1   2   3   4   NA
6. The curriculum allows for differentiation for gifted learners who are at different levels of sophistication.   1   2   3   4   NA
7. Problem solving using the methodologies of professionals in this discipline is included.   1   2   3   4   NA
8. Recognition, analysis, and revisions of the process used to generate products receive as much focus as the evaluation of the product itself.   1   2   3   4   NA
9. Authentic problems are included when appropriate.   1   2   3   4   NA
10. Authentic or real products are encouraged as appropriate.   1   2   3   4   NA
11. Opportunities are provided for gifted and talented students to pursue areas of their own selection—individually or collectively   1   2   3   4   NA
12. Content reflects a level of abstraction appropriate for gifted learners.   1   2   3   4   NA
13. Content reflects a level of depth and complexity appropriate for gifted learners.   1   2   3   4   NA
14. The process dimension of instruction reflects a level of depth and complexity appropriate for gifted learners.   1   2   3   4   NA
15. Pacing of learning is appropriate for gifted learners.   1   2   3   4   NA
16. The curriculum allows for students of different ethnic, socioeconomic, or racial backgrounds to become engaged in learning.   1   2   3   4   NA
17. The content, process, and product dimensions of the curriculum reflect learning experiences that other students either could not, would not, or should not do.   1   2   3   4   NA
18. Students will have a better understanding of the epistemology of the discipline.   1   2   3   4   NA
19. Learning experiences require students to engage in the transformation of information, rather than mere memorization.   1   2   3   4   NA
20. Creative productivity is encouraged.   1   2   3   4   NA

Figure 13: A rating scale for use by experts in assessing curricular quality

like to sit near? With whom would you most like to play? With whom would you most like to work? Ask the student to list their three top choices (with all names written on the blackboard so fear of misspelling does not influence choice). Then, ask the same three questions in the negative form. Who would you least like to sit near? and so forth. The strategies for analyzing sociograms can be found in most introductory assessment textbooks (e.g., Gronlund, 1985).

Qualitative data collection. Interviews and observations form the basis for nearly all qualitative data collections. The process may be highly structured with specific interview questions or guides for observation, or they may be more open-ended, leaving the structure of the interview or observation open to the discretion of the person collecting the data. The choice of a structured interview and observation is most appropriate when there are specific areas about which the evaluator is seeking data. When the purpose is to explore a more general sense of overall effectiveness and process, then a more open-ended approach should be used.

Data Analysis

The analysis of quantitative and qualitative data is the subject of whole courses in statistical and qualitative evaluation design courses. Questionnaire data is usually analyzed by presenting descriptive statistics or frequency counts of responses. And, on rating scales, the mean and standard deviation of responses is presented if there is a sufficiently large number (more than 25 respondents) to make interpretation meaningful. These same strategies are used to report on ratings of curricula and other elements of a gifted program.

For reporting student outcome data, inferential statistics comparing the learning of students receiving services with similar groups not receiving services may be used if there is a control or comparison group. However, most often, results are compared to a standard or norm established by the program.

The issues involved in using qualitative data has been the subject of many books, and those who are interested in pursuing this line of data collection and analysis should consult Guba and Lincoln (1981) or Yin (1990).

Decision Making

Whichever line of data collection and analysis is used for exploring program evaluation, the critical element is the use of the data. The evaluation data must reach appropriate decision makers for their use in evaluating the degree to which the program is functioning as intended. It must be presented in such a way that decision makers can assess the degree to which results achieved match the program's goals. And it should be clear enough that they can use the information to direct the program toward improvement in delivering appropriate curricula and high-quality learning experiences to gifted students.

All of these evaluation efforts, either at the classroom or program level, are to no avail unless the data is fed back into the decision-making process to allow for the teacher or administrator to do the most effective instructional and program planning. Further, the most effective planning will occur when the evaluation processes in the classroom and across program components are carried out regularly and systematically. Hence, planning for instruction and for program modification must begin and end and begin again with effective evaluation.

The Instructional Circle

Too often, evaluation is viewed as the end process of instruction or the inevitable evil that accompanies schooling. Effective educators adopt a different framework. The effectiveness of efforts to provide the highest quality services to gifted students will be greatest when

- the assessment and evaluation process becomes part of a cycle where information is used to provide feedback to teachers on the effectiveness of instruction and for planning the next stage of instruction;
- the assessments provide students with useful information on how they are growing and changing;
- parents are given meaningful information on the accomplishments of their children; and
- decision makers are able to use valid and reliable data to adjust program parameters to ensure the maximum effectiveness of services offered.

For these goals to be accomplished, each of the individuals responsible for the delivery of services—teachers and administrators—must assume responsibility for specifying the expected outcomes of instruction, defining quality in programming, and selecting or designing and then using assessment tools that will assess the important learning outcomes and the effectiveness of related program components. To educate without systematically assessing the program's readiness for instruction and to fail to evaluate the results of instructional efforts is an injustice to students and the community.

Teacher Statement

As Carolyn Callahan points out, educators of the gifted, like others in the field of education, all too often view the evaluation process as a necessary evil, a course of action that must be carried out, but one that is not fully understood. When these educators become involved in an evaluation process that is properly utilized, however, they understand its impact upon the entire learning community.

When is an evaluation process properly utilized in gifted education? First of all, an effective evaluation process directly impacts the focus of gifted education: the gifted learner. An effective evaluation process enables teachers of the gifted to ensure that the learning of new material is taking place at the appropriate level. Whether the material is new in terms of depth, difficulty, or originality, the gifted learners are required to build upon prior knowledge to achieve. Effective evaluation also enables teachers of the gifted to recognize that gifted students perform at different levels and possess different interests, which, in turn, helps these teachers plan appropriate instruction. Additionally, a properly utilized evaluation process helps students, their parents, and their teachers monitor the students' progress.

How can a properly utilized evaluation process directly impact instruction? Teachers and administrators who use the evaluation process effectively choose curricular models that lend themselves to the evaluation of their effectiveness with individual learners and learner groups in the cognitive, affective, and psychomotor domains. Selected curricular models contain appropriate objectives that are measurable and utilize a wide array of assessments that are valid and reliable.

What other gains result from properly utilizing the evaluation process? An effective evaluation process goes beyond the achievement of the individual gifted learner and the effectiveness of classroom instruction to an evaluation of the gifted program as a whole. This evaluation examines the effectiveness of the identification process, the appropriateness of the curriculum, the skill of the teachers, the quality of the instructional delivery, and the effectiveness of communication with the entire learning community.

Educators and other stakeholders in gifted education wanting to develop and maintain strong and effective gifted programs monitor the learning outcomes of the students in their programs and make the necessary modifications to ensure the programs' continued success. Ultimately, effective educators of the gifted view the evaluation process as a way to make the most of their instructional efforts.

—Trudy P. Cook

Discussion Questions

1. What are some examples of performance assessment that you have experienced in your school career? What were the positive and negative aspects of your experience with performance assessments as compared to traditional testing? When could assessment data that are collected for student evaluation also be used for program evaluation?

2. Consider a unit you might teach. What do professionals in that discipline do with the knowledge, skills, and understandings in that unit? How can you use that information in constructing a performance assessment?

3. Consider a product that you might ask students in your classroom to produce. What would be the most important dimensions of that product to assess? Describe at least three levels of performance on one of those dimensions.

4. What do you consider as important cognitive learning outcomes for a gifted program? How could you measure those outcomes?

5. List at least four affective outcomes of instruction for gifted programs. How could you measure those outcomes reliably and validly?

6. How do you grade gifted students in a heterogeneously grouped classroom fairly? In a special pull-out program for gifted students?

References

American Association for the Advancement of Science. (1993). *Benchmarks for science thinking.* New York: Author.

Baker, E. L., & Schacter, J. (1996). Expert benchmarks for student academic performance: The case for gifted children. *Gifted Child Quarterly, 40,* 61–65.

Betts, G. T. (1986). The autonomous learner model for the gifted and talented. In J. S. Renzulli (Ed.), *Systems and models for developing programs for the gifted and talented* (pp. 27–56). Mansfield Center, CT: Creative Learning Press.

Burns, D. E. (1993). *The teaching of thinking skills in the regular classroom: A six-phase model for curriculum development and instruction* (Handouts to accompany an interactive satellite broadcast). Storrs: The National Research Center on the Gifted and Talented, University of Connecticut.

Burns, D. E., & Reis, S. M. (1991). Developing a thinking skills component in the gifted education program. *Roeper Review, 14,* 72–79.

California Department of Education. (1996). *Differentiating the core curriculum for advanced and gifted students.* Sacramento: Author.

Callahan, C. M., & Caldwell, M. S. (1986). Defensible evaluation of programs for the gifted and talented. In C. J. Maker (Ed.), *Critical issues in gifted education: Vol. 1: Defensible programs for the gifted* (pp. 277–296). Rockville, MD: Aspen.

Callahan, C. M., & Caldwell, M. S. (1993). *A practitioner's guide to evaluating programs for the gifted.* Washington, DC: National Association for Gifted Children.

Cohen, E. G., Lotan, R. A., Whitcomb, J. A., Balderrama, M. V., Cossey, R., & Swanson, P. E. (1994). Complex instruction: Higher order thinking in heterogeneous classrooms. In S. Sharon (Ed.), *Handbook of cooperative learning methods* (pp. 82–96). Westport, CT: Greenwood.

Consortium of National Arts Education Associations. (1994). *National standards for art education: What every young American should know and be able to do in the arts.* Reston, VA: Music Educators National Conference.

Dow, C. (1978). *Lunchroom waste: As study of "How Much and How Come."* Mansfield Center, CT: Creative Learning Press.

Ennis, R. H. (1985). A logical base for measuring critical thinking skills. *Educational Leadership, 43*(2), 44–48.

Ennis, R. H. (1993). Critical thinking assessment. *Theory Into Practice, 32*(1), 79–86.

Ennis, R. H., Gardiner, W. L., Guzzeta, J., Morrow, R., Paulus, D., & Ringel, L. (1964). *Cornell conditional reasoning test.* Champagne: Illinois Critical Thinking Project.

Ennis, R. H., Millman, J., & Tomko, T. (1985). *Cornell critical thinking test.* Pacific Grove, CA: Midwest Publications.

Fimian, M. J., Fastenau, P. A., Tashner, J. H., & Cross, A. H. (1989). The measure of classroom stress and burnout among gifted and talented students. *Psychology in the Schools, 26,* 139–153.

Gronlund, N. E. (1985). *Measurement and evaluation in teaching.* New York: Macmillan.

Harter, S. (1982). The Perceived Competence Scale for Children. *Child Development, 53,* 87–97.

Guba, E. G., & Lincoln, Y. S. (1981). *Effective evaluation.* San Francisco: Jossey-Bass.

Hoge, R. D., & Renzulli, J. S. (1991). *Self-concept and the gifted child.* Storrs: The National Research Center on the Gifted and Talented, University of Connecticut.

Kaplan, S. N. (1986). The grid: A model to construct differentiated curriculum for the gifted. In J. S. Renzulli (Ed.), *Systems and models for developing programs for the gifted and talented* (pp. 180–193). Mansfield Center, CT: Creative Learning Press.

Karnes, K. A., & Bean, S. M. (2004). *Process skills rating scales–Revised*. Waco, TX: Prufrock Press.

Libernetz, M. (n.d.). *Rubric for scoring a poetry unit*. Unpublished manuscript, National Research Center on the Gifted and Talented, University of Virginia, Charlottesville.

Marsh, H. W., & O'Neil, R. (1984). Self-Description Questionnaire III: The construct validity of multi-dimensional self-concept ratings by late adolescents. *Journal of Educational Measurement, 21,* 153–174.

Marzano, R. J., Pickering, D., & McTighe, J. (1993). *Assessing student outcomes: Performance assessment using the dimensions of learning model*. Alexandria, VA: Association for Supervision and Curriculum Development.

Morse, H. T., McCune, G. H., Brown, L. P., & Cook, E. (1971). *Selected items for the testing of study skills and critical thinking*. Washington, DC: National Council for the Social Studies.

National Council for History in the Schools. (1995). *National standards for history*. Los Angeles: Author.

National Council of Teachers of Mathematics. (1993). *Curriculum and education standards for mathematics*. Reston, VA: Author.

National Research Council. (1995). *National science education standards*. Washington, DC: Author.

Piers, E. (1984). *Piers-Harris Self-Concept Scale: Revised manual*. Los Angeles: Western Psychological Service.

Reis, S. M. (1984). Avoiding the testing trap: Using alternative assessment instruments to evaluate programs for the gifted. *Journal for the Education of the Gifted, 7,* 45–59.

Renzulli, J. S. (1977). *The enrichment triad model: A guide for developing defensible programs for the gifted and talented*. Mansfield Center, CT: Creative Learning Press.

Renzulli, J. S., & Reis, S. M. (1997). *The schoolwide enrichment model: A how-to guide for educational excellence* (2nd ed.). Mansfield Center, CT: Creative Learning Press.

Robinson, N. M. (2002). Individual differences in gifted students' attributions for academic performances. In M. Neihart, S. M. Reis, N. M. Robinson, & S. M. Moon (Eds.), *The social and emotional development of gifted children: What do we know?* (pp. 61–69). Waco, TX: Prufrock.

Ross, J. D., & Ross, C. M. (1976). *Ross test of higher cognitive processes*. Navato, CA: Academic Therapy.

Schack, G. D. (1994). Authentic assessment procedures for secondary students' original research. *Journal of Secondary Gifted Education, 6,* 38–43.

Sharan, Y., & Sharan, S. (1992). *Expanding cooperative learning through group investigation*. New York: Teachers College.

Shipman, V. (1983). *New Jersey test of reasoning skills*. Upper Montclair, NJ: Institute for the Advancement of Philosophy for Children.

Slavin, R. E. (1994). Student-teams-achievement divisions. In S. Sharon (Ed.), *Handbook of cooperative learning methods* (pp. 3–19). Westport, CT: Greenwood Press

Torrance, E. P., & Ball, O. E. (1984). *Torrance tests of creative thinking: Revised manual, figural A and B*. Benesville, IL: Scholastic Testing Service.

Treffinger, D. J. (1986). Fostering effective, independent learning thorough individual programming. In J. S. Renzulli (Ed.), *Systems and models for developing programs for the gifted and talented* (pp. 429–460). Mansfield Center, CT: Creative Learning Press.

Vygotsky, L. S. (1986). *Thought and language* (A. Kozuin, Trans.). Cambridge MA: MIT Press. (Original work published 1934)

Watson, G., & Glaser, E. M. (1980). *Watson-Glaser critical thinking appraisal.* San Antonio, TX: The Psychological Corporation.

Wiggins, G. P. (1993). *Assessing student performance: Exploring the purposes and limits of testing.* San Francisco: Jossey-Bass.

Wiggins, G. P. (1996). Anchoring assessment with exemplars: Why students and teachers need models. *Gifted Child Quarterly, 40,* 66–69.

Virginia Department of Education. (2001). *Science standards of learning: Sample scope and sequence, grade 2.* Richmond, VA: Author. Retrieved February 19, 2004, from http://www.pen.k12.va.us/VDOE/Instruction/solscope

Yin, R. K. (1990). *Case study research.* Newbury Park, CA: Sage.

Author Note

The work reported herein was supported under the Education Research and Development Centers Program, PT/Award Number R206R5001, as administered by the Office of Educational Research and Improvement, U.S. Department of Education. The findings and opinions expressed do not reflect the positions or policies of the National Institute on the Education of At-Risk Students, the Office of Educational Research and Improvement, or the U.S. Department of Education. Permission to reproduce this material has been granted by The National Research Center on the Gifted and Talented, Joseph S. Renzulli, director.

Strategies for Best Practices

Teaching Analytical and Critical Thinking Skills in Gifted Education

by **Sandra Parks**

ne common trait that differentiates gifted students from their age peers is their capacity to perceive information and use it productively to an unusual degree. Their analytical thinking skills are evaluated in the various cognitive ability instruments. To assess their cognitive abilities, students are given a variety of analysis tasks. They compare, contrast, or classify objects or ideas and recognize what part of a whole is missing, give definitions by stating categories and differentiating attributes, put objects or events in the correct order, and look for connections among facts. Because they analyze information intuitively and efficiently, they are able to learn quickly and effectively.

Students' critical thinking skills are seldom effectively measured in most assessment procedures. While they may be asked some "common sense" questions like, "What would you do if . . .," tests do not often assess their abilities to make well-founded judgments. Critical thinking tasks, such as evaluating the reliability of a source of information or deciding whether an inference is supported by evidence, are not commonly practiced in gifted student identification.

Once students are placed in gifted programs, their teachers must organize and implement instruction appropriate to the higher order thinking capacities and needs of gifted students. While educators have shown considerable interest in critical thinking during the last decade, processes and principles of sound reasoning are seldom developed meaningfully in curricular guides or textbooks. Thus, teachers of the gifted must select or design instruction that addresses inferential reasoning processes that are abstract, sometimes requiring a technical understanding of logic.

While educators tend to differentiate between critical and creative thinking, in everyday thinking tasks these mental processes are functionally interrelated. As shown in Figure 1, skillful decision making and effective problem solving require thoughtful analysis of an issue by considering creative alternatives and evaluating the reasonableness of alternatives or options (Swartz & Perkins, 1990). The methods, materials, and programs described in this chapter promote analytical and critical thinking, decision making, and problem solving.

Analytical and Critical Thinking Instruction for Gifted Students

Instruction in thinking processes addresses and extends the unusual cognitive abilities of gifted students. The analytical skills that have warranted differentiated instruction are refined and used effectively in academic tasks. They practice creative and critical thinking skills that may not have been assessed or that may be underdeveloped. They apply all these types of thinking processes in complex tasks. Students with creative or artistic talents employ critical or analytical thinking in order to critique and explain their work more effectively. Students with leadership talent learn to be more organized and skillful in making judgments and to consider more original solutions.

Since gifted education curricula are focused on higher order thinking, the teaching of analytical and critical thinking processes is an essential aspect of instruction. For analysis, synthesis, and evaluation tasks to be meaningful learning, students must utilize cognitive skills that underlie these types of content objectives. Students must not only employ important knowledge, comprehension, and application processes in content lessons, but also be skillful at various analysis and evaluation processes.

Meaningful analysis involves many knowledge-level skills, according to Bloom's (1956) Taxonomy of Educational Objectives:

1.20   Knowledge of the ways of organizing, studying, judging and criticizing ideas and phenomena;

1.21   Knowledge of conventions, knowledge of characteristic ways of treating and presenting ideas and phenomena;

1.22   Knowledge of the processes, directions, and movements of phenomena with respect to time;

1.23   Knowledge of the classes, sets, divisions, and arrangements which are regarded as fundamental or useful for a given subject field, purpose, argument, or problem. (pp. 69–71)

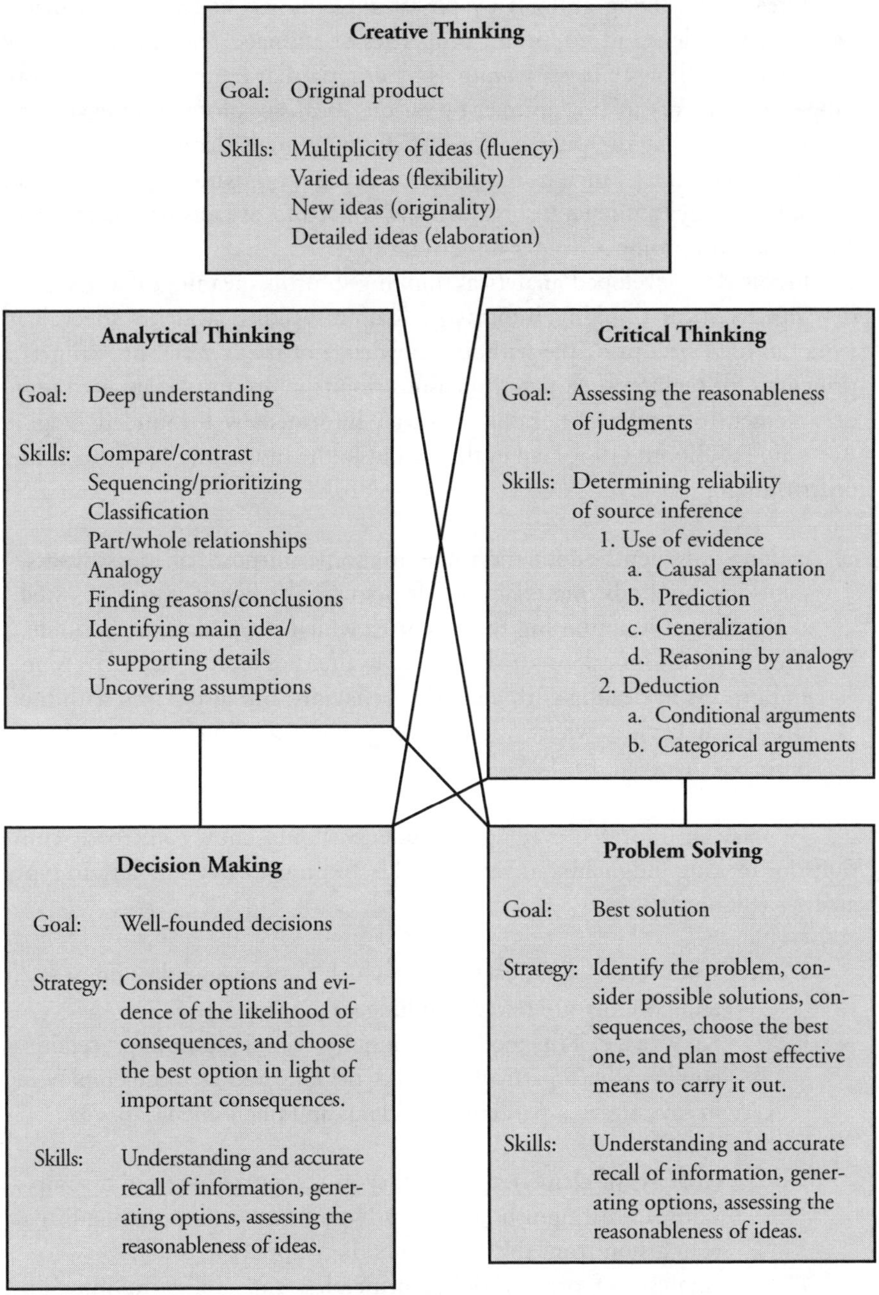

Creative Thinking

Goal: Original product

Skills: Multiplicity of ideas (fluency)
Varied ideas (flexibility)
New ideas (originality)
Detailed ideas (elaboration)

Analytical Thinking

Goal: Deep understanding

Skills: Compare/contrast
Sequencing/prioritizing
Classification
Part/whole relationships
Analogy
Finding reasons/conclusions
Identifying main idea/
supporting details
Uncovering assumptions

Critical Thinking

Goal: Assessing the reasonableness
of judgments

Skills: Determining reliability
of source inference
1. Use of evidence
a. Causal explanation
b. Prediction
c. Generalization
d. Reasoning by analogy
2. Deduction
a. Conditional arguments
b. Categorical arguments

Decision Making

Goal: Well-founded decisions

Strategy: Consider options and evidence of the likelihood of consequences, and choose the best option in light of important consequences.

Skills: Understanding and accurate recall of information, generating options, assessing the reasonableness of ideas.

Problem Solving

Goal: Best solution

Strategy: Identify the problem, consider possible solutions, consequences, choose the best one, and plan most effective means to carry it out.

Skills: Understanding and accurate recall of information, generating options, assessing the reasonableness of ideas.

Figure 1. Map of the thinking domain

Note. From *Teaching Thinking: Issues and Approaches* (p. 133), by R. J. Swartz and D. N. Perkins, 1990, Pacific Grove, CA: Critical Thinking Press and Software (800) 458-4849. Copyright ©1990 by Critical Thinking Press and Software. Adapted with permission.

Already classifying animals by phyla, students use at least one schema by which they understand important properties of animals. Teaching analysis skills shows students how to classify animals by criteria that examine other important properties (e.g., organizing animals by various means of protection; see Figure 2). Students learn that the purpose for classifying animals determines the kind of properties one selects, such as those shown in Figure 3. Knowing how to classify skillfully prepares students to organize any collection of facts or objects by categories that will promote deeper understanding.

Just as well-developed analytical thinking informs meaningful analysis, well-developed critical thinking informs evaluation. Asking students to evaluate a work, an idea, or a principle without knowledge of the criteria, procedures, and principles for making such determinations results in an unsubstantiated opinion or statement of preference, rather than an informed, well-founded judgment. According to Bloom (1956), an evaluation task, the most complex form of higher order thinking, involves

> making judgments about the value, for some purpose, of ideas, works, solutions, methods, materials, etc. It involves the use of criteria, as well as standards for appraising the extent to which particulars are accurate, effective, economical, or satisfying. . . . Evaluation represents not only an end process in dealing with cognitive behaviors, but also a link with the affective behaviors where values, liking, and enjoying are the central processes involved. (p. 185)

To make an informed evaluation, students should know some basic conventions for making judgments in various fields and must carry out certain types of analysis (Bloom, 1956):

1.24   Knowledge of the criteria by which facts, principles, opinions, and conduct are tested and judged;

1.25   Knowledge of the methods of inquiry, techniques, and procedures employed in a particular subject field, as well as those employed in investigating particular problems and phenomena. (p. 71)

4.1   Analysis of elements: the ability to recognize unstated assumptions, to distinguish facts from hypotheses, and to distinguish a conclusion from the statements that support it; and

4.2   Analysis of organizational principles: the ability to infer an author's purpose, point of view, or traits of thought and feeling as exhibited in his work or to infer the author's concept of science as exemplified in his practice. (p. 146)

In critical thinking instruction, students use knowledge and analysis principles to learn how to assess whether or not an evaluation report is reliable. The

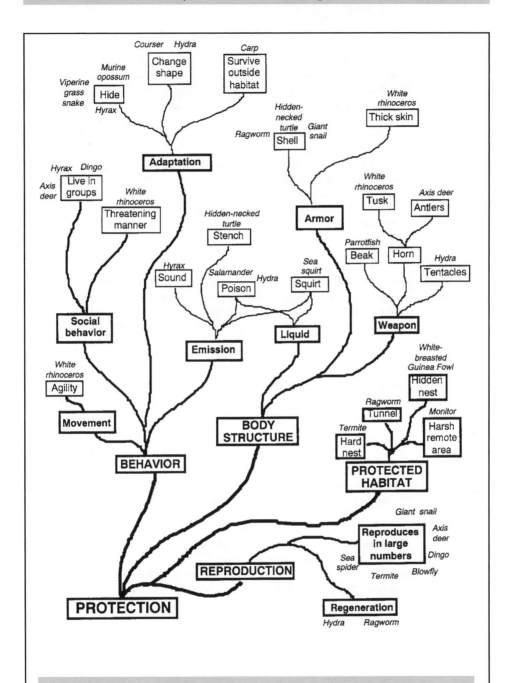

Figure 2. Classifying animals by types of protection

Ways to Classify	Purpose of the Classification	Who Would Use It and Why
Location	To indicate which animals inhabit a particular region. To indicate where in the world a particular animal can be found.	Traveler who wants to know what animals can be seen in an area. People who find animals for zoos.
Ecosystem	To indicate what kind of environment the animal needs to survive. To indicate what kinds of animals are likely to be found in a type of environment.	Environmentalists and government officials who try to preserve animals. Naturalists who want to find and observe animals in their natural environment. Zoo and aquarium workers who keep animals healthy.
Habitation (nest, den, hive, shell, etc.)	To indicate what kind of environment the animals need to survive. To indicate in what type of home the animal can be found.	Naturalists who want to find and observe animals in their natural environment. Zoo and aquarium workers who keep animals healthy. Architects who create homes and buildings based on natural principles of design. People who cultivate animals.
Outer covering	To indicate what kind of protection the animal needs to survive.	Environmentalists who try to preserve animals. Designers who create clothing based on natural design principles.
Body structure and functioning	To provide information about the bodies of animals. To indicate how animals function in their environment.	Biologists who explain diversity and evolution of animals. Doctors who treat ill animals. Zoo and aquarium personnel who keep animals healthy.
Benefit or harm to man	To indicate which animals can be used to benefit man. To indicate how various animals can benefit man. To indicate from which animals we need to protect ourselves.	Ranchers who cultivate animals for food. People who hunt animals for food (e.g., fishermen). Travellers who are going into the wilds. People who train animals.
Population/ species stability	To indicate size of population. To indicate which animals are endangered.	Environmentalists who try to preserve species of animals. People who hunt animals for food.

Figure 3. Purposes for classifying animals

Note. From *Infusing the Teaching of Critical and Creative Thinking Into Content Instruction: A Lesson Design Handbook for the Elementary Grades* (p. 161), by R. Swartz and S. Parks, 1994, Pacific Grove, CA: Critical Thinking Books and Software (800) 458-4849. Copyright ©1994 by Critical Thinking Books and Software. Reprinted with permission.

Questions   **Types of Questions**

	Observer	Observation	Corroboration	Report
What is his background?				
What is his scientific reputation?				
For whom was the report written?				
What kind of equipment did he use?				
Did he use the same equipment for all sightings?				
What was his state of mind? Was he clear-headed?				
Where was he when he made his observation?				
Did other accounts corroborate his report?				
In what form or publication did the report appear?				
Was the report a translation or his own words?				
What were the weather conditions?				
In what year did he make the observation?				
When did he write the report?				
Did he have normal sight?				
Was the equipment appropriately maintained?				
Was he typically trustworthy?				
What did he expect to see?				
Did he know how to use the equipment?				
How often did he observe it?				
Is the lens scratched?				
How long did he observe it?				
Did he believe in life on Mars prior to the observation?				
Did he make accurate observations of other planets?				
Was he drinking before he made the observations?				
Was a model made to verify how formations should look?				
Was he paid for this account? If so, by whom?				

Figure 4. Questions about reliability of source information

Note. From *Infusing the Teaching of Critical and Creative Thinking into Content Instruction: A Lesson Design Handbook for the Elementary Grades* (p. 159), by R. Swartz and S. Parks, 1994, Pacific Grove, CA: Critical Thinking Books and Software (800) 458-4849. Copyright ©1994 by Critical Thinking Books and Software. Reprinted with permission.

example in Figure 4 shows questions students generated about Percival Lowell's observations of Mars, in which he reported seeing lines on Mars that he described as canals. Students listed questions they wanted satisfied in order to decide whether the observation report was reliable. From their list of questions, they generated a strategy map of the factors they would take into account when they evaluated the reliability of any observation report.

Using lines and color, students created a strategy map by "lining up" their questions with the types of questions represented on their list. Questions generally fell in four main categories: (1) questions about the observer (capacity, expertise, background, objectivity, etc.), (2) the observation itself (the conditions, procedures, equipment, etc.), (3) the nature of the report (type of publication, the reputation of the publication, audience, use of pictures or tables, etc.), and (4) evidence that other observers have corroborated the findings.

Once the types of questions were established and criteria for reliability were clarified, students then applied the strategy to evaluate the reliability of Lowell's observation. The example in Figure 5 shows that students decided the technology available to Lowell and his predisposition to believe that there were canals on Mars biased his observation and outweighed his credentials and other scientific achievements.

While analytical and critical thinking is essential for meaningful content learning, these thinking processes promote students' decision making and problem solving. Developing students' analytical and critical thinking is not only one goal of the academic curriculum for the gifted, but is also integral to their personal growth and the development of leadership skills.

Approaches to Teaching Analytical and Critical Thinking

Deciding which approach to use is determined primarily by the gifted and talented service model employed in a specific gifted program, whether it be in a homogeneous class, in cluster groupings, in a resource room, or in a mixed-ability classroom. The three approaches in the teaching of analytical and critical thinking, further summarized in Figure 6, include

- teaching thinking processes directly in a structured course of study or separate lessons;
- infusing analytical and critical thinking into content instruction; and
- using methods that promote thinking about content learning (Swartz & Parks, 1994).

These approaches have also proven effective in gifted education classes for different reasons, with different emphases and different results.

Teaching Analytical and Critical Thinking Directly in a Structured Course of Study or Separate Lessons

Two formats are commonly used for the direct teaching of thinking in gifted programs: (a) using separate courses with a clearly developed structure and objectives and (b) teaching a thinking process explicitly as a single, supplemental les-

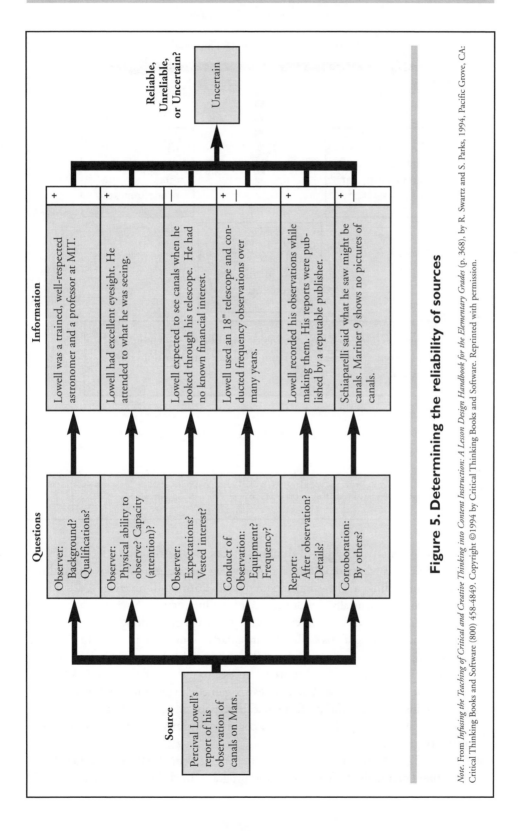

Figure 5. Determining the reliability of sources

Note. From *Infusing the Teaching of Critical and Creative Thinking into Content Instruction: A Lesson Design Handbook for the Elementary Grades* (p. 368), by R. Swartz and S. Parks, 1994, Pacific Grove, CA: Critical Thinking Books and Software. Copyright ©1994 by Critical Thinking Books and Software. Reprinted with permission.

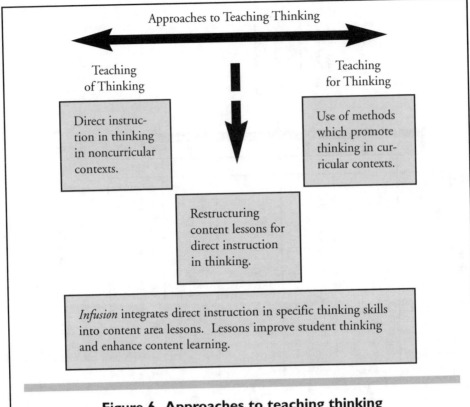

Figure 6. Approaches to teaching thinking

Note. From *Infusing the Teaching of Critical and Creative Thinking into Content Instruction: A Lesson Design Handbook for the Elementary Grades* (p. 9), by R. Swartz and S. Parks, 1994, Pacific Grove, CA: Critical Thinking Books and Software (800) 458-4849. Copyright ©1994 by Critical Thinking Books and Software. Reprinted with permission.

son. The systematic teaching of thinking processes is particularly effective for special populations whose development or language acquisition needs warrant direct instruction. Bilingual, hearing-impaired, and learning-disabled gifted students benefit from sequentially developed cognitive instruction. Such programs offer practice in metacognition and employ the language of thinking.

Instruction in analysis skills is particularly significant in making sure that special populations of gifted students (learning-disabled, sensorially impaired, or minority students) have appropriate access to gifted, honors, or Advanced Placement (AP) programs. Once access is gained, these students learn the academic skills for successful performance. The pool of potentially gifted minority students can be enlarged by the use of cognitive stimulation programs in the elementary grades.

The TEAM program in Dade County Public Schools (Rito & Moller, 1989) and the Potentially Gifted Minority program in Palm Beach County, FL,

(Howells, 1992) have demonstrated for more than a decade that analysis instruction can increase the number of minority students placed in gifted programs. Both programs identified minority students who exhibited the behaviors of being gifted, but scored only in the fifth and sixth stanines in achievement testing. These students were placed in classes where they received daily instruction in analysis skills. In both programs, after 1 year of instruction, approximately 25–30% of these students scored the 130 IQ required for placement in Florida's gifted programs.

Both programs used Building Thinking Skills (Black & Parks, 1985), a cognitive development curriculum of figural and verbal lessons that develop key analysis skills: compare and contrast, sequencing, classification, and analogy. Lessons are sequenced by increasing complexity and provide cognitive stimulation and vocabulary acquisition for learning-disabled gifted students or those with limited English proficiency. Building Thinking Skills provides cognitive objectives, practice exercises, content transfer, and suggestions for metacognition. It is evaluated using normed cognitive skills tests and the Mathematics Comprehension, Mathematics Problem Solving, and Reading Comprehension subtests of the Stanford Achievement Test (Harcourt-Brace Educational Measurement, 1996).

In a similar secondary program in Jacksonville, FL, which also implemented analysis instruction, the number of minority students in AP classes tripled in a 5-year period. Enrollment in AP classes for one predominately minority high school increased 3,000%. After program implementation, one third of the district's AP students were African American. SAT scores of these students in this school district topped the national average by 31 points—43 points above the state average (Potter & Dawson, 1988).

Critical thinking instruction as a separate course usually involves teaching logic, ethics, or aesthetics. *Critical Thinking Book One* (Harnadek, 1976) and *Critical Thinking Book Two* (Harnadek, 1980) are two student books for specialized instruction in formal and informal logic. While the symbolic logic lessons may be taught in mathematics classes and the informal logic taught in English instruction, the actual implementation of the complete course requires at least 60 hours of instructional time. *Critical Thinking Book One* and *Book Two* have been widely used in 5th- through 9th-grade gifted education classes for more than 20 years. *Critical Thinking* (Ennis, 1996) is more appropriate for secondary gifted education instruction in English or humanities classes.

Philosophy for Children (Lipman, 1979) involves specialized instruction (primary grades through high school) in courses on logic, ethics, aesthetics, and scientific reasoning. It assists teachers in conducting class discussion of student novels, although training is necessary to teach the courses meaningfully. This program, featured on the National Diffusion Network, a nationwide education dissemination system (http://www.ed.gov/pubs/EPTW/eptwndas.html), is evaluated using a critical thinking test developed for it by Education Testing Service.

Analytical and critical thinking courses have three common features. First, they contain objectives that are cross-disciplinary in content or application.

Secondly, they involve a structured sequence of instruction to build competence in thinking skills. And, third, they rely heavily on class discussion of specialized student materials. Thinking objectives are clearly stated and measurable with cognitive abilities or critical thinking tests or performance assessment, such as debate or writing tasks.

Thinking courses are used primarily in resource rooms or enrichment centers because of their versatility across the curriculum and because a dedicated amount of time can be spent on them on a regular basis. A variety of direct instruction programs are listed in the summary of centers and networks in the appendix of this chapter.

Teaching Thinking Processes Explicitly as Single, Supplemental Lessons

Analytical and critical thinking may be taught in single lessons scheduled within the academic year as the content requires. Such instruction involves teaching a specific thinking strategy that supplements a content lesson. For example, teachers may teach a short lesson using a graphic organizer "scaffolding" to clarify various thinking or learning processes. Students may then utilize the strategy to make the content lesson more effective and meaningful. Students may modify the diagrams to fit individual styles, purposes, and interests. The goal of such instruction is self-initiated thinking and learning where the learner is proactive in conducting and managing his or her own mental tasks.

The graphic organizer shown in Figure 7 depicts the content of a lesson on information literacy. The strategy involves a variety of analytical and critical thinking skills and prompts the learner to reflect on (1) how to determine the type, quality, and availability of needed information; (2) how to retrieve and evaluate it; and (3) how to express or depict it for more effective understanding and decision making. The information explosion has made information literacy a timely curricular initiative, particularly for independent study and research skills objectives for gifted curricula.

Students use a blank version of the diagram in Figure 7 to take notes, applying the strategy to a specific research inquiry of key questions: How does one define the type of information that is needed? How does one select a search strategy? How does one locate resources? How does one retrieve the needed data? How does one assess the accuracy and quality of information? How does one interpret, evaluate, and communicate that information? How does one draw well-founded judgments? How does one produce creative products based on one's research?

A second example of teaching an analysis strategy involves using a modification of Hilda Taba's concept development model as a review tool (Eggen, Kauchek, & Harder, 1979). This process helps students assess how well they understand a concept. Each step of the process involves an analysis task: comparison and contrast, attribution, exemplification, and classification. If a student can answer six basic questions about a concept, he or she can be confident of his or

How do I find and use information well?

What information do I need?
What kind? Statistics, facts, observation reports, interpretations, depictions, creative works, explanations?
What form? Text, tables, lists, maps, diagrams, outlines, pictures, interviews, speeches, diaries?
What medium? Print, film, videotape, videodisc, photograph, microfiche?

How do I find it?
What resources show where information like this is located? Internet search engine, *Books in Print, Reader's Guide*, etc.
What search plan will offer adequate information efficiently? Steps in search and retrieval?

Where is the information located?
Type of source? Public libraries, specialized libraries, research or government agencies, computer file, Internet, CD-ROM
Specific source? Title, author, publication, date, file name, volume, e-mail listing, publisher's address, telephone number?

How do I obtain it?
Policies? Authorization for access and use, limitations on volume and application, restrictions on photocopying, royalties, access fees?
How transmitted? Print material, computer disk, fax, e-mail? Time necessary? How converted? Technological compatibility?

How reliable is this information?
Primary or secondary?
Reliability of observation report? Observer? Procedures? Corroborated? Report documented?
Regarded in this field?
Fits key factors in this use? Timeliness, comparable definitions, compatible procedures?

How can I show what I learned from this information?
Type of product? Text display, performance, computer file?
Audience? Reader, listeners, size and background of audience?
Criteria for reporting? Documentation, standards for this type of product, citation, format, user-friendliness?

Figure 7. Graphic organizer

Note. From *Learning on Purpose* (p. 132), by B. Juarez, H. Black, & S. Parks, 1999, Pacific Grove, CA: Critical Thinking Books and Software (800) 458-4849. Copyright ©1999 by Sandra Parks. Reprinted with permission.

her own conceptualization. The money example in Figure 8 shows how using the concept development model yields clear definitions. Lack of clarity about any of these questions shows the student the omissions or incomplete understandings that should be corrected.

While all students profit from using strategies such as this one, gifted students utilize these techniques in independent study and advanced academic programs. These strategies are useful in any gifted education service model and are particularly valuable when teaching gifted students in heterogeneous classrooms.

Infusing the Teaching of Analytical and Critical Thinking Into Content Instruction

The direct instruction examples described in the previous section involve either a structured course of study taught independently from content or cross-disciplinary lessons involving nonacademic exercises. The infusion approach involves the clarification and application of thinking processes within content lessons. It involves structured questions to form various kinds of judgments and graphic organizers to hold evidence and to guide students' thinking. The diagram in Figure 9 shows the key questions in the decision-making strategy and the steps in thoughtful decision making that can be taught in any discipline.

The decision-making graphic organizer in Figure 10 depicts students' research on Harry Truman's decision regarding the ending of World War II. Truman's options, the consequences of one option, information about the likelihood of various consequences, and consideration of the value of the consequences are summarized on the diagram. Students then evaluate each option to arrive at a judgment regarding the best alternative to end the war.

By "picturing" the decision-making process, the graphic organizer displays evidence for or against the likelihood of various consequences and records students' deliberations about their relative significance. By comparing graphics for several options, students "see" which options have significant positive and negative consequences.

The infusion approach emphasizes systematic thinking and metacognition about the thinking strategies students have experienced. Infusion lessons also employ the instructional methods described in the next section using cooperative or problem-based learning, using graphic organizers, and asking higher order questions. Clarity about the thinking processes, as employed by the infusion approach, allows for clear transfer, in contrast to the more situation-specific character of techniques so embedded in content that students may not recognize or remember the thinking involved.

Unlike separate courses, the infusion approach involves redesigning content lessons to employ the thinking strategy fully. Teachers also plan sufficient transfer applications to assure that students are competent in using the strategy independently. This approach is more commonly used in homogeneous classes or

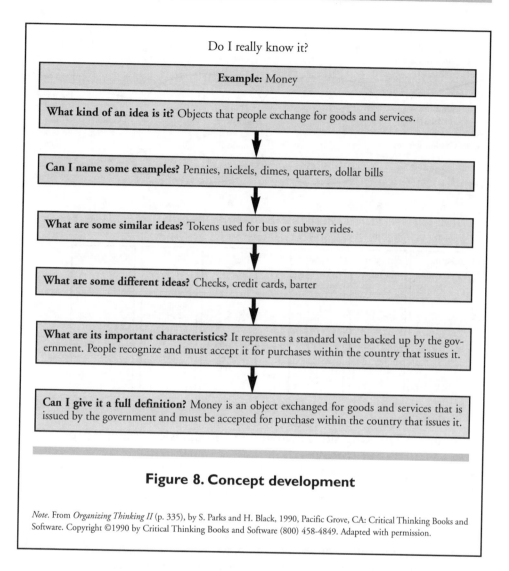

Figure 8. Concept development

Note. From *Organizing Thinking II* (p. 335), by S. Parks and H. Black, 1990, Pacific Grove, CA: Critical Thinking Books and Software. Copyright ©1990 by Critical Thinking Books and Software (800) 458-4849. Adapted with permission.

cluster-grouped classes because of the depth of understanding, research, and discussion of content involved in infusion lessons. Enrichment units (e.g., global studies, technology, anthropology), generally not offered in the general elementary grades curriculum, provide thought-provoking contexts that are easily modified for infusion lessons.

Using Methods That Promote Thinking About Content

Using instructional methods to stimulate students' thinking about content is commonly practiced in gifted education. Staff development for teachers of the gifted frequently includes using cooperative learning, depicting content by graphic organizers, asking higher order questions, employing Socratic dialogue or

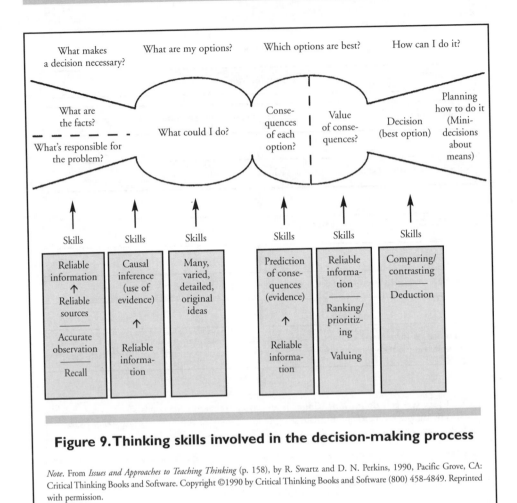

Figure 9. Thinking skills involved in the decision-making process

Note. From *Issues and Approaches to Teaching Thinking* (p. 158), by R. Swartz and D. N. Perkins, 1990, Pacific Grove, CA: Critical Thinking Books and Software. Copyright ©1990 by Critical Thinking Books and Software (800) 458-4849. Reprinted with permission.

shared inquiry, using interactive computer software, designing instruction to honor various learning styles, implementing hands-on mathematics and process science, and engaging in inquiry or problem-based learning and integrating art into other content areas.

While these instructional methods may be used in any gifted education service model, they are especially useful in heterogeneous classes and cluster-grouped classes. Such methods promote deep understanding of content for all students, resulting in stimulating classroom activities. However, gifted students may utilize them at a more advanced level and with greater effectiveness. Gifted students demonstrate more complex applications of these techniques in classroom activities, discussions, and assessment tasks.

For more than two decades, teachers of the gifted learned to ask higher order questions and conduct meaningful dialogue through training in the Junior Great Books Program. Teachers facilitate discussions in which students examine great

Options
What can I do?

- Demonstrate the bomb on or near the Japanese homeland, but not in a populated area
- Surrender
- Capture the Emperor
- Embargo/blockade
- Terrorist attacks
- Subversive activities
- Change demands and negotiate
- Bribe the Japanese
- Increase conventional bombing

- Incite Japanese people against their government
- Use chemical weapons
- Invade Japan
- Drop A-bomb on populated military target
- Cease fire
- Tell the Japanese about the A-bomb and threaten its use
- Resign as President
- Declare victory and withdraw

Option Considered:
Invade Japan

Consequences What will happen if I take this option?	Support Why do I think each consequence will occur?	Value How important is the consequence? Why?
− Heavy U.S. casualties ✓	Japanese military officers claim preparedness for an invasion. Iwo Jima and Okinawa reports indicate heavy U.S. and Japanese casualties. U.S. lost 300,000 men breaking through the perimeter islands. Kamikaze attacks kill 13,000 U.S. men in 2 days off Okinawa. Stimson predicts 1,000,000 U.S. military killed in total invasion. Marshall estimates that 63,000 of 190,000 landing force will be killed. 5,000,000 in Japanese army.	**Very Important** Loss of life is the most important consideration. Preservation of life is our highest value.
− War prolonged	✓ Invasion scheduled for November, 1945. Fierce fighting on Iwo Jima and Okinawa shows slow gains.	**Very Important** Prolonged war means more loss of life and material costs.
− High economic costs and loss of equipment ✓	Iwo Jima and Okinawa report fierce fighting destroying tanks and losses of 15 ships and damage to 200 others.	**Very Important** Such losses affect ability to wage war and U.S. economy.
− Worsen morale and lose public support	✓ Brutality of Pacific fighting was abhorrent to public. Letters to newspapers and officials show opposition.	**Important** Public support needed for congressional funding.
+ War contractors do well	✓ Iwo Jima and Okinawa reports indicate heavy losses of tanks and ships. Invading the mainland will result in more fierce fighting and losses. Prolonged war requires more equipment.	**Not Important** They are a special interest group. The war affects the whole country.
− Heavy Japanese casualties	✓ Cultural disposition to "fight-to-death." Heavy Japanese losses on Iwo Jima and Okinawa.	**Very Important** Loss of life is the most important factor.
− Destroy Japanese cultural and economic resources	✓ Heavy bombing had already destroyed cities and industrial plants and created fire damage. Invasion in Europe led to great destruction.	**Important** Industries can be rebuilt, but shrines may be lost forever.
− Invasion fails	Military reports indicate massive destruction of cities and dwindling food and resources. Fierce fighting on Iwo Jima and Okinawa shows Japanese determination.	**Very Important** Successful end to war requires that invasion succeeds.
− Soviet Union invades Japan	✓ At Potsdam, the Soviets said that they would invade Japan by August 8, 1945.	**Important** Soviet presence in Japan will affect U.S. influence in Pacific.
− Truman loses election	Letters to newspapers and officials show opposition to the war. Election is 3 years away.	**Important** Truman's policies are sound.

Figure 10. Decision-making graphic organizer

Note. From *Infusing the Teaching of Critical and Creative Thinking into Social Studies Instruction: A Lesson Design Handbook for the Secondary Grades* (in process), by R. Swartz and S. Parks, in process. Copyright ©1999 by Sandra Parks. Reprinted with permission.

works of children's literature, using techniques of shared inquiry about the novels. While Junior Great Books is commonly employed in single-language, advanced academic programs, it has been effectively implemented in the Dade County, FL, gifted program, which includes large numbers of gifted students whose primary language is not English.

Using Graphic Organizers

In previous examples, strategy maps have been supplemented by graphic organizers. Specialized diagrams depict how information is related, "picturing" issues so we can make informed interpretations or judgments. By using graphic organizers, teachers and students can access, organize, and display complex information involved in evaluating issues, solving problems, or making decisions. Graphic organizers may also be used to guide or stimulate thinking, to plan projects, and to assess students' learning.

Specially designed graphic organizers depict questions that thoughtful people ask and answer when they think critically: assessing the reliability of sources of information, evaluating reasons for conclusions, reasoning by analogy, evaluating causal explanations, making informed predictions, evaluating or forming generalizations, and using conditional or categorical reasoning. Notations on the graphic organizer summarize the information or evidence required in making such judgments and depict the steps in the evaluation process by symbols and design elements (arrows, circles, boxes, colors, etc.).

Graphic organizers may be used for several purposes:

- to hold and organize information for research and evaluation;
- to show relationships;
- to stimulate or guide thinking; and
- to assess thinking and learning.

Graphics That Hold and Organize Information. Matrices are commonly used in textbooks, newspapers, and periodicals to organize complex information. The matrix in Figure 11 contains information involved in considering what energy sources our nation should develop and use. This matrix on alternative energy sources serves as a data retrieval chart—a graphic organizer to guide students' research and observations for conducting inductive reasoning. Students are not given this data but, instead, use the matrix to organize their research. The empty cells of the diagram in Figure 12 remind students of the kind of data needed in order to make an informed judgment.

In Figure 11, students listed their options (various types of energy sources) down the left side of the diagram. They labeled each column with a kind of consequence that should be considered in deciding energy use (availability, impact on the environment, cost to use and produce, etc.). After each student group reported its findings about an energy source, their information was added to the

Options	Relevant Consequences			
	Ease of Production	Environment	Cost	Availability
Solar Active Passive Photovoltaic	• Easy, if location, latitude, and weather conditions are favorable. • Little maintenance. • Limited service for repairs. • Photovoltaic not cost-effective until improved technology makes it more efficient.	• No undesirable air or water pollution. Unsightly equipment or circular fields of mirrors. • Loss of trees. Environmental impact of manufacturing materials and equipment or disposing of batteries.	• Start up is costly (could be reduced by mass manufacture). • Low maintenance and repair. • Operation costs are minimal. • Research and development costly.	• Limited by location, latitude, and weather. • Seasonal in some areas. • Distributing and storing resulting electricity is limited. • Renewable.
Nuclear	• Complex, requiring sophisticated instruments, specialized technicians, and unusual safety measures. • Waste disposal is risky and requires long-term safeguards.	• Radiation danger. • Mining erosion and toxic tailings are produced to secure uranium. • Storage of waste may result in radiation contamination. • Production structures are huge.	• Protective measures in operation and start-up costs are high. • Licensing, certifying, and inspecting plants are expensive. • Maintenance costs.	• Uranium is scarce. • Breeder reactors are controversial and limited.
Petrochemical	• Complex, but commonly practiced.	• Risk of oil spills. • Depletion of the oil supply. • Hydrocarbons pollute the air, damage the ozone layer, and create acid rain. • Processing pollutes air.	• Exploration, research, distribution, and clean-up costs are high. • Importing is costly; depends on international pricing. • Valuable for uses other than energy.	• Limited regional supplies. • Nonrenewable.
Coal	• Complex, but commonly practiced.	• Strip and shaft mining scars the land. • Use creates a grey film in the surfaces. • Particulate emissions pollute air. • Acid rain pollutes air and water.	• Research and development of soft coal use is costly. • Labor, transportation, and conservation are costly.	• Diminishing supply. • Underutilize soft coal.

Figure 11. Completed decision-making matrix

Note. From *Infusing the Teaching of Critical and Creative Thinking into Content Instruction: A Lesson Design Handbook for the Elementary Grades* (p. 62), by R. Swartz and S. Parks, 1994, Pacific Grove, CA: Critical Thinking Books and Software (800) 458-4849. Copyright ©1994 by Critical Thinking Books and Software. Reprinted with permission.

Options	Relevant Consequences			
	Ease of Production	Environment	Cost	Availability

Solar
  Active
  Passive
  Photovoltaic				

Nuclear				
Petrochemical				
Coal				

Figure 12. Blank decision-making matrix

Note. From *Infusing the Teaching of Critical and Creative Thinking into Content Instruction: A Lesson Design Handbook for the Elementary Grades* (p. 62), by R. Swartz and S. Parks, 1994, Pacific Grove, CA: Critical Thinking Books and Software (800) 458-4849. Copyright ©1994 by Critical Thinking Books and Software. Reprinted with permission.

matrix. A huge bulletin board can be used to organize and display the class's combined research on sources of energy.

Having organized this mass of information, students must interpret its meaning. Individually, in small groups, or as a whole class, students summarized information in each row and created a summary statement to synthesize the important information about each particular form of energy. Then, students summarized the information in each column to state a generalization that addresses the next important question: What kinds of consequences are more important than others? This summary statement addresses which factors in considering energy use warrant greater weight than others. By reflecting on the summary statements for the rows and the columns, students prepared a recommendation about which types of energy sources our nation should utilize.

Graphics That Show Relationships. Most of the graphic organizers featured in textbooks or magazines are designed to show how information is related. Common graphics, such as matrices, flowcharts, Venn diagrams, branching diagrams, and concept maps, depict analysis: sequence, rank, classification, subdivision, analogy, part-to-whole relationships, or attribution.

Concept maps, also called "bubble maps" or "web diagrams," can be used to show a variety of relationships (attribution, classification, and part-to-whole relationships), can stimulate creative thinking, and are versatile for numerous instructional or personal uses. In the example in Figure 13, the concept map shows some key ideas students learn about in a unit on the Civil Rights Movement. This concept map may be the teacher's planning tool to design the course, a preinstruction assessment instrument, an advanced organizer for students (a framework to depict the concepts they will learn in the course), or a review tool to summarize instruction when the unit is completed.

In this case, the concept map for the Civil Rights Movement is a mental model for any struggle for equality: the struggle against apartheid in South Africa, the labor movement, the women's movement, and so forth. Because gifted students tend to look for similar connections and applications, mental models that are as clearly "visible" as this one become a powerful tool for efficient learning and organized thought.

Graphics That Stimulate or Guide Thinking. Graphic organizers can be used to analyze or create a metaphor. Class discussions recorded on graphic organizers show how metaphors serve as idea bridges to convey other characteristics or images with playfulness and richness. Consider the cat metaphor in Carl Sandburg's (1916/1993) poem "Fog":

The fog comes
on little cat feet

It sits looking

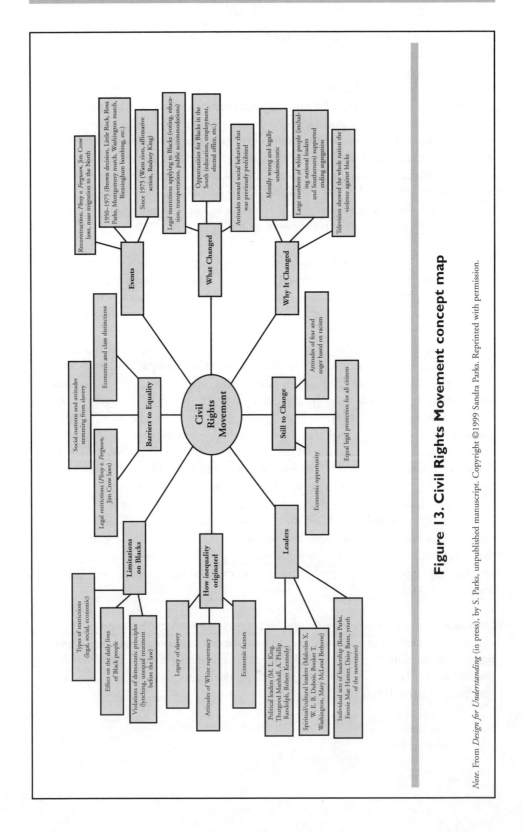

Figure 13. Civil Rights Movement concept map

Note. From *Design for Understanding* (in press), by S. Parks, unpublished manuscript. Copyright ©1999 Sandra Parks. Reprinted with permission.

over harbor and city
on silent haunches
and then moves on. (p. 1268)

Using the diagram shown in Figure 14, students named a characteristic of a cat that was also true of fog, such as "silence." Students brainstormed words for silence, associated with either a cat or fog, and wrote these details or descriptors in the boxes on each side of the diagram. They then used the information on the graphic to critique the effectiveness of the cat metaphor and created a poem that used fog as a metaphor for a cat.

Graphic Organizers for Assessment. Portfolio and performance assessments increasingly include graphic organizers for teachers' evaluations and students' self-assessments. Graphics allow students to assess what they know, what they have learned, and what questions remain unanswered about concepts in an instructional unit. Using graphics to show what they know is particularly important for language-limited students whose knowledge and level of understanding may not be expressed well in writing.

Using graphic organizers allows teachers and students to depict learning quickly and easily, appealing to the cognitive styles of holistic, visual learners. While graphics are well-suited to show gains in learning factual information, the validity of inferences that can be drawn from using graphics in assessment warrants further investigation. Rubrics for the scoring of individual products and guidelines for interpreting graphics should be clarified and carefully reviewed before making quantitative judgments. However, as one indicator for broad interpretation of students' learning, concept maps provide helpful information.

Computer Software and Technology Tools

Computer technology offers access to an array of information resources, promotes interactivity among people, and allows users to manipulate images and information on a scale unprecedented in human thought. CD-ROMs hold enormous databases that make information available to us in word-processing format that can be reorganized. Classroom teachers are only beginning to understand the richness of using databases and videodiscs to access and hold information that students can manipulate and from which they may draw interpretations.

Interactive software allows the user to engage in inductive thinking in situations that cannot be modeled with concrete objects. For example, the software Gertrude's Puzzles (The Learning Company, 1983) simulates using attribute blocks and Venn diagrams to show characteristics. However, students are not told the attributes of various sets and must inductively infer the characteristics of a set by observing whether their placement of the figures remains in the circle or falls out—an activity that one cannot carry out placing the actual blocks on a flat surface. Thus, concept attainment is superimposed to a classification task.

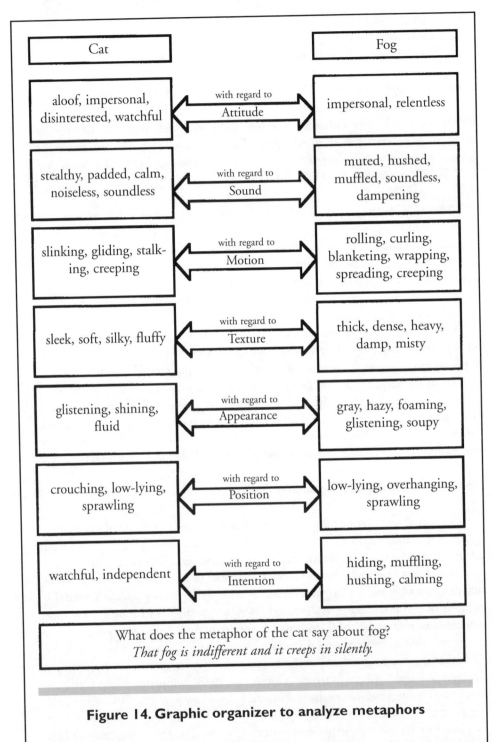

Figure 14. Graphic organizer to analyze metaphors

Note. From *Organizing Thinking II* (p. 90), by S. Parks and H. Black, 1990, Pacific Grove, CA: Critical Thinking Books and Software (800) 458-4849. Copyright ©1990 by Critical Thinking Books and Software. Reprinted with permission.

The HOTS program, featured on the National Diffusion Network, demonstrates the effectiveness of using computer software with higher order questioning to increase the basic skills development of low-performing students. Discussing the thinking involved in interacting with carefully selected interactive software involves both thinking skill development and metacognition. Designed for middle school and high school students, HOTS has also been used effectively with elementary gifted students.

One of the key benefits of using computer software to stimulate ideas is demonstrated by Mindlink (Mauzy, 1991). This software is designed to guide the user, even if one has not been trained in creative thinking, through the synectics process. One principle of synectics is that the user has an enormous bank of background information that can be applied to a specific problem, if accessed analogically; the software is designed to access the user's stored, often unconscious, memory.

Mindlink prompts the user to generate new ideas in much the same way that "think tanks" work. The software is programmed to prompt metaphoric thinking as the user applies both the synectics process and his or her own background information to a particular problem. As an individual interacts with the software, he or she is guided to think and uncover new perspectives, different speculations, and more ideas than if he or she were working independently. Since the software takes the user down different lines of inquiry and provides different stimuli, at certain points in the process the software also guides the user on a creative "bird walk." This is an imagery experience, seemingly unrelated to the problem, that diverts the user from the content of the specific problem and prompts analogical connections that one would perhaps not access if focused on the issue only.

Since using graphic organizers allows us to depict ideas quickly and easily, computer software helps us "download" ideas onto diagrams. These diagrams become an aid to creative thinking, critical thinking, decision making, and planning. Some graphics software, such as Inspiration (Inspiration Software, 1994; see Figure 15), is programmed to reproduce standard design elements of graphic organizers (flowchart symbols, arrows, boxes, ovals, icons, clip art, etc.) so that one can "doodle" with a computer. Templates to depict various analysis tasks are included in the software.

Because some spacing and size features are standardized, one can "draw out" his or her thought almost as quickly on the computer as he or she could sketch it on paper, thus producing a first-draft diagram of surprisingly good craftsmanship. Helping students use computer drawing to depict their thinking and learning improves their motivation to show what they know and models the "thinking with computer" skills that are becoming increasingly common in the workplace.

Video technology can provide the context for students to develop problem-solving skills contextualized in real-world problems. The Vanderbilt Learning Technology Center developed a series of videodiscs that present complex, but

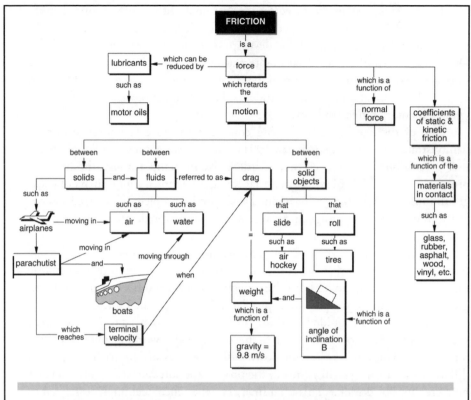

Figure 15. Organizer created with graphic software

Note. From *Inspiration.* (p. 10), by Inspiration Software, graphic created by Paul Rutherford, Science Coordinator, Lee's Summit R–7 School District, Lee's Summit, MO, 1997, Portland, OR: Inspiration Software. Copyright 1997 by ©Inspiration Software. Reprinted with permission.

authentic, problems in which students must generate and solve many subproblems in order to resolve the larger issue. For example, *The Adventures of Jasper Woodbury: Episode One* (Vanderbilt Learning Technology Center, 1996) presents a situation in which Jasper must decide what to do to get his boat home late in the afternoon, realizing that his boat has no lights. Based on a principle of embedded data design, the videodisc provides relevant and irrelevant data (time of sunset, a river map, weather conditions, etc.) that middle school students use to define and solve Jasper's problem. The design features of this videodisc (embedded data, a videodisc format with random access capability, a context in which students must define problems, mathematics operations, and problem-solving skills) provide a rich source of data not commonly available in middle school mathematics classes and offer an authentic, cooperative problem-solving experience for students.

Assessing Analytical and Critical Thinking

Analytical and Critical Thinking Tests

Analytical thinking programs are commonly evaluated by cognitive abilities tests, such as those listed in the teacher resources. The Developing Cognitive Abilities Test (American College Testronics, 1990) provides data about the Bloom's taxonomy-related cognitive abilities in figural, symbolic, and verbal form. The Ross Test of Cognitive Processes (Ross & Ross, 1976) contains some analysis subtests and some inferential reasoning items. It is easily administered and is used commonly in gifted education programs.

Evaluating critical thinking by creating one's own objective tests requires considerable skill and background in test design and critical thinking. Guidelines for creating such assessment instruments, as well as an annotated bibliography of critical thinking tests, are available in *Evaluating Critical Thinking* (Ennis & Norris, 1980).

Assessing Students' Thinking in Writing

The effectiveness of analytical and critical thinking instruction is demonstrated dramatically in the quality of students' writing. Our writing is the hard copy of our thinking. If a student's thinking is fuzzy, disorganized, and incomplete, his or her writing will be similarly fuzzy, disorganized, and incomplete. Improvement in the quality of students' writing is the most dramatic and direct evidence of the efficacy of analytical and critical thinking instruction. Figure 16 shows the correlation of thinking processes to various kinds of writing prompts. While the questions in the thinking strategy may serve as standards for creating rubrics, students' thinking is often implicit, rather than explicit. Unless teachers review students' prewriting notes, one may not always know whether or not students have considered the key questions of various thinking strategies when preparing their papers.

Writing assessment increasingly involves using graphic organizers. Students frequently submit prewriting material so that the teacher can understand the process of their composition, as well as the final product. While we must guard against the artificial standardization of diagrams (such as proper or improper design of a student-generated graphic organizer), we can make assessment tasks more flexible by incorporating these tools into portfolio and performance assessment.

Assessing Thinking and Learning

One of the most complex issues in evaluating students' critical thinking and content learning involves planning appropriate assessment tasks (including performance assessments) and weighing students' work to assign a grade. For teachers

Types of Writing	Thinking Strategy
Narrative Create a story about this situation: _____.	Decision Making
Expository Compare and contrast _____ and _____. Describe the events that lead to _____. What caused _____. What would happen if _____.	Compare and Contract Sequencing Causal Explanation Prediction
Persuasive Why should _____ do _____? Why did _____ do _____? Develop an argument for _____? What should be done to _____?	Reasons/Conclusions Causal Explanation Reasons/Conclusions and Uncovering Assumptions Decision Making
Creative Create a poem or story about _____.	Create a metaphor Generating possibilities
Descriptive Describe a _____. Describe how to _____.	Parts of a Whole or Classification Sequencing

Figure 16. Correlated thinking strategies to types of writing

Note. From *Design for Understanding*, by S. Parks, in process, Pacific Grove, CA: Critical Thinking Books and Software. Copyright ©1999 by Sandra Parks. Reprinted with permission.

of gifted classes in core content subjects, grading is always difficult, especially when class time and students' assignments have emphasized critical thinking. The diagram in Figure 17 shows examples of assessment tasks in a unit on the Civil War. Since higher order thinking is best demonstrated in the performance of skillful thinking and content understanding, which requires considerable time and preparation for the students, such evaluation procedures should be weighted accordingly:

- Evaluation tasks that involve critical or creative thinking require products that take considerable time and preparation and, therefore, receive the most credit.

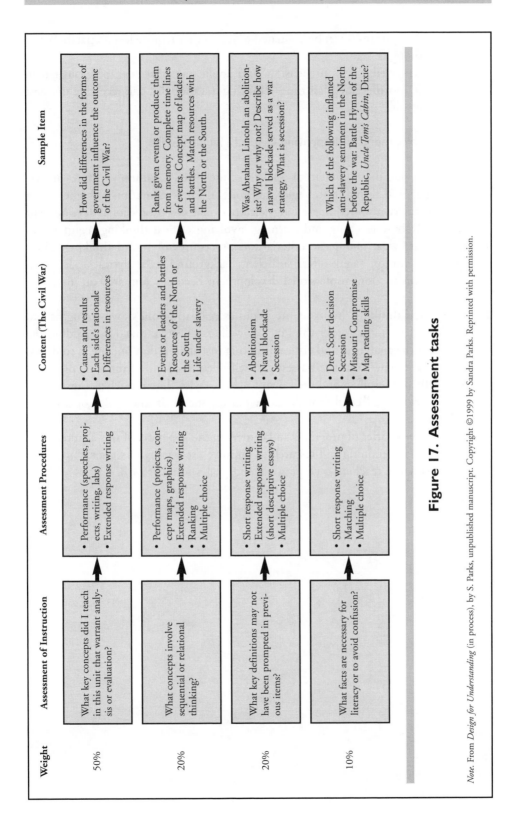

The table in the figure reads as follows:

Weight	Assessment of Instruction	Assessment Procedures	Content (The Civil War)	Sample Item
50%	What key concepts did I teach in this unit that warrant analysis or evaluation?	• Performance (speeches, projects, writing, labs) • Extended response writing	• Causes and results • Each side's rationale • Differences in resources	How did differences in the forms of government influence the outcome of the Civil War?
20%	What concepts involve sequential or relational thinking?	• Performance (projects, concept maps, graphics) • Extended response writing • Ranking • Multiple choice	• Events or leaders and battles • Resources of the North or the South • Life under slavery	Rank given events or produce them from memory. Complete time lines of events. Concept map of leaders and battles. Match resources with the North or the South.
20%	What key definitions may not have been prompted in previous items?	• Short response writing • Extended response writing (short descriptive essays) • Multiple choice	• Abolitionism • Naval blockade • Secession	Was Abraham Lincoln an abolitionist? Why or why not? Describe how a naval blockade served as a war strategy. What is secession?
10%	What facts are necessary for literacy or to avoid confusion?	• Short response writing • Matching • Multiple choice	• Dred Scott decision • Secession • Missouri Compromise • Map reading skills	Which of the following inflamed anti-slavery sentiment in the North before the war: Battle Hymn of the Republic, *Uncle Tom's Cabin*, Dixie?

Figure 17. Assessment tasks

Note. From *Design for Understanding* (in process), by S. Parks, unpublished manuscript. Copyright ©1999 by Sandra Parks. Reprinted with permission.

- Analysis tasks can be evaluated in forms that require less preparation and thought.
- Knowledge, comprehension, and application tasks can be evaluated in test form, taking less time, requiring less thought, and receiving the least credit.

Staff Development on Improving Critical Thinking Skills

While staff development for teachers of the gifted commonly features analytical and critical thinking strategies, meaningful implementation of higher order thinking instruction requires a long-term personal and professional development process. Robust teaching and learning involving critical thinking requires that teachers are clear about the criteria and procedures of sound thinking. Since teacher education rarely offers sufficient background in analytical and critical thinking instruction, professional development becomes primarily an in-service function.

Critical thinking, by its nature, requires evaluating one's own strengths and weaknesses in higher order thinking, as well as reflective practice regarding the quality of the analytical and critical thinking instruction that one offers students. Individual teachers must self-assess and self-select the kind of thinking processes that fit their disciplines and their own teaching styles. Then, teachers must invest in their own intellectual growth, as well as expand their knowledge of teaching techniques.

The summaries of programs and centers in the appendix of this chapter indicate sources of training and research to improve the quality of students' thinking and to enhance teachers' own personal and professional growth.

Teacher Statement

In our all-day pull-out gifted program, my 5th graders participate in shared inquiry discussions using Junior Great Books. After reading a piece of literature from Junior Great Books, the students basically lead their own thorough discussion of the piece and write an essay requiring critical thinking, creative thinking, or a combination of the two. Their favorite part? The discussions—and they would continue for much longer if our class met daily.

We also study an interdisciplinary thematic unit called "Our Germanic Roots." In it, the students are introduced to many aspects of the country: its history, geography, language, people, animal life, plant life, natural resources, education systems, economy, politics, arts, music, sports, foods, and even its hopes for the future. They investigate these topics through intensive research using many resources in our school's media center. The students work in small groups creating projects to present their research findings. If two or more students find opposing facts about a topic, they must consider the reliability and biases of the sources and reach a consensus as to which side to rely upon for their information. Students critically evaluate their projects and presentations using rubrics they create in class. They score their peers, themselves, and the class as a whole. They also make suggestions about how to improve both the projects and the presentations for future reference.

In another learning unit, the children study economy, business, and advertising techniques. They create their own imaginary business within budgetary guidelines I provide, then they make a Web site to advertise it. The Web sites must meet guidelines the students select prior to beginning their technological projects. The culminating activities include class presentations of the Web sites followed by peer- and self-evaluations of the sites according to the criteria and guidelines the students chose as their standards for acceptable projects.

My students also enjoy matrix logic puzzles. Whenever they enter our gifted program (even in early primary grades), they are taught to solve these types of puzzles. By the 5th grade, the children are very comfortable solving relatively complex ones. To stretch their critical thinking skills, I also ask the students to create original matrix logic puzzles of their own. Each must make the matrix, a suitable introduction, a set of clues, and an answer sheet, then they test each other's puzzles for solvability and logic.

—Tina Goggans Gay

Discussion Questions

1. Why is it important for teachers to incorporate analytical and critical thinking skills into the curriculum for gifted students?

2. Why do you think analytical and critical thinking skills have been neglected in the curriculum? What is your strategy for changing this?

3. Compare and contrast various strategies for incorporating analytical and critical thinking skills into the curriculum for gifted students. Which strategies would work best for your program and your population of gifted learners?

4. What are the most important concepts you want your gifted learners to master in terms of their critical and analytical thinking skills?

5. Examine the screening and identification instruments you use for identifying critical and analytical thinking skills in your gifted students. Which one(s) are most appropriate for your needs?

Teacher Resources

Web Sites

Tim van Gelder's Critical Thinking on the Web—http://www.austhink.org/critical
A comprehensive directory of online resources.

Critical Thinking Consortium—http://www.criticalthinking.org
Provides resources and information for teaching critical thinking on the college, primary, and secondary levels.

Mission: Critical—http://www2.sjsu.edu/depts/itl
This is an interactive tutorial for critical thinking in which you will be introduced to basic concepts through sets of instructions and exercises.

The Critical Thinking Co.—http://www.criticalthinking.com
Products for home and classroom use in mathematics, science, language arts, social studies, and more.

Critical Thinking Across the Curriculum Project—http://www.kcmetro.cc.mo.us/longview/ctac/index.htm
The resources on this site are managed or created by the faculty of Longview Community College for use in integrating critical thinking into all areas of the college curriculum.

The National Council for Excellence in Critical Thinking—http://www.critical-thinking.org/ncect.html
The goal of the NCECT is to articulate, preserve, and foster intellectual standards in critical thinking research, scholarship, and instruction. The NCECT is a creation of the Foundation for Critical Thinking. The council presently consists of about 8,000 leading educators.

The National Diffusion Network—http://www.ed.gov/pubs/EPTW/eptwndas.html
The National Diffusion Network offers proven educational programs that have demonstrated their effectiveness in improving student performance. The NDN also offers technical assistance to schools in identifying needs, matching programs to needs, and developing effective school-improvement strategies.

Teaching Critical Thinking—http://www.dartmouth.edu/~compose/faculty/pedagogies/thinking.html
The Dartmouth College Composition Center Web site provides resources to faculty and students interested in writing and writing instruction in critical thinking.

The Maryland Community College Consortium for Teaching Reasoning—http://
academic.pg.cc.md.us/~wpeirce/MCCCTR
This Web site contains a number of valuable resources for teachers in a variety of
disciplines, such as articles, workshop handouts, lists of books on teaching students to think critically (including publishers' URLs and telephone numbers),
and links to other Web sites on teaching thinking.

Publications

The College Board & Academic Testing Service. (2002). *The academic profile.*
    Princeton, NJ: Educational Testing Service.
Facione, P. (1998). *The test of everyday reasoning.* Millbrae, CA: California Academic
    Press.
Nosich, G. M. (2004). *Learning to think things through: A guide to critical think-
    ing in the curriculum* (2nd ed.). Upper Saddle River, NJ: Prentice Hall.
Paul, R., & Elder, L. (2000). *Critical thinking handbook: Basic theory and instruc-
    tional structures.* Dillon Beach, CA: Foundation for Critical Thinking.
Paul, R., & Elder, L. (2001). *The miniature guide to critical thinking: Concepts
    and tools.* Dillon Beach, CA: Foundation for Critical Thinking.
Paul, R. & Elder, L. (2001). *The international critical thinking test.* Dillon Beach,
    CA: Foundation for Critical Thinking
Paul, R., & Elder, L. (2002). *Instructors manual to critical thinking: Tools for
    taking charge of your learning and your life.* Upper Saddle River, NJ: Prentice
    Hall.
Paul, R. & Elder, L. (2004). *The miniature guide on the nature and functions of
    critical and creative thinking.* Dillon Beach, CA: Foundation for Critical
    Thinking

References

American College Testronics. (1990). *Developing cognitive abilities test.* Iowa City, IA: Author.

Black, H., & Parks, S. (1985). *Building thinking skills.* Pacific Grove, CA: Critical Thinking Books & Software.

Bloom, B. S. (Ed.). (1956). *Taxonomy of educational objectives: The classification of educational goals. Handbook I: Cognitive domain.* New York: Longman.

Eggen, P. D., Kauchek, D. P., & Harder, R. (1979). *Strategies for teachers: Information processing models in the classroom.* Englewood Cliff, NJ: Prentice-Hall.

Ennis, R. (1996). *Critical thinking.* New York: Prentice-Hall.

Ennis, R., & Norris, S. (1980). *Evaluating critical thinking.* Pacific Grove, CA: Critical Thinking Books & Software.

Harcourt-Brace Educational Measurement. (1996). *Stanford achievement test–9th edition (SAT).* San Antonio, TX: Author.

Harnadek, A. (1976). *Critical thinking book one.* Pacific Grove, CA: Critical Thinking Books & Software.

Harnadek, A. (1980). *Critical thinking book two.* Pacific Grove, CA: Critical Thinking Books & Software.

Howells, R. F. (1992). Thinking in the morning, thinking in the evening, thinking at suppertime. *Phi Delta Kappan, 74,* 223–225.

Inspiration Software. (1994). *Inspiration.* Portland, OR: Author.

The Learning Company. (1983). *Gertrude's puzzles.* Palo Alto, CA: Author.

Lipman, M. (1979). *Philosophy for children.* Montclair, NJ: Institute for the Advancement of Philosophy for Children.

Mauzy, J. (1991). *Mindlink internelis.* North Pomfret, VT: Mindlink.

Parks, S. (1999). *Design for understanding.* Unpublished manuscript.

Parks, S., & Black, H. (1990). *Organizing thinking II.* Pacific Grove, CA: Critical Thinking Books & Software.

Potter, P., & Dawson, J. W. (1988, October). National merit scholars by design, not by chance. *Educational Leadership,* 54–56.

Rito, G. R., & Moller, B. W. (1989). Teaching enrichment activities to minorities: TEAM for success. *Journal of Negro Education, 58,* 212–219.

Ross, J. S., & Ross, K. T. (1976). *Ross test of cognitive processes.* San Raphael, CA: Academic Therapy.

Sandburg, C. (1993). Fog. In D. McQuade (Ed.), *The Harper American literature, Vol. 2* (2nd ed., p. 1268). New York: HarperCollins College Publishers. (Original work published 1916)

Swartz, R., & Parks, S. (1994). *Infusing the teaching of critical and creative thinking into content instruction: A lesson design handbook for the elementary grades.* Pacific Grove, CA: Critical Thinking Press & Software.

Swartz, R., & Parks, S. (in process). *Infusing the teaching of critical and creative thinking into social studies instruction: A lesson design handbook for the secondary grades.* Unpublished manuscript.

Swartz, R., & Perkins, D. (1990). *Issues and approaches to teaching thinking.* Pacific Grove, CA: Critical Thinking Press & Software.

Vanderbilt Learning Technology Center. (1996). *The adventures of Jasper Woodbury: Episode one* [Videodisc]. Nashville, TN: Vanderbilt University.

Author Note

The summaries of programs, centers, and networks were prepared by the author and are updated on the Web site of the Teaching Thinking Network of the Association for Supervision and Curriculum Development.

Chapter 10

Adapting Problem-Based Learning for Gifted Students

by **Shelagh A. Gallagher**

 ducational reform has spawned much experimentation in both curricula and instruction. One approach that has gained popularity over the past decade is problem-based learning (PBL; Barrows, 1985; Stepien & Gallagher, 1993). With explicit attention to authentic problem solving, hands-on learning, and self-directed learning, many teachers have embraced PBL as a way to improve curricula and instruction for all their students. Others have claimed that PBL is perfect for gifted students. Can both these viewpoints be true? Of course they can. However, although it is true that PBL is appropriate for all students, it does not necessarily follow that PBL is exactly the same for all students. Certainly, a fundamental similarity will always be evident because the *structural elements* of PBL are the same in any setting. The *substance* inside a PBL unit, however, can and should be adapted to meet the individual needs of the students who will be working with the problem.

The purpose of this chapter is to present unique characteristics of gifted students as problem solvers and to show how PBL units can be adapted to extend their potential.

Matching Curriculum and Characteristics: Gifted Students and Problem Solving

Gifted students have cognitive and affective characteristics that distinguish them from the regular population of students.

Interestingly enough, many of these traits are similar to those that distinguish experts from novice problem solvers. The characteristics that gifted students and expert problem solvers share in common provide a set of guidelines to use when thinking about adapting PBL for gifted students. Essentially, the goal of modifying PBL for the gifted is to narrow the gap between the special potential possessed by the child and the actual practice of expert adults. The similarities between expert problem solvers and gifted students are observed in four broad areas: knowledge base, conceptual reasoning, problem-solving strategies, and dispositions.

Gifted Students Have the Capacity to Build an Expert's Knowledge Base

The cornerstone of an expert problem solver's expertise is a large knowledge base (Rabinowitz & Glaser, 1985). Experts acquire and retain large bodies of information by making connections among different facts. The large knowledge base serves to make experts both better informed and more creative: The more they know, the more opportunity they have to see unusual associations (Bruer, 1993). For example, an expert ecologist might remember the facts *fish*, *water*, and *aquatic plants* by connecting them all to a fishbowl. Using *fishbowl* as a central point of reference, experts can also use the idea to make associations with new information like *gravel* or *fish food*. In the future, when the expert needs this information, she need only recall the fishbowl, and all of the associated information will be retrieved, as well.

The capacity to learn quickly and then retain information is also one of the most frequently cited characteristics of gifted children (Clark, 1996; Gallagher & Gallagher, 1994). However, to make effective use of their knowledge, gifted students need to learn how to use their information like an expert, making connections among pieces of information and creating new knowledge by making new associations.

Gifted Students Practice Conceptual Reasoning

Expert problem solvers and gifted students alike tend to look beyond the surface of the problem to find an underlying meaning. When searching for a helpful way to represent a problem, experts tend to look for its *deep structure*, using abstract concepts or principles to describe the heart of the dilemma. By contrast, novices tend to work with surface characteristics that may be more obvious, but are less essential to developing an understanding of the heart of the problem. To go back to the previous example, the novice would try to solve a problem of dying fish in a fishbowl by looking at the fish food and the water in the tank—obvious targets, but perhaps not the right ones. The expert, on the other hand, would look at the fishbowl as a water ecosystem. Recognizing that the elements in systems interact, the expert might look for interactions in the fishbowl and find that the gravel reflects sunlight, raising the water to a dangerously high temperature for the fish (Chase & Simon, 1973; DeGroot, 1965).

Gifted students give evidence of conceptual and abstract reasoning at an earlier age than their agemates (Berliner, 1986; Bransford & Vye, 1989; Sternberg & Davidson, 1985). Similar to expert problem solvers, gifted students show the early promise of being able to develop skill in deep structure thinking.

Gifted Students Have Early Capacity for Problem Solving

Experts also tend to have *more* problem-solving tools at their disposal than novices, and they know how to select among those skills according to their needs (Minstrell, 1989). While solving the problem of the fishbowl, the expert can switch easily from a content analysis of the water, to a dissection of a dead fish, to consultation with resources to fill in gaps in understanding. Without a similar repertoire of skills, the novice may simply conduct different variations of water analysis. Having looked at the data from many perspectives, the expert is also more likely to come up with a more creative or sophisticated problem definition. The expert's capacity for creative problem definition, or problem finding, provides the foundation for unique solutions (Getzels, 1979). Throughout the problem-solving process, experts make greater use of metacognitive reflection by monitoring and controlling their thinking (Bransford & Vye, 1989) by reflecting on questions like "Have I considered all the possibilities?," "What assumptions am I making about the effect of lamp light on the fishbowl water?," and "Is this strategy working?" By contrast, novices might doggedly pursue the same unsuccessful strategy, unable to find their way out of a dead end.

Gifted students are more adept at problem finding than average-ability students (Runco, 1986). Rogers (1986) found other similarities between the problem-solving behaviors of experts and gifted students, including careful selection of strategies. While solving problems, gifted students also use metacognitive skills spontaneously, learning them more quickly and transferring them to new situations more readily than average-ability students (Carr & Borkowski, 1986).

Gifted Students Have Expert-Like Dispositions

Eminent authors, scientists, and historians all emphasize the importance of exploration and the disposition to seek the unknown to their success (Judson, 1980; O'Connor, 1962; Tuchman, 1966). With the inclination to search for the unknown, experts are more likely to use forward problem solving, since they assume that the answer to their problem does not exist. Novices, on the other hand, would be more likely to pursue more predictable questions with verifiable solutions.

Taking an open-ended approach to problem solving requires believing that some problems have no predetermined "right" answer. Students who believe that all problems have a single, absolute right answer are not likely to look for many alternative answers in an ill-structured problem. The belief that some questions

Table 1

**Shared Qualities of Expert Problem Solvers
and Gifted Students**

Expert Problem Solver Qualities	Gifted Student Qualities
• Has broad knowledge base	• Acquires information quickly
• Looks for "deep structure" of problems	• Gives early evidence of conceptual thinking
• Has a large tool kit of skills; uses skills flexibly	• Carefully selects problem-solving strategies
• Monitors the problem-solving process	• Spontaneously uses metacognitive skills
• Uses dispositions supporting open-ended problem solving; uses forward thinking problem solving	• Recognizes that many questions have no single, absolute right answer

have no single right answer is one factor that might determine a student's success in open-ended assignments. A few studies investigating student dispositions have shown that gifted students are more likely to believe that some questions have no predetermined answers (Goldberger, 1981; Murphy & Gilligan, 1980). In this attribute, gifted students are similar to adult experts.

Taken together, these research data give evidence that gifted students have a head start on their peers in developing expert problem-solving capabilities, as demonstrated in Table 1. At the same time, there is no doubt that gifted students have a long way to go in refining their raw potential into sophisticated skill. Having a head start is no guarantee of achieving the level of problem solving that a gifted student could well acquire. What must intervene is an education that moves gifted students from potential to skill and, hopefully, expertise along these dimensions.

While there is not, as of yet, a clear path from potential to expertise (Callahan, 1996), there are some hints as to how to begin developing an expert problem solver (Bransford & Vye, 1989; Bruer, 1993; Rabinowitz & Glaser, 1985). There is evidence that information is retained better when it is presented in a context that is meaningful to students (Brown, Collins, & Duguid, 1989). Students will learn to look for underlying concepts when they are confronted with many representations of the same problem (Shoenfeld, 1989). Conceptual reasoning is enhanced when a teacher models the kind of thinking that reveals the conceptual level of activities (Bransford & Vye). Conversely, we know that expert-like understanding will not develop in environments where instruction is oversimplified, presented from a single perspective, context-independent, rigidly compartmentalized into structures, and passively transmitted (Spiro, Carlson, Feltovich, & Anderson, 1988). In other words, success in complex thinking happens only with repeated practice in complex learning environments.

Problem-Based Learning: A Promising Road to Expertise

Problem-based learning (PBL) provides the kind of complex learning environment that is well suited to developing expertise. The complex learning environment is created through the combined impact of the structural components of PBL: the ill-structured problem, the student as stakeholder, the self-directed learner, and the teacher as coach.

The Ill-Structured Problem

Perhaps the most noticeable difference between traditional instruction and PBL is that a PBL unit begins with the presentation of an ill-structured problem. The differences between traditional well-structured problems and ill-structured problems are embodied in the following two examples:

Problem A

You have two dozen oranges in your store. Mary comes in and buys six. Charles thinks about buying three but then changes his mind and gets six. If Teresa buys four oranges and Ryan buys eight, is Brenda justified when she complains to you about not being able to find any oranges in the produce department?

Problem B

You are the owner of the local food co-op. Your favorite customers have all come in complaining about the insufficient supply of oranges. What should you do?

These two problems have some surface similarities: They both deal with oranges, shortages, and customer dissatisfaction. Their differences are far more important than their similarities, for they are the characteristics that distinguish a well-structured problem from an ill-structured one. Characteristics of the ill-structured problems include the following:

- *More information than is initially available is needed to understand the problem.* In the example, Problem A can be solved quite easily once the appropriate formula is in place. In Problem B, much more is needed to understand the problem. Why is there an insufficient supply of oranges? What do the clients mean by *insufficient?* Did we run out? What are some ways of keeping oranges (and other fruit) in stock? The quality of the ill-structured problem is frequently referred to a *generative.* That is, the ill-structured problem actually generates questions.

- *No single formula exists for conducting an investigation to resolve the problem.* In Problem A, there is a specific set of operations to conduct in order to solve the problem; and, while some of the operations are reciprocal, there isn't much room for creative structure. In Problem B, however, there may be any number of different ways to deal with the client's complaints, depending, in part, on the exact nature of the problem.
- *As new information is obtained, the problem changes.* In this case, Problem A has all the information needed to solve the problem supplied in the brief paragraph. In Problem B, the problem could shift considerably if students were to find either that there were restrictions on the import of citrus fruit or, on the other hand, that a new "orange diet" had caused a run on the fruit.
- *Students can never be 100% sure they have made the "right" decision.* Problem A has a single, correct answer. In Problem B, the many possible options would have to be weighed to select the most reasonable one; and, even then, there would likely be negative, as well as positive, consequences to the solution. Only rarely would an answer be absolutely right.

An important point to be made about PBL is that students are solving problems that are central to a field of study and designed around specific educational goals. Indeed, one of the reasons why PBL is considered defensible by many medical school programs is the care that is taken to create an apt reflection of learning and problem solving as they occur in the discipline (Boud & Feletti, 1991). Because an important goal of PBL is to integrate core content with authentic problem solving, the ill-structured problems used in the PBL classroom must meet additional criteria. To be considered educationally sound, PBL problems must

- be designed to ensure that students cover a predefined area of knowledge, preferably integrated from many disciplines;
- help students learn a set of important concepts, ideas, and techniques;
- successfully lead students to (parts of) a field of study; and
- hold intrinsic interest or importance or represent a typical problem faced by the profession (Ross, 1991).

Thus, PBL is considered to be a more effective way to teach the core curriculum. In Problem B, students would run into much substantial content while trying to figure out why there are no oranges, including the growing cycle and different varieties of oranges, import-export laws, or diseases that might infest oranges. All of these are associated with basic learning objectives at different grade levels. Taken together, the qualities of the ill-structured problem lead students to pursue questions and, in the process, extend their knowledge base in a meaningful context.

Student as Stakeholder

A second feature of PBL is the practice of placing students in a carefully selected stakeholder position. The stakeholder in a PBL unit is a person who has some level of authority, accountability, and responsibility for resolving some aspect of the problem. Students are assigned a specific role in each problem they encounter: a political advisor in a problem about district gerrymandering; a journalist in a problem about media in the courtroom; a golf course groundskeeper in a problem about improving golf through grass selection. The goal of placing students in the shoes of a person actually involved in the problem is to make them an "apprentice" in that area. Like an artist's apprentice, students in a PBL problem experience the entire world of the problem solver and learn to adopt the appropriate dispositions, as well as content and skills. While in their apprenticeships, students learn many valuable lessons about problem solving from inside a discipline, including

- the way problem solving is approached in different disciplines;
- the role of bias and perspective in the problem-solving process;
- the subjective nature of all real-world problem solving;
- the need to understand many different ways to solve a problem (economic, scientific, political, ethical); and
- the intricate process of weighing the priorities of different points of view in a complex problem.

The Self-Directed Learner

The third change incorporated into the PBL classroom is that students are encouraged to take control of the learning process, thus becoming increasingly capable, self-reliant, and responsible learners. Teachers assist in this process by becoming a "tutor" who focuses on helping students develop a good tool kit of problem-solving skills, assisting students as they learn to use them, and engaging students in a process of reflection about their own performance and the nature of problem solving.

The tutor also allows students to take on an increasing set of responsibilities, including setting the learning agenda, facilitating the group process, and setting timelines or deadlines. Using metacognitive questioning and modeling good inquiry, the tutor reveals to students how professionals approach similar problems, helps students focus on a problem's central concepts, and probes to ensure that they understand all the data they gather. By reflecting on and evaluating their own thinking, students acquire better control over their thinking and feeling processes, ultimately resulting in better reasoning.

Adapting PBL for Gifted Students:
New Applications of Familiar Recommendations

PBL is not inherently appropriate for gifted students. Rather, it must be adapted and designed to match their unique needs. The appropriateness of PBL for gifted students depends on the kinds of adaptations that are built into the problem design and instruction. For average-ability students, the first order of business in PBL might be to acquire the basics of metacognition and self-direction, the nature of concepts, and the skills of problem solving. Gifted students, on the other hand, need a different level of challenge in PBL, one that refines and extends existing skills that are already in place. The five adaptations recommended here may sound quite familiar, since the same recommendations are made for all sorts of curricula for gifted students (Kaplan, 1986; Maker, 1982; VanTassel-Baska, 1988). Recommended modifications of PBL for gifted students include

- ensuring advanced content;
- working with complex concepts;
- demonstrating interdisciplinary connections;
- practicing good reasoning, habits of mind, and self-directed action; and
- discussing conflicting ethical appeals.

Changes in any one of these five dimensions makes PBL problems more appropriate for gifted students; the benefits in learning accumulate, and the number of adaptations increase. Perhaps the best way to demonstrate how a problem can be modified for instruction with gifted students is to work with a concrete example. For the purpose of discussion, consider the introduction to a problem involving an old oil platform, presented in Figure 1.

Students in this problem are in the stakeholder of the panel of scientists facing the problem of finding something to do with the defunct oil platform. After thinking about the problem, a group of gifted middle school students might develop a Learning Issues Board that looks something like the version presented in Figure 2.

Modification 1: Ensuring Advanced Content

One essential component of any PBL curriculum is a problem designed around an important and worthy body of knowledge. More specifically, the problems designed for gifted students should lead to advanced investigations that

The 40-story oil storage tank, named Brent Spar by its owner, the Shell Oil Company, is easy to spot, even in the cold choppy water of the North Sea. Its giant carcass, towering more than 90 feet above the surface and extending 370 feet below it, is temporarily anchored at $60°$ degrees north latitude, 50 kilometers west of the Shetland Islands. It has been there since June 1995. According to plans by Shell Oil, the storage tank should have been disposed of by now. But, Greenpeace became involved, and now the obsolete tank is riding the waves off Scotland.

The Brent Spar is now your problem! Shell Oil and Greenpeace have agreed to allow an impartial team of scientists to decide what to do with the platform. This is where you and your team come in.

Shell Oil no longer wants to use the old storage tank, or any of the more than 100 of the old platforms, built in the 1970s. Last June, Shell Oil and the British government agreed to allow the oil company to scuttle the platform and let it settle to the bottom of the ocean. When Greenpeace heard of the plan, it organized a boycott against Shell Oil gasoline in Europe and landed protesters on the platform itself. A small group of protesters are still on the tank.

You and your team must decide what to do with the Brent Spar. As the boat approaches the platform, your team assembles to begin discussing the situation. What are your first thoughts about the situation? What do you think the group should know more about to solve the problem of the Brent Spar?

Figure 1. Brent Spar problem

Note. From *Problem-Based Learning Across the Curriculum: An ASCD Professional Inquiry Kit* (Folder 4, Activity 1, p. 2), by W. J. Stepien & S. A. Gallagher, 1997, Alexandria, VA: Association for Supervision and Curriculum Development. Copyright ©1997 by ASCD. Reprinted with permission. All rights reserved.

broaden and deepen their knowledge base. Teachers can ensure the presence of complex information by choosing problems that require the study of advanced information. For example, middle school students will be more challenged by the Brent Spar problem than by a problem about building a playground. Teachers can also arrange for students to "discover" resources with appropriately challenging information. In the case of the Brent Spar problem, this might take the form of prompting a guest speaker to raise issues about regulating ocean waters that might not otherwise emerge.

The content in a PBL problem can even be differentiated in a heterogeneous classroom. For example, in the Brent Spar problem, all students will encounter a foundation of understanding about the effects of oil on the ocean. During the course of small-group research, the teacher/coach could help a small group of

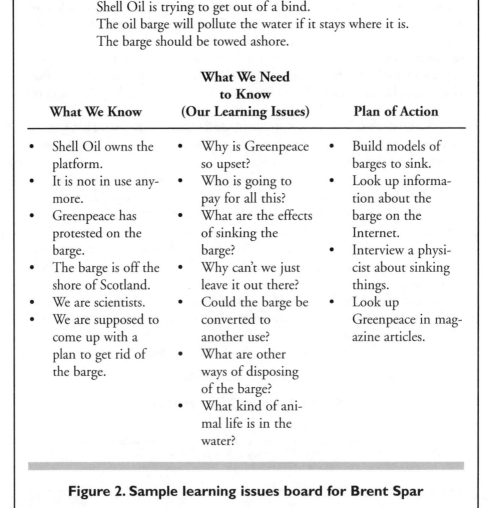

Hunches: What seems to be going on here?
Shell Oil is trying to get out of a bind.
The oil barge will pollute the water if it stays where it is.
The barge should be towed ashore.

What We Know	What We Need to Know (Our Learning Issues)	Plan of Action
• Shell Oil owns the platform. • It is not in use anymore. • Greenpeace has protested on the barge. • The barge is off the shore of Scotland. • We are scientists. • We are supposed to come up with a plan to get rid of the barge.	• Why is Greenpeace so upset? • Who is going to pay for all this? • What are the effects of sinking the barge? • Why can't we just leave it out there? • Could the barge be converted to another use? • What are other ways of disposing of the barge? • What kind of animal life is in the water?	• Build models of barges to sink. • Look up information about the barge on the Internet. • Interview a physicist about sinking things. • Look up Greenpeace in magazine articles.

Figure 2. Sample learning issues board for Brent Spar

gifted students understand more challenging information about the physics involved in different approaches to sinking the platform.

Modification 2: Complexity of the Concept

Problem-based learning and a concept-centered curriculum go hand in hand. In Brent Spar, the concept *change* is used to help students organize and think about the different components of the problem (Gallagher & Stepien, 1996). Discussion of the concept should not be reserved just for gifted students, since all students need to learn the fundamental nature of change. However, gifted stu-

PBL in Action: Planet X

When pilot testing the PBL science units, commonly referred to as "the William and Mary units," "Planet X"* was of special interest to us. Students were placed in the role of "mission specialists," charged with the job of creating a plant ecosystem that would help save the dying planet. It was the first time PBL had been tested with very young children, so we were eager to document as much as possible. A graduate assistant was in the classroom nearly every day to videotape the problem at work. Initially, we would have been satisfied with a very modest success; but, before long, we realized that we were onto something very, very special. The teachers working with the 2nd graders were natural PBL coaches, and soon they were all on an adventure in plant ecosystems.

One day, the students were discussing how they might communicate with personnel on Planet X. The planet was just opposite the Earth on the other side of the sun, and it had exactly the same tilt and rotation. Being on the other side of the sun, the children were faced with the dilemma of how to send messages to their colleagues on the planet. They knew that sound travels in a straight line, which means that messages "beamed" to the planet would always bump into the sun. Their coach gently encouraged students to consider alternatives—drawing the Earth on a chalkboard and marking the path of a sound wave; and in a corner of the room, barely audible, you could hear someone murmur, ". . . mirror . . ."

"What?" exclaimed the coach, seizing on the teachable moment. "What do you mean? Here, come up to the board and show us."

He handed the chalk to the 2nd grader and stood back. The boy shuffled up to the chalkboard and drew a line above the picture of the Earth.

He said, "If we put a mirror up here . . ."

"Yes! Yes!" the nearest girl shouted. "This will work because when we experimented with light, we bounced light!"

"Ah," the coach stepped in. "You mean that sound might reflect like light reflects? Could we use something like a satellite to get sound by the sun to Planet X? Would that work?"

"Yes!" shouted the class, overjoyed with their own cleverness.

That was just one moment in an amazing four months of PBL. That's right: four months. The unit lasted that long; not because the problem got out of control but because the teachers and students were both enjoying it and learning so much, they decided to keep it going for as long as they could. Even after four months, the students were disappointed when the adventure ended.

* "Planet X" has since been revised into the problem "Dust Bowl."

dents will be ready to appreciate the power of the concept at a more advanced level. Where regular students might benefit from a discussion centering around the fact that "Change causes change," gifted students are ready for a more sophisticated application of the problem, such as "Change is irreversible because it interacts with time." Concepts can be drawn into the problem as a part of coaching, in Problem Log assessments, or during problem debriefing. At a more advanced level, teachers can use a concept to tie several problems together and let the concept develop as students transfer it from one problem to the next. Seeing the same concept in action in several problems should also help students develop the habit of looking for a conceptual structure to the problem (Gallagher, Sher, Stepien, & Workman, 1995; Stepien, Gallagher & Workman, 1993).

Modification 3: Interdisciplinary Connections and Interactions

Most real-world problems are interdisciplinary (Carter, 1988), which makes the goal of revealing connections and interactions among disciplines quite natural. However, the degree to which a problem is interdisciplinary can vary as a function of problem design and tutor guiding. A likely goal for teachers of the gifted would be to help gifted students explore intricate interconnections. As with the development of the concept, several layers of interdisciplinary interactions could be explored in Brent Spar. For example, while regular students think about the interactions of the energy use on the environment, gifted students might investigate other kinds of interactions, including the multifaceted interactions of energy dependence, global governmental regulation, and territoriality.

Modification 4: Higher Order Thinking Skills

A well-designed problem provides an environment where tutors can help students acquire sound inquiry skills (Schmidt & Moust, 1995). PBL provides an environment where students can be coached to improve their skills along many dimensions of good reasoning.

Critical Thinking Skills. Just as the problem can be designed to rely on more or less complex applications of a concept, so can students be encouraged to use more complex kinds of reasoning. Different phases of the problem draw on various kinds of reasoning skills. The first lesson of a problem, filling in the Learning Issues Board, requires analytical reasoning, discriminating between fact and inference, recognizing gaps in understanding, and prioritizing. Problem definition, on the other hand, requires skills that include analysis and synthesis of information, determining bias, and summarizing understanding.

Beyond the basic problem-solving and critical thinking skills, students will have an opportunity to learn discipline-specific skills related to the content matter of the problem. In Brent Spar, students have a natural opportunity to learn about posing scientific hypotheses, experimentation, and reporting. Students will

PBL in Action: Student Perspectives

One of the questions that perpetually pesters teachers is whether or not students "get it." In the case of PBL, we might ask whether or not students "get" the idea of complex problem solving. Recently, in Project P-BLISS (Problem-Based Learning in the Social Sciences), we became *very* interested in this question. We were working with disadvantaged gifted high school students, looking for curricula that would excite them and motivate them to engage in complex thought. To see if the students "got" the idea of complex problem solving, we used this question in their Problem Log: "What do you know about problem solving that you didn't know before?" Here are some representative responses:

- This unit taught me that if you want to be a good problem solver, you must be totally unbiased and look at both sides of the problem. I also learned that everything in a problem is not always as it seems, and many times you have to look into the facts deeper before you can come to a conclusion.
- This unit taught me that the solving process takes a while and is also a lot of work; but, once you get into the flow, it's fun. This process taught me how to compare and contrast and how to choose the right one. It also taught me how not to take sides in the matter because before you can understand what's going on, you have to get both sides of the story.
- I learned that, to solve a problem, it helps to break it down into a bunch of smaller problems that can be solved one at a time. And, doing this, you make it so you don't miss any parts of the problem that could play a good part in making it right. I also learned that, if you try to solve a problem without breaking it down, you can end up with a huge mess.
- You have to have lots of patience. Because everyone might not agree, everyone is not going to agree, and you have to stop and see it in two ways. Sometimes, when you think you've got somewhere, you have to go back 'cause you might have overlooked something.
- I did not realize the extent of how hard it is to make everyone agree on one topic, even though we all wanted essentially the same outcome.

also learn firsthand why it is important for scientists to be able to communicate with a variety of audiences, from other people in the science community, to the lay public, as they try to explain to the press the rationale behind their decision.

Standards. Self-regulation is an integral part of self-directed learning, and becoming attentive to the standards of good reasoning is an integral part of becoming a self-regulating thinker. Paul (1992) provided a list of standards for good reasoning, including being clear, specific, relevant, logical, precise, accurate, consistent, and complete. With a list like Paul's as a point of reference, teachers could select a couple to emphasize with gifted students as they assess their own work. For example, teachers could raise the issue of standards with their students as they begin their experiments in Brent Spar. Particularly important to scientific research are standards of precision and accuracy. Assessments of the experiment could be designed to make the standards of clarity and precision a priority. As students become increasingly self-directed, they should be expected to adopt not only skills, but standards, as well.

Dispositions. Stakeholder positions, or the roles students take during the problem, can provide more than career exposure. Experts often emulate the behaviors of a mentor before they create on their own (Storr, 1989). For this reason, mentorships are an often mentioned recommendation for gifted students (Clark, 1996; Gallagher & Gallagher, 1994; Maker, 1982; Renzulli, 1977).

While it may be impossible to provide all students with mentorship opportunities, teachers can help students understand different professions by judiciously selecting stakeholder positions. Immersion in the stakeholder point of view can be used to full benefit by requiring some reflection specifically about their role. As scientists sent to investigate the Brent Spar, students should be encouraged to think like scientists and have firsthand experience with the difficulties of conducting science in a politically heated arena. Tutors maximize the apprenticeship by asking students to reflect about the scientist's dispositions: "As a member of the science team investigating Brent Spar, what are your priorities?" "Why is careful data recording so important?" "What are you learning about the way scientists work?" Other questions could engage students in dialogue about the role of people who are involved in both science and community life: "What happens when business or government interferes in the course of science?" "If you are a scientist who works for the government or business, where is your first obligation: to the company or to the data?" Questions like these maximize the nature of the mini-apprenticeship created in the PBL classroom.

Metacognition. From the very beginning, students should be encouraged to reflect on their own problem-solving practices. Metacognition is important for all students. That is, all students need to learn how to self-assess their success in selecting priorities, implementing good problem-solving strategies, and using positive individual and cooperative work habits. As a part of the goal to promote self-directed learning, gifted students could be asked, either during discussion or in Problem Log activities, to reflect on their own attitudes toward problem solving and on key dispositions by asking them questions such as "How do your own personal biases affect your problem solving?," "Is it ever possible that the least supported idea is the right idea?," "What happens when we close off our options too early or too late?," "What does it mean to have intellectual courage?," and "Why would that be important while solving a problem?"

Modification 5: Discussing Ethical Appeals

Complex, real-world problems often involve ethical dilemmas, and all students need to explore some dimensions of this side of any problem. Gifted students are unusually attuned to ethical issues and can benefit from discussions involving right, wrong, and best options. However, gifted students also appreciate complexity and realize that ethical discussions presenting one perspective as right are often too simplistic. Rather than point to one preferable perspective, an effective way to discuss ethics with gifted students is to look at the different ethical appeals evoked in the problem. Brody (1988) defined six ethical appeals: to rights, to consequences, to justice, to virtues, to benefit/cost, and to personhood. Each presents a different paradigm from which to view the problem. By looking at the problem through these different vantage points, students learn how problems become more complicated when different parties are using a different basis for their actions. In the problem of the Brent Spar, students/scientists would first see that the ethical appeal of their own perspective is an appeal to consequences: "What will happen if the oil platform isn't removed?" In order to develop a reasonable solution, they might also have to see that others involved with the problem use different ethical appeals. Environmentalists might be more interested in personhood—in this case, the right of the individual to live in a clean, safe environment—and the owner of Shell Oil might be concerned about the benefit/cost of the spill.

Putting the Pieces Together

As mentioned above, changes in any one of the five recommended areas make the PBL environment more appropriate for gifted students. The degree of adaptation depends on the usual variables: teacher comfort and skill, student age and ability level, type of classroom adaptation, and everyone's familiarity with the PBL environment. Some teachers, working in heterogeneous groups, may only be able to adapt Problem Log activities for their gifted students, focusing on different kinds of self-reflection for different ability groups. Teachers in pull-out or self-contained settings may want to try more ambitious adaptations. A summary of all of the adaptations described above is presented in Table 2.

Where and When to Use PBL

Complexity, especially the kind found in PBL curricula, can be fun; but, it's not always easy. Because it is built to be multifaceted and complex, PBL requires a certain amount of time and continuity. Teachers of gifted students, on the other hand, work in a number of different program configurations. Resource teachers can use PBL effectively, but it takes a little more organization and effort. The following section provides a brief set of guidelines to use when considering PBL for your classroom.

Table 2

Summary of Adaptations of PBL Problems for Gifted Students

Area of Adaptation	Baseline Goals for Regular-Ability Students	Additional Goals for Gifted Students
Content	• Roles governing ocean territories • Monetary conversions (pound to dollar) • Three alternative strategies to discard the Brent Spar • The impact of pipeline technologies • The impact of oil on the surrounding ocean ecosystem • Water flow rates	• Chemical composition of metals and oils • Radio nuclides • Differences between intensity and duration effects • Physics of fast and slow release options
Concept	• Most things change • Change causes change	• Adaptation and transformation are two different kinds of change and have different effects. • Change is irreversible because of its interaction with time.
Interdisciplinary	• Interaction of science (methods of sinking the barge; environmental impact) and social science (economics of each disposal option; business interest in benefit/cost)	• More complex interactions of social science (global regulation versus local regulation of water/local decision making impacts global arena) and economics (monetary versus human and/or animal costs) • Long-term effect of dependence on oil
Critical Thinking and Habits of Mind	• Experimentation, selection of problem solving strategies, and progress through the problem, including collaborative group work	• Additional reflection about the nature of problem solving, about the biases and assumptions of people with different points of view

Continuous-Instruction-Classroom (Regular Classroom, Self-Contained Gifted Classroom, Daily Pull-Out Program)

PBL can be used in any setting when students and teachers are together daily. While the regular classroom and self-contained classrooms offer different kinds of challenges to teachers, they are no different from the challenges presented by any curriculum. In the regular classroom, all students of varying abilities need to be stimulated. Making judicious use of the Learning Issues Board helps to differentiate, as the coach can help students find problems they will find appropriately challenging. In the self-contained classroom or daily pull-out program, the challenge is in the design of the problem, since the whole problem should be made more advanced along the dimensions described above.

Resource Consultation

Another ideal configuration for PBL is resource consultation. Building on the collaborative relationship between the regular classroom teacher and the resource teacher, the two adults can build the program together and then share responsibility for differentiating instruction. While in the classroom, the resource teacher could either work with the gifted students on a specific aspect of the problem or assist the regular classroom teacher with coaching strategies. The resource teacher could also help the regular classroom teacher develop assignments and activities to keep the high-ability students engaged with the problem between visits.

Pull-Out Program, Occasional

The PBL model has been adapted successfully for pull-out programs where students meet less frequently, but modifications must be made. The nature of the problem must be adapted along at least two dimensions. First, the story must be a little more episodic. Especially important is the use of "kickers" or "twists" to keep the story alive for students from week to week. Research tasks assigned for the periods between meetings can help provide a link from one session to the next. Second, the problem must be somewhat less complex, since a huge, multi-faceted problem would take the majority of the school year when students only meet once a week. Teachers who only see their students for an hour once a week may not be able to use PBL, but those with half-day blocks once a week will probably be successful if they think ahead about keeping the problem lively.

These guidelines are not meant to seem prescriptive, restrictive, exclusive, or exhaustive, but rather to serve as a helpful blueprint as teachers experiment with PBL. Most of all, they are designed to answer the question, "Isn't this for *all* kids?" Yes, PBL is for all students, but adaptations help maximize its usefulness for different groups of students. It is true that all students should learn important concepts, but concepts differ in levels of abstraction and complexity. Gifted students are likely to need more complex applications of concepts to be appropriately challenged. All students need to understand relationships among disciplines, but they interact with each other in different ways. All students should be taught to self-assess their ability to analyze information, but gifted students will be ready earlier to think about their capacity to show intellectual honesty or integrity in their reasoning. With careful adaptation, teachers of the gifted can successfully use PBL to open the doorway to rich, challenging, and exciting learning experiences for gifted children.

Teacher Statement

Although I've had many experiences using problem-based learning, my first one is special to me. At the time I learned about PBL, I was teaching in a multiage (grades 4–6) Montessori classroom. As one of two teachers in the room, I had the opportunity to take a small group of gifted students to try out a PBL unit. The group, all girls, had a strong interest in environmental issues and science, a perfect combination for the ill-structured problem I had designed around their science curriculum. PBL can be either real or simulated; this problem was real and centered on a nonprofit botanical forest overpopulated with deer. The deer were enjoying all the vegetation they could get, so the board decided to put up a fence to keep the hungry animals out. Of course, the girls knew nothing of this when one day they received a "fax" informing them that, as members of the board's Subcommittee on Fencing Recommendations (their stakeholder role), they had to present their fence design to the board in 2 weeks.

The girls wasted no time. With fax in hand, they immediately began to re-read the details, take notes, and talk about the assignment. A key element of an ill-structured problem is that information presented is just vague enough to encourage students to ask natural questions: "What kind of fence?" "How high will it need to be?" "Will it keep other wildlife out, too?"

As the students contacted deer experts at zoos, salesmen at fence companies, and relearned (this time with a purpose) mathematical concepts like perimeter and costs per foot, they received a rather heated fax from the "Deer Lovers of America" insisting the fence would prevent these beloved creatures from enjoying their own natural habitat. The reaction to this PBL "kicker" was not at all what I expected. Despite their love of animals, the students had been assigned an important job: to design a fence that would protect the plants and trees of this forest. They had no intention of hurting any of the wildlife, nor were they going to cave into the pressures of an animal-lovers group. As one of the girls said, "There's plenty for them to eat *outside* the fence." Indeed, a trip to the forest (a true field trip) proved just that. The area owned by the nonprofit contained 200-year-old beech trees and other fragile vegetation that needed protection to survive. Plenty of forest remained for the deer to inhabit outside the property lines.

However, the kicker helped the girls recognize one new concern: the risk of injury to the deer should they try to jump the fence. Through careful research, the students became real experts in the abilities and tendencies of these animals. They also learned that no fence company had the perfect fence, so they designed their own. More importantly, they learned to be problem solvers in a world where sometimes problems have no predetermined right answer.

We all learned a lot with this unit. The girls learned content and worked with meaningful thinking skills. They learned how to act professionally outside of the classroom. They even learned how to present at a conference; their enthusiasm was so infectious I took them to the state gifted education conference to share their excitement about their PBL experience. For my part, I learned that even a novice PBL teacher can have a huge success. Every extra minute I spent in preparation was returned in extra enthusiasm and investment by my students.

—Christine H. Weiss

Discussion Questions

1. Inquiry-based approaches such as problem-based learning have consistently demonstrated that students learn the same amount of content, if not more, than when they are taught through more traditional approaches. Even so, many teachers balk at the idea of using these highly effective strategies for fear that students will not perform as well on standardized tests. What do you think it would take to convince teachers that the data regarding inquiry and content acquisition is true and reliable?

2. Why is it important to think of problem-based learning as a curriculum *and* instruction model, rather than simply a new way to write curricula?

3. Teachers who are most successful trying PBL for the first time have generally put some effort into planning and support. What kind of advanced planning do you think you would need to do to before teaching a PBL unit? What kind(s) of support would you need and from whom?

4. Which of the following words do you think best describes problem-based learning: *model, framework,* or *strategy*? Why?

5. The chapter presents five ways of adapting PBL to make it more appropriate for gifted students: ensuring advanced content, complexity of the concept, interdisciplinary connections and interactions, higher order thinking skills, and discussing ethical appeals. Which of these do you think would be the best place to start making modifications?

6. Problem-based learning is an important part of any teacher's repertoire. However, debate continues over how frequently PBL should be used. Some medical school programs use PBL exclusively. Most K–12 teachers find this comprehensive approach extreme and unfeasible. Ideally, how many times a year do you think a teacher should use PBL?

7. What are the similarities and differences between problem-based learning and other approaches to problem solving (i.e., Parnes' creative problem solving)?

8. Given that PBL is only one of a number of ways to differentiate curricula and instruction for gifted students, think about which strategies would complement PBL in a well-rounded program for gifted students. How are the models you choose to go alongside PBL in your hypothetical program model complementary to PBL?

Teacher Resources

Publications

Barrows, H. (1985). *How to design a problem-based curriculum for preclinical years.* New York: Springer.

Barrows, H. (1988). *The tutorial process.* Springfield: Southern Illinois University School of Medicine.

Barrows, H. (1994). *Practice-based learning.* Springfield: Southern Illinois University School of Medicine.

Benoit, B., McClure, T., & Kuinzle, R. (1997). Problem-based learning: Meeting real-world challenges. In J. H. Clarke & R. M. Agne (Eds.), *Interdisciplinary high school teaching: Strategies for integrated learning* (pp. 208–235). Boston: Allyn and Bacon.

Boyce, L. N., VanTassel-Baska, J., Burruss, J. E., Sher, B. T., & Johnson, D. T. (1997). A problem-based curriculum: Parallel learning opportunities for students and teachers. *Journal for the Education of the Gifted, 20,* 363–379.

College of William and Mary Center for Gifted Education. (1997a). *Acid, acid everywhere.* Dubuque, IA: Kendall/Hunt.

College of William and Mary Center for Gifted Education. (1997b). *Dust bowl.* Dubuque, IA: Kendall/Hunt.

College of William and Mary Center for Gifted Education. (1997c). *What a find.* Dubuque, IA: Kendall/Hunt.

College of William and Mary Center for Gifted Education. (1997d). *Electricity city.* Dubuque, IA: Kendall/Hunt.

College of William and Mary Center for Gifted Education. (1997e). *The Chesapeake Bay.* Dubuque, IA: Kendall/Hunt.

College of William and Mary Center for Gifted Education. (1997f). *No quick fix.* Dubuque, IA: Kendall/Hunt.

College of William and Mary Center for Gifted Education. (1997g). *Hot rods.* Dubuque, IA: Kendall/Hunt.

Cuozzo, C. C. (1996/7). What do lepidopterists do? *Educational Leadership, 53,* 34–37.

Delisle, R. (1997). *How to use problem-based learning in the classroom.* Reston, VA: Association for Supervision and Curriculum Development.

Dods, R. F. (1997). An action research study of the effectiveness of problem-based learning in promoting the acquisition and retention of knowledge. *Journal for the Education of the Gifted, 20,* 423–437.

Gallagher, S. A. (1997). Problem-based learning: What did it come from, what does it do, and where is it going? *Journal for the Education of the Gifted, 20,* 332–362.

Gallagher, S. A. (2000). Project P-BLISS: An experiment in curriculum for gifted disadvantaged high school students. *NAASP Bulletin, 84*(615), 47–57.

Gallagher, S. A., Romanoff, B., Crossett, B., & Stepien, W. J. (1998a). *Gateways*. Charlotte: University of North Carolina.

Gallagher, S. A., Romanoff, B., Crossett, B., & Stepien, W. J. (1998b). *Kids at work*. Charlotte: University of North Carolina.

Gallagher, S. A., Romanoff, B., & Stepien, W. J. (1998). *A just prosecution: The adjudication of violent juveniles*. Charlotte: University of North Carolina.

Gallagher, S. A., Sher, B. T., Stepien, W. J., & Workman, D. (1995). Implementing problem-based learning in the science classroom. *School Science and Mathematics, 95*, 136–146.

Gallagher, S. A., Stepien, W. J., & Romanoff, B. (1998). *Impasse*. Charlotte: University of North Carolina.

Gallagher, S. A., Stepien, W. J., & Rosenthal, H. (1994). The effects of problem-based learning on problem solving. *Gifted Child Quarterly, 36*, 195–200.

Hmelo, C. E., & Ferrari, M. (1997). The problem-based learning tutorial: Cultivating higher order thinking skills. *Journal for the Education of the Gifted, 20*, 401–422.

Kain, D. (2003). *Problem-based learning for teachers, grades K–8*. Boston: Allyn and Bacon.

Kain, D. (2003). *Problem-based learning for teachers, grades 6–12*. Boston: Allyn and Bacon.

Ronis, D. L. (2000). *Problem-based learning for math and science*. Arlington Heights, IL: Skylight.

Stepien, W. (2002). *Problem-based learning with the internet: Grades 3–6*. Tucson, AZ: Zephyr Press.

Stepien, W. J. (1997). *Problem-based learning across the curriculum* [Cassette Recording]. Reston, VA: Association for Supervision and Curriculum Development

Stepien, W. J., & Pyke, S. L. (1997). Designing problem-based learning units. *Journal for the Education of the Gifted, 20*, 380–400.

Stepien, W. J., & Gallagher, S. A. (1993). Problem-based learning: As authentic as it gets. *Educational Leadership, 50*(7), 25–29.

Stepien, W. J., & Gallagher, S. A. (1997). *Problem-based learning across the curriculum*. Reston, VA: Association for Supervision and Curriculum Development.

Stepien, W. C., Gallagher, S. A., Romanoff, B., & Stepien, W. J. (1998). *To farm or not to farm*. Charlotte: University of North Carolina.

Stepien, W. J., Gallagher, S. A., & Workman, D. (1993). Problem-based learning for traditional and interdisciplinary classrooms. *Journal for the Education of the Gifted, 16*, 338–357.

Stepien, W. J., Senn, P., & Stepien, W. C. (2001). *The Internet and problem-based learning: Developing solutions through the web*. Tucson, AZ: Zephyr Press.

Torp, L., & Sage, S. (2002). *Problems as possibilities: Problem-based learning in K–12 classrooms* (2nd ed.). Reston, VA: Association for Supervision and Curriculum Development.

Films

Johnson, T. (Producer), & Murphy, M. (Regional Director). (1998a). *Problem-based learning: Using problems to learn* [Film]. (Available from Association for Supervision and Curriculum Development, 1703 N. Beauregard St., Alexandria, VA 22311–1714)

Johnson, T. (Producer), & Murphy, M. (Regional Director). (1998b). *Problem-based learning: Designing problems for learning* [Film]. (Available from Association for Supervision and Curriculum Development, 1703 N. Beauregard St., Alexandria, VA 22311–1714.)

Web Sites

Association for Supervision and Curriculum Development Education Topics: Problem-Based Learning—http://www.ascd.org/cms/index.cfm?TheViewID=1766
ASCD provides resources in the form of both publications and online answers to basic questions about PBL. See the Illinois Mathematics and Science Academy Web site for information regarding ASCD's PBL Net.

Exploring the Environment: Problem-Based Learning—http://www.cotf.edu/ete/teacher/teacherout.html
Part of NASA's Classroom of the Future initiative, this site gives a nice overview of the theory and structure of PBL along with several model science units.

The Illinois Mathematics and Science Academy (IMSA) PBL Net—http://www2.imsa.edu/programs/pbl/pbln/index.html
The IMSA hosts a number of resources for teachers through the IMSA Center for Problem-Based Learning. Included on their Web site are descriptions of the PBL process, sample problems, and, perhaps most importantly, access to ASCD's PBL Net, a network, newsletter, and listserv for teachers and other professionals involved with PBL.

Problem-Based Learning Initiative—http://www.pbli.org
Generally recognized as the modern father of PBL, Howard Barrows works at the Medical School at Southern Illinois University. Anyone who is interested in PBL should be familiar with Dr. Barrow's work and philosophy of PBL. This site describes the work of Barrows and his colleagues at SIU and in K–12 classrooms.

SCORE: Problem-Based Learning—http://score.rims.k12.ca.us/problearn.html
SCORE (Schools of California Online Resources for Education) has been a source of a number of innovations in California's educational system. This Web site includes several examples of PBL units.

Project P-BLISS: Problem-Based Learning in the Social Sciences—http://www.uncc.edu/sagallag/pbliss
This project, sponsored by the Jacob K. Javits Gifted and Talented Program, is underway at the University of North Carolina at Charlotte to develop PBL science units, social studies units, or both for use with gifted disadvantaged students. The project Web site describes the program model and the use of PBL to identify gifted disadvantaged students, and it includes sample activities.

University of Delaware Problem-Based Learning—http://www.udel.edu/pbl
This Web site is for people interested in the application of PBL in higher education (or for people looking for problems to use with advanced high school students). The University of Delaware presents an example of an undergraduate institution that is proactive in its support of the transformation from traditional to PBL-structured classrooms. The Web site offers an impressive list of classes offered using the PBL model.

College of William and Mary Center for Gifted Education—http://cfge.wm.edu
The College of William and Mary Center for Gifted Education has the only project to date that has resulted in nationally published PBL units. Information about these science units can be found at the Center for Gifted Education web page.

References

Barrows, H. (1985). *How to design a problem-based learning curriculum in the preclinical years.* New York: Springer-Verlag.

Berliner, D. (1986). Catastrophes and interactions: Comments on the mistaken metaphor. In C. J. Maker (Ed.), *Critical issues in gifted education: Defensible programs for the gifted* (pp. 31–38). Rockville, MD: Aspen.

Boud, D., & Feletti, G. (1991). *The challenge of problem-based learning.* New York: St. Martin's Press.

Bransford, J. D., & Vye, N. J. (1989). A perspective on cognitive research and its implications for instruction. In L. B. Resnick & L. E. Klopfer (Eds.), *Toward the thinking curriculum* (pp. 173–205). Reston, VA: Association for Supervision and Curriculum Development.

Brody, B. A. (1988). *Life and death decision making.* New York: Oxford University Press.

Brown, J. S., Collins, A., & Duguid, P. (1989). Situated cognition and the cultures of learning. *Educational Researcher, 18*(1), 32–45.

Bruer, J. T. (1993, Summer). The mind's journey from novice to expert. *American Education,* 6–46.

Callahan, C. M. (1996). A critical self-study of gifted education: Healthy practice, necessary evil, or sedition? *Journal for the Education of the Gifted, 19,* 148–163.

Carr, M., & Borkowski, J. (1986). Metamemory in gifted children. *Gifted Child Quarterly, 31,* 40–44.

Carter, M. (1988). Problem solving reconsidered: A pluralistic theory of problems. *College English, 50,* 551–565.

Chase, W. G., & Simon, H. A. (1973). Perception in chess. *Cognitive Psychology, 4,* 55–81.

Clark, B. (1996). *Growing up gifted* (3rd ed.). Columbus, OH: Merrill.

DeGroot, M. (1965). *Thought and choice in chess.* The Hague, The Netherlands: Mounton.

Gallagher, J. J., & Gallagher, S. A. (1994). *Teaching the gifted child* (4th ed.). Boston: Allyn and Bacon.

Gallagher, S. A., Sher, B. T., Stepien, W. J., & Workman, D. (1995). Implementing problem-based learning in the science classroom. *School Science and Mathematics, 95,* 136–146.

Gallagher, S. A., & Stepien, W. J. (1996). Depth versus breadth in problem-based learning: Content acquisition in American studies. *Journal for the Education of the Gifted, 19,* 257–275.

Getzels, J. (1979). From art student to fine artist: Potential, problem finding, and performance. In A. Passow (Ed.), *The gifted and the talented* (pp. 372–388). Chicago: University of Chicago Press.

Goldberger, N. R. (1981). Developmental assumptions underlying models of general education. *Liberal Education, 67,* 233–243.

Judson, H. F. (1980). *The search for solutions.* Baltimore, MD: Johns Hopkins University Press.

Kaplan, S. N. (1986). The grid: A model to construct differentiated curriculum for the gifted. In J. S. Renzulli (Ed.), *Systems and models for developing programs for the gifted and talented* (pp. 180–193). Mansfield Center, CT: Creative Learning Press.

Maker, C. J. (1982). *Curriculum development for the gifted.* Rockville, MD: Aspen Systems.

Minstrell, J. (1989). Teaching science for understanding. In L. B. Resnick & L. E. Klopfer (Eds.), *Toward the thinking curriculum* (pp. 129-149). Reston, VA: Association for Supervision and Curriculum Development.

Murphy, J. M., & Gilligan, C. (1980). Moral development in late adolescence and adulthood: A critique and reconstruction of Kohlberg's theory. *Human Development, 23,* 77–104.

O'Connor, F. (1962). *Mystery and manners.* New York: The Noonday Press.

Paul, R. (1992). *Critical thinking: What every person needs to survive in a rapidly changing world.* Rohnert Park, CA: Foundation for Critical Thinking.

Rabinowitz, M., & Glaser, R. (1985). Cognitive structure and process in highly competent performance. In F. D. Horowitz & M. O'Brien (Eds.), *The gifted and talented: Developmental perspectives* (pp. 75–98). Washington, DC: American Psychological Association.

Renzulli, J. S. (1977). *The enrichment triad model: A guide to developing defensible programs for the gifted and talented.* Mansfield Center, CT: Creative Learning Press.

Rogers, K. (1986). Do the gifted think and learn differently: A review of recent research and its implications. *Journal for the Education of the Gifted, 10,* 17–40.

Ross, B. (1991). Toward a framework for problem-based curricula. In D. Boud & G. Feletti (Eds.), *The challenge of problem-based learning* (pp. 34–41). New York: St. Martin's Press.

Runco, M. A. (1986). Maximal performance on divergent thinking tests by gifted, talented, and nongifted children. *Psychology in the Schools, 23,* 308–315.

Schmidt, H. G., & Moust J. J. (1995). What makes a tutor effective? A structural-equations modeling approach to learning in problem-based curricula. *Academic Medicine, 70,* 708–714.

Shoenfeld, A. H. (1989). Teaching mathematical thinking and problem solving. In L. B. Resnick & L. E. Klopfer (Eds.), *Toward the thinking curriculum: Current cognitive research* (pp. 83–103). Reston, VA: Association for Supervision and Curriculum Development.

Spiro, R. J., Carlson, R. L., Feltovich, P. J., & Anderson, D. K. (1988). *Cognitive flexibility theory: Advanced knowledge acquisition in ill-structured domains.* Hillsdale, NJ: Erlbaum.

Stepien, W. J., & Gallagher, S. A. (1993). Problem-based learning: As authentic as it gets. *Educational Leadership, 50,* 25–29.

Stepien, W. J., & Gallagher, S. A. (1997). *Self-study kit: Problem-based learning* (Folder 4, Activity 1). Alexandria, VA: Association for Supervision and Curriculum Development.

Stepien, W. J., Gallagher, S. A., & Workman, D. (1993). Problem-based learning for traditional and interdisciplinary classrooms. *Journal for the Education of the Gifted, 16,* 338–357.

Sternberg, R. J., & Davidson, J. E. (1985). Cognitive development in the gifted and talented. In F. D. Horowitz & M. O'Brien (Eds.), *The gifted and talented: Developmental perspectives* (pp. 37–74). Washington, DC: American Psychological Association.

Storr, A. (1989). *Solitude: A return to the self.* New York: Ballantine Books.

Tuchman, R. (1966, March). Historian as artist. *New York Herald Book Week,* 14.

VanTassel-Baska, J. (1988). *Comprehensive curriculum for gifted learners.* Boston: Allyn and Bacon.

Chapter 11

Developing Creative Thinking

by **Bonnie Cramond**

hen describing the impact that others can have on an individual's creativity, former U.S. Secretary of Health, Education, and Welfare, John W. Gardner, told the following story about creativity:

> When Alexander the Great visited Diogenes and asked whether he could do anything for the famed teacher, Diogenes replied: "Only stand out of my light." Perhaps some day we shall know how to heighten creativity. Until then, one of the best things we can do for creative men and women is to stand out of their light. (*Quotations Page*, n.d.)

It's quite possible that Diogenes would have agreed that the most important thing we can do to encourage creativity is to get out of its way. The ancient Aztecs and Greeks viewed creativity as mystical, an inspiration "breathed in" from gods or muses (Rothenberg & Hausman, 1976). Many contemporary people and cultures feel the same way. Singer/songwriter and Grammy Award winner Lionel Richie described the composition process this way:

> It's like radio stations playing in my head. I'm in the shower singing along to this great song, and then I stop one moment and go, "Hey, it's not on the radio." What's fright-

ening about it is I'm not singing a song, I'm singing *along* with the song that's playing in my head. (Rader, 1993, p. 20)

He went on to say that he considered God his cowriter.

There are many other examples of this spiritual view, both ancient and modern. Elmer Bernstein, the Oscar-winning composer of movie scores, responded to the question of where he got the inspiration for his melodies this way: "Sometimes the melodies come from playing around on the piano, sometimes I awaken with one in my head, and sometimes they just come like a miracle from God" (Scott, 2003, p. 1).

A collection of essays by creators as diverse as Federico Fellini, Maurice Sendak, Isadora Duncan, Carl Jung, and Maya Angelou illuminates the range of views of the creative process (Barron, Montuori, & Barron, 1997). From opening up their hearts and minds, to use of imagination, dedication to mastery, creation within a system, and courage to create, these musicians, writers, philosophers, directors, scientists, dancers, and composers describe the creative process, or a part of the creative process, according to their individual experiences.

Another excellent collection of original writings on various views of creativity (Rothenberg & Hausman, 1976) illustrates the diversity of conceptions of the nature of creativity. There is the psychoanalytic view of creativity as described by Freud and others, which explains creative expression as a regression to a childlike way of thinking or as a way to express aggressive or sexual thoughts safely. Conversely, humanists such as Rogers or Maslow differentiate self-actualizing creativity as part of optimal mental health from special talent creativity that may accompany mental problems. Behaviorists, led by Skinner, have argued that creativity is simply a learned response to stimuli, and many cognitive psychologists, such as Weisberg, believe that creativity is a way of thinking that can be taught. Other views include the physiological view that creativity is related to brain organization or brain wave functions (Diamond, 1988; Ferguson, 1977; Restak, 1993). Piirto (1992, pp. 316–322) has compiled a helpful listing of theories of creativity divided into four groups (philosophical, psychological, psychoanalytical, and domain-specific), which indicates the number and diversity of the theories that exist. There is probably some truth to all of these views, yet each one is insufficient to explain the complexity that is creativity.

Some scholars prefer to think of creativity as a system that incorporates the person, process, product, and the environment (e.g., Feldman, Csikszentmihalyi, & Gardner, 1994; Sternberg, 1988). Such system views grant that, within each of the four dimensions listed above, there are many variables that determine the if, when, how, who, what, where, and why of creativity. For example, a person may be born with perfect pitch, a good auditory memory, and the creative capacity to write new music, but not have the opportunity for music lessons, the manual dexterity to play an instrument, or the time, money, and encouragement to

Emergenative Creativity—entirely new principles or assumptions around which new schools, movements, and the like can flourish.

Innovative Creativity—improvement through modification involving conceptualizing skills.

Inventive Creativity—ingenuity is displayed with materials, methods, and techniques.

Productive Creativity—artistic and scientific products within restrictions.

Expressive Creativity—spontaneous drawings of children.

Figure 1. Taylor's levels of creativity

Note. From "The Nature of the Creative Process," in P. Smith (Ed.), *Creativity*, (pp. 51–82), by I. A. Taylor, 1959, New York: Hasting House. Copyright ©1959 by Hasting House.

pursue a musical interest. Such a person would have some of the components necessary for the expression of musical creativity, but not others. So many variables must coincide at the same time for creativity to be expressed—inborn talent, creative motivation, opportunity, environmental supports, persistence, creativity, and so forth. It is no wonder great creative accomplishments are so rare!

On the other hand, such a person may create tunes for his children, pick out some songs on the harmonica at a party, and sing with a local group. He may think of imaginative ways to make his everyday job more interesting and his paycheck stretch. Everyday examples of creativity surround us.

Some people differentiate between big "C" creativity, that of the eminent, and little "c" creativity, such as in the examples given above. Others believe that creativity can be viewed hierarchically (Taylor, 1959). In Taylor's model, outlined in Figure 1, the expressive artwork of a child can be considered creative; however, it is not as high on the scale as a creative invention. The highest level, emergenative creativity, involves changing the structure of the field or starting a new field or movement. Freud's work in psychotherapy could be considered in such a category.

Sometimes, the only difference between the great and the everyday creatives is that someone has discovered and promoted the former. For example, Boorstin (1992) has made the case that Shakespeare owes his success to the affection of his fellow actors, as well as to his unquestionable talent.

> About three-fourths of the prolific output of playwrights in his lifetime has disappeared. But Shakespeare's fellow actors, as a token of friendship to him, did us the great service of preserving the texts of his plays when they arranged publication of the First Folio in 1623. (p. 317)

Luck plays a big part in creativity, too. However, luck and inspiration are not the only, or even the most important parts, of creativity. The hard work that is central to creativity was addressed when Louis Pasteur said, "Chance favors the prepared mind."

Not surprisingly, then, there is some confusion in schools about the concept of creativity. One source of confusion arises from the assumption that creativity is limited to artistic expression and doesn't include problem solving. In recognition of this bifurcated conceptualization, I have divided creativity into two types for definition purposes: expressive and adaptive (Cramond, 2002). Expressive creativity is the type that is used to communicate the creator's emotional and aesthetic senses. It is creative if it is judged to be original and valuable. On the other hand, adaptive creativity is the type that addresses a worthwhile problem and results in a novel and appropriate solution. Torrance (1988) has said, "when a person has no learned or practiced solution to a problem, some degree of creativity is required" (p. 57). This is the type that is used to make scientific discoveries, solve social problems, and keep restless children entertained on a rainy day. In fact, there are indications that the personalities of creative artists and scientists differ in many ways (cf. Piirto, 1992).

However, the creative process may not be as dichotomous as defined here. There is certainly the aesthetic experience in the realization of an elegant solution to a problem, and there are many problems to be solved in the completion of any artistic work. Sometimes, a product is a combination of both types, as when an architect creates a new building that is aesthetically pleasing (expressive), but also fits well into the environment (adaptive). Freeman Dyson, indicating the degree to which the scientists, artists, and philosophers at the 16th Nobel Conference, held in 1980, agreed on the universality of creativity, said,

> [T]he analogies between science and art are very good as long as you are talking about the creation and the performance. The creation is certainly very analogous. The aesthetic pleasure of the craftsmanship of performance is also very strong in science. (cited in Root-Bernstein & Root-Bernstein, 1999, p. 11)

Another source of confusion arises from the use of the words *talented* or *gifted* along with *creative*. In some uses, *talent* refers to a point on the continuum of ability that is less than giftedness, for example, when one believes there are many talented musicians, but few truly gifted ones (Cox, Daniel, & Boston, 1985, p. 122). At other times, *giftedness* is used to refer to general intellectual ability and *talent* to specific ability. For example, a person who is very intelligent overall may be called gifted, while a person who has a specific aptitude in mathematics is called a talented mathematician (Feldhusen, 1986; MacKinnon, 1978).

Still another view is Gagné's (1985), which conceptualized giftedness as ability and talent as performance. This is similar to Bloom's (1985) definition of talent as a high level of *demonstrated* ability, rather than *aptitude* in a certain field of study or interest. It seems that, in order for someone to demonstrate giftedness at the highest levels in any field, there is a need for the confluence of creativity, talent (or skill in a particular domain), and motivation.

Who is Creative?

There has been a great deal of interest over the years in describing the creative personality. Much of our information in this regard comes from retrospective research that has examined the lives of eminent creative people such as Wolfgang Amadeus Mozart, Sigmund Freud, Charles Darwin, Albert Einstein, and others. Another line of research has compared the personality characteristics of creative people in a specific field, such as architecture, with less creative people in the same field (MacKinnon, 1976). A third line of research has examined the personality characteristics of individuals who score high on a measure of creativity or produce something judged to be creative. From such research studies we have amassed a compendium of creative characteristics (see Figure 2).

Because so many of the behaviors that have been listed as indicative of creative individuals may also be used in identifying learning and behavior problems, teachers should be wary of attributing a negative cause to a child's "differentness." For example, an examination of the similarity in the behaviors attributed to both highly creative individuals and those diagnosed with Attention-Deficit Hyperactivity Disorder (ADHD) indicates the possibility of an overlap in the conditions (Cramond, 1994, 1995). Both individuals who are creative and those who have been diagnosed with ADHD may manifest similar characteristics, such as daydreaming, high energy, impulsiveness, risk taking, preoccupation, difficult temperament, and poor social skills. In addition, there is evidence from both groups of mixed laterality and anomalies in cerebral dominance, more spontaneous ideation, higher levels of sensation seeking behavior, and higher energy or activity than in normal populations.

The best way to think of creativity may be analogous to our modern conceptions of intelligence. Psychologists generally agree that intelligence can be expressed in many ways, is affected by genetics and environment, may be nurtured or hindered by experiences, is at least partly defined by the culture, and is measured inexactly by any test. Substitute the word *creativity* for *intelligence* and it would be largely the same. Both creativity and intelligence are multidimensional constructs that all humans demonstrate to some degree. Although people readily admit they have no creativity, they rarely would claim to have no intelligence. It is our job as teachers to help students find and enhance their abilities in both areas.

The single best way to nurture creativity in anyone may be to recognize and value it. In his 22-year follow-up of individuals first tested in elementary school, Torrance (1981) found that the "teachers who made a difference" were those who enabled their students to hold on to their creativity. These teachers were not always the most creative individuals themselves, but they recognized that spark in

Cognitive	Personality
• relatively high intelligence	• willingness to confront hostility and take intellectual risks
• originality	
• articulateness and verbal fluency	• perseverance
• good imagination	• curiosity
• metaphorical thinking	• openness to new experience
• flexibility	• driving absorption
• independence of judgment	• discipline and commitment to one's work
• ability to cope well with novelty	
• logical thinking skills	• high intrinsic motivation
• internal visualization	• tolerance for ambiguity
• ability to escape perceptual sets	• a broad range of interests
• ability to find order in chaos	• tendency to play with ideas
• questioning	• unconventionality in behavior
• alert to novelty and gaps in knowledge	• tendency to experience deep emotions
• ability to use existing knowledge as a base for new ideas	• intuitiveness
	• seeking interesting situations
• aesthetic ability that allows recognition of good problems in the field	• opportunism
	• conflict between self-criticism and self-confidence

Figure 2. Characteristics of creative individuals

Note. From "What Do We Know About Creativity," by T. Z. Tardiff & R. J. Sternberg, in R. J. Sternberg (Ed.), *The Nature of Creativity: Contemporary Psychological Perspectives* (pp. 434–435), 1988, Buffalo, NY: Creative Education Foundation. Copyright ©1988 by Creative Education Foundation, 1050 Union Rd., Buffalo, NY 14224. Reprinted with permission.

their students and encouraged it. As parents, teachers, colleagues, and friends (even to ourselves), we can refrain from joining the "murder committees" who try to kill every new idea with negativism and instead maintain an open mind for new possibilities. There are other more active ways to nurture creativity.

Enhancing Creativity Through the Environment

Psychological Safety

One way to enhance creativity is to maintain an environment conducive to it. Rogers (1954) pointed out that creativity is more likely to be expressed in a situation where there is *psychological safety*. Because coming up with an original idea requires taking a risk—that you'll be wrong, make a fool of yourself, be rejected—the less severe the consequences, the more likely the risk will be assumed. In other words, a classroom where ideas are valued as highly as answers and mistakes are viewed as learning opportunities is more encouraging of innovation than one where humiliation and punishment are frequently used.

Rewards

There is some debate about the role of rewards in the fostering of creativity. Amabile (1983) found that *any* evaluation of performance, even positive evaluation, can diminish creativity because the expectation of a possible positive evaluation also carries with it the possibility of a negative one next time. In some cases, the more positive the first evaluation, the harder it is to live up to it on subsequent tries. Thus, we have the writer who's blocked after one bestseller or the artist who releases one hit recording and is never heard from again. Also, the reward can have a role in shaping the behavior. A person who is seeking a reward may opt to do that which is perceived to be most likely to be rewarded again, rather than that which is truly creative. So, we have the artists who "sell out" to commercialism and the writers who continue to write books according to a hackneyed formula.

But, the relationship between reward and creativity is not so simple. There are individuals who are rewarded for their work and continue to produce creatively. In fact, some of them may not be so moved to be prolific without the financial incentive. Amabile (1983) conceded that the expectation of reward and other factors, such as self-esteem and the degree of intrinsic motivation, affect how the reward state is perceived. Other researchers have concluded that rewards do not dampen intrinsic motivation (Cameron & Pierce, 1994). For teachers, the key seems to be helping students find what they love and encouraging them to do it well. Students with strong self-esteem and strong intrinsic motivation are resistant to the possible deleterious effects of rewards (Amabile).

Balancing Stimulation and Reflection

Another environmental factor that can affect creativity is the amount and timing of stimulation. Although most parents and teachers know about the positive effects on brain development that are attributed to a stimulating environment, many are not aware that individuals also need quiet time to reflect and fantasize. Elkind (1989) warned against the stress that results when children are overscheduled. In the 1960s, Taba (1962) explained that a good lesson has proper pacing, alternating active lessons and quiet lessons. More directly related to this discussion, Torrance (1981; Torrance & Safter, 1990) advised that stimulation be alternated with times for quiet reflection. Without both, individuals lack the impetus for creative ideas or the time to develop them.

Wallas (1976) described the creative process as occurring in four parts: preparation, incubation, illumination, and verification. During preparation, materials and information are gathered. This phase may include the stimulation that could inspire a creative response. During incubation, the individual is not visibly working on the problem, but may be fooling around with the materials. When illumination occurs, there is an idea, a solution to a problem, or a sentiment to express. Finally, during verification, the idea is carried out, the solution is applied, or the art is completed. Two of these, preparation and verification, are outwardly active periods. The other two, incubation and illumination, are introspective. These may coincide roughly with the need for stimulation and peace, although the four stages do not occur so linearly as presented. They may occur out of order, be repeated, or vary in length and intensity.

Flow

A leading creativity theorist, Csikszentmihalyi (1990; Csikszentmihalyi & Csikszentmihalyi, 1988), has studied the emotional and motivational aspects of creativity. After interviewing more than 300 people involved in creative activities, he concluded that they described their experiences during the creative process with the same phenomenological characteristics. Because several talked about being swept along or other such terms, he called the experience *flow*. There are eight key conditions, all or many of which are necessary for flow to occur.

1. The challenges of the activity are well-matched to the individual's skills. If the activity is too easy, the individual is bored. If it is too difficult, anxiety is the result.
2. There are clear goals and clear feedback.
3. There is a merging of action and awareness; the individual often reports feeling like a conduit of the work.
4. Still, the individual feels a sense of control. There is motivation to continue, but a feeling that one can stop at will.
5. The individual is concentrating only on the relevant stimuli and giving the task full attention.
6. There is an absence of self-awareness because of the focused attention on the task that sometimes, at its most challenging levels, becomes a transcendence of self.
7. Because of a change in consciousness, there is a distorted sense of time. One can work for hours without realizing how much time has gone by or feel that an eon has passed in just a few seconds.
8. The process is an exhilarating experience that creates intrinsic motivation to engage in the same sort of activity again. However, the activity and the skills must continue to become more complex in order to engage the individual fully. Thus, flow may be seen as a dynamic force in evolution.

Most teachers can readily see that it is difficult, if not impossible, to create such conditions in the regular school classroom. For example, the first condition, matching the task to the student's ability, is quite challenging with a heterogeneously grouped class. However, we can create flow experiences with which children can continue to work outside of school. These would include activities that come from the students' interests, have some degree of self-selection, and are extended over time, but have continual feedback.

Summary

In summary, an environment that is conducive to creativity is one that is psychologically safe, where the intrinsic rewards of accomplishment are emphasized over extrinsic rewards and controls, where students have opportunities to learn about their interests and pursue them with some autonomy, where there is a balance of stimulation and quiet time, and where challenges are matched to the abilities of the learners. Such an environment can be created for students at least some of the time, and they can learn to create such environments for themselves.

Space does not permit more detail about how to provide such an environment. Interested individuals could look at some curricular models that would assist in providing a good environment for creativity, such as the Schoolwide Enrichment Model (Renzulli & Reis, 1985), the Autonomous Learner Model (Betts, 1986), or the Incubation Model (Torrance & Safter, 1990), which will be described later because of its emphasis on creativity development.

Strategies for Promoting Creativity in the Classroom

Although providing the proper environment is crucial for nurturing creativity, there are more active ways to promote creativity in the classroom. Through the use of specific creativity strategies, teachers can help students develop thinking skills and attitudes that are conducive to the creative process. It is important to note that such skills and attitudes should be infused throughout the curriculum, rather than taught separately. Just as with critical thinking activities, creative thinking activities should be ingrained in all subjects if students are to see their worth and apply them when suitable.

Warm-Up

Before any activity is undertaken, individuals should first participate in a warm-up activity. Just as it is important to warm up your muscles before any vigorous exercise, so too is it important to warm up our brains, especially for creative thinking. You could use just about any creative activity as a warm-up. It's a good idea to use multimodal approaches—verbal, visual, musical, and physical activities can all be effective.

One example of a good warm-up activity is to have groups of four students sitting at a table with a fountain pen cartridge that has a small pin prick in one end, four sheets of art paper, and four pencils. Students should be instructed to number each edge of one side of the paper 1–4. The students should then be instructed to squeeze a drop of ink in the center of the paper, fold the paper in half, and smooth it to create an ink blot. With edge #1 facing them, give students 30 seconds to list all of the things the shape could be. At the end of 30 seconds, have each student pass his or her sheet to the next student on the right, who will turn it to edge #2. Students again have 30 seconds to imagine what the ink blot could be from this angle. Repeat until all four edges have been titled. Then, have students show the pictures and share some of the titles.

A good, active, kinesthetic movement warm-up is one based upon complex contraptions. Explain that such a machine is like the one in the popular game *Mousetrap*, or show pictures of Rube Goldberg's (1968) inventions. Students are asked to volunteer to get in front of the group and make a repeated machine-like movement. Then, other students can come up one by one and add a motion to the machine. When all volunteers are up and moving, remaining students are asked to brainstorm what the machine is and how the various movements work together. For example, students may decide that it is a baby-washing machine with a washer, dryer, powderer, and diaperer.

Humor is always a good warm-up. A simple use of humor is to share appropriate jokes or cartoons with the class. Another idea is to have students propose captions for cartoons chosen from children's magazines (Ziv, 1983).

The ideas for warm-ups are almost limitless. The main criteria for a good warm-up activity are that it is enjoyable, engages the students, gets them to think creatively, and promotes a relaxed atmosphere.

Ideation

There are several ideation strategies that can be used to warm up or restart creative thinking when things get bogged down. Perhaps the best known of these is brainstorming.

The principles of brainstorming are simple: (1) There must be deferred judgment, and (2) quantity breeds quality. That is, while producing ideas, we must resist the urge to criticize our own ideas, as well as those of others. The goal is to produce as many ideas as possible so that at least one good creative idea will be generated. Sometimes, even one person's silly idea will spark a creative idea in another. In accordance with these principles are the following four rules of brainstorming:

1. Criticism is ruled out. All evaluative comments, both positive and negative, must be withheld during the brainstorming process.
2. Free wheeling is welcomed. Individuals are encouraged to use free association to elicit as many different ideas as possible.

3. Quantity is wanted. All ideas are recorded.
4. Combination and improvement are sought. Individuals are encouraged to hitchhike or piggyback—embellish, adapt, or connect the ideas of others to create new ideas.

Starters for brainstorming can be as simple as "Name all the things that you can think of that are green" or as thought-provoking as "Just suppose teachers did have eyes in the backs of their heads. What are some things that might happen?" Some other brainstorming starters include: "Name all the words you can think of that begin with a B." "What are some ways that we could make zoos better for animals?" "Name some things you can make with an old shoe box." There are many ways to start this process that are appropriate for the age and sophistication of the group.

One simple technique for encouraging ideation is called SCAMPER (Eberle, 1996). The letters of the word stand for the different methods for considering things in order to think of new ideas. For example, take the question, "What are some ways that we could make zoos better for animals?" We might use the SCAMPER method to brainstorm:

Substitute (put the people in enclosures and let the animals run free);
Combine (have the birds from the aviary in the same place with the monkeys);
Adapt (use climate control domes and vegetation to simulate their natural environment);
Magnify or minify (make zoos larger with more space; breed smaller versions of animals so that the space seems larger);
Put to other uses (give the animals activities to occupy them);
Eliminate (remove as many unnatural sensations as possible—sights, sounds, smells, foods, textures, and so forth; and
Reverse or rearrange (group animals and vegetation together as in the wild and let them hunt or forage for their own food).

Many of these ideas have been incorporated in some form or another in modern zoos. Other ideas may be unfeasible. The point at this juncture is just to generate as many, and as varied, ideas as possible. Ideally, many ideas could be listed under each category and sorted out in a subsequent step. The same process could be applied to a social studies topic such as, "What are some ways that we could make the election process better?"

Metaphorical or Analogical Thinking

Other creative strategies use metaphorical or analogical thinking. One technique is to begin with a stem: (Something) is like _____ because _____. Then, participants complete the phrase with an unlikely object and tell how they are

323

alike. Here is a stem and some sample responses from *A Whack on the Side of the Head* (von Oech, 1983):

> Life is like . . .
> . . . a jigsaw puzzle, but you don't have the picture on the front of the box to know what it's supposed to look like. Sometimes you're not even sure you have all the pieces.
> . . . riding an elevator. It has a lot of ups and downs and someone is always pushing your buttons. Sometimes you get the shaft, but what really bothers you are the jerks. (pp. 40–41)

A variation would be to have participants choose nouns at random by drawing word cards from a hat, picking words from a dictionary, and so forth. Then, they would have to find ways to force-fit the two nouns to answer the question of how they are alike. For example, a student who chose *book* and *sponge* might say, "A book is like a sponge because they both can be absorbing." This would be a good way to involve students in using the vocabulary for a new unit of study. For example, when studying geometry, the students may be asked to pick the name cards of two geometrical shapes and compare them (e.g., a *rhombus* is like a *triangle* because they both have straight sides with connecting angles). It could even be a game with points for the most correct comparisons per pair.

Synectics

Gordon (1961) developed a method of systematically applying analogies in problem solving that he called "synectics." Such thinking has been used in business for creating new products or improving existing products. One famous example is the Pringles potato chip. The problem was, "How can we package chips to minimize breakage and maximize the number of chips we can fit into a compact container?" The answer came from an analogy in nature. Leaves that are wet and pressed together dry together in a compressed shape. It wasn't too big a leap to figure how to apply this to chips. Science, too, has used analogies from nature to create products like the hypodermic needle (snake's fang) or the submarine (fish's swim bladder).

The idea of synectics is to solve problems using analogies and opposites to associate comparable responses and then to force-fit generated responses into a realistic solution for the problem. There are four types of analogies used: (1) *direct*, with the goal of making actual comparisons with similar situations in nature or elsewhere; (2) *personal*, with the goal of having the problem solver identify with some aspect of the problem in order to look at it in an unfamiliar way; (3) *symbolic*, with the goal of using an objective and impersonal image to represent some component of the problem, perhaps through putting two conflicting aspects of the problem together; and, (4) *fantasy*, which uses imaginary ideas to find ideal solutions (Gordon, 1961).

How could this be applied? Let's say the problem is how to reduce the noise in the school cafeteria, and we want a solution other than the age-old one of having students eat in silence. The analogies need not be used in any particular order.

- Direct: What materials muffle noise in nature?
    Brainstorm: cotton, water, earth
    Force-fit: Use some soundproof materials on the walls to absorb some of the noise.
- Personal: How would I like to be captured if I were a noise?
    Brainstorm: in a soft cloud, in an open field, with a close group of friends
    Force-fit: Noise is diminished if it is absorbed, allowed to be in wide-open spaces, or divided into smaller segments. We've already suggested an absorbent material for the walls, so change the configuration of the room so that there is more or less space.
- Symbolic: Take two conflicting aspects of the analogy and put them together into a short phrase or image.
    Force-fit: We want to create a quiet noise. Perhaps we can teach children to speak quietly at lunch.
- Fantasy: Eat like at a picnic or a restaurant.
    Force-fit: Eat outside on nice days or in smaller groups in smaller rooms.

Through this method, several possible solutions may be proposed that can be used singularly or in conjunction. If our goal is to allow children to eat in the cafeteria and socialize with their friends without creating a great deal of noise, then we could put some absorbent, soundproofing material on the walls; reconfigure the room with dividers so that there are smaller, more intimate dining areas; incorporate lessons on speaking softly at the table; and eat outside on nice days.

Visualization

Another kind of exercise that can range from simple to complex is visualization. One way to promote visualization skills is through guided imagery. With this technique, students relax and close their eyes while the teacher verbally leads them through a succession of images. One language arts teacher in the Midwest took a group of middle school students on an imaginary trip to the beach. These students, who had never seen an ocean, were led to imagine what the ocean looked and smelled like, the salt of the water, the soft heat of the sand, and the cawing of gulls overhead. The teacher used vivid sensory images to describe the scene. Then, she had the students write a story about a trip to the beach. She was amazed at the length of the stories and the students' use of descriptive words and phrases.

Another activity that uses visualization is the encounter lesson. Encounter lessons are activities to stimulate creativity and positive feelings of worth. They are active lessons, lasting from 15 to 20 minutes, that involve sensory imagination. The structure of the lesson consists of five questions with lengthy pauses for the students to imagine their answers. Soft music can be played in the background. The type and order of the questions are (1) question of identity; (2) question of awareness; (3) question of isolation; (4) question of risk or danger; and (5) question of wisdom.

The following is an example of an encounter lesson that could be used with a class studying about Native Americans:

Imagine you are a Native American . . .

- What tribe do you belong to? (identity)
- What do you hear . . . see . . . feel . . . smell . . . taste? (awareness)
- You are away from the rest of the tribe. How do you feel? (isolation)
- You've been captured by an enemy. How do you feel? (danger)
- What have you learned from these experiences? What would you like to tell the world for posterity? (wisdom)

Then, students can take turns telling about their experiences. This would be a good introductory activity for the teacher to assess each student's background knowledge and preconceived ideas about a topic. It would also be a good cumulative activity whereby students use what they have learned to imagine the details of different Native American cultures.

Focusing on Attributes

Attributes are categories of characteristics. For example, attributes of people include hair color, eye color, height, weight, temperament, ethnicity, talents, and so forth. Attributes can include the physical, psychological, social, and other. According to Koberg and Bagnall (1991), "Attribute listing is easiest when you begin with general categories and work your way down to specifics" (p. 59). By focusing on attributes, we can solve problems in several ways. Four techniques that use attributes are attribute listing, attribute analogy chains, morphological analysis, and morphological synthesis.

To use attribute listing, list all of the components or elements of the given problem in one column. List all the attributes or characteristics of each component in a second column. Generate ideas for improvement in a third and positive and negative features in a fourth. The problem should be stated in "how-to" fashion, for example, "How to improve the playground" (see Table 1). Using this model, each positive and negative feature can then be translated into a new element of the problem to be run through the entire process again, making the creative activity self-perpetuating (see Table 2).

Another way to use attributes in problem solving is to look for a relationship between two extremely different things, even if this relationship has to be some-

Table 1

Attribute Listing Chart

Element	Attribute	Ideas for Improvement	Positive/Negative
1. Swings	Too high	Lower them	Small kids can swing; if too low, little kids can get hurt easier
2. Ground	Blacktop	Soften with mats, artificial turf	Safety; increases number of games playable and cost; effects of weather on mats

Table 2

Second Attribute Listing Chart

Element	Attribute	Ideas for Improvement	Positive/Negative
1. Children	Different ages	Separate in areas	Safer for small ones; less interaction
2. Cost	High	Fund raiser	Effective; work

what forced. Then, create attribute analogy chains. For example, if we wanted to improve the design of a television set, we could list its basic attributes.

- Name: television
- Form: geometric, angular, cube
- Function: entertain, educate, accompany

To each of these attributes we might tag analogy ideas.

- Name: videotube, idiot box, entertainment cube
- Form: prism, sphere, semicircle
- Function: live theater, school, conversation

From these, we might produce alternative views.

- Change name to Entertainment Prism (EP).
- Try prism forms that allow for different screens at different angles—with ear phones, families can view different shows in the same room.
- Use at school to send different lessons to different groups within the same classroom—called Educational Prism (EP).

Morphological analysis is another technique that uses attributes to develop new ideas. With this checkerboard technique, attributes from one dimension of the object are listed along the top and attributes of another dimension along the side. The new ideas are created when combinations are forced to fill in the squares of the grid (see Figure 3).

Morphological synthesis is a similar technique that requires you to list the attributes of the situation. Then, below each attribute, brainstorm as many alternatives as you can. When completed, make many random runs across the lists of alternates, picking up a different one from each column and combining them into original forms. Here is one way to do this to get an idea for writing a story:

- *List the main attributes that you want to use for the story starter:* main character, supporting characters, conflict, setting.
- *Brainstorm as many ideas as you can under each attribute.* In this case, I have listed six under each, but there are many more possibilities (see Figure 4).
- *Randomly pick one option from each of the columns.* One way to do this is to use the last four digits of a phone number. For example, using the phone number 4246, I would choose the fourth option in column one, the second in column two, and so on. (If you're going to use this method, it helps to come up with at least 10 options in each column. Otherwise, with larger numbers, you have to count down and then begin again at the top.)
- *Put your combination together.* In this case, I would have a beauty queen involved in an international plot with circus acts at a TV station. Some television plots have been written this way. Author Terry Kay, who wrote *To Dance With the White Dog,* has used a method somewhat similar to this in writing scenes for television programs or chapters for books (T. Kay, personal communication, November 16, 1997).

Lateral Thinking

Certainly, one of the most prolific authors in the area of creativity strategies has been Edward de Bono, who coined the term "lateral thinking" and defined it as pattern switching, a new way of looking at the world (de Bono, 1985a). He explained that lateral thinking is not the same as creativity; rather, it is valueless, but it comprises both an attitude and a number of defined methods (de Bono, 1970).

Grain			
	Corn	**Barley**	**Kasha**
Kiwi	Kiwi corn	Kiwi barley	Kiwi kasha
Mango	Mango corn	Mango barley	Mango kasha

Fruit (row label)

Figure 3. Morphological analysis grid

Main Character	Supporting Characters	Conflict	Setting
dog	farm hands	property	mountain town
detective	circus acts	jealousy	Old West
murderer	talking animals	theft	New York
beauty queen	school children	international plot	Ancient Egypt
super hero	a family	war	farm
rock star	bikers	personal	TV station

Figure 4. Morphological synthesis grid

Each of these methods is named with key letters that stand for the first letters in the words of the method. For example, EBS is a method that has participants *examine both sides* of an argument. A follow-up method called ADI has participants list the issues of the argument under the columns *agreement, disagreement,* and *irrelevance.* This might be a good way to have students look at a concern in social studies or science and prepare to discuss it based on the issues.

Some of these methods are as complex as PISCO, which outlines the steps in a planning operation: *purpose, input, solutions, choice,* and *operation.* As you will see, this problem-solving method is similar in many ways to the Osborn/Parnes Creative Problem Solving process and the Japanese Quality Circles to be discussed later. One that I have found particularly useful for students when reading some new information is to have them list in columns ideas they think are positive, those they think are negative, and those that have no particular value, but are worth noting. This method is called PMI for *plus, minus, interesting.* Although simple, it is an effective way to get students to interact with the reading and consider how they feel about what they are reading.

Another method de Bono has used is from his book *Six Thinking Hats* (1985b). In 1991, he published *Six Action Shoes,* with a similar technique. The six hats represent six different ways of thinking. White is worn by the neutral and objective thinker who is concerned with facts and figures. Red represents the emotional, intuitive view that acts on hunches and impressions, rather than on logical reasons. Black points out the negative aspects of a situation, the errors in logic, and possible consequences of a course of action. Yellow maintains optimistic, positive thinking and focuses on benefits and constructive ideas. Green represents creativity, deliberate innovation, and new approaches to problems. Blue stands for control and organization of the thinking and of the other thinkers.

Students can be divided into groups and each given a hat made from construction paper in one of the six colors. When presented with a problem to solve or an issue to discuss, the students must stay in the role according to the hat they are wearing. This method helps them to be aware of some of the ways in which people think about issues and to focus on deliberate thinking.

One variation on this is to pair the students—white and red, black and yellow, green and blue—to discuss the issue. Another is to have them discuss for a certain amount of time, then switch hats. The Six Hats Method is particularly effective when students get to "try on" methods of thinking that are not natural to them.

The beginning of such a discussion might sound something like this:

White: Our problem is to decide whether it is ethical for scientists to continue to conduct research with live animals.

Red: Oh, the poor little monkeys!

Black: You can't just consider the animals. Without animal research, many medical discoveries would not have been made. Many people are alive today because of such discoveries.

Red: Thank goodness for that!

Yellow: Perhaps there is a way we can still get the benefits of animal research without too much pain and suffering.

Blue: Let's stick to our problem at hand: Is research on live animals ethical?

Green: There wouldn't be such an ethical dilemma if we could think of a way to do the same quality of research without sacrificing animals. Let's think about how might we simulate animal reactions realistically so that we can conduct research without using live animals.

Such a discussion might lead into a creative problem solving exercise to attempt to solve Green's stated question.

Creative Problem Solving

The Osborn/Parnes Creative Problem-Solving process (CPS) is composed of five steps: fact finding, problem finding, idea finding, solution finding, and acceptance finding (Parnes, 1981). This process incorporates both *divergent thinking*, or thinking of many possibilities, and *convergent thinking*, or thinking of the one right or best solution. During *fact finding*, information is gathered about the situation. *Problem finding* means identifying the central or most salient problem and any underlying subproblems. *Idea finding* refers to the process of generating many possible solutions (usually by brainstorming). The *solution finding* step involves applying criteria to choose the best solution. And *acceptance finding* involves "selling" the solution to the key individuals involved in decision making.

Although these steps are presented in a logical order, in real problem solving, they do not always occur in this order. Sometimes, we are presented with a problem and have to go back and research the facts. Other times, we may be in a position to sell an idea to a constituency and find that the correct problem was not identified, so we have to go back to the problem finding step. This was the case in the 1970s when the Detroit automakers lost money trying to sell luxury cars to a public that was seeking more energy-efficient and reliable vehicles. Therefore, strict adherence to an order or insistence in completing every step every time is artificial after students have learned the process.

There are some techniques, activities, and devices that have been found helpful in training others to use CPS. One standard device is the use of IWWMW during problem finding. When students begin the problem statement with "In what ways might we . . . ." it is left open for creative attack.

Another standard device is the use of a criteria grid for evaluating solutions. The one in Figure 5 is shown with space to list five ideas along the left side, but many more are possible and desirable. It is also illustrated with spaces for six criteria across the top; but, again, this is an arbitrary number.

Here is an example. Suppose some high school students used CPS to solve the dilemma of what to do to celebrate their graduation. They worded the problem as, "In what ways might we celebrate our graduation?" During the fact finding step, they discovered that most of them did not have much money to spend, they wanted to involve as many graduates as possible, they wanted to do something fun and informal, and they had to plan it quickly. During idea finding, they brainstormed many possibilities (see Figure 5).

331

Ideas	Fun	Inexpensive	Interactive	Location	Weather	Total
1. picnic	3	5	4	5	1	18
2. party	5	4	5	2	3	19
3. dance	4	3	3	1	4	15
4. dinner	1	2	2	3	5	13
5. go out	2	1	1	4	2	10

Figure 5. Creative problem-solving solution evaluation grid

During solution finding, they chose the top five to consider further and listed them along the left side of the grid. They chose criteria based upon their fact finding and the realities of planning. Then, they applied each criterion to each idea and rank ordered the ideas with the highest number going to the best idea in that category. So, they decided the party would be the most fun and the dinner the least. The dance was the hardest to find a location, and the picnic was most dependent on the weather. When all criteria had been used to rank all ideas, the numbers were totaled across the rows and entered in the last column.

The idea with the highest total is the best idea according to the listed criteria. In this case, the party was rated slightly higher than the picnic. The major considerations seem to be the possibility of inclement weather for the picnic and the possibility of finding a location to hold the party. At this point, the students could go back to fact finding and check the weather reports and availability of a party locale. Or, they could choose to go back to the problem finding step: "In what ways might we plan for the picnic so that weather would not ruin it?" Then, ideas might be generated about securing a shelter, picking the best date based on the forecast, and so forth.

Quality Circles

Like CPS, Quality Circles is a problem-solving process that is primarily used by groups. Developed by Japanese industrialists, it was brought to U.S. industry in the 1960s (Bellanca, 1984; Dewar, 1980). Also like CPS, it requires shifting back and forth from divergent to convergent thinking. However, Quality Circles differs in its emphasis on convergent thought and analytical thinking and its formality. With CPS, members just call out ideas as they occur. With Quality Circles, members take turns around the circle, with each member saying one thing or opting to pass. There is a designated leader and a rotating role as recorder. The brainstorming ends when everyone passes. The basic steps for Quality Circles are these:

1. *Problem selection by formal brainstorming.* This step is further broken down into problem listing, problem clarifying, discussion of the pros, discussion of the cons, participant voting, and data collection to ensure that the problem is the correct one to choose.
2. *Cause-effect analysis.* Participants attempt to determine the causes of the problem situation and target the main cause. Once again, there is problem clarifying, discussion of the pros and cons, participant voting, and data verification in an orderly, round robin fashion.
3. *Solution identification.* In this step, participants use formal brainstorming and costs-benefits analysis, with the impediments to the solution as the costs and the expected positive outcome as the benefit. Then they vote.
4. *The recommendation.* This is a formal presentation to decision makers that should include as much documentation of the project's history and the proposed plan as possible. This might include the goal, data gathered, action steps, timelines, responsibilities, obstacles, and a plan of evaluation.
5. *Implementation.* If the plan is approved, then each member of the circle takes on a specific responsibility to implement the plan. If not, the circle goes back to address the problem again.
6. *Evaluation.* Circle members conduct the evaluation and provide a final report.

Role-Playing

Role-playing can be a wonderful outlet for creative expression, as well as an effective creative problem solving technique. Role-playing and creative dramatics have been recommended as part of the curriculum for gifted children, especially in the language arts (Cramond, 1993; VanTassel-Baska, 1998). Most teachers are well aware that children enjoy such activities. In fact, a survey of a group of gifted middle school students indicated that role-playing and creative dramatics were among their favorite activities in school (Martin & Cramond, 1983).

However, fewer teachers seem to be aware of the need and methods for teaching problem solving through role-playing (Torrance, Murdock, & Fletcher,

1997). Based upon the techniques of sociodrama or psychodrama, role-playing in creative problem solving differs from each in the type of problem that is addressed and the depth of emotional involvement and disclosure of the participants. Although psychodrama can be a powerful tool for individuals to address serious psychological problems, sociodrama can be the same for groups. Problem solving through role-playing can use many of the same techniques with less personal problems. For example, students could role-play to convince the principal to consider their bid for a change in cafeteria rules.

Using the terms of psychodrama (Blatner, 1973), the main roles are *protagonist(s)*, the main character in the problem situation; *director*, usually the teacher, who guides the action and ensures that rules are followed and that the situation does not touch on matters too serious or sensitive for the classroom; and *auxiliaries*, others who take part in the enactment in supporting roles. There are three main parts to the enactment:

1. *Warm-up* may include group-building activities, as well as defining the problem; discussing the logistics, time, and rules; and choosing roles.
2. *Action* is where the protagonist(s) and auxiliaries enact the situation as if it were happening in the "here and now." The director monitors the action, adding other roles and players as they become necessary. The director also uses other techniques to move the problem along, such as the *mirror technique*, whereby other actors play the role of the protagonist to show him how he is behaving; *modeling* by other group members to show how they would act in the same situation; *role reversal* of the protagonist and his antagonists to enable individuals to see both sides of a conflict; and *repeat role-playing* with the protagonist trying a different solution each time.
3. *Closure* is when the group discusses the action and evaluates the possible solutions that were generated. In some cases, this may begin another role-playing scenario during which members attempt to predict the outcome of the proposed solution.

There are many more techniques and variations on this basic creative problem solving method through role-playing (Torrance, Murdock, & Fletcher, 1997). Teachers are cautioned to be alert during the action for any sensitive matters or strong emotional reactions from students that may warrant professional counseling. If these arise, the action should be stopped until the matter is addressed. The key to this method is having students act out and be emotionally involved in the problem at hand, not to cause stress.

Removing Blocks

Another effective way to encourage creativity is to remove blocks to individuals' creativity. These blocks are described, with exercises designed to help remove them, in Adams' (1986) book *Conceptual Blockbusting: A Guide to Better Ideas.* *Perceptual blocks* include:

- seeing what you expect to see—stereotyping;
- difficulty in isolating the problem;
- tendency to delimit the problem area too closely;
- inability to see the problem from various viewpoints;
- saturation; and
- failure to utilize all sensory inputs.

One exercise that illustrates how perceptual blocks can limit our thinking uses common materials. Give students a sheet with nine illustrations of a penny. Only one should have all of the elements correct and in the actual locations as on the penny. Most people, although we see pennies every day, are not able to complete the task of identifying the correct one. We handle pennies all the time, but we no longer really see them. The same point could be made by asking students to draw a computer keyboard. How many could place all the letters and symbols correctly? When we don't pay attention to details, we can miss clues to solving a problem.

Emotional blocks include

- fear of making a mistake, failing, risking;
- inability to tolerate ambiguity—overriding desires for security, order, with "no appetite for chaos";
- preference for judging ideas, rather than generating them;
- inability to relax, incubate, and "sleep on it";
- lack of challenge—problem fails to engage interest;
- excessive zeal, overmotivation to succeed quickly;
- lack of access to areas of imagination;
- lack of imaginative control; and
- inability to distinguish reality from fantasy.

How many students, especially bright ones, have difficulty suspending disbelief long enough to consider that the improbable may be possible? Torrance (1974) reported that the great psychologist Thorndike presented prospective graduate students with an unlikely hypothetical situation and asked them to "just suppose" the outcome. Those who were unable to conjecture were considered too incurious for graduate study. As an exercise, try a "just suppose" activity with students or friends. Or, discuss how often each of you has missed an opportunity because of fear of failure. These blocks prevent us from exercising our creativity.

Cultural blocks include

- fantasy and reflection are a waste of time, lazy, even crazy;
- playfulness is for children only;

- problem solving is serious business, and humor is out of place;
- reason, logic, utility, and practicality are good, while feelings, intuition, qualitative judgments, and pleasure are bad;
- tradition is preferable to change;
- any problem can be solved by scientific thinking and lots of money; and
- taboos.

An example of an activity that illustrates the power of taboos in hindering problem solving is given by Adams (1986). The problem may be shown as a visual or described accordingly:

Imagine that you are one of a group of six people in a bare room along with the following objects: 100 feet of clothesline, a carpenter's hammer, a chisel, a box of Wheaties, a file, a wire coat hanger, a monkey wrench, and a light bulb. A steel pipe is stuck vertically in the concrete floor with a ping-pong ball lying at the bottom of the pipe. The inside diameter of the pipe is just slightly larger than the diameter of the ping-pong ball. Your task is to get the ball out of the pipe without damaging the ball, tube, or floor. How many ways can you think of to do this? (p. 54)

Depending on the nature of the group and the setting, participants can usually think of several possible solutions. However, the solution of urinating in the pipe to float the ball out is rarely suggested. When it is suggested, it is typically by a male, and it is often after there has been some whispering among the participants and laughing. Once that boundary has been breached, many other ideas come forth. This is not to say that these are the best ideas, but only that taboos can keep us from even considering some ideas and can limit our creativity.

Environmental blocks include

- lack of cooperation and trust among colleagues;
- autocratic boss who values only his or her own ideas and does not reward others;
- distractions (phone, easy intrusions, etc.); and
- lack of support to bring ideas into action.

It is easy to demonstrate environmental blocks if you work in a school setting. Have students discuss the things they find most distracting when they are trying to concentrate at home and at school. Then, have them sit silently for a prescribed amount of time in each location and record the number and types of distractions they observe. Finally, address how they may eliminate or mitigate against most distractions.

Another good activity to illustrate environmental blocks is to think of a new idea—maybe an invention or new way of doing things—that seems reasonably plausible. Then, seriously propose this idea to friends and, if you are brave, colleagues and others you meet from time to time. Note their reactions. Most often, people immediately form the murder committees discussed earlier and tell you all of the reasons your idea won't work. This activity is especially potent in a faculty meeting.

Intellectual and expressive blocks include

- solutions formed by solving the problem using an incorrect language;
- inflexible or inadequate use of intellectual problem-solving strategies;
- lack of, or incorrect, information and inadequate language skill to express and record ideas (verbally, musically, visually, etc.).

Most of us have favorite languages (verbal, mathematical, visual, psychomotor) with which we attempt to solve most problems. For most people, verbal or mathematical skills are used most often to solve problems, probably because these are the kinds of problems we usually solve in school. Few of us are equally adept in all areas or are even capable of identifying problems that require a different language to solve.

A favorite example is the Buddhist monk problem (Sternberg, 1986). I've seen a couple of variations of this problem, but the essence is that a Buddhist monk walks up a mountain path to a temple at the top to pray. He leaves the bottom at 6 a.m., stops to eat lunch along the way, then continues until he reaches the top by 6 p.m. He prays and meditates through the night, then leaves at 6 a.m. the next morning to return to the bottom along the same path. Once again, he stops to rest and eat before arriving at the bottom near 6 p.m. The question: Is there a point along the path that the monk passes at the same time of day on both the days of his trip?

I have used the problem in my class and seen extremely bright adults struggle with the semantics or the numbers in trying to answer the question. The answer is "yes," and the proof is visual. Instead of 2 days, imagine that there are two monks on 1 day. Of course they would meet somewhere along the narrow path as one ascended and the other descended. Another way to visualize this is to draw a graph (see Figure 6).

The key is not whether that graph exactly represents the path that the monk took, but whether it is possible to draw any representative graph of his trip in which the lines do not intersect.

Here is another example from Adams (1986).

Picture a large piece of paper, the thickness of this page. In your imagination, fold it once (now having two layers), fold it once more (now having four layers), and continue folding it over upon itself 50 times. How thick is the 50-times folded paper? (pp. 71–72)

If you answered that it is impossible to fold a piece of paper, no matter how big or thin, 50 times, you are correct; but, you need to practice suspending disbelief.

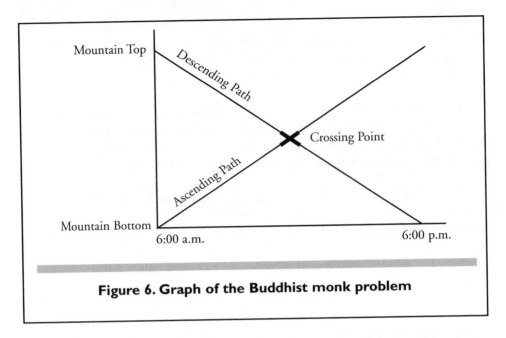

Figure 6. Graph of the Buddhist monk problem

Your first fold would result in a stack two times the original thickness, your second would give you a stack 2 x 2 times the original thickness, and so on. So, the solution is 2^{50} times the original thickness or about 1,100,000,000,000,000 times the original thickness. According to Adams, "if the paper is originally the thickness of typing paper, the answer is some 50,000,000 miles or over half the distance from the earth to the sun" (p. 72). If you tried to use visualization on this problem, it probably did not work. Nor would verbal strategies be likely to result in a correct answer. Although it sounded like a problem that you should solve by doing or visualizing, the correct language for this problem was mathematics.

There are many problems that require expertise at verbal ability in books of riddles. A problem that requires spatial ability is to use six drinking straws to make four equilateral triangles with no overlap and no extraneous figures. Most people will struggle with this for some time before an enterprising individual realizes that the key is in "breaking the plane" and creating a three-dimensional pyramid with three straws as the base and three rising up as the pyramid.

The point of these exercises is to get people to realize that expert problem solvers spend time assessing the problem and devising a suitable strategy, rather than attacking every problem in the same way. Such flexibility in problem solving is an asset to creativity.

Competitions

Another important way that students can exercise their creative thinking is through competitions. For some people, the idea of competition is an anathema to the idea of creativity; for many students, competitions motivate, enhance their creativity, and provide them with opportunities that they would not have otherwise (Karnes & Riley, 1996; Torrance & Sisk, 1997).

Future Problem Solving

One of the best known competitions is the Future Problem Solving (FPS) program. Begun by E. Paul Torrance in 1974, it is based on the CPS model described previously. Students compete at the local, state, and international levels in teams of four or as individuals at one of three age levels: Junior (grades 4–6), Intermediate (grades 7–9), or Senior (grades 10–12). Students practice and train on "fuzzy" situations that are based on projected problems of the future. Some past "fuzzies" have dealt with prisons in space, famine, international terrorism, and the like.

Students brainstorm the many possible problems inherent in the fuzzy, select and write one problem statement, then do research on the topic to gain as much information as possible. They then apply the other steps of the CPS process to find possible solutions, apply criteria to choose the best solution, and devise a plan for selling their idea. Evaluation teams give students written feedback throughout the year on the three practice problems. The fourth problem is a qualifying problem, and teams that do well are invited to compete in the state bowl. Teams don't know ahead of time what the topic of the fuzzy will be at the bowl, just that it will be on one of the four areas they've researched that year.

Other newer components of the FPS program include the Scenario Writing Competition, where students write stories set in the future about one of the four fuzzy topics, and the Community Problem Solving Competition, where students identify a problem in their community and implement their solution.

Each state runs its own competitions a little differently and with different dates for the bowl; but, the state bowl winners, as well as those from Australia, New Zealand, and Canada, are then invited to compete at the International FPS Bowl held in the United States in June. (There are other countries, including China, South Africa, and Korea, that participate in FPS, but have not sent teams to compete.)

Odyssey of the Mind

This competition, begun in New Jersey in 1979 by Samuel Micklus, is similar to the Future Problem Solving program in that there are problems that teams work on all year in order to prepare for the local, state, and world competitions. However, it differs from FPS in some key ways.

Although there are levels of competition, with Odyssey of the Mind (OM), there are four age divisions from kindergarten through college. Perhaps most important, OM presents problems in a variety of domains. There are always five problems, one for each of the following categories: structure, mechanical/vehicle, technical performance, performance, and classics. There is also a noncompetitive primary problem. This diversity may be the reason that it is the most popular of the national and international competitions; it appeals to children who express their creativity in many different ways. The content of the problems from 2003–2004 competition (Odyssey of the Mind, n.d.) reflects this diversity:

1. *Envirover.* The team's problem is to build and drive a human-powered Envirover vehicle that will collect trash and deliver it to a factory, where it will be used to manufacture a product of the team's design.
2. *Strategy Sphere.* This technical problem requires teams to design and build two devices that will mechanically propel balls through a circular rim.
3. *Fantastic Art.* In this problem, teams will create and present a performance that includes works of art that come alive when no one can see them and return to their original state when others are around.
4. *Balancing Act.* This problem calls for the team to design, build, and test an asymmetrical structure made of balsa wood and glue.
5. *Featured Creature.* The problem is to create and present an original performance about mythological animals.

Teams of no more than seven children work together on one of the problems throughout the year. Winners at the lower levels are qualified to present their winning product at the World level.

Other Competitions

Although FPS and OM are the only large-scale creative problem solving competitions, there are many competitions for individuals who are creative in specific domains. Some of these include competitions for writing poetry, prose, and plays, as well as news articles and editorial cartoons. There are competitions in business, mathematics, science, social studies, leadership, service, and technology, as well as in the performing and fine arts. For detailed information about competitions in all of the above categories, see Karnes and Riley (1996).

The Incubation Model

The Incubation Model is, as the name says, a model, rather than a strategy for teaching creative thinking (Torrance & Safter, 1990). It was conceived as a way of addressing the whole of creativity, both rational and supra-rational.

A supra-rational view of creativity suggests that individual consciousness transcends the boundaries of the deliberately rational creative process and experiences an altered state of consciousness, a holistic state of awareness, a state of instant communication among all the parts. (p. vii)

It is a challenge to become a great teacher and go beyond teaching students the rational creative thinking techniques and engage their curiosity, intuition, and emotions. Because incubation is often considered a vital part of the creative process, this model has the goal of fostering incubation in students by encouraging them to continue thinking about the lessons beyond the classroom. For example, many lesson plan formats have an initial activity, some developmental activities, and a culminating activity that is often some type of evaluation. With this type of lesson, the students' minds are opened up with the initial activity, then closed with the final, closing, or evaluation activity. The point of the Incubation Model is to open the students' minds and keep them open to learning about the topic when the formal lesson is ended. Following are the steps of the Incubation Model and some short descriptions of instructional activities for each.

Stage 1: Heightening Anticipation

1. Confront ambiguities and uncertainties.
2. Question to heighten expectation and anticipation.
3. Create awareness of a problem to be solved, a possible future need, or a difficulty to be faced.
4. Build on the learners' existing knowledge.
5. Heighten concern about a problem or future need.
6. Stimulate curiosity and desire to know.
7. Make the strange familiar or the familiar strange.
8. Free from inhibiting mind sets.
9. Look at the same information from different viewpoints.
10. Question proactively to make the learner think of information in new ways.
11. Predict from limited information.
12. Make the purposefulness of the lesson clear by showing the connection between the expected learning and present problems or future career.
13. Provide only enough structure to give clues and direction.
14. Take the next step beyond what is known.
15. Warm up physically or bodily to the information to be presented.

In using activities of the kind listed above, the teacher must keep in mind the purpose of such experiences. In essence, they are

- to create the desire to know;
- to heighten anticipation and expectation;
- to get attention;
- to arouse curiosity;
- to tickle the imagination; and
- to give purpose and motivation.

341

Stage 2: Encountering the Expected and Unexpected and Deepening Expectations

1. Heighten awareness of problems and difficulties.
2. Accept limitations constructively as a challenge, rather than cynically, improvising with what is available.
3. Encourage creative personality characteristics or predispositions.
4. Practice creative problem solving in a disciplined, systematic manner, with the problem and information at hand.
5. Deliberately and systematically elaborate upon the information presented.
6. Present information as incomplete and have learners ask questions to fill gaps.
7. Juxtapose apparently irrelevant elements.
8. Explore and examine mysteries and try to solve them.
9. Preserve open-endedness.
10. Make outcomes not completely predictable.
11. Predict from limited information.
12. Search for honesty and realism.
13. Identify and encourage the acquisition of new skills for finding information.
14. Heighten and deliberately use surprises.
15. Encourage visualization.

Stage 3: Going Beyond and "Keeping It Going"

1. Play with ambiguities.
2. Deepen awareness of a problem, difficulty, or gap in information.
3. Acknowledge a pupil's unique potentiality.
4. Heighten concern about a problem.
5. Challenge a constructive response or solution.
6. See a clear relationship between the new information and future careers.
7. Accept limitations creatively and constructively.
8. Dig still more deeply and go beneath the obvious and accepted.
9. Make divergent thinking legitimate.
10. Elaborate the information given.
11. Encourage elegant solution, the solution of collision conflicts, unsolved mysteries.
12. Require experimentation.
13. Make the familiar strange or the strange familiar.
14. Examine fantasies to find solutions to real problems.
15. Encourage future projections.
16. Entertain improbabilities.
17. Create humor and see the humorous in the information presented.

18. Encourage deferred judgment and the use of some disciplined procedures of problem solving.
19. Relate information to information in another discipline.
20. Look at the same information in different ways.
21. Encourage the manipulation of ideas, objects, or both.
22. Encourage multiple hypotheses.
23. Confront and examine paradoxes.

The Incubation Model was presented last under techniques for creative thinking because it could be used as an organizing framework within which the various activities described earlier could be incorporated. For example, in teaching a lesson on density in a science class, the teacher *heightens anticipation* by showing the students a tub of water and two cans of soda of the same brand—one regular and one diet. She asks the students to speculate about whether the cans will float or sink, questioning them about some of the principles they've learned about density. After the students have discussed their predictions and reasons, the teacher drops the regular can of soda in the water and it sinks. By doing this, the teacher guides the students to *encounter the expected* (for those who guessed correctly) *and unexpected* (for those who did not) *and deepen their expectations* by predicting whether the can of diet soda will sink or float. When the students have made their predictions, the teacher drops the diet soda into the tub and it floats.

Most lessons would conclude at this point with a wrap-up and summary of why the two cans reacted differently. However, the idea of the Incubation Model is to *keep it going*, rather than wrap it up. So, before class ends, the students may be asked to think about another test they could do to discover the principle behind the density difference. If students are intrigued enough, they will continue to think about the problem outside of class. Some may try to discover at home why some sodas sink and others float. Other students may propose another test to be done in class. At this point, the teacher may incorporate other creativity and problem-solving strategies by having the students brainstorm the differences in the diet and regular sodas and create an attribute listing chart to compare them. With guidance, and a touch of drama, the teacher should be able to lead the students to discover that the sugar in the regular soda is what makes it denser than the diet soda. The students have learned about density, but they have also learned about problem solving, hypothesizing, testing ideas, and persisting with an idea beyond the boundaries of the classroom.

Summary

A number of creative strategies have been described, and some illustrative activities provided, but the preceding is not an all-inclusive list. There are many sources of activities designed to enhance creativity that are available to teachers.

Some are from educational publishers, others are available from various sites on the Internet. A sample of these is listed in the Teacher Resources section at the end of this chapter; however, these change, appear, and disappear so quickly that they should be reviewed frequently. Then there are materials that are available to educators from companies that have provided grants. One of the best is the four-part film *The Creative Spirit* (Perlmutter, 1992), which was broadcast on PBS and was funded by IBM. There is a book to accompany it (Goleman, Kaufman, & Ray, 1992) and a teacher's guide with activities and a computer disk. The teaching materials are available from The Creative Spirit, c/o TELED Inc., P.O. Box 933022, Los Angeles, CA 90099-2199.

Conclusion

In order to nurture creativity in ourselves or others, we must first show that we value creativity by recognizing and respecting it in ourselves and others. Also, we can create a climate that is conducive to creativity, one that is psychologically safe and provides stimulation, as well as time for quiet reflection. Then, there are several techniques we can use, first as warm-up, but also exercises to promote ideation, visualization, analogical thinking, lateral thinking, group and individual problem solving, and going beyond the rational for incubation. We can help identify and remove blocks to creativity, find competitions and other outlets for children's creativity, and provide opportunities and encouragement for expressive and problem-solving creativity whenever possible. If we do all of these things in the classroom, then we can be confident that we have become, like those reported in Torrance's (1981) longitudinal study, the "teachers who made a difference."

Teacher Statement

How can we prepare children for the future? Teach them how to solve problems. The Future Problem Solving Program (FPSP) is the only program that teaches children step by step the creative problem solving process.

I like to begin by leading primary-age children through community problem solving. We tackle a problem that arises in our classroom. For example, "In what ways might we encourage children to arrive to class on time?" As children mature, I broaden their scope of influence by tackling problems within the school and, finally, within the local community.

By 4th grade, students have internalized the process and are able to communicate effectively their ideas to their teammates. They also begin writing their ideas themselves. By completing the FPSP booklet, students learn to brainstorm ideas, answer open-ended questions, find the main problem/conflict, identify stakeholders, learn questioning techniques, evaluate ideas using a grid, and learn how to sell/promote their solution. When students are allowed to practice their skills and receive feedback before they enter into competition, they grow and build their cooperative and leadership skills. After participating in the six-step process, children have the skills to tackle any problem.

As a reading teacher, I often have students who enjoy working and writing alone. The scenario competition is perfect for their unique abilities. Scenario writing allows creative writers the opportunity to stretch their imaginations while perfecting their writing skills.

I also use the FPSP in the classroom because it encourages children to find positive solutions to futuristic problems. Students feel empowered to make a difference in their community. By teaching them how to solve difficult problems, they realize that they are an integral part of our community and that they have the skills to tackle any problem that arises in their future.

—Susan Winstead

Discussion Questions

1. What do you think creativity is, and where does it come from? Do you think that there is a difference in the creative process between "C" and "c" creativity, or does the culture decide which creations are major? Is there a difference in the creative process in the sciences and in the arts?

2. What situations, events, people, etc. have helped you nurture your creativity? What things have hindered it?

3. Design a classroom for optimal development of creativity. Keep in mind both the emotional and the physical climate.

4. Create a warm-up activity for creative thinking. Why would it be a good warm-up?

5. Think of another example for applying one of the strategies described in another content area or for another age student. What strategies could be effectively incorporated into classrooms in different content areas and with students of different ages?

6. How do you see the role of competition in education? Is it motivating or intimidating? In what ways might it be used most effectively?

7. Is creativity something that can and should be taught? Where does it fit into the curriculum?

Teacher Resources

Publishers

The Creative Education Foundation
289 Bay Road
Hadley, MA 01035
http://www.cef-cpsi.org

Creative Learning Press, Inc.
P.O. Box 320
Mansfield Center, CT 06250
http://www.creativelearningpress.com

Free Spirit Publishing, Inc.
217 Fifth Ave. N, Ste. 200
Minneapolis, MN 55401-1299
http://www.freespirit.com

Prufrock Press, Inc.
P.O. Box 8813
Waco, TX 76714-8813
http://www.prufrock.com

Zephyr Press
3316 N. Chapel Ave.
P.O. Box 66006-C
Tucson, AZ 85728-6006
http://www.zephyrpress.com

Competitions

Future Problem Solving Program
2028 Regency Road
Lexington, KY 40503
http://www.fpsp.org

Odyssey of the Mind Association
c/o Creative Competitions Inc.
1325 Rt. 130 S, Ste. F
Gloucester City, NJ 08030
http://www.odysseyofthemind.com

Web Sites

A recent search of the Internet for sites on creativity listed 285 sites. On any given day, there may be more or less. Many of these deal with creativity in business or some other specific domain. Still others are more age-specific, designed for adults or sophisticated older children. However, some of the ones that looked best are included below.

Cyberkids—http://www.cyberkids.com
Cyberteens—http://www.cyberteens.com
These are connected sites that feature age-appropriate games, contests, a magazine, and various outlets for creative expression. The launchpad links visitors to sites for art, business, child safety, children's books online, computers, educational resources, entertainment, various academic subjects, museums and libraries, music, nature, sports, and more.

Creativity Café—http://creativity.net
This site features, for example, Storytellers of the New Millennium; live and cyberspace interactive programs like "KidCast For Peace" which are designed to "bring the community together and to create and enjoy evolutionary entertainment"; an Earthday Broadcast and KidCast Multicast; a Creativity Camp which teaches Digital Storytelling tools, and a "living gallery" where all artists can show their art.

Kid-Safe Sites—http://www.thwww.com/mrwizard/kids.htm
This site has many fun and safe links for kids, as well as homework helpers in various content areas. With cool animated graphics, kids are sure to enjoy this one.

The American Creativity Association—http://www.amcreativityassoc.org
This site is a resource for learning about the latest work in applied creativity and innovative problem solving.

Project Zero at the Harvard Graduate School of Education—http://pzweb.harvard.edu
Project Zero is an educational research group committed to understanding and enhancing learning, thinking, and creativity across disciplines.

Enchanted Mind—http://enchantedmind.com
This wonderful site has links and resources on creativity and innovation.

Creativity-Based Information Resources (CBIR)—http://www.buffalostate.edu/orgs/cbir
For research, there is database maintained by The International Center for Studies in Creativity at Buffalo State College. Currently, the database contains over 10,300 annotated references of works focusing on creativity. You can actually search the database online.

References

Adams, J. L. (1986). *Conceptual blockbusting: A guide to better ideas*. Reading, MA: Addison-Wesley.

Amabile, T. M. (1983). *The social psychology of creativity*. New York: Springer-Verlag.

Barron, F., Montuori, A., & Barron, A. (1997). *Creators on creating: Awakening and cultivating the imaginative mind*. New York: Tarcher/Putnam.

Bellanca, J. (1984). Can quality circles work in classrooms of the gifted? *Roeper Review, 6*, 199–200.

Betts, G. T. (1986). The autonomous learner model for the gifted and talented. In J. S. Renzulli (Ed.), *Systems and models for developing programs for the gifted and talented* (pp. 27–56). Mansfield Center, CT: Creative Learning Press.

Blatner, H. A. (1973). *Acting-in: Practical applications of psychodramatic methods*. New York: Springer.

Bloom, B. S. (Ed.). (1985). *Developing talent in young people*. New York: Ballantine Books.

Boorstin, D. J. (1992). *The creators: A history of heroes of the imagination*. New York: Random House.

Cameron, J., & Pierce, W. D. (1994). Reinforcement, reward, and intrinsic motivation: A meta-analysis. *Review of Educational Research, 64*, 363–423.

Cox, J., Daniel, N., & Boston, B. (1985). *Educating able learners: Programs and promising practices*. Austin: University of Texas Press.

Cramond, B. (1993). Speaking and listening: Key components of a language arts program for the gifted. *Roeper Review, 16*, 44–48.

Cramond, B. (1994). Attention-Deficit Hyperactivity Disorder and creativity—What is the connection? *The Journal of Creative Behavior, 28*, 193–210.

Cramond, B. (1995). *The coincidence of ADHD and creativity* (Research-Based Decision-Making series). Storrs: National Research Center for the Gifted and Talented, University of Connecticut.

Cramond, B. (2002). The study of creativity in the future. In A. G. Alienikov (Ed.), *The future of creativity* (pp. 83–86). Bensenville, IL: Scholastic Testing Service.

Csikszentmihalyi, M. (1990). *Flow: The psychology of optimal experience*. New York: Harper.

Csikszentmihalyi, M., & Csikszentmihalyi, I. S. (Eds.). (1988). *Optimal experience: Psychological studies of flow in consciousness*. New York: Cambridge University Press.

de Bono, E. (1970). *Lateral thinking*. New York: Harper & Row.

de Bono, E. (1985a). *de Bono's thinking course*. New York: Facts on File Publications.

de Bono, E. (1985b). *Six thinking hats*. Boston: Little, Brown.

de Bono, E. (1991). *Six action shoes*. New York: HarperCollins.

Dewar, D. L. (1980). *The quality circle guide to participation management*. Englewood Cliffs, NJ: Prentice-Hall.

Diamond, M. C. (1988). *Enriching heredity: The impact of the environment on the anatomy of the brain*. New York: The Free Press.

Elkind, D. (1989). *The hurried child: Growing up too fast too soon*. Reading, MA: Addison-Wesley.

Eberle, B. (1996). *Scamper: Creative games and activities for imagination and development*. Buffalo, NY: D.O.K.

Feldhusen, J. F. (1986). A conception of giftedness. In R. J. Sternberg & J. E. Davidson (Eds.), *Conceptions of giftedness* (pp. 112–127). Cambridge, England: Cambridge University Press.

Feldman, D. H., Csikszentmihalyi, M., & Gardner, H. (1994). *Changing the world: A framework for the study of creativity.* Westport, CT: Praeger.

Ferguson, M. (1977). "Mind mirror" EEG identifies states of awareness. *Brain/Mind Bulletin, 2*(30), 1–2.

Gagné, F. (1985). Giftedness and talent: Reexamining a reexamination of the definitions. *Gifted Child Quarterly, 29,* 103–112.

Goldberg, R. (1968). *Rube Goldberg vs. the machine age: A retrospective exhibition of his work with memoirs and annotations.* New York: Hastings House.

Goleman, D., Kaufman, P., & Ray, M. (1992). *The creative spirit.* New York: Dutton.

Gordon, W. J. (1961). *Synectics.* New York: Harper & Row.

Karnes, F. A., & Riley, T. L. (1996). *Competitions: Maximizing your abilities.* Waco, TX: Prufrock Press.

Koberg, D., & Bagnall, J. (1991). *The universal traveler: A soft-systems guide to creativity, problem solving, & the process of reaching goals.* Menlo Park, CA: Crisp.

MacKinnon, D. W. (1976). Architects, personality types, and creativity. In A. Rothenberg & C. R. Hausman (Eds.), *The creativity question.* (pp. 175–189). Durham, NC: Duke University Press.

MacKinnon, D. W. (1978). *In search of human effectiveness.* Buffalo, NY: Creative Education Foundation.

Martin, C. E., & Cramond, B. (1983). Creative reading: Is it being taught to the gifted in elementary schools? *Journal for the Education of the Gifted, 6,* 70–79.

Odyssey of the Mind. (n.d.). *2003–2004 Odyssey of the Mind long-term problem synopsis.* Retrieved March 6, 2004, from http://www.odysseyofthemind.com/materials/2004synopsis1.php

Parnes, S. J. (1981). *The magic of your mind.* Buffalo, NY: Creative Education Foundation.

Perlmutter, A. H. (Producer). (1992). *The creative spirit* [Motion picture]. (Available from The Creative Spirit, c/o TELED Inc., P.O. Box 933022, Los Angeles, CA 90099-2199)

Piirto, J. (1992). *Understanding those who create.* Dayton: Ohio Psychology Press.

Quotations page: Quotations by author. (n.d.). Retrieved January 30, 2004, from http://www.quotationspage.com/quotes.php3?asearch=John+W.+Gardner&x=43&y=1

Rader, D. (1993, January 31). Why I walked away. *Parade,* 20–21.

Renzulli, J. S., & Reis, S. M. (1985). *The schoolwide enrichment model: A comprehensive plan for educational excellence.* Mansfield Center, CT: Creative Learning Press.

Restak, R. (1993). The creative brain. In J. Brockman (Ed.), *Creativity* (pp. 164–175). New York: Simon & Schuster.

Rogers, C. R. (1954). Toward a theory of creativity. *ETC: A Review of General Semantics, 11,* 249–260

Root-Bernstein, R., & Root-Bernstein, M. (1999). *Sparks of genius: The 13 thinking tools of the world's most creative people.* Boston: Houghton Mifflin.

Rothenberg, A., & Hausman, C. R. (Eds.) (1976). *The creativity question.* Durham, NC: Duke University Press.

Scott, W. (2003, January 4). Walter Scott's personality parade. *Parade,* 1.

Sternberg, R. J. (1986). *Intelligence applied: Understanding and increasing your intellectual skills.* New York: Harcourt, Brace, Jovanovich.

Sternberg, R. J. (Ed.). (1988). *The nature of creativity: Contemporary psychological perspectives.* New York: Cambridge University Press.

Taba, H. (1962). *Curriculum development: Theory and practice.* New York: Harcourt, Brace.

Taylor, I. A. (1959). The nature of the creative process. In P. Smith (Ed.), *Creativity* (pp. 521–82). New York: Hastings House.

Torrance, E. P. (1974). *Norms-technical manual: Torrance Tests of Creative Thinking.* Lexington, MA: Ginn.

Torrance, E. P. (1981). Predicting the creativity of elementary school children (1958–80) and the teacher who "made a difference." *Gifted Child Quarterly, 25,* 55–62.

Torrance, E. P. (1988). Creativity as manifest in testing. In R. J. Sternberg (Ed.), *The nature of creativity* (pp. 43–75). New York: Cambridge University Press.

Torrance, E. P., Murdock, M., & Fletcher, D. (1997). *Creative problem solving through role-playing.* Pretoria, South Africa: Benedic Books.

Torrance, E. P., & Safter, H. T. (1990). *The incubation model of teaching: Getting beyond the aha!* Buffalo, NY: Creative Education Foundation Press.

Torrance, E. P., & Sisk, D. (1997). *Gifted and talented children in the regular classroom.* Buffalo, NY: Creative Education Foundation Press.

VanTassel-Baska, J. (1998). *Excellence in educating gifted and talented learners* (3rd ed.). Denver: Love.

Von Oech, R. (1983). *A whack on the side of the head: How to unlock your mind for innovation.* New York: Warner Books.

Wallas, G. (1976). Stages in the creative process. In A. Rothenberg & C. R. Hausman (Eds.), *The creativity question.* (pp. 69–73). Durham, NC: Duke University Press.

Ziv, A. (1983). The influence of humorous atmosphere on divergent thinking. *Contemporary Educational Psychology, 8,* 68–75.

Chapter 12

Developing Research Skills in Gifted Students

by **Barbara Moore**

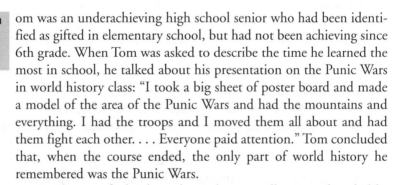

om was an underachieving high school senior who had been identified as gifted in elementary school, but had not been achieving since 6th grade. When Tom was asked to describe the time he learned the most in school, he talked about his presentation on the Punic Wars in world history class: "I took a big sheet of poster board and made a model of the area of the Punic Wars and had the mountains and everything. I had the troops and I moved them all about and had them fight each other. . . . Everyone paid attention." Tom concluded that, when the course ended, the only part of world history he remembered was the Punic Wars.

Keisha, a gifted 8th-grade student, vividly remembered 4th-grade science when the students created an ant farm and incubated chicken eggs. As the students observed the behavior of the ants and eggs, they speculated about the meaning of what they saw, created hypotheses based on their observations, tested these hypotheses by further observation, and read books on the subject from their school library.

Gifted students of all ages, whether they achieve or perform poorly in academic settings, share many characteristics that make them enjoy group or individual projects that allow them to be active investigators (Clark, 1988; Piirto, 1994). They are frequently interested in topics that are beyond the interests or capabilities of their age peers, and their task commitment allows them to investigate a subject of interest for extended periods of time. Their high degree of curiosity makes them want to probe, ask questions, and discover reasons why. Because of their ability to synthesize disparate information, they can work on complex projects, and their insight allows them to find answers where others do not perceive questions. Yet, because of their precocious ability to learn and retain information easily, they are often impatient with the pace of the regular classroom curriculum and are bored in class.

The opportunity for gifted students to study topics in-depth is often limited to library searches. These "research" assignments usually consist of compiling information from encyclopedias and library books about a topic. This patchwork quilt variety of research projects often results in excruciatingly dull reports and does little to help gifted students experience the joy of discovery that true research can bring. Unless, of course, creative students like Tom look beyond the school library for source material and find innovative ways to present their projects.

The science fair project, similar to Keisha's whole-class investigations of ants and eggs, is the kind of research familiar to all students and teachers beginning in elementary school. With this kind of project, students' investigative endeavors are framed by the scientific method, beginning with a question that leads to a hypothesis, a research design, data collection, analysis, findings, and conclusions. Gifted students, who have a propensity to think in terms of "why" and "what if" can find this kind of project enjoyable as they test their theories about a variety of science-related topics, such as the ability of goldfish to survive subfreezing temperatures, the relative effectiveness of various insulators, or the kinds of mold spores produced by different foods. One added benefit of this kind of assignment is that students' parents can become involved in the planning and implementation of the project. Any minor inconveniences that parents might have to endure, such as dead goldfish, moldy cheese, or other foreign objects in their refrigerators, are overshadowed by the opportunity to participate in their child's education in a meaningful way.

Original research can also be used to enrich curricula in gifted students' social studies, mathematics, and language arts classes. Just as these highly curious and motivated students can function as biological or physical scientists, they can also function as social scientists—creating surveys, observing, interviewing, and analyzing primary documents. Yet, few programs for gifted students include research projects based on the social sciences.

Gifted students have been described as those who will be our future inventors, creators, and leaders in their fields. Yet, many students do not understand how professionals in various fields related to social sciences conduct their work. What *does* a cultural anthropologist do all day? Who uses social studies in their careers? How are language arts skills used outside the fields of journalism and fiction writing? Students who begin to think and work like social scientists discover that history is not a collection of dates and events, but rather a complex interaction of human beings and their visions, values, strengths, and frailties.

A large part of the problem may be that many teachers, including teachers of the gifted, are unfamiliar with the research process as it relates to the social sciences. When teachers rely on textbooks that present a multitude of historical events that are to be covered in a short period of time, students may lose the colorful details of the era and the individual human trees that make up the historical forest.

The social science research process is like scientific research in some ways, but in others it is notably different. Like science research, social science research begins with a question: "What was education like 70 years ago?" "How were advertisements in magazines different during World War II?" "How do preschool children play?" Unlike science research, though, social science researchers do not form a hypothesis at this point. Instead, they gather data by interviewing people, observing, or looking at primary documents. After they have categorized and analyzed the data, they form a hypothesis based on that data.

Collected data for social science researchers usually take the form of transcripts of interviews, field notes of observations, or collections of primary documents. This information is analyzed using a different methodology from that of science research. Numbers are usually avoided. Instead, the researcher reads through the material and, in the margins, writes a one- or two-word description of meaningful sentences. These descriptions are called "codes." The following is an example of an interview with a senior citizen about what school was like when she was a child, and includes the student-researcher's codes in parentheses:

> Now, one thing that was different, girls had to wear dresses [clothing]. Girls were not allowed to wear pants, but we were allowed to smoke [changing customs]. . . . We took government classes where you learn about voting. And I wonder how a student taking these classes could have been ignorant of the fact that Black people could not vote [discrimination]. . . . When I got to high school, I did not want to take home economics, but that was all the females could take [gender discrimination].

Once the documents have been coded, the researcher looks at all the codes and determines how they relate to each other, often changing the names of the codes during that process. Sometimes, if the researcher finds data that do not fit any codes, he or she creates a new code that will incorporate the coded and new data. The process is much like assembling a crossword puzzle—organizing bits and pieces until they form a complete picture. However, the nice part of social science research is that the researcher is not trying to assemble someone else's "picture," but is creating one that is new and original. Thus, the goal of social science research is to discover themes, patterns, and relationships. Based on these, the researcher creates a hypothesis.

The findings of social science research can become extremely important in connecting the community to the classroom and helping our society understand itself (Chapdelaine & Chapman, 1999; Crocco, 1998). In 1993, two youngsters from a Chicago housing project were equipped with microphones and tape recorders. Their task was to create "sound portraits of growing up in poverty"

(Jones & Newman, 1997, p. 17). The project was so successful it became a documentary that was aired on the Public Broadcasting System(PBS) and published in a book entitled *Our America* (Jones & Newman).

Primary documents found in the local library or on the Internet can be an excellent source of information for young social science researchers. McCoach (2002) cautioned, however, that one must be careful about the authenticity of information found on the Internet. For that reason, it is probably best to use only reliable sources such as those connected to the government such as the Library of Congress, those on reputable media Web sites such as PBS, or those on college or university Web sites. McCoach's article has an extensive listing of these sites.

Teachers of the gifted are fortunate to have examples of television programs that use primary documents to tell a historical story. PBS frequently airs programs that include the rich use of primary sources to capture an event in history. The most well-known examples of this kind of programming are Ken Burns' documentaries on the Civil War, the history of jazz, and the history baseball, as well as his investigations into the lives of Thomas Jefferson and Lewis and Clark. In a trailer to his Lewis and Clark series, Burns described a methodology different from the step-by-step linear process used by the traditional scientist. He talked instead of a more intuitive, holistic approach in which gathering data, creating a script, and finding background music were accomplished simultaneously. LaRue (1995) described this process as being more like our everyday experience of history.

> We are brought to our history in just this fashion—story, memory, anecdote. . . . These emotional connections become a kind of glue, which makes the most complex of past events stick in our minds and, particularly, in our hearts. (p. 1)

Thus, gifted students can pursue two paths to research. Like scientists, they can create experiments to test theories; or, like social scientists, they can observe, interview, and analyze written documents to arrive at generalizations about their world.

Historical Perspective

The concept of student as researcher is more than a century old. At the basis of Dewey's (1897) educational philosophy was the idea of students exploring their environment. Education, he stated, was not a succession of studies, but the development of new attitudes and interests in children toward the world around them (Dewey, 1901). He noted that, in textbook-driven education, the content is preselected, there is usually one method of dealing with that content, and students have little opportunity to experiment or try new ideas. The ideal student in such a learning environment is passive and willing to submit to another's agenda.

The child, Dewey (1901) argued, is a complex being who learns best when content is presented in a complex manner that mirrors real life. Dewey proposed a concept of education in which children carry out projects that are generated by their own curiosity. He believed that a school whose function is to give information, teach lessons, and form correct habits in children is not truly educational. The aim of education should be the growth of children, not the acquisition of skills they will need as adults. One attains power, he reasoned, by determining a personal issue or problem, selecting the means and materials needed to deal with that problem, and then using the processes of testing and experimentation to resolve the problem.

Piaget, in describing the behavior of children in terms of problem solving and internal motivation, reasoned, "A person won't ever solve a problem if the problem doesn't interest him" (Bringuier, 1980, p. 50). Piaget, too, was opposed to the concept of teaching as a transfer of knowledge from adult to child: "Everything one teaches a child prevents him from inventing and discovering" (p. 102). Although much attention has been paid to Piaget's stages of learning, Bruner (1977) noted that the focus of Piaget's observations was the way children learn—by actively exploring and interacting with their environments and by relying on trial and error to reach understandings.

Bruner (1977) believed that teaching should shift from the transfer of skills and understandings related to a field toward an understanding of the structure of the discipline being studied. Educators should "talk physics" to students, rather than "talking about physics" (p. ix). He felt that it is more important for students to understand the underlying concepts, principles, attitudes, and problems of a field than to learn factual information related to that field. Like Dewey, Bruner noted that events in life are not isolated. Our physical and social world is made of a complexity of interwoven factors. Therefore, isolated facts are not easily remembered. To be retained, information must be placed in a meaningful structure or pattern. Bruner described the act of learning as a continuous process of problem solving in which the child acquires new information that often contradicts what the child already knows, manipulates the information to figure out why there is an apparent contradiction, and then checks to determine whether the manipulation of the information accomplished the task for which it was designed.

Ward (1961) was one of the first educational theorists to apply these principles to the field of gifted child education. Ward believed that gifted children differed from other children in the degree of their intrinsic motivation and in their ability to learn *about* content. One of his important contributions to the field of gifted education was to shift the focus from differentiating the content studied by gifted students to changing the process through which they learned. He viewed gifted students as needing to have academic experiences that teach them to become producers of knowledge because, when these students become adults, they will be the ones to change and redefine the world. He wrote, "Gifted students are those who will advance their culture, not just participate in it.

Therefore, their education must be qualitatively different" (p. 80). He also stipulated that the education of gifted students needs to include opportunities to work alone, to use advanced resources and materials, to be allowed unstructured time, to be mentally and physically active, to try individualistic approaches to problems, and to exhibit creative behavior.

Renzulli's (1988) Multiple Menu Model incorporates many of the above ideas. He stated that students need to have *Knowledge Of*, a superficial familiarity of a subject; *Knowledge About*, a deeper understanding of the principles and theories related to a subject; and, *Knowledge How*, the understandings and tools needed to make a meaningful contribution to the field related to that subject. His Knowledge Menu includes the process of identifying problems within a subject area, gathering and analyzing data, drawing conclusions, and reporting findings.

From Dewey to Renzulli, educational theorists have emphasized the importance of helping students create real-world products. They believe in the importance of students' understanding and using a variety of methodologies that may be different for each content area. Practice in applying knowledge of one setting to a specific problem can give students the tools they need to examine other problems in various fields.

Program Models

Renzulli was one of the first theorists in gifted education to create a program model that included the concept of gifted students as researchers. His Enrichment Triad Model, developed in the 1970s, is based on his Three-Ring Conception of Giftedness, which describes gifted behaviors as resulting from the combination of above-average ability, task commitment, and creativity (Renzulli, 1988). Influenced by Bruner and Ward, Renzulli's Enrichment Triad Model focuses on helping gifted students develop behaviors exhibited by gifted adults who are successful in their fields. Because of this behavioral emphasis, Renzulli's model defines the gifted student in active terms: as a researcher, inventor, or creator.

Renzulli and Reis (1985) divided the research process into three phases or types of activities. Type I Enrichment activities consist of experiences that expose all students to professionals in a variety of fields. Each Type I activity concludes with a debriefing in which students brainstorm current issues or problems that those with an intense interest in that field can pursue. For example, after listening to a Type I speaker describe the problem of water pollution, a group of students in Torrington, CT, decided to study water quality in their area. Type II Enrichment activities prepare students to function as professionals, teaching them the skills they will need to pursue their group or individual investigations. For example, the students studying water pollution needed to know ways of testing and analyzing water samples. During Type III Enrichment activities, students actually conduct their research and present their findings to a real audience. The students who studied water quality discovered that a river in their area was polluted and created a petition that was presented to their state legislature. This presentation to a real audience of legislators helped the students understand the connection between science and social science. In addition, they were able to understand how their research could benefit their community. Possibly the greatest benefit to this kind of project is that, in addition to teaching students the skills needed to research issues within a particular area, the inclusion of real products for real audiences helps the students function as true researchers.

The Autonomous Learner Model (Betts, 1985) builds on Renzulli's concept of allowing gifted students to pursue areas of intense interests. Betts, too, believes that learning for gifted students should be self-directed and that the teacher of the gifted must help facilitate the pursuit of these interests. Like Renzulli, he described Explorations, Investigations, and In-Depth Study in which students develop knowledge, skills, and products within a particular field. His model differs from Renzulli's in that Betts places a greater emphasis on the affective results of independent learning, such as increased self-direction and self-understanding, that can result from the student being an active learner and researcher. Both models rely strongly on teaching gifted students the skills—such as problem solving, organization, decision making, writing, interviewing, and using computers— they will need to be successful creators of knowledge.

Most educational models for gifted students recognize the need to teach gifted students how to become researchers. For example, Tannenbaum (1986) included the use of mentors and apprenticeships in his model. The Purdue Model, developed by Feldhusen and Kolloff (1986), includes teaching gifted students independent study skills so they can conduct independent investigations. In the latter model, students are encouraged to brainstorm problems their communities will face in the near future and, by using the creative problem solving process, arrive at a solution to one of these problems.

The Research Process

Student research can occur in a variety of classroom environments. Some teachers prefer to have science research projects conducted by an entire class. Deal and Sterling (1997) described using questions such as "Why do apples float and grapes sink?" to begin a unit on mass, volume, and density. Students were encouraged to use their senses to investigate the physical properties of a variety of objects, but were also encouraged to read related reference materials and access experts by telephone or the Internet to increase their background knowledge about the subject.

In other instances, gifted students in either mixed-ability classes or resourced-out classes can conduct their own independent or small-group investigations. One class of middle school gifted students decided to research individual landmarks in their town. One student discovered the remains of an old mill, and another found that the office building in which her mother worked was formerly a hospital where her father had been born. The students shared their findings in PowerPoint presentations.

Steps in the Research Process

As discussed earlier, student researchers, like their adult counterparts, can follow two paradigms, depending on the question they are researching. The quantitative paradigm uses the scientific method, consisting of creating and testing hypotheses. The qualitative paradigm, originating in social science research, uses observations, interviews, and document analysis to arrive at generalizations or hypotheses. With either paradigm, the student researchers will follow similar steps in the process of their independent or group investigations (Curry & Samara, 1991; VanTassel-Baska, 1997):

1. *Selecting a topic.* Students explore topics related to a field through activities such as reading, brainstorming, discussing, and making webs.
2. *Finding a question or problem to research.* Students generate a list of many possible questions and choose one that is interesting and has not already been answered.
3. *Developing a plan of action.* Students investigate how others in the field carry out research on similar problems, determine how they will collect and analyze data, and decide on a way to record their progress.
4. *Gathering information.* Students determine sources of information; create a file of potential resources; determine guidelines for conducting interviews, observations, experiments, or surveys; locate existing information; and record their progress in meeting objectives.
5. *Analyzing information.* Students analyze the data they have collected along with their notes, determine relevant findings, and organize all information.
6. *Reporting findings.* Students determine an audience and decide on a product form.

Selecting a Topic

The first step in the research process is most important because it determines the direction in which the project will go and the quality of the research study. Sometimes, it is helpful for students to talk to a teacher or other adult who shares an interest. For example, when Elvin was assigned a research project in his high school social studies class, he and his teacher discussed his interests during an after-school meeting. Because the teacher knew that Elvin was interested in music, he suggested that Elvin talk to his music teacher. During their conversation, Elvin revealed that he had once attempted to make his own guitar and was curious about how stringed instruments were made. The music teacher provided Elvin with the addresses of instrument makers in the area and enlisted the support of Elvin's parents as drivers. Thus, Elvin's project was born.

Finding a Question or Problem to Research

Once students have decided their area of interest, they need to determine a question or problem to research within that area. Elvin's topic, "Instrument Makers in Maine," became "How Are Stringed Instruments Made by Instrument Makers in Maine?" The problem needs to be stated in such a way that student researchers can not answer it by merely reading what others have said about it. There are several ways in which students can change a topic into a problem:

- Students can use brainstorming techniques to list problems they perceive at school and in their community.
- They can interview the principal and other school personnel or invite them into the classroom to determine what they perceive to be problems. In one school, gifted students learned that the cafeteria workers were interested in knowing what foods served on a regular basis students really liked. The gifted students created a survey and administered it to all students in the school. When the cafeteria workers received the gifted students' analysis of the survey responses, they were surprised to learn that few of the students liked macaroni and cheese, so they discontinued serving it.
- Students can interview people in the community to determine problems that need innovative solutions. Olenchak (1996) used the Future Problem Solving process to help teams, consisting of two adult members of the community and four students, identify a community problem and create an innovative solution to that problem. One such team found a historic building that was about to be demolished so the land could be used for commercial purposes. The winning team's solution was adopted by the town, and the building is now a historical museum.
- One form of Renzulli and Reis' (1985) Type I general exploratory experience involves inviting community members and experts in a variety of endeavors into the school to share their areas of expertise on topics related to the regular classroom curriculum. Type I speakers might include people knowledgeable about such diverse topics as robotics, acid rain, astronomy, or physical disabilities. As part of the debriefing process after the Type I activity, students determine problems that continue to exist in the field.
- College and university professors, especially those in the fields of social studies or science, are excellent sources of questions one might ask about the local community. These questions might include the impact a new regional industry has on people and the environment, the reasons why certain groups migrated to a region, or the origins of local weather tales.

- Students can look for local landmarks that might merit their investigation, including old cemeteries, historical buildings, or historical events that took place in their area, but have no marked site. Cooper (1985) suggested taking students on field trips through their local town and asking tantalizing questions such as the following: "How did the town get its name?" "How did your street get its name?" "Why did a particular industry decide to locate in your town?" "What famous people were born in your area?" "What was life in your town like a 100 years ago?" "Why was your town settled?" "Where is the oldest cemetery in town?" "Who was the first doctor in your community?" "How did your community change when the railroad came?" "Has your area ever experienced a natural disaster?"

Developing a Plan of Action

Although one goal of gifted education is to create students who are self-directed, independent learners, most students have few opportunities in the classroom to develop the skills that will allow them to reach that goal. Therefore, it is important for the teacher to help student researchers divide their projects into manageable steps.

Working with student researchers to create a structure and timeline for research projects allows students to work efficiently and effectively, minimizing off-task time. Winebrenner (1992) suggested creating a learning contract with each student (see Figure 1). These contracts should include a section that stipulates the conditions under which the student agrees to work. These stipulations may include: (1) recognizing that the teacher is not to be bothered when working with another group of students (one elementary school teacher solved this problem by wearing a colorful necklace when she was working with a small group and did not want to be disturbed); (2) using acceptable ways to obtain help when the teacher is busy; (3) knowing what to do if no help is immediately available; and (4) acknowledging that students working on projects are not to bother other students or call attention to themselves. These rules are important in any classroom, but are especially important in a mixed-ability class where gifted students have been compacted out of the regular assignments and are conducting individual or group research as a form of enrichment.

Tomlinson (1995) and Curry and Samara (1991) have suggested several guidelines that can help the regular classroom teacher successfully implement a research program for gifted students:

- Each student needs to have a clear understanding of his or her project's objectives and the criteria that will be used to evaluate these objectives.
- Independent or group investigations need to be set up in small steps to ensure success. Help students plan projects carefully and allow for frequent check-in dates when the teacher and students can discuss the progress of their projects.

Chapter: _____

Name: _____

✓ Page/Concept	✓ Page/Concept	✓ Page/Concept
__ _____	__ _____	__ _____
__ _____	__ _____	__ _____
__ _____	__ _____	__ _____
__ _____	__ _____	__ _____
__ _____	__ _____	__ _____

Enrichment options: _____

Special Instructions

_____

_____

_____

Your idea: _____

Working Conditions

_____

_____

_____

Teacher's Signature: _____

Student's Signature: _____

Figure 1. Learning contract

Note. From *Teaching Gifted Kids in the Regular Classroom* (p. 24), by S. Winebrenner, 1992, Minneapolis, MN: Free Spirit. Copyright ©1992 Free Spirit. Reprinted with permission.

- Skills need to be mastered before content acquisition (e.g., students need to be comfortable with interviewing skills before conducting an interview). Research skills can be introduced through whole-group instruction.
- Parents need to understand about their child's projects, why they are being undertaken, when they are to be completed, how they can help, and how they should not help. This cannot be overemphasized. Parents who are informed can be a teacher's biggest fan. They need to know from the teacher of the gifted—indeed, from all teachers—the types of work the child will be doing and the rationale for this work.

Independent or group investigations that are carefully planned by the teacher and take into account the above considerations can be meaningful, challenging experiences for student researchers and will interfere minimally with the management of learning for other students in the class.

Gathering Information

Not all research studies will use the scientific method. Students and teachers must be aware of the kinds of research conducted by people in the field most closely related to the topic the student wishes to study. Some of these kinds of data collection methods are described below.

Surveys. If students are going to construct surveys, there is a great deal they must understand first. Considerations include the following:

- Surveys need to be short for two reasons. First, a lengthy survey given to every student in a school can quickly become an overwhelming experience for student researchers. The process of recording responses to a long survey can take weeks of class time. When seniors at a high school in Maine were told that the school board was considering eliminating senior week before graduation, one senior decided to survey principals at the other high schools in the state to determine senior week practices in their schools. Although the survey ultimately provided the school with valuable information, the simple task of addressing more than 100 envelopes demanded a great deal of the student's time. The second reason for keeping surveys short is that most people do not have the time to complete a lengthy survey. The response rate for a short survey can be far greater than for a longer one.
- Students need to decide who will be surveyed and under what conditions. Surveys can be administered to students in school during lunch time or to adults at a public place (such as a shopping mall). In any case, arrangements and permission need to be completed in advance.
- Students need to determine whether they want to use open-ended questions ("My favorite novel is . . .") or Likert-scale questions in which, for

example, people respond to statements on a scale from *strongly agree* (SA) and *agree* (A) to *disagree* (D) and *strongly disagree* (SD).

- Students need to pilot their survey on a small sample of the population from whom they want information to determine if the questions make sense, if the instructions are clear, whether people have difficulties with individual questions, and whether their survey will give them the information they need.
- Students need to decide how they will analyze the data once they receive it.
- Students need to decide in advance with whom they will share the results of the survey. Product forms can include a report to the school board, the state legislature, the local historical society, or some other interested group; an article for the student newspaper; a bulletin board for the school; or a newsletter to parents.

Interviews. Interviews are another method of obtaining data for a research study. Students need a number of skills in order to conduct smooth interviews. First, they need to be at ease telephoning or writing to the person they will be interviewing. Indeed, interviews are a wonderful way to teach these skills. A student who is about to telephone the local veterinarian is usually highly motivated to practice telephoning in class.

Carey and Greenberg (1983) suggested the following checklist for student interviewers: (1) decide on the source, then contact the person to establish a date, time, and place for the interview; (2) conduct background research before the interview in order to have some familiarity with the topic; (3) make a list of questions and practice asking them; (4) decide what equipment you will use and practice using it; and (5) prepare an introduction that will explain the purpose of the interview and how it will be used.

Student interviewers need to consider several aspects related to the use of tape recorders, including replacing batteries, testing the tape recorder at the beginning of the interview to determine whether it is working properly, determining the best placement for the tape recorder during the interview, and obtaining permission in advance to have the interview taped. Cooper (1985) gave several tips for recording interviews: (1) use a good quality tape and an external microphone, if you have one; (2) interview the person in a quiet place; (3) don't switch the recorder on and off; (4) help the person relax by talking about a childhood experience or asking about some object in the room; (5) give the person plenty of time to think or even give him or her the interview questions in advance; and (6) listen carefully and probe for more information about an interesting story.

Students need to write their interview questions ahead of time and ask peers and teachers to critique them. Students should practice asking questions that are broad and general ("Tell me about your school"), rather than questions that require only short answers, ("Did you like school?") or that tend to suggest an answer. For example, "What did you like about school?" assumes that the respondent liked something about school. Students will also want to practice ways to begin and end interviews smoothly.

Once an interview is taped, students need to transcribe the interview or know someone who can. Parent volunteers or students in high school keyboarding classes will sometimes agree to do this laborious task. Students may also wish to photograph the person being interviewed and will need experience using a camera. A student with a camcorder may wish to use this equipment with the participant's permission. Although the skills needed to use this equipment seem basic, we cannot assume that all students are capable of using technology skillfully. Teachers need to build into the student researcher's curriculum opportunities to practice the many skills related to the interviewing process.

Primary Documents. If students are interested in examining primary documents, they need to know where they can be found. A trip to the local library can be extremely helpful for students researching local topics. If the librarian is notified in advance, he or she can pull books and documents for the students to peruse. A field trip to the county clerk's office is also helpful. Most students are not aware of the vast numbers of documents that can be found in county offices. Students may also be able to find primary documents by contacting local organizations such as the local historical society and national organizations such as National Geographic or by searching the Internet. Internet sites change regularly, but sites such as The Library of Congress (http://www.loc.gov) or The Smithsonian (http://www.si.edu) are rich sources for primary documents and artifacts.

Students may also want to check with older residents in their communities about letters, diaries, photographs, and other documents that can help them in their searches. Teachers cannot assume that students know how to talk to a senior citizen, even if that person is the child's grandparent. Role-playing in class can make these contacts much less stressful for student and elder alike.

If students want to research one particular time period, a number of inexpensive books containing actual letters and diaries of individuals from that period can be found in college libraries or purchased through catalogues. For example, the Perspectives on History Series (published by Discovery Enterprises; see Teacher Resources at the end of the chapter) publishes letters from Civil War soldiers in both armies and women who worked as nurses and spies.

Analyzing Information

Students do not have to be statisticians to analyze the data they collect. However, they do need to know how to organize information so they can draw conclusions about their research. A variety of methods used by professionals can also be incorporated into student research projects.

Analyzing Surveys. With Likert-scale questions, students can look for frequencies or percentages for each response (e.g., 46% agreed and 54% disagreed) and report the frequencies in a bar graph or percentages on a pie chart. The students who surveyed their classmates about cafeteria foods reported the percent of students who selected each category response to their Likert-scale questions. Other students have used graphing software or books such as *Chi Square, Pi Charts, and Me* (Baum, Gable, & List, 1987) to organize their findings.

Responses to open-ended questions need to be analyzed using a more qualitative approach in which responses are labeled and separated into categories, with categories and category names continuously changing as new responses are analyzed. For example, one student researcher who asked about people who had influenced high school students' career choices began her analysis with three categories: Politicians, Actors, and Athletes. Later, she realized that all the responses in those three categories were related to people the students had seen on television, so she generated a new category called Television Personalities.

Analyzing Primary Documents. Research related to social science or literature frequently relies on a content analysis of primary documents such as letters, diaries, or newspapers from a particular period. The purpose of the content analysis may be as diverse as looking for a theme in a writer's body of work, to analyzing letters and diaries in order to determine factual information or personal reactions to a historical event. Students can also analyze the content of many forms of current written and oral communication such as advertising, graffiti, song lyrics, television shows, or movies. They can look at how written or visual communications have changed over time, such as the portrayal of women in advertisements found in *Life* or *Look* magazines over a 30-year period; changes in cartoons before, during, and after World War II; or changes in comic strips over the years.

Fraenkel and Wallen (1996) described three main types of content analysis: (1) frequency counts in which the researcher looks for a particular category of information, such as acts of violence in a movie, and counts the number of times that category appears; (2) nonfrequency analysis, in which the researcher looks for the presence of a category, but does not count the instances, such as movies in which people smoke; and (3) combinations of events in a communication, such as movies with violence and characters who smoke.

A fourth, more qualitative, approach to document analysis, described earlier, involves the researcher reading the document or viewing the communication without any predetermined categories in mind, looking to see what themes or concepts emerge. For example, a group of students reading firsthand accounts about slave ships determined that the writer's point of view greatly influenced the interpretation he or she placed on the events described. A ship's doctor and a sailor described similar events in completely different ways.

Students need to understand that, no matter what method they use, they can improve the reliability and validity of their findings by asking other student researchers to be peer reviewers, by dividing a document in half to determine whether a theme found in one half is also in the other half, by having two people analyze the same document separately, or by determining whether two aspects of the document (e.g., text and advertisements in a newspaper) reflect the same themes (Fraenkel & Wallen, 1996).

Individuals or groups of students can also research a particular time period by analyzing the paintings or photographs from that era. As with letters and diaries from another time period, students can create hypotheses about the period by analyzing the image. They might want to discuss how the people are dressed, what they seem to be doing, and what emotions they seem to be feeling. They might want to speculate about the purpose of any objects in the picture. When an exhibit of artifacts from Versailles came to Mississippi, a class of students in that state examined Rigaud's painting of Louis XIV, concluding that Louis' primary concern was for people to see him as being wealthy and powerful. They then speculated about why he would want himself portrayed in this manner. These observations led to a deeper understanding of absolute monarchy when the students later studied Versailles and its kings.

Reporting Findings

Research products can take a variety of written and oral forms. Many lists of possible products can be found in the curriculum literature. One of the most handy lists is by Forte and Schurr (1996), who have created easy-to-use curricular planners for each subject area that include lists of product forms divided according to Gardner's (1983) multiple intelligences.

A social studies teacher at the Mississippi School for Mathematics and Science had his students research the local cemetery. The project began with a class field trip to the cemetery. Before the trip, the teacher listed the names of all the people buried in the cemetery and gave the list to the local librarian. She checked through her archives to determine which individuals were on record. Each student selected a gravestone from the list and began a search of the library's archives at the county courthouse. After the students gathered biographical information, they synthesized and wrote it in the form of a monologue. After several weeks of practice, the students performed their monologues in character and appropriate period dress (often supplied by the local historical society). Judges reviewed these performances, and the winners made up the cast for that year's "Tales of the Crypt." People from around the country who visited the town during Pilgrimage each spring to tour the antebellum homes were also able to be audiences for "Tales" performances, which took place at night in the cemetery.

Foxfire, a journal begun by an English teacher from a school district in the Appalachian South, consists of the "recollections and reminiscences of living people about their past" (Sitton, Mehaffy, & Davis, 1983). Early *Foxfire* articles included topics such as "Moonshining as a Fine Art" and "Log Cabin Construction." Ultimately, the collection of articles was published by the editors of Doubleday, who were amazed when the book sold more than 100,000 copies in the 1st month of publication (Sitton, Mehaffy, & Davis). Since then, many other *Foxfire*-type publications have chronicled history and folklore of communities around the country. Sitton, Mehaffy, and Davis told about a 3-year-old girl who was brought to the *Foxfire* offices by her parents to hear the tape of an interview with her grandfather who had died before she was born. The authors suggested that product forms can be written in the *Foxfire* format, dramatized, or simply kept as a tape archive in a local library.

Evaluating Student Researchers

When adults conduct research, their evaluations may be in the form of a publication in a distinguished journal or the response of peers after a presentation at a national conference. Often, the most important evaluator is the researcher. A study that may be deemed unsuccessful by others may, nonetheless, have been meaningful to the researcher.

Evaluation of student research projects often has to be tied to grades, yet all the elements in evaluation of adult products also need to be present. Students must be allowed to fail. They need to understand that research is a kind of risk-taking behavior that may not result the way they had anticipated. It is important to determine in advance with students what the criteria will be to evaluate their projects and who the evaluators will be. An elementary school teacher in Maine not only establishes in advance with her students the criteria that will be used to evaluate the students' projects, but also works with students to describe behavioral characteristics for each criterion. For example, if students decide they want to be evaluated on the quality of content and amount of creativity in their projects, they must determine what attributes constitute an A, B, C, D, or F (or outstanding, acceptable, not acceptable) for each criterion. In other words, how is A creativity different from B creativity? Although these discussions can become quite lengthy, they serve a variety of purposes. They teach students the skill of establishing criteria, force students to look at the standards of the field, and allow students to agree on specific concrete definitions of abstract concepts. Incidentally, this practice also helps the teacher develop the same skills. Karnes and Stephens (2000) have developed many rubrics for the student evaluation of products.

Wiggins (1989) suggested that any authentic assessment of student products should include the following criteria:

- skills of inquiry, which consist of the abilities to ask questions, analyze information, make decisions, and solve problems; and
- skills of expression, which consist of the abilities to communicate orally and in writing and to interact with others.

If the research project is replacing a curriculum that has been compacted in the regular classroom, Reis, Burns, and Renzulli (1992) suggested that it be evaluated because evaluation and feedback are important for the growth of any researcher, but it should not be graded. At the time the regular curriculum is compacted, students who compact out of certain skills or content should receive a grade of A for knowing that subject matter, but do not need to receive an additional letter grade for the enrichment activities that replace the curriculum they already have mastered.

Research and Gifted Students With Learning Disabilities

Teaching gifted students to be active researchers can be especially helpful when working with atypical gifted students, particularly those who have been identified as having a learning disability. West (1991) speculated that students with learning disabilities may have neurological organizations that create difficulties with traditional educational tasks such as memorization, short answer, or multiple-choice assessments. He quoted Einstein's statement, "As a pupil I was neither particularly good or bad. My principal weakness was a poor memory and especially a poor memory for words and texts" (p. 119).

The brains of learning-disabled gifted students may be more suited to tasks that involve finding and solving problems or creating original ideas. West (1991) noted that, when a subject is approached in a more holistic manner, it more accurately reflects the world outside school. For example, he described mathematics as "a way of looking at and talking about the way plants grow, the way a bridge is stressed, the way music flows" (p. 207). West cited many famous people, such as Albert Einstein, Lewis Carroll, and Leonardo da Vinci, whose self-education, driven by their curiosity, led to their success in life.

Baum's (1988) description of her work with learning-disabled gifted students supports West's theoretical observations. The traditional curriculum for students with learning disabilities, regardless of the students' level of intelligence, usually focuses on remediation in the deficit area. As a result, these students frequently experience high levels of frustration in school, which may lead to disruptive behavior in the classroom and negative feelings about school and their own abilities (Baum & Owen, 1988). Baum observed, however, that in nonacademic settings, gifted students with learning disabilities are frequently productive and are able to learn rapidly. Using Renzulli's Triad Model, Baum helps learning-disabled gifted students investigate real problems. First, they explore various areas of interest; next, they are taught the skills they need to conduct their own investigation; and, finally, they investigate a real problem, creating an authentic product for a real audience. Baum described one elementary school student with severe writing problems who audiotaped her research notes and created her own slide show called "A Day in the Life of Drusella Webster," which has been shown repeatedly at the Noah Webster House.

Baum and Owen (1988) noted two major benefits of this kind of research project for students: Students who completed projects (1) expressed increased feelings of self-efficacy and (2) demonstrated a great increase in time on task. The authors concluded that the students' feelings of self-efficacy increased because they had been successful in meaningful and challenging situations.

Baum, Renzulli, and Hébert (1995) reported successfully using research projects with underachieving gifted students. They found that students not only made positive academic gains after the project, but also strengthened their relationships with teachers and peers.

Conclusions

Diffily (2002) described project-based learning as a powerful tool to help students connect their work in the classroom with the world outside. Research projects can become a meaningful part of curricula for gifted students, whether students are homogeneously grouped or in a mixed-ability classroom. Research projects that investigate real problems allow gifted students to be excused from curricula they already have mastered. These projects also give gifted students an understanding of how adults work in various fields of study. In addition, as the students work to complete research projects, they develop the many process skills, such as problem solving, observing, categorizing, and analyzing, that they will need in order to become independent learners.

Many articles in contemporary journals stress the need for problem-based learning, thematic instruction, and authentic assessment. On the other hand, some critics of these interdisciplinary strategies note that there is a vast array of knowledge that can be explored and used within each discipline. Prawat (1995), who is concerned with the superficiality of some project-based instruction, cited a statement Dewey made in 1931:

> Many so-called projects are of such short time span and are entered upon for such casual reasons, that extension of acquaintance with facts and principles is at a minimum. In short they are too trivial to be educative. (p. 15)

Prawat concluded that, although students can benefit from studying interdisciplinary concepts such as power or conflict, they also need to be aware of the powerful ideas that are contained within each discipline. Student research projects can accomplish this task.

Teacher Statement

As a teacher at the Mississippi School for Mathematics and Sciences, the task of designing research activities that challenge my students is a great one. In that regard, this chapter on developing research skills has helped me have a clearer understanding of what it means to conduct original research with my students that will truly enrich both of our lives.

After posing the question, "What was it like to be an immigrant to the United States at the turn of the century?," the classroom was filled with a flurry of hands eager to answer. Little did they know that this question was not to be answered by simply looking in the textbook, but that it would take an array of sources and experiences for them to truly understand.

By using this chapter as a model, I was able to structure the research project in a clear and concise manner that would act as a framework for each individual student. The process itself also allowed for flexibility with those students who had minor learning disabilities. Before they could began researching, each student had to first understand the steps in the research process. Many were familiar with research, but only in the manner of the scientific method. After we completed our study of the steps and I was certain that they were ready to proceed, we began the research project itself.

The results of the project were phenomenal. The students were able to create presentations, dramatizations, artwork, and papers that were excellent examples of their abilities to make the emotional connections that are so crucial in social science research. When it was time for grading, the students knew exactly what to expect because they had played an active role in the evaluation process and were aware of the risks involved when the research began.

Having read this chapter ahead of time, I was better prepared to present the research process to my students as an attractive way of studying history. By following the steps in the research design, I believe that each student was able to attain a level of self-direction and understanding that would have only been possible by using this method.

—Sarah E. Sumners

Discussion Questions

1. What are the names and telephone numbers of 10 people in your community who could be guest speakers in your social studies or science classroom? Be sure to include faculty from nearby colleges and universities.

2. What are the names and telephone numbers of 10 people in your community whom you could contact regarding a field trip for your students related to your social studies or science curriculum? Be sure to include the county courthouse, cemeteries, library archive rooms, and historical buildings.

3. What are the occupations of your students' parents? Which ones relate to social studies (parents who work in retail, banks, law offices, etc.)? Which relate to the field of science and mathematics?

4. What are some ways in which your students could share the results of their research? What are some real audiences of adults or students with whom they could share their understandings? How can they incorporate multimedia in their presentations?

Teacher Resources

Publications

Baum, S., Gable, R. K., & List, K. (1987). *Chi square, pie charts, and me.* Monroe, NY: Trillium Press.

Burns, D. E. (1990). *Pathways to investigative skills.* Mansfield Center, CT: Creative Learning Press.

Carey, H. H., & Greenberg, J. E. (1983). *How to use primary sources.* New York: Watts.

Cooper, K. (1985). *Who put the cannon in the courthouse square?* New York: Walker.

Forte, I., & Schurr, S. (1996). *Curriculum and project planner for integrating learning styles, thinking skills, and authentic assessment.* Nashville, TN: Incentive Publications.

McCoach, D. B. (2002). Using the web for social studies enrichment. *Gifted Child Today, 25*(3), 48–53.

Shack, G. D., & Starko, A. J. (1998). *Research comes alive: A guidebook for conducting original research with middle and high school students.* Mansfield Center, CT: Creative Learning Press.

Sitton, T., Mehaffy, G. L., & Davis, O. L. (1983). *Oral history: A guide for teachers (and others).* Austin: University of Texas Press.

Starko, A. J., & Shack, G. D. (1990) *Looking for data in all the right places.* Mansfield Center, CT: Creative Learning Press.

VanTassel-Baska, J. (1997). *Guide to teaching a problem-based science curriculum.* Dubuque, IQ: Kendall/Hunt.

Winebrenner, S. (1992). *Teaching gifted kids in the regular classroom.* Minneapolis, MN: Free Spirit.

Addresses

Discovery Enterprises, Ltd.
31 Laurelwood Dr.
Carlisle, MA 01741
(800) 729-1720
http://www.ushistorydocs.com

Foxfire
P.O. Box 541
Mountain City, GA 30562
(706) 746-5828
http://www.foxfire.org

The Library of Congress
101 Independence Ave. SE
Washington, DC 20540
(202) 707-5000
http://www.loc.gov

National Geographic Society
1145 17th St. N.W.
Washington, DC 20036–4688
(800) 647-5463
http://www.nationalgeographic.com

Public Broadcasting System
1320 Braddock Pl.
Alexandria, VA 22314
(703) 739-5000
http://www.pbs.org

The Smithsonian Institute
P.O. Box 37012
SI Bldg., Rm. 153, MRC 010
Washington, DC 20013-7012
(202) 357-2700
http://www.si.edu

Web Sites

U.S. National Archives and Records Administration—http://www.archives.gov/research_room/index.html (Click on "Digital Classroom and Teaching With Documents")

This Web site contains reproducible copies of primary documents from the holdings of the U.S. National Archives, teaching activities correlated to the National History Standards and National Standards for Civics and Government, and cross-curricular connections.

References

Baum, S. (1988). An enrichment program for gifted learning-disabled students. *Gifted Child Quarterly, 32,* 226–230.

Baum, S., Gable, R. K., & List, K. (1987). *Chi square, pie charts, and me.* Monroe, NY: Trillium Press.

Baum, S., & Owen, S. V. (1988). High ability/learning-disabled students: How are they different? *Gifted Child Quarterly, 32,* 321–326.

Baum, S. M., Renzulli, J. S., & Hébert, T. P. (1995). Reversing underachievement: Creative productivity as a systematic intervention. *Gifted Child Quarterly, 39,* 224–235.

Betts, G. T. (1985). *The autonomous learner model for the gifted and talented.* Greeley, CO: Autonomous Learner Publications.

Bringuier, J. C. (1980). *Conversations with Jean Piaget.* Chicago: University of Chicago Press.

Bruner, J. (1977). *The process of education.* Cambridge, MA: Harvard University Press.

Carey, H. H., & Greenberg, J. E. (1983). *How to use primary sources.* New York: Watts.

Chapdelaine, A., & Chapman, B.L. (1999). Using community-based research projects to teach research methods. *Teaching of Psychology, 26*(2), 101–106.

Clark, B. (1988). *Growing up gifted: Developing the potential of children at home and at school.* New York: Macmillan.

Cooper, K. (1985). *Who put the cannon in the courthouse square?* New York: Walker.

Crocco, M.S. (1998). Putting the actors back on stage: Oral history in the secondary school classroom. *Social Studies, 89*(1), 19–25.

Curry, J., & Samara, J. (1991). *Curriculum guide for the education of gifted high school students.* Austin: Texas Association for the Gifted and Talented.

Deal, D., & Sterling, D. (1997). Kids ask the best questions. *Educational Leadership, 45*(6), 61–63.

Dewey, J. (1897). My pedagogic creed. *School Journal, 54,* 77–80.

Dewey, J. (1901). *Psychology and social practice.* Chicago: University of Chicago Press.

Diffily, D. (2002). Project-based learning: Meeting social studies standards and the needs of gifted learners. *Gifted Child Today, 25*(3), 40–45.

Feldhusen, J., & Kolloff, P. B. (1986) The Purdue three-stage enrichment model for gifted education at the elementary level. In J. S. Renzulli (Ed.), *Systems and models for developing programs for the gifted and talented* (pp. 126–152). Mansfield Center, CT: Creative Learning Press.

Forte, I., & Schurr, S. (1996). *Curriculum and project planner for integrating learning styles, thinking skills, and authentic assessment.* Nashville, TN: Incentive Publications.

Fraenkel, J. R., & Wallen, N. E. (1996). *How to design and evaluate research in education.* New York: McGraw-Hill.

Gardner, H. (1983). *Frames of mind: The theory of multiple intelligences.* New York: BasicBooks.

Jones, L., & Newman, L. (1997). *Our America.* New York: Scribner.

Karnes, F. A., & Stephens, K. R. (2000). *The ultimate guide to student product development and evaluation.* Waco, TX: Prufrock Press.

LaRue, W. (1995, September 19). Ken Burns tries to "present the variety of existence." *Syracuse Herald-Journal.* Retrieved August 25, 2004, from http://caolan.tripod.com/kenburns/burns.html

McCoach, D. B. (2002). Using the web for social studies enrichment. *Gifted Child Today, 25*(3), 48–53.

Olenchak, R. (1996). *Rearing our village's children: Problem-solving partners*. Paper presented at the annual convention of the National Association for Gifted Children, Indianapolis, IN.

Piirto, J. (1994). *Talented children and adults: Their development and education*. New York: Macmillan.

Prawat, R. S. (1995). Misreading Dewey: Reform, projects, and the language game. *Educational Researcher, 24*(7), 13–22.

Reis, S. M., Burns, D. E., & Renzulli, J. S. (1992). *Curriculum compacting: The complete guide to modifying the regular curriculum for high ability students*. Mansfield Center, CT: Creative Learning Press.

Renzulli, J. S. (1988). The multiple menu model for developing differentiated curriculum for the gifted and talented. *Gifted Child Quarterly, 32*, 298–309.

Renzulli, J. S., & Reis, S. M. (1985). *The schoolwide enrichment model: A comprehensive plan for educational excellence*. Mansfield Center, CT: Creative Learning Press.

Sitton, T., Mehaffy, G. L., & Davis, O. L. (1983). *Oral history: A guide for teachers (and others)*. Austin: University of Texas Press.

Tannenbaum, A. J. (1986). The enrichment matrix model. In J. S. Renzulli (Ed.), *Systems and models for developing programs for the gifted and talented* (pp. 391–428). Mansfield Center, CT: Creative Learning Press.

Tomlinson, C. A. (1995). *How to differentiate instruction in mixed-ability classrooms*. Alexandria, VA: Association for Supervision and Curriculum Development.

VanTassel-Baska, J. (1997). *Guide to teaching a problem-based science curriculum*. Dubuque, IQ: Kendall/Hunt.

Ward, V. S. (1961). *Educating the gifted: An axiomatic approach*. Columbus, OH: Merrill.

West, T. G. (1991). *In the mind's eye*. Buffalo, NY: Prometheus Books.

Wiggins, G. (1989). Teaching to the (authentic) test. *Educational Leadership, 46*, 41–46.

Winebrenner, S. (1992). *Teaching gifted kids in the regular classroom*. Minneapolis, MN: Free Spirit.

Chapter 13

Teaching Gifted Students Through Independent Study

by **Susan K. Johnsen** and **Krystal K. Goree**

A 3rd-grade teacher announced to a small group of gifted students that they were going to begin their first independent study. She asked, "Does anyone know about independent study?"

A proud little girl immediately raised her hand and blurted, "It's when you write a research report!"

Most students might define an independent study in the same way as this 3rd grader, but it is much more than reading books and writing papers. Independent studies may be used for solving community problems; uncovering new questions; writing histories; and, most importantly, helping a student create a lifelong love affair with learning.

Independent study is the most frequently recommended instructional strategy in programs for gifted students and is included in the majority of introductory texts as a means for differentiating and individualizing instruction (Clark, 2002; Colangelo & Davis, 2003; Davis & Rimm, 1998; Feldhusen, VanTassel-Baska, & Seeley, 1989; Gallagher & Gallagher, 1994; Parker, 1989; Swassing, 1985; Treffinger, 1986). Independent study is also preferred by gifted students (Dunn & Griggs, 1985; Renzulli, 1977a; Stewart, 1981). When compared to learning styles of more average students, gifted students like instructional strategies that emphasize independence such as independent study and discussion. However, while gifted students like these methods, they do not always have the necessary skills that are essential to self-directed learning; consequently, they need to learn them. Once they have acquired the critical independent strategies, gifted students are able to become lifelong learners, capable of responsible involvement and leadership in a changing world (Betts, 1985).

Johnsen and Johnson (1986b) defined independent study as "the process that you apply when you research a new topic by yourself or with others" (p. 1). Along with research, Kitano and Kirby (1986) added the important elements of planning and teacher involvement: "Students conduct self-directed research projects that are carefully planned with the teacher and are monitored frequently" (p. 114). Both Betts (1985) and Renzulli and Reis (1991) have emphasized the importance of "real-world investigations" in their definitions. "In-depth studies are life-like for they provide an opportunity to go beyond the usual time and space restrictions of most school activities" (Betts, p. 55). Type III research projects are "investigative activities and artistic productions in which the learner assumes the role of a first-hand inquirer—thinking, feeling, and acting like a practicing professional" (Renzulli & Reis, p. 131).

In summary, independent study is a planned research process that (a) is similar to one used by a practicing professional or authentic to the discipline; (b) is facilitated by the teacher; and (c) focuses on lifelike problems that go beyond the regular class setting.

Independent Study Models

Models such as Renzulli's Enrichment Triad Model (1977a; Renzulli & Reis, 1997), Feldhusen and Kolloff's (1986) Three-Stage Model, Treffinger's (1975, 1978, 1986) Self-Initiated Learning Model, and Betts and Kercher's (1999) Autonomous Learner Model have inspired teachers to include independent study as an important component of their programs.

Renzulli's (1977a) model contains three qualitatively different phases: Type I enrichment or general exploratory activities introduce the student to a variety of topics and interest areas; Type II group training activities develop creativity and research skills; and Type III investigations encourage students to pursue real problems of personal interest to them (see Figure 1). Students move among and between the three types of activities as based upon their interest in a particular question, topic, or problem. When students arrive at Type III activities, the teacher helps them identify specific questions and methods to use in pursuing their independent studies. The teacher also provides feedback and helps the student find resources and audiences who might be interested in their products (Renzulli, 1979). Renzulli (1979) emphasizes the importance of finding "real" problems and using "authentic" methods during the Type III activities.

Feldhusen and Kolloff's (1986) Purdue Three-Stage Enrichment Model focuses on the development of basic divergent and convergent thinking abilities at Stage 1, more complex creative and problem-solving activities at Stage 2, and independent learning abilities at Stage 3 (see Figure 2). In the independent learn-

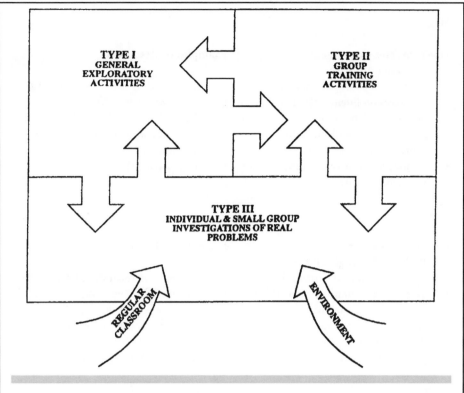

Figure 1. The Enrichment Triad Model

Note. From *The Enrichment Triad Model: A Guide for Developing Defensible Programs for the Gifted and Talented* (p. 14), by J. S. Renzulli, 1977. Mansfield Center, CT: Creative Learning Press. Copyright ©1977 by Creative Learning Press. Reprinted with permission.

ing stage, gifted students are involved in research projects that focus on defining problems, gathering data, interpreting findings, and communicating results. At this stage, the students' own interests and knowledge base serve "to stimulate a deep intrinsic interest in an area of investigation" (p. 131). More recently, Feldhusen (1995) proposed the Purdue Pyramid (see Figure 3). Included in the wide array of learning experiences needed to develop talent and still occupying a prominent position is "independent study and original investigations" (p. 92).

Treffinger (1975) developed a four-step plan for teaching increasing degrees of independent, self-initiated learning (see Figure 4). At the Teacher-Directed Level, the teacher prescribes all the activities for individual students. At Level 1, the teacher creates the learning activities and the student chooses the ones he or she wants to do. At Level 2, the student participates in decisions about the learning activities, goals, and evaluation. And, at Level 3, the student creates the choices, makes the selection, and carries out the activity. The student also evaluates his or her own progress.

Stage I

Divergent and Convergent Thinking Abilities

- Teacher-led short span activities
- Emphasis on fluency, flexibility, originality, elaboration
- Application of skills in various content areas
- Balance between verbal and nonverbal activities

Examples of Resources

- *Basic Thinking Skills* (Harnadek, 1976)
- *New Directions in Creativity* (Renzulli & Callahan, 1973)
- *Purdue Creative Thinking Program* (Feldhusen, 1983)
- *Sunflowering* (Stanish, 1977)

Stage II

Development of Creative Problem-Solving Abilities

- Teacher-led and student-initiated
- Techniques of inquiry, SCAMPER
- morphological analysis, attribute listing, synectics
- Application of a creative problem-solving model

Examples of Resources

- *CPS For Kids* (Stanish & Eberle, 1996)
- *Problems! Problems! Problems!* (Gourley & Micklus, 1982)
- *Design Yourself!* (Hanks, Belliston, & Edwards, 1977)
- *Hippogriff Feathers* (Stanish, 1981)

Stage III

Development of Independent Learning Abilities

- Student-led, teacher-guided individual or small group work on selected topics
- Application of research methods
- Preparation of culminating product for an audience

Example of Resources

- *Big Book of Independent Study* (Kaplan, Madsen, & Gould, 1976)
- *Self-Starter Kit for Independent Study* (Doherty & Evans, 1980)
- *Up Periscope!* (Dallas Independent Schools, 1977)
- *Interest-A-Lyzer* (Renzulli, 1977b)

Figure 2. Purdue Three-Stage Model

Note. From "The Purdue Three-Stage Enrichment Model for Gifted Education at the Elementary Level," by J. F. Feldhusen and P. B. Kolloff, 1986, in J. S. Renzulli (Ed.), *Systems and Models for Developing Programs for the Gifted and Talented* (p. 131), Mansfield Center, CT: Creative Learning Press. Copyright ©1986 by Creative Learning Press. Reprinted with permission.

More recently, Treffinger (2003) has identified self-directed learning as one "style" that might be observed in a classroom (p. 14; see Figure 5). The emphasis in the student-teacher contract style (i.e., contracting) and self-directed learning

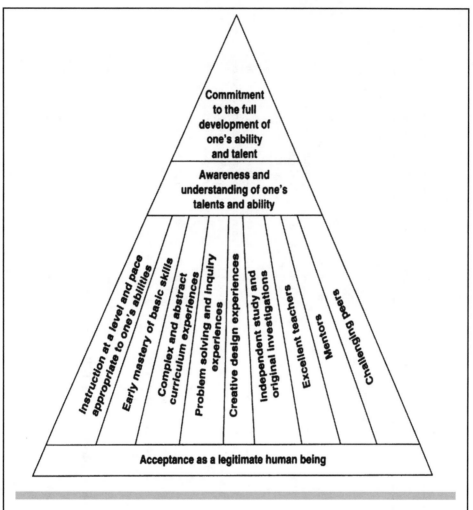

Figure 3. The Purdue Pyramid

Note. From "Talent Development: The New Direction in Gifted Education" by J. F. Feldhusen, 1995, *Roeper Review, 18,* p. 92. Copyright ©1995 by Roeper Review, P.O. Box 329, Bloomfield Hills, MI 48303. Reprinted with permission.

style (i.e., exploring) is on student-led or student-managed activities where the teacher acts as a facilitator of independent and group efforts. The other styles are controlled either by the teacher (i.e., command and task styles) or by the group (i.e., peer partner styles).

Betts and Kercher (1999) divided their Autonomous Learner Model into five major dimensions: orientation, individual development, enrichment activities, seminars, and in-depth study (see Figure 6). During orientation, the students learn about themselves and what the program has to offer. In individual development, the student focuses on developing skills, concepts, and attitudes that pro-

Levels of Self-Direction

Decisions to Be Made	Teacher-Directed	Self-Directed—Level 1	Self-Directed—Level 2	Self-Directed—Level 3
Goals and objectives	Teacher prescribes for total class or individuals.	Teacher provides choices or options for students.	Teacher involves learner in creating options.	Learner controls choices; teacher provides resources and materials.
Assessments of entry behaviors	Teacher tests, then makes specific prescription.	Teacher diagnoses, then provides several options.	Teacher and learner hold diagnostic conference; tests employed individually if needed.	Learner controls diagnosis; consults teacher for assistance when unclear about some need.
Instructional procedures	Teacher presents content, provides exercises and activities, arranges and supervises practice.	Teacher provides options for student to employ independently at his or her own pace.	Teacher provides resources and options, uses contracts that involve learner in scope, sequence, and pace decisions.	Learner defines project and activities, identifies resources needed, makes scope, sequence, and pace decisions.
Assessment of performance	Teacher implements evaluation procedures, chooses instruments, and gives grades.	Teacher relates evaluation to objectives and gives student opportunity to react or respond.	Peer partners used to provide feedback; teacher and learner conferences used for evaluation.	Learner does self-evaluation.

Figure 4. Model for self-directed learning

Note. From "Teaching for Self-Directed Learning: A Priority for the Gifted and Talented," by D. J. Treffinger, 1975, *Gifted Child Quarterly, 19*, p. 47. Copyright ©1975 by the National Association for Gifted Children. Reprinted with permission.

Teacher–Directed Styles	Group–Directed Styles	Self–Directed Styles
Command Style *Emphasis: Directing* The teacher controls decisions about goals and objectives, diagnostics, learning activities, and evaluation. This style is beneficial when the goals emphasize conveying information, teaching specific skills, or communicating basic declarative knowledge and concepts within a prescribed curriculum area. It may be appropriate for "enthusiastic beginners" who need considerable task direction. **Task Style** *Emphasis: Enabling* The teacher controls decisions about goals, objectives, diagnostics, and evaluation. The students have some choices regarding learning activities. This style is beneficial when the goals include content at varying levels of difficulty, or varying themes within a broad topic area. It still provides considerable task direction while offering some support for student choices. It is appropriate when the teacher begins teaching the students how to make choices and deal with mobility and freedom of movement.	**Peer Partner Styles with two substyles** **(Peer teaching and Cooperative)** *Emphasis: Collaborating* These styles are highly interactive, as the teacher begins to involve the students in shared decisions about goals and objectives, diagnostics, learning activities, and evaluation. *Peer Teaching or Tutoring.* Members of the groups are dissimilar in relation to the task on which they are working. One (who is proficient in relation to the task) serves as the "teacher partner" or tutor, and the other is the "learner partner," for whom the task represents a new and important goal. The students begin to define and carry out the "teacher" role with a peer, before undertaking it for themselves. *Cooperative groups.* The group members are relatively similar in relation to the task at hand. The group members work together in planning, carrying out, and evaluating learning activities, after conferencing with the teacher. The major purpose is to serve as a "prelude" for self-direction.	**Student-Teacher Contract Style** *Emphasis: Contracting* The student takes increasing control and responsibility for decisions about goals and objectives, diagnostics, and evaluation. Students negotiate specific contracts or learning agreements with the teacher, including all four areas of instructional decisions. There will be specific curriculum relevance or "pay-off" in the contracts; the teacher will involve students in individual and group evaluation, but retains final "approval" and evaluation authority. **Self-Directed Learning Style** *Emphasis: Exploring* Individuals, or student-initiated teams pursue projects they have designed. They assume leadership for goals and objectives, diagnosis, activities, and evaluation. They are responsible for demonstrating the appropriateness and relevance of their plans in relation to acceptable educational goals or requirements and for documenting the quality and quantity of their work and results. They may involve outside resources or mentors.

Figure 5. Classroom teaching styles

Note. From *Independent, Self-Directed Learning: 2003 Update* (p. 14), by D. J. Treffinger, 2003, Sarasota, FL: Center for Creative Learning. Copyright ©2003 by Center for Creative Learning. Reprinted with permission.

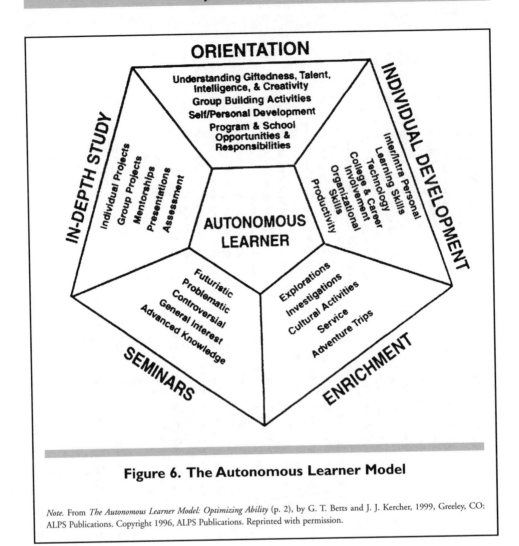

Figure 6. The Autonomous Learner Model

Note. From *The Autonomous Learner Model: Optimizing Ability* (p. 2), by G. T. Betts and J. J. Kercher, 1999, Greeley, CO: ALPS Publications. Copyright 1996, ALPS Publications. Reprinted with permission.

mote lifelong independent, autonomous learning. Enrichment activities assist students in deciding what they want to study independently. Seminars provide a forum for students in small groups to present their research to the rest of the group. Students learn how to promote understanding of their topics and facilitate the discussions. During the final in-depth study, students pursue areas of interest in long-term individual or small-group studies similar to Renzulli's Type III projects.

While these and other models of independent study exist, empirical research is limited, with most of the studies focusing on Renzulli's model. For example, students who completed Type III investigations reported that they were better prepared for research assignments, "were able to manage their time efficiently, and plan their work to meet their desired goal" (Hébert, 1993, p. 27). They have higher self-efficacy with regard to creative productivity and are more likely to pursue creative productivity outside of school (Starko, 1988). Delcourt (1993) found that students were more internally motivated toward projects they wanted to do and viewed other types of projects such as regular and gifted class assignments as "routine" or "regular" and not a part of creative activities. Olenchak and Renzulli (1989) found that students enrolled in Schoolwide Enrichment Model (SEM) schools had numerous creative products that exceeded the norm of typical student creative production. Gifted students who have participated in these programs feel that independent study has a positive influence on their motivation and career, their study habits and thinking processes, the degree of challenge, and the opportunity for self-expression in school (Renzulli & Gable, 1976; Zimmerman & Martinez-Pons, 1990).

Using Kuhlthau's Information Search Process Model, Bishop (2000) reported that the most difficult stage in independent study is exploring and forming a focus for the project. This stage appears critical to the success of the process and shows the importance of the teacher's guidance in framing the problem and organizing information.

Guidelines for Independent Study

While independent study is frequently used by teachers of gifted students, it is also one of the most abused strategies. Parents often find themselves struggling with their children's September-assigned research projects that are due in the spring. In these cases, teachers provide only grades, with limited instruction and support. In effective independent studies, teachers are actively involved, facilitating each phase of the study as a student's interest emerges and develops. Teachers therefore need to remember the following guidelines when initiating independent studies with their students.

1. *Don't confuse aptitude with skill.* While gifted students have a great aptitude for performing at a high level and producing complex products, they may not have the necessary skills for completing an independent study project. For example, they may not know how to identify good study questions, select a sample, use a systematic study method, or gather information from a variety of sources. The teacher will need to teach many of these skills, particularly during the first independent study.
2. *Identify independent study skills.* To facilitate the independent study, the teacher must be aware of the skills that are involved in every step of the process. For example, if the student is going to be conducting historical research, the teacher needs to know the specific steps in this method or be able to identify a historian who could serve as a resource or mentor.
3. *Adapt as the student changes.* While the teacher needs to have a thorough understanding of the steps in the process, the student's interest *must* guide the study. An interest cannot always be "turned on" according to

schedule. Some flexibility must be built into the process so that students have choices of what, when, how, and how much they want to explore a topic.

4. *Use different types of research.* "Don't take away my encyclopedia" is quickly being replaced with "Don't take away the Internet!" While both of these are great resources, students also need to learn about firsthand or hands-on learning such as interviewing, experimenting, conducting field studies, observing, surveying, discussing, and brainstorming with others. The type of research should match the question and method of study and be authentic to the discipline. For example, if the student is interested in roller coasters, then he might study them using the tools of a physicist.

5. *Make it a part of a regular program, not an addition.* Sometimes, independent study is something that students do when they finish the rest of their regular work. When this occurs, the student may never have enough time to pursue something of interest, may lose continuity, or, worse yet, may view research as extra work. The teacher may wish to use curriculum compacting to buy class time for independent study (Renzulli & Reis, 1997).

6. *Monitor progress and products.* Establish a regular time to meet with students to facilitate various phases and stages as they become more involved with their areas of study. This one-on-one time is important to identify needed research skills and to maintain each student's interest.

7. *Develop an appropriate evaluation.* The evaluation should match the characteristics of each step in the process and the student's experience with independent study. If the student is pursuing a topic independently for the first time, the teacher should consider this novice-level and evaluate accordingly. Evaluations should improve a student's study skills, encourage his or her interests, and increase a love of learning. If evaluations are too harsh initially, students will quickly lose motivation and follow teacher rules rigidly to receive the desired grade.

8. *Believe in the student's ability and be a model.* Nothing is more stimulating to students than others' interest in their independent studies. Teachers should make a point of noticing improvements and new ideas. Teachers who are engaged in their own research provide a model and can discuss their challenges in a collegial fashion with their students.

9. *Remember that independent study is only one way of meeting the needs of gifted students.* Programs for gifted students are often synonymous with independent study because it is the only strategy that is used. However, students quickly become bored with a repetition of projects leading to more and more products. Teachers will want to include many different strategies in their programs and limit independent studies to student-driven interests.

Steps in Independent Study

This section will describe nine steps that might be used in independent study. All of the steps may or may not be used in every independent study since the teacher and the student may already have defined some steps. For example, the teacher may present a problem and the students are responsible primarily for gathering information and sharing their results. Teachers who want students to find problems in their own interest areas may discover that all of these steps are helpful in teaching the process of independent study.

Step 1: Introducing the Independent Study

In introducing the independent study, the teacher defines the process and gives each student a plan to manage his or her work. At this stage, the teacher describes (a) various steps that will be used during the study; (b) the dates when different stages of the study are due; and, if known, (c) the audience who will be interested in the results of their study. As mentioned earlier, the steps may vary depending upon the nature of the study. If the teacher has already identified the questions, the students may be focusing primarily on collecting information, developing and sharing a product, and evaluating the process.

At this initial step, the teacher must help students learn how to meet deadlines by establishing due dates. While researchers often dream of unlimited time to pursue topics of interest, reality generally dictates such a timeline.

Students also will be more involved in the independent study if the topic is of genuine interest to them and if they know it will be used or heard by an authentic audience. For example, when a 2nd-grade gifted class was introduced to the problem of limited recycling in their community, they immediately pinpointed the lack of curbside services as a contributing factor. With the help of their teacher, they identified the city council as an important audience because the members held the budgetary power to make changes in the current recycling program. Their entire study then focused not only on researching various aspects of recycling, but also on how to sell their ideas to the council. Their enthusiasm and their professional video were rewarded with the desired change. Curbside recycling indeed improved the recycling program within their community.

Step 2: Selecting a Topic

At this step, the students select something to study. It may be a problem they want to solve, an issue they want to debate, an opinion they want to prove, something they want to learn how to do, or simply something they want to know more about. Interesting ideas may be pursued immediately or collected over a period of time. For example, a bulletin board of expressed classroom opinions might be developed with the purpose of proving or disproving them later. Newspaper headlines can become issues or problems for community action studies. Ideas and new questions that grow from classroom units can be researched immediately or stockpiled for future investigations.

When students have difficulty selecting a single area for study, they may want to consider some of these questions: Which topic is most interesting to me? Which topic do I know the least about? Which topic do I know the most about? Which topic will be easy to find information? Which topic is the most unusual? Which topic will be the most useful to me? Which topic will be the most interesting to the audience?

This step frequently involves gathering more information about the topic. Students may investigate by contacting museums, agencies, universities, and state or national departments. They may send home letters to parents, put bulletins that request topic information in the teacher's lounge, interview experts in the field, call public radio and television stations, or, of course, browse through the school library. The teacher may also help by inviting experts to discuss their fields of study with the class, taking the class on field trips, or setting up learning centers that provide an overview of a specific topic. During this process, students may discover that they cannot locate information about their topic, that the information is too technical or too difficult to understand, that the information is really not very interesting to them after all, or that another topic is more interesting. Throughout, the teacher lets the students know that seemingly good ideas don't work and that new ideas may appear accidentally or in unusual places. This step is important. If students are energized by their topics, the teacher may assume the role of facilitator, rather than dictator.

For example, Alice happened to be in a 4th-grade resource room with five other gifted children—all of whom were boys. The boys were interested in discovering methods for designing new video games. Alice could care less about games; instead, she was interested in penguins. While her choice created some difficulty for the teacher who had wanted a group-designed project, she eventually acquiesced to Alice's interest. The result was a beautifully designed zoo for Emperor Penguins.

Step 3: Organizing the Study

Sometimes, the teacher assists students in organizing or "mapping" their topics to help them find specific questions or problems. For example, if the teacher asks the students to brainstorm problems related to space explorations and the result includes only questions about UFOs and aliens, then this step is needed.

Organizational structures may include (a) descriptions, (b) comparisons, (c) causes and effects, or (d) problems and solutions. In *describing* space exploration, for example, the teacher might want to begin by creating categories for brainstorming. These categories may include space exploration's contributions, its future, its features, its history, its changes, its stages, or people's beliefs, feelings, or criticisms about it. Each of these broader categories form the hub of a wheel of student ideas and, eventually, questions.

Any of the descriptors generated about space exploration can be *compared* to other topics, models, theories, or rules. For example, the teacher might encourage the students to compare technological and human space exploration, historical and current beliefs about space exploration's contributions to science, or the features of early spacecraft with current or future ones. Again, questions begin to emerge from these comparisons and may lead to other organizational structures such as causes and effects or problems and solutions.

For example, if people have changed their feelings about space exploration, the student may want to consider the *causes and effects* of such a shift in attitudes. What might happen to space exploration's financial support? To scientific advances? To educational benefits? To scientists involved in cosmology? These effects may generate future *problems*. If financial support is withdrawn from space exploration, then the understanding of our solar system and the creation of a broader knowledge base may be limited.

All of these ways of examining a topic should lead to the most important step in the process: asking questions.

Step 4: Asking Questions

After doing some preliminary research and organizing their topics, the students are ready to ask questions. Good questions lead to quality independent studies, so it is crucial that teachers instruct students about the criteria for selecting good study questions.

One criterion relates to the question's complexity. Can it be answered by a simple "yes" or "no" or by facts from a reference book? If so, the question may not be one that requires much research. Good study questions often produce several possible answers and may be pursued differently by various researchers. Two other criteria relate to practicality. Does the student have the time or resources to study the question? Finally, is the question useful or beneficial to the student or others? These criteria should help students evaluate their questions.

Students may use their organizational categories to generate questions related to these stems: who, what, when, where, why, how, how much, how many, how long, and how far, along with what might happen if? For example, if a student were studying seals, he or she might ask descriptive questions such as, "What does a seal look like?" "Where does a seal live?" "When do seals breed?," or comparison questions such as, "How are seals and penguins alike or different?," or cause and effect questions such as, "How do treaties protect seals?," or problem questions such as, "Why is there a disagreement among countries over the hunting of seals?" The process of including categories with "W + H" stems should produce a great many questions (e.g., who, what, when, where, why, how, how much, how many, how long, and how far). The teacher might wish to have the student select several questions for study or have the student examine the level of thinking required by each question.

In the latter case, some teachers choose to teach their students a framework for asking questions such as Bloom's taxonomy (Bloom, 1956). In this way, the student can determine the complexity of the question. One approach is to teach them the differences among "little thinking," "more thinking," and "most thinking" questions (Johnsen & Johnson, 1986a, p. 19). "Little thinking" (i.e., knowledge and comprehension) questions are those that the student can answer by simply copying or redoing something that someone else has done. "More thinking" (i.e, application and analysis) questions are those that can be answered if the student uses the information in new situations. "Most thinking" questions are those that can only be answered if the student creates and evaluates new information. Giving students these evaluation tools helps them create more complex questions that, in turn, influence the overall quality of the independent study.

For example, in Alice's study of Emperor Penguins, she asked several "little thinking" questions such as, "What are the characteristics of Emperor Penguins?," "Where do they live?," "How do they breed?," and "What do they eat?" One "more thinking" question was, "How does the zoo in our city provide a habitat similar to the natural habitat of Emperor Penguins?" And one "most thinking" question was, "What might be an ideal zoo for an Emperor Penguin?"

Step 5: Choosing a Study Method

Most of the time, students are aware of only a limited number of methods for gathering information to study a question in an area of interest: the library and, more recently, the Internet. In both cases, students often feel that their research is not quite complete without referring to the venerable encyclopedia. This one-type-of-method approach may not even address their study questions. How might Alice answer the question, "How does the zoo in our city provide a habitat similar to the natural habitat of Emperor Penguins?" by gathering information in the library? Alice is going to need to visit the city zoo, talk to the zookeepers, and interview experts who know about Emperor Penguins. In Alice's and other students' studies, the questions should determine the study method.

There are many different kinds of study methods. Some of these methods include descriptive, historical, correlational, developmental, ethnographic, action, experimental, and quasi-experimental research (Issac & Michael, 1995). For example, if students want to know how different schools in their town were named, they would be interested in an historical study method. First, they might contact primary sources such as the principals of the different schools and people who were either at the school building when it was dedicated or know the person or place for whom/which the school was named. Second, they might locate secondary sources, such as newspaper stories that were written about the people or places for whom/which the schools were named. Third, they would interview their primary sources and take notes from their secondary sources. Fourth, they would review their interviews and notes, focus on facts, and delete biased or exaggerated information. Finally, they would verify information with their primary sources before sharing it with others.

Teachers will want to become acquainted with the research methods that address different kinds of questions so that their students will use authentic approaches that are frequently practiced by experts in each field. In addition, teachers will want to engage experts as mentors when students pursue topics in greater depth. What better way to study paleontology than to visit a dig with a practicing archaeologist? Or to learn about theater with a director of drama? Or to visit a courtroom with a practicing attorney? Authenticity is supported through the use of scientific methods, experts in various disciplines, a genuine student interest, and multiple approaches to gathering information, which is addressed in the next section.

Step 6: Gathering Information

Both the study method and the information are related to the questions. If a student is interested in the relationship between the number of study hours at home and grades in school, then he or she will use a correlational method of research and gather information from students related to "study hours" and "grades." If students are interested in how an engineer spends his or her time during a workday, they will use a more ethnographic method of research to observe engineers during their workdays.

There are many ways of gathering information. Some of these include note taking, writing letters, surveying, interviewing, observing, reading, listening to focus groups, brainstorming with others, locating information on the Internet, going on field trips, and conducting controlled experiments in a laboratory. In each case, the teacher needs to clearly specify and teach the steps involved with the approach. For example, when interviewing, the student needs to know (a) how to select a person to interview; (b) how to make the initial contact and set up an appointment; (c) how to locate background information and prepare questions for the interview; (d) how to make a good impression during the interview; (e) how to ask questions and record information; (f) how to summarize interview notes; and (g) how to provide information to the interviewed person. With the advent of e-mail, interviews with experts are much more accessible for students. With the Web, the interested researcher may even be able to take virtual tours of museums all over the world. Again, the teacher plays a valuable role by assisting the student in using search engines, locating reliable sources of information and experts, and critically evaluating the information.

Younger gifted children often gather information through hands-on activities, oral interviews, or surveys. For example, in learning about structures, children might build bridges with various materials, testing the strength of each design by placing toy cars or other objects on top. In deciding what businesses are needed in a classroom "city," they might conduct a "market analysis" through a survey of their classmates.

Remember that gathering information or paraphrasing written materials is a difficult task and should be taught to older students before they begin the process of independent study. In this way, interest in the topic and pacing of the project are not delayed by the frequently perceived drudgery of writing notes and outlining information. If students are already proficient in these tasks, then their studies can flow at a rate that maintains their enthusiasm.

In summary, information that is gathered should relate to the question, be authentic within the field of study, be clearly defined and taught to the students, and be appropriate for the age of the researcher.

Step 7: Developing a Product

While most students believe that "independent study" is synonymous with "written report," information may be organized in a variety of ways. Products include books, diagrams, dioramas, videos, computer programs, games, graphs, posters, puppet shows, reports, tape recordings, timelines, debates, dramatizations, models, newspapers, poems, speeches, and many others.

If the product is an option, then students may select one or more that match their original questions. For example, Albert had several questions that related to his topic of interest, "bees." They included "What are the parts of a bee?," "What are the different kinds of bees?," and "Which wild flowers in my neighborhood do bees prefer?" Albert might have answered all of these questions with a written report or a PowerPoint presentation, but he wanted to organize a display for parent open house. To answer the questions related to parts and kinds of bees, he drew a diagram of each one—comparing and contrasting coloration, size, and shape. He mounted these on a poster along with some photos of the bees in their natural habitats and labeled each part. For his study question that examined wild flower preferences among bees, he displayed his field notes, presenting the results in a series of graphs. He then prepared an audiotape in which he enthusiastically described the entire process of his independent study.

Similar to the step of gathering information, the product should be authentic within the field of study. For example, what product(s) might a naturalist develop to share his or her work? Did Albert share his bee study in a similar way? Indeed, a naturalist would keep a scientific journal, attach pictures or photos as examples, summarize results in a graph, and present information orally or in written form.

The teacher will want to teach each step of product development. For example, in designing a timeline, the student might (a) determine which years will be included; (b) decide whether the timeline will be horizontal or vertical; (c) decide whether to use pictures, drawings, special lettering, or other graphic designs; (d) decide the length of the line and each time period; (e) draw the line manually or use the computer; (f) divide the line into specific time periods; (g) write the dates and information beside the timeline and attach any pictures or drawings; and (h) write a title.

Finally, the way that the information is organized should again match the age of the student. Hands-on, visual, and oral products are easier than written ones for younger children. For example, in presenting information gathered about an ancient culture, a class of young gifted students created a museum of artifacts with videos of "experts" describing each display. The teacher will find many resources to help in organizing information into products (see Teacher Resources at the end of this chapter).

Step 8: Sharing Information

While information may be shared informally, students need to learn that there is life beyond the product. The teacher might discuss with the students some of these reasons for sharing information: Students can learn from one another; students can improve their products; others can help evaluate the product; and students can gather support for the product.

There are two major ways of sharing information with an audience: through oral presentation or in a display. The best approach should be determined by the audience. Each step needs to be outlined and taught. For example, in designing an oral report, the student will need to (a) plan the report; (b) practice the report; (c) arrange materials in order; (d) stand in a visible spot; (e) introduce him- or herself; (f) look at the audience; (g) speak loudly enough to be heard; (h) hold the product or visuals where they can be seen; (i) state major points; (j) keep the talk short; (k) ask for questions; (l) have the audience complete the evaluation; and (m) thank the audience.

For an oral report, students should practice before their peers. During these practice sessions, each student should provide at least two positive comments to every one improvement comment that relates to specific criteria. In this way, students' self-esteems and performances will improve.

Sometimes, the process of independent study stops with the completion of a product. Products are graded, taken home, and eventually discarded. For products to *live*, students need to share their ideas, garner support, and develop new ideas that might intensify or create fresh interests in their topics. For example, Albert, who studied bees, might contact entomologists via e-mail or at a local university to discuss the results of his field study. He might improve his techniques through these communications or by actually working with an expert in planning his next study.

Step 9: Evaluating the Study

The evaluation of independent studies is both formative and summative. With formative evaluation, students examine their performance in terms of the overall process. Criteria might include the following statements:

- I had a well planned independent study.
- I used my time efficiently.
- I wrote a probing study question.
- I used varied resources.
- My research was extensive.
- I developed a fine product.
- My class presentation was effective.
- I have good feelings about the independent study. (Johnsen & Johnson, 1986b, p. 22)

Similar criteria may be developed for other evaluators, such as the teacher, peers, or both. The audience may also contribute their evaluation comments. All of the evaluations can be collected and reviewed at a final teacher-student conference.

In addition to these types of formative evaluations, the student and teacher will want to use summative evaluation in judging the independent study products. Checklists or rubrics can be designed with specific criteria listed for each type of product. For example, an evaluation of a pictograph might include the following questions:

- Did the picture relate to the collected data?
- Did the picture reflect the kind of information being expressed? For example, if the graph is about money, money signs ($) or pictures of coins might be used.
- Did each symbol represent the same amount?
- Did partial symbols represent fractions of the amount?
- Were the symbols the same size?
- Were the symbols aligned next to the labels?
- Did the graph have a title that represented the question?
- Was each line of pictographs labeled?
- Was there a key that indicated the amount that each pictograph represented?
- Was the overall graph neat and attractive?

Evaluations in independent studies should focus on what the student has learned and what he or she might do to improve the next research project. If evaluations are positive, the student will be encouraged to continue his or her study, looking for new questions or new areas. There are many evaluations that may be accessed in the literature. One example is the Student Product Assessment Form (Renzulli & Reis, 1997), which examines the statement of the purpose; problem focus; level, diversity, and appropriateness of resources; logic, sequence, and transition; action orientation; and audience.

Conclusion

This chapter has provided a brief overview of the critical steps involved in independent study and research. The reader is encouraged to use the Teacher Resources at the end of the chapter to learn more about this important instructional strategy with gifted students.

Teacher Statement

As a teacher in a heterogeneously grouped classroom of 2nd graders, differentiating the curriculum to meet the needs of individual learners was one of my greatest challenges. For me, independent study was the most effective strategy to use in addressing the needs of gifted learners in the group. It provided an opportunity for students to study topics of interest in-depth while learning and practicing a variety of skills. It also set the stage for lifelong learning, confidence, and success.

I quickly discovered that the most efficient way to introduce the independent study process was to take the entire classroom through the process as a group. As we worked together through the process, every child in the classroom became excited about the contribution he or she would make to the project.

After navigating the project together, children were prepared to delve into independent research on their own. I often involved mentors from the community to meet with students and provide expertise in the area chosen for study, making the experience more meaningful for the young researcher and validating their area of interest.

After completion of the study and sharing the products with selected audiences, children were listed in the campus library resource guide as experts on the topics they had studied. Then, teachers would invite them into classrooms to share their knowledge when the class was studying the topic on which they had become an expert.

One student, Todd, was particularly excited about engaging in an independent study. He was a 2nd grader who was immensely talented in the area of art and immediately decided that he wanted to study a topic that would enhance his understanding of art in society. As he began to gather information on the wide array of topics that could be considered, he became interested in studying the art of origami. Due to the fact that I was no expert in the field of art, I immediately began looking for someone who could be a valuable resource for Todd. I called the art center associated with a community college in the area and found that the director of the center was interested in origami and had studied it extensively. He was thrilled to have the opportunity to share his passion with a young person and agreed to meet with Todd two times, once to introduce Todd to the topic and once during the study to answer any questions that had come up since the initial meeting.

Having gone through the entire independent study process with his class as a group, Todd was familiar with the process and could work on the study independently during the school day. He learned a great deal as he conducted his study and proudly chose his class as the audience for his product presentation when the study was complete. The art center director was in attendance for the presentation, and Todd proudly presented his findings related to the art of origami.

Following the presentation, Todd's mentor talked to Todd's mother and me about Todd sharing his expertise with other children. Several months later, Todd appeared on the local PBS station, presenting short segments about origami between *Sesame Street* and *Mr. Roger's Neighborhood.*

Several years later, I walked into the high school Todd attended. It was Christmas time and, as I entered the building I immediately noticed a beautiful Christmas tree decorated from top to bottom with intricately crafted origami ornaments. At the bottom of the tree was a small sign that said, "The ornaments on this tree were made by Todd Smith." Todd is now studying architectural design.

—Krys Goree

Discussion Questions

1. In comparing each of the models, how might the implementation of independent study be similar and different?

2. From the perspective of the classroom teacher, what are the positive and negative aspects of implementing independent study as an instructional strategy for gifted learners? How might the negative aspects you listed be addressed?

3. There are nine steps of the independent study process described in the chapter. Which step do you think would be most difficult to facilitate as a teacher? Why?

4. Given a typical classroom with gifted and general education students, how might the teacher include independent study in the curriculum?

5. How might you design a community project that would include independent study?

6. What teacher characteristics are important in facilitating independent studies?

7. How might involving mentors who are experts in the fields chosen by students to study enhance the independent study experiences of the students? How might a teacher find mentors to work with students on independent study projects?

8. What might be your philosophy and rationale for including independent study in a comprehensive curriculum?

9. Interview several gifted high school students. How do they describe their independent study experiences from elementary through high school? How are their experiences the same or different?

Teacher Resources

Publications

Betts, G. T., & Kercher, J. K. (2001). *The autonomous learner model: Optimizing ability.* Greeley, CO: ALPS.
This 336-page book is a guide to the Autonomous Learner Model. It describes each of the five dimensions of the model and includes essential activities.

Blair, C. (2003). *Let your fingers do the searching.* Dayton, OH: Pieces of Learning.
This book for grades 7–12 guides students in using 40 reference sources to conduct research. Grading tally sheets and record-keeping assignments are included.

Blandford, E. (1998). *How to write the best research paper ever.* Dayton, OH: Pieces of Learning.
This student workbook for grades 6–12 provides a framework for organizing a well-written research paper. Topics include choosing a subject, works cited, locating and using resources, developing a thesis sentence, outlining, evaluating opposing evidence, and constructing effective conclusions.

Burns, D. E. (1990). *Pathways to investigative skills: Instructional lessons for guiding students from problem finding to final product.* Mansfield Center, CT: Creative Learning Press.
This resource book contains 10 lessons designed to teach students how to initiate a Type III investigation. Lessons focus on interest finding, problem finding, topic webbing, topic focusing, and creative problem solving.

Doherty, E. J. S., & Evans, L. C. (2000). *Self-starter kit for independent study.* Tucson, AZ: Zephyr Press.
This resource book offers tools to guide students through complete independent investigations that target individual interests. It includes ideas for maintaining organized records.

Draze, D. (1986). *Blueprints: A guide for independent study projects.* San Luis Obispo, CA: Dandy Lion.
This book for students in grades 4–8 provides directions for a written report, speech, model, debate, experiment, poster, book, survey, demonstration, learning center, multimedia project, problem solution, science project, game, special event, and display.

Draze, D. (1989). *Project planner: A guide for creating curriculum and independent study projects.* San Luis Obispo, CA: Dandy Lion.
This 48-page book includes suggestions for high-interest topics, hands-on

methods of investigation, techniques for processing information, and product ideas that guide teachers and students through project design and independent study.

Heuer, J., Koprowicz, C., & Harris, R. (1980). *M.A.G.I.C. K.I.T.S.* Mansfield Center, CT: Creative Learning Press.
This activity book presents a collection of theme-based activities for Type I and Type II Enrichment experiences.

Johnsen, S. K., & Johnson, K. (1986). *Independent study program.* Waco, TX: Prufrock Press.
This program for students in grades 2–12 includes a teacher's guide with lesson plans for teaching research skills; student workbooks that correlate to the guide and are used for organizing the student's study; and reusable resource cards that cover all the steps of basic research.

Kaplan, S., & Cannon, M. (2001). *Curriculum starter cards: Developing differentiated lessons for gifted students.* Waco, TX: Prufrock Press.
This book includes guidelines for independent study, creative student products, and higher level thinking skills as tools for building units of instruction that emphasize depth and complexity of curricula for gifted students in grades K–12.

Kramer, S. (1987). *How to think like a scientist.* New York: Crowell.
This book teaches students in grades 2–5 the steps in the scientific method: asking a question, collecting data/information, forming a hypothesis, testing the hypothesis, and reporting the results.

Laase, L., & Clemmons, J. (1998). *Helping students write the best research reports ever.* New York: Scholastic.
This book contains mini-lessons that help students select meaningful topics, navigate references, take effective notes, paraphrase, organize materials, and write research reports that verify learning. Creative product ideas are also included.

Leimbach, J. (1986). *Primarily research.* San Luis Obispo, CA: Dandy Lion.
This 64-page book includes eight units for primary-age children. Each unit presents a different animal or pair of animals and includes interesting facts and activities for structuring research.

Leimbach, J., & Riggs, P. (1992). *Primarily reference skills.* San Luis Obispo, CA: Dandy Lion.
This 64-page book helps students in grades 2–4 learn how to use the library. Reproducible worksheets teach the parts of a book, alphabetical order, dictionaries, encyclopedias, and how to find books.

Lester, J. D., & Lester, J. D. (1992). *The research paper handbook.* Mansfield Center, CT: Creative Learning Press.
This book for students in grades 7–12 targets the writing process, from selecting a topic, to writing a polished paper. Examples and models that illustrate how to examine various subjects and sources, as well as tips on using computer searches and databases, are included.

Meriwether, N. W. (1997). *12 easy steps to successful research papers.* Mansfield Center, CT: Creative Learning Press.
This resource for grades 7–12 guides students through the process of writing a research paper, from choosing a subject and taking notes, to organizing the structure of the paper and preparing the final copy.

Merritt, D. (2003). *Independent study.* Dayton, OH: Pieces of Learning.
This book for grades 4–12 provides students with tools for planning studies, researching topics, presenting information, and assessing learning experiences. An overview to guide teachers in using the tools to design independent study experiences for students is included.

Mueller, M. (2002). *Great research projects step by step.* Portland, ME: Walch.
This book, which is recommended for grades 7–12, presents research as a thorough process that involves steps including topic selection, finding what students need to know, navigating systems that will help provide needed information, and conducting meaningful research.

Nottage, C., & Morse, V. (2000). *Independent investigation method: Teacher manual.* Mansfield Center, CT: Creative Learning Press.
This manual for teachers working with children in grades K–8 provides instructions for two skill levels, reproducible workpages and assessment tools, sample research studies, and teacher resource pages. A poster set (sold separately) reinforces the vocabulary and flow of the process.

Polette, N. (1984). *The research book for gifted programs, K–8.* Dayton, OH: Pieces of Learning.
This 176-page book provides more than 150 projects for primary, middle, and upper grades. Critical thinking skills are stressed.

Polette, N. (1991). *Research without copying for grades 3–6.* Dayton, OH: Pieces of Learning.
This 48-page book describes practical approaches for reporting on topics in diverse ways. Different types of research are illustrated along with models.

Polette, N. (1997). *Research reports that knock your teacher's socks off!* Dayton, OH: Pieces of Learning.

This book for grades 3–8 gives specific models and examples to show students different ways to organize information about animals, people, places, and events.

Polette, N. (1998). *The research project book.* Dayton, OH: Pieces of Learning.
This book for grades 4–9 presents more than 100 models for reporting research in divergent ways. The text focuses on models designed to stimulate analysis of information.

Redman, L. T. (2002). *Choosing and charting: Helping students select, map out, and embark on independent projects.* Mansfield Center, CT: Creative Learning Press.
This book for grades 3–6 guides students step-by-step through the process of choosing a topic, finding information, taking and keeping track of notes, conducting interviews, developing appropriate products, and deciding on an audience for presentation. Guidelines and forms to help teachers assess and understand student interests and learning are included.

Renzulli, J. S., & Reis, S. M. (1997). *The schoolwide enrichment model: A how-to guide for educational excellence* (2nd ed.). Mansfield Center, CT: Creative Learning Press.
This resource book includes a collection of useful instruments, checklists, charts, taxonomies, assessment tools, forms, and planning guides to organize, implement, maintain, and evaluate different aspects of the SEM in grades K–12.

Roets, L. (1994). *Student projects: Ideas and plans.* Mansfield Center, CT: Creative Learning Press.
More than 250 pages of project and independent investigation ideas are covered in this book on independent study and research for grades 3–12. The text includes models of outstanding student work.

Rothlein, L., & Menbach, A. (1988). *Take ten . . . steps to successful research.* Mansfield Center, CT: Creative Learning Press.
Appropriate for grades 5–8, this book presents the research process in 10 logical steps that include choosing the subject, selecting suitable reference materials, writing an outline, and writing the final copy.

Wishau, J. (1985). *Investigator.* San Luis Obispo, CA: Dandy Lion.
This step-by-step guide for students in grades 4–7 includes activities in completing and presenting an in-depth research project. Specific information is provided for using the library, selecting a research topic, writing a business letter, writing a biography, conducting an interview, taking a survey, and making a speech.

Woolley, S. (1992). *Writing winning reports.* San Luis Obispo, CA: Dandy Lion.
This set of guides for students in grades 4–7 includes instructions about how to write reports on specific topics such as animals, planets, countries, and explorers. Point breakdowns for grading are also included.

Web Sites

These Web sites will provide teachers and students with information about independent study topics.

Best Environmental Resources Directories—http://www.ulb.ac.be/ceese/meta/cds.html
This site highlights timely topics and publications that focus on environmental and energy issues in society.

iLoveLanguages: Your Guide to Languages on the Web—http://www.june29.com/HLP
This page is a catalog of language-related Internet resources. You may find online language lessons, translating dictionaries, native literature, translation services, software, language schools, or language information.

Internet Resources for Children & Educators—http://www.monroe.lib.in.us/~lchampel/childnet.html
Many references and resources are easily accessed through this Web site, which is sponsored by the Children on the Internet Conference. The Library of Congress, NASA, the National Science Foundation, and the University of California–Berkeley Museum of Paleontology are among the host sites that are linked to this page and provide valuable research information.

KidsOLR: Kids' Online Resources—http://www.kidsolr.com
Numerous resources are provided on this page, including links to information sources that focus on discipline areas such as art, music, geography, history, language arts, math, science, and health.

Kids Web: The Digital Library for K–12 Students—http://www.npac.syr.edu/textbook/kidsweb
This Web site is simple to navigate and contains information at the K–12 level. Categories include the arts, sciences, social studies, miscellaneous, and other digital libraries.

The Math Forum—http://forum.swarthmore.edu
This forum contains math resources organized by subject. Broad topics include numbers, chaos, cellular automata, combinatorics, fractals, statistics, and topology. When exploring numbers, you will find Archimedes' constant, Devlin's angle, Pi, favorite mathematical constants, and many other interesting topics that will link to other sites.

Martindale's The Reference Desk— http://www.martindalecenter.com
Great science discoveries are included among the thousands of science links at

this page. ExtraSolar planets, genome mapping, genetic testing, global ecosystem, and top quark may become interesting topics for students interested in science.

Ivy's Search Engine Resources for Kids—http://www.ivyjoy.com/rayne/kidssearch.html
This page offers links to more than 10 search engines and more than 80 Web sites that are appropriate for children and young adults. Research sources are presented according to search engines, Web guides, and specialized searches for kids.

History/Social Studies for K–12 Teachers—http://home.comcast.net/~dboals1/boals.html
The major purpose of this site is to encourage the use of the Internet as a tool for learning and teaching and to help teachers locate and use resources. A wide selection of topics are included under the general headings of archaeology, genealogy, humanities, economics, history, government, research, critical thinking, and more.

ThinkQuest—http://www.thinkquest.org
This page provides an opportunity for students and educators to work collaboratively in teams to learn as they create Web-based learning materials and share research.

WWW Virtual Library: Museums Around the World—http://www.comlab.ox.ac.uk/archive/other/museums/world.html
This site provides a comprehensive directory of online museums and museum-related resources. Museums are organized by country and by exhibitions. The USA link also lists the 57 top museum Web sites.

Yahoo!—http://www.yahoo.com
You may search for specific topics using this page or use the listed resources to help you find information. Listed resources relate to arts and humanities, business and economy, computers and Internet, education, entertainment, government, health, news and media, recreation and sports, reference, regional, science, social science, and culture.

Yahooligans!—http://www.yahooligans.com
A search engine designed especially for elementary children. Sites include around the world, art and entertainment, computers and games, school bell, science and nature, and sports and recreation.

References

Betts, G. T. (1985). *The autonomous learner model for gifted and talented.* Greeley, CO: ALPS.

Betts, G. T., & Kercher, J. K. (1999). *The autonomous learner model: Optimizing ability.* Greeley, CO: ALPS.

Bishop, K. (2000). The research processes of gifted students: A case study. *Gifted Child Quarterly, 44,* 54–64.

Bloom, B. S. (Ed.). (1956). *Taxonomy of education objectives: The classification of educational goals. Handbook I: Cognitive domain.* New York: Longmans Green.

Clark, B. (2002). *Growing up gifted: Developing the potential of children at home and at school* (6th ed.). Upper Saddle River, NJ: Prentice Hall.

Colangelo, N., & Davis, G. A. (Eds.). (2003). *Handbook of gifted education* (3rd ed.). Needham Heights, MA: Allyn and Bacon.

Dallas Independent School District. (1977). *Up periscope! Research activities for the academically talented student.* Dallas, TX: Author.

Davis, G. A., & Rimm, S. B. (1998). *Education of the gifted and talented* (4th ed.). Needham Heights, MA: Allyn and Bacon.

Delcourt, M. A. B. (1993). Creative productivity among secondary school students: Combining energy, interest, and imagination. *Gifted Child Quarterly, 37,* 23–31.

Doherty, E. J., & Evans, L. C. (1980). *Self-starter kit for independent study.* Austin, TX: Special Education Associates.

Dunn, R., & Griggs, S. (1985, November/December). Teaching and counseling gifted students with their learning style preferences: Two case studies. *G/C/T, 40–43.*

Feldhusen, J. F. (1983). The Purdue creative thinking program. In I. S. Sato (Ed.), *Creativity research and educational planning* (pp. 41–46). Los Angeles: Leadership Training Institute for the Gifted and Talented.

Feldhusen, J. F. (1995). Talent development: The new direction in gifted education. *Roeper Review, 18,* 92.

Feldhusen, J. F., & Kolloff, P. B. (1986). The Purdue three-stage enrichment model for gifted education at the elementary level. In J. S. Renzulli (Ed.), *Systems and models for developing programs for the gifted and talented.* Mansfield Center, CT: Creative Learning Press.

Feldhusen, J. F., VanTassel-Baska, J., & Seeley, K. R. (1989). *Excellence in education of the gifted.* Denver: Love.

Gallagher, J. J., & Gallagher, S. A. (1994). *Teaching the gifted child* (4th ed.). Boston: Allyn and Bacon.

Gourley, T. J., & Micklus, C. S. (1982). *Problems! Problems! Problems!* Glassboro, NJ: Creative Competitions.

Hanks, K., Belliston, L., & Edwards, D. (1977). *Design yourself.* Los Altos, CA: Kaufmann.

Harnadek, A. (1976). *Basic thinking skills: Critical thinking.* Pacific Grove, CA: Midwest.

Hébert, T. P. (1993). Reflections at graduation: The long-term impact of elementary school experiences in creative productivity. *Roeper Review, 16,* 22–28.

Issac, S., & Michael, W. (1995). *Handbook in research and evaluation: A collection of principles, methods, and strategies useful in the planning, design, and evaluation of studies in education and the behavioral sciences* (3rd ed.). San Diego, CA: Edits.

Johnsen, S. K., & Johnson, K. (1986a). *Independent study program.* Waco, TX: Prufrock Press.

Johnsen, S. K., & Johnson, K. (1986b). *Independent study program: Student booklet.* Waco, TX: Prufrock Press.

Kaplan, S., Madsen, S., & Gould, B. (1976). *The big book of independent study.* Santa Monica, CA: Goodyear.

Kitano, M., & Kirby, D. F. (1986). *Gifted education: A comprehensive view.* Boston: Little, Brown.

Olenchak, F. R., & Renzulli, J. S. (1989). The effectiveness of the schoolwide enrichment model on selected aspects of elementary school change. *Gifted Child Quarterly, 33,* 36–46.

Parker, J. P. (1989). *Instructional strategies for teaching the gifted.* Boston: Allyn and Bacon.

Renzulli, J. S. (1977a). *The enrichment triad model: A guide for developing defensible programs for the gifted and talented.* Mansfield Center, CT: Creative Learning Press.

Renzulli, J. S. (1977b). *The Interest-a-lyzer.* Mansfield Center, CT: Creative Learning Press.

Renzulli, J. S. (1979). The enrichment triad model: A guide for developing defensible programs for the gifted and talented. In J. C. Gowan, J. Khatena, & E. P. Torrance (Eds.), *Educating the ablest: A book of readings on the education of gifted children* (2nd ed., pp. 11–127). Itasca, IL: Peacock.

Renzulli, J. S., & Callahan, C. (1973). *New directions in creativity: Mark 3.* Mansfield Center, CT: Creative Learning Press.

Renzulli, J. S., & Gable, R. K. (1976). A factorial study of the attitudes of gifted students toward independent study. *Gifted Child Quarterly, 20,* 91–99.

Renzulli, J. S., & Reis, S. M. (1991). The schoolwide enrichment model: A comprehensive plan for the development of creative productivity. In N. Colangelo & G. A. Davis (Eds.), *Handbook of gifted education* (pp. 111–141). Needham Heights, MA: Allyn and Bacon.

Renzulli, J. S., & Reis, S. M. (1997). *The schoolwide enrichment model: A how-to guide for educational excellence* (2nd ed.). Mansfield Center, CT: Creative Learning Press.

Stanish, B. (1977). *Sunflowering.* Carthage, IL: Good Apple.

Stanish, B. (1981). *Hippogriff feathers.* Carthage, IL: Good Apple.

Stanish, B., & Eberle, B. (1996). *CPS for kids.* Waco, TX: Prufrock Press.

Starko, A. J. (1988). Effects of the revolving door identification model on creative productivity and self-efficacy. *Gifted Child Quarterly, 32,* 291–297.

Stewart, E. D. (1981). Learning styles among gifted/talented students: Instructional techniques preferences. *Exceptional Children, 48,* 134–138.

Swassing, R. H. (1985). *Teaching gifted children and adolescents.* Columbus, OH: Merrill.

Treffinger, D. (1975). Teaching for self-directed learning: A priority for the gifted and talented, *Gifted Child Quarterly, 19,* 46–49.

Treffinger, D. (1978). Guidelines for encouraging independence and self-direction among gifted students. *Journal of Creative Behavior, 12*(1), 14–20.

Treffinger, D. (1986). Fostering effective, independent learning through individualized programming. In J. S. Renzulli (Ed.), *Systems and models for developing programs for the gifted and talented* (pp. 429–460). Mansfield Center, CT: Creative Learning Press.

Treffinger, D. (2003). *Independent, self-directed learning: 2003 Update.* Sarasota, FL: Center for Creative Learning.

Zimmerman, B. J., & Martinez-Pons, M. (1990). Student differences in self-regulated learning: Relating grade, sex, and giftedness to self-efficacy and strategy use. *Journal of Educational Psychology, 82,* 51–59.

Chapter 14

Affective Education:

Addressing the Social and Emotional Needs of Gifted Students in the Classroom

by **Stephanie A. Nugent**

---

he affective characteristics of gifted individuals, as well as the social and emotional needs related to those characteristics, have been well documented by researchers in the field of gifted education (Clark, 2002; Cohen & Frydenberg, 1996; Cross, 2003; Delisle, 1987; Roeper, 1995; Silverman, 1993). However, despite the evidence and support provided by the literature, proactive attention to the affective domain is still overlooked in many schools unless that attention is in reaction to some overt problem identified by teachers or the administration (Peterson, 2003).

What Is Affective Education?

"To be nobody-but-myself—in a world that is doing its best, night and day, to make you everybody else—means to fight the hardest battle which any human being can fight, and never stop fighting."

—e.e. cummings

Theories Supporting the Affective Domain and Its Development

Theories advancing the social and emotional aspects of human development and their connection to cognitive processing are numerous. Many of these have direct influence on educational practices even though they may or may not have been developed with gifted individuals in mind.

Not all students arrive at the school's door ready to focus on the day's tasks. Maslow (1971) developed a hierarchy of human needs in which the primary needs of food, shelter, safety, and a sense of love and belonging must be met in order for the more complex needs of self-concept, self-actualization, and transcendence to be addressed. If a need at any level goes unmet, then all energies that would have been spent moving up in the hierarchy are refocused to fill the void. Thus, students who arrive at school hungry or homeless, as well as those who are experiencing familial discord or dysfunction, will have difficulty self-actualizing, let alone developing a positive self-concept. Gifted students who wonder where they fit into the schema of school and the social cliques and hierarchies may have trouble forming a positive self-concept and reaching self-actualization.

The theory of positive disintegration (Dabrowski, 1964) and theory of overexcitabilities (Dabrowski & Piechowski, 1977) both address affective development. Dabrowski's theory of positive disintegration highlights the role emotions and struggles play in human development (Silverman, 1993). The theory suggests that tension created by inner conflict moves an individual toward higher levels of emotional development (See Figure 1). The levels of development progress from rigid, stereotypical structures and actions at the lowest level, through the emergence of an understanding of the difference between "what is" and "what ought to be," to the highest level manifested in altruism, compassion, and integrity (Mika, 2002).

The relationship between emotion and cognition are emphasized in Dabrowski's explanation of overexcitabilities (OEs; Silverman, 1993). An OE is a higher-than-average capacity (sensitivity) for experiencing stimuli, both internal and external, involving both psychological factors and nervous system sensitivity (Mika, 2002). Dabrowski identified five OEs:

- psychomotor, which is characterized by needing movement, having difficulty quieting one's mind in order to rest, or both, and may manifest in fast talking, gesturing, or nervous tics;
- sensual, which is characterized by powerful reactions to sensory stimuli (e.g., tastes, smells, sights, sounds, textures) and may manifest in profound aesthetic awareness (e.g., crying in reaction to a television commercial);
- imaginational, which is characterized by visual or metaphorical thinking and may manifest through daydreaming or vivid memories of nightly dreams;
- intellectual, which is most identified with classic definitions of giftedness, characterized by logical prowess and reasoning skills, and may manifest in aptitude for puzzles and logic games; and
- emotional, which is characterized by an intensity of emotion, a wider range of emotions, empathy, compassion, and a need for deep connec-

Level V: Secondary Integration

organization, harmonization, and actualization of the personality and the personality ideal; the integration of personal values and ideals into one's everyday life; characterized by personal responsibility, compassion, authenticity, autonomy, and empathy

Self-aware

Altruistic

Level IV: Organized Multilevel Disintegration

conscious shaping and categorization of personal behavior; deliberate self-transformation and movement toward self-actualization; clarity of values and goals

Metacognitive Transformation

Level III: Spontaneous Multilevel Disintegration

Emerging hierarchy of values and goals; awareness of inner conflict between "what is" and "what ought to be"; aspirations to grow toward the ideal

Positive Maladjustment

Level II: Unilevel Disintegration

influence stems from external societal mainstream values and peer group; ambivalence due to ambiguous internal values

Moral Relativity

Level I: Primary Integration

no inner conflicts; lack of empathy or self-reflection; impulsive actions characterized by lack of responsibility for one's actions

Egocentric
Nonreflective

Figure 1. Dabrowski's theory of positive disintegration

tions with others and may manifest in the creation and prolonged maintenance of imaginary friends (Mika, 2002; Silverman, 1993; Tolan, 1999).

Table 1 provides descriptions, possible manifestations, and suggested strategies for each OE.

Both positive disintegration and OEs provide a context with which to interpret common characteristics associated with giftedness such as asynchronous development; intensities of interest, emotion, creativity, and movement; perfectionism; interpersonal dynamics; and some maladaptive behaviors.

Table 1

Dabrowski's Overexcitabilities, Manifestations, and Strategies

OE	Description	Possible Manifestations	Suggested Strategies
Psycho-motor	A heightened tendency toward being active and energetic, either mentally, physically, or both.	• Less need for sleep • Action oriented; restless • Gesturing • Rapid talk • Preference for violent or fast games and/or sports • Delinquent behavior • Nervous tics • Self-injurious behavior	• Promote constructive release of excess energy (e.g., organized sports, trips, community activity) • Employ relaxation and sensory integration techniques
Sensual	An increased capacity to experience sensory pleasure or displeasure	• Strong aesthetic interests • Need for physical contact; attention; companionship • Dislike of loneliness • Keen interest and curiosity in food • Early signs of sexual interest and development	• Promote empathy • Teach techniques for desensitization to overwhelming stimuli • Encourage self control and reflection
Imag-inational	A strong ability to produce creative thought and visualization	• Associates images and impressions • Visual thinking • Adept use of imagery and metaphor in expression • Visualization skills • Vivid day dreams, dreams, nightmares • Developed sense of humor • Mixing of truth and fiction • Highly developed internal fantasy world (e.g., imaginary friends) • Maladjustment to external reality	• Encourage adaptive creativity strategies rather than maladaptive isolation • Teach the difference between reality and fantasy • Provide time for creative production and relaxation
Intellectual	A capacity for sustained intellectual effort	• Inquiry skills • Theoretical thinking • Search for truth; moral concern • Extensive reading	• Balance by encouraging the development of emotional and physical domains
Emotional	A heightened capacity for emotional depth and sensitivity	• Need for connections with people, places, or things • Empathy; compassion • Heightened sense of responsibility • Self-examination • Need for security • Exclusive relationships	• Develop talents and encourage creativity • Encourage healthy friendships • Provide contact with nature • Employ bibliotherapy • Teach relaxation techniques

Note. Adapted from *Theory of Positive Disintegration*, by E. Mika, 2002, Retrieved March 31, 2003, from http://www.nswagtc. org.au/ozgifted/conferences/TPD.html and *Dabrowski's Over-excitabilities: A Layman's Explanation*, by S. Tolan, 1999, Retrieved October 22, 2003, from http://www.stephanietolan.com/dabrowskis.htm. Adapted with permission.

Piaget (1936/1965) constructed a model of moral development that incorporated the individual's situation and point-of-view. Kohlberg (1974) extended the Piaget's work by examining the reasoning that leads to moral decisions. Kohlberg's six stages of moral development are grouped into three levels (see Figure 2):

1. *Pre-conventional.* This level emphasizes the "Might makes right" and "You scratch my back, I'll scratch yours" mindsets where consequences or punishment are integral to the choices one makes (Stage 1) and adherence to the rules is contingent upon having one's own needs met (Stage 2).
2. *Conventional.* This level revolves around law, order, conformity, and social conventions where there is a need to meet the expectations of others (Stage 3) and the maintenance of social order is based upon fulfilling one's obligations (Stage 4).
3. *Post-conventional.* This level examines personal, societal, and universal moral principles where the relative rules of one's own group or culture are upheld for the benefit of the group as a whole (Stage 5), and self-defined or chosen ethics are rooted in universal principles such as justice, truth, and equality (Davis & Rimm, 2004; Nugent, 2002).

Rest (1979) and Gilligan (1993) both expanded and adapted Kohlberg's stages in an attempt to explain further the process individuals undergo in their orientation from self to others. The literature suggests that, from an early age, many gifted children show evidence of acute sensitivity to moral issues (Lovecky, 1997; Silverman, 1993). According to Sisk (1982), the importance of the moral development of all children cannot be overstated, but the need to address the moral development of gifted children is essential if they are to develop and utilize their potential.

Krathwohl, Bloom, and Masia (1964) developed the Affective Taxonomy to provide criteria with which to classify educational objectives according to the depth, complexity, and thinking skills required. As addressed in the taxonomy, the affective domain involves the manner in which individuals deal with emotions—demonstrating feelings, personal values, appreciation, enthusiasm, motivations, attitudes, and sensitivities to other people, things, or ideas (see Figure 3). The Affective Taxonomy is comprised of five categories:

1. receiving (awareness and passive or selective attention);
2. responding (complying with given expectations, willingness to respond, and satisfaction in responding);
3. valuing (assessing worth of a person, thing, situation, or idea, ranging from acceptance to preference and, finally, commitment to a value or belief system);
4. organizing (categorizing and prioritizing values and resolving conflicts among competing values by comparing, relating, and synthesizing them); and

Level 1: Pre-conventional
emphasizes an adherence to rules and norms whose
origins and reasons are not fully understood

Stage 1: Heteronomous Morality—obedience and punishment orientation; egocentric deference to superior power or authority; trouble or punishment avoidance mindset; individuals avoid breaking rules due to the consequence of punishment; morality seated in external source; consequences determine whether actions are good or bad; decisions made without considering the needs or feelings of others

Stage 2: Instrumental Relativism—personal reward orientation; characterized by the desire to follow rules only when those rules serve one's own purpose; orientation to exchange and reciprocity; recognition of more than one point of view; morality determined by self-interest

---

Level 2: Conventional
emphasizes conformity to the rules, conventions,
and expectations of the established society

Stage 3: Interpersonal Concordance—good boy/good girl orientation; evidenced by the need to meet the expectations set by others; conformity to stereotypical images of the majority; morality is determined by society's point of view

Stage 4: Law and Order Orientation—related to the maintenance of the social order where an individual seeks to fulfill agreed upon duties; regard for earned expectations; differentiates actions out of a sense of obligation to rules from actions based on other motives

---

Level 3: Post-conventional or Principled Moral Development
emphasizes moral principles

Stage 5: Social-Contract Legalistic Orientation—relative rules of one's own group or culture must be upheld for the benefit of the group; valuing the rights of others, upholding values regardless of majority; awareness of the relativism of personal values; rules can be changed when they no longer meet society's needs

Stage 6: Universal Ethical Principles—manifested when an individual discards social or legal mores when such laws violate universal moral principles, such as justice; ethics and morals transcend societal rules; action is controlled by internalized ideals that exert pressure to act accordingly regardless of the reactions of others

Figure 2. Kohlberg's stages of moral development

Note. Adapted from *A Study of Moral Development and Self-Concept in Academically Talented Residential High School Students* by S. Nugent, 2002, unpublished doctoral dissertation, The University of Southern Mississippi, Hattiesburg. Adapted with permission.

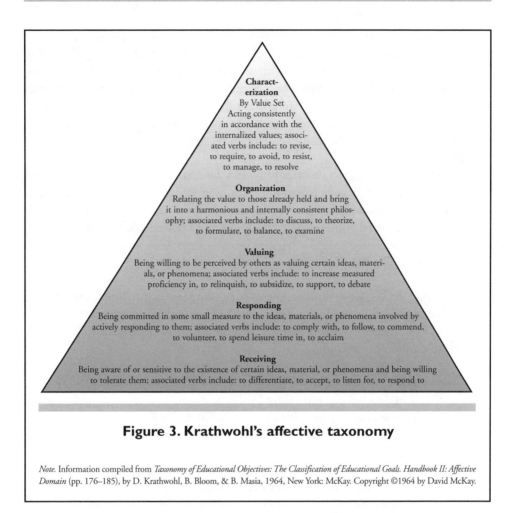

Figure 3. Krathwohl's affective taxonomy

Note. Information compiled from *Taxonomy of Educational Objectives: The Classification of Educational Goals. Handbook II: Affective Domain* (pp. 176–185), by D. Krathwohl, B. Bloom, & B. Masia, 1964, New York: McKay. Copyright ©1964 by David McKay.

5. characterizing (internalizing the established value system and behaving in a manner that is consistent with that system; Maker & Nielson, 1995).

Since emotions are not directly measurable, the criteria related to each category focus upon the demonstrated presence or absence of an emotion or attitude as it guides or controls one's behavior.

Two of Gardner's (1983) theorized multiple intelligences are associated with the affective domain: the intrapersonal and interpersonal. Intrapersonal intelligence is demonstrated by people who are able to determine moods, feelings, and other mental states within themselves, whereas interpersonal intelligence involves making distinctions among the moods, temperaments, motivations, and intentions of other individuals. With both intrapersonal and interpersonal intelligences, the information obtained is used as a guide for behavior. The interplay between these two intelligences impacts the group dynamics within any given situation.

Expanding upon the concept of the intrapersonal and interpersonal intelligences, Goleman (1995) proposed the idea of emotional intelligence (EQ). Defined as the ability to connect with and work with others, EQ helps individuals use the skills they have to the best of their abilities (Johnson, 2000). Goleman suggested that EQ is even more important than raw intelligence (IQ) for humans to reach their full potential because, when individuals are emotionally upset or off-center, they have difficulty remembering, learning, or making appropriate decisions.

The aforementioned theories provide a foundation upon which definitions of affective education have been built. However, just as there is no standard definition of giftedness upon which all interested parties can agree, there are multiple facets associated with affective education, but no single definition.

Operationalizing the Definition of Affective Education

While the cognitive domain encompasses intellectual processes, the affective domain addresses emotional aspects. Because researchers interpret the components of the affective domain differently, there are many elements associated with affective education, including:

- individualized value systems (Krathwohl, Bloom, & Masia, 1964);
- attitudes, beliefs, and values (Sellin & Birch, 1980);
- interests and appreciations (Carin & Sund, 1978);
- persistence, independence, and self-concept (Levey & Dolan, 1988);
- feelings, emotions, and awareness of self and others (Piechowski, 1997);
- interpersonal relations (Piechowski, 1997);
- humanitarianism (Weinstein & Fantini, 1970);
- curiosity, risk taking, complexity, and imagination (Williams, 1970); and
- character and leadership (Delisle, 2001).

With so many factors linked to affective education, it is a wonder that schools continue to neglect the affective domain. Prior to crises or overt threats, schools have traditionally paid little attention to the social and emotional needs of the student body in general and gifted students in particular (Peterson, 2003).

Reasons Schools Neglect the Affective Domain

Researchers cite numerous causes behind schools choosing not to include the affective domain within their gifted curricula:

- the lack of acknowledgement that the gifted have specific affective needs (Delisle, 1992; VanTassel-Baska, 1989);
- the traditional lack of concern in education for the affective domain (Tannenbaum, 1983);

- attitudes on the part of adults that emotions are to be dealt with at home, rather than in the school (Elgersma, 1981);
- fear of indoctrination (Bloom, Hastings, & Madaus, 1971);
- the position that, if the school meets the child's cognitive needs, affective development will automatically follow (Mehrens & Lehman, 1987);
- lack of reliable and valid tools for assessing affective functioning (Levey & Dolan, 1988);
- lack of clarity as to the optimal level of affective functioning to be attained (Levey & Dolan, 1988); and
- the belief that healthy emotional development among the gifted is automatic (Blackburn & Erikson, 1986).

Whatever reasons schools may give for not addressing the affective needs of gifted students within the curriculum, ultimately the effects of such shortsightedness will be evident in gifted students who do not reach their full potential (Galbraith, 1985; Lovecky, 1997; Roeper, 1988; Silverman, 1993; Sisk, 1982).

Why Include Affective Education in the Curriculum?

"I really must learn to read, except I'm afraid it will make it awfully hard for me in school next year if I know things. I think it will be better if people just go on thinking I'm not very bright. They won't hate me quite so much."

—Charles Wallace, from *A Wrinkle in Time*
by Madeleine L'Engle

Morelock (1992) defined asynchronous development in gifted individuals as an uneven rate of development in the cognitive, affective, and physical domains. When the school curriculum focuses solely upon the cognitive realm, the uneven development of the other domains may be enhanced, thus emphasizing the gifted child's feeling of being out of sync with his or her peers (Silverman, 1993). Roeper (1995) contended that, if asynchronous development is left unchecked, the adoption of unhealthy lifestyles (e.g., perfectionism, self-criticism, poor self-concept) or maladjustment (e.g., depression, eating disorders, antisocial behavior) may ensue. However, when affective issues are addressed and social and emotional needs are met, gifted students face their challenges with emotional balance and appropriate coping mechanisms that promote success in reaching personal potential (Roeper).

Issues Facing Gifted Students in the Affective Domain

Gifted individuals undergo the same developmental stages as others, but often earlier and at a faster rate (Webb, 1994). Although all children face affective and developmental challenges, gifted children, due to their unique characteristics in the affective domain, may also face issues that their agemates may not. Table 2 provides affective characteristics as articulated by Clark (2002), Webb (1994), Seagoe (1975), and VanTassel-Baska (1998), social and emotional needs associated with specific characteristics, and possible negative behaviors that may appear if the social and emotional needs are not addressed.

All too often in school, gifted students are asked to put their emotions aside and focus on the cognitive task at hand. In the current atmosphere of accountability in education, many administrators and educators feel as though there aren't enough hours in the school day to address the academic standards set forth by local, state, and federal authorities. However, research suggests that there is a connection between cognitive and affective functioning (Goleman, 1995). This relationship has the potential to impact school performance on a variety of levels. Katz (1994) purported that perceived social status, perception of teachers, perception of peers, participation in class discussions, and self-direction in learning can be linked to either a positive or negative self-concept depending upon how those impressions are internalized and processed. Frey and Sylvester (1997) contended that successful exposure to affective education strategies can aid in the development of a positive self-concept.

As further support for addressing the affective domain in the curriculum, Landrum, Callahan, and Shaklee (2001) incorporated affective components into the National Association for Gifted Children (NAGC) pre-K–12 gifted program standards. The standard relating to socio/emotional guidance and counseling promotes the need to "establish a plan to recognize and nurture the unique socio-emotional development of gifted learners" (Nevitt, 2001, p. 27). Within this standard, guiding principle #4 states, "Gifted learners must be provided with affective curriculum in addition to differentiated guidance and counseling services" (Nevitt, p. 34), the rationale being that the inclusion of affective components within the curriculum enhances the whole student, rather than merely focusing upon cognitive development.

How Can the Affective Domain Be Addressed in the Classroom?

"You have brains in your head. You have feet in your shoes. You can steer yourself in any direction you choose."
—Dr. Seuss, *Oh! The Places You'll Go*

Addressing the affective domain within the context of the academic curriculum does not have to be an arduous task (Johnson, 2000). Strategies addressing the affective domain may be integrated into students' daily activities. Such strategies may be used individually within content areas, or multiple strategies may be combined to form entire units focusing upon a specific affective aspect (e.g., self-knowledge and exploration of giftedness). However, it should be noted that the

Table 2

Affective Characteristics, Needs, and Manifestations of the Gifted

Affective Characteristic	Social/Emotional Needs	Negative Manifestations
Keen interest in understanding one's self and feelings of being 'different'	To understand differences and similarities between themselves and others; To assert personal needs; To share with self and others as a means of self-clarification and validation	Tendency toward introversion, isolation; May result in peer rejection
High expectations of self and others	To learn to clarify one's own feelings as well as the expectations of others; To set reasonable goals and communicate feelings	Tendency toward intolerance, perfectionism, criticism, depression, distorted self-concept; Being overwhelmed by competing expectations
Highly developed sense of humor	To learn how one's own behavior may affect the feelings or behavior of others	May be misunderstood or misinterpreted by peers; Tendency toward verbal attacks on others
Early sense of idealism, emphasizing truth, justice, equity	To reconcile 'what should be' with 'what is'; To find causes to which one can commit and promote; To develop personal value system	Tendency toward altruistic worrying or humanitarian concerns resulting in undue stress; Attempts toward unrealistic endeavors resulting in frustration
Development of inner locus of control; internal motivation and satisfaction	To self-monitor motivational issues; To prioritize personal value system in order to address potential conflicts	Tendency toward nonconformity, which may be perceived as a challenge to authority; Rejects external motivators
Heightened emotional intensity and depth; sensitivity; empathy	To process cognitively the emotional meaning of experience; To learn healthy ways of expressing emotions	Sensitivity to criticism and rejection; Vulnerable to giving too much to others without ensuring that one's own needs are met
Strong need for self-actualization	To pursue interests and seemingly divergent directions; To understand the process and demands of self-actualization	Lack of challenge, frustration, loss of undeveloped or underutilized talents
Ability to address and conceptualize societal, social, and environmental problems	To learn various problem solving frameworks; To experience meaningful involvement in real world societal, social, and environmental problems	Tendency toward developing quick solutions without addressing the depth and complexity of the problem at hand; Those in authority may not value the contributions of children
Attraction to the aesthetic facets of society at large (e.g., truth, beauty, justice)	To explore and experience the highest levels of human thought, potential, and production	Tendency to be drawn to obscure organizations with questionable, narrow, or perfectionistic value systems

success of many affective strategies relies heavily upon the attitude, development, and comfort level of the teacher (Clark, 2002). Teachers of the gifted have a unique opportunity to help their students address their own affective needs through classroom activities (Nugent, 2000).

Affective Instructional Strategies

Classroom Climate. Once a comfortable classroom climate has been established, students are much more willing to share their own insights. An atmosphere of acceptance and personal responsibility, rather than fear of retribution or negativity, provides students with a safe haven where risk taking and personal reflection can take place. One method for creating such an atmosphere within the classroom is the exploration and development of class parameters. Instead of dictating a set of rules and consequences to be used within the classroom, engage students in an open discussion about what kinds of behaviors promote their individual learning success and what types of behaviors undermine their learning. Have students brainstorm a list of acceptable and unacceptable behaviors. Combine and restructure the brainstormed items into a positively stated set of classroom parameters (see Table 3). Then, follow the same process to develop the consequences for not adhering to the established parameters. In so doing, students become stakeholders in the classroom community. If parameters are exceeded, the students themselves have taken part in the development of the guidelines or rules, as well as the consequences.

Another strategy to aid in the establishment of an affective classroom community is the identification of banished or dead words, words that are not acceptable to use in the classroom. Often, gifted students are inundated with a barrage of negative terms that their peers use as synonyms for *gifted*, such as *nerd*, *brainiac*, and *bookworm*. These and other offensive words (e.g., *stupid, dumb, idiot, retard*) are written on slips of paper and placed on a bulletin board or wall display. For a banished words theme, a jail cell motif could be used to imply that these words have been "put away." For a dead words topic, a headstone with "rest in peace" or a cemetery effect may be used.

Arts Incorporation. Sometimes, no matter how inviting and nonthreatening a classroom environment is, some gifted students may not be comfortable verbalizing their affective needs. Others may not even be cognitively aware that they have affective issues to address and, thus, are at a loss during activities that require affective verbal disclosure.

Incorporating art into a content area activity is one method that can be used to access the affective domain of gifted students when verbal strategies are ineffective or as a companion to verbal activities. The use of collage is one strategy that allows students of all artistic skill levels to participate in a creative activity that may be used as an affective outlet. For example, when a discussion on the real versus the ideal develops during a unit on justice, you can ask students to cre-

Table 3
Transforming Negative Statements Into Positive Parameters

Negative Statements	**Positive Parameters**
Do not criticize.	Provide positive, constructive feedback.
Do not speak out of turn.	Use respect and exercise good judgment.
Do not cheat.	Adhere to the school's academic honesty policy.
Lateness is not acceptable.	Show responsibility for your own learning by being prompt.

ate individual collages using discarded magazines to depict what ought to be on one side and what is on the other. The pictures students choose to incorporate into their collages may reveal more about their perception of the real and the ideal than their discussion. Upon completion of the collages, allow students the opportunity to share their observations about their own work and the work of other students in the class. Debrief students on the applicable affective aspects of reconciling the real and the ideal, such as perfectionism, body image, and multipotentiality.

Bibliotherapy. Bibliotherapy is the use of literature to help understand and resolve personal issues (Frazier & McCannon, 1981). The interaction between the reader and the story through identification or universal experience, catharsis, and insight appeals to many gifted students (Nugent, 2000). Gifted students whose strengths lie in their ability to conceptualize and generalize often find success through bibliotherapeutic reading (Adderholt-Elliot & Eller, 1989). It is one of the most valuable affective strategies available to teachers, parents, counselors, and gifted students (Silverman, 1993). After careful selection of a book or short story, develop activities and guided inquiry questions to aid students in the understanding and internalization of the book and the bibliotherapeutic process.

Planning activities prior to the bibliotherapy session, like the sample provided in Figure 4, helps to ensure that guided discussion, structured activities, or both take place. Short stories or novels used within the curriculum may also be used with bibliotherapeutic goals in mind depending on the themes or issues presented within the context of the plot.

Cinematherapy. Like bibliotherapy, cinematherapy engages viewers in an interaction with the medium to examine specific issues. Using films portraying the gifted as characters, either major or minor, to address the affective needs of gifted students has been the focus of several articles within the field of gifted edu-

Book: L'Engle, M. (1962). *A wrinkle in time*. New York: Dell.
Grade Level: upper elementary, junior high

Major Characters:
- *Meg Murray*: An awkward, highly intelligent, but underachieving high school student who is insecure about her physical appearance and abilities and displays social immaturity, particularly not taking responsibility for her own actions.
- *Charles Wallace Murray*: The extraordinarily intelligent 5-year-old brother of Meg who has a strong interpersonal connection with Meg and his mother. He exhibits uncanny empathy and entelechy. He hides his brilliance from most of society.
- *Calvin O'Keefe*: A popular and athletic boy in Meg's high school. He is also very intelligent, but has never felt truly accepted for who he really is.
- *Mr. and Mrs. Murray*: Both brilliant scientists (a physicist and an experimental biologist, respectively) who instill a thirst for learning and independence in their children.
- *Sandy and Dennys Murray*: Meg and Charles Wallace's twin brothers, who are very athletic and popular in school.

Themes:
A Wrinkle in Time is a classic retelling of the battle between good and evil and the ultimate triumph of love. Additional motifs are encountered through the life lessons Meg learns as she completes her quest to find her father. They include overcoming her desire for conformity and appreciating her own uniqueness; realizing and accepting that one person cannot know everything; and understanding the importance of communication even when words are inadequate.

Suggestions for Use in Bibliotherapy:
Understanding Giftedness: Charles Wallace realizes he is different. While he is intellectually gifted, he lacks the physical ability to do things like other boys in his class.
1. Have students define asynchronous development and give examples from their own life experiences when they have been touched by it.
2. Have students brainstorm the characteristics of an intellectually gifted child. Then, make a chart for each of the Murray children and Calvin O'Keefe and cite evidence from the book that indicates his or her giftedness.
3. Have students comment on the following quote from Charles Wallace: "I really must learn to read, expect I am afraid it will make it awfully hard for me in school next year if I know things. I think it will be much better if people go on thinking I'm not very bright. They won't hate me quite so much." Have they ever felt the way Charles Wallace does as evidenced by this quote? What coping skills do they use to combat it?

Ownership of the Gift: Meg, Charles Wallace, and Calvin all have issues dealing with conformity and others' expectations of themselves.
1. Have students discuss or journal about the pressures they face to be like everyone else. Then, discuss, brainstorm, or present coping skills that can be employed to combat such pressures.
2. Using collages, poetry, or some other form of personal expression, have students illustrate their unique abilities, the things that make them special.

Figure 4. Sample bibliotherapy guide

cation (Nugent & Shaunessy, 2003). Milne and Reis (2000), Hébert and Neumeister (2001), and Newton (1995) concur that teachers can effectively use film to help students understand themselves and cope with being gifted. Figure 5 provides a sample plan for using film clips in the classroom as a way to address specific affective issues. When selecting film clips, teachers should identify which affective characteristics are to be targeted during instruction. As with bibliotherapy, film clips from cinematic versions of short stories or novels used in the curriculum may be applicable to cinematherapeutic strategies.

Character Education. Anne Frank wrote in her diary, "The final forming of a person's character lies in their own hands" (as cited in Lewis, 1998, p. 226). Teachers of the gifted can help their students develop character not only through modeling positive character traits, but also through the integration of those traits in the content of daily curricula.

For example, try regrouping the selections presented in the literature text by character themes like tolerance, justice, equality, and honesty. Use each theme as a prereading activity by defining it and then having students describe what such behavior looks like and give examples of that character trait in action through current events or daily activities. If the content area's scope and sequence is not flexible enough to allow the reordering of selections, then be sure that a positive character theme is unveiled in the discussion of each selection. In subjects other than language arts, character themes can be identified in units being covered in social studies (e.g., justice, loyalty), science (e.g., ethics, integrity), and physical education (e.g., cooperation, fairness).

Service Learning. One affective characteristic that many gifted students share is a heightened emotional intensity and sensitivity toward social problems (Clark, 2002). One way for students to address those feelings is to become proactive and "do something" about their chosen cause (e.g., homelessness, elder care, pollution).

Service learning is a way to incorporate such proactive measures into the curriculum. Service learning is a method whereby students learn and develop through active participation in thoughtfully organized service experiences that meet community needs while being integrated into the students' academic curriculum. It provides structured time for students to think, talk, or write about what they did and saw during the service activity and to use newly acquired skills and knowledge in authentic situations, thereby enhancing what they have learned in school by extending it beyond the classroom (Belbas, Gorak, & Shumer, 1993). The benefits of service learning extend to the students, the school, and the community (see Table 4).

Making a difference is a need for many gifted students. Often, they bear the weight of the world on their shoulders as they empathize with the woes of our society and our environment. Through service learning, they have the opportunity to help. Because service learning activities are open-ended, gifted students are

Film: Van Sant, G. (Director). (2000). *Finding Forrester* [Motion Picture]. United States: Columbia Pictures.

MPAA rating: PG-13 for brief strong language and some sexual references.

Major Characters:
- *Jamal Wallace* (Rob Brown): An intellectually gifted African American high school student who prefers to hide his intellect in lieu of basketball with his friends in his New York City neighborhood.
- *William Forrester* (Sean Connery): A famous writer-turned-recluse who befriends Jamal and helps him with his writing and self-discovery.

Summary:
Jamal Wallace is an inner-city kid from the Bronx who has an aptness for basketball and a genius at writing. While always a C student, Jamal comes to the attention of a prestigious New York City prep school when he scores highly on his standardized tests. While Jamal is given a heavy load at his new school, both he and the school know that the real reason they took him on is for his prowess on the court. Befriended by a fellow student, Claire, and helped along by Pulitzer Prize-winning author and recluse, William Forrester, Jamal pursues his dreams both on and off the court while overcoming obstacles placed by his bitter literature teacher. As Jamal is shaped by Forrester, he finds that he is changing the old writer as well, forcing him to confront his past and his future.

Pertinent Scenes and Suggested Uses:
Conformity and Masking Talent: In the scene where Jamal's mother meets with his English teacher to discuss his standardized test results, there is a contrast between what the scores show and Jamal's behavior in school versus his behavior at home. He tends to hide his intellect in order to fit in with his friends, but he is a voracious reader and writer at home.
1. Share through discussion or journaling instances when each student has hidden his or her gift in order to conform. Discuss the context of the conformity and alternate coping mechanisms that could be used in the future.
2. Operationally define the term *potential*. Have students share through discussion, writing, or artistic creation what they feel their potential contribution to society is. Discussion goal-setting strategies to help students reach their potential.

Empathy and Challenge to Authority: After viewing the scenes where Jamal defends his fellow student during English class by correcting the English teacher's grammatical error and where Jamal engages in a quoting battle with the English teacher, discuss methods of teaching that are not effective with students in the class and analyze possible reasons for their ineffectiveness. Then, present or discuss coping skills that could be employed by students when faced with inappropriate teaching methods.

Stereotyping: After viewing the scene where Jamal is accused of cheating on his essay, discuss the role that stereotyping plays in prejudice. What is the root of prejudice? How can we combat it?

Figure 5. Sample film clip usage guide

Note. From "Using Film in Teacher Training: Viewing the Gifted Through Different Lenses," by S. Nugent & E. Shaunessy, 2003, *Roeper Review, 25*, p. 134. Copyright ©2003 by The Roeper Institute. Reprinted with permission.

Table 4

The Benefits of Service Learning

Benefits to Students	Benefits to the School	Benefits to the Community
• Improve self-esteem • Become active citizens • Exercise leadership • Positive relationship between peers and adults • Apply academic and social skills in a real-world setting • Gain relevant skills and experience • Explore careers	• Engender positive relationships with community • Create positive images of students within the community • Provide a vehicle for positive public relations • Become positive, active learners • Develop partnerships within the community	• Students provide a needed service • Schools become a resource to the community • Students become stakeholders in the community

often excited by the possibilities and experience the full effect of their creativity. In Massachusetts, a group of middle school students solved a community conundrum of stockpiling sludge from liquid wastes, in the process saving the community about $120,000 (Nugent, 1998).

Self-Understanding. In order to reach their potential and move toward self-actualization, gifted students need to understand themselves and their abilities, both relative strengths and weaknesses. One way to begin the self-discovery process is to use a student questionnaire. Although many teachers use such questionnaires or inventories at the beginning of the school year to learn about their students and their interests, by using those instruments as a springboard for discussion, teachers can promote reflective and metacognitive behaviors, as well as identify coping strategies in use or in need of instruction. Have students complete several open-ended statements (see Figure 6). Then, use their responses as a means to open sharing and group discussion (see Figure 7). Upon completing the questionnaire, a discussion on reasons behind the responses and possible coping strategies would be appropriate. Coupling self-exploration activities with appro-

Complete the following phrases to make true statements. Write your first instinctual response after reading the phrase.

I don't know why _____

If no one helps me _____

Some teachers_____

I hope I'll never_____

It makes me angry when_____

I'm happy when_____

Most people don't know_____

I'm tired of_____

I'm good at_____

I believe that_____

Figure 6. Open-ended response form

priate bibliotherapy, cinematherapy, character education, service learning activities, or some combination, teachers could develop an entire unit on the discovery of the gifted self.

Closing Thoughts

Addressing the affective domain within the curricula is appropriate for all students, but it is essential for gifted students whose affective traits may include divergent thinking, overexcitabilities, sensitivities, perceptiveness, and entelechy (Lovecky, 1992). In order to meet the program standards set forth by NAGC, gifted programs must incorporate the affective domain. Specific strategies to meet students' affective needs can be integrated into any subject area through individual activities, lessons, curricular units, or separate units. It is essential, however, that teachers who endeavor to address the affective aspects of giftedness be willing to follow up on issues that are inadvertently revealed. Whenever classroom

I don't know why . . .
> *People make things harder than they are.*
> *I can't sit still.*
> *Nobody understands me.*
> *Life's not fair.*

If no one helps me . . .
> *I do it myself.*
> *I do a whole lot better.*
> *I'll be smarter.*

Some teachers . . .
> *Don't teach to your level.*

I hope I'll never . . .
> *Lose hope.*
> *Become like my mom.*
> *Get brain damage.*

It makes me angry when . . .
> *People cheat off other people who do the work.*
> *I get picked on.*

I'm happy when . . .
> *It's complicated.*

Most people don't know . . .
> *How smart I am.*
> *How to reason.*
> *The real me.*
> *How to feel.*

I'm tired of . . .
> *People asking stupid questions.*

I'm good at . . .
> *Whatever I put my mind to.*

I believe that . . .
> *People can do a lot if they are determined.*
> *People can make the world better.*

Figure 7. Sample responses of junior high school gifted students

activities touch upon the affective realm, it is important to remember that most teachers are not trained counselors, and therefore they may not be prepared for all that is disclosed. A support system must be in place in the form of school counselors, school psychologists, or therapists.

Teacher Statement

This chapter on affective education is well organized and covered the topics that are of main concern to me as an educator of gifted students. I was particularly delighted with the affective instructional strategies section. It included several adaptable examples of how to put the strategies into action. When I read, I like to walk away feeling as though I can use what I read within my own classroom. This chapter certainly enables me to do that while still giving me the theoretical base to understand the "why," as well as the "how" in order to enhance my own instruction.

—Susan Panzavecchia

Discussion Questions

1. With respect to Maslow's hierarchy of needs, what programs are currently in place to help meet students' primary needs so that learning can take place? How could you help students move from primary need concerns to more complex needs within the context of your classroom?

2. By applying your knowledge of general characteristics of the gifted, which of Dabrowski's overexcitabilities seems to be the most common? Justify your response.

3. Develop your own comprehensive definition of affective education, describing what it is and how it can be incorporated into the curriculum. Which theories, methods, and strategies did you include? Why?

4. Examine your own school setting (either the school you attended, your work setting, or your postsecondary school experience). How are/were students' affective needs met within the curriculum? Provide an example that illustrates the integration of the affective domain. If the affective domain is/was not addressed, suggest a way that it might be integrated.

5. Select one of the strategies provided in the chapter and develop an activity that addresses at least one of the affective characteristics listed in Table 2. How would you integrate this strategy into a specific content area? What are the goals and objectives? How would you assess the activity?

6. Select one of the three quotes presented in the chapter. Explain how the selected quote applies to educational issues within the affective domain.

Teacher Resources

Affective Education Books

Beane, J. (1990). *Affect in the curriculum: Toward democracy, dignity, and diversity.* New York: Teachers College Press.
This book outlines important ways in which the subjects of morals, values, and citizenship can be reintroduced to students, detailing how this emphasis may contribute to a more humane future.

Blymire, L., Jones, C., Brunner, T., & Knauer, D. (1998). *Affective cognitive thinking: Strategies for the gifted.* Harrisburg, PA: Penns Valley.
The strategies included in this workbook for gifted students are based upon cognitive thinking theory and affective process skills. The workbook is photocopy-ready and contains specific activities for language arts, social studies, mathematics, and science.

Cohen, J. (Ed.). (1999). *Educating minds and hearts: Social emotional learning and the passage into adolescence.* New York: Teachers College Press.
With chapters detailing best practices in creating a positive school climate, social decision making and problem solving, emotional learning in middle school, conflict resolution, and tolerance, this book shows how several schools have been successful at implementing programs that effectively address the affective domain.

Kirschenbaum, H. (1995). *One hundred ways to enhance values and morality in schools and youth settings.* Needham Heights, MA: Allyn and Bacon.
This text provides easily adaptable activities that integrate aspects of the affective domain.

Affective Education Web Sites

Kieve Affective Education Inc.—http://www.kieve.org
Started in 1926, as a summer camp in Maine, Kieve has grown to include summer camps for both boys and girls, an ocean discovery program, science and wilderness programs, and a leadership program. They offer a free e-mail newsletter that is packed with informative strategies and suggestions.

The Ethics Resource Center (ERC)—http://www.ethics.org
The Ethics Resource Center (ERC) is a nonprofit, nonpartisan educational organization whose vision is a world where individuals and organizations act with integrity. This site provides information that can be used in classrooms to prompt ethical dilemma discussions.

Classroom Climate Books

Canfield, J., & Wells, H. (1994). *One hundred ways to enhance self-concept in the classroom.* Needham Heights, MA: Allyn and Bacon.
This book offers more than 100 practical, class-tested exercises that can be integrated into the school day or used in specific self-esteem programs. The authors provide suggestions for organizing and sequencing the activities, which are based upon solid learning and psychological research.

Shoop, L., & Wright, D. (1999). *Classroom warm-ups: Activities that improve the climate for learning and discussion.* San Jose, CA: Resource Publications.
These easy-to-use and enjoyable activities are quickly adaptable and easy to incorporate into a classroom.

Freiberg, H. (1999). *School climate: Measuring, improving, and sustaining healthy learning environments.* New York: RoutledgeFalmer.
This book provides a framework for educators to look at school and classroom climates using both informal and formal measures. Each chapter focuses on a different aspect of climate and details techniques that may be used by heads or classroom teachers to judge the health of their learning environment.

Classroom Climate Web Sites

Tribes Learning Community—http://www.tribes.com
Tribes is an organization dedicated to promoting caring, safe, and comfortable learning environments. This site provides information and suggested bibliographies, as well as staff development opportunities regarding the Tribes program.

Arts Incorporation Books

Gelb, M. (1998). *How to think like Leonardo da Vinci.* New York: Delacorte Press.
The author presents strategies for approaching challenges through problem solving, creative thinking, self-expression, aesthetic recognition, and goal setting.

McAuliffe, J., & Stoskin, L. (1993). *What color is Saturday?* Tucson, AZ: Zephyr Press.
Using analogies, this book encourages both cognitive and affective aspects of creativity. The strategies used in the book lend themselves well to arts incorporation in the curriculum.

Arts Incorporation Web Sites

Americans for the Arts—http://www.artsusa.org
This advocacy organization provides information on how to increase the cover-

age of arts in education. The site provides a wealth of information to help justify arts incorporation, as well as links to local arts associations and agencies.

National Arts Council—http://www.nac.gov.sg
This site provides links and information on grants and innovative funding ideas for arts education.

Bibliotherapy Books

Halsted, J. (1994). *Some of my best friends are books: Guiding gifted readers from pre-school to high school.* Scottsdale, AZ: Gifted Psychology Press.
Halsted provides background and research on the affective and cognitive needs of gifted students along with their typical reading patterns. Also included is an annotated bibliography of more than 300 books appropriate for gifted readers, indexed by topic.

Gold, J. (2002). *Read for your life: Literature as a life support system.* Allston, MA: Fitzhenry & Whiteside.
Offering a wide range of familiar books, Gold illustrates the ways daily reading can lead to sound mental health and personal empowerment. The book includes sections on reading for children and adolescents, as well as recommendations for reading in times of crisis, stress, and anxiety.

Odean, K. (1998). *Great books for boys.* New York: Ballantine.
More than 600 titles have been carefully selected and annotated. Organized by reader age and genre, this is an excellent resource for parents, teachers, and librarians.

Odean, K. (1997). *Great books for girls.* New York: Ballantine.
This resource provides more than 600 titles selected to encourage, challenge, and nurture girls. Each book is annotated and provided with a reading level range by grade. The selected books are indexed by author, title, and category.

Stanley, J. (1999). *Reading to heal: How to use bibliotherapy to improve your life.* Boston: Element.
The first nonacademic book about bibliotherapy, this is an accessible, useful, and engaging tool that informs readers how to choose and use books for bibliotherapeutic processes.

Bibliotherapy Web Sites

Bibliotherapy Bookshelf—http://www.carnegielibrary.org/kids/booknook/ bibliotherapy
A service of the Carnegie Library of Pittsburgh, PA, this site provides an extensive list of books categorized by issue. The site is updated frequently.

Cinematherapy Books

Hesley, J., & Hesley, J. (2001). *Rent two films and let's talk in the morning: Using popular movies in psychotherapy* (2nd ed.). New York: Wiley.
This book provides concise descriptions of dozens of popular films and shows how they can be used to address specific issues (e.g., divorce, substance abuse, personal responsibility). The volume also offers suggestions for selecting films and creating assignments.

Solomon, G. (2001). *Reel therapy: How movies inspire you to overcome life's problems.* New York: Lebhar-Friedman.
Solomon suggests films to address life's emotional problems and also provides analyses to aid viewers in comprehending the films on deeper, more emotional levels.

Cinematherapy Web Sites

Cinematherapy.com—http://www.cinematherapy.com
This site, authored and hosted by Dr. Birgit Woltz, provides an index of films with suggestions for use as cinematherapy.

Character Education Books

DeRoche, E., & Williams, M. (1998). *Educating hearts and minds: A comprehensive character education framework.* Thousand Oaks, CA: Corwin Press.
This guide provides a framework to help design, organize, implement, and maintain a character education program that is successful for students, staff, and the community. The suggestions provided are easily adaptable and implemented, and the book includes standards to aid in assessment of the program.

Lewis, B. (1998). *What do you stand for?: A kid's guide to building character.* Minneapolis, MN: Free Spirit.
This user-friendly book guides the reader through units grouped by character traits such as courage, honesty, sincerity, honor, and cooperation. Each chapter includes character dilemmas and activities promoting problem solving and the clarification of values.

Ryan, K., & Bohlin, K. (1999). *Building character in schools: Practical ways to bring moral instruction to life.* San Francisco: Jossey-Bass.
This book outlines the principles and strategies of effective character education and explains what schools and teachers must do to teach students the habits and attitudes that combine to define a person of character.

Character Education Web Sites

Character Counts!—http://www.charactercounts.org
This organization promotes the six pillars of character: trustworthiness, responsibility, respect, fairness, caring, and citizenship. The Web site offers free teaching materials and suggestions.

Good Character.com—http://www.goodcharacter.com
This Web site offers free teaching guides specifically designed for high school, middle school, and elementary school students. In addition, the site provides specific information on character in sports, opportunities for action, school-to-work ethics, and links to other character education organizations.

Character Education Partnership (CEP)—http://www.character.org
The Character Education Partnership (CEP) is a nonpartisan coalition of organizations dedicated to developing moral character and civic responsibility. The site contains resource lists, virtual bulletin boards, and current news events related to character education.

Center for the 4th and 5th Rs—http://www.cortland.edu/www/c4n5rs
This center, directed by Dr. Thomas Lickona, author of *Educating for Character*, is based at the State University of New York at Cortland and promotes the "4th and 5th Rs": respect and responsibility. The site contains valuable links to information and best practices for character education.

The School for Ethical Education—http://www.ethicsed.org
This organization offers strategies for putting ethics into action and offers assistance and staff development for educators interested in character education.

Service Learning Books

Lewis, B. (1998). *The kid's guide to social action* (Rev. ed.). Minneapolis, MN: Free Spirit.
Beyond providing real-life vignettes of students who have made a difference, Lewis outlines the skills and steps needed in developing, enacting, monitoring, and evaluating social action projects.

Eyler, J., & Giles, D. (1999). *Where's the learning in service-learning?* San Francisco: Jossey-Bass.
This book explores service learning as a valid learning activity. Eyler and Giles present data from two national research projects. Their studies include a large national survey focused on attitudes and perceptions of learning, intensive student interviews before and after the service semester, and additional comprehensive interviews to explore student views of the service learning process. The book

433

provides ideas for those interested in promoting service learning projects in their own settings.

Service Learning Web Sites

The Strawberry Point School Service Learning Primer—http://www.goodcharacter.com/SERVICE/primer-1.html
This guide offers step-by-step instructions on how to create, implement, and assess service learning projects.

The Big Dummies Guide to Service Learning—http://www.fiu.edu/%7Etime4chg/Library/bigdummy.html
This site provides solid answers to common questions about service learning—a vast amount of information in an easy-to-use format. The topics are categorized into faculty concerns, program concerns, student issues, administrative concerns, and nonprofit issues.

Learn and Serve—http://www.learnandserve.org
This is a comprehensive information system that focuses on all dimensions of service learning, covering kindergarten through higher education and school-based, as well as community-based, initiatives.

Self-Understanding Books

Galbraith, J. (1999). *The gifted kids' survival guide: For ages 10 and under* (Rev. ed.). Minneapolis, MN: Free Spirit.
This book helps young gifted children construct their own understanding of what it means to be gifted. The book is filled with contributions from gifted kids written to gifted kids providing insight and advice.

Galbraith, J., & Delisle, J. (1996). *The gifted kids' survival guide: A teen handbook* (Rev. ed.). Minneapolis, MN: Free Spirit.
This book, arranged by issues, is filled with strategies, advice, and insights from gifted adolescents from all over the country.

Kincher, J. (1995). *Psychology for kids*. Minneapolis, MN: Free Spirit.
This book provides 40 Personality Style Inventories to help students learn about their own attitudes, opinions, beliefs, habits, choices, memories, ideas, feelings, and abilities.

Kincher, J. (1995). *Psychology for kids II*. Minneapolis, MN: Free Spirit.
This second volume presents 40 experiments to help students learn about the beliefs, attitudes, perceptions, differences, and styles of learning of others. The tests are presented in a student-friendly format and provide debriefing infor-

mation, as well as resources for further information if students' interest is sparked.

Coping Strategies Books

Cohen, L., & Frydenberg, E. (1996). *Coping for capable kids: Strategies for parents, teachers, and students.* Waco, TX: Prufrock Press.
This book provides practical strategies for those who need to find positive ways to cope with the social and emotional issues that confront gifted kids. One half of the book is written for parents and teachers and the other half is written for gifted kids.

Forman, S. (1993). *Coping skills interventions for children and adolescents.* San Francisco: Jossey-Bass.
The author details specific techniques for educators and parents to use and share with students.

Coping Strategies Web Sites

Coping.org—http://www.coping.org
This site provides online manuals for coping strategies in a number of areas, including trauma/crises (separate section for 9/11 issues), stress, communication, anger, personal growth, loss, and self-esteem.

References

Adderholt-Elliot, M., & Eller, S. (1989). Counseling students who are gifted through bibliotherapy. *Teaching Exceptional Children, 22*(1), 26–31.

Belbas, B., Gorak, K., & Shumer, R. (1993). *Commonly used definitions of service-learning: A discussion piece.* Retrieved on August 31, 2004, from http://www.west.asu.edu/volunteers/service_learning_definitions.htm

Blackburn, C., & Erikson, D. (1986). Predictable crises of the gifted student. *Journal of Counseling and Development, 64,* 552–554.

Bloom, B., Hastings, J., & Madaus, G. (1971). *Handbook of formative and summative evaluation.* New York: McGraw-Hill.

Carin, A., & Sund, L. (1978). *Creative questioning: Sensitive listening techniques: A self-concept approach.* Columbus, OH: Merrill.

Clark, B. (2002). *Growing up gifted* (6th ed.). Upper Saddle River, NJ: Merrill/Prentice Hall.

Cohen, L., & Frydenberg, E. (1996). *Coping for capable kids: Strategies for parents, teachers, and students.* Waco, TX: Prufrock Press.

Cross, T. (2003). *On the social and emotional lives of gifted children* (2nd ed.). Waco, TX: Prufrock Press.

Dabrowski, K. (1964). *Positive disintegration.* Boston: Little, Brown.

Dabrowski, K., & Piechowski, M. (1977). *Theory of levels of emotional development* (Vols. 1 & 2). Oceanside, NY: Dabor Science.

Davis, G., & Rimm, S. (2004). *Education of the gifted and talented* (5th ed.). Boston: Allyn and Bacon.

Delisle, J. (1987). *Gifted kids speak out.* Minneapolis, MN: Free Spirit.

Delisle, J. (1992). *Guiding the social and emotional development of gifted youth: A practical guide for educators and counselors.* New York: Longman.

Delisle, J. (2001). Affective education and character development: Understanding self and serving others through instructional adaptations. In F. A. Karnes & S. M. Bean (Eds.), *Methods and materials for teaching the gifted* (pp. 471–494). Waco, TX: Prufrock Press.

Elgersma, R. (1981). Providing for affective growth in gifted education. *Roeper Review, 3*(4), 6–8.

Frazier, M., & McCannon, C. (1981). Using bibliotherapy with gifted children. *Gifted Child Quarterly, 25,* 81–85.

Frey, K., & Sylvester, L. (1997). *Research on the second step program: Do student behaviors and attitudes improve?* Seattle, WA: Committee for Children.

Galbraith, J. (1985). The eight great gripes of gifted kids: Responding to special needs. *Roeper Review, 8,* 15–18.

Gardner, H. (1983). *Frames of mind: The theory of multiple intelligences.* New York: BasicBooks.

Gilligan, C. (1993). *In a different voice: Psychological theory and women's development.* Cambridge, MA: Harvard University Press.

Goleman, D. (1995). *Emotional intelligence: Why it can matter more than IQ.* New York: Bantam Books.

Hébert, T., & Neumeister, K. (2001). Guided viewing of film: A strategy for counseling gifted teenagers. *Journal of Secondary Gifted Education, 12,* 224–227.

Johnson, K. (2000). Affective component in the education of the gifted. *Gifted Child Today, 23*(4), 36–41.

Katz, E. (1994). *Self-concept and the gifted student.* Boulder, CO: Open Space Communications.

Kohlberg, L. (1974). The child as moral philosopher. In G. A. Davis & T. F. Warren (Eds.), *Psychology of education: New looks* (pp. 144–154). Lexington, MA: D.C. Heath.

Krathwohl, D., Bloom, B., & Masia, B. (1964). *Taxonomy of educational objectives: The classification of educational goals. Handbook II: Affective domain.* New York: McKay.

Landrum, M., Callahan, C., & Shaklee, B. (Eds.). (2001). *Aiming for excellence: Annotations to the NAGC Pre-K–12 gifted program standards.* Waco, TX: Prufrock Press.

Levey, S., & Dolan, J. (1988). Addressing specific learning abilities in gifted students. *Gifted Child Today, 11*(3), 10–11.

Lewis, B. (1998). *What do you stand for?: A kid's guide to building character.* Minneapolis, MN: Free Spirit.

Lovecky, D. (1992). Exploring social and emotional aspects of giftedness in children. *Roeper Review, 15,* 18–25.

Lovecky, D. (1997). Identity development in gifted children: Moral sensitivity. *Roeper Review, 20,* 90–94.

Maker, C. J., & Nielson, A. (1995). *Teaching models in education of the gifted* (2nd ed.). Austin, TX: PRO-ED.

Maslow, A. (1971). *The farther reaches of human nature.* New York: Viking.

Mehrens, W., & Lehman, I. (1987). *Using standardized tests in education.* New York: Longman.

Mika, E. (2002). *Theory of positive disintegration.* Retrieved March 31, 2003, from http://www.nswagtc.org.au/ozgifted/conferences/TPD.html

Milne, H., & Reis, S. (2000). Using videotherapy to address the social and emotional needs of gifted students. *Gifted Child Today, 23*(1), 24–29.

Morelock, M. (1992). Giftedness: The view from within. *Understanding Our Gifted, 4*(3), 1, 11–15.

Nevitt, H. (2001). Socio-emotional guidance and counseling. In M. Landrum, C. Callahan, & B. Shaklee (Eds.), *Aiming for excellence: Annotations to the NAGC Pre-K–12 gifted program standards* (pp. 27–37). Waco, TX: Prufrock Press.

Newton, A. (1995). Silver screens and silver linings: Using theater to explore feelings and issues. *Gifted Child Today, 18*(2), 14–19, 43.

Nugent, S. (1998, June). *Service learning and technology.* Paper presented at the annual meeting of High Schools That Work, Tulsa, OK.

Nugent, S. (2000). Perfectionism: Its manifestations and classroom-based interventions. *Journal of Secondary Gifted Education, 11,* 215–221.

Nugent, S. (2002). *A study of moral development and self-concept in academically talented residential high school students.* Unpublished doctoral dissertation, The University of Southern Mississippi, Hattiesburg.

Nugent, S., & Shaunessy, E. (2003). Using film in teacher training: Viewing the gifted through different lenses. *Roeper Review, 25,* 128–134.

Peterson, J. (2003). An argument for proactive attention to affective concerns of gifted adolescents. *Journal of Secondary Gifted Education, 14,* 62–70.

Piaget, J. (1965). *The moral judgment of the child* (M. Gabin, Trans.). New York: Free Press. (Original work published in 1936)

Piechowski, M. (1997). Emotional giftedness: The measure of interpersonal intelligence. In N. Colangelo & G. A. Davis (Eds.), Handbook of gifted education (2nd ed., pp. 366–381). Boston: Allyn and Bacon.

Rest, J. (1979). *Development in judging moral issues.* Minneapolis: University of Minnesota.

Roeper, A. (1988). Should educators of the gifted and talented be more concerned with world issues? *Roeper Review, 11,* 12–13.

Roeper, A. (1995). How the gifted cope with their emotions. In *Annemarie Roeper: Selected writings and speeches* (pp. 74–84). Minneapolis, MN: Free Spirit.

Seagoe, M. (1975). *Terman and the gifted.* Los Altos, CA: Kaufmann.

Sellin, D., & Birch, J. (1980). *Psychoeducational development of gifted and talented learners.* Rockwell, MD: Aspen.

Silverman, L. (Ed.). (1993). *Counseling the gifted.* Denver: Love.

Sisk, D. (1982). Caring and sharing: Moral development of gifted students. *Elementary School Journal, 82,* 221–229.

Tannenbaum, A. (1983). *Gifted children: Psychological and educational perspectives.* New York: Macmillan.

Tolan, S. (1999). *Dabrowski's over-excitabilities: A layman's explanation.* Retrieved March 22, 2004, from http://www.stephanietolan.com/dabrowskis.htm

VanTassel-Baska, J. (Ed.). (1989). *A practical guide to counseling the gifted in a school setting* (2nd ed.). Reston, VA: Council for Exceptional Children.

VanTassel-Baska, J. (1998). Counseling talented learners. In J. VanTassel-Baska (Ed.), *Excellence in educating gifted and talented learners* (pp. 489–509). Denver: Love.

Webb, J. (1994). *Nurturing the social-emotional development of gifted children.* Arlington, VA: ERIC Clearinghouse on Disabilities and Gifted Education. (ERIC Digest No. E527)

Weinstein, G., & Fantini, M. (1970). *Toward humanistic education: A curriculum of affect.* New York: Praeger.

Williams, F. (1970). *Classroom ideas for encouraging thinking and feeling* (2nd ed.). Buffalo, NY: D.O.K.

Chapter 15

Developing the Leadership Potential of Gifted Students

by **Suzanne M. Bean** and **Frances A. Karnes**

 group of preschoolers negotiating the use of playground equipment . . . elementary-age students working on group projects . . . teenagers planning special events for the school.

These are examples of the experiences through which leadership potential is developed. Although the concept of *leadership* is often misunderstood and the process for developing good leaders is still debated, it is resolved that leadership skills can be developed and more intentional endeavors must be made to cultivate bright, young leaders.

Of all the types of giftedness set forth in the various state and federal definitions, leadership is one of the least recognized areas. The Marland report (1972) gave the first formal federal definition of giftedness, which included "leadership ability" as one of six domains of giftedness. The more recent federal definition of gifted and talented students (Javits, 1988) states:

> The term "gifted and talented students" means children and youth who give evidence of high performance capability in such areas as intellectual, creative, artistic, or leadership capacity, or in specific academic fields; and who require services or activities not ordinarily provided by the schools in order to develop such capabilities fully. (P.L.100–297, Sec. 4103. Definitions)

While most states accept this federal definition in their legislation and in their written program plans, the majority of special programs focus primarily on intellectual, academic, creative, and artistic capabilities. Stephens and Karnes (2000) found that only 18 of the states recognize leadership as a part of the state definition. Although leadership has been included in formal definitions for more than 30 years, many agree that it remains the most neglected and least served of the areas of giftedness (Chan, 2000; Hays, 1993; Huckaby & Sperling, 1981; Karnes & Bean, 1996; Roach, Wyman, Brookes, Chavez, Heath, & Valdes, 1999; Smith, Smith, & Barnette, 1991). This may be due to the intricate nature of the concept of leadership (Bass & Stogdill, 1990) and the lack of agreement it yields (Edmunds & Yewchuk, 1996; Simonton, 1995). Others have indicated that the inattention to leadership may be due to the lack of valid and reliable measures of leadership ability (Edmunds, 1998; Jarosewich, Pfeiffer, & Morris, 2002) or the lack of research connecting youth leadership behavior/training with adult leadership performance (Foster, 1981; Huckaby & Sperling; Roach et al.).

Whatever reasons may exist, there are too few studies devoted to leadership and giftedness, too few states identifying leadership gifted, and too few in-school leadership development programs designed for students with strong leadership potential. Furthermore, every year, millions of dollars are spent for leadership training in business and industry, the military, government, religion, and sports, but few dollars are spent for leadership education and development of children and youth in elementary and secondary schools.

The process of becoming a leader holds many valuable lessons in life. Interpersonal skills are necessary in every aspect of human endeavor—at home, school, work, and in the social arena. As one's leadership potential is nurtured, the ability to relate to others improves and skills in communication, conflict resolution, decision making, and goal achievement are refined. Initiative and responsibility increase, and self-concept and personal fulfillment flourish. Basic human needs of belonging, accomplishment, and reaching one's potential can be realized through the development of leadership. Leadership skills can make the difference between talents being fully utilized or unfulfilled.

The personal rewards for developing one's leadership potential are many, but the societal benefits of effective leaders may be even more significant. The call for more effective leaders must not be ignored. Perhaps at no other time in history has there been a greater challenge for positive human interaction and ethical leadership. These goals are critical to the progress of humankind.

Definitions of Leadership

The word *leadership* means different things to many people. Most of the disagreement stems from the fact that leadership is a complex phenomenon involving the leader, the followers, and the situation. Some researchers have focused on the personality, physical traits, or behaviors of the leader; others have addressed the relationships between leaders and followers; still others have studied how aspects of the situation affect leaders' actions. According to Burns (1978), leadership is one of the most observed and least understood phenomena on Earth. It involves a range of experiences in the life of a person, which suggests the changing nature of this elusive concept.

Leadership has been defined in the following ways:

1. the directing and coordinating of the work of group members (Fiedler, 1967);
2. leadership over human beings is exercised when persons with certain motives and purposes mobilize, in competition or in conflict with others, institutional, political, psychological, and other resources so as to arouse, engage, and satisfy the motives of followers (Burns, 1978);
3. the process of persuasion or example by which an individual (or leadership team) includes a group to pursue objectives held by the leader or shared by the leader and his or her followers (Gardner, 1990);
4. an interpersonal relation in which others comply because they want to, not because they have to (Hogan, Curphy, & Hogan, 1994);
5. an activity or set of activities, observable to others, that occurs in a group, organization, or institution involving a leader and followers who willingly subscribe to common purposes and work together to achieve them (Clark & Clark, 1994); and
6. a deeply felt sense of mission, of private purpose, of inevitability which may be so powerful that one has little control (Lee & King, 2001).

Although the definitions differ in many ways, it is important to remember that there is no single *correct* definition. This variety points to the multitude of factors that affect leadership and the different perspectives from which to view it.

Unique parallels exist between the concepts of giftedness and leadership. Definitions in both areas are expanding, becoming more inclusive, and considering cultural and situational factors. Identification and assessment procedures for both giftedness and leadership have also developed to reflect the complexity and multidimensionality of the concepts.

Theories of Leadership

One of the earliest leadership theories was the Great Man theory, which maintained that leaders were distinguishable from followers by fixed, inborn traits that were applicable across all situations (Galton, 1869). Research focused on identifying these abilities and traits believed to separate leaders from followers; but, for the most part, these efforts failed to find conclusive evidence that leaders and followers were truly different (Stogdill, 1974).

Since the Great Man theory, research efforts have fluctuated with respect to issues like the behavior of leaders, the modifications they make based on the followers and the situation, and the characteristics and effects of transactional and transformational leaders. Situational Leadership theory inspired further analysis of the relationship among leader behaviors, followers' satisfaction and performance, and the situation of the leadership experiences (Blake & Mouton, 1985; Hersey & Blanchard, 1982). Stogdill (1974) and Bass (1981) supported the notion that leadership effectiveness is highly dependent on the relationship between leader characteristics and the demands of specific situations. The past two decades have seen an interest in Transactional and Transformational leadership theories (Bennis & Nanus, 1985; Hollander & Offerman, 1990; Yammarino & Bass, 1990). The basic difference in these two models is in the process by which the leader is thought to motivate followers. Transactional leaders motivate through contingency rewards and negative feedback, while transformational leaders inspire performance beyond ordinary expectations as they create a sense of mission and encourage new ways of thinking.

Changing Generations and Paradigms

In addition to the changing theories of leadership, it is important to consider the changing thought and behavioral patterns of generations and how those changes may affect their perspective on leadership. For example, Bennis and Thomas (2002) investigated how one's formative era shapes the character of the leaders. Lee and King (2001) indicated that attitudinal changes between generations show differences in people's willingness to respect formal authority, indicating that today, more than ever, leadership is more about *influence* than *authority*. This generational change means that leaders of today will need to find new ways to motivate and meet the needs of this generation and those to follow. As a result of these and other generational changes, there are multiple definitions and theories of leadership operating in a multitude of ways. Leaders are often harder to recognize by their titles, and job descriptions of leaders may indicate a wide range of expectations for what the person in that job will actually do or the style he or she will use to lead.

Bennis and Thomas (2002) reported that, despite the varied backgrounds of the generations they analyzed, four competencies were common to all of them:

- adaptation (resilience and learning how to learn);
- engagement (the ability to create shared meaning);
- voice (emotional intelligence and perspective); and
- integrity (a strong moral compass).

While commonalities across generations of leaders do exist, from Baby Boomers, to Generation X, to the Millennials, each generation has developed its own paradigm of life and distinctive voice (Elmore, 2001; Howe & Strauss, 2000). Figure 1, inspired by George Barna of the Barna Research Group and

	Seniors	Builders	Boomers	Generation X	Millennials
1. Era They Were Born	1900–1928	1929–1945	1946–1964	1965–1983	1984–2001
2. Worldview	Manifest destiny	Be grateful you have a job	You owe me	Relate to me	Life is a cafeteria
3. Attitude to Authority	Respect them	Endure them	Replace them	Ignore them	Choose them
4. Role of Relationships	Long-term	Significant	Limited; useful	Central; caring	Global
5. Value Systems	Traditional	Conservative	Self-based	Media	Shop around
6. Role of Career	Loyalty	Means for living	Central focus	Irritant	A place to serve
7. Schedules	Responsible	Mellow	Frantic	Aimless	Volatile
8. Technology	What's that?	Hope to outlive it	Master it	Enjoy it	Employ it
9. Market They Introduce	Commodities	Goods	Services	Experiences	Transformations
10. View of Future	Uncertain	Seek to stabilize	Create it!	Hopeless	Optimistic

Figure 1. Generational changes

modified by Elmore (2001), depicts changing generations of thought since 1900. According to Elmore, the youth of today have always lived with fast-paced change. They can process visuals much faster than adults, are accustomed to multitasking, and get bored quickly. To Millennials, life is like a smorgasbord from which they may pick and choose as well as mix and match everything from music, to courses, to religion. With so many options available, the youth of today may need more guidance in critical thinking and decision making as they develop themselves as leaders. This generation is already engaged in community problem solving, and they want to fix the world. This view may cause them to seek out experiences that transform them, such as leadership development.

Current Research on Leadership and Youth

Although the majority of research in the area of leadership addresses adults, studies focusing on leadership and youth are increasing.

Studies pertaining to leadership and gender in youth have indicated some differences. Nemerowicz and Rosi (1995) found that both 4th- and 5th-grade boys and girls preferred to depict their own gender as the leader; however, boys did so 95% of the time as compared to 53% for girls. In a study of students in grades 6–11, Karnes and D'Ilio (1989, 1990) found that the girls in both groups perceived most leadership roles to be suitable for either gender, whereas the boys held more traditional stereotypical views. Karnes and D'Ilio (1989) also found significant differences favoring girls on emotional stability, dominance, and the secondary factor of independence using the High School Personality Questionnaire (HSPQ; Cattell, Cattell, & Johns (1984) with gifted students in grades 6–11. Karnes and Riley (1996) found that, when asked, "Who are the three greatest leaders of this century?," 29.1% of the 6th- through 11th-grade girls participating in the Leadership Gifted Studies Program listed their mother, while 2.9% of the boys in the program listed their father. The most frequent response made by boys in the Leadership Studies Program sample was Martin Luther King, Jr. Aside from mothers and teachers, female leaders were not frequently mentioned, which indicates more traditional views of leadership were reflected in this study.

Studies have shown that psychological type can be a good predictor of leadership style and behavior (Barr & Barr, 1989; Campbell & Velsor, 1985; Lawrence, 1982; McCaulley & Staff of the Center for Applications of Psychological Type, 1990; Myers & Myers, 1980). Alvino (1989) reviewed data collected using the Myers-Briggs Type Indicator (MBTI) with gifted students and young adults. He found that high school student leaders who were not necessarily identified as gifted fell predominantly into a group described as analytical managers of facts and details, practical organizers, imaginative harmonizers of people, and warmly enthusiastic planners of change. Leaders in student government activities fell predominantly into a group described as independent, enthusiastic, intuitive, aggressive, and innovative.

Several studies have indicated that participation in extracurricular/community activities provides unique opportunities for students to belong and contribute to a group, as well as to experience success (Bass, 1981; Bennett, 1986; McNamara, Haensly, Lupkowski, & Edlind, 1985; Stogdill, 1974). Using the Leadership Strengths Indicator (Ellis, 1990) with disadvantaged youth ages 10 to 15, Riley and Karnes (1994a) found that students' scores fell within the normal range. A significant difference favoring boys was found in the scale High Level Participator in Group Activities. Slight nonsignificant differences were found among the Enjoys Group Activities, Journalistic, and Courageous scales. The same measure was administered to intellectually gifted students in grades 4–6, and significant differences were found favoring girls on two scales, Sympathetic and Conscientious, and the total score (Riley & Karnes, 1994b). Intellectually gifted students in grades 6–12 in suburban and rural settings also were administered the same instrument, and no significant differences were found (Abel & Karnes, 1993). Wade and Putnam (1995) found that the willingness of gifted high school sophomores and juniors to participate in extracurricular/community activities would be increased by providing them opportunities for input, choice, responsibility, and meaningful influence. These studies emphasized the importance of extracurricular activities and group work in the development of leadership potential.

Leadership and Giftedness

Although gifted students are often deemed the future leaders at local, state, national, and international levels, little has been or is being undertaken to identify young leaders and help them develop their leadership potential. According to Wade and Putnam (1995), all cultures need role models, and most professions depend upon people who exercise intelligence, creativity, and critical judgement in decision making. Unfortunately, leadership is the most controversial and neglected area in gifted education (Lindsay, 1988), with few gifted programs incorporating leadership into their curriculum (Florey & Dorf, 1986). Schools must go beyond educating the gifted for followership and must become involved in understanding the fundamentals of leadership and incorporating it into the school curriculum (Foster & Silverman, 1988).

There are many connections between the characteristics used to describe an effective leader and a gifted individual. Both are often highly verbal, socially sensitive, visionary, problem solvers, critical and creative thinkers, initiators, responsible, and self-sufficient (Black, 1984; Chauvin & Karnes, 1983; Plowman, 1981). Terman's (1925) classic study of the gifted revealed that gifted students were often the leaders in school. Hollingworth (1926) indicated that, among a group of children with average intelligence, the IQ of leaders was likely

445

to fall between 115 and 130. Schakel (1984) found that, in comparison with nonintellectually gifted students, intellectually gifted students could be characterized as visionary leaders, whereas nongifted students seemed to be organizational leaders.

Using the High School Personality Questionnaire (HSPQ; Cattell et al., 1984) with students attending a self-contained high school for the intellectually gifted, Karnes, Chauvin, and Trant (1984) found that it failed to discriminate between individuals who held an elected leadership position and those who did not. Elected leaders, however, tended to be more tender-minded (sensitive, intuitive, tense, driven, group-dependent, and conscientious) than the nonelected group. In addition, females scored significantly higher than males on excitability, and males scored significantly higher on sensitivity.

Although the need for more effective leaders is clear and gifted students typically possess the characteristics to become effective leaders, the development of leadership skills in gifted youth is often neglected.

Screening and Identification of Gifted Leaders

Identifying students for leadership training is a complex task. Conradie (1984) and Hensel (1991) urged that leadership potential be identified early. The following leadership behaviors are often seen in preschool children: high verbal ability; sensitivity to the needs and concerns of others; popularity with their peers for companionship, ideas, and opinions; easy interaction with peers and adults; and easy adjustment to new situations, problem solving, and conflict resolution (Hensel). Fukada, Fukada, and Hicks (1994) examined preschool children's leadership behavior during free play. Behaviors were recorded on a checklist consisting of items such as initiating play, giving directions to others, monitoring the play, encouraging others, peacemaking, and so fourth. Results from this study indicated that leadership behavior is multidimensional and the relationship between children's attributes and leadership behavior may depend on the dimension of leadership. Thus, more than one measure should be utilized to measure children's leadership.

Conradie (1984) also indicated the need for the identification of leadership potential to be continuous because, as children develop, social changes and leadership ability may emerge. A variety of methods may be utilized to identify leadership potential: parent/teacher/self-rating checklists or nomination forms, sociometric devices, observation of leadership behaviors in group tasks, and commercially prepared screening and identification instruments.

Friedman, Jenkins-Friedman, and Van Dyke (1984) examined whether self-, peer, or teacher nominations were more effective in selecting students with leadership ability. They found that students who had self-nominated, either singly or in combination with other types of nominations, scored more highly on leadership than students nominated by peers or teachers or both.

Feldhusen and Pleiss (1994) compared teachers' ratings of leadership on a composite measure from three published leadership scales with their ratings of creativity and dramatic ability using the Scales for Rating Behavioral Characteristics of Superior Students. The study involved 54 teachers and the 54 students in grades K–12 identified by the teachers as high in leadership. Leadership scores were not significantly correlated with creativity, but were moderately and significantly correlated with dramatics.

Sociograms, a formal peer rating method of identifying behaviors and characteristics, were used by Perez, Chassin, Ellington, and Smith (1982) to investigate leadership giftedness among kindergarten and preschool children. Students with the highest verbal scores on the Peabody Picture Vocabulary Test (PPVT) were selected by their classmates as leaders. Teacher observations reflected the same identifications made through the sociogram data and PPVT scores.

Hamback (1988) used four group leadership development activities to help identify student leadership behaviors. The study indicated the importance of verbal fluency in emergent leadership, the tendency of leaders to "take over" a situation, the influence of task-specific skills in gaining leader status, and the decrease in the number of emergent leaders as group size increases.

Using Fiedler's model of situational leadership (1967), Myers, Slavin, and Southern (1990) conducted a study to identify leadership behaviors of 122 rising 10th and 11th graders at a Governor's School program for gifted students. The students were placed in groups of eight and given an ill-defined task with a 1-week time frame for completion. Individual and group evaluations were conducted through program staff, peer ratings, and group product ratings completed by independent observers. Staff observations classified leadership behaviors as Active, Participative, Passive, or Process/Product-oriented. Peer ratings indicated that dominant leaders were perceived as strong, implying that verbal skills were viewed as more important to leadership than the quality of the group's final product. Product ratings found that groups with Participative leaders who had strong interpersonal skills developed the best products, Active or Authoritarian leadership generated less creative and less effective products, and Passive leadership produced the lowest quality outcomes.

The status of screening and identification instruments in leadership for elementary and secondary youth is limited and in its infancy (Karnes & Meriweather-Bean, 1991). Instruments with validity and reliability are limited in number. All vary on several aspects, including grades or ages, number of items specific to leadership, response modes, scoring procedures interpretation, and scores rendered. Current measures include:

- The Eby Gifted Behavior Index (Eby, 1989);
- The Gifted and Talented Evaluation Scale (GATES; Gilliam, Carpenter, & Christensen, 1996);
- The Gifted Education Scale–Second Edition (GES-2; Henage, McCarney, & Anderson, 1998);

- The High School Personality Questionnaire (Cattell, Cattell, & Johns, 1984);
- Khatena-Morse Multitalent Perception Inventory (Khatena & Morse, 1994);
- Leadership: A Skill and Behavior Scale (Sisk & Rosselli, 1987);
- The Leadership Characteristics (Part IV) of the Scales for Rating the Behavioral Characteristics of Superior Students (SRBCSS; Renzulli, Smith, White, Callahan, & Hartman, 1976) and The Leadership Characteristics (Part IV) of the Scales for Rating the Behavioral Characteristics of Superior Students: Revised Edition (SRBCSS-R) (Renzulli, Smith, White, Callahan, Hartman, & Westberg, 2002);
- Myers-Briggs Type Indicators (Myers & McCaulley, 1985);
- Murphy-Meisgeier Type Indicator for Children (Meisgeier & Murphy, 1987);
- The Gifted Rating Scales (GRS; Pfeiffer & Jarosewich, 2003)
- Roets Rating Scale for Leadership (Roets, 1986); and
- Student Talent and Risk Profile (Institute for Behavioral Research in Creativity, 1990).

Two additional standardized measures are commercially available, both of which have been designed for purposes other than screening and identification: the Leadership Skills Inventory (Karnes & Chauvin, 2000a) and the Leadership Skills Indicator (Ellis, 1990). The former was developed to be a diagnostic/prescriptive measure for instruction in leadership, and the latter was designed to serve as a basis for discussion on the topics of leaders and leadership by counselors and teachers.

The Gifted Education Scale–Second Edition (GES-2; Henage, McCarney, & Anderson, 1998) was constructed to assist in the screening, identification, and educational planning for children and youth in K–12. There are 48 items across the five areas of giftedness in the federal definition: intellectual ability, creativity, specific academic aptitude, leadership, and performing and visual arts. Ten items are included in the leadership segment. An optional scale on motivation has been developed. The total time to complete the instrument is 20 minutes. It may be completed by anyone familiar with the student to be rated, such as the teacher or other school/clinical personnel. The items are rated on a five-point scale from (1) *Does not demonstrate the behavior or skill* to (5) *Demonstrates the behavior or skill at all times.*

There were 1,439 students ages 5–18 in the standardization sample. Information is available in the technical manual, which gives internal consistency data along with test-retest reliability. Statistical comparisons with the Gifted and Talented Evaluation Scales indicated significant correlations of the five subscales of the GES-2. Scores rendered for each scale are frequency-rated for each item, subscale raw score, subscale standard score, and quotient score.

The Scales for Rating the Behavioral Characteristics of Superior Students (SRBCSS; Renzulli et al., 1976) was originally published to assist teachers in assessing the characteristics of high-ability students. The original scales consisted of four rating areas or components: learning, motivation, creativity, and leadership. A criterion of the scales accepted early in the development process was that at least three separate studies in the literature had to specify the importance of a specific observable characteristic for it to be included in the instrument. In the first experimental edition, several districts offering programs for gifted and talented youth were involved. Validity and reliability studies were undertaken on all four scales. Part IV, Leadership Characteristics, was validated by comparing teachers' and peers' ratings through sociometric techniques (Hartman, 1969). The correlations were high for teachers and 4th-, 5th-, and 6th-grade students' ratings. By correlating the individual items with the total leadership ratings, the internal consistency of the leadership scale was verified. Further studies included the investigation of the factor-analytical structure of the SRBCSS (Burke, Harworth, & Ware, 1982), which found that the Leadership Characteristics assessed many behavioral characteristics that typify leadership, but concluded that they were descriptive of the type of leader who conforms and adapts to traditional expectations in a school setting.

Roets Rating Scale for Leadership (Roets, 1986) is a self-rating measure for students in grades 5–12. A five-point scale (*almost always, quite often, sometimes, not very often,* and *never*) is employed to rate 26 items. The instrument was administered to 1,057 youth living in the continental limits of the United States in both public and private schools. The validity was established by administering to 631 students in the standardization group two other measures of leadership with correlations of $r = .71$ and $.77$, respectively. The Spearman-Brown split-half formula established the reliability and correlation for the total sample at $r = .85$. Further investigation of reliability of the measure with the leadership scale of the SRBCSS indicated a correlation of $r = .55$.

Chan (2000) conducted a study using Chinese versions of the Roets Rating Scale for Leadership (RRSL) and the Scales for Rating the Behavioral Characteristics of Superior Students (SRBCSS). He found that parent and teacher ratings on the SRBCSS subscales were significantly correlated with the students' self-rated scores on the RRSL and that parent and teacher ratings were also significantly correlated with one another.

After extensive revisions of the scales were conducted, the Scales for Rating Behavioral Characteristics of Superior Students–Revised (SRBCSS-R; Renzulli et al., 2002) were published. There are 10 scales to identify student strengths in the areas of learning, creativity, motivation, leadership, artistic characteristics, musical characteristics, dramatics, communication-precision, communication-expressiveness, and planning. The leadership scale contains seven items. Although the authors have not developed national norms, detailed information is provided on how to develop local norms. The manual contains information on construct validity, alpha reliability, and interrater reliability. The SRBCSS-R was field tested twice. In the first field test, 921 students were administered the scales, and 572 students were used in the second field test.

Leadership: A Skill and Behavior Scale is a self-rating instrument developed by Sisk and Rosselli (1987). It contains the areas of positive self-concept, decision-making skills, problem-solving skills, group dynamics skills, communication skills, organizing, implementing skills, planning skills, and discerning opportunities. *Never*, *seldom*, *sometimes*, *often*, and *always* are the dimensions of the rating scale. Validity and reliability data are not provided.

The Khatena-Morse Multitalent Perception Inventory (Khatena & Morse, 1994) is a self-rating scale that contains the areas of artistry, musical, creative imagination, initiative, and leadership. The two forms of the instrument, A and B, contain four and six items in leadership, respectively. The standardization data, including extensive information on validity and reliability, are contained in the technical manual.

Seven checklists are contained in The Eby Gifted Behavior Index (Eby, 1989), six of which identify the behavioral processes of elementary and secondary gifted youth in different talent areas: verbal, math/science/problem solving, musical, visual/spatial, social/leadership, and mechanical/technical/inventiveness. An additional area was developed to provide criteria for the rating of original student products. Twenty items on the social/leadership checklist include active interaction with the environment, reflectiveness, perceptiveness, persistence, goal orientation, originality, productivity, self-evaluation, independence, and the effective communication of ideas. A five-point Likert-type rating format is provided for the teacher. The responses are evidence of the behavior is shown rarely or never in social activities to evidence of the behavior is shown consistently in most social activities. The validity and reliability studies on the social/leadership checklist are reported in the manual.

The High School Personality Questionnaire (HSPQ; Cattell, Cattell, & Johns, 1984) yields the Leadership Potential Score (LPS). Fourteen bipolar traits of personality are assessed: warmth, intelligence, emotional stability, excitability, dominance, enthusiasm, conformity, boldness, sensitivity, withdrawal, apprehension, self-sufficiency, self-discipline, and tension. The instrument, which was designed for students ranging in age from 12 to 18, is a self-rating form that may be given individually or in groups. The 142-item instrument requires approximately 45 to 60 minutes to administer. Numerous studies attesting to validity and reliability of the instrument with a variety of youth samples are described in the manual.

The LPS score is predicted from the HSPQ by an equation derived empirically by combining scores on the 14 primary scales using a specific formula (Johns, 1984). The LPS has been employed in several studies with intellectually gifted, creative, and leadership students. The mean scores of the subjects in each study were above those of the norming group (Karnes, Chauvin, & Trant, 1984, 1985; Karnes & D'Ilio, 1988a, 1988b).

The Student Talent and Risk (STAR) Profile (The Institute for Behavioral Research in Creativity, 1990) is based on Form U, Biographical Inventory, which was developed in 1976. Seven performance measures are provided: academic performance, creativity, artistic potential, leadership, emotional maturity, educational orientation, and at-risk. The student responds to 150 items based on the answer that is most like him- or herself. Analysis on each student in the seven performance areas and on the group as a whole by percentile scores are provided through computer feedback. Validity, reliability, and research studies are provided in the technical manual.

Psychological type information, based on Carl Jung's theory of observable differences in mental functioning, is provided by the Myers-Briggs Type Indicator (MBTI; Myers & McCaulley, 1985). Individuals create their "type" through the exercise of their individual preferences. Type theory provides a model for understanding the nature of differences among leaders (McCaulley et al., 1990). Each person has a predisposed preference for one of the bipolar attitudes (extroversion/introversion, judging/perceiving) and functions (sensing/intuition, thinking/feeling). The MBTI provides an interpretation of type as it relates to how an individual best perceives and processes information and how that individual prefers to interact socially and behaviorally with others. Psychological type is the combination of the two attitudes and functions preferred by the individual; therefore, all eight preferences are combined in all possible ways, with 16 types resulting. To administer the 166-item measure, approximately 45 to 60 minutes are needed. The instrument was designed and standardized to be a self-rating instrument for adolescents and adults. Reliability, validity, and other data are reported in the manual.

The Murphy-Meisgeier Type Indicator for Children (MMTIC; Meisgeier & Murphy, 1987) was also developed based on Jung's theory of psychological type. The 70-item instrument, which was designed for students in grades 2–8, measures the same four preference scales as the MBTI. A total of 4,136 students in grades 2–8 were included in the standardization process. Estimates of concurrent and content validity, reliability, and other data are reported in the manual.

The Pfeiffer-Jarosewich Gifted Rating Scale (GRS; Pfeiffer & Jarosewich, 2003) has two forms. The GRS for Preschool and Kindergarten and the GRS-School form both have subscales focusing on intellectual, academic, creative, and artistic talent and motivation. The leadership scale is only on the GRS-School form. Validity and standardization studies are described in the manual.

The Gifted and Talented Evaluation Scale (GATES; Gilliam, Carpenter, & Christensen, 1996) was designed to identify gifted students ages 5–18. It was based on the most current federal and state definitions, including intellectual ability, academic skills, creativity, leadership, and artistic talent. Ten items are included in the leadership portion of the GATES. The rating scale has nine points divided into three areas: below (1–3), average (4–6), and above (7–9). Teachers, parents, and others who are knowledgeable about the child may use the GATES. The instrument was normed on a national sample of 1,000 people who had been identified as gifted and talented. Studies of test-retest reliability and internal consistency produced .90+ coefficients. In the examiner's manual, there are additional studies confirming the content, construct, criterion-related, and concurrent validity.

These screening and identification instruments yield information about many leadership attributes and behaviors of developing young leaders. Because of the complex and multidimensional nature of leadership, it is recommended that more than one measure be used to assess students' leadership potential. The type of instructional program for leadership should be considered when selecting appropriate screening and identification instruments.

Instructional Programs and Materials for Leadership

The acquisition and application of the necessary leadership concepts and skills based on those identified as necessary to function as an adult leader in society is the basis for The Leadership Development Program (Karnes & Chauvin, 2000b). The Leadership Skills Inventory (LSI; Karnes & Chauvin, 2000a), a diagnostic-prescriptive instrument, has nine subscales: fundamentals of leadership, written communication, speech communication, character building, decision making, group dynamics, problem solving, personal development, and planning. Eight samples of students in grades 4 through junior college in seven states were included in the standardization. Criterion and content validity studies have been conducted (Karnes & D'Ilio, 1988a, 1988b; Karnes & Chauvin, 2000a). Reliability data are reported in the manual.

Upon beginning a leadership program, the students are administered the LSI, which is a self-rating and self-scoring instrument. After they complete the inventory, scores are plotted on the Leadership Skills Inventory Profile Sheet, which graphically depicts their strengths and weaknesses in leadership concepts and skills on the nine subscales. The concepts and skills that have been acquired and those in need of strengthening are immediately apparent. This information provides the teacher with the necessary data to assist the student in planning the appropriate instructional activities for every item on the LSI. One or more instructional strategies for each item are provided in The Leadership Development Program. The teacher does not have to incorporate all the activities, only those that will provide the improvement necessary to become an effective leader based on the student's self-perceived strengths and weaknesses. Group discussions, simulations, and role-playing activities are the primary vehicle for learning, and they are student-centered rather than teacher-directed.

Crucial to the program is the application of the acquired leadership concepts and skills, which is facilitated through developing and implementing a "Plan for Leadership." After the completion of the instructional component, each student identifies an area in which he or she may initiate something new or change an already existing area of need in his or her school, community, or religious affiliation. The plan must have two major purposes: (a) to bring about desirable changes in the behavior of others and (b) to solve a major problem or work toward major improvements. Within the abilities of the students, it should be realistic, well-sequenced, and comprehensive. The student writes a plan with an overall goal with accompanying objectives, activities, resources, timelines, and methods for evaluation. Each plan developed is presented in class for peer review. An example of a completed plan and the types of plans prepared by male and female students for the school, community, and religious affiliation and the numbers of plans developed during each year of the program have been described (Karnes & Meriweather, 1989).

The instrument and the materials are the foundation of the Leadership Studies Program, a 1-week summer residential experience, which has been validated (Karnes, Meriweather, & D'Ilio, 1987). The statistical analysis of the data collected in the programs indicates pre- and postassessment gains to be significant ($p = .01$).

After a careful analysis of all the program components, including the nine instructional areas necessary for being a leader and the plan for leadership, teachers, administrative decision makers, and community leaders can readily select the format of the program appropriate for their school and town. It may be an ongoing component of a resource enrichment program, conducted as a separate class at the junior or senior high school level, or the appropriate components may be included in English, speech, social studies, and other academic courses. Mentorship and internship provisions for leadership growth should also be made readily available to students after the completion of the instructional activities.

Another approach to examining leadership in youth is The Leadership Strengths Indicator (Ellis, 1990), a 40-item self-report questionnaire designed to obtain students' evaluations of their leadership traits and abilities. Eight cluster scores and an overall total leadership score are rendered on the 40-item self-report instrument. The eight clusters contain two to six items within the following areas: enjoys group activities, key individual in group activities, high-level participator in group activities, journalistic, sympathetic, confident, courageous, conscientious, and self-confident. The response choices on the rating scale are *excellent, very good, better than most, okay,* and *not so good*. The indicator is intended to be a discussion starter for guidance and leadership development classes designed for students in grades 6–12. The psychometric properties, including validity and reliability, are reported in the manual.

Research has been conducted using the indicator with gifted. Disadvantaged gifted students ranging in age from 10 to 15 had scores within the normal range. A significant difference on Cluster Scale III, High-Level Participator in Group Activities, was found favoring boys (Riley & Karnes, 1994a). Rural and suburban gifted high school youth were compared with no significant differences found (Abel & Karnes, 1993).

Parker (1989) proposed a leadership model designed to serve as the foundation for gifted programs. According to the theory on which her Leadership Training Model is based, leadership potential can be developed through the strengthening of four essential components: cognition, problem solving, interpersonal communication, and decision making. In their book, *Developing Creative Leadership*, Parker and Begnaud (2003) included an overview of leadership theory, suggested strategies for developing creative leadership in gifted students, and a variety of leadership units designed for use with gifted students of all ages.

For almost two decades, commercially prepared instructional materials for teaching leadership have been available. As early as 1980, Magoon and Jellen designed 25 strategies for developing leadership. Designed, according to the authors, to assist students in becoming future leaders by acquiring the skills of leading, the materials offer such instructional assistance as a checklist for committee work, a group observation scale, and a listing of references.

The Leadership Series, which contains six instructional units in analyzing leadership, group skills, self-esteem, communication skills, values and goal setting, and social responsibility, was designed by House (1980). Based on Bloom's Taxonomy of Educational Objectives (1956), each unit contains 30 instructional activities with reproducible worksheets. Objectives with emphasis on the high thinking levels of analysis, synthesis, and evaluation are the basis of the program.

A curricular unit on leadership for upper elementary and junior high school gifted youth was developed by Gallagher (1982). Content specialists and teachers of the gifted worked to construct the instructional lessons, which had three specific objectives: to illustrate a particular leadership concept, to provide opportunities for the students to understand and internalize the concepts, and to develop the students' higher level thinking skills. Three types of leaders were highlighted in the lesson plans: traditional, legal-rational, and charismatic. The activities in each lesson are grouped at three levels: awareness, instructional, and extension. Reproducibles for student use are included in the materials. An annotated bibliography on leadership and evaluation forms for students and parents are provided for the teacher.

Leadership: A Skills Training Program (Roets, 1997) is an instructional program for students ages 8–18. The instructional activities are based on four themes: people of achievement, language of leadership, project planning, and debate and discussion. Suggested readings for young people, both fiction and nonfiction, and a listing of readings for adults are provided.

Several books directed to elementary and secondary school youth and teachers are available, and each contains many instructional activities for leadership training. The goals of the leadership materials presented in *Leadership Education: Developing Skills for Youth* (Richardson & Feldhusen, 1987), which had previously been developed by Feldhusen, Hynes, and Richardson (1977) with a grant in vocational-technical education, are to develop the social skills of leadership and an understanding on the part of the student as a potential leader. The 11 chapters include an introduction to leadership, outcomes of leadership education, personal characteristics of effective leaders, skills of a group leader, communication skills for leaders, leadership skills for group members, group goals development, group activity plans, committee organization, parliamentary procedure skills, and leadership and special abilities. Feldhusen and Kennedy (1986) reported evaluation results on the use of the materials in a summer leadership program with secondary gifted youth.

Sisk and Shallcross (1986) developed a guide, *Leadership: Making Things Happen,* to help clarify the meaning of leaders and leadership. The book is divided into 10 chapters: What is Leadership, Self-Understanding, Intuitive Powers, Visual Imagery, Communication, Motivation, Creative Problem-Solving Process, Futuristics, Women in Leadership Positions, and Learning Styles. Activities presented in each chapter may be used in a wide variety of instructional situations within schools. References for each topic are presented at the end of each chapter.

Sisk and Roselli (1987) coauthored *Leadership: A Special Kind of Giftedness* to assist in the understanding of the concepts of leadership and in applying current theories to personal lives and teaching. The book includes a definition of leadership, the theories, a model for planning and developing leadership training activities, a succinct summary of teaching/learning models, and a discussion on issues and trends in leadership. The four elements of the model developed by Sisk are characteristics of gifted leadership, selected teaching strategies, teaching/learning models, and key concepts. Twenty lessons are provided.

Lead On (Hagemann & Newman, 1999) helps educators and students address leadership problems more effectively. The book offers strategies for students and teachers to work together as they develop interpersonal and intrapersonal skills. Objectives, procedures, and extended activities provide cross-curricular connections, best practices, and real-life leadership applications for the 21st century.

The outstanding leadership stories of girls are highlighted in *Girls and Young Women Leading the Way* (Karnes & Bean, 1993). Twenty biographies of girls from elementary school through college are provided as role models for leadership. Each story contains personal information followed by a detailed overview of leadership accomplishment. There are questions to challenge the reader to leadership and a listing of appropriate agencies/organizations from which to gain more information. Quotations from nationally known female leaders are included to provide motivation and inspiration. Suggestions for actions to record in a leadership notebook and an extensive reading list on female leaders from kindergarten to the young adult level are provided.

Leadership for Students: A Practical Guide (Karnes & Bean, 1995), a book for young leaders ages 8–18, contains guidance and advice about moving into leadership positions in the home, school, and community. The book contains chapters on leadership definitions, self-assessment of leadership, opportunities and training for leadership, influence and encouragement from others, great leaders, and advice to others. Figures 1–4 are examples of activities from the book that help extend students' views of leadership and assist them in planning for leadership. The book was designed to be interactive through the use of the Leadership Action Journal, which allows students to record their thoughts and actions pertaining to leaders and leadership. Stories of young leaders offer examples of peers and explain how they became leaders. Also featured is a listing of resources and addresses on leadership opportunities.

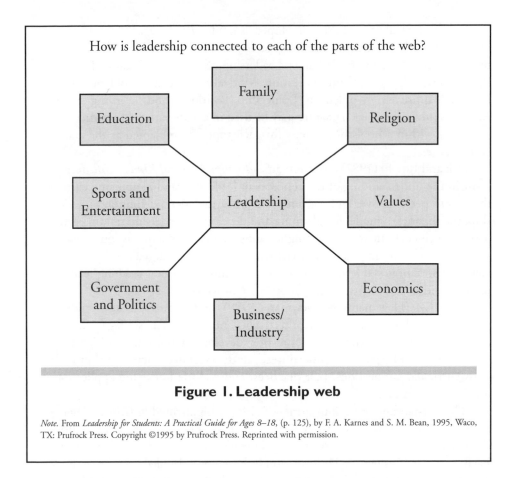

How is leadership connected to each of the parts of the web?

Figure 1. Leadership web

Note. From *Leadership for Students: A Practical Guide for Ages 8–18*, (p. 125), by F. A. Karnes and S. M. Bean, 1995, Waco, TX: Prufrock Press. Copyright ©1995 by Prufrock Press. Reprinted with permission.

Incorporating Leadership
Into the Curriculum for Gifted Students

The goal of cultivating young leaders is of such critical importance to the individual and to society that it should be made an integral part of school and community programs for youth. Without more purposeful and intentional approaches to developing young leaders, only a few students are likely to emerge as effective adult leaders, and the world will continue to be in need of more. Given the parallels between characteristics of effective leaders and gifted individuals, leadership education is a natural fit. And, with the flexibility that often exists in the curriculum for gifted learners, programs and services for the gifted present environments that are most conducive to leadership development.

Toward this end, the concept of leadership must be a more direct part of the curriculum. It must also be broadened from the narrow view of leadership as elected or appointed positions in politics, government, business, or industry, to an expanded view of leadership permeating all dimensions of life, across all disciplines, ages, cultures, and levels of society. Leadership can and should be infused

	Education	Government	Humanities	Mathematics	Medicine	Politics	Religion	Science/ Technology	Sports	Performing Arts	Business/ Industry
Community/ Regional											
State											
National											
International											

Figure 2. Leadership matrix

Note. From *Leadership for Students: A Practical Guide for Ages 8–18*, (p. 166), by F. A. Karnes and S. M. Bean, 1995, Waco, TX: Prufrock Press. Copyright ©1995 by Prufrock Press. Reprinted with permission.

into the broad-based concepts, themes, and issues of the curriculum for gifted students. Leadership should be explored as it connects to power, symbols, culture, patterns, relationships, and values. The conceptual frameworks for thinking about leadership are valuable parts of one's leadership development.

There are many approaches that could prepare gifted learners for leadership roles. Instructional units on leadership should be taught in programs for the gifted. These units could include the study of the history of leadership, great leaders, ethical dimensions of leadership, theories and styles of leadership, leadership across cultures, leadership and futurism, and so on.

Education about leadership is important, but it is not enough. Even those individuals with extensive knowledge about leadership may be poor leaders. Knowing what to do is not the same as knowing when, where, and how to do it. The *skills* of leadership are significant, too. Leadership through experience begins with the development of intrapersonal and interpersonal skills. Gifted students need guidance in self-understanding and access to their own feelings and emotions, examining individual strengths and limitations, accepting those that cannot be changed, and setting goals to develop areas needed for personal growth and human relations. Also critical to leadership skills is the ability to see

---

Changes in Leadership Over Time

Tribal Leadership _____

_____

_____

Leadership in Royalty _____

_____

_____

Democratic Leadership _____

_____

_____

Cooperative or Shared Leadership _____

_____

_____

Positive Aspects of Leadership in Today's Society _____

_____

_____

Figure 3. The history of leadership

Note. From *Leadership for Students: A Practical Guide for Ages 8–18,* (p. 129), by F. A. Karnes and S. M. Bean, 1995, Waco, TX: Prufrock Press. Copyright ©1995 by Prufrock Press. Reprinted with permission.

---

events from the perspective of another, understand and relate to others, and perceive human needs and motivations. Gardner (1990) referred to these skills as the crowning capacity of the human condition, which supersedes and presides over other forms of intelligence. Teachers may use journaling, bibliotherapy, and other strategies for self-reflection and analysis. For interpersonal skills to flourish, teachers should intentionally plan group discussions and collaborative work. Problem-solving skills, conflict resolution, role-playing, and creative

My Goal _____

_____

_____

Objectives _____

_____

_____

Resources/People _____

_____

_____

Other _____

_____

_____

Timeline _____

_____

_____

Figure 4. Leadership development plan

Note. From *Leadership for Students: A Practical Guide for Ages 8–18*, (p. 176), by F. A. Karnes and S. M. Bean, 1995, Waco, TX: Prufrock Press. Copyright ©1995 by Prufrock Press. Reprinted with permission.

drama are all strategies that can be used to develop the seeds of early leadership development.

Schools should also offer structured courses on leadership for which credit is granted. Within these courses, students may assess their own leadership potential and develop plans of leadership to be implemented in schools, communities, and religious organizations. Students need the opportunity to examine areas of interest to which leadership experiences could be applied.

Mentorships and internships offer real-life experiences for adult leaders to collaborate with the schools for the purpose of developing young leaders. Pairing adult leaders with students interested in developing their leadership potential can be a positive practice for student and adult leaders, as well as the school and community.

Riley and Karnes (1996) recommended competitions as a vehicle for incorporating leadership in the curriculum and for recognizing and inspiring young leaders. Competitions such as the I Dare You Leadership Award and the J. C. Penney Golden Rule Award recognize those who have achieved in the area of leadership and reward promising young leaders with scholarships to attend an international leadership conference. These and other such competitions can not only help inspire and recognize young leaders, but can promote goal setting and a sense of autonomy and provide the opportunity for students to meet other young leaders with similar interests and abilities.

Teachers must also be prepared to expose gifted learners to the array of choices for leadership opportunities outside the school. Youth leadership conferences, seminars, and weekend and summer programs are offered through colleges and universities, civic organizations, and business and industries across the nation. Such services and programs often serve as a spark to ignite the desire for becoming a leader and a boost in self-confidence, which is critical to effective leadership.

Educators must seek every opportunity to identify potential leaders at an early age and infuse leadership concepts and skills into the learning environment for gifted students. The ultimate goal is for each gifted student to understand the importance of leadership, realize his or her potential for leadership, gain the knowledge and skills necessary to be an effective leader, and be exposed to all avenues of leadership development within and outside the school environment.

Summary

Researchers are still struggling to generate appropriate definitions and theories of leadership. These conceptual frameworks for thinking about leadership bring meaning and relevance to one's leadership development. Although the majority of research on leadership centers around adults, studies focusing on leadership development of children and youth have emerged over the last decade. In particular, the similarities of characteristics and behaviors of effective leaders and gifted learners have been recognized. Leadership screening and identification instruments have been identified, and strategies for incorporating leadership into the curriculum for gifted learners have been discussed.

The primary goal is to heighten students' interest in the concept of leadership and help them to become more reflective and active in their individual pursuits of leadership potential. This goal requires support and commitment from all educators and other interested adults. Purposeful and creative approaches to leadership development must be pursued vigorously by those interested in the challenge.

Teacher Statement

As a teacher of gifted learners, one of my primary goals has been to help these bright young people learn skills of leadership, as well as the value of developing themselves as leaders. I have used the information in this chapter to guide me as I help students discover what their own personal strengths and limitations are and how to develop themselves as both followers and leaders. I have found that some of my students may be able to tell others what to do, but they have tremendous difficulty in the role of follower. With my unit on leadership, we discuss the importance of good leaders being good followers, too. Through various group activities, my students engage in followership, team building, collaboration, and leadership experiences, and with all of these, the debriefing, reflection, and self-assessment sessions are critical.

In addition to the skills of leadership, I have used the resources in this chapter to help me know how to infuse some aspect of leadership into all of the units I teach. For instance, in our study of Europe, the students explored the influence of European leaders in many areas, such as artists, inventors, mathematicians, and politicians. Learning about leaders themselves is of great value. At the conclusion of our units, we reflect on what new understandings we have about leadership and how it changes in different times, with different types of people, and in different lands.

—Beverly Alexander

Discussion Questions

1. Why is it important to incorporate leadership development into programs and services for gifted children and youth?

2. Why do you think leadership has been one of the most neglected types of giftedness?

3. How has society's concept of leadership changed over time and how do these changes affect the ways educators should approach leadership development with children and youth?

4. How are the qualities, characteristics, and behaviors of gifted learners similar to those of strong leaders?

5. Examine the screening and identification instruments for young gifted leaders. Which one(s) are most appropriate for your needs?

6. Compare and contrast various strategies for incorporating leadership into the curriculum for gifted students. Which strategies would work best for your program and your population of gifted learners?

7. Analyze the materials available for leadership development. Which materials match your students' needs?

8. What are the most important concepts and skills of leadership you want your gifted learners to gain?

Teacher Resources

Publications

Boccia, J. A. (Ed.). (1997). *Students taking the lead: The challenges and rewards of empowering youth in schools.* San Francisco: Jossey-Bass.
Contributors to this volume suggest that broader integration of leadership training and opportunities into school programs will allow educators to tap into the rich networks of peer influence that exist among adolescents and reach the goal of citizenship education. As a student educational goal, leadership development encompasses lessons from civics, communications, critical thinking, history, and a host of other disciplines. As an institutional value, student leadership reflects the practice of democratic principles that underlie U.S. public education. And, as an administrative structure, student leadership provides a dynamic, renewable resource for feedback and ideas about teaching, learning, and living in a school.

Delisle, D., & Delisle, J. (1996). *Growing good kids: 28 activities to enhance self-awareness, compassion, and leadership.* Minneapolis, MN: Free Spirit.
Created by teachers and classroom-tested, these fun and meaningful enrichment activities build children's skills in problem solving, decision making, cooperative learning, divergent thinking, and communication while promoting self-awareness, tolerance, character development, and service. Many activities include extensions and variations for use at school, at home, and in the community. The book includes 33 reproducible handout and transparency masters.

Ellis, J., Small-McGinley, J., & DeFabrizio, L. (2002). *Caring for kids in communities: Using mentorship, peer support, and student leadership programs in schools.* New York: Peter Lang.
Caring for Kids in Communities invites schools to consider the use of mentorship, peer support, and student leadership programs to support the growth and learning of all students. It presents research on successful programs spanning kindergarten through grade 12 and includes a wealth of case studies of individual programs, as well as individual pairs of mentors and mentees. Thus, this book provides insight into the experiences of students, mentors, teachers, and coordinators from these programs, as well as descriptive, practical material for implementing similar programs.

MacGregor, M. G. (1997). *Leadership 101: Developing leadership skills for resilient youth (Facilitator's guide).* Denver: Youthleadership.com.
Leadership 101 is a foundational curricular guide for adolescent and young adult leaders. The facilitator's guide consists of eighteen 90-minute lessons or more than thirty 50-minute lessons. Topics include defining leadership, qualities of leaders/leadership, self-assessment, power/influence/authority, communication and listening, consensus building, ethical leadership, team building, gender and

leadership, tolerance and diversity, motivation, risk taking, decision making, and creative thinking. Other topics are addressed in the debriefing and application of each activity/lesson. An accompanying student workbook is also available.

MacGregor, M. G. (1999). *Designing student leadership programs: Transforming the leadership potential of youth.* Denver: Youthleadership.com.
Designing Student Leadership Programs arose as a result of an ongoing effort to prepare adults who work with educating youth leaders. It is set up as a "guidebook" to be used within staffs or as part of focus groups or discussions as a program/school evaluates or establishes their youth leadership program. As a guidebook, there are pages that consist of lists of ideas and/or statements that have been gathered and tested in various youth leadership programs. There are also pages that consist of questions to consider when establishing a program or evaluating existing efforts.

Marx, J. (1999). *How to win a high school election.* New York: Jeff Marx Books.
This book contains advice and ideas from more than 1,000 high school seniors about how to win a high school election. Via e-mail, the seniors contributed input for this book about things they observed that worked or didn't work, things that were memorable or funny, mistakes they made or watched someone else make, ideas for platforms, issues, promises, posters, campaign speeches, advice on how to speak in front of peers without appearing nervous, and having the right attitude.

Project Adventure. (1994). *Youth leadership in action: A guide to cooperative games and group activities.* Dubuque, IA: Kendall/Hunt.
This is a how-to guide that prepares young people to lead experiential programs that teach team and leadership skills to other youth and adult groups. It includes directions to 52 activities, sample programs, and comprehensive overviews of critical facilitation skills.

van Linden, J. A., Fertman, C. I., & Long, J. A. (1998). *Youth leadership: A guide to understanding leadership development in adolescents.* San Francisco: Jossey-Bass.
Based on 15 years of work with teens and the adults in their lives, the authors of *Youth Leadership* identify the three major stages of adolescent leadership development. It outlines practical tactics for developing leadership skills through experiences at home, school, community, and work; and, most importantly, it shows how adults in these settings can have a positive impact. The authors provide flexible strategies that can be used with adolescents in any program and in varied settings and offer diagrams, tables, and charts to clarify recommendations and processes.

Web Sites

Congressional Youth Leadership Council—http://www.cylc.org
An organization that offers conferences on educational leadership for youth from the United States and abroad.

CyberSisters—http://www.cyber-sisters.org
An online mentoring program designed to provide gender equitable leaders, such as teachers and college mentors to middle school girls.

Do Something—http://www.dosomething.org
An organization that encourages children and teenagers to take an active role in public affairs.

Free The Children—http://www.freethechildren.org
An organization dedicated to empowering children with the skills necessary to become effective leaders that make a global impact.

G.U.T.S. (Guys/Gals Utilizing Their Strengths)—http://www.presentation-style.com/guts/default.html
G.U.T.S. is an international, social-leadership society that brings youth from all around the world together in a nonthreatening, noncompetitive setting to build socially conscious leaders of the future.

Hugh O'Brian Youth Leadership—http://www.hoby.org
The mission of this foundation is to seek out, recognize, and develop leadership potential commencing with high school sophomores.

Leadership Village—http://www.leadershipvillage.com
Devoted to the improvement of leadership skills in children and families.

National Council on Youth Leadership—http://www.lzrnews.com/articles/22&1
This organization recognizes and fosters high ideals of leadership and integrity among the youth of America.

National Youth Leadership Council—http://www.nylc.org
The National Youth Leadership Council's mission is to build vital, just communities with young people through service learning.

National Youth Leadership Forum—http://www.nylf.org
Founded in 1992, the National Youth Leadership Forum (NYLF) is a tuition-based 501 (c)(3) nonprofit educational organization established to help prepare extraordinary young people for their professional careers.

National Youth Leadership Network—http://www.nyln.org
The National Youth Leadership Network (NYLN) is dedicated to advancing the next generation of leaders.

The Points of Light Youth Leadership Institute—http://www.pyli.org
The goal of this institute is to provide youth with the encouragement, peer networks, and leadership skills necessary for them to make meaningful contributions to their communities and begin a lifelong journey of leadership and service.

Youthleadership.com—http://www.youthleadership.com
Youthleadership.com is dedicated to providing current, creative, and dynamic youth leadership education information and serving as a resource clearinghouse for individuals who work with youth leaders.

Youth Leadership Institute—http://www.yli.org
The Youth Leadership Institute (YLI) works with young people and the adults and systems that impact them to build communities that invest in youth.

The Youth Leadership Support Network—http://www.worldyouth.org
The Youth Leadership Support Network is a violence prevention, arts, education, media and training network based in Washington, DC. Its mission is to empower youth to express themselves and to have a voice in society through intergenerational and diverse leadership opportunities and civic engagement.

References

Abel, T., & Karnes, F. A. (1993). Self-perceived strengths in leadership abilities between suburban and rural gifted students using the Leadership Strength Indicator. *Psychological Reports, 73,* 687–690.

Alvino, J. (1989). Psychological type: Implications for gifted. *Gifted Children Monthly, 10*(4), 1–2, 23.

Barr, L., & Barr, N. (1989). *The leadership equation.* Austin, TX: Eakin Press.

Bass, B. M. (1981). *Stogdill's handbook of leadership: A survey of theory and research.* New York: Free Press.

Bass, B. M., & Stogdill, R. M. (1990). *Bass and Stogdill's handbook of leadership: Theory, research, and managerial applications* (3rd ed.). Riverside, NJ: Simon and Schuster.

Bennett, W. J. (1986). *What works: Research about teaching and learning.* Washington, DC: U.S. Department of Education.

Bennis, W. G., & Nanus, B. (1985). *Leaders: The strategies for taking charge.* New York: Harper & Row.

Bennis, W. G., & Thomas, R. J. (2002). *Geeks and geezers: How era, values, and defining moments shape leaders.* Boston: Harvard Business School Press.

Black, J. D. (1984). *Leadership: A new model particularly applicable to gifted youth* (Report No. EC171399). (ERIC Document Reproduction Service No. ED 253 990)

Blake, R. R., & Mouton, J. S. (1985). *The managerial grid III.* Houston, TX: Gulf.

Bloom, B. (Ed.). (1956). *Taxonomy of educational objectives. Handbook I: Cognitive domain.* New York: McKay.

Burke, J. P., Harworth, C. E., & Ware, W. B. (1982). Scale for rating behavioral characteristics of superior students: An investigation of factor structure. *Journal of Special Education, 16,* 477–485.

Burns, J. M. (1978). *Leadership.* New York: Harper & Row.

Campbell, D., & Velsor, E. V. (1985). *The use of personality measures in the leadership development program.* Greensboro, NC: Center for Creative Leadership.

Cattell, R. B., Cattell, M. D., & Johns, E. F. (1984). *Manual and norms for the High School Personality Questionnaire.* Champaign, IL: Institute for Personality & Ability Testing.

Chan, D. W. (2000). Assessing leadership among Chinese secondary students in Hong Kong: The use of the Roets Rating Scale for Leadership. *Gifted Child Quarterly, 44,* 115-122.

Chauvin, J. C., & Karnes, F. A. (1983). A leadership profile of secondary gifted students. *Psychological Reports, 53,* 1259–1262.

Clark, K. E., & Clark, M. B. (1994). *Choosing to lead.* Charlotte, NC: Iron Gate Press.

Conradie, S. (1984). The identification of leadership potential. In J. Cawood et al. (Eds.), *Climbing the ladder to leadership: A panel discussion* (Report No. ED20210). (ERIC Document Reproduction Service No. ED 292 228)

Eby, J. W. (1989). *Eby gifted behavior index (Administration manual).* East Aurora, NY: D.O.K.

Edmunds, A. L. (1998). Content, concurrent, and construct validity of the Leadership Skills Inventory. *Roeper Review, 20,* 281–284.

Edmunds, A. L., & Yewchuk, C. R. (1996). Indicators of leadership in gifted grade twelve students. *Journal of Secondary Gifted Education, 7,* 345–355.

Ellis, J. L. (1990). *Leadership strengths indicator: A self-report leadership analysis instrument for adolescents.* Monroe, NY: Trillium Press.

Elmore, T. E. (2001). *Nurturing the leader within your child: What every parent needs to know.* Nashville, TN: Thomas Nelson.

Feldhusen, J. F., Hynes, K., & Richardson, W. B. (1977). Curriculum materials for vocational youth organizations. *Clearinghouse, 50,* 224–226.

Feldhusen, J. F., & Kennedy, D. (1986). Leadership training for gifted and talented youth. *Leadership Network Newsletter, 1*(2), 1–2.

Feldhusen, J. F., & Pleiss, M.K. (1994). Leadership: A synthesis of social skills, creativity, and histrionic ability? *Roeper Review, 16,* 292–293.

Fiedler, F. E. (1967). *A theory of leadership effectiveness.* New York: McGraw-Hill.

Florey, J. E., & Dorf, J. H. (1986). *Leadership skills for gifted middle school students.* (ERIC Document Reproduction Service No. ED 273 404)

Foster, W. (1981). Leadership: A conceptual framework for recognizing and educating. *Gifted Child Quarterly, 25,* 17–25.

Foster, W. H., & Silverman, L. (1988). Leadership curriculum for the gifted. In J. VanTassel-Baska, J. Feldhusen, K. Seeley, G. Wheatley, L. Silverman, & W. Foster (Eds.), *Comprehensive curriculum for gifted learners* (pp. 356–360). Boston: Allyn and Bacon.

Friedman, P. G., Jenkins-Friedman, R., & Van Dyke M. (1984). Identifying the leadership gifted: Self, peer, or teacher nominations? *Roeper Review, 7,* 91–94.

Fukada, S., Fukada, H., & Hicks, J. (1994). Structure of leadership among preschool children. *Journal of Genetic Psychology, 155,* 389–395.

Gallagher, J. J. (1982). *A leadership unit.* New York: Trillium Press.

Galton, F. (1869). *Hereditary genius: An inquiry into its laws and consequences.* London: Macmillan.

Gardner, J. W. (1990). *On leadership.* New York: Free Press.

Gilliam, J. E., & Carpenter, B. O. (1996). *Gifted and talented evaluation scales.* Austin, TX: PRO-ED.

Hagemann, B., & Newman, C. (1999). *Lead on.* Marion, IL: Pieces of Learning.

Hamback, D. (1988). Finding leadership in the G/C/T classroom. *Gifted Child Today, 11*(6), 49–50.

Hartman, R. K. (1969). *Teachers' identification of student learners.* Unpublished paper, University of Connecticut, Storrs.

Hays, T. S. (1993). An historical content analysis of publications in gifted education journals. *Roeper Review, 16,* 41–43.

Henage, D., McCarney, S. B., & Anderson, P. D. (1998). *Gifted evaluation scale* (2nd ed.). Columbia, MO: Hawthorne Educational Services.

Hensel, N. H. (1991). Leadership giftedness: Social leadership skills in young children. *Roeper Review, 14,* 4–19.

Hersey, P., & Blanchard, K. H. (1982). Leadership style: Attitudes and behaviors. *Training and Development Journal, 36*(5), 50–52.

Hogan, R. J., Curphy, G. J., & Hogan, J. (1994). What do we know about personality: Leadership and effectiveness? *American Psychologist, 49,* 493–504.

Hollander, E. P., & Offerman, L. (1990). Power and leadership in organizations: Relationships in transition. In K. E. Clark & M. B. Clark (Eds.), *Measures of leadership* (pp. 83–97). West Orange, NJ: Leadership Library of America.

Hollingworth, L. S. (1926). *Gifted children: Their nature and nurture.* New York: Macmillan.

House, C. (1980). *The leadership series.* Coeur D'Alene, ID: Listos.

Howe, N., & Strauss, W. (2000). *Millennials rising.* New York: Vintage Books.

Huckaby, W. O., & Sperling, H. B. (1981). Leadership giftedness: An idea whose time has not yet come. *Roeper Review, 3*(3), 19–22.

Institute for Behavioral Research in Creativity. (1990). *Student talent and risk profile.* Salt Lake City, UT: Author.

Jarosewich, T., Pfeiffer, S. I., & Morris, J. (2002). Identifying gifted students using teacher rating scales: A review of existing instruments. *Journal of Psychoeducational Assessment, 20,* 322–336.

Javits, J. K. (1988). *Gifted and Talented Students Education Act* (Title IV, Part B of P.L. 100–297).

Johns, E. F. (1984). The relationship of personality and achievement to creativity and leadership behavior. In R. B. Cattell, M. D. Cattell, & E. Johns (Eds.), *Manual and norms for the High School Personality Questionnaire* (pp. 35–56). Champaign, IL: Institute for Personality and Ability Testing.

Karnes, F. A., & Bean, S. M. (1993). *Girls and young women leading the way.* Minneapolis: Free Sprit.

Karnes, F. A., & Bean, S. M. (1995). *Leadership for students: A practical guide for ages 8–18.* Waco, TX: Prufrock Press.

Karnes, F. A., & Bean, S. M. (1996). Leadership and the gifted. *Focus on Exceptional Children, 29*(1), 1–12.

Karnes, F. A., & Chauvin, J. C. (2000a). *Leadership skills inventory.* Scottsdale, AZ: Gifted Psychology Press.

Karnes, F. A., & Chauvin, J. C. (2000b). *The leadership development program.* Scottsdale, AZ: Gifted Psychology Press.

Karnes, F. A., Chauvin, J. C., & Trant, T. J. (1984). Leadership profiles as determined by the HSPQ of students identified as intellectually gifted. *Roeper Review, 7,* 46–48.

Karnes, F. A., Chauvin, J. C., & Trant, T. J. (1985). Validity of the leadership potential score of the High School Personality Questionnaire with talented students. *Perceptual and Motor Skills, 61,* 163–166.

Karnes, F. A., & D'Ilio, V. (1988a). Assessment of concurrent validity of the Leadership Skills Inventory with gifted students and their teachers. *Perceptual and Motor Skills, 66,* 59–62.

Karnes, F. A., & D'Ilio, V. (1988b). Assessment of criterion-related validity of the Leadership Skills Inventory. *Psychological Reports, 62,* 263–267.

Karnes, F. A., & D'Ilio, V. (1989). Leadership positions and sex-role stereotyping among gifted students. *Gifted Child Quarterly, 33,* 76–78.

Karnes, F. A., & D'Ilio, V. (1990). Sex-role stereotyping of leadership positions by student leaders. *Perceptual and Motor Skills, 70,* 335–338.

Karnes, F. A., & Meriweather, S. (1989). Developing and implementing a plan for leadership: An integral component for success as a leader. *Roeper Review, 11,* 214–217.

Karnes, F. A., Meriweather, S., & D'Ilio, V. (1987). The effectiveness of the Leadership Studies Program. *Roeper Review, 9,* 238–241.

Karnes, F. A., & Meriweather-Bean, S. (1991). Leadership and gifted adolescents. In M. Bireley & J. Genshaft (Eds.), *Understanding the gifted adolescent: Educational, developmental, and multicultural issues* (pp. 122–138). New York: Teachers College Press.

Karnes, F. A., & Riley, T. L. (1996). *Competitions: Maximizing your abilities.* Waco, TX: Prufrock Press.

Khatena, J., & Morse, D. T. (1994). *Khatena-Morse multitalent perception inventory.* Bensonville, IL: Scholastic Testing Service.

Lawrence, G. (1982). *People types and tiger stripes: A practical guide to learning styles.* Gainesville, FL: Center for the Applications of Psychological Type.

Lee, R. J., & King, S. N. (2001) *Discovering the leader in you: A guide to realizing your personal leadership potential.* Greensboro, NC: Center for Creative Leadership and Jossey-Bass.

Lindsay, B. (1988). A lamp for Diogenes: Leadership, giftedness, and moral education. *Roeper Review, 11,* 8–11.

Magoon, R. A., & Jellen, H. G. (1980). *Leadership development: Democracy in action.* Poquoson, VA: Human Development Press.

Marland, S. P., Jr. (1972). *Education of the gifted and talented: Report to the Congress of the United States by the U.S. Commissioner of Education and background papers submitted to the U.S. Office of Education,* 2 vols. Washington, DC: U.S. Government Printing Office. (Government Documents, Y4.L 11/2: G36)

McCaulley, M. H., & Staff of the Center for Applications of Psychological Type. (1990). The Myers-Briggs Type Indicator and leadership. In K. E. Clark & M. B. Clark (Eds.), *Measures of leadership* (pp. 381–418). New York: Center for Creative Leadership.

MacGregor, M. G. (1997). *Leadership 101: Developing leadership skills for resilient youth facilitator's guide.* Denver: Youthleadership.com.

MacGregor, M. G. (1999). *Designing student leadership programs: Transforming the leadership potential of youth.* Denver: Youthleadership.com.

McNamara, J. F., Haensly, P. A., Lupkowski, A. E., & Edlind, E. P. (1985). *The role of extracurricular activities in high school education.* Paper presented at the meeting convention of the National Association for Gifted Children, Denver.

Meisgeier, C., & Murphy, E. (1987). *Murphy-Meisgeier type indicator for children.* Palo Alto, CA: Consulting Psychologists Press.

Myers, I. B., & McCaulley, M. (1985). *Manual: A guide to the development and use of the Myers-Briggs Type Indicator.* Palo Alto, CA: Consulting Psychologists Press.

Myers, I. B., & Myers, P. B. (1980). *Gifted differing.* Palo Alto, CA: Consulting Psychologists Press.

Myers, M. R., Slavin, M. J., & Southern, W. T. (1990). Emergence and maintenance of leadership among gifted students in group problem solving. *Roeper Review, 12,* 256–261.

Nemerowicz, G., & Rosi, E. (1995). *Children's perceptions of leadership: A report of preliminary findings.* Aurora, NY: Women's Leadership Institute.

Parker, J. P. (1989). *Instructional strategies for teaching the gifted.* Boston: Allyn and Bacon.

Parker, J. P., & Begnaud, L. G. (2003). *Developing creative leadership.* Englewood, CO: Teacher Ideas Press.

Perez, G. S., Chassin, D., Ellington, C., & Smith, J. A. (1982). Leadership giftedness in preschool children. *Roeper Review, 4*(3), 26–28.

Pfeiffer, S. I. (2003). Challenges and opportunities for students who are gifted: What experts say. *Gifted Child Quarterly, 47,* 161–169.

Pfeiffer, S. I., & Jarosewich, T. (2003). *Gifted rating scales.* San Antonio, TX: The Psychological Corporation.

Plowman, P. D. (1981). Training extraordinary leaders. *Roeper Review, 3,* 13–16.

Renzulli, J. S., Smith, L. H., White, A. J., Callahan, C. M., & Hartman, R. K. (1976). *Scales for rating the behavioral characteristics of superior students (SRBCSS).* Wethersfield, CT: Creative Learning Press.

Renzulli, J. S., Smith, L. H., White, A. J., Callahan, C. M., Hartman, R. K., & Westberg, K. L. (2002). *Scales for rating the behavioral characteristics of superior students–Revised edition (SRBCSS-R)*. Mansfield Center, CT: Creative Learning Press.

Richardson, W. B., & Feldhusen, J. F. (1987). *Leadership education: Developing skills for youth*. New York: Trillium.

Riley, T. L., & Karnes, F. A. (1994a). Intellectually gifted elementary students' perceptions of leadership. *Perceptual and Motor Skills, 79,* 47–50.

Riley, T. L., & Karnes, F. A. (1994b). A leadership profile of disadvantaged youth based on Leadership Strengths Indicator. *Psychological Reports, 74,* 815–818.

Riley, T. L., & Karnes, F. A. (1996). *Competitions as an avenue for inspiring and recognizing young leaders*. Unpublished manuscript, The University of Southern Mississippi, Hattiesburg.

Roach, A. A., Wyman, L. T., Brookes, H., Chavez, C., Heath, S. B., & Valdes, G. (1999). Leadership giftedness: Models revisited. *Gifted Child Quarterly, 43,* 13–24.

Roets, L. (1986). *Roets rating scale for leadership*. Des Moines, IA: Leadership Publishers.

Roets, L. S. (1997). *Leadership: A skills training program* (8th ed.). New Sharon, IA: Leadership Publishers.

Schakel, L. (1984). *Investigation of the leadership abilities of intellectually gifted students*. Unpublished doctoral dissertation, University of South Florida, Tampa.

Simonton, D. K. (1995). Personality and intellectual predictors of leadership. In D. H. Saklofske & M. Zeidner (Eds.), *International handbook of personality and intelligence* (pp. 739–757). New York: Plenum Press.

Sisk, D. A., & Rosselli, H. C. (1987). *Leadership: A special kind of giftedness*. New York: Trillium.

Sisk, D. A., & Shallcross, D. J. (1986). *Leadership: Making things happen*. Buffalo, NY: Bearly Limited.

Smith, D. L., Smith, L., & Barnette, J. (1991). Exploring the development of leadership giftedness. *Roeper Review, 14,* 7–12.

Stephens, K. R., & Karnes, F. A. (2000). State definitions for the gifted and talented revisited. *Exceptional Children, 66,* 219–238.

Stogdill, R. M. (1974). *Handbook of leadership*. New York: Free Press.

Terman, L. M. (1925). *Genetic study of genius: Vol. 1. Mental and physical traits of a thousand gifted children*. Stanford, CA: Stanford University Press.

Wade, R. C., & Putnam, K. (1995). Tomorrow's leaders? Gifted students' opinions of leadership and service activities. *Roeper Review, 18,* 150–151.

Yammarino, F. J., & Bass, B. M. (1990). Long-term forecasting of transformational leadership and its effect among naval officers: Some preliminary findings. In K. E. Clark & M. B. Clark (Eds.), *Measures of leadership* (pp. 151–169). West Orange, NJ: Leadership Library of America.

Author Note

Portions of this chapter were previously published in "Leadership Education: Resources and Web Sites for Teachers of Gifted Students," by A. Bisland, F. A. Karnes, and Y. B. Cobb, 2004, *Gifted Child Today 27*(1), pp. 50–56.

Chapter 16

Extending Learning Through Mentorships

by Del Siegle and D. Betsy McCoach

"If I have seen farther [than you and Descartes] it is by stand-ing upon the shoulders of Giants."

—Sir Isaac Newton,
in a letter to Robert Hooke, 1675

ow often does a high school student have an opportunity to study the diet of hummingbirds in the far reaches of Chili? Search a local archeological site for native artifacts? Shadow a photojournalist? Use advanced research skills to collect and analyze data on gender bias?

High school students in Connecticut experienced these oppor-tunities because altruistic mentors were willing to share their time, passion, and resources during a summer mentoring program at their state university (Palmer, 2002; Purcell, Renzulli, McCoach, & Spottiswoode, 2001; Wray, 2002). Not all gifted children want or need such mentoring experiences, nor should all adults serve as men-tors. However, when both parties are ready, willing, and able, men-torships such as these can be an extraordinary experience for all parties involved.

"The idea of mentoring is old. At its core, a mentorship reflects the way in which humans have always passed on their legacy, their artistry" (Tomlinson, 2001, p. 5). Parents, classroom teachers, and teachers of the gifted cannot be all things to the young people in their charge. The nature and diversity of gifted students' interests demand resources beyond the confines of the school and demonstrate the need for mentors and other resource people. Mentors provide content sophistication that normally would not be accessible from traditional resources (Siegle, 2001).

Mentoring has been incorporated into gifted education since the beginning of the movement (Milam & Schwartz, 1992). What distinguishes mentoring from other programs for the gifted is that it is essential when students have skills and interests that are "so advanced or divergent from the typical school resources that they need to be placed in situations where those resources are available" (Colemen & Cross, 2001, p. 325). Gifted students need mentors when they have interests that their peers are not yet ready to explore. They need this special contact with others who are interested in their ideas (Roberts & Inman, 2001). Gifted students benefit from mentorships because they often master content and skills sooner than their peers. Through mentorships they can learn more deeply and at an accelerated pace with meaningful and personal feedback (Purcell et al., 2001). In effect, mentoring provides the benefits of both enrichment (Nash, 2001) and acceleration (Nash; Rogers & Kimpston, 1992).

> Educators of the gifted realize that possessing seeds of a talent or ability is one thing; nurturing and developing a talent to fruition is quite another. Not many people are capable of "blooming" alone. Mentors can help one persevere when burdens seem the greatest. (McGreevy, 1990, p. 6)

Gifted students demonstrate career awareness at an earlier age than their peers and benefit from exposure to a variety of careers (Silverman, 2000). Considering that many gifted and talented students deal with multipotentiality, the opportunity to explore at least one area of strong interest before entering college helps them make more effective course and career selections (Davalos & Haensly, 1997). Mentors who are involved in the work world can provide special details on the demands of future jobs and the preparation they require. In addition to providing information about their careers, mentors serve as role models for students who wish to enter a career field (VanTassel-Baska & Baska, 2000). Mentorships may be the most fertile form of career education for the gifted because the mentor is often the chief factor in a successful person's career (Merriam, 1983). For example, most Westinghouse winners and Nobel laureates have had mentors (Winner, 1996).

While career identification and investigation have been the primary focus of many mentoring experiences, another crucial role is making mentees' school experiences more meaningful. Mentors share unique knowledge and talents that cannot be experienced within the confines of the four walls of the classroom by bringing real-world learning to the mentee. This gives the mentee an opportunity to study something beyond the traditional classroom (Davalos & Haensly, 1997), where it is possible to focus intensely on an emerging interest in a ceilingless learning environment (Purcell et al., 2001).

A mentorship usually involves a one-on-one relationship between someone younger and an older expert or someone with knowledge or passion in a field (Roberts & Inman, 2001). One-on-one relationships can be one of the best educational approaches for meeting the needs of gifted and talented children. Mentoring is one of the three most popular one-on-one approaches, the other two being independent study and tutoring (Coleman & Cross, 2001). Developmental psychologists and educators have indicated that youth require more individual attention and one-on-one time from significant adults than they have been receiving (Davalos & Haensly, 1997). Mentoring is one way to meet that need for gifted students.

Definition of a Mentorship

Mentoring is a relationship based on one person helping another person reach a major life goal (Goff & Torrance, 1999). Mentoring can be a formal arrangement that is carefully planned and executed (Nash, 2001; Tomlinson, 2001), in which case the mentor is given the title, often by a third party, in anticipation of what he or she might do (Bennetts, 2001). It can also be a serendipitous meeting of like-minded souls who have a common interest (Nash; Tomlinson), which is usually retrospectively called a mentorship (Bennetts). Finally, it can be a quiet attempt by someone with more experience to reach out to someone less experienced (Tomlinson).

When educators attempt to arrange mentoring, they must carefully plan the union and prepare the student and mentor for it (Reilly, 1992b). The mentoring relationship differs from the typical teacher-student relationship in that mentors and mentees form a partnership to explore their passion, interest, or career (Roberts & Inman, 2001). A mentorship differs from an internship in that it is not limited to specific tasks or jobs (Swassing & Fichter, 1991). The mentor and mentee can explore a variety of interests over several years or even a lifetime. "Mentoring is a creative endeavor where there must be a willingness to let one thing lead to another. It is a relationship based upon trust and sincere desires for growth and learning" (Goff & Torrance, 1999, p. 53).

Being a mentor goes beyond being a role model (Rimm, 2003). A mentor is a role model with considerable knowledge who teaches, counsels, engages, and inspires students with similar interests (Nash, 2001). More than providing skills, the mentor helps the student develop a vision for his or her future, while offering a combination of support and challenge to help the student in his or her quest for that vision (Kaufmann, 2003). A mentor also serves as a friend who helps to advance the student's knowledge of a particular field (Silverman, 2000). Mentorships generally involve development of in-depth academic projects, exploration of strong personal interests and hobbies, or examination of career opportunities (Nash, 2001).

Mentoring is necessary when students cannot find sufficient support and information at home or at school to pursue an area of interest (Forster, 1994).

Expertise in a specific domain of knowledge often requires going beyond the classroom teacher, outside the school system to the community and the world of work where productive professionals with specific expertise can extend the process of inquiry. (Davalos & Haensly, 1997, p. 207)

The value of teachers also serving as mentors should not be overlooked. In reviewing her research on Presidential Scholars, Kaufmann (2003) noted that 66% of her respondents reported their most significant mentor had been a secondary or graduate school teacher.

The Effectiveness of Mentorships

Torrance (1984) documented that mentors make a difference in the creative achievement and educational attainment of mentees. Individuals with mentors complete more education than those without, and having a mentor is significantly related to adult achievement. Study and program evaluation reports consistently show positive results for mentorships (Beck, 1989; Ellingson, Haeger, & Feldhusen, 1986; Hamilton & Hamilton, 1992; Prillaman & Richardson, 1989; Swassing & Fichter, 1991; Wright & Borland, 1992).

Generally, mentorships produce additional academic benefits for bright high school students, although the additional benefit may be small or difficult to measure.

> When a student is matched to someone with more knowledge and equal levels of interest in a specific topic, it makes sense that there will be positive outcomes for that student. But when a study is set up, the performance of mentored students will be compared to that of non-mentored students more likely on some general subject area test, rather than on the specific topic the mentored students explored. Likewise, the student's increased knowledge on a specific topic may not flow over into measurable psychological changes with so complex a construct as self-concept. (Rogers & Kimpston, 1992, pp. 60–61)

The benefits of a mentorship transcend career awareness and an academic or topic focus and may include increased self-confidence, self-awareness (Nash, 2001), commitment, self-trust, empathy (Tomlinson, 2001), responsibility, future-mindedness (Purcell et al., 2001), exceptional production (Nash), and positive self-images (Davalos & Haensly, 1997; Goff & Torrance, 1999). Students in telementoring programs also report improved technology and telecommunication skills and increased school attendance (International Telementoring Program, n.d.). Mentorships also provide improved work and study skills for mentees, including improved organization skills, time management, and responsibility (Davalos & Haensly).

"Powerful mentorships help prepare young people to live with greater purpose, focus, and appreciation at a younger age by drawing not only on the knowledge of the past, but on its wisdom as well" (Tomlinson, 2001, p. 27). For example,

> When Eleanor Roosevelt [1884–1962] was of high school age, she attended Allenswood, a boarding school in England dedicated to giving a broad education emphasizing responsibility in society and personal independence. It was a collegiate environment that took the education of women seriously. The founder and headmistress of Allenswood was Mlle. Marie Souvestre, a passionate humanist committed to human justice. She believed that young women should develop an independent vision and the means to defend that vision. She demanded that her students take themselves seriously and encouraged them to become politically engaged. Eleanor was one of her favorite students, chosen to sit beside her at dinner and to travel with her during several vacations. These were the happiest years of Eleanor's life. For the rest of her life she kept Marie Souvestre's portrait on her desk. Her life reflected Souvestre's influence and spirit. (Geiger, 2001, p. 347)

It naturally followed that Eleanor would later become an activist for human rights. Likewise, Charles Darwin reported that his mentor, John Stevens Henslow, influenced his career more than any other circumstance (McGreevy, 1990).

Benefits to Mentors

There are benefits to the mentor, as well as to the mentee. Corporations that support mentoring programs report that employees who volunteer as mentors have better teamwork skills, improved moral and self-worth, and improved employee retention. In one study, 75% of the Allstate Insurance Company's employees who served as mentors said participation in the mentorship improved their attitude at work (National Mentoring Partnership, 2003). Roberts and Inman (2001) described one mentors' reflection on mentoring:

> The joy in mentoring is that it doesn't feel at all like real work. Gifted kids learn independently, usually acquire an interest in ideas for their own sake, and are nourished more by the mentor's enthusiasm than by smoothness in the mentor's teaching technique. (p. 10)

Mentoring adds spark to the mentors' lives, appeals to their altruistic streak, identifies someone who cares about what they do (Nash & Treffinger, 1993), perpetuates interest and knowledge in their passion area, and develops pleasure of knowing and working with a young person on a personal basis (Roberts & Inman, 2001). As one mentor reflected,

> When I heard about Jon and received some of his work in the mail, it was almost like a case of déjà vu. I remembered the years I spent as a youth in which my interests and thoughts didn't quite fit. I remembered inventing board games while my peers were tinkering with cars. I recalled visualizing elaborate scenes on imaginary planets while listening with one ear to monotone chemistry lectures. I saw myself in Jon, and I wanted to help him discover and treasure his strengths before they atrophied in the midst of an unappreciative society. (Ambrose, Allen, & Huntley, 1994, p. 133)

Mentoring at Different Ages

Mentorships are particularly effective in the later elementary, middle, and high school years (Roberts & Inman, 2001), although young children benefit from them, as well (Shaughnessy, 1989). Early mentorships can help young students recognize and validate their creativity, develop respect for their own uniqueness, grow in self-esteem, act in a trustworthy matter that gains respect, and explore opportunities for creative achievement (Bennetts, 2001). Participating in a mentorship at an early age provides the emotional support and encouragement that children need to pursue their talents. Many creative young people suffer and actually have their skill development retarded because they do not have access to a mentor (Torrance, 1984).

During adolescent age, even young people who enjoy parental mentoring begin to seek relationships apart from their parents. Interestingly, having a school or community mentor does not negate the effects of a parental mentor (Bennetts, 2001). Adolescents benefit from opportunities for collaboration and personal achievement, assistance with the transition from youth to adulthood and from school to college, esoteric resources and inspiration to feed creativity, and respect for the mentees' choices (Bennetts).

At the adulthood level, mentors take their mentees' creative work seriously, provide a critical review of their work, listen to the their ideas and give feedback (Bennetts, 2001), and open doors of opportunity. For example, the National Association for Gifted Children (NAGC) has a mentoring program for its members. In this program, teachers, parents, and counselors who are interested in developing their expertise in some aspect of gifted and talented education are paired for 2 years with professionals within the organization with expertise in the mentee's interest area. Together, the mentor and mentee set goals for (1) increasing the mentees' knowledge of the chosen area, (2) reflecting on the newly acquired knowledge base, (3) solving problems in the mentee's environment using the newfound knowledge, and (4) sharing what the mentee has learned throughout the mentorship through presentations and written disseminations (NAGC, 2003).

Mentoring Underserved Populations

Three groups of gifted and talented students are in greatest need of mentorships: highly gifted, disadvantaged, and underachieving. The highly gifted require challenges well beyond the school's capability; the disadvantaged benefit from important role models, college and career guidance, and possible summer employment and scholarship opportunities; and the underachieving benefit from meaningful learning experiences, individual attention, and a change from the status quo (VanTassel-Baska, 2000). In his 2003 State of the Union address, President George W. Bush called for $450 million over 3 years to recruit and train 1 million mentors for disadvantaged middle school children and children whose parents are incarcerated. His proposal also included support for the training and recruiting of mentors.

In this section, we will discuss the mentoring of gifted females, culturally diverse students, and economically disadvantaged populations.

Gifted Females

Providing gifted females with mentors is one of the suggested strategies for helping gifted females succeed (Reis, 1998). Mentorships are particularly valuable for gifted women in the early stages of their careers and have been shown to produce higher earnings for women (Kaufmann, Harrell, Milam, Woolverton, & Miller, 1986).

Several special issues confront women who are interested in finding mentors. First, men tend to avoid female mentors. Second, women who have worked their way up in male-dominated fields are often reluctant to server as mentors for other women. Third, social pressure and concern about appearance limit older men serving as mentors for younger women. Fourth, limited numbers of female mentors exist because young women fail to find mentors and they are then less likely to later serve as mentors. Finally, male chauvinism still exists in some organizations (Shaughnessy & Neely, 1991).

Females tend to express stronger support for mentorships than males (Shaughnessy & Neely, 1991). Females may be better role models for other females, but the limited number of female mentors often results in males serving as their mentors. Females with male mentors report a greater need for more personal and friendship relations than females with female mentors. Females also tend to be less satisfied with their mentors than men (Torrance, 1984), which may be due to the limited number of available female mentors. While females do not often report strong mentoring relationships during their formal schooling years, when they do encounter significant teachers, their lives are greatly influenced (List & Renzulli, 1991). Also, once young women reach their college years, mentors often powerfully influence their future careers (Leroux, 1994).

Culturally Diverse Students

Both society and the education system frequently penalize children who are raised with different values and attitudes from those of the dominant culture (Goff & Torrance, 1999). Mentors can be positive role models and can encourage protégés who face alienation, exclusion, and disenfranchisement caused by societal stereotypes. For this reason, mentors must be willing to take risks and be willing to acquire a broad knowledge of human differences and similarities. This may also involve extra creativity on the mentor's part (Goff & Torrance).

It is possible that more students from underrepresented populations might qualify for gifted and talented programs if they were exposed to mentorships because mentors act as talent scouts who recognize, acknowledge, and develop students' strengths. They use students' potential to build success, skills, and abilities, rather than focus on their deficits. The premise that "giving attention to successful behavior motivates the attainment of potential" has been the foundation of gifted education since its inception (Goff & Torrance, 1999, p. 14). Mentoring capitalizes on the mentee's strengths and the mentor's expertise (Forster, 1994). This is achieved by instilling pride, aiding in creating a positive self-image, providing adventure, and building prestige with peers (Goff & Torrance).

As for race, the research findings suggest that race by itself does not play a significant role in determining whether or not a mentor and mentee form a strong relationship and the extent to which that relationship leads to positive changes for the youth. In one study, there were a few differences in outcomes when the same-race and cross-race groups were further differentiated by gender, but those differences did not seem to suggest a pattern (Jucovy, 2002). In fact, the findings suggest that the effects of race on relationships are subtle and act in combination with other factors (such as gender and the mentor's interpersonal style) to shape the ultimate influence of mentoring. Nevertheless, many programs are committed to same-race mentoring, which can be problematic because 15–20% of adult volunteers are members of a racial minority, while approximately 50% of the students who apply for programs are from a racial minority. For programs committed to same-race matches, the result is that minority youth may spend a long time on a waiting list until a mentor becomes available (Rhodes, 2002).

Jucovy (2002) suggested that mentors adhere to three suggestions when mentoring diverse students:

1. *Mentors are the experienced one in the relationship* and it is their responsibility to make the mentee feel comfortable in the relationship.

2. *Mentors should be themselves.* Mentees can see through a mentor who is trying to be someone else by using the mentee's slang, for example.

3. *Mentors should learn about the mentee's culture, lifestyle, and age group*, but they never will be from that group, so they should avoid trying to over-identify with it.

Mentors should honestly examine their own prejudices and stereotypes, make a personal commitment to be culturally sensitive, see the mentee first and foremost as a valuable and unique person, and approach cultural differences as an opportunity to expand their own understanding. All mentors, regardless of whether they are matched with youth of the same race, can benefit from training in cultural understanding. For mentors who are of a different race than their mentee, this training is essential (Jucovy, 2002).

Educators can also be key agents in affirming students' cultural and linguistic identity by mentoring and advocating for their academic success. "The challenge is for educators to discover and link personal and school lives of bicultural students to a meaningful and high-quality instructional program" (Gonzalez, 2003, p. 93).

Economically Disadvantaged Students

Mentorships are highly recommended for gifted students from economically disadvantaged backgrounds (Olszewski-Kubilius & Scott, 1992; Wright & Borland, 1992). College and career guidance is a valuable mentoring outcome for underserved populations. Gifted economically disadvantaged students are as motivated to attend college as their middle class peers, and they receive similar support; however, they report being less prepared to go to college (Olszewski-Kubilius & Scott). The mentoring process can facilitate that preparation. For example, students in the summer mentoring program at the University of Connecticut (Purcell et al., 2001) assume roles similar to graduate research assistants. As a result, these students leave their summer campus experiences much better prepared for the transition from high school to college life.

Economically disadvantaged students can also serve as mentors for younger students. In one innovative project, disadvantaged adolescents tutored young able children from extremely disadvantaged backgrounds (Wright & Borland, 1992). Since mentorships positively impact both mentors and mentees, using older students to mentor younger students can have a positive effect on both parties in the relationship.

Telementoring is also an important mentoring option for low-income communities. First, it increases technological literacy among members of low-income communities, and second, it addresses the inability of youth programs to find enough adults willing to serve as mentors (Buery, n.d.). Telementoring is discussed in more detail in the next section.

Telementoring

Not all mentoring occurs in person. Mentoring experiences can also occur over the Internet or through books and other resource materials. One of the fastest growing areas of mentoring is telementoring, also known as virtual mentoring, e-mentoring (Nash, 2001), or iMentoring (Buery, n.d.). The National Mentoring Partnership (http://www.mentoring.org) features an extensive Web site on all aspects of organizing and running mentorship programs. In addition to the program information, the site also includes information about telementoring and links to telementoring organizations such as the International Telementor Program (http://www.telementor.org).

By developing interesting classroom projects centered on the use of e-mail and the World Wide Web, telementoring helps bridge the digital divide separating those who regularly use new information technologies from those who don't. It also allows mentor volunteers to use their limited time effectively and efficiently.

Telementoring can be divided into three types of programs:

- mentor experts who agree to respond to questions;
- mentors who are paired with a single learner; and
- mentors who work in partnerships (Riel, n.d.).

Mentor Experts

Mentor experts usually have short interactions with students. This often involves topical focus Web sites that are sponsored by corporations or organizations. Students e-mail their questions to the organization and an expert on the topic e-mails a reply. The interaction is usually limited to the exchange of an e-mail with a possible follow-up message. Many of these sites keep archives of the questions and answers, which often provide interesting reading for students. One of the more well-known mentor expert sites is the MadSci Network (http://www.madsci.org). Pitsco's Ask an Expert site (http://www.askanexpert.com) provides an index of experts sites in a variety of subject areas.

Mentor Pairs and Partnerships

Many businesses provide telementoring as a service option. Hewlett Packard was an early supporter of telementoring, providing support for their employees to participate in e-mail mentoring programs. The HP program is now part of the larger International Telementor Program (ITP), which provides academic mentoring support from professionals of sponsoring companies. All student-mentor communication is project-focused and facilitated by a teacher or parent (ITP, n.d.).

The most successful telementoring programs are usually partnerships that include a three-component design that involves students, their teachers, and mentors. Students in these programs may not participate unless a teacher sponsors them (some programs allow parents to sponsor their children). The teacher works with the student to design a mentoring proposal. Together they submit the student's proposal to an online mentoring organization that posts it for consideration by potential mentors (Dahle, 1998). Once a mentor match is made, the teacher usually monitors the student's participation. E-mail is the most common communication format for the mentor and mentee to use. Many larger telementoring organizations offer secure online discussion forums for mentors and mentees to use (ITP, n.d.). Organizations with these systems often limit all communication between the mentor and mentee to their secure system. A secure system maintains the privacy of all parties and also allows the telementoring organization to monitor the mentor and mentee interactions, which is necessary to safeguard the mentee and limit the liability of the telementoring organization.

One reason why programs such as HP's telementoring program, after which ITP is fashioned, have been so effective is that they require specific commitments from everyone involved. Students must be sponsored by a teacher who, in turn, must agree to certain ground rules. Teachers must devise lesson plans for mentoring projects, coordinate those projects with traditional class work, and guarantee that the students will have e-mail access. For their part, mentors agree to own the relationship. Mentors respond to every e-mail and stay with their mentees even if they waiver. This type of mentorship isn't a substantial sacrifice for mentors; most send and receive one to three e-mail messages per week in such programs (Dahle, 1998).

Telementoring has some unique advantages over traditional mentoring. It

- provides a means of connecting thousands of professionals with students on a scale that is impractical in traditional face-to-face mentoring;
- matches students with appropriate mentors without geographic limitation;
- allows convenient, consistent, weekly communication between students and mentors and creates an archive of all communication;
- eliminates scheduling problems between mentors and students because an e-mail communication can be sent any time; and
- provides the opportunity for students to work on long-term projects with their mentors and allows mentors to see the impact they are having on students. (ITP, n.d.).

Telementoring provides four major benefits for teachers.

- With telementoring projects, students become fully engaged in projects, which makes teachers' jobs much easier. Teachers can then act to facilitate learning, rather than trying to convince students that they need to learn.
- Students are responsible for developing their own special projects based on their interests. When students are encouraged to explore their own

curiosities, they are much more likely to engage in effective, multidimensional learning. Students focus on their particular interests and learn to incorporate a variety of skills into a project. For example, these may include research, writing, math, and experimentation.

- Telementoring utilizes the skills and knowledge of adult professionals. By tapping into these specialists, teachers are provided a vast new resource of expertise that brings the world into the classroom. Likewise, students receive instruction from field professionals and gain access to significant new role models.
- The value of students interacting with people outside the classroom is beyond measure. They learn about different careers, lifestyles, and cultures. And, by working with a mentor to whom they are accountable, students develop a new understanding of the importance of being responsible. (ITP, n.d.).

Much of the selection criteria for telementors is similar to that for in-person mentors and is discussed in a later section.

Establishing a Mentorship Program

Mentoring programs are usually organized and conducted by schools, universities, parent groups, service organizations, businesses and corporations, or spiritual groups. The suggestions presented in this chapter are applicable to all of these, although we place an emphasis on programs organized by schools.

Programs must be able to recruit, screen, and train mentors; match them with youth; monitor the matches; and identify and help resolve problems as they arise. Prior to planning a mentoring program, visit the National Mentoring Partnership's extensive Web site (http://www.mentoring.org), which includes a myriad of information ranging from developing plans, to training mentors, to evaluating program outcomes. The free material from this site would fill several textbooks on the topic. Veterans and neophytes alike will gain valuable information from the hundreds of pages of useful information posted there. Mentorship coordinators will also want to consult *Mentorship: The Essential Guide for Schools and Business* (Reilly, 1992a), a standard book in the field on organizing and implementing mentoring programs.

A successful program requires a coordinated effort from planning through evaluation. The following section describes a detailed six-step plan for planning, operating, and evaluating a mentorship program.

1. Developing a Plan

A planning committee is usually formed to develop and implement a mentoring program. Aside from the program coordinator, the committee should include teachers, a school administrator, the school psychologist or counselor, parents, students, and community members. The teachers build support for the program within the school. The administrator offers insight into program operations and school budgets. The school psychologist is helpful when evaluating students and mentors. Student input is invaluable when selecting the type of program to offer. Parents and community members can assist in building community support and gaining access to future mentors.

The first priority of the planning committee is determining what type of mentoring program to establish. Although many mentorships are a combination of the following, mentorships usually fall into one of three categories based on their purpose.

1. *Interest area mentoring* is a way of expanding or enriching the curriculum to enable students with special skills, knowledge, and interests to work with others who have expertise in those areas.
2. *Career investigation mentoring* provides opportunities for career exploration.
3. *Affective development mentoring* focuses on issues of self-esteem, values, and emotional support and seeks to provide role models for students (Milam, 2001, p. 527).

One or a combination of these purposes can be achieved through academic tutoring, job shadowing, career exploration, job and life skills development, or participation in internships (National Mentoring Center, n.d.).

Mentors who assist students on a regular basis with classwork or special projects fall into the academic tutoring category. They may work with their students at school or at the mentor's workplace. This type of mentoring may abate as soon as a special project is completed or may continue throughout the student's school career. The Study of Mathematically Precocious Youth's (SMPY) Diagnostic–Prescriptive Instruction model is an advanced example of academic tutoring. With this model, the mentor is more responsible for directing the student's learning. The mentor analyzes student errors on a standardized achievement test and then works with the student on the principles (not the items) he or she did not understand. As the model title states, the mentor diagnoses and prescribes. Mentors for this model need not be teachers, but they do need expertise in the subject area (in this case, mathematics) so that they are intellectually able, fast-minded, and well versed in the subject (Lupkowski, Assouline, & Stanley, 1990). For example, because young gifted mathematicians want to know why something works, the mentor must be well versed in theory (Emerson-Stonnell & Carter, 1994). The mentor sets the learning pace, stimulates interest, clarifies principles, and extends knowledge (Lupkowski et al.). Once the student demonstrates understanding of a topic, the mentor can move onto another (Emerson-Stonnell & Carter).

Job shadowing is usually a short-term option where the student spends from 1 or 2 days to several weeks at the mentor's workplace learning about a given career. Job shadowing can develop into a career exploration mentorship. Under this option, the student spends a substantial amount of in-depth time on location with the mentor. One of our students spent a semester job shadowing a veterinarian at an animal clinic, where she was able to assist with several animal surgeries.

Mentors can also assist young people in developing job and life skills that will help them gain employment and be successful in the workplace. Finally, students may participate in paid internships where they provide assistance and develop their talents simultaneously.

In addition to the type of program, the scope of the program must also be considered. Typical programs match mentors and mentees for 6 months to a year (National Mentoring Partnership, n.d.), although many young people can benefit from longer relationships. The frequency of meetings between mentors and mentees also should be considered. Finally, the depth to which the organization wishes to develop mentorships should be discussed.

Ultimately, the mentoring program that is established should be based on the needs of the students and the resources of the school and community. These will drive the program goals. Unfortunately, planners often take shortcuts when establishing program goals. Many program handbooks contain lofty program goals that have very little to do with what actually happens in the program. The time spent discussing student needs and the resources the program will have available is time well spent. Selection of mentors, mentees, program activities, and program evaluation will be much easier once clearly defined goals are established.

Student needs. Schools with a variety of accelerated classes and an extensive honors and Advanced Placement program have different needs than those with a pull-out enrichment program or no program at all. As stated earlier, mentorships can serve to provide more depth through advanced content or greater breadth through enrichment opportunities.

Available resources. Planners should ask how current resources can be used and what additional resources are necessary. Resources and support are necessary to create a successful program. Mentorship programs sometimes appear to be an attractive alternative for schools because they seem to cost less than other services for gifted students (Coleman & Cross, 2001). Unfortunately, mentorship programs have traditionally received low funding priority in schools. Districts support is often limited to funding a teacher to coordinate and manage the mentoring program (Davalos & Haensly, 1997).

Three questions to ask about available resources are:

1. *Is there already a sufficient, trained staff to plan and implement the program without significantly restructuring or adding new staff?* The staff may exist, but funds may be needed for training.
2. *What type of administrative support and overhead is available?* While most

mentorships occur onsite, space is needed for program files and the coordinator. Obviously, any program requires some type of administrative support on a regular basis.

3. *What are the program costs and how will they be funded?* Mentoring programs often operate under existing programs. Even if the mentoring program is part of a larger program for gifted and talented students, additional funds are necessary for promotion, training, daily operations, and evaluation (National Mentoring Partnership, n.d.).

Liability. Liability must also be well thought-out during the planning phase. As with any relationship outside the school, safety and security need to be considered. The safety and well-being of the students is the first priority, and it must be discussed with parents, mentors, and mentees at orientation meetings. Many schools conduct criminal checks on mentor volunteers (Roberts & Inman, 2001). One mentor program uses the following guidelines to address liability:

- Parents are required to sign a statement that they will stay with students during meetings.
- Mentors must be known to or recommended by a reliable source.
- All mentors are met face-to-face by a selection committee.
- Security checks are conducted for all mentors who are linked with mentees.
- Legal advice is sought from legal services regarding the operation of the program (Forster, 1994, p. 27).

The National Mentoring Partnership (2003) also recommends that a "Mentor's Code of Conduct" that addresses appropriate activities for mentors, explicit rules about drug and alcohol use, and boundaries of mentor/mentee relationships be written and shared with anyone involved in the program. An organization's insurance company should be consulted regarding how the current liability coverage specifically applies to mentoring efforts. The coverage should shield mentors from claims by participants, as well as shield the organization from claims by mentors and mentees.

The Nebraska Work-Based Project (Nebraska Department of Education, 1998) suggests the following insurance considerations for parents, school administrators, and employers:

- *Health/life insurance*–provided by student's family; however, employers are responsible for offering coverage for students in paid work site learning experiences if similarly classified employees are eligible for these benefits.
- *Automobile accident insurance*–provided by the student/parent (for travel to and from activities) unless the district provides transportation.
- *Accident/liability insurance*–insurance for personal injury or property

damage should be carried by the employer, school district, and family; additional liability (malpractice) insurance may be advisable in the health care field.

- *Worker's compensation*–students participating in paid work site experiences are covered by worker's compensation and may be covered by the school district's policy or the employer. Students participating in unpaid work site experiences are not covered by worker's compensation; but, if they are injured at the work site, they may be covered by the school district or business's liability insurance, their family insurance, or both.
- *Medical treatment waiver*–parents sign a waiver for student's participation in a work site learning experience.

2. Recruiting Mentors

Any recruitment of participants should portray accurate expectations and benefits (National Mentoring Partnership, n.d.). Presentations to local organizations and businesses, articles in the local school newspapers, radio and television news coverage, Web sites, school newsletters, and brochures are effective ways to promote the program. Promotional material should include:

- history of the program;
- program philosophy;
- program components;
- student selection process;
- mentor role;
- student role;
- parent role; and
- coordinator role (Nash & Treffinger, 1993).

Mentors can be found in area colleges and universities (professors and university students); K–12 schools; service groups and community organizations; research institutes; cultural institutes (art, science, music, history); government agencies; media (television, radio, newspaper, publishing, advertising); area businesses; area libraries; sports organizations; outdoor/environmental associations; professions (medicine, law, education, engineering, literature, architecture, art); and senior citizen centers (Nash & Treffinger, 1993). The Community Talent Miner (see Figure 1) is an excellent tool to collect information from potential mentors, and Figure 2 is an example of a mentor application form.

Beyond the traditional pool of mentors from community resources and service clubs, there may be willing volunteers within the school (VanTassel-Baska & Baska, 2000). Many teachers have worked in other professions before earning their teaching certificates and can use that expertise mentoring students. Many universities offer teacher certification programs for people with other degrees, and these individuals bring a myriad of real-world experiences with them.

Recruiting mentors from the community can be time-consuming and expensive. Initially, it may be easier to recruit mentors from a single source, such as a particular service organization. Mentors from a single source may already enjoy a sense of team spirit that can help new mentoring relationships grow. It may also be easier to recruit mentors who work or live in close geographic proximity to the program. This eases their commuting time. Once the program begins, existing mentors make the best recruiters for future mentors (National Mentoring Partnership, n.d.).

Many program coordinators make a habit of scanning newspaper articles for stories about interesting people and then contact them about joining the mentoring pool. While a mass mailing or leaving brochures at various locations is an option, we found personal contact was superior. We left brochures at our local college and senior citizen center and experienced a low return rate. However, when we approached individuals and asked them to participate or made presentations to organizations, we were successful. The National Mentoring Center (n.d.) created an attractive postcard to give to potential mentors. The card begins with a catchy introduction: "You have received this postcard because somebody believes that you would make a great mentor." Individuals involved in the mentoring program should be encouraged to distribute such cards personally to potential mentors they know.

Don't overlook senior citizens. What they may lack in current career connections, they more than make up for it in their willingness to share. The elderly woman serving fries at the local fast food restaurant may be a retired textile conservator or a former journalist who would love to share her knowledge with an eager young person.

Skill in an area is not sufficient for someone to be a mentor. The mentor must have the desire and the ability to establish a nurturing relationship (Roberts & Inman, 2001).

> In order to appreciate and perceive the artistry of the traditional mentor relationship it is essential to perceive and sense the whole. Mentors do not so much teach as live the process . . . and in so doing provide for others a foundation for learning and living throughout the lifespan. (Bennetts, 2001, p. 260)

Mentors must be secure and confident in their own skills and abilities; be aware of their own jealousy, competitiveness, and frustration tolerance; have higher order and creative teaching strategies; be motivational; and exhibit excellent assessment skills (Shaughnessy & Neely, 1991). A quality mentors almost always

- understands and appreciates the general and specific giftedness of the mentee;
- is generous with his or her time;
- is caring;

Name _____ Date _____
Address _____
Telephone _____
E-mail: _____ Fax: _____
Place of Business _____

Instructions

In filling out this questionnaire, please keep in mind:

1. There are no predetermined responses. Be as original as you like in your replies.
2. Take as much space as you need to respond to any item. Use the back of the sheet if necessary.
3. If there are sections or questions you'd rather omit, simply skip them.

I. Trips, Safaris, and Excursions

1. Have you traveled "off the beaten track"—to any unusual or out-of-the-way places?
2. Where did you go (include dates)?
3. What sorts of records do you have of your travels (e.g., photographs, local products, or other artifacts)?

II. Academic Experience

1. If you attended college, business school, or had technical training, what subject was your major emphasis?
2. Did it have any unusual aspects (e.g., an interdisciplinary major, involvement in original research, publications, or presentations)? Please list.

III. Intercultural Experiences

1. Have you lived in another culture? If so, where?
2. For how long and under what circumstances did you live in the culture?
3. Describe one meaningful experience you had during your visit.

IV. Hobbies, Collections, and Competitions

1. What are your hobbies?
2. Are you a collector? If so, what sorts of things do you collect?
3. How did you become involved with your hobby or collection?
4. Do you belong to an organized group of people with like interests (e.g., Stamp Collectors of America, Flat Earth Society)? Please list.
5. Have you entered your collection or hobby in a competition (include details and outcomes)?
6. Have you ever entered any other unusual competitions or contests (e.g., a frog jumping contest, limerick competition, model sailboat race)? What sort? Is this something in which you participate on a regular basis?

V. Esoteric Topical Interests

Most of us know people who describe themselves as history buffs, computer whizzes, ecology nuts, science fiction freaks, committed health food faddists, or hopeless Sherlock Holmes addicts. Could you think of a special interest of yours for which you'd give yourself a similar label? Please include area of interest and labels.

1. In what ways have you followed up on your interests?
2. Do you meet with other people who have similar interests (include group names, any organized activities, etc.)?

VI. Community-Related Activities

Directions: For each item, include group name(s), positions held, dates of involvement, and how you became involved.

Have you ever:
1. Lobbied for something?
2. Belonged to an interest group?
3. Campaigned for a cause or a person?
4. Been involved in a religious group?
5. Joined a community action group?
6. Donated time to a "charitable" organization?

VII. Professional Experiences

1. What do you do for a living?
2. How long has it been your career?
3. What other career(s) have you explored? How?
4. How did you select your current career?
5. How long have you worked at your present job? Please provide a short description of your position.
6. Which unique or creative aspects of your profession would you like to communicate to a young person who might be interested in entering your field (e.g., skills you have had to learn "the hard way")?

Of those areas explored in this questionnaire, the following are ones about which I am especially enthusiastic:

I would be willing for the teacher(s) of _____ to contact me regarding possible applications of some of my interests and talents with students.

_____
(Your Signature)

Figure 1. The Community Talent Miner:
A survey for locating community resources

Note. From *The Enrichment Triad Model: A Guide for Developing Defensible Programs for the Gifted and Talented*, by J. S. Renzulli (pp. 84–86), Mansfield Center, CT: Creative Learning Press. Copyright ©1977 by Creative Learning Press. Reprinted with permission.

University
YWCA

YOUTH MENTOR PROGRAM
2600 Bancroft Way, Berkeley, CA 94704
(510) 848-6370; ywcaymp@earthlink.net

Mentor Application

Name: _____ Gender: M / F Date: _____

Local Address: _____

_____

Permanent Address: _____

_____

Local Phone #: _____ Permanent #: _____

Mobile Phone #: _____ Other #: _____

E-mail Address: _____ Do you check your e-mail? Y / N

Other E-mail Addresses: _____

Date of Birth: _____ Ethnicity: _____

Do You Speak Any Languages Other Than English? _____

Current Class Level: _____ Expected Graduation Date: _____

Major/Minor: _____

Will you be employed during the current academic year? If so, please note how many hours and days.

What other programs, clubs, or activities will you be involved in during the current year? How much time do you expect to commit to them?

Will you be able to commit three hours a week to meet your mentee and participate in group activities for the rest of the academic year? Y / N

Do you have a car? Y / N   Would you like to carpool with other mentors? Y / N

How did you learn of the Youth Mentor Program?

What interested you most about being a mentor for the Youth Mentor Program? Why do you want to be a mentor?

What skills would you contribute to the program? How will they enhance your ability to be a youth mentor?

Please describe any prior experience you have had working with youth and why it would prepare you to be an effective and positive mentor.

What are your interests and how do you enjoy spending your time?

Please describe any additional information that would be helpful in the selection and matching process.

To complete your application we require 2 references, one from a current /previous employer, instructor, or other professional who can validate your skills and abilities; and one from a person who has known you for at least two years (not a relative). Please list below the name, relationship to you, phone number, and email address of each person from whom you are using as a reference.

1. Name _____
    Relationship _____
    Phone _____ E-mail _____

2. Name _____
    Relationship _____
    Phone _____ E-mail _____

Have you ever been convicted of a criminal act? Y / N
If yes please explain:

Your Signature: _____ Date: _____

Figure 2. Sample mentor application

Note. Retrieved June 8, 2004, from http://www.ywca-berkeley.org/mentor.html. Copyright ©2004 YWCA at U.C. Berkeley. Reprinted with permission.

- is respectful of the mentee's right to make his or her own choices;
- is a good listener;
- is open and willing to accept different ideas and points of view;
- holds the mentee to high standards;
- extends the mentee's experiences;
- can provide constructive, rather than critical, feedback; and
- is comfortable being a role model for the mentee.

Mentors frequently seek out mentees, cultivating friendship, sharing their lives, and offering advice and support (Geiger, 2001).

Questions to consider about potential mentors:

1. Does the mentor like working with gifted youngsters?
2. Is the mentor's teaching style compatible with the student's learning style?
3. Is the mentor willing to be a role model by sharing his or her excitement and joy of learning?
4. Is the mentor optimistic and positive about the future? (Berger, 1990)

3. Selecting Mentees

Not all students want or need mentors. The following four questions (Berger, 1990), each of which will be discussed in more depth below, should guide the decision to find a mentor for a student:

- Does the mentee want a mentor, or simply some exposure to a particular subject or career field?
- What type of mentor does the student need?
- Is the student willing to invest a significant amount of time with the mentor?
- Does the student fully understand the purpose, benefits, and limitations of a mentoring relationship?

Does the mentee want a mentor, or simply some exposure to a particular subject or career field? A mentorship is appropriate for a student who has a clear goal, such as an in-depth investigation of an issue. It may not be appropriate if the student simply wants some advice on a school project (Kaufmann, 2003). Students with idle curiosity in a topic or who are seeking quick answers to their questions are not candidates for mentoring. Mentoring is a sustained relationship over time with a more knowledgeable advisor. Successful mentor-student relationships involve students with high levels of self-motivation and a demonstrated commitment to a particular field of endeavor (Forster, 1994). Prior to considering a mentorship, students should reflect on the following questions:

- What do I hope to get from this relationship?
- What type of adult would I get along with best?
- Are there any special skills or interests that I want my mentor to have?
- What can I do to help my mentor bring out the best in me?
- How can I help my mentor in return? (Rimm, 2003, p. 91)

Students who are disenfranchised within their educational program sometimes indicate that they wish to work on their own with a mentor. However, just because a students indicates that he or she wants to work on his or her own doesn't necessarily mean a mentorship is the best arrangement. Reilly (1992b) noted that "on my own" can depict a desire to study a topic of interest not covered in the curriculum, to move more or less rapidly through the curriculum, to work individually instead of in a group, to produce a different product than was assigned, or to see connections between the content and the real world. She cautioned that, because schools have the primary responsibility to educate children, they should investigate a variety of available resources within the school before asking others for a long-term mentoring commitment.

An authentic mentorship is more than a student receiving supplemental information. It can provide the student with opportunities for real-world application of his or her passion or interest, self-confidence, expanded possibilities for learning, increased knowledge base, continuous progress, deepened enthusiasm for a subject, extension or enrichment of the curriculum, a role model, and growth in an area of giftedness (Roberts & Inman, 2001). Because of the demanding level of interaction between a mentee and mentor, other sources of information or other types of interaction between the student and a knowledgeable adult may be more appropriate. For example, the telementoring option of asking an expert that is discussed elsewhere in this chapter may be more appropriate. Perhaps one or two meetings with a knowledgeable adult who is willing to share resources with the student will suffice. In one of our school districts, the formal mentorship program at the high school represented the culmination of a variety of independent enrichment and career awareness opportunities. Students were encouraged to participate in job shadowing, independent study, and enrichment seminar options prior to enrolling in a mentorship program.

Students who have independent work habits, a strong grasp of subject matter, and a desire for mentoring are the strongest candidates (Roberts & Inman, 2001). These students are also goal-driven and can articulate a clear purpose for their mentorship.

What type of mentor does the student need? A mentor can serve five different roles:

- Mentors serve as models for their mentees. Mentees may seek to emulate the talents, skills, or personality characteristics of their mentors.
- Mentors provide a knowledge base for mentees.
- Mentors help students formulate future plans and ways to achieve them.

- Mentors help students think about the world differently and look at the world through new eyes.
- Mentors help students better understand themselves (Shaughnessy & Neely, 1991, p. 131).

Reilly (1992a) developed a resource chart (see Figure 3) for identifying and using resources with students. Start at the bottom of the chart and move upward toward mentorship.

Selecting the right mentor is a difficult task. Torrance's (1984) research indicates that females mention the following positive characteristics of mentors (in order of most frequently cited): (1) encouraging, praising; (2) skilled, expert; (3) a friend; (4) inspiring, energizing; (5) supportive; (6) acknowledged talent; (7) confidence giving; (8) caring, interested; and (9) persistent. Men mention (1) skilled, expert; (2) a friend; (3) encouraging, prodding; (4) respectful; (5) guiding; (6) caring, interested; (7) motivating; (8) committed, dedicated; (9) hardworking; and (10) honest. Mentor characteristics are discussed in more detail in another section of this chapter.

The mentor's teaching style should be compatible with the student's learning style (Berger, 1990; Kaufmann, 2003). Potential mentors and mentees may wish to complete a learning style inventory to assess their compatibility. Table 1 contains a list of some commonly available inventories and what they measure.

The mentee must also identify with the mentor. Identification with a role model is based on three variables: "(1) *nurturance*, or the warmth of the relationship between the child and a particular adult; (2) *similarities* that children see between themselves and an adult; and (3) the *power* of the adult as perceived by the child" (Rimm, 2001, p. 27).

Effective mentors are usually older than their mentees. At least a 15-year difference "affords the psychological and developmental distance needed for the mentor to guide from a 'higher' perspective while minimizing the possibilities for competition between the mentor and the student" (Kaufmann, 2003, p. 5). Mentors should avoid trying to lead their young mentees down the path they wished they had taken. The point is to forge the path that develops based on the student's interests (Roberts & Inman, 2001). Therefore, careful consideration to the student's and mentor's interests and goals is essential for a successful match. When students are passionate about a topic, an informal interview typically reveals much about their interest and understanding of a topic. A variety of interest assessment instruments are available. The *Interest-A-Lyzer* (Renzulli, 1997) is commonly used by schools.

Selecting a mentor for students is not simply finding the most knowledgeable person in a student's area of interest and considering compatible learning styles. An appraisal of the student's expertise or performance level is warranted. Bloom (1985) and his colleagues conducted a 4-year study of 150 world-class pianists, sculptors, tennis champions, research mathematicians, and research neurologists. They discovered that all the individuals progressed through three dis-

Start at the Lowest Level That Will Serve the Student

11 Arrange for a mentorship or internship, a long-term commitment from both the student and the expert. Best done during school time or during the summer so the experience is not tacked on the the end of a full day.

10 Arrange for the student to meet with experts at their workplace. Meeting can be a short conversation and/or an observation, or shadowing, experience.

9 Ask a specialist to visit the classroom to offer enrichment to all students while directly serving the one with a more in-depth need. Some programs arrange for specialists to visit schools regularly over a span of time.

8 Ask a specialist within your school district to assist the student. With minimal inquiry, you will be amazed at the range of expertise within your district.

7 Ask someone within the student's school to help the student one-on-one.

6 Brainstorm possible activities and resources that will allow the student to advance his learning as independently as possible. Consider public libraries or specialized libraries located within museums, wildlife centers, or even businesses; community education classes; zoos, art, history, and science museums or galleries and/or their classes; local theaters and public park systems and/or their classes; private lessons such as dance, musical instruments or voice, theater, foreign language, or computer instruction. Local colleges and universities, businesses, human service agencies, clubs, or organizations may also offer resources for students from preschool through high school. Television and videotaped programs may offer information, culture, or a perspective on an issue. They are also helpful to those who prefer alternatives to reading.

5 Add a list of what the student has already accomplished to your student profile. Include courses, clubs, books read, related activities, independent research, and work experiences.

4 Ask parents how they have helped the student to date. Inquire about their availability and willingness to assist the student in pursuing new opportunities. Can they provide transportation? Field trips? Supplies and appropriate equipment? Space? If parents can't, who might be able to provide these resources?

3 Find out what the student's needs are. What does he want to learn? How does she think would be the best way for her to learn? How much time and energy can he devote? Develop a student profile.

2 Who perceives the need for additional enrichment? The student? The parent? The teacher?

1 Decide who should be involved in the process of identifying the students' needs and planning for further learning and development.

START HERE!
Don't move up a level until you have exhausted the potential of the current level. Remember this chart has been designed to give you ideas.
There are additional levels and opportunities not shown!

Mentor Program Identifying and Using Resources

Figure 3. Mentorship flow chart

Note. From *Mentorship: The Essential Guide for Schools and Businesses* (p. 15), by J. M. Reilly, 1992, Scottsdale, AZ: Gifted Psychology Press (formerly Ohio Psychology Press). Copyright ©1992 by Gifted Psychology Press. Reprinted with permission.

Table 1

Common Learning and Thinking Style Inventories

Instrument	Preference Assessed
My Way: An Expression Style Inventory (Kettle, Renzulli, & Rizza,1998)	Mode of expression (e.g., drama, written)
Learning Style Inventory (Renzulli, Rizza, & Smith, 2002)	Method of instruction (e.g., peer teaching, projects)
Learning Style Inventory (Dunn, Dunn, & Price, 2000)	23 learning styles (e.g., motivation, visual-auditory-tactile)
Thinking Styles Questionnaire (Sternberg, 1994)	Sternberg's Mental Self-Government Model (e.g., judicial)
Gregorc Style Delineator (Gregorc, 1985)	Gregorc's Mind Styles (e.g., concrete sequential)
Myers-Briggs Type Indicator (Briggs & Myers, 1977)	Jung-Myers-Briggs typological approach to personality

tinct phases of learning and that the length of these phases, the type of interaction involved at each phase, and the sequence of the phases were instrumental in talent development.

> [N]o matter what the initial characteristics (or gifts) of the individuals, unless there is a long and intensive process of encouragement, nurturance, education, and training, the individuals will not attain extreme levels of capability in . . . [their] fields. (Bloom, p. 3)

Based on this work, Bloom (1985) identified three different types of mentors/instructors. Students who are new to a topic or talent field require mentors who help them develop a passion for the field of study. These mentors are less concerned with right and wrong and measurable objectives than they are with sharing the field and having fun with it. This initial phase of talent development is characterized by "enormous encouragement of interest and involvement, stimulation, freedom to explore, and immediate rewards." The effect of this is that the student becomes involved, captivated, and eager for more information and expertise. The first mentors' talent abilities are less important than the mindset they help develop in their young charges. This first instructor probably falls between the traditional role of a teacher and a mentor.

Students who have already fallen in love with a discipline require a different type of mentor. These mentors are selected for their expertise in the talent area. Mentoring at this level focuses on technical skill development and perfecting the small details of the talent field. The personal bond between the mentor and mentee is based on respect. Skill, technique, and the habit of accuracy are dominant. Self-discipline becomes a factor as students interact with their mentors at this level.

Most students will never reach or require the third type of mentor. Mentors at this phase are masters who help their mentees transition from technical precision to personal expression. This is the mentor who helps Michelle Kwan skate differently than any other figure skater. Bloom (1985) proposed that only a handful of mentors exist at this level within a given talent field.

The following sequence of questions can guide what level mentor is needed:

- Is the student already passionate about the topic?
- If the student is passionate, is he or she ready for more advanced training?
- Has the student mastered the topic and is he or she ready to discover how he or she can uniquely participate in it?

Carefully considering this placement increases students' enthusiasm and mastery of their skills. Failure to consider the match between a student's mastery level and the mentor's demands may actually hamper the student's interest and talent development. Mentors have to be willing to let go and move on when the mentee has outgrown them (Shaughnessy & Neely, 1991).

Is the student willing to invest a significant amount of time with the mentor? While some mentoring experiences are short-term, the classic mentorship can't be hurried and takes time (Edlind & Haensly, 1985). Effective mentorships demand passionate commitments from mentees. Students who demonstrate the following characteristics are likely to invest the time and energy that are necessary for a successful mentorships:

- can sustain curiosity and interest;
- have the ability to focus and exert extended effort on tasks of personal interest;
- ask many questions that are not being answered by classes or the present curriculum;
- are not being challenged by traditional methods and activities;
- show evidence of previous and current active involvement with the topic (products, accomplishments, active participation in an area);
- possess extensive vocabulary in the field;

- can communicate with adults;
- are receptive to new ways of learning;
- know or are willing to learn process and methodological skills;
- display a personal sense of responsibility and autonomy (Nash & Treffinger, 1993, p. 49);
- are intellectual risk takers; and
- are open to guidance (Minority Engineering and Computer Science Program, n.d.).

Students who have exhausted their available resources are likely candidates for mentoring since this indicates they have the necessary interest and motivation. Coordinators ought to screen students for successful experiences. This includes a review of the students' intent, expectations, and motivation; depth of background on the topic; ability to learn as evidenced by previous grades; and school attendance. Likely candidates have a clear understanding of their interest area and have demonstrated past initiative in independently expanding their knowledge of it (Reilly, 1992a).

Does the student fully understand the purpose, benefits, and limitations of a mentoring relationship? A successful mentorship provides benefits for both the mentor and the mentee, evidenced by the fact that those who have been recipients of mentoring relationships often become mentors themselves (Bennetts, 2001). The mentor and mentee work together as a team to develop objectives and goals for the mentoring experience. An end product or final goal then guides the mentoring relationship (Roberts & Inman, 2001). The mentor and mentee must be flexible and willing to modify or even change these goals as their investigation develops. Mentorships die when the pace is too slow or too fast (likely too fast); the mentor demonstrates too much personal sacrifice in his or her career; the mentor has a limited perspective; sex and race barriers exist; or the mentor doesn't approve of the mentee's behavior (Torrance, 1984).

"It seems certain that both persons in a mentorship must continue to grow and contribute to each other's growth" in order to sustain a mentorship (Torrance, 1984, p. 19). A mentoring relationship evolves through various stages. One adult mentee described how a teacher of hers became a mentor and then a friend. Their relationship ultimately formed a never-ending circle in which they nurtured each other (Meador, 1992).

Rimm (2003) suggested that mentees show their appreciation to their mentors by being respectful, being prompt, and providing assistance to the mentor. She also warned young people that even role models have their weaknesses.

Role models can help you identify the traits you admire, but even people you look up to exhibit some qualities you'd rather not have. . . . You can still learn from these people. The trick is to take the best from each person. (p. 94)

4. Matching Mentors and Mentees

The match between mentor and mentee is crucial. These matches are particularly important because one of the roles of mentors is the transmission of values and attitudes (Kaufmann, 2003). As one of Kaufmann's Presidential Scholars noted,

> He [The mentor] had an absolute passion for teaching! Nothing seemed to excite him like having a student suddenly grasp something. It is that excitement, rather than the specific subjects he taught, that has stayed with me and emerged as the most significant contribution of his mentorship. (p. 5)

Mentors, mentees, and parents ought to be interviewed prior to making a match. A committee of at least three ought to participate in interviews. The special skills and insight of school psychologists may be useful in matching potential mentors and mentees (VanTassel-Baska & Baska, 2000). Interviews can be time-consuming, and it may be difficult to coordinate the interview and interviewee's schedules. Advance long-term planning facilitates more efficient scheduling of everyone's time (Forster, 1994).

Aside from considering the ability levels of the mentor and mentee, the following areas are also worth exploring during the interviews:

- *Level of interest in the program.* This involves all parties: student, parents, teacher, and school.
- *Reason for involvement.* What does each party hope to achieve? Parents may want to raise the child's self-esteem; the teacher may be concerned about boredom the child is enduring at school.
- *Level of interest in the area.* What has the student/mentor already done in this area?
- *Standards of work.* What is the quality of previous work in the area of interest?
- *Learning style.* Is the mentee comfortable working with adults? What characteristics would the mentee like in a mentor and vice versa? Is humor important? Gender? Ethnicity?
- *Recommendation.* What have others said about the mentor/mentee? (Forster, 1994).

The following points of compatibility should be considered when making a match:

- *Personal preferences.* Mentors and youth may request someone of the same gender, a certain age range, or other characteristic. These requests should be honored whenever possible.

- *Temperament.* Try to ensure that personality and behavior styles mesh. Does the mentor have a nurturing, familial approach or a more businesslike, impersonal one? Match each mentor with a young person who responds best to his or her particular style.
- *Life experiences and interests.* Do the potential mentor and mentee share hobbies, lifestyles, or family makeup? (National Mentoring Partnership, n.d.)

Mentors and mentees should have an opportunity to express a preference regarding a match, understand how matching decisions are made, and be given an opportunity to request a different match if the their original match is not satisfactory after reasonable effort.

5. Training and Orientation Meetings

Mentor Training. In some organizations, as many as 7 out of 10 mentors drop out within the first 3 months. The primary reasons are lack of training and inadequate screening (Mentoring Partnership of Minnesota, 2002). Generally, interested mentors attend an orientation meeting that covers an overview of the program. If they are interested and selected as mentors, they usually later attend a 2- to 3-hour training session. Most organizations hold separate initial training for mentors and mentees. For advanced training, however, they may conduct combined events. Some of the topics (e.g., career development and cross-difference mentoring) may actually be more stimulating and beneficial if both groups attend (Phillips-Jones, n.d.).

The first mentor training includes an explanation of the purpose, benefits, and limitations of mentorships and an explanation of the mentee's rights and responsibilities. This 2- to 3-hour training session provides volunteer mentors with the skills they'll need to start and maintain a successful mentoring relationship. During this session, mentors can address their concerns and expectations, explore boundary issues, discuss communication styles, and learn about the stages of the mentoring relationship through a combination of role-playing, interactive exercises, and lecture (Mentoring Partnership of Minnesota, 2002).

At a minimum, the following topics should be covered during mentor training:

- steps of the formal mentoring process (a more detailed discussion of the process appears in the next section);
- how to negotiate various aspects of a mentoring partnership;
- how to assist mentees in developing goals and planning activities;
- key mentor and mentee process skills (listening actively, building trust, encouraging, identifying goals and current reality, instructing/developing capabilities, inspiring, opening doors, managing risks, providing corrective feedback, acquiring additional mentors, learning quickly,

showing initiative, following through, managing the relationship, career awareness);

- how to conduct some basic evaluation of the mentee's progress and the relationship;
- unexpected challenges and solutions (Phillips-Jones, n.d.); and
- an understanding of diversity and cultural awareness.

Upon completion of their training, mentors should exhibit a clear understanding of their role in the areas listed below. These guidelines are meant to help mentors avoid situations that might negatively reflect on themselves or the organization that they serve in the community.

1. *Preparedness.* Mentors are prepared to be a friend to a young person and demonstrate consistent, dependable, trustworthy, accepting, honest, and respectful behaviors.
2. *Integrity.* Mentors consistently act in ways that are ethical, earning the respect and trust of their mentees and supporting community partners.
3. *Commitment.* Mentors are steadfast in their commitment to the policies and procedures of the guiding organization.
4. *Knowledge builder.* Mentors actively seek out shared opportunities that enhance the knowledge, skills, and abilities of their mentees.
5. *Inclusive attitude.* Mentors value the diverse racial, economic, cultural, and religious traits of their mentees.
6. *Maintain confidentiality.* Mentors act in the best interest of the mentoring organization and ensure confidentiality, taking care to protect against inadvertent disclosure.
7. *Accountability.* Mentors make regular contact with the mentoring organization to ensure effective mentoring practices.
8. *Appropriate behavior.* Mentors refrain from profanity, criticism of school faculty or staff, inappropriate physical contacts, and violations of laws or school codes of conduct.
9. *Eligibility.* Mentors authorize the completion of required background checks to cover criminal history, driving records, personal interviews, and other forms of screening as deemed appropriate.
10. *Service to community.* Mentors maintain a steady presence in the lives of youth and in community efforts that strive to encourage others toward participation in volunteer efforts. (Letting Education Achieve Dreams, n.d.)

To maintain momentum, build camaraderie among participants, and share wisdom, many programs offer a second training once mentorships begin. Following are some possible topics for this follow-up training:

- building trust, managing risks, and giving corrective feedback;
- ideas for successful cross-difference (gender, race, culture, style) mentoring;

- career development topics such as career planning, helping mentees promote themselves, and helping mentees with informational interviews;
- challenging the mentee;
- successes and dilemmas mentors are experiencing and what they've learned; and
- keeping the mentorship stimulating (for mentor and mentee). (Philllips-Jones, n.d.)

Mary Jones (n.d.), a former engineer at Hewlett-Packard, prepared these comments for mentors. While she was a telementor, her suggestions apply to a variety of mentoring situations.

1. *Building a genuine mentor relationship.* At the beginning of the process, be sure to let the student know who you are, what you do, and how you got there, and tell them about some of your outside interests. Let them know what you hope to learn from the mentor relationship. Be open and candid—this will show them you are a real person and give them the courage to be open and honest. Be an example to them, show them how you use math and science and other basic academic skills in your work and life.

2. *Be professional in all communication.* Doing so will encourage the student and teachers to respect time. Mentor sessions should not be gossip sessions. If discussions are off track, respond in a professional manner stating that the session must focus on learning. Don't forget to check your spelling and grammar before sending your messages. This sets an important example for students.

3. *Promptly respond to all messages.* Be proactive in sending out messages and respond quickly to messages from the student and teacher. Sending two or more messages a week shows the student you are interested and committed. Even basic messages—"Heads up," "How's it going," "Here are a few ideas to work on"—are very effective.

4. *Keep the school contact in the loop.* At least twice a month, send a project/communication update to the teacher. Ask the teacher for advice to be more effective with your particular student. Teachers appreciate communication from the mentors.

5. *Collaborate with other mentors.* Find out if there are mentors working with other students in the same class. Mentors can learn from each other what is effective.

6. *Resolve all communication problems immediately.* Creating a successful relationship has its challenges. If a problem arises that can't be resolved through regular communication with your student, ask for help from the teacher or program coordinator. Don't be afraid to ask for help.

7. *Seek to understand the entire academic experience.* It's helpful for mentors to know how students are doing in other classes. Knowing this can help you be more effective in reaching them and enabling them to succeed at school in general. Try to instill that their education is their responsibility and in their control. Explain to them how they have the power to do anything and everything they can imagine. This is a great motivator, especially for those teens who are frustrated with adult supervision.

8. *Share the importance of teamwork.* The ability to work with others and establish professional teamwork relationships are critical factors in the world of work. Developing these skills in a student is just as important as teaching academic subjects. Talk to your mentee about teamwork, how to work with others, and interpersonal communications.

9. *Switch mentor/student roles.* Expect to learn from your mentee. For instance, I found it fun to ask my student for advice on how to teach math to my own daughter or what Web sites to share with her. Letting your student know that you value his or her input and opinions will go far in building a strong, supportive relationship.

10. *Create a development plan with your student.* Build a monthly development plan with your student to identify long-term and short-term goals with monthly objectives. These might include learning about a math, science, or personal interest topic; improving test scores; or developing better homework habits. This will help focus discussions.

Mentee Training. Mentees also require an introduction to the mentoring process. Their training should prepare them to understand the purpose of and their responsibilities in the relationship. This should include a discussion of the following topics:

- setting important goals;
- evaluating their progress;
- appropriate mentor/mentee relations;
- providing feedback to mentors;
- showing appreciation to mentors; and
- options for an unsuccessful match.

6. Monitoring and Evaluating the Mentorship

Mentorships grow through four stages. An understanding of these stages and clear communication during them is essential for a successful mentoring relationship. Inadequate communication flow is often cited as an obstacle to program success (Berger, 1990).

In the first stage, mentors and mentees become acquainted and identify their common interests and goals. Communication tends to be awkward since neither party has developed trust at this stage. Relationships remain at this stage from one to six meetings. During stage two, mentors and mentees begin sharing and confiding in each other. As confidence develops, they establish attainable expectations for the relationship. This stage usually lasts from 1 to 3 months. The two begin to accomplish their goals during the third stage. New goals may develop as old ones are met and new challenges emerge. The final stage involves closure of the mentorship. The relationship may be redefined. This may also include defining next steps (Letting Education Achieve Dreams, n.d.).

After initially linking the mentor and mentee and setting a time, further meeting arrangements should be made by the mentor, mentee, and parents. The next location and time should be firmly set following each meeting between the mentor and mentee. All parties should understand who will be making the next contact. During the early stages of the NAGC Professional Achievement Certificate program, clear guidelines were not set regarding communication. After the initial pairing, there were cases of mentors waiting for mentees to contact them while the mentees were waiting for the mentors. Ultimately, the mentor was held responsible for maintaining contact with the mentee. The coordinator should check to ensure that contact is made. E-mail is an efficient alternative to phone calls when contacting mentors and mentees. All parties should feel free to contact the coordinator if problems arise (Forster, 1994).

The coordinator should also periodically contact mentors and mentees regarding their progress and whether they are satisfied with the match. Students and mentors may be asked to evaluate the experience at the end of the first month to make sure that both parties are interested in continuing their relationship. The coordinator should also monitor whether the mentee is identifying with the mentor, how well his or her self-esteem and confidence are developing, and whether any unrealistic expectations have risen (Berger, 1990).

"People associated with mentoring programs tend to believe implicitly that mentoring benefits young people and that, therefore, expensive evaluations are an unnecessary drain on precious resources" (National Mentoring Partnership, n.d.). Evaluations need not be expensive. They can be as simple as asking mentors and mentees about their experiences. Three initial program concerns that warrant early evaluation are the effectiveness of the match, the mentor's willingness to recognize and develop the mentee's talent, and the mentee's satisfaction with the experience. Evaluations can also be included as part of a follow-up activity in which students write or talk about their experiences.

More formal evaluations cover the processes and the outcomes of a program. Process information pertains to the number of mentor/mentee matches, types of activities that were held, length of the mentorship relations, frequency and duration of meetings, and perceptions of the relationship. Outcome information might include such data as the mentee's grades, behaviors, and attitudes; the teacher's reports of the mentee's classroom behaviors; the mentor's reflections on his or her experiences; the mentee's optimism about the future; parent-child relationships; and graduation rates (National Mentoring Partnership, n.d.).

If the program goals were clearly articulated at the start of the program, evaluating them is an easy task. Without clearly defined goals, deciding how to define program success can be difficult.

An Example of a Secondary Level Mentoring Program Design

When gifted students are asked what they like best about being in a special program for the gifted and talented, the first response usually deals with the greater freedom allowed in selecting topics of study. Conversely, when they are asked about their greatest objection to the regular curriculum, students' comments frequently refer to the limited opportunities to pursue topics of their own choosing.

Providing gifted students with options for studying areas that interest them in secondary education involves some unique problems that are often not present when providing elementary services. Not only must the material be differentiated at a more advanced level, it must be available in a variety of talent areas. As gifted students enter high school, they demonstrate more understanding and depth in specific content areas, resulting in a need for individualized educational opportunities related to these interest areas. Unfortunately, this is occurring at a time when class schedules are less flexible and personnel resources may be limited. Beneficially, it is also occurring when their teachers are more subject-oriented and are better equipped to delve in-depth into specific disciplines. Thus, while the diversity of talents exhibited by high-achieving students at the secondary level warrants a multitude of educational options, the educational system that serves the secondary level, while often lacking flexibility in scheduling options, does have many of the resources necessary to provide a richer educational experience.

One option for serving gifted and talented students at the secondary level is a mentoring model based on Student Developed Courses (SDC). The SDC model was developed to provide students with opportunities for further study in their talent areas (Siegle, 1998). Based on the Schoolwide Enrichment Model (Renzulli & Reis, 1985) and the Autonomous Learner Model (Betts, 1985), the SDC model fits well within the traditional high school schedule and can be easily implemented in both small and large high school settings.

The SDC model provides secondary students with the option to study topics that match their interests and talents through a two-step process. First, students learn about their talents, weaknesses, and learning styles in a one-semester SDC class. They also learn about the mentoring process and how to design an independent study course. Students cannot be expected to possess already the skills necessary to design and conduct an independent study. The SDC class teaches them how to design and execute an independent study based upon their unique strengths and interests.

Following completion of the SDC class, students are encouraged to register for a one-semester mentoring experience that they design. A student with a special interest in photography might elect to document historic homes in the community and publish a Web site featuring her work. A student interested in creative writing might wish to write and produce a play, or a student interested in science might build a laser or study the effects of radiation on tissue development. Although not all students will wish to develop an independent study mentoring option after completion of the SDC class, many elect to design and complete one.

After completing the SDC class and prior to beginning a mentoring option, students develop proposal outlines for their studies. The outlines include learning objectives, a list of proposed activities and a timeline, a list of resources needed to complete the project, a description of the final product and audience, and a description of how the project will be evaluated. Their plan will later be modified once they connect with a mentor who will supervise their independent study.

Once the independent study proposal is complete, the student contacts one of the secondary teachers or a community person to mentor him or her through the project. The mentor's role is to guide the student's progress during the semester. Initially, the mentor will assist the student in refining his or her mentorship plan and finding a place to work. The working location may be within the school, or, if the mentor is a community member, it may be at his or her place of business. Once the project begins, the mentor and student meet at least once a week to share knowledge, discuss the student's progress, and resolve any roadblocks the student might be encountering. The mentor's role is to

1. become aware of gaps in knowledge, disharmonies, or problems calling for new solutions;
2. identify the difficulty or gap in knowledge;
3. think of possibilities and formulate hypotheses;
4. test, modify, retest, and predict;
5. puzzle over it and fit the pieces together; and
6. communicate the results. (Torrance, Goff, & Satterfield, 1998, p. 37)

At the completion of the project, the mentor and student jointly review the student's progress and final product. This evaluation is based on the goals the mentor and student developed at the start of the program.

Students receive one semester credit for their projects. They register for this credit as they would register for any regularly scheduled class and work on their project during a scheduled time just as they would other courses. Traditionally, independent project credits serve as elective credits within the content area that the student has chosen to investigate. Thus, the photography project mentioned earlier could count as an art elective, while the laser project would serve as a science elective.

While one staff member is responsible for teaching the SDC class that prepares students for their independent projects, the secondary faculty and screened community members are eligible to mentor students through their projects. This serves three purposes: It capitalizes on faculty and community interests and skills within the subject areas where they have expertise, it does not unnecessarily burden a single faculty member, and it creates broad ownership for educating gifted and talented students.

The independent study mentoring option is one viable means of meeting the needs of many students. It affords students an opportunity to expand their understanding of specific disciplines through self-directed inquiry under the mentorship of adults with similar interest while providing minimum interruption in the secondary schedule.

Conclusion

E. Paul Torrance (1984) stated it best:

The Most Important Things Mentors Can Do for Creatively Gifted Youth

Help them to:

Be unafraid of "falling in love with something" and pursue it with intensity and in-depth. [People are] motivated most to do the things they love and can do best.

Know, understand, take pride in, practice, use, exploit, and enjoy their greatest strengths.

Learn to free themselves from the expectations of others and to walk away from the games that others try to impose upon them.

Free themselves to play their own game in such a way as to make the best use of their strengths and follow their dreams.

Find some great teachers and attach themselves to these teachers.

Avoid wasting a lot of expensive, unproductive energy in trying to be well-rounded.

Learn the skills of interdependence and give freely of the infinity of their greatest strength. (pp. 56–57)

"Often the gifted do not fail intellectually, but emotionally. Obstacles or circumstances become so overwhelming that even the best consider giving up" (McGreevy, 1990, p. 8). Because they have years of experience, mentors know the roadblocks talented students face. They also know the incremental nature of talent development and are able to advance students along it (Purcell et al., 2001). They accomplish this by changing students from reactive to proactive learners (Nash, 2001).

Mentoring works. It works at all age levels. It works under a variety of conditions. It works because mentors recognize young people's talents and interests and provide them with opportunities to explore and develop them. Each year, hundreds of thousands of young people benefit from the wisdom and dedication of adult mentors. Mentorships make a difference in lives. In their simplest form, mentoring programs can begin with one child working with one adult. From that simple beginning, the possibilities are limitless.

Mentorship in Action

Anne has been my mentor for 2 years in junior high. She has been both a great teacher and a great friend as long as I have known her. She has enabled me to progress at the speed that I feel I need while making sure that I know what I am doing and that I don't get ahead of myself. I think that what makes her an extraordinary instructor is the way she relates to students in order to help them better understand what they are doing in both school work and general life decisions. Anne gives her students more freedom than other instructors by using trust. When teachers can build the kind of trust that she can, they will realize results immediately with students.

Anne served as Tracy's mathematics mentor for grades 8 and 9. Tracy was identified as highly gifted in mathematics, and the Lincoln Public Schools in Lincoln, NE, recruited and supported Anne to mentor her in developing her exceptional mathematics talent. The two collaborated for up to 5 hours each week during their 2-year mentorship.

Lincoln Public Schools has a pool of several hundred carefully selected mentors who work with highly gifted students in grades 1–12. A committee screens each mentor prior to being assigned to a student. The mentors have earned academic majors, have extensive training in the discipline (e.g., mathematics) in which they are mentoring students, or both. More rigorous academic credentials are required for those who mentor students in junior high and high school. The mentors are compensated for their time, travel, and any special materials. Mentoring occurs during regular school hours, and students receive regular progress reports.

Parents are involved in selecting and evaluating their children's mentors. Parents are also responsible for notifying the mentor when a student will miss school. Parents, the mentor, and the student develop a Personal Learning Plan that guides the mentorship. The mentoring program in Lincoln is successful because it is a collaborative effort among teachers, parents, mentors, and students that is supported by the district's gifted and talented program.

— Tom Hays

Discussion Questions

1. What makes a good mentor?

2. Why do gifted students need mentors? Which types of gifted students are especially likely to need mentors?

3. What is the difference between a mentorship and an internship?

4. How is a mentor relationship beneficial for the mentor?

5. What are the advantages and disadvantages of telementoring programs?

6. What are the three main categories of mentorship programs? How would your approach to setting up a mentorship program differ depending on the category of mentorship you envision using?

7. What are the steps to creating a successful mentorship program?

8. How can you tell whether a student will benefit from a mentorship experience? What are the qualities that make someone a good mentee?

9. What legal and ethical considerations should you address when starting a mentorship program?

10. What kind of training should you provide for mentors, mentees, or both?

Teacher Resources

Publications

Nash, D., & Treffinger, D. (1993). *The mentor kit: A step-by-step guide to creating an effective mentor program in your school.* Waco, TX: Prufrock Press.

Reilly, J. (1992a). *Mentorships: The essential guide for schools and business.* Dayton: Ohio Psychology Press.

Torrance, E. P. (1984). *Mentor relationships: How they aid creative achievement, endure, change, and die.* Buffalo, NY: Bearly Limited.

Torrance, E. P., Goff, K., & Satterfield, N. B. (1998). *Multicultural mentoring of the gifted and talented.* Waco, TX: Prufrock Press.

Web Sites

International Telementor Program—http://www.telementor.org
The International Telementor Program is a leader in telementoring. Students and potential mentors can register at this site, which also includes valuable information on the telementor process.

Letting Education Achieve Dreams—http://www.uhv.edu/lead/mentoring.htm
LEAD is an initiative of the University of Houston–Victoria. The Web site contains background information on mentoring, information about mentor ethics, and a list of frequently asked questions.

MadSci Network—http://www.madsci.org
MadSci Network is an interactive site where students can post questions related to science that are answered by a pool of scientists.

National Mentoring Partnership—http://www.mentoring.org
The National Mentoring Partnership is probably the most extensive mentorship-related site on the Internet. It contains step-by-step instructions for developing and running a mentoring program, as well as links to established mentoring programs.

Nebraska State Department of Education's Work-Based Learning—http://www.nde.state.ne.us/TECHPREP/WBL/index.htm
This site contains pages of useful forms for beginning mentoring programs.

Northwest Regional Lab's National Mentoring Center—http://www.nwrel.org/mentoring
This site features publications and Web resources on mentoring.

Pitsco's Ask an Expert—http://www.askanexpert.com
This is a student-friendly site the features hundreds of experts who field student questions.

The Mentoring Center—http://www.mentor.org
This is a 501(c)(3) tax-exempt private nonprofit organization in the San Francisco Bay area. This site contains information on mentoring and links to mentoring programs.

References

Ambrose, D., Allen, J., & Huntley, S. B. (1994). Mentorship of the highly creative. *Roeper Review, 17,* 131–134.

Beck, L. (1989). Mentorships: Benefits and effects on career development. *Gifted Child Quarterly, 33,* 22–28.

Bennetts, C. (2001). Fanning the aesthetic flame: Learning for life. *Gifted Education International, 15,* 252–261.

Berger, S. L. (1990). *Mentor relationships and gifted learners* (Digest #E486). (ERIC Document Reproduction Service No. ED321491)

Betts, G. (1985). *The autonomous learner model.* Greeley, CO: Autonomous Learning Publications Specialists.

Bloom, B. S. (Ed.). (1985). *Developing talent in young people.* New York: Ballantine Books.

Briggs, K. C., & Myers, I. B. (1977). *Myers-Briggs type indicator form G.* Palo Alto, CA: Consulting Psychologists Press.

Buery, R. (n.d.). *Building electronic bridges to connect mentors and young people.* Retrieved May 25, 2004, from http://www.uwnyc.org/technews/v3_n6_a2.html

Bush, G. W. (2003). President delivers "State of the Union." Retrieved May 25, 2004, from http://www.whitehouse.gov/news/releases/2003/01/20030128-19.html

Coleman, L. J., & Cross, T. L. (2001). *Being gifted in school: An introduction to development, guidance, and teaching.* Waco, TX: Prufrock Press.

Dahle, C. (1998). *HP's mentor connection.* Retrieved May 25, 2004, from http://www.fastcompany.com/online/19/hpmentor.html

Davalos, R. A., & Haensly, P. A. (1997). After the dusk has settled: Youth reflect on their high school mentored research experience. *Roeper Review, 19,* 204–207.

Edlind, E., & Haensly, P. (1985). Gifts of mentorships. *Gifted Child Quarterly, 29,* 55–60.

Ellingson, M. K., Haeger, W. M., & Feldhusen, J. F. (1986). The Purdue mentor program. *G/C/T, 9*(2), 2–5.

Emerson-Stonnell, S., & Carter, C. (1994). Math mentor programs. *Gifted Child Today, 17*(1), 34–36, 41.

Forster, J. (1994). Mentor links program. *Gifted Education International, 10,* 24–30.

Geiger, R. (2001). Nurturing for wisdom and compassion: Influencing those who influence. In N. Colangelo & S. Assouline (Eds.), *Talent development IV: Proceedings from the 1998 Henry B. and Jocelyn Wallace National Research Symposium* (pp. 345–349). Scottsdale, AZ: Great Potential Press.

Goff, K., & Torrance, E. P. (1999). Discovering and developing giftedness through mentoring. *Gifted Child Today, 22*(3), 14–15, 52–53.

Gonzalez, V. (2003). Biracial and bicultural gifted students. In J. A. Castellano (Ed.), *Special populations in gifted education: Working with diverse gifted learners* (pp. 79–96). Boston: Allyn and Bacon.

Gregorc, A. F. (1985). *Gregorc style delineator: A self-assessment instrument for adults.* Columbia, CT: Gregorc Associates.

Hamilton, S. F., & Hamilton, M. A. (1992). Mentoring programs: Promise and paradox. *Phi Delta Kappan, 73,* 546–550.

Howley, C. B. (1989). Career education for able students. *Journal for the Education of the Gifted, 12,* 205–217.

International Telementoring Program (ITP). (n.d.). Retrieved May 25, 2004, from http://www.telementor.org

Jones, M. (n.d.). *Mentor tips for successful telementoring.* Retrieved March 20, 2003, from http://www.telementor.org/itp/info/mentoring_tips.html

Jucovy, L. (2002). *Same-race and cross-race matching* (Technical Assistance Packet #7). Retrieved May 24, 2004, from http://www.nwrel.org/mentoring/pdf/packseven.pdf

Kaufmann, F. (2003, Winter). Mentorships for gifted students: What parents and teachers need to know. *PAGE Update,* pp. 1, 5, 11.

Kaufmann, F. A., Harrel, G., Milam, C. P., Woolverton, N., & Miller, J. (1986). The nature, role, and influence of mentors in the lives of gifted adults. *Journal of Counseling and Development, 64,* 576–578.

Kettle, K. E., Renzulli, J. S., & Rizza, M. G. (1998). My Way: An expression style inventory. *Gifted Child Quarterly, 42,* 48–61.

Leroux, J. A. (1994). A tapestry of values: Gifted women speak out. *Gifted Education International, 9,* 167–171.

Letting Education Achieve Dreams (LEAD). (n.d.). *Mentoring.* Retrieved May 25, 2004, from http://www.uhv.edu/lead/mentoring.htm

List, K., & Renzulli, J. S. (1991). Creative women's developmental patterns through age thirty-five. *Gifted Education International, 7,* 114–122.

Lupkowski, A. E., Assouline, S. G., & Stanley, J. C. (1990). Applying a mentor model for young mathematically talented students. *Gifted Child Today, 13*(2), 15–19.

McGreevy, A. (1990). Darwin and teacher: An analysis of the mentorship between Charles Darwin and professor John Henslow. *Gifted Child Quarterly, 34,* 5–9.

Meador, K. (1992). My teacher, my mentor, my friend. *Gifted Child Today, 15*(3), 14.

Mentoring Partnership of Minnesota. (2002). *News and events: MPM training director brings new energy and expertise to help programs run more successfully.* Retrieved April 2, 2003, from http://www.mentoringworks.org/news_events/Full_News.cfm?ID=30

Merriam, S. (1983). Mentors and protégés: A critical review of the literature. *Adult Education Quarterly, 33,* 161–173.

Milam, C. P. (2001). Extending learning through mentorships. In F. A. Karnes & S. M. Bean (Eds), *Methods and materials for teaching the gifted* (pp. 523–558). Waco, TX: Prufrock Press.

Milam, C. P., & Schwartz, B. (1992). The mentorship connection. *Gifted Child Today, 15*(3), 9–13.

Minority Engineering and Computer Science Program (n.d.). *Mentorship program.* Retrieved May 25, 2004, from http://mecsp.cecs.ucf.edu/mentor.htm

Nash, D., (2001, December). Enter the mentor. *Parenting for High Potential,* 18–21.

Nash, D., & Treffinger, D. (1993). *The mentor kit: A step-by-step guide to creating an effective mentor program in your school.* Waco, TX: Prufrock Press.

National Association for Gifted Children (NAGC). (2003). *Professional achievement certificate program guide.* Washington, DC: Author.

National Mentoring Center. (n.d.). *Mentor recruitment postcards.* Retrieved May 24, 2004, from http://www.nwrel.org/mentoring/postcard.html

National Mentoring Partnership. (n.d.). Retrieved May 25, 2004, from http://www.mentoring.org

Nebraska Department of Education. (1998). *Nebraska work-based learning manual.* Retrieved May 25, 2004, from http://www.nde.state.ne.us/TECHPREP/WBL/WBL%20Manual.htm

Olszewski-Kubilius, P., & Scott, J. M. (1992). An investigation of the college and career counseling needs of economically disadvantaged minority gifted students. *Roeper Review, 14*, 141–148.

Palmer, J. (2002, February 4). Mentoring program helps teen make research connection. *UConn Advance*. Retrieved March 1, 2003, from http://www.advance.uconn.edu/02020412.htm

Phillips-Jones, L. (n.d.). *Ideas about mentoring*. Retrieved May 25, 2004, from http://www.mentoringgroup.com/advancedtrng.html

Prillaman, D., & Richardson, R. (1989). The William and Mary mentorship model: College students as a resource for the gifted. *Roeper Review, 12*, 114–118.

Purcell, J. H., Renzulli, J. S., McCoach, D. B., & Spottiswoode, H. (2001, December). The magic of mentorships. *Parenting for High Potential*, 22–26.

Reilly, J. (1992a). *Mentorships: The essential guide for schools and business*. Dayton: Ohio Psychology Press.

Reilly, J. (1992b). When does a student really need a professional mentor? *Gifted Child Today, 15*(3), 2–8.

Reis, S. M. (1998). *Work left undone: Choices & compromises of talented females*. Mansfield Center, CT: Creative Learning Press.

Renzulli, J. S. (1977). *The enrichment triad model: A guide for developing defensible programs for the gifted and talented*. Mansfield Center, CT: Creative Learning Press.

Renzulli, J. S. (1997). *Interest-A-Lyzer family of instruments: A manual for teachers*. Mansfield Center, CT: Creative Learning Press.

Renzulli, J. S., & Reis, S. M. (1985). *The schoolwide enrichment model: A comprehensive plan for educational excellence*. Mansfield Center, CT: Creative Learning Press.

Renzulli, J. S., Rizza, M. G., & Smith L. H. (2002). *Learning styles inventory (Version III): A measure of student preferences for instructional techniques*. Mansfield Center, CT: Creative Learning Press.

Rhodes, J. E. (2002, March). *Research corner: What's race got to do with it?* Retrieved May 25, 2004, from http://www.mentoring.org/research_corner/mar_background.adp

Riel, M. (n.d.). *Tele-mentoring over the net*. Retrieved May 25, 2004, from http://edc.tech-leaders.org/LNT99/notes_slides/presentations/riel-tues/telement.htm

Rimm, S. (2001, December). Parents as role models and mentors. *Parenting for High Potential*, 14–15, 27.

Rimm, S. (2003). *See Jane win for girls: A smart girl's guide to success*. Minneapolis, MN: Free Spirit.

Roberts, J., & Inman, T. (2001, December). Mentoring and your child: Developing a successful relationship. *Parenting for High Potential*, 8–10.

Rogers, K. B., & Kimpston, R. D. (1992). Acceleration: What we do vs. what we know. *Educational Leadership, 50*(2), 58–61.

Shaughnessy, M. F. (1989). Mentoring the creative child, adult, and prodigy: Current knowledge, systems and research. *Gifted Education International, 6*, 22–24.

Shaughnessy, M. F., & Neely, R. (1991). Mentoring gifted children and prodigies: Personological concerns. *Gifted Education International, 7*, 129–132.

Siegle, D. (1998, Spring). An independent study model for secondary students. *The National Research Center on the Gifted and Talented*, 14–15.

Siegle, D. (2001, December). "One size fits all" doesn't work when selecting a mentor. *Parenting for High Potential*, 7, 11.

Silverman, L. K. (2000). Career counseling. In L. K. Silverman (Ed.), *Counseling the gifted and talented* (pp. 215–238). Denver: Love.

Starko, A. J. (1986). *It's about time: Inservice strategies for curriculum compacting.* Mansfield Center, CT: Creative Learning Press.

Swassing, R. H., & Fichter, G. R. (1991). University and community-based programs for the gifted adolescent. In M. Bireley & J. Genshaft (Eds.), *Understanding the gifted adolescent: Educational, developmental, and multicultural issues* (pp. 176–185). New York: Teachers College Press.

Tomlinson, C. A. (2001, December). President's column. *Parenting for High Potential, 5,* 27.

Torrance, E. P. (1984). *Mentor relationships: How they aid creative achievement, endure, change, and die.* Buffalo, NY: Bearly Limited.

Torrance, E. P., Goff, K., & Satterfield, N. B. (1998). *Multicultural mentoring of the gifted and talented.* Waco, TX: Prufrock Press.

VanTassel-Baska, J. (2000). Academic counseling for the gifted. In L. K. Silverman (Ed.), *Counseling the gifted and talented* (pp. 201–214). Denver: Love.

VanTassel-Baska, J., & Baska, L. (2000). The roles of educational personnel in counseling the gifted. In L. K. Silverman (Ed.), *Counseling the gifted and talented* (pp. 181–200). Denver: Love.

Winner, E. (1996). *Gifted children: Myths and realities.* New York: BasicBooks.

Wray, J. (2002, April 1). Where are they now? Success stories from UConn Mentor Connection students. *UConn Advance,* p. 5.

Wright, L., & Borland, J. H. (1992). A special friend: Adolescent mentors for young, economically disadvantaged, potentially gifted students. *Roeper Review, 14,* 124–129.

Chapter 17

Cooperative Learning and Gifted Learners

by Mary Ruth Coleman

ooperative learning (CL) is not an entirely new idea. The use of a variety of forms of group work for problem solving and learning dates back to early proponents of education, including John Dewey (Ellis & Whalen, 1990). However, cooperative learning has come to mean much more than just small groups of students working together on a shared task. Although cooperative learning can take many forms, there are several common denominators that usually distinguish it from other small-group work:

- positive interdependence among group participants;
- individual accountability for content, skills, and concept mastery;
- face-to-face interaction among group members;
- development of appropriate socialization skills; and
- group processing of learning and interactions (Johnson, Johnson & Holubec, 1990; Neber, Finsterwald, & Urban, 2001).

Other differences between small-group work and cooperative learning may include the ways in which the groups are structured. Many proponents of CL recommend that groups be created with mixed abilities to include high-, middle-, and low-ability students (Johnson & Johnson, 1991; Sharan, 1990). The grouping strategy, however, does not always have to include mixed ability levels (Nelson, Gallagher & Coleman, 1993). Slavin (1990) pointed out that "cooperative learning has been used successfully within ability-grouped classes for very high achievers" (p. 7). The use of CL with high-ability groups has also proven to be successful in addressing these students' learning preferences and learning styles (Baytops & Reed, 1997) and in facilitating their achievement (Heinz et. al., 2001; Ramsay, & Richards, 1997).

Cooperative Learning Models

Three widely used models for cooperative learning were developed by David and Roger Johnson (1987), Robert Slavin (1988), and Spencer Kagan (1990). Most teachers who use cooperative learning pull from each of these three models, as well as from others to create methods that work for them in their classrooms (Coleman, Gallagher, & Nelson, 1997). A brief overview of each shows how diverse cooperative learning approaches can be.

Johnson and Johnson's Model

The Johnson and Johnson model strongly emphasizes social skills and group dynamics as key goals for cooperative learning (Johnson & Johnson, 1990, 1993). Students are assigned to groups that reflect the diversity of the overall classroom, and heterogeneity of the CL group is stressed. The ideal task is one that requires interdependence of the group, with every member making a meaningful contribution to the learning process. Students are assigned (or they may select) roles within the CL group to ensure smooth operating. These roles usually include functional jobs like materials gatherer or recorder, but may also include social responsibilities like designated encourager (Ellis & Whalen, 1990). Groups are assessed regularly on both academic growth and social dynamics, and progress is recognized through group rewards (and sometimes group grades).

Slavin's Model

Robert Slavin's approaches to cooperative learning are highly content-driven and emphasize shared responsibility of learning with individual accountability for mastery. Competition across the CL groups, or teams, is frequently used to motivate and reward students. Team members work to support each other's learning while earning points for team progress and effort. Slavin has designed several specific methods, including Team Games Tournaments (TGT), Student Teams Achievement Division (STAD), Team Accelerated Instruction (TAI), and Cooperative Integrated Reading and Comprehension (CIRC). In addition to the strategy of blending competition with cooperation, Slavin has also focused on developing curricular materials in math and reading to support his methods. In addition to helping teammates learn, students are also encouraged to move through the materials at a self-paced rate, allowing them to accelerate when appropriate (Slavin, 1980, 1981, 1994).

Kagan's Model

Spencer Kagan's model relies on a variety of structures to organize interactions among students (Kagan, 1990). Examples of structures include Think-Pair-Share, where students reflect individually, discuss in pairs, and share with their CL group or the class; Round Robin, where each group member shares in turn; Numbered Heads Together, where students consult (all heads in) to ensure that everyone in the group understands the answer; and Jigsaw, where individual members work across teams to become experts on a topic and then return to their home team to share their knowledge. The use of structures gives teachers a number of ways to shift classroom "talk patterns" so that more students can be actively involved in each lesson. Student learning is assessed individually, but group rewards are used to build incentive.

Cooperative Learning With Gifted Students

The controversy over the use of cooperative learning with gifted students stems primarily from a heavy reliance on mixed-ability CL groups in heterogeneous classrooms (Allan, 1991; Gallagher & Coleman, 1994; Johnson, & Johnson, 1993; Melser, 1999; Robinson, 1990; Sapon-Shevin & Schniedewind, 1993). When CL is used as the predominate method of instruction and groups are configured heterogeneously, gifted students may experience frustration (Mills & Durden, 1992; Robinson, 1991). Under these circumstances, gifted students in a national study expressed the following concerns:

- worry when others in the group wouldn't listen to them or help complete the work;
- anxiety that, if they took over, others wouldn't like them;
- frustration that they were being dragged down by students who were not interested in learning;
- annoyance at always being "bugged" for the answers; and
- anger when their grades were lowered as a result of the lack of effort on the part of others (Coleman & Gallagher, 1995).

These dilemmas have been aptly described as "the sucker effect," where the high-ability student carries the group, and the "free-rider effect," where some learners are allowed to remain passive and therefore do not gain much from the cooperative learning activity (Ross & Smyth, 1995). Robinson (1990) captured the feeling of the gifted students in this situation with a single word: *exploitation*.

However, in spite of the difficulties gifted students often experience in cooperative learning, they also indicate that work in CL groups gives them a chance to feel helpful, to be a leader, and to get help when they need it. Furthermore, they have said that they are not always perfect and that sometimes they are the ones in trouble (Gallagher, Coleman, & Nelson, 1993; Matthews, 1992).

The problems experienced by gifted students in these settings likely stem from a misuse of CL, rather than an appropriate use of a viable teaching/learning strategy (Coleman, 1994). In December 1996, the National Association for Gifted Children issued a position paper that captures the main ideas of the controversy (see Figure 1).

When cooperative learning is used with groups of high-ability students—in either advanced classes or in classes for gifted students—many of the difficulties disappear completely (Coleman et al., 1997; Heller, 1999; Neber et al., 2001). Gifted students working in CL groups with others of similar abilities seem to thrive on the interactive dynamic exchanges this format promotes (Baytops, & Reed, 1997; VanTassel-Baska, 1998). The only drawback expressed by students regarding CL in these settings is that there never seems to be enough talk time for everybody to share their ideas fully.

Special Factors to Consider

As our understanding of the use of cooperative learning becomes more sophisticated, we have recognized some of the nuances that impact how successful this method can be. The following four factors need to be considered when planning to incorporate cooperative learning in the classroom.

The Structure of the Task

Tasks that work best for CL groups are those that are rich and open-ended (Chizhik, 2001; Cohen, Lotan, Scarloss, & Arellano, 1999). These tasks give students multiple entry points and require a variety of types of input for successful completion. Complex CL tasks are especially appropriate for addressing the needs of gifted students. To complete these tasks, students must engage in multileveled discussions, and this increases the likelihood that "authentic interdependence" will emerge. Because they provide fewer opportunities for input, single-answer tasks offer a less equitable platform for students whose abilities have historically been overlooked. This means that using complex tasks is even more essential in today's increasingly diverse classrooms.

Needs of Culturally and Linguistically Diverse Students

CL has been used successfully to create a classroom environment that encourages student-to-student interactions. This seems to be a particularly effec-

The National Association for Gifted Children (NAGC) periodically issues policy statements dealing with the issues, policies, and practices that have an impact on the education of gifted and talented students. Policy statements represent the official convictions of the organization.

All policy statements approved by the NAGC Board of Directors are consistent with the organization's belief that education in a democracy must respect the uniqueness of all individuals, the broad range of cultural diversity present in our society, and the similarities and differences in learning characteristics that can be found within any group of students. NAGC is fully committed to national goals that advocate both excellence and equity for all students, and we believe that the best way to achieve these is through differentiated educational opportunities, resources, and encouragement for all students.

Cooperative learning (CL) encompasses a variety of classroom practices which include the following attributes: group interdependence built around common goals, a focus on social skills or group dynamics, and individual accountability for material learned. Cooperative learning experiences can provide valuable opportunities to share ideas, practice critical thinking, and gain social skills.

When heterogeneous CL groups are the primary strategy in the classroom, gifted students' needs may not be met. Cooperative learning advocates often stress forming CL groups with students intentionally clustered by mixed-abilities. When gifted students are included in these CL groups, special care must be taken to differentiate the tasks appropriately. Cooperative learning is more likely to be effective for gifted learners when group tasks and goals:

- take into account differences in students' readiness levels, interests, and learning modes;
- focus on high-level tasks that require students to manipulate, apply, and extend meaningful ideas;
- ensure appropriate and balanced work responsibilities for all participants;
- ensure balanced opportunities for learners to work with peers of similar, as well as mixed readiness levels; and
- are balanced with opportunities for students to work independently and with the class as a whole.

When differentiation does not happen, gifted students may feel overburdened and responsible for the entire "workload."

Teachers who use CL with heterogeneous groups need additional support and preparation in how to structure the learning tasks to ensure that the instructional activities meet the cognitive and social needs of the most able students in the group. NAGC believes that cooperative learning should be viewed within a range of instructional strategies that may enhance some learning objectives for some gifted students some of the time but should not be used as a panacea to replace differentiated services addressing the educational needs of gifted students. When used in conjunction with an array of services to differentiate the education of gifted students, CL can be an appropriate strategy.

Figure 1. NAGC Position Paper on Creative Learning

tive strategy for involving students from culturally and linguistically diverse families in active learning (Baytops & Reed, 1997; Hansman, Spencer, Grant, & Jackson, 1999; Klingner, Vaughn, & Schumm, 1998; Tam & Gardner, 1997). CL seems to be especially appropriate for students who are English language learners (Calderon, Hertz-Lazarowitz, & Slavin, 1998; Kagan, 1986; Klingner et al.; Lampe, Rooze, & Tallent-Runnels, 1996).

There are also specific benefits for gifted students from culturally and linguistically diverse families. Samaha and de Lisi (2000) found that CL activities facilitated peer support for the development of critical thinking in groups of inner-city African American students, and Calderon et al. (1998) noted that the opportunities to interact around meaningful topics of high interest led to greater engagement for Latino students. One purpose for using CL that has often been overlooked is the creation of observation opportunities to help teachers spot students with outstanding potential (Baytops & Reed, 1997). Used as observation platforms, complex CL tasks give teachers a chance to see students in action. Through this we can note problem solving, creative thinking, leadership, and motivation, all of which are indicators of outstanding potential. For CL to be truly useful as an observation platform, however, we must make sure that all students have opportunities to be equally engaged in the group's work.

Issues of Status and Voice

Some students in any given classroom will have more status with peers than other students (Cohen et al., 1999). Variables that can affect a student's status include race, economic level, gender, and successfulness in school. Because of differences in status, students will participate in CL activities in different ways. Low-status students tend to contribute less often and tend to have their ideas incorporated less frequently when they work in CL groups, which in turn limits the benefits they receive from the group work (Chizhik, 2001). To mitigate the effects of low status, teachers must intentionally intervene to assign higher status to vulnerable students (Cohen et al.). This can be done simply by commenting that a particular student has a good idea or by publicly noting that the student has a strength that will be a real asset to the group's work. Attention to status is essential because the voice of students without some degree of status will never be heard (Lotan, 1997). The structuring of CL tasks, as noted earlier, is also critical to ensure that all students will have opportunities to become involved. CL tasks that are more complex facilitate student involvement better than tasks with a single answer (Chizhik; Lampe et al., 1996).

Use of Technology to Enhance Cooperative Learning

One additional factor that should be considered when planning CL activities for gifted students is the use of technology (Ciges, 2001). Online or virtual CL groups extend the possibilities well beyond the classroom and school. This is especially important for gifted students attending rural schools or schools where they have few peers who are working at their cognitive level. Access to the Internet provides opportunities for e-mail exchanges, discussions in chat rooms, and the use of virtual experts to enhance the group's thinking. Online CL groups can also be used in combination with problem-based learning to allow students to engage in meaningful exchanges of information. The use of online formats can help to reduce some stereotypes, thereby equalizing status for students. In short, by incorporating technology, we can enhance CL, making it more meaningful and far-reaching for our students (Ciges). There are several Web sites provided at the end of this chapter that support this approach to CL.

Strategies for Cooperative Learning With Gifted Students

The question is not "Should we use CL with gifted students?," but "How can we effectively use CL in both its heterogeneous and homogeneous forms so that all students, including gifted learners, will benefit?" A variety of strategies can be used to increase the likelihood that cooperative learning will meet the needs of gifted students. The following ideas should be considered:

- Offer some CL experiences in groups of high-ability students, such as honors and advanced classes, pull-out or gifted resource classes, and similar-ability clusters within heterogeneous classrooms.
- Make sure that CL assignments reflect tasks that are differentiated for students' learning levels. For instance, if the group is finding locations on a globe using latitude and longitude, the locations should reflect a variety of difficulty levels to match a range of student needs.
- Plan open-ended tasks so that all students can make meaningful contributions. Examples of open-ended tasks that allow student contributions include creating a travel brochure for your state or designing a collage representing an African country. Tasks like these allow students to contribute ideas and information in multiple ways.
- Use the jigsaw method to regroup students by specific task, by interest, or by level of difficulty. With the jigsaw method, students are first placed in "home teams" that are usually formed with heterogeneous grouping. The home team is responsible for completing the primary assignment. It is then separated into secondary topic/task teams to complete part of the group's work. This "jigsaw" allows members of the home team to work with others on specific tasks that will contribute to the home team's work. These secondary workgroups can easily be used to differentiate for students' interests, skills, or ability levels. An example of this would be the creation of a multimedia presentation on the Vietnam War. The home team would be responsible for pulling the final presentation together, while the jigsaw groups would allow students to explore specific

topics (e.g., political precursors to the war, economic impacts of the war, role of women in the military during the war, social implication of war protests, or music that evolved during this time period that reflected social feelings about the war).

- Create CL groups as expert groups on a given topic, where students are allowed to self-select tasks to explore in greater depth. This is a particularly good option for students who have mastered the basic curriculum before their classmates. In a U.S. history class, groups may form to study the roles of African Americans during the Civil War or analyze early gospel music for themes and messages of freedom.
- Form CL groups across grade levels. This allows advanced students to work with older students on projects of interest or to work with younger students in support roles in an area of strength. Students might join together to write computer programs or to create a nature path for the school.
- Use a variety of self-paced materials that encourage CL team members to move at their own learning rate while earning "progress points" for their team. Slavin (1991) designed several instructional materials that are appropriate for students in these settings.
- Use flexible CL groups so that students can accomplish large tasks through the efforts of smaller strength and interest groups. For example, when putting on a class performance, students can choose from working on the sets; designing costumes; working on the programs, advertisements, and concessions; or writing, producing, and acting in the play.
- Form CL groups around problem-based learning activities (Gallagher, 1997; Hmelo & Ferrari, 1997) where students engage in working through an ill-structured problem. Problems focusing on high-interest concerns and curricular content are integrated into the solution-building process. For example, a science class could be asked to explain and make recommendations regarding a series of fish kills in a local water system.
- Provide a safety net for students who either do not want to work in a group (Li & Adamson, 1992) or who are experiencing great difficulty in group participation by planning alternatives for completing the assignments. Alternatives should be used as a natural part of the continuum of learning options and should not be seen as a punishment. Students who may have difficulty working in a group of four, for example, may do well working with a partner to complete a given task or might need to complete their part of the CL group work alone, bringing their section back to the team for inclusion with the final product. Some students who may need to be considered for this type of differentiation include students with Asperger's Syndrome and students with intense interest who are working at a substantially higher level than their classmates.
- Use technology to form virtual CL groups with students at different schools. These multisite CL groups expand the ability of students to

complete complex learning tasks with others and can facilitate learning because they increase motivation. An example of this is the creation of virtual CL groups in a high school foreign language class to explore the cultural differences between the U.S. and Spain. The groups are formed with partner schools in Spain, and students exchange e-mails to get to know each other and discuss cultural differences related to specific topics they have selected (e.g., music, dating customs, college entrance and expectations, families, clothes, etc.). These exchanges give all the students an authentic reason to use the language they are learning.

- Plan assessment strategies that recognize and reward group problem solving, innovation, and group dynamics. Do *not* assign individual grades for students based on the group's efforts. CL members can earn points or rewards for their team by working well and creating innovative solutions to given tasks, but individual learning must be evaluated through individual means.

The major theme of all of these strategies is building flexibility, choice, and challenge into the CL activities. CL tasks that work well for a variety of student needs are those that are rich and complex (Cohen et al. 1999; Neber et al. 2001). This means that, when we design CL lessons, we should try to incorporate multiple levels of difficulty, thus giving students a variety of meaningful ways to contribute to the task. Complex tasks provide several opportunities for students to make decisions regarding the completion of the task/project, and thus the participation of all students is facilitated. This kind of CL takes a lot of planning and preparation, but the benefits are worth the extra effort. The next sections contain outlines of ideas and examples for CL activities.

Sample CL Activities for Different Grades and Settings

The following descriptions are meant to be used as examples of how CL activities might be structured to meet students' needs at multiple levels. Although the activities have been organized by subject area and grade level, they can be modified to fit different grades depending on the needs of the students. The first description, "Room for Improvement," is presented in detail from the preparation through assessment phases. The remaining activities are briefly described.

3rd-Grade Measurement and Area: Room for Improvement

The purpose of these activities is to reinforce measurement and the calculation of area. Students will work on both a CL home team (four to five students) and in jigsaw groups to gather information. The CL home team will be responsible for completing the main task and developing a proposal to redecorate the classroom. Each jigsaw group will work on a specific task to be folded into the home team proposal.

The difficulty levels of the individual tasks can be adjusted by assigning students to jigsaw groups. Students' choices are incorporated as they select the materials and design their proposal; individual students' strengths should be used in the preparation of the proposal itself. Time needed for completion of these activities will vary from a week to 10 days, depending on the amount of time designated each day.

Task Description For Teacher. This is a simulation lesson where the class is asked to develop a plan to redecorate the classroom. The CL groups are responsible for developing a proposal to improve the classroom. The principal (or a panel of teachers) will review the proposals and select one for the class. You may also want to establish different categories so that several proposals can be recognized; these might include "most beautiful," "most practical," or "most creative."

To develop their proposals, students will need a great deal of information. Here are some options you can discuss with them: paint or wallpaper the walls, carpet part or all of the floor, put shelf-lining paper on the desks, get new window blinds, and add some bookshelves. You can brainstorm with your students a variety of ideas that they can consider incorporating in their proposals.

Each CL group is responsible for developing a proposal for the changes. The proposal serves as a "bid" for the job so it must contain complete information on choices of colors, design ideas, time to complete the redecoration, and costs. The proposal must include enough information to complete the redecoration if it is the one selected.

The key components of the proposal should include a brief description of the proposed changes, a fact sheet with specific cost information (including the cost to paint the walls with the number of gallons of paint selected and the price per gallon), a timeline showing how the work would progress, a design board that shows all the colors and combinations used, and a drawing of the room with the new changes.

Preparation. In the weeks before you begin, visit a hardware store and gather materials to build a resource bank for the project (this could be a field trip). You can use sample paint chips (make sure you list on each the cost per gallon and how much wall a gallon will cover—are two coats recommended?), wallpaper samples with cost/coverage information, swatches of carpet with price per square foot (does it need a carpet backer?), samples of shelf-liner paper with cost and dimensions per roll, and window blind options with prices. If you want your students to look at bookshelves, you will also need information on boards, nails, and paint for these. Many hardware stores will donate yardsticks (and even hats with their logo) if you tell them it is for a school.

You will also need several measurement tools, such as tape measures, rulers, and yardsticks, as well as graph paper, pencils, and calculators. Materials for the proposals should also be handy (poster board, paper, colored pencils, or crayons).

CL Activities. Assign students to mixed-ability CL home teams (four to five per team). Present the "Room for Improvement" simulation task and discuss the bidding process along with the principal's role in ultimately selecting the proposal (make sure your students know this is a simulation). Assign students to jigsaw groups of appropriate difficulty level for data collection. Members of the jigsaw group will figure out how to calculate the area and cost of the items in their proposal, including floor area, type of carpet needed, and carpet prices. The five jigsaw groups (bookshelves, floor covering, desk tops with shelf paper, windows, and wallpaper and paints) will carry this information back to their home CL team. You may want to design a worksheet for each group to record its data (see Figure 2).

Students in jigsaw groups should figure out how to measure and calculate the cost of the various options on which they are working (the more challenging tasks, such as calculating wall area and paint and paper cost, should be assigned to your top math students). During the process, students can explore a variety of problem-solving approaches to get the needed information. Once the jigsaw groups have their summary sheets, students return to their CL home team and share what they have learned.

The CL home team then selects the options it wants for its proposal. Once the options have been agreed on, the team assigns tasks for the proposal development (fact sheets, description, timelines, cost analysis, design board, and drawing).

Assessment of the CL Task. A sample rubric is included to present the CL home team's success in completing the assigned tasks (see Figure 3). The areas included in the sample assessment are:

- group dynamics (ability of the students to work in harmony and ensure that all members make meaningful contributions);
- content of the proposal (comprehensiveness, accuracy, and integration of ideas);
- presentation (neatness, organization, and beauty); and
- innovation (ability to incorporate originality and uniqueness of style).

These areas may change depending on what you want to emphasize. The teams can be given special recognition or rewards for their work based on the review of their success. The ultimate recognition would be the selection of their proposal by the principal as the winning bid.

Individual assessment of learning must be done using students' work samples, tests, and demonstrated mastery of content (in this case, measurement and calculation of area). Students may be given a smaller version of this task to complete independently, or they may be asked questions like "How many different methods can you use to figure out how much carpet will be needed to recarpet

Name: _____

Surface area of walls (sq. ft.): _____ Home team: _____

Paint:

	Color	Cost per gallon	Sq. ft. covered per gallon	2 coats? Yes No	Total cost
1.					
2.					
3.					
4.					
5.					

Wallpaper:

	Color	Cost per roll	Sq. ft. covered per roll	Total cost
1.				
2.				
3.				
4.				
5.				

**Figure 2. Room for improvement:
Sample worksheet for data collection**

the principal's office?" Grades for math should reflect students' knowledge and mastery of the content and must be assigned through individual assessments.

6th-Grade Social Studies

Many social studies classes in the middle grades are heterogeneously grouped with students of wide-ranging abilities. The ideas here are designed to

Title: Sample CL rubric for "Room for Improvement"　　Date: _____
Topic: Math measurement and calculation of area　　Grade level: _____

Level	Group dynamics	Content of proposal	Presentation	Proposal
5	Individuals worked in harmony and made meaningful contributions to group. Problems were handled in a positive manner.	Proposal incorporates all required elements and reflects accuracy and continuity of group thinking (integration of components).	Proposal presentation is neat, well organized, colorful, and aesthetically pleasing.	Proposal ideas reflect original designs with unique style and/or combine existing components in an unusual fashion; has "flare."
4	The group worked well together completing the task and resolved problems in a positive manner.	Proposal is complete and accurate, and some attempt has been made to integrate parts.	Proposal is neat, well-organized, and colorful.	Ideas reflect some originality and unique combinations of components.
3	The group was able to complete task with minimum conflicts and was able to solve problems that arose with some support.	Proposal is complete and accurate, but is somewhat disjointed (segments were not integrated).	Proposal is neat and well-organized.	Ideas reflect some originality.
2	The group was able to complete task with support to help them resolve conflicts.	Proposal is complete, but information is incorrect.	Proposal is well-organized but messy.	Ideas reflect little originality.
1	Group was unable to work together and problems overwhelmingly lead to conflicts.	Proposal is incomplete, and information is incorrect.	Proposal presentation is messy and poorly organized.	Ideas reflect little originality and represent a "copy."

Figure 3. Rubric Planner

allow the teacher to incorporate a variety of CL strategies to meet a range of student needs.

1. Create mixed-ability study teams to review material, compete in quiz bowls (make sure you offer challenge questions of increasing difficulty), and compete for accomplishment/improvement points. You can also award team points for homework completion as an extra incentive (Slavin, 1988).

2. Use pretests to assess mastery of basic information and allow students to "challenge out" of work they have mastered so they can pursue an area of interest. CL groups should be formed around topics related to the curriculum (e.g., study of the role of individuals in the early exploration of the West or changes in fashion across history). Products developed by the CL group can be shared with the class. Grades for these students should reflect individual mastery of the core content (pretest results) and success in completion of their part of the CL group work (student contracts can help clarify expectations). If several students contribute to one product, ask that each student initial his or her contributions.

3. Structure a large event—such as History Day, creation of an interactive history museum, or a period play/reenactment—and form CL groups around students' interests and areas of strength to make contributions.

4. Complete an analysis of historical periods by developing a "cosmic calendar" that shows the major event in politics, literature, the arts, science, inventions, fashion, and education. A cosmic calendar is a matrix that gives the time periods down the side and categories across the top. Each cell in the matrix reflects key events in that category for that time period (these actually look like *Jeopardy!* boards and can be used as bulletin boards for the classroom). The organization of information in this way allows students to think about and discuss history as a series of interrelated events across different categories. Using the cosmic calendar approach, you can ask questions like "How did the political events (Category #1) during the Vietnam War shape the social culture (Category #2)?" You can also ask questions about a given category over time. For example, your students look at access to college educations (within the category of "Education"), and you can ask them to discuss how the presence of different conflicts influenced the numbers of college graduates at various points in history and what impact this had on society at large. Your CL groups can select the topic to research and contribute their information to the overall calendar, or you can form home teams to create the calendars and they can jigsaw out into the area study groups.

High School Physical Science

Most high school science classes are already leveled by ability or student self-selection. Within this setting, CL groups can provide motivation by capitalizing on students' interests. Whenever possible, students should be allowed to select the groups in which they will work. If this is not possible, then the group members should be randomly assigned. Some ideas for CL activities include:

1. CL groups may form to study areas of high interest that are not usually included in the curriculum, such as chaos theory, the Tao of Physics, the physics of baseball, the portrayal of physics in science fiction, or the history of physics. Students should self-select groups and contract to complete specific work assignments.

2. Science labs offer an ideal opportunity for CL groups to collaborate on problem solving. In addition to traditional labs, students can be given puzzlers and can be asked to design experiments to test, explain, or explore solutions. Puzzlers might include fairly straightforward physics applications like "What is the optimal wall covering for a music hall that accommodates for sounds during performances?" or more complex applications such as "Design an energy-efficient dwelling that is as self-sustaining as possible" (this may be a space station or an underwater ecosphere).

3. High school science classes provide the perfect opportunity to infuse problem-based learning (PBL) activities. In a biology class, students may be asked to wrestle with problems as large as global warming or as close as a new shopping mall going up in the community. When CL groups are formed around PBL activities, students work together as a team to research, debate, and present solutions to their problem.

4. Service learning opportunities are being provided for many high school students, which in some districts are a requirement for graduation. Cooperative learning groups are an ideal vehicle for the development of service projects for the community or school. Service projects focus on needs and involve things like developing a playground for younger students, working with an after-school tutorial program, or monitoring the environment of a river for runoff and other pollution. These projects allow students to make meaningful contributions while exploring interests and career options.

Classes for Gifted Students

Special classes for gifted students offer a unique setting for CL. Students can be given the chance to pursue areas of high interest through CL groups, and the use of CL often reduces competitiveness through collaboration (Joyce, 1991). Although most students identified as gifted are socially competent (unlike the myth of the complete nerd), it may be necessary to review group dynamics and teach some skills to help build group cohesion (Joyce). These skills may be part of a leadership unit, or they may be built into a self-study approach as students get to know their learning and interaction styles (Ross & Smyth, 1995).

Role of the Teacher

The teacher's role in CL activities is different from his or her role in direct instruction. The primary work of the teacher actually happens before the CL activity takes place—the planning. Investment in planning time is essential to successful CL. Designing high-quality CL lessons takes time. When planning to use cooperative learning, the same kinds of decisions need to be made as with any other teaching strategy. As teachers, we continually reflect on questions like the following: Is the time going to be well spent? Does the topic lend itself to group work? Can I structure the task so that all students can make meaningful contributions? What can I do for those who either will not or cannot work in groups? How can I make sure that all of my students will contribute to the CL group—and ensure that they will be heard? Is there a better way to engage my students?

During the CL lesson, teachers monitor the group work, help students troubleshoot, and, when necessary, intervene to help resolve group conflicts. Rules of thumb, such as "Ask three before me," help students understand that they should rely on their group first and the teacher second. Teachers' informal observations of students can often be done best when CL groups are meaningfully engaged. One strategy for this is to tell students that part of their grade for the project will be based on their participation in their group and that, during the course of the project, you will be doing two or three observations of each of them. Each day, you can use sheets of mailing labels on a clipboard to record observations and grades for specific students (peel off the sticker and place it in the student's portfolio or file). If you do not tell your students when you are observing them specifically for their grade, you will find that they notice whenever you walk around with your clipboard!

Conclusion

When used appropriately, cooperative learning is a wonderful way to engage students in learning. Unfortunately, the misuses of CL, as either a teacher convenience or as a replacement for a variety of differentiated learning experiences, has caused problems for some gifted students. I hope this chapter will help to provide optimal learning experiences for all students. Creating opportunities to engage students in exciting learning and allowing them to generate and share ideas is what schooling should be about. Cooperative learning is one option we have to reach and teach our students; we should use it wisely.

Teacher Statement

Since its inception within my classroom, cooperative learning (CL) has worked well for me. While CL does a wonderful job of offering flexibility and various challenges to students, I feel that its best aspect is its ability to personalize each student's education. It has definitely invigorated the learning process for my students and for myself.

I have created primary and secondary CL groups for most of my classroom activities. The primary groups are determined by ability level. Class performance, informal observation, and pretests aid in my selection. I have also developed secondary CL groups, or home teams, that are more heterogeneous in terms of ability and learning styles. My seating arrangement is reflective of these secondary groups. Thus, I can put my primary groups on a specific task, and when kids return to their assigned seats, they are already placed in their home teams, ready to share new knowledge.

During a recent short story unit, I assigned the top-tier primary group to read ahead and individually formulate 15 questions they might use in a group discussion. These five students were then instructed to work collectively to make a top 10 list of interpretive, open-ended questions. As the students examined their questions, they began to arrive at new and more intriguing queries. The group escaped from the story itself and questioned the author's motives; they also connected their own lives to the text. After I demonstrated a small-group discussion with their top 10 list, each student returned to his or her home team and led the group in a discussion of the short story.

As opposed to one teacher asking good questions to 30 students (wherein only the most communicative students will participate), CL helped me personalize the learning process by creating an atmosphere in which each learner could share his or her opinions. The role of the leaders was not to answer the questions, but to merely ask them. Leaders also reminded students to back up their ideas with evidence.

A postactivity survey revealed that the leaders believed that the assignment was definitely challenging. They also expressed surprise at the amount of new knowledge they gained through the final group discussions. I believe that the CL grouping worked in this jigsaw activity not only because the secondary groups learned new ideas about the story, but because the discussion leaders gained new perspectives, as well.

—J. J. Eagleston

Discussion Questions

1. What does a complex CL task look like? What criteria could you use to judge the complexity of the CL tasks you create?

2. How can you influence students' perceptions of other students' status to enhance equitable participation in CL groups for all students?

3. What student behaviors could you observe during CL activities to help you do the following:
   a. Identify students who might be gifted?
   b. Identify students who seem low status?
   c. Identify students who are bored or frustrated with the CL task?
   d. Identify students who are having a difficult time working in a group?

4. How can you use technology to enhance CL activities?

5. What criteria would you use to determine if a given topic or lesson is really suited to CL?

6. How can you assess group work and still base grades on an individual student's learning?

Teacher Resources

Publications

Churchill, R. (1992). *Amazing science experiments with everyday materials*. New York: Sterling.
More than 60 science experiments can be replicated at home so students (grades 2–8) can share their learning with family members.

Coffin, M. (1996). *Team science*. Tucson, AZ: Zephyr Press.
The outlines of science labs, appropriate for groups of students in grades 4–8, foster cooperation while students learn about Earth, life, or physical science topics.

Davidson, N., & Worsham, T. (Eds.). (1992). *Enhancing thinking through cooperative learning*. Williston, VT: Teachers College Press.
Practical ideas for implementation have been included to give the reader several ideas on how to build cooperative thinking into group activities.

Fogarty, R. (1997). *Problem-based learning*. Arlington Heights, IL: SkyLight.
While providing a variety of curricular frameworks, this book uses real-world problems to promote students' learning and thinking.

Addresses

Center for Gifted Education
The College of William and Mary
P.O. Box 8795
Williamsburg, VA 23187-8795
(757) 221-2362; (757) 221-2184 (fax)
cfge@facstaff.wm.edu
http://www.cfge.wm.edu
The William and Mary Center for Gifted Education's curriculum units for gifted students provide an excellent platform for cooperative learning groups. Many of these units involve problem-based learning activities.

Shelagh A. Gallagher
The University of North Carolina at Charlotte
9201 University City Blvd.
Charlotte, NC 28223-0001
(704) 687-3757
sagallag@email.uncc.edu
Contact Shelagh Gallagher in the Counseling and Special Education Department at UNC-Charlotte for additional problem-based learning materials for middle school and high school students.

Prufrock Press
P.O. Box 8813
Waco, TX 76714–8813
(800) 998-2208
http://www.prufrock.com

SkyLight Professional Development
2626 S. Clearbrook Dr.
Arlington Heights, IL 60005
(800) 290-6600
http://www.skylightedu.com

Teachers College Press
P.O. Box 20
Williston, VT 05495–0020
(800) 575-6566
http://www.teacherscollegepress.com

Zephyr Press
P.O. Box 66006
Tucson, AZ 85728–6006
(800) 232-2187
http://www.zephyrpress.com

Web Sites

Concept to Classroom: Resources—http://www.thirteen.org/edonline/concept2
class/w5-resources.html
This site provides quick links to books, articles, and Web sites on cooperative
learning for educators, parents/caregivers, and students.

PIGS Space: Cooperative Learning Modules—http://cspace.unb.ca/nbco/pigs/
modules
This site offers cooperative learning lesson plans for language arts, math, science
and social studies.

Cooperative Learning Lessons—http://www.henry.k12.tn.us/teachersworkshop/
cooplearn/lessons.html
This site offers more cooperative learning lesson plans and other sites for cooperative learning such as Math Stories, Archive to Cooperative Lessons, and
Educator's Reference Desk, just to name a few.

International Institute for Communication and Development: The Global Teenager Project—http://www.iicd.org/globalteenager
The Global Teenager Project was launched in 1999 to bring the full potential of information and communication technologies (ICT) into the classroom. Its aim is to enhance secondary pupils' ICT skills while increasing their understanding of other cultures. Students can exchange information on specific topics via global classrooms.

Pitsco's Ask an Expert—http://www.askanexpert.com
This Web site can facilitate question-and-answer activities, encouraging students to exchange and share their opinions and information actively.

KIDPROJ's Multicultural Calendar—http://www.kidlink.org/KIDPROJ/MCC
This site is an example of a database created and made available to others via the Internet where secondary schools can join global projects.

Basic Support for Cooperative Work—http://bscw.gmd.de
Basic Support for Cooperative Work provides online cooperative learning resources and enables collaboration over the Web.

References

Allan, S. (1991). Ability grouping research reviews: What do they say about grouping for the gifted? *Educational Leadership, 48*, 60–65.

Baytops, J. L., & Reed, D. (1997). Making connections: Developing strategies to teach African-American gifted learners effectively. In B. A. Ford (Ed.), *Multiple voices for ethnically diverse exceptional learners* (pp. 45–49). Arlington, VA: Council for Exceptional Children.

Calderon, M., Hertz-Lazarowitz, R., & Slavin, R. (1998). Effects of bilingual cooperative integrated reading and composition on students making the transition from Spanish to English reading. *The Elementary School Journal, 99*, 153–165.

Chizhik, A. W. (2001). Equity and status in group collaboration: Learning through explanations depends on task characteristics. *Social Psychology of Education, 5*, 179–200.

Ciges, A. S. (2001). Online learning: New educational environments in order to respect cultural diversity through cooperative strategies. *Intercultural Education, 12*, 135–147.

Cohen, E. G., Lotan, R. A., Scarloss, B. A., & Arellano, A. R. (1999). Complex instruction: Equity in cooperative learning classrooms. *Theory in Practice, 38*, 80–86.

Coleman, M. R. (1994). Using cooperative learning with gifted students. *Gifted Child Today, 17*(6), 36–37.

Coleman, M. R., & Gallagher, J. J. (1995). The successful blending of gifted education with middle schools and cooperative learning: Two studies. *Journal for the Education of the Gifted, 18*, 362–384.

Coleman, M. R., Gallagher, J., & Nelson, S. M. (1997). *Cooperative learning and gifted students: Report on five case studies.* Washington, DC: National Association for Gifted Children.

Ellis, S. S., & Whalen, S. F. (1990). *Cooperative learning: Getting started.* New York: Scholastic.

Gallagher, S. A. (1997). Problem-based learning: Where did it come from, what does it do, and where is it going? *Journal for the Education of the Gifted, 20*, 332–362.

Gallagher, J. J., & Coleman, M. R. (1994). Cooperative learning and gifted students: Five case studies. *Cooperative Learning, 14*, 21–25.

Gallagher, J. J., Coleman, M. R., & Nelson, S. (1993). *Cooperative learning as perceived by educators of gifted students and proponents of cooperative education.* Chapel Hill: University of North Carolina, Gifted Education Policy Studies Program.

Hansman, C. A., Spencer, L., Grant, D., & Jackson, M. (1999). Beyond diversity: Dismantling barriers in education. *Journal of Instructional Psychology, 26*, 16–22.

Heinz, N., Finsterwald, M., & Urban, N. (2001). Cooperative learning with gifted and high-achieving students: A review and meta-analysis of 12 studies. *High Ability Studies, 12*, 199–215.

Heller, K. A. (1999). Individual (learning and motivational) needs vs. instructional conditions of gifted education. *High Ability Studies, 9*, 9–21.

Hmelo, C. E., & Ferrari, M. (1997). The problem-based learning tutorial: Cultivating higher-order thinking skills. *Journal for the Education of the Gifted, 20*, 401–422.

Johnson, D., & Johnson, R. (1987). *Learning together and alone.* Englewood Cliffs, NJ: Prentice Hall.

Johnson, D., & Johnson, R. (1990). Social skills for successful group work. *Educational Leadership, 47*, 29–32.

Johnson, D., & Johnson, R. (1991). What cooperative learning has to offer the gifted. *Cooperative Learning, 11*, 24–27.

Johnson, D., & Johnson, R. (1993). Gifted students illustrate what isn't cooperative learning. *Educational Leadership, 50*, 60–61.

Johnson, D., Johnson, R., & Holubec, E. (1990). *Circles of learning: Cooperation in the classroom* (3rd ed.). Edina, MN: Interaction Book.

Joyce, B. (1991). Common misconceptions about cooperative learning and gifted students. *Educational Leadership, 48*, 72–74.

Kagan, S. (1986). Cooperative learning and socio-cultural factors in schooling. In California State Department of Education, *Beyond language: Social and cultural factors in schooling language minority students* (pp. 231–298). Los Angeles: California State University, Evaluation, Dissemination, and Assessment Center.

Kagan, S. (1990). The structural approach to cooperative learning. *Educational Leadership, 47*, 12–15.

Klingner, J. K., Vaughn, S., & Schumm, J. S. (1998). Collaborative strategic reading during social studies in heterogeneous fourth-grade classrooms. *The Elementary School Journal, 99*, 3–22.

Lampe, J. R., Rooze, G. E., & Tallent-Runnels, M. (1996). Effects of cooperative learning among Hispanic students in elementary social studies. *The Journal of Educational Research, 89*, 187–191.

Li, A., & Adamson, G. (1992). Gifted secondary students' preferred learning style: Cooperative, competitive, or individualistic? *Journal for the Education of the Gifted, 16*, 46–54.

Lotan, R. (1997). Principles of a principled curriculum. In E. G. Cohen & R. A. Lotan (Eds.) *Working for equity in heterogeneous classrooms: Sociological theory in action* (pp. 105–116). New York: Teachers College Press.

Matthews, M. (1992). Gifted students talk about cooperative learning. *Educational Leadership, 50*, 48–50.

Melser, N. (1999). Gifted students and cooperative learning: A study of grouping strategies. *Roeper Review, 21*, 315.

Mills, C., & Durden, W. (1992). Cooperative learning and ability grouping: An issue of choice. *Gifted Child Quarterly, 36*, 11–16.

National Association for Gifted Children. (1996). *Position paper on cooperative learning.* Washington, DC: Author.

Neber, H., Finsterwald, M., & Urban, N. (2001). Cooperative learning with gifted and high-achieving students: A review and meta-analysis of 12 students. *High Ability Studies, 12*, 199–214.

Nelson, S., Gallagher, J., & Coleman, M. R. (1993). Cooperative learning from two different perspectives. *Roeper Review, 16*, 117–121.

Ramsay, S., & Richards, H. (1997). Cooperative learning environments: Effects on academic attitudes of gifted students. *Gifted Child Quarterly, 41*, 160–167.

Robinson, A. (1990). Cooperation or exploitation? The argument against cooperative learning for talented students. *Journal for the Education of the Gifted, 14*, 9–27, 31–36.

Robinson, A. (1991). *Cooperative learning and the academically talented student.* Storrs: National Research Center on the Gifted and Talented, University of Connecticut.

Ross, J. A., & Smyth, E. (1995). Differentiating cooperative learning to meet the needs of gifted learners: A case for transformational leadership. *Journal for the Education of the Gifted, 19*, 63–82.

Samaha, N. H., & de Lisi, R. (2000). Peer collaboration on a nonverbal reasoning task by urban, minority students. *Journal of Experimental Education, 69*, 5–22.

Sapon-Shevin, M., & Schniedewind, N. (1993). Why (even) gifted children need cooperative learning. *Educational Leadership, 50*, 62–63.

Sharan, S. (1990). Cooperative learning and helping behavior in the multi-ethnic classroom. In H. Foot, M. J. Morgan, & R. Shute (Eds.), *Children helping children* (pp. 151–176). New York: Wiley.

Slavin, R. E. (1980). Cooperative learning. *Review of Educational Research, 50*, 315–342.

Slavin, R. E. (1981). Synthesis of research on cooperative learning. *Educational Leadership, 38*, 655–700.

Slavin, R. E. (1988). *Student team learning: An overview and practical guide.* Washington, DC: National Education Association.

Slavin, R. E. (1990). Ability grouping, cooperative learning, and the gifted. *Journal for the Education of the Gifted, 14*, 3–8, 28–30.

Slavin, R. E. (1991). What cooperative learning has to offer the gifted. *Cooperative Learning, 11*, 22–23.

Slavin, R. E. (1994). Student teams-achievement divisions. In S. Sharan (Ed.), *Handbook of cooperative learning methods* (pp. 3–19). Westport, CT: Greenwood Press.

Tam, B. K. Y., & Gardner, R. (1997). Developing a multicultural and student-centered educational environment for students with serious emotional disturbances. In B. A. Ford (Ed.), *Multiple voices for ethically diverse exceptional learners* (pp. 8–18). Arlington, VA: Council for Exceptional Children.

VanTassel-Baska, J. (1998). *Excellence in educating gifted and talented learners* (3rd ed.). Denver: Love.

Chapter 18

Teaching the Gifted Through Simulation

by **Dorothy Sisk**

braham Maslow once said, "If the only tool you have is a hammer, every problem looks like a nail." Teachers and administrators want to improve the ability of gifted students to solve problems in a variety of situations, and simulation is an important teaching tool to help accomplish this objective. Simulation provides opportunities for students to develop awareness, knowledge, and skills, as well as meaningful practice opportunities. However, simulation isn't the only teaching tool educators and administrators have. This chapter will suggest guidance on when it is the right tool, and, more importantly, it will offer action steps to design and use simulation.

Background and Definitions

Simulation as a teaching tool is not new by any means. As a way of learning, it has been used for centuries, and it is thought that board games like chess and draughts were initially devised to teach the art of war (Drummer, 2002). Simulation is a natural activity in which most young children engage as they pretend and role-play. In these activities, children build an understanding of the world around them, simulating interactions with other people, animals, and objects. As they construct reproductions of objects and situations, children build an understanding of reality and all of its intricacies.

There is little consensus on the terms used in the literature to define simulation, and a few of the terms are often used interchangeably, such as *simulation, game, role-play, simulation game, computer simulation*, and *role-play simulation*. Yet, there is considerable agreement that simulation is a much broader concept than role-playing. Simulation is more complex, lengthy, and relatively inflexible, while role-playing is usually quite simple, brief, and flexible. In simulations, the participants simulate real-life situations, while in role-playing the participants represent and experience a character or type known in everyday life. However, simulations, also include elements of role-playing.

Simulation is a powerful tool to teach content, thinking, and reasoning skills that are necessary to solve problems in the real world. Simulation simplifies reality to highlight certain key ideas (Renzulli, Leppen, & Hays, 2000). There are three areas in which simulation is useful: work, education, and play. In the work environment, simulation is given an important role in research and development (Romme, 2003). Two examples of simulation use are on-the-job training flight simulation to train pilots and training simulations for doctors and dentists to learn about and practice new techniques.

Role-playing in simulation, particularly if it is computer-based, is a widely used teaching tool in business and government. Considerable initiative has been demonstrated in higher education in the use of simulation to enhance the initial academic stage of education in university and college classrooms, particularly science. Simulation is also used by prelaw students in moot courts and in case-study demonstrations. Many elementary and secondary students participate in mock political conventions and United Nations simulations to expand their knowledge of content and skills.

Computer simulations are widely used for entertainment and play, and numerous computer games employ simulation, including *Barbie's Fashion Make-Over, G.I. Joe and the Combat Mission, Jeopardy!*, and *Name That Tune*. Students learn how to manage a small business, command troops in a Civil War battle, conduct a series of chemistry experiments, and travel to Jupiter using computer simulation programs. Students interact with the World Wide Web and move beyond the classroom walls to visit the White House, see NASA's latest expedition, learn about current exhibits at the Smithsonian, check the status of the stock market, and interact with other students in classrooms throughout the world (Lewis & Doorlag, 2003).

Reporter Project, a computer simulation that encourages students to be writers, uses a simulated newspaper format. A student reporter is placed in a situation where choices must be made concerning which sections of the paper target a story. This decision influences the way the story must be written and which facts need to be highlighted. For example, if a student reporter is covering a sports story for the Sports section, details about the game, the players, and the score are most important. Yet, the same game covered by the People and Style section of the paper would highlight the dignitaries attending and include some fashion information. Students role-play a reporter and search for pertinent facts and write their stories. Later, the reporter may role-play a writer who submits the story to the editor (the computer), who checks key words in the story and then provides feedback about the logic of the facts. Real news footage is used in this computer simulation, courtesy of NBC News. *Reporter Project* software also enables students to print their stories.

Brozo and Simpson (2003) shared how a secondary history teacher had his class participate in a simulation activity called *Government Experiment*. The students were divided into two groups, the Oros and the Bindus. Each group had a set of directions for electing representatives to make laws or rules. The Bindus could only make rules that applied to themselves, whereas the Oros could impose rules on the Bindus. Each group was given a lump sum of $100 for its treasury.

The teacher as a leader of the Oros immediately began imposing laws on the Bindus that roughly paralleled the Stamp Act and the Tea Act. He levied the Paper and Pencil Rule, which taxed every Bindu $5 for every pencil, pen, and piece of paper used. He also created the Pop Rule, which taxed the Bindus $10 for having a soda. Soon the Bindus challenged the authority of the Oros by drinking soda and using the materials without paying taxes.

In a debriefing, the students began to analyze the situation. The Bindus argued that it was extremely unfair for a separate group of people to tell them what to do. They said they wanted and were able to take care of themselves. One student said, "What gives you the right to tax us?" The students listed the rules imposed by the Oros and the Bindus' reactions to those rules. As they discussed the list, they soon began to see the similarity between their view and the Colonial American view during the Revolutionary War.

Simulation techniques are experiencing significant growth in development and use in education as a result of the growing emphasis on teaching higher order thinking. Consequently, a primary objective for teachers is to prepare students for the world of tomorrow. Heward (2003) noted that simulation encourages students to think critically and analytically, make decisions, and solve problems; and computer simulation provides guided discovery of real-world situations and hands-on experiences. Learning by simulating motivates further learning of content, and, as students encounter complex questions they want to explore in greater depth, they discover they need additional information.

Simulation represents an operating imitation of a real process.
A game includes:

- Play
- Players
- Rules

A game is defined as any contest (play) among adversaries (players) operating under constraints (rules) for an objective (winning, victory, or consensus building). The term *game* is applied to a simulation that works wholly or partly on the basis of decisions made by players because the environment and participants' activities have the characteristics of a game. Players have goals, sets of activities to perform, constraints on what can be done, and payoffs (good and bad) as consequences of action.

Adventure games are quite similar to simulations except that the situations portrayed are selected for entertainment value, rather than educational value. In adventure games, participants engage in role-playing, and decisions made by the players alter the course of the adventure. Adventure games are found in arcade-type computer games, and they are quite popular outside the classroom. Players earn points by skillful maneuvering and careful aim as they battle with an opponent, make their way through a maze or labyrinth, or play an electronic version of a sport or conventional arcade game.

Simulations contribute to the richness of the learning environment for gifted students in numerous ways. Some of these have just been described, while others can be found in publications such as *Technology & Learning* and *Instructor*, both of which are magazines for teachers that are published in two formats: a standard print version and an abbreviated online version. For example, the Web site for *Technology & Learning* reprints articles in the current issue of the magazine, including recent columns from departments such as Editor's Desk, Trend Watch, Web Sightings, and What's New. Searchable databases list technology products, grants related to technology, and technology conferences and events.

There are many exciting simulation games available; however, the examples provided in this chapter were primarily selected as examples of simulations successfully used by the author in gifted programs and in the training of teachers of the gifted: *BaFá BaFá, Barnga, Infotactics, Land of the Sphinx and Land of the Rainbow, Parlé, Star Power,* and *Tag Game.* Several publishing companies have numerous simulation materials available, including Broderbund, Interact, and Prufrock Press. Many of these simulations are listed in the Resources section at the end of the chapter.

Example of a Simulation Game

To better understand what a simulation game actually is, each part of a sample simulation will be examined: (1) the activity, (2) the simulation, and (3) the game.

The Activity. Most teachers are familiar with small-group activities in which teachers and students discuss or "process" a completed exercise or activity that provides opportunities to learn by doing. For example, an activity used in group dynamics training is *Puzzle Activity.* The leader asks a small group to put a puzzle together, gives each student a few of the pieces, and the students set about completing the task. After about 5 minutes, the leader is instructed to stop the activity and ask the students what they have learned from it. Students are usually frustrated because everyone doesn't share their pieces and no specific directions were given—no directions saying, "You can share." Concepts identified in this type of activity include cooperation, power, leadership, and the need for strategic planning.

The Simulation. This activity can be converted into a simulation by asking the students, "What workplace roles would be appropriate for putting the puzzle together?" The students might suggest "puzzle assemblers," "assembly managers," "timekeepers," and "group leaders." Following this interchange, the leader can ask for volunteers to play each of the identified roles and give each student an appropriate identification badge. The students continue to put the puzzle together, but now with designated ways of relating to each other while completing the task. This activity now represents a simulation.

The Game. To turn this simulation into a simulation game, game-like elements and rules need to be added. Some of the puzzle assemblers can be given specific constraints such as "blindfolds," or a rule can be imposed that "You can only touch inside pieces, not edges." Chips can be given to the assembly managers to be used as rewards or to the timekeepers to reward fast assembly. These chips can also be taken away when the students make errors. The group leader can be given the puzzle box with the picture of what the completed puzzle looks like, or the group leader can be given a separate puzzle to complete. Payoff chips can be distributed for each puzzle that is correctly put together.

At the completion of the simulation game, the leader engages in debriefing, and the discussion is usually quite revealing. Comments made by a group of middle school gifted students on completion of a similar simulation game included the following: "Even though you said the group leader could see the puzzle picture, the group leader didn't share that information"; "Every time someone got chips for finishing a puzzle, I became so frustrated I couldn't think. It's like knowing who is the best in your class or something"; "The timekeeper bothered me. I don't work well under pressure"; and "This activity was more inviting with the roles and rules. I liked it. Can we do another?"

Why is Simulation Effective for Gifted Students?

Teaching at its most fundamental level is task-focused on the creation of an environment in which students are able to interact and to learn how to learn (Dewey, 1916; Joyce, Weil, & Calhoun, 2003). Simulation creates an environment in which gifted students learn because they see a useful reason to learn: to succeed and to win. Playing to win a simulation game engages the competitive nature of many gifted students, and the gaming aspect provides opportunities for them to develop and enhance higher level thinking and problem-solving skills. Social values are also enhanced through simulation, as gifted students realize that cooperation is necessary to win the game. Gifted students build empathy for real-life situations in simulations, particularly when they make difficult decisions in games.

> Simulation is effective for gifted students because it
>
> * provides for collective decision making;
> * develops language skills;
> * builds cross-cultural understanding;
> * develops decision-making skills;
> * builds a realistic paradigm of the world; and
> * provides opportunities for experimenting with ideas.

Island Game, developed by Crookall and Oxford (1991), illustrates the collective decision making that simulation can provide for gifted students. In *Island Game,* a group of individuals have been stranded on an island, and a volcano is to erupt in 30 to 60 minutes. The group must devise an escape plan to be implemented quickly. There are lifeboats to carry all of the group to safety on neighboring islands, but an overall group consensus must be reached on who will go where and with whom. All the students complete personal profiles with accurate information on their sex, age, nationality, background, and practical skills, and then they identify their top three preferred islands. In debriefing the simulation, students are asked to identify and rank order the five main factors that influenced decision making in forming groups and choosing islands and escape boats. These factors are discussed in the debriefing to provide opportunities for gifted students to experience and build individual tolerance and acceptance for different points of view.

Crookall and Oxford (1991) strongly endorsed the use of simulation to learn the highly developed language skills that gifted students need, including the ability to express agreement and disagreement, persuade, defend a point of view, elicit cooperation, analyze data, and make judgments. Other communication skills enhanced through the use of simulation include listening, understanding directions, initiating, speaking, writing, and reading. Simulations such as *Island Game* also provide gifted students opportunities to practice these important language skills in an exciting format.

Simulations of political and societal situations encourage gifted students to use authentic tools and concepts within content study and to build cross-cultural understanding. One of the more popular social studies programs is *The Oregon Trail,* in which students simulate the journey of the pioneers across the United States.

Simulation provides information about a situation students will encounter and then asks them to make decisions. Student space travelers, for example, need to select provisions for a journey and chart the route they plan to follow. When a simulation begins, events unfold and more choices must be made. Many simulations have an element of chance, so that students may be unsuccessful despite careful planning and prudent decisions. Because students learn through experience by perceiving the consequences of decisions, simulations, unlike tutorials and drills, represent discovery learning activities.

In *All Around Frippletown*, a computer-based program, students are provided a set of devices with which to manufacture cookies that match the model presented by the program. The order in which the devices are used affects the outcome, so students must experiment in order to come up with the right product. Students are posed with a problem and then directed to gather information about the program, suggest alternative solutions, and evaluate the effectiveness of the solutions.

Simulation experiences provide rich content and opportunities for gifted students to build a more realistic paradigm of the world through exploring issues and examining the multiple perspectives and experiences of specific events or situations. Several simulations developed by Charlotte Beeler (listed in the Resources section at the end of the chapter) provide this type of learning experience: *American Nostalgia, Earth Friendly, Endangered Species, Medieval Destination,* and *Western Exploration. Ancient China: The Middle Kingdom,* is another example of a simulation that explores specific issues (Sandling, 2003).

In the nonjudgmental environment of simulation, gifted students can practice new behaviors and experiment with new attitudes and points of view. They act and interact, becoming involved in the facts, the processes, and the key concepts to be learned in the game. It is this dynamic interaction that becomes a legitimate vehicle for learning. Powerful and deep learning takes place as gifted students engage in exciting and satisfying play, using the scenarios in the simulation for problem solving (Gregory, 2000).

Friend and Cook (2000) said that teams go through a life cycle, as do simulations and their players. The cycle includes:

Forming: Students examine the task in a simulation, learn about each other, and clarify the objective of the game.

Storming: Students work to resolve issues of power, leadership, procedures, and goals.

Norming: Students establish role relationships and procedures for accomplishing the task in the simulation.

Performing: Students align themselves and work toward achieving the goal.

Adjourning: Having completed the task and the game, the groups debrief and disband.

Major Benefits for Gifted Students
Derived From Simulation Games

Gifted students learn on three levels when they participate in simulation games. They learn (1) facts and information embodied in the context and dynamics of the game; (2) processes that are simulated in the game; and (3) the relative costs, benefits, risks, and potential rewards of using alternative strategies for decision making. This interaction of information, processes, and strategies provides gifted students the experience of simultaneously operating on all three levels and reinforces the idea that decision making is not a simple process (Lewis & Doorlag, 2003). Many gifted students operate on several levels simultaneously, and they enjoy the engaging nature of simulation.

Major Benefits of Simulation for Gifted Students

It provides opportunities for:

- critical thinking;
- questioning of assumptions and exploration of diverse opinions;
- integrating higher order thinking;
- building personal responsibility;
- understanding the role of change;
- enhancing knowledge and skills;
- understanding of social systems;
- leadership skills;
- independence in action and thought; and
- group dynamics.

Use of Critical Thinking

Simulation games motivate and reward the critical thinking of gifted students as they analyze possible decisions, reflect on the probable consequences of those decisions, and then plan and think through countermoves and strategies. Simulation games also encourage and develop the intuitive thinking of gifted students as they engage in spontaneous decision making. Critical thinking empowers gifted students to take charge of their learning and life (Paul & Elder, 2001). As they use critical thinking in simulations, logical gifted students become more spontaneous and spontaneous gifted students become more logical.

Questioning of Assumptions and Exploration of Diverse Opinions

Simulation games provide opportunities for gifted students to encounter different points of view and to explore the social values of cooperation, empathy, and compassion. In the simulation game *Parlé*, students soon realize that players must cooperate in order to win and that, through cooperation, problems can be solved and goals of the game achieved.

Opportunities for Integrating Higher Order Thinking Processes and Building Personal Responsibility

Players make choices and receive rapid feedback from other players; in this lively interchange, gifted students immediately realize the consequences of decisions. They learn that their actions affect others, as well as themselves, both in the present and in the future. Simulation games provide opportunities for gifted students to recognize the importance of personal responsibility in dealing constructively and effectively with the environment and in influencing action in the future.

Understanding the Role of Chance

Simulation games demonstrate that life is not always predictable, nor is it guided by logical plans. Gifted students learn that most individuals are rarely, if ever, completely in control of their lives. As a result, they learn the importance of flexibility in life decisions and action. Most designers of simulations include "chance variables" to provide experiences for the players to adapt to chance and change.

Knowledge and Skills Enhancement

Simulation games build upon the knowledge and skills that gifted students bring to the simulation. And, in the intense interaction of the games, students learn from one another. Simulations also increase gifted students' knowledge of specific terms, concepts, facts, structures, and relationships.

Understanding of Social Systems

Teachers can assist gifted students in developing social skills in simulation as they guide them through the process of examining individual and group opinions and attitudes. Simulation games also provide opportunities for gifted students to think about and ask the kinds of questions that expand understanding of social systems in a global situation.

Leadership Skills

Simulation games provide a safe and structured situation for gifted students to experiment, try new ideas and new behaviors, develop leadership skills to persuade others about their point of view, and initiate actions.

Independence in Action and Thought

In simulations, learning is turned over to the students, which gifted students with a strong sense of individuality and a need for independence thrive on. Because the teacher acts as a facilitator in simulation games, gifted students enjoy the intellectual freedom inherent in the gaming process. The rules of the game are there to direct the students; as a consequence, the teacher is not viewed as a judge or jury, but as an assistant in the gaming process. This teacher-role encourages students to focus attention on what is happening in the game and to relinquish the "push-pull" for control that sometimes exists between gifted students and their teachers. As a result, simulation games build and reinforce the close teacher-student working relationship that is needed for maximum learning.

Group Dynamics

Simulation creates a sense of community among the student participants, thus creating a low-risk environment in which gifted students build greater self-awareness. The problem-solving scenario in simulations actively engages gifted students, and requires considerable group interaction and communication. Active group interaction builds a sense of trust and community in gifted students, and develops a high degree of individual and group motivation because the students enjoy the group roles.

According to James Coleman, former director of the Johns Hopkins Center for Developing Simulation Games, the use of simulation reverses a common situation for the learner. Instead of having learning as the primary goal, the student now has learning material as a secondary motivation, a process necessary to reach the main goal of doing well in the simulation game (Coleman, 1996). In simulation games, students assimilate content material in order to carry out actions efficiently toward the goal of the game. With skillful debriefing, teachers can link game behavior to real-life problem solving.

Simulation games are used at the highest levels of international policy study. One example is Project IDEELS, an international interdisciplinary collaborative of diverse groups of educators and researchers from five higher education institutions in four European countries. IDEELS is engaged in developing, testing, evaluating, and implementing simulation scenarios, mathematical models, a software platform, and supporting materials. The goal of IDEELS is to provide Europeans with an effective means of harnessing the power, creativity, and richness of cultural diversity to address current challenges facing Europe. IDEELS owes much of its operating procedure to Project IDEALS, a telematics simulation directed by David Crookall at the University of Alabama and funded by the U.S.-based National Science Foundation (NSF), and from ICONS, an outstanding telematics simulation program with an international relations focus directed by Jonathan Wilkenfeld at the University of Maryland. As college and university students participate in IDEELS simulations, they learn to use computers and the Internet as tools for communication and collaboration as they are used in the workplace in Europe and in the global community. Students report learning to accept responsibility for their own learning and for the success of their team. Moreover, they gain experience in working together to accomplish shared goals and to experience conflict resolution.

A Teacher's Checklist for Effective Simulations

Powerful and deep learning takes place as gifted students engage in exciting and satisfying simulations. Effective simulations

- motivate and reward creative thinking;
- provide opportunities to encourage different points of view;
- demonstrate that life is not always predictable;
- provide experiences to deal constructively and effectively with the environment;
- build on student knowledge and skills;
- provide a safe and structured opportunity to experiment;
- build and reinforce close teacher-student working relationships; and
- create a sense or community.

Examples of Simulation Games

One way to better understand simulation games is to examine several different games, with differing key concepts, props, number of participants, and time involvement.

BaFá BaFá

In *BaFá BaFá*, developed by Gary Shirts (1974), players are divided into two cultures: Alpha and Beta. Separately, each group learns the rules specific to its own culture. Alpha is an in-group/out-group, a touching culture, and Beta is a foreign language-speaking, task-oriented culture. Once players learn and practice the rules of their own culture, observers and visitors are exchanged. After each exchange, the players return to their culture and try to describe their experiences in observing and interacting with the other culture. *BaFá BaFá* demonstrates that what seems irrational, contradictory, or unimportant in one culture may seem rational, consistent, and terribly important to another culture. Shirts developed *BaFá BaFá* for the Navy to help military personnel successfully coexist within different cultures.

Barnga

Barnga was created by Sivasailam Thiagarajan (1989), and the key concept is that cultural differences exist in subtle forms that are often covered up by obvious similarities. Players in groups of four are taught to play a quick card game. Each group thinks all the players are learning the same game, but each game is slightly different. After 5 minutes, the players are asked to play the games silently and to settle any disagreements by communicating through gestures. After 5 additional minutes, two players from each table are moved to the next table under the guise of a tournament. Because there are two sets of rules now in operation, there is heated discussion expressed through gestures. After 5 minutes of play at this table, the players shift once more to the next table. The game is terminated after another 5 minutes.

Infotactics

Infotactics, developed by Dorothy Sisk (1999), focuses on the problem of information overload that many people are experiencing in the Information Age. As people encounter more knowledge and become immersed in knowledge, it is increasingly difficult to really know "what is going on." In *Infotactics*, students participate in one of four leadership teams: Azul, Verde, Rojo and Amarillo. Each team follows a brief scenario to role-play and interact with the other teams. Each team has one "infotactic" to use in communicating with the other teams and one piece of information the other teams don't have. The goal of the simulation game is to communicate as a team and to convince the other teams of each individual team's leadership and point of view. The four infotactics used are Vapor tactic, Double Channel tactic, Need-to-Know tactic, and Generalizing tactic.

Land of the Sphinx and Land of the Rainbow

Land of the Sphinx and Land of the Rainbow was developed by Dorothy Sisk (1983) to assist a group of psychologists in understanding and experiencing cerebral differences and learning preferences. Although the game can take up to a half day with debriefing, it has been played successfully in two class periods with secondary gifted students.

The setting for the game is the year 2050, and a minimum of four travelers are selected to visit the two different lands: the Land of the Sphinx and the Land of the Rainbow. Each land is asked to develop three projects to shape the future of their land: (1) Education, (2) Research, and (3) Environment. In small groups, the students identify and develop their projects, and then each group receives the travelers. The scenario for the Land of the Sphinx describes it as being inhabited by people who trust logic, objectivity, and implicit action. Order is very important to them, particularly schedules and routine. The Land of the Rainbow is described as being inhabited by people who are interested in a deeper, larger, all-embracing reality, and they follow their hunches. Students in one land do not have the description or scenario of the people in the other land.

The travelers generate questions to ask the citizens of the two lands, which elicit many different reactions. The travelers are instructed to ask questions with enthusiasm and curiosity; to be bold, open, and courageous; and to find out as much about each land as possible. In the debriefing, the students discuss whether or not they felt welcome or comfortable in their assigned land, and the travelers are asked to select the land they would choose to remain in as a citizen. This game can be played with as many as 100 students. Large numbers of students will require the creation of several Lands of the Sphinx and Lands of the Rainbow to accommodate at least six citizens in each land and to provide a sufficient number of travelers to visit all of them.

In the debriefing, discussion will center around which environment is more conducive to aspiration, curiosity, and individual goal attainment. Students from different cultures quickly identify the similarities between the simulated lands and their home countries, and many of these students want to discuss the ways in which their homeland shapes their future. This simulation game has been used in leadership seminars with middle school and high school gifted students and as an opening exercise to build a sense of community in the residential Texas Governor's Honors program for gifted students. Gifted students quickly identify the similarity of the characteristics of the travelers and the characteristics of gifted students.

Parlé

Parlé was developed by Dorothy Sisk (1976) to provide gifted students an opportunity to experience leadership by simulating different roles in 10 imaginary countries: Shima, Myna, Ila, Usa, Pam, Bonay, Shivey, Lani, Ranu, and Bili. Each country has three factors to be considered: Defense, Resources, and Demography. The major theme of *Parlé* is the importance of negotiation and interdependence between and among countries. Several crisis incidents are introduced, such as a revolution in Ranu. The teacher/leader can vary the point of time to reflect the past or present, or the game can be projected into the future. The only way a country can win in this simulation is through cooperation and sharing of resources.

Tag Game

Tag Game, developed by Garry Shirts (1992) at Simulation Training Systems, is a short, highly participative game that encourages players to focus on similarities and differences and to discuss these openly in debriefing. Players wear tags of different shapes and colors, walk around silently, and observe each other. Then, without any talking, the teacher/leader asks the students to group themselves. After a couple of rounds, the players hand in their tags and receive new, very unique tags. Again, the students are asked to observe one another, but not to talk before deciding on how to form groups. Game time and debriefing combined usually takes less than an hour. Gifted students quickly list the obvious similarities and differences among people, but they soon begin to identify deeper, more abstract similarities and differences.

Elements of Simulation Games

- Time
- Props
- Number of Participants
- Debriefing

A Comparison of Elements of Simulations Games

A comparison of the selected simulation games across a range of gaming characteristics—time, props, number of participants, and debriefing—can be helpful in building greater understanding of simulation as a teaching strategy.

Time

Simulation games can take a short period of time; some, like *Tag Game*, *Parlé*, and *Barnga* can be accomplished in an hour. Or, they can take a longer extended period of time, as in *Land of the Sphinx and Land of the Rainbow* and *BaFá BaFá*, which can take from several hours to a half a day for completion.

Props

Some games use simple props or artifacts such as the paper clips and construction paper used in *Tag Game*, while other use more sophisticated props like those used in *BaFá BaFá*. Other games, such as *Land of the Sphinx and Land of the Rainbow*, use only the instructions. In addition, simulation games can simulate whole cultures or only specific aspects of a culture, as in *Parlé* and *BaFá BaFá*.

Number of Participants

Parlé can be played with 40 to 80 participants, or it can be played with as few as 14 individuals, although much of the rich interaction and involvement of the game is lost with the use of small numbers of participants. *Tag Game* can be played with 9 people, but it is more effective with 16 to 20. It can also be played in a large area using tables and chairs with 100 to 200 people. Most games have an optimum number for playing, but with ingenuity on the part of the teacher, the games can be reduced or expanded to accommodate varying numbers of participants. One simple way to expand a game is to run several games simultaneously.

Debriefing Issues

Parlé is a nonthreatening simulation game that can be used as an introduction to gaming for gifted students and to help them learn how to discuss sensitive issues. When the game ends, the teacher can debrief what occurred in the simulation and encourage students to draw analogies to real life. For example, a group of gifted high school students identified biased perception as a communication problem, and they listed a number of misconceptions they had experienced because of viewing another culture from the viewpoint of their own.

Teachers will need to encourage gifted students to identify and discuss specific real-life situations that are simulated in the games that focus on multicultural issues. For example, after playing *Land of the Sphinx and Land of the Rainbow*, the teacher can ask students to address what might be done when someone is placed in a situation of not knowing the rules in a new culture—but thinking they do. "Processing" is the heart of simulation games, and debriefing focuses on what happened, what the consequences of the actions were, how misperception can lead to mistakes, and how certain strategies are effective. Brozo and Simpson (2003) stressed the importance of teachers observing and debriefing stereotyping and dealing with content issues such as cultural biases, values, and the need for adaptation and accommodation.

Using Simulation Effectively

In using simulation games effectively with gifted students, it is important for the teacher to motivate the students with "warm-ups," including a brief introduction of the game and a simple explanation of the rules and the patterns of play. It is important that the presentation be clear, and the teachers needs to move on to accommodate the impatience and eagerness that gifted students may exhibit in wanting to get started in the gaming process. However, clarity of the expectations is essential for the game to progress. When the students begin to play the game, the role of the teacher is to be observant, alert, and unobtrusive. In calling for the game to halt for debriefing, a simple bridge from the game to debriefing can be "Let's talk about what happened during the past half-hour or so . . ."

Flexibility and imagination are essential in organizing gifted students for a successful experience in simulation games. The high degree of student-to-student communication in simulations requires an atmosphere that encourages physical and intellectual mobility. To facilitate this atmosphere, the teacher will need to develop a sense of timing—to be able to know or sense when it is appropriate to offer aid and support and when to interrupt the simulation for processing or debriefing of the action.

The debriefing or processing phase of simulation is an essential element; by analyzing experiences, gifted students capitalize on the full learning potential of the strategy. The importance of processing is reflected in Brozo and Simpson's (2003) assertion that, until the students have an opportunity to reflect, total learning has not taken place. Students learn and remember best when they fully participate in the debriefing. Gifted students can inductively arrive at a consensus of ideas, and the role of the teacher is to direct critical attention to the concepts and processes simulated in the game.

The open debriefing format of simulation encourages gifted students to share experiences, and initially they may need to describe what happened. However, it is helpful for them to hear the experiences of others, as well be able to share their own experiences. As the students discuss the beliefs and feelings they experienced during a simulation game, the teacher can then encourage them to analyze why certain things happened and identify the basis for their decisions. With a little teacher guidance and encouragement, debriefing sessions will naturally move to summarizing, generalizing, and identifying the big idea of the simulation game. "What we're talking about here is the need for negotiation," said one student, spontaneously identifying the organizing concept of the game after playing *Parlé*.

Another effective debriefing technique is to ask students to list and share specific ideas generated during the discussion and to make further generalizations based on these ideas. This process helps them draw meaningful conclusions and make broader generalizations since they are student-generated.

Clark (2002) cautioned teachers to be aware that the sensitivity and empathy gifted students experience in simulation games may cause them to lose their critical sense. Games can trigger intense emotional feelings, and disagreements may occasionally lead to expressions of personal hostility. A skillful and sensitive teacher can help prevent these outbursts by closely observing the group during the simulation, making special effort to resolve ill feelings as they emerge during the debriefing, and helping students leave their roles. In discussing disagreements, the teacher can ask the students to identify which rules were being ignored and why and encourage them to analyze their behavior during the game. This self-reflection will build on the interpersonal and intrapersonal behaviors of giftedness (Gardner, 1983).

Teachers need to ensure that simulation games are culturally appropriate since participative learning is not traditional in all cultures. Unfortunately, there is no set rule for making decisions on whether or not to use a simulation game. The factors that seem to be correlated with successful use of simulation include the comfort level of the teacher with the method, the degree of trust developed between the teacher and the students, and the effectiveness of the teacher in framing the game in terms that are meaningful and relevant to the students' maturity level. When these factors are considered, simulation games can be used successfully in cross-cultural training when there appears to be little or no chance for their success.

Designing a Simulation Game

A simulation game takes a real-life situation as a model and draws out the key features—the struggles, roles, and dilemmas. Simulation games imitate reality, and the players experience walking in the shoes of another. Rules, symbols, goals to be achieved, and the timeframe all motivate gifted students to become involved quickly from the very beginning of a simulation game.

Designing a simulation game is a complicated procedure and is not to be taken lightly. The following are six steps that are helpful for a designer:

1. Identify the key concepts or big ideas upon which the game will focus, then select the real-life situation the game will simulate.
2. Identify the structure of the game and the roles or characters.
3. Decide on a point in time for the simulation.
4. Establish the goals to be accomplished.
5. Identify needed resources or props.
6. Decide on the sequence of events.

Questions to be considered include:

- Are there external factors that need to be considered?
- Will there be some sheets, tables, graphs, chance cards, spinners, dice, board tokens, and similar devices to add to the structure of the game?

Once these six steps are addressed, then the rules can be written. What is the order of play? What do the players do? How does the game end?

In designing a game, it is essential to test, retest, and revise it. Adjust the game to reality, comprehensiveness, playability, and validity. Trying out a game with participants is important in troubleshooting potential problems. The International Simulation and Gaming Association (ISAGA) encourages its members and participants to field-test new games at association meetings with veteran gamers. *Infotactics* was introduced at an ISAGA meeting, and many new ideas and suggestions for revising it were offered by the participating players. Gifted students will enjoy assisting in the design and subsequent revision of games. This involvement provides a sense of ownership in the emerging game, and the involvement activates one characteristic of giftedness: being critical.

A format for designing games developed by Avis Reid (1987) can be quite helpful (see Figure 1). Reid suggested starting with a problem base and deciding on a concise statement of the problem, such as, "A communicable disease virus has broken out in a community." Then, the objectives of the simulation game are identified, such as (1) students will experience group dynamics in reaching consensus; (2) students will develop insight into their personal value system and the value system of others; and (3) students will experience a variety of decision-making methods.

After the objectives are identified, the scenes or scenario can be written, including past events, background information, point in time, setting, and any conditions that will affect the game. Such conditions might include the fact that the community is culturally diverse, including citizens who are Anglo, Hispanic,

---

Name of the Game

- **Statement of the Problem:** Be brief and precise.

- **Objectives:** Be specific. What do you plan to achieve?

- **Scenario:** Include past events, background information, the present time, setting, and conditions that may affect the game.

- **Characters:** Give a brief description of the physical characteristics, personality, and goals of the players in the game.

- **Point in Time:** The exact place and time the game begins.

- **Resources:** Props for the game—physical, social, economical, political, or personal.

- **Rules:** Rules that govern the players, the game pattern, scoring, and implementation.

- **Debriefing and Evaluation:** What did you experience in the process? What did you learn? Were the objectives reached and how can the game be improved?

Figure 1. Design Your Own Simulation

Note. From "Turn to Page 84," by Avis Reid, in *Creative Teaching of the Gifted* (p. 114), by D. Sisk, 1987, New York: McGraw-Hill. Copyright ©1987 by McGraw-Hill. Reprinted with permission.

Asian, and African American. The community is comparatively isolated and it is midwinter, so the decision concerning what to do about the communicable disease must be made in 24 hours.

Characters and their roles are then identified: doctors, nurses, parents, teachers, principals, students, community members and citizens who will be involved in the decision-making process. Brief descriptions can be written concerning the physical and personality characteristics of the characters. Keeping these descriptions brief will encourage students to use their creativity in role-playing the characters. Descriptions can be as brief as the following: "The doctor is the only one who knows how the cure or antidote must be used. He is to be assisted by an advisory panel of citizens, parents, teachers, principals, and students, including two nurses who are adamantly against using the antidote or serum." Roles can be more specific, leaving little opportunity for improvisation, or they can leave considerable opportunity for gifted students to add their own ideas and values to the characters.

After the characters and their goals have been established, Reid (1987), who was passionate about the use of simulation with gifted students, would announce, "Now you can decide on the point in time, then the action will begin." Physical, social, economical, political, or personal resources may need to be added, since resources add greater complexity to simulations and heighten students' interest.

Rules and rules administration (including rules that govern the student players), the game pattern, the scoring, and the implementation are the last to be added. In the case of the communicable disease simulation game, the rules are as follows:

> Several people (15) have been exposed to a communicable disease, and there is serum for only eight people. How can a decision be made to save eight people and to sacrifice the lives of seven others? Each person is given a role on the advisory panel and a certain number of points. A consensus is required for a decision to be made, and there is a time constraint of 1 hour.

The last step in devising a simulation game is the debriefing or processing. In the debriefing, the students examine how decisions were made and how they feel about the decision-making process. They can be encouraged to ask deeper questions, analyze the situation thoroughly, and search for more knowledge. For many gifted students, the empathy developed in simulations may lead to a more profound commitment to justice and development concerns. During debriefing, the teacher can reinforce the positive social attitudes that were observed and arrange follow-up experiences for the students to gather information to build greater understanding of the issues involved in decision making. Analogies can be drawn to present and past situations and from observations the gifted students share. Debriefing is an important part of simulation, and the time allotment is usually 25% of the total time allotted to a game. In the case of the communicable disease simulation, 1 hour is allotted, so the debriefing time would be 15 minutes.

In debriefing, the teacher will need to guide the students to ask themselves the following questions:

- Will the person understand me?
- Will the person be able to accept my feedback?
- Will the person be able to use the information?

The most significant consideration in the debriefing session is that feedback be constructive. Reflecting on the above three questions will help maximize the effectiveness of the students in giving positive feedback to one another.

Situations in Which Simulation Games Are Useful

Simulations have been useful in preparing students for exchange programs in which students experience living in different cultures. *BaFá BaFá* is most helpful in building an understanding of the importance of keen observation and flexibility in interacting and responding appropriately with people from different cultures.

Simulation games have also proved useful with foreign exchange graduate students in preparation for reentry to their home countries. At the Center for Creativity, Innovation, and Leadership (CCIL) at Lamar University, simulation games were used in the United States Agency for International Development (USAID) training programs for graduate students studying at major universities and colleges throughout the U.S. These students, who were mostly from under-developed countries, readily responded to simulations like *Land of the Sphinx and Land of the Rainbow*, and they quickly identified areas of misunderstanding that they anticipated encountering on return to their countries. In open discussions, they discussed these expected problems, including generalizations and expectations from families and friends concerning work and family relations. Most of the students had spent 2 to 4 years in the United States, and they had learned, accepted, and assimilated many aspects of Western culture. They realized how difficult it was going to be to return home and to reexperience the culture of their countries. Simulation provided opportunities for them to step outside the real dilemma of reentry and analyze the return in the safety of a simulation. *BaFá BaFá* was particularly helpful in stimulating a healthy exchange of ideas and generating positive strategies for successful reentry.

Simulation games are useful with a broad age span of students, and most games require little alteration or change in operating format to accommodate age differences. For example, *Parlé* can be played with middle school students studying environmental science to learn the importance of the interrelationship between the environment and humankind. Secondary students can play *Parlé* to focus on problems and issues dealing with foreign policy and the importance of personal diplomacy and individual responsibility in transforming sensitive international relationships. Recently, a group of sophomore students playing *Parlé* identified similarities to the Middle East controversy, and elementary gifted students successfully played *Parlé* to develop an understanding of the importance of leadership and the interaction of resources and demography in the political dilemma in Middle Eastern countries.

Simulation has been employed by schools and school districts to gather information and identify community attitudes toward proposals or changes being considered that impact the total system. For example, *Land of the Sphinx and Land of the Rainbow* was used to assist a school district in planning and hosting an international educational seminar. The simulation helped the district personnel to understand and appreciate the complexities of different cultures and the many different ways in which people respond and behave. The organizers of the conference who participated in the simulation said they gained many useful insights from playing it, particularly in how to organize the seminar to make it more meaningful and successful. They decided to incorporate different cultural aspects of the participating countries as resources, including specific customs of greeting, food, music, art, and dance.

Simulation games can be great levelers in assisting gifted students in facing new experiences and challenges, such as moving from elementary school to middle school. By playing *Tag Game*, for example, gifted students learn how to interact more effectively and how to become contributing members of a new and older group of students. In simulation games, gifted students also develop an awareness of their strengths and weaknesses, as well as the strengths and weaknesses of others. They also experience the power of being able to help others reach common group goals. Leu and Kinzer (2003) defined meaningful simulations as the ones in which students role-play and put themselves in the place of others to experience walking in their shoes.

Benefits and Outcomes From Using Simulation Games

In a discussion on the use of simulation games, Phil Phenix, professor emeritus at Columbia University, stressed that play is one of the more fundamental factors in the creation of culture and that simulation games can provide a means for making the topic at hand relevant to students' current reality (Phenix, 1987). Phenix emphasized the importance of reflection skills in simulation games, particularly when players role-play future roles in the limited time and space framework of a simulation. The players make choices to follow certain courses of action and reflect on those choices, and in that moment in time, gifted students turn the present into the future in order to sample it.

Manipulation of time and space is one of the more meaningful and motivating experiences of simulation. In simulations, gifted students eliminate the interval between learning concepts, skills, and application. Students blend the skills, values, and knowledge of the present and the future together to experience relevant and useful learning. Simulations provide gifted students opportunities to practice leadership and creative behavior in the context of a safe classroom environment under the guidance of their teachers (Lewis & Doorlag, 2003).

Comparison With Other Teaching Methods

Using the selected variables of responsiveness and variety of input modes to compare simulation with other teaching methods, including lectures, workbooks, textbooks, and computer-assisted presentations, it can be noted that simulation games require an active response from each student to the actions of other students. This interaction cycle is dynamic, and the pace of learning is more accelerated than learning with other teaching methods. A survey of more than 350 students in a school for gifted students found that the students overwhelmingly preferred the collaborative experiences in the group work of simulation games to more individual experiences (Christensen, 1994). Simulation games incorporate a wide variety of input methods and ways in which information can be presented, including speeches, prints, pictures, charts, maps, and diagrams, which broadens the appeal and positive learning for both teachers and students. The use of a number of props depends on the players and the teachers. A group of middle school gifted students playing *Land of the Sphinx and Land of the Rainbow* created songs, wrote histories of each land, and devised unique greetings for the visitors; one group of students even created a constitution that was dramatically presented to the travelers.

Some simulations present information through the physical positioning of tokens on a board, furniture in the room, or even the students themselves. Simulation games may take a longer period of time than more overtly didactic methods, but the learning in simulation is quick and often more insightful and meaningful for gifted students since the games are more active and intense than other teaching methods. The list of advantages and disadvantages in Figure 2 can be helpful for teachers to use in deciding if a simulation is an appropriate tool for a given lesson or area of study.

Conclusion

The highly motivating nature of simulation makes it a complementary teaching tool for gifted programs, and the intellectual jolt it provides gifted students in learning how to learn can be amazing. In debriefing sessions with their teachers and classmates, gifted students reflect on the content, skills, and values learned and relearned in simulation games. Gifted students learn how to make more intelligent decisions about life as they experience the variety of processes employed in simulation games, including interactive negotiation, persuasive communication, decision making, and creative problem solving. One of the more effective outcomes of simulation for gifted students is its positive effect on the study of issues.

Simulations have been used for decades in business, the military, government, and higher education. The potential use of simulation in K–12 programs is immense, and this potential is growing daily as witnessed by the increase in the number of simulation games and computer-based programs available for use in education. Simulation meets all five of the essential factors VanTassel-Baska and Little (2003) suggested for educators to keep in mind when assessing curricula for gifted students: complexity, depth, challenge, creativity, and acceleration.

Advantages	Disadvantages
• Active involvement • Fun and challenging • Encourages risk taking and creativity in a safe environment • Promotes change of learning pace • Builds community and shared experience • Promotes problem-solving skills and the development of analytical and critical thinking skills • Provides opportunities for practice • Employs social construction of knowledge • Simplifies complicated issues or concepts • Encourages empathy • Uses prior knowledge • Blends theory and strategy in a realistic experience • Promotes student-student interaction • Encourages students to expand their relationship with people • Enables students to make and act on their own choices	• Time-consuming • May require special space or equipment requirements • Expense of commercial games • Not considered legitimate training • Students may act and react immaturely • Cultural issues may arise with multicultural groups • Unsophisticated learners may not monitor their understanding • Intense enthusiasm for active learning may cause student resistance to more traditional learning • Can oversimplify complex issues and concepts • Not all students are metacognitively aware • Momentum of game may mask objectives • Students may have trouble or refuse to relinquish game roles • All students may not have the same experience • Some students may monopolize.

Figure 2. Advantages and disadvantages of simulation games

Note. Compiled from Brozo & Simpson (2003), Heward (2003), Leu & Kinzer (2003), Lewis & Doorlag (2003), Turnbull, Turnbull, Shank, Smith, & Leak (2003).

Teacher Statement

Through the use of simulations, my students have had the opportunity to gain a deeper understanding of big concepts. With my gifted elementary-age students, I've used a variety of simulations, ranging in length from a brief 10-minute impromptu simulation of an assembly line during a study of economics, to a 2-week *Mysterious Machines* simulation to explore and build machines and develop hypotheses for their uses.

One especially powerful simulation experience for my 4th- and 5th-grade gifted students was a 50-minute game of *Parlé* played during the time of Operation Iraqi Freedom. Through this simulation, my students gained a better understanding of the importance of relationships between countries and began to understand better the complexity of the issues leading to war. It was interesting to observe students during the initial moments of the simulation as they negotiated with other "countries" to develop allies "just in case they ever had problems." When the country of Shima experienced a famine, students from several other countries came forward with aid stating, "It was the right thing to do" or "We would want help if it were us," while others made the comment that they were holding back aid because "they did not want Shima to have too much and become too powerful." During the debriefing session following the simulation, one student commented on how his country had made an alliance with another powerful country and had sent them natural resources in exchange for an agreement that "they would be protected in case of future war, just like the United States and Great Britain." Through playing the simulation game *Parlé*, my students practiced cooperation, competition, empathy, and trust—skills that will help prepare them for their future.

—Lauri Kirsch

Discussion Questions

1. One consequences of an interdependent world is that people in any one country have to learn to think in intercultural terms. There are far too few opportunities for such learning on today's schools. What are some of the ways that simulations like *Parlé* could be used in a local school district's efforts to encourage students to be more aware of our growing multicultural society? In social studies? In language arts?

2. There are times when simulation games can become charged with heightened emotion. When students are debriefing, they may be quite candid with one another and make statements like, "That was just plain stupid." At that point, the teacher needs to intervene and make sure that hurt feelings are handled. Discuss how humor might be used to soothe the tension.

3. Climate setting for simulation is essential, and teachers must be cautious in attempting to hurry the game by skipping this aspect. The teacher can talk briefly about the value of simulation, of trying on new roles and "walking in someone else's shoes." Discuss the importance of climate setting, particularly the importance of legitimizing feelings and individual perceptions.

4. Processing is a key aspect of simulation, and the teacher needs to avoid close-ended questions because they tend to limit discussion. Discuss processing one of the games and list several open-ended questions that might be used. Remember to maintain a sense of "play" and that it is fun to act in simulation. Then, discuss what occurred even though the learning may be substantial and serious. For example, "When you were the leader in *Land of the Sphinx and Land of the Rainbow*, how did you feel when the travelers came to your country?"

5. Think of a situation that could be made into a simulation. Using the guidelines included in Figure 1, outline the beginning of a simulation.

6. There are cultural differences in interacting with others, and some of your students may be reluctant or unwilling to enter into a simulation game. Discuss how you would handle this situation. What are some roles the student or students might play, such as observer, time keeper, and so forth?

Teacher Resources

Language Arts Publications

Arner, B. (1995). *Library detective.* Carlsbad, CA: Interact.
This is a simulation game of solving a mystery while learning how to find library information. A precious library manuscript has been stolen, and students join in cooperative learning teams and work to find the missing manuscript. Appropriate for grades 4–8.

Beeler, C. (1992). *American nostalgia.* Waco, TX: Prufrock Press.
American Nostalgia is a simulation that explores the literature of early 20th-century America. Students create a communications corporation and develop and communicate their ideas about the drama of the early 1900s. Students produce exciting and creative projects as a part of their corporation activity. Appropriate for grades 7–12.

Jaffe, C. (1991). *Enchanted castle.* Carlsbad, CA: Interact.
In this simulated journey through a fantasy world of fairy tales, students receive a Story Guide Map and Travel Tickets and plan a journey to an enchanted castle. Along the way, they stop to read fantasy fairy tales and complete intriguing activities. Appropriate for grades 2–4.

Jaffe, C., & Liberman, M. (1989). *Odyssey.* Carlsbad, CA: Interact.
In this simulated journey through the world of classic Greek mythology, student teams meet heroes, heroines, gods, and goddesses. Students read at least eight classical myths in teams. They also work to climb Mt. Olympus by working through each level, with team members analyzing the myths cooperatively, then completing a comprehension worksheet for group evaluation. Appropriate for grades 4–8.

Math Publications

Bippert, J., & Steiger, J. (1989). *Shopping spree.* Carlsbad, CA: Interact.
As contestants on a game show, students reinforce their calculator skills, make purchasing decisions, and spend game show money in six different shops. Appropriate for grades 3–8.

Day, M. (1980). *Stock market.* Carlsbad, CA: Interact.
In this math and economics simulation, students have an imaginary $100 to invest. They try to make wise decisions by researching their purchases. Appropriate for grades 6–12.

Middendorf, C. J., & White, F. (1991). *Math quest.* Carlsbad, CA: Interact.
This is an adventure simulation focusing on problem-solving techniques in which cooperative learning groups explore four strange worlds in search of great treasure. Students apply several math problem-solving strategies while trekking through Dinosaurland, Fantasyland, Sportland, and Numberland. Appropriate for grades 3–8.

Science Publications

Beeler, C. (1992). *Earth friendly.* Waco, TX: Prufrock Press.
Earth Friendly is a simulation designed around environmental protection issues. Students engage in small-group work to create an ecologically sound city—an environment to provide a safe dwelling for all wildlife and plant life, pollution-free air, and freedom from the threat of toxic waste and nuclear disaster. In this simulation, gifted students solve problems, set and achieve goals, and develop an in-depth understanding of environmental issues related to environmental protection. Appropriate for grades 4–10.

Beeler, C. (1992). *Endangered species.* Waco, TX: Prufrock Press.
Students learn about endangered species, the fragile nature of ecologies, and the impact humans have on nature. They solve ecological problems and develop a deeper appreciation of ecological responsibilities. Appropriate for grades 4–10.

Bippert, J., & Vanding, L. (1995). *Project polaris.* Carlsbad, CA: Interact.
In cooperative learning space pods, students use estimation and hands-on measurements at each of 10 constellation stopping points in space. The mission is to build a space station where everyone can convene in a united effort to ensure galactic peace. Appropriate for grades 3–6.

Flindt, M. (1990). *Zoo.* Carlsbad, CA: Interact.
In this simulation, the mayor and city council members plan to close Zooland because it is outdated, the animals are poorly treated, and attendance is declining. The students want to save Zooland by taking action. Appropriate for grades 2–5.

Libetzky, J., & Hildebrand, J. (1993). *Adapt.* Carlsbad, CA: Interact.
Students become geographers examining the importance of the physical environment to the lives of past and present human beings living in hunting and gathering societies. Appropriate for grades 6–9.

Wallace, D. (1991). *Clone.* Carlsbad, CA: Interact.
In this simulation of a congressional hearing on genetic engineering, students explore what makes us human. They also explore such issues as, if a human is cloned, does the clone have human rights? Appropriate for grades 6–12.

Wesley, J. (1993). *Ecopolis*. Carlsbad, CA: Interact.
In this simulation of a community struggling to solve ecological problems, students study a 150-year ecosystem history and then examine ecological issues in the imaginary city of Ecopolis, whose population has soared to 225,000. Appropriate for grades 6–9.

Social Studies Publications

Beeler, C. (1992). *Western exploration*. Waco, TX: Prufrock Press.
Western Exploration provides opportunities for students to journey through the Old West by taking the part of historical characters. Students research and create visual and written representations of this period of American history, exploring its literature, history, culture, and art. Appropriate for grades 4–10.

Beeler, C. (1992). *Medieval destinations*. Waco, TX: Prufrock Press.
Medieval Destinations is a simulation that engages students in exploring the history and literature of the European Middle Ages. Students take a flight across England during the Middle Ages in a variety of "flying machines." They accumulate mileage by studying the history of the period, completing drawings of the architecture, and exploring the literature as they complete research projects.

Broderbund/Learning Company. (1985). *Where in the world is Carmen San Diego?* San Rafael, CA: Author.
Students learn facts and skills in geography while tracking Carmen across the globe. Appropriate for grades 5–12.

Lacey, B. (1998). *Calhoun vs. Garrison*. Carlsbad, CA: Interact.
This simulation uses a confrontational talk show format between Southern advocate John C. Calhoun and abolitionist William Lloyd Garrison. They debate whether or not Americans should allow slavery to remain in the nation. Appropriate for grades 7–12.

Plantz, C., & Callis, J. M. (1995). *Pacific Rim*. Carlsbad, CA: Interact.
This simulation helps students understand the growing importance of Pacific Rim countries, lands, peoples, and cultures. Students complete research projects and written reports. They also simulate travel on a ship from Japan to New Zealand. Appropriate for grades 5–9.

Addresses and Web Sites

Association for Business Simulations and Experimental Learning (ABSEL)
http://www.absel.org

Broderbund
500 Redwood Blvd.
P.O. Box 6121
Novato, CA 94948
(800) 521-6263
(415) 382-4582 (fax)
http://www.broderbund.com

Electronic Arts
http://www.ea.com

Elyssabeth Leigh, President
Faculty of Education
University of Technology, Sydney
P.O. Box 123
Broadway NSW 2007 Australia
Elyssebeth.Leigh@uts.edu.au
http://www.education.uts.edu.au/ostaff/staff/elyssebeth_leigh.html

Intercultural Press
P.O. Box 700
Yarmouth, ME 04096
(866) 372-2665
(207) 846-5181 (fax)
http://interculturalpress.com

International Simulation and Gaming Association (ISAGA)
Markus Ulrich, General Treasurer, SAGSAGA Representative
Ulrich Creative Simulations (UCS)
Blaufahnenstr. 14
CH-8001 Zuerich, Switzerland
+41-1-253-1335
+41-1-251-3869 (fax)
markus.ulrich@ucs.ch
http://www.isaga.info

INTERACT
P.O. Box 900
Fort Atkinson, WI 53538
(800) 359-0961
(800) 700-5093 (fax)
interact@highsmith.com
http://www.teachinteract.com

North American Simulation and Gaming Association (NASAGA)
P.O. Box 78636
Indianapolis, IN 46278
(317) 387-1424
(317) 387-1921 (fax)
info@nasaga.org
http://www.nasaga.org
Prufrock Press
P.O. Box 8813
Waco, TX 76714-8813
(800) 998-2208
(800) 240-0333 (fax)
http://www.prufrock.com

Gary R. Shirts
BaFá BaFá
Simile II
218 Twelfth Street,
P.O. Box 910
Del Mar CA 92014

Simulation Training Systems
P.O. Box 910
Del Mar, CA, 92014
(800) 942-2900
(858) 792-9743 (fax)
http://www.stsintl.com

S. Thiagarajan
Barnga
4423 E. Trailridge Rd.
Bloomington, IN 47408-9633
(812) 332-1478
(812) 332-5701 (fax)
thiagi@thaigi.com
http://www.thiagi.com

References

Brozo, W., & Simpson, M. (2003). *Readers, teachers, learners: Expanding literacy across the content areas.* Columbus, OH: Merrill/ Prentice Hall.

Christensen, P. (1994). An investigation of gifted students' perceptions involving competitive and noncompetitive learning situations. In N. Colangelo, S. G. Assouline, & D. L. Ambroson (Eds.), *Talent development II: Proceedings of the 1993 Henry B. and Jocelyn Wallace National Research Symposium on Talent Development* (pp. 505–507), Dayton: Ohio Psychology Press.

Clark, B. (2002). *Growing up gifted: Developing the potential of children at home and at school* (6th ed.). Columbus, OH: Merrill.

Coleman, J. S. (1996). In defense of games. *American Behavioral Scientist, 10,* 3–4.

Crookall, D., & Oxford, R. L. (1991). *Simulation, gaming, and language learning.* New York: Newbury House.

Dewey, J. (1916). *Democracy and education.* New York: Macmillan.

Drummer, L. J. (2002). *Computer simulation in education.* Springfield: University of Illinois at Springfield. Retrieved June 11, 2004, from http://students.uis.edu/ldrum01s/papers.html

Friend, M., & Cook, L. (2000). *Interactions: Collaboration skills for school professionals* (3rd ed.). New York: Longman.

Gardner, H. (1983). *Frames of mind: The theory of multiple intelligences.* New York: BasicBooks.

Gregory, T. (2000). *Social studies curricula for gifted learners in elementary and middle school.* Unpublished master's thesis, College of William and Mary, Williamsburg, VA.

Heward, W. (2003). *Exceptional children: An introduction to special education.* Columbus, OH: Merrill/Prentice Hall.

Joyce, B. R., Weil, M. E., & Calhoun, E. (2003). *Models of teaching* (7th ed.). Boston: Allyn and Bacon.

Leu, D., Jr., & Kinzer, C. K. (2003). *Effective literacy instruction K–8: Implementing best practice* (5th ed.). Columbus, OH: Merrill/Prentice Hall.

Lewis, R. B., & Doorlag, D. H. (2003). *Teaching special students in general education classrooms* (6th ed.). Columbus, OH: Merrill/Prentice Hall.

Paul, R., & Elder, L. (2001). *Critical thinking: Tools for taking charge of your learning and your life.* Upper Saddle River, NJ: Prentice Hall.

Phenix, P. (1987). *Views on the use, misuse, and abuse of instructional materials.* Paper presented at the annual meeting of the National Leadership Training Institute for Gifted and Talented, Houston, TX.

Reid, A. (1987). Turn to page 84. In D. Sisk, *Creative teaching of the gifted* (pp. 116–117). New York: McGraw-Hill.

Renzulli, J., Leppen, J., & Hays, T. (2000). *The multiple menu model: A practical guide for developing differentiated curriculum.* Mansfield Center, CT: Creative Learning Press.

Romme, G. A. (2003). *Microworlds for management education and learning.* Tilburg, The Netherlands: Tilburg University.

Sandling, M. M. (2003). Adapting social studies curricula for high-ability learners. In J. VanTassel-Baska & C. A. Little (Eds.), *Content-based curriculum for high-ability learners* (pp. 219–257). Waco, TX: Prufrock Press.

Shirts, R. G. (1974). *BaFá BaFá.* Del Mar, CA: Simulation Training Systems.

Shirts, R. G. (1992). *Tag game.* Del Mar, CA: Simulation Training Systems.

Sisk, D. (1976). *Parlé. A simulation game:* Washington, DC: Department of Health, Education, & Welfare.

Sisk, D. (1983). *Land of the Sphinx and Land of the Rainbow.* Beaumont, TX: Center for Creativity, Innovation, and Leadership, Lamar University.

Sisk, D. (1987). *Creative teaching of the gifted.* New York: McGraw-Hill.

Sisk, D. (1999). *Infotactics.* Beaumont, TX: Center for Creativity, Innovation, and Leadership, Lamar University.

Thiagarajan, S. (1989, June). *Barnga: A simulation game on cultural diversity.* Yarmouth, ME: Intercultural Press.

Turnbull, R., Turnbull, A., Shank, M., Smith, S., & Leal, D. (2002). *Exceptional lives: Special education in today's schools.* Columbus, OH: Merrill/Prentice Hall.

VanTassel-Baska, J., & Little, C. A. (2003). *Content-based curriculum for high-ability learners.* Waco, TX: Prufrock Press.

Supporting and Enhancing Gifted Programs

Chapter 19

Teaching Gifted and Talented Students in Regular Classrooms

by **Tracy L. Riley**

frequently suggested means of giving gifted and talented students a variety of options is a "menu approach," which is an appropriate analogy for examining methods and materials for teaching gifted students in regular classrooms. A menu is a bill of fare, *carte de jour*, or list of choices most commonly associated with restaurants. The menu may be written on a blackboard, printed on a card, or explained by a hostess. Prices may or may not be included, and there may be different menus for different purposes and people. These may feature appetizer, main courses, desserts, and special. Kids' meals, vegetarian options, and senior citizens' discounts, as well as mouth-watering descriptions of culinary delights, might be offered. All of this is to provide customers with enough options and information that they can make informed decisions and leave the restaurant satisfied and with full stomachs.

The key terms that appear time and again in gifted education match those of a good restaurant's menu: *choice, variety, flexibility, appropriateness, relevance, comprehensively planned*. But, behind any good restaurant menu is the staff, the chefs who prepare the meals and wait staff who serve them, both of whom have one goal: to satisfy the customer. This translates to classroom practice through the work of the teacher, who must not only provide a good menu, but also facilitate the selection, preparation, and consumption of a feast. To do this, he or she must know the customers, the raw ingredients on hand, his or her own skills and abilities in the kitchen, and ways of measuring customer satisfaction. In delivering the classroom menu, other key terms begin to take on importance: *enriched, accelerated, real, meaningful, inclusive, integrated, stimulating, depth,* and *breadth.* Just as the owner of a five-star restaurant knows his or her clientele and aims to provide just what they want, teachers in regular classrooms must begin by understanding gifted and talented students, their strengths and interests, the theory behind qualitative differentiation, and its translation into classroom practice.

This chapter describes the relationship between gifted and talented students and the principles of qualitative differentiation embedded in both enriched and accelerated strategies within regular classrooms. The strategies described use individualized assessment to identify strengths, interests, skills, and abilities so that responsive educational options can be flexibly delivered. The principles and practices of schoolwide strategies and those based in individual classrooms are shared. Finally, answers to some frequently asked questions regarding regular classroom practices are contemplated, and materials designed to support gifted and talented students and their teachers are recommended.

Not Just Gifted on Wednesdays

Gifted and talented students are characterized by their unique cognitive and affective strengths, abilities, qualities, and interests. Educators and parents of gifted and talented students can quickly rattle off their distinctive behaviors: an advanced vocabulary, quick wit, inquisitive thinking, emotional sensitivity, rapid pace of learning, high energy levels, leadership skills, and so on. It is recognized that these students have exceptional abilities or the potential for exceptional abilities in relation to their peers, be they of the same age, culture, socioeconomic background, or gender. From these behaviors, many definitions or concepts of giftedness, along with tools for identification, have developed and continue to be hotly debated. But, more importantly, special provisions are made to help create a better match between gifted and talented students and their unique learning characteristics.

There is a continuum of approaches, ranging from withdrawal programs to full-time schools. Many of these are described in this textbook, and they are theoretically sound, research-driven, and practically plausible. But, when reading between the lines, it becomes clear that they are often part-time solutions to full-time problems. In other words, though these provisions aim to meet the needs of gifted and talented students, unless they are full-time special schools, they probably fall short of doing so. The skills, abilities, strengths, and interests of gifted and talented students, just like those of all individuals, are present 24 hours a day, 7 days a week. Exploring ideas in a resource room, working alongside a mentor, preparing for a competition, or being accelerated for one subject for *part* of one's education does not address these ever-present special abilities.

Even when special provisions are in place, gifted and talented students continue to spend the majority of their education in heterogeneous, mixed-ability classrooms. This has always been the case, but when coupled with cutbacks to gifted education funding and the inclusive education movement of the early 1990s (Willard-Holt, 1994), the push for even more time in regular classrooms increases. For specialists in gifted education who have long advocated for special provisions for gifted and talented students, many of which are outside mainstreamed classrooms, the result of this wake-up call seems to have been twofold. Firstly, there has been the application of many gifted education principles and practices, particularly those associated with differentiation, to all students (George, 1997; Heacox, 2002; Renzulli, 1999; Tomlinson, 1999, 2001a). Secondly, the ways in which teachers can understand and address the needs of gifted and talented students within regular classrooms have been articulated (Smutney, Walker, & Meckstroth, 1997; Winebrenner, 2001).

Differentiation is the "process of assessing individual needs and responding with appropriate learning experiences" (George, 1997, p. 10). When differentiating instruction, "teachers begin where students are" (Tomlinson, 1999, p. 2), meaning that educators must recognize the many variances in students: learning styles, rates of learning, activities, interests, expectations, motivation, outcomes, abilities, resources, skills, tasks and parental or family support (George). "Differentiating instruction means changing the pace, level, or kind of instruction . . . in response to individual learners' needs, styles, or interests" (Heacox, 2002, p. 5).

Renzulli (1999) best summed up the rationale for the emergence of differentiated approaches for all students, not just for the gifted:

> respect for the abilities, interests, and learning styles of all students, would: (1) guard against charges of elitism and undemocratic practice, (2) provide a flexible vehicle for developing the talents of students who might otherwise go unrecognized, and (3) allow us to continue to serve our highest achieving students. In other words, a consistent democratic philosophy of education for all students legitimizes differentiation for all students. (pp. 28–29)

The principles of differentiation are indeed important considerations for all students, including gifted and talented students. However, recognition that one size doesn't fit all and responding to that with differentiation for all is *only* of value to gifted and talented students when their uniqueness is put into the formula. Otherwise, there is the danger that this philosophy will negate the need for other provisions for gifted and talented students—and this should not be the case. As Renzulli (1999) stated in regard to the Schoolwide Enrichment Model, "I would be extremely disappointed if someone said, 'We don't have a gifted program because we use Schoolwide Enrichment'" (p. 41).

Delisle (2000) takes this a step further with his belief that educators have made an erroneous assumption that "what is good for the gifted is good for all learners" (p. 36), and he raises fears that differentiation for all, even with the best of intentions, may quickly be interpreted as the old one-size-fits-all solution.

"Everyone benefits somewhat, but the gifted child benefits somewhat less than others in the classroom" (Delisle, p. 36). Without examining the unique needs of gifted and talented learners and providing appropriate educational interventions for meeting those, "'differentiation for all' may masquerade itself as the panacea for meeting their potential—but it will clearly be a façade" (Riley, in press).

Therefore, it is the combination of strategies that enable differentiation for all students and those aimed at gifted and talented students that holds the most promise. Acknowledgement of the different and varied learning and emotional needs of gifted and talented students, alongside the reality factor that they are first and foremost being educated in regular classrooms, necessitates changes or modifications to the content, processes, and products of learning in all classrooms, for all gifted and talented students, by all teachers, all the time. But, "educators today can respond successfully . . . by bringing the considerable resources, research, and experience of educators of the gifted to bear on the regular classroom" (McDaniel, 2002, p. 112). This begins by remembering that gifted students are not just gifted on Wednesdays; rather, they exhibit qualitatively different behaviors and characteristics everyday.

Qualitative Differentiation

The response to giftedness and talent is not simply differentiation, but qualitative differentiation: doing different kinds of things, not more of the same things. In other words, students who are provided with a qualitatively different education are not working their way up the same ladder, but *changing ladders*. Modifications to learning experiences are made in degree and kind, marked by dissimilarity, not similarity. In a practical sense, this means gifted students may need modifications that are of a different type altogether from what works for other students. As Tomlinson (2001b) said, "Differentiated instruction is not just 'tailoring the same suit of clothes'" (p. 3).

So, what do teachers tailor? As stated earlier, adjustments are made to content, processes, and products to better suit individual student needs. *Content* refers to what students are taught and learn; *processes* refer to how students are taught and learn; and *products* refer to the outcomes, or ways in which students demonstrate what they have learned. The New Zealand Ministry of Education (2000) expanded on these ideas:

- Content: concepts, information, ideas, and facts;
- Processes: how new material is presented, what activities students are involved in, and what teaching methods are used;
- Products: tangible or intangible results of student learning, "real" solutions to "real" problems. (p. 36)

A synthesis of best practices associated with qualitative differentiation for gifted and talented students is presented in Table 1. It should serve as the

Table 1

Principles of Qualitative Differentiation

Content should be	Processes should be	Products should be
• Abstract, centered around broad-based themes, issues, and problems • Integrated, making multi-disciplinary connections • In-depth and with breadth • Self-selected based upon student interests and strengths • Planned, comprehensive, related, and mutually reinforcing • Culturally inclusive, appropriate, and relevant • Advanced in both complexity and sophistication • Gender-balanced and inclusive • Enriched with variety, novelty, and diversity • Embedded within methods of inquiry, emulating the work of professionals • Inclusive of moral, ethical, and personal dimensions • Explored through the study of the lives of gifted people	• Independent and self-directed, yet balanced with recognition of the value of group dynamics • Inclusive of a service component, or opportunity to share outcomes for the good of others, like the community or family • Stimulating higher levels of thinking (analysis, synthesis, and evaluation) • Creative, with the chance to problem find and problem solve • Accelerated in both pace and exposure • An integration of basic skills and higher level skills • Open-ended, using discovery or problem-based learning strategies • Real—mirroring the roles, skills, and expertise of practitioners • Designed to develop research skills; time management, organizational and planning abilities; decision-making processes; and personal goal setting • Metacognitive, allowing students to reflect upon their own ways of thinking and learning • Created with the aim of developing self-understanding, specifically in relation to giftedness • Facilitated by mentors, as well as teachers	• The result of real problems, challenging existing ideas, and creating new ones • Developed using new and real techniques, materials, and ideas • Evaluated appropriately and with specific criteria, including self-evaluation • Self-selected • Wide in variety • Designed for an appropriate audience • Transformations of ideas, shifting students from the role of consumers to producers of knowledge

Note. Adapted from "Qualitative Differentiation for Gifted and Talented Students" by T. Riley, in D. McAlpine & R. Moltzen (Eds.), *Gifted and talented: New Zealand perspectives* (2nd ed.), in press, Palmerston North, New Zealand: Massey University. Copyright © Massey University. Adapted with permission.

roadmap for *all* educational opportunities for gifted students in the regular classroom, enriched or accelerated. It is important to remember that the adaptations made to content, processes, and products should be qualitative, not quantitative. Qualitative differentiation is not about more of the same; rather, it incorporates "well-thought-out, meaningful learning experiences that capitalize on students' strengths and interests" (Ministry of Education, 2000, p. 36). Finally, without evidence of quality determined by the unique nature of gifted students, differentiation is merely a security blanket that provides no real safety.

These principles should be woven through both enriched and accelerated educational options. *Enrichment* refers to the horizontal broadening of the curricular aims and objectives, and *acceleration* is the vertical movement through those. Ideally, both of these options are used in tandem, as opposed to an either/or approach. Thus, in regular classrooms, both enrichment-based and acceleration-based approaches should be used and should involve modification to content, processes, and products. Again, the goal here is not to offer more of the same, but something qualitatively different. For example, a child completing his vocabulary words should not be given yet another 20 words or even a set of harder words on a similar worksheet. By applying the strategies discussed later in this chapter, this child's learning experiences can quickly move away from being boring and repetitive to being flexible, relevant, choice-filled, appropriate, and challenging.

Getting to Know Gifted and Talented Students

Understanding gifted and talented students entails ongoing assessment and the many methods identifying special abilities, including formal and informal assessment, parent nomination, observation by teachers, peer nomination, and self-inventories of interests and strengths. The combination of all these ingredients results in a profile of the student as an exceptional individual and serves as the "trigger that activates the differentiated curriculum" (Braggett, 1994, p. 71).

In order to "pull the trigger," educators must rely on both identification and assessment and, in doing so, must undertake the following steps:

1. Determine appropriate identification and assessment methods and use a variety of them. The methods used should reflect the goals and objectives of learning experiences; the nature of the classroom environment; the student's age, culture, and gender; and so on.
2. Use the data gathered to differentiate the content, processes, and products of planned individual and group learning experiences.
3. Actively seek better fitting learning experiences for gifted and talented students by using identification and assessment data in curricular decision making (Riley, 2000).

In short, assessment of any nature should be purposeful. Teachers in differentiated classrooms "study the results," seriously considering the implications for themselves and their students (Tomlinson, 1999). By continuously gathering information about the strengths and interests of gifted and talented students from a variety of sources, assessment and instruction become inseparable—another key principle of differentiation (Tomlinson).

Identification of Giftedness and Talent

An all-too-often overlooked tool for regular classroom teachers wanting to understand gifted and talented students better is the identification process for special programs. Sometimes, its only purpose seems to be the provision of a label or placement in gifted and talented programs, which is short-sighted. Identification is a "means to an end and not an end in itself" (Ministry of Education, 2000, p. 27). Data collected should not be used just for identification, but also as the basis of planning learning experiences for gifted and talented students. Educators need to unpack the objective and subjective information obtained through the identification process, using it as evidence to create a relevant and effective plan for differentiation (Rogers, 2002). Thus, regular classroom teachers need to be privy to the means, reasons, and results of any identification procedures for gifted programs.

In order for this to happen, gifted education specialists must create transparent plans for screening and identification, and they must share this information with regular classroom teachers. For example, it is not particularly useful to know that a child is included in a withdrawal program because his or her achievement test score is in the top ranges. What *is* useful is looking behind the score by analyzing the individual subtests and the student's strengths and weaknesses on those. In this scenario, it is also important to remember the value of off-grade-level, or above-grade-level, testing, which aims to remove the ceiling that grade-level tests can create. Similarly, information gathered from other sources, such as parents, teachers, and the students themselves, should be readily available to all teachers.

Many schools document identification information in students' cumulative folders. As Smutney et al. (1997) noted, "Documentation showing what the child knows and is able to do should be maintained and passed along from teacher to teacher" (p. 121). Additionally, Winebrenner (2001) has pointed out the value of cumulative records as greater assurance of consistency in provision as students make the transition from one classroom or school to another. This also applies to the relationship between specialized gifted programs and the regular classroom. All teachers need to understand why and how students have been identified. However, in many cases, only the gifted education specialist pays much attention to this information; in these instances, then a more transparent, less fragmented system of identification is clearly needed.

Ongoing Assessment

The second tool for getting to know gifted and talented students is ongoing assessment. There are three types of assessment that are critical in understanding gifted students:

1. preassessment;
2. formative assessment; and
3. cumulative assessment.

Preassessment is one of the most recommended practices in gifted education. This simply means that a student's level of ability and interest is determined *before* teaching even begins. It may be nothing more than utilizing typical assessment tools planned for the end of a unit of study at the start. Tests, checklists, quizzes, class discussions, journal entries, and portfolios intended to measure the achievement of learning objectives should not only be used for assessing mastery, but also for planning. Preassessment using everyday approaches means educators "don't have to reinvent the wheel, just rotate and realign it" (Riley, 2000, p. 3).

There are additional strategies recommended for predetermining the knowledge and skills of gifted and talented learners. Roberts and Roberts (see Chapter 7) and Winebrenner (2001) have recommended several strategies as appropriate for gifted and talented students. The first is called "Five Most Difficult First." A teacher simply asks the five most difficult questions to be answered at the end of a unit or lesson at the beginning. If a student can answer those prior to the start, then a differentiated learning experience is warranted. The second strategy is allowing students the opportunity to design a mind map, visually sharing information they know and the interrelationships they grasp before a unit of study is undertaken. By giving students key words, the teacher can allow them to share their knowledge, experiences, and interests with a graphic design. A third technique is a KW chart. On a KW chart, students detail what they know (K) and what they want to find out (W). The information students give in K can be analyzed in relation to core goals and objectives, and their questions in W can be used as the basis for differentiated learning experiences.

Formative assessment refers to daily checks on achievement, and cumulative (or summative) assessment takes place at the end of a unit, term, or year of study. These types of assessment can be used similarly to preassessment to determine what students know and do not yet know. Careful documentation and analysis of both cumulative and formative assessment scores give insight into the strengths and weaknesses of students. For example, by charting a student's daily scores on timed mathematics quizzes, one teacher quickly realized the mismatch between his expectations and the performance of a bright mathematician. The consistent scores of 100% over several weeks was an indicator that the child was well beyond the aims and objectives. Using assessment for more than marks in a grade book means that teaching decisions and plans are informed and subsequently more relevant to gifted and talented learners.

Interest and Learning Preferences

Many of the strategies discussed so far profile student readiness (strengths and needs), but how do educators determine their interests and learning preferences? Tomlinson (1999) recommended that all students in a differentiated classroom should be given an opportunity to examine and share their individual differences early on. The strategies she suggested are:

- graphing their perceived strengths and weaknesses of skills, understandings, and the like;
- writing autobiographies about themselves as learners; and
- answering questions about positive and negative school experiences, best and worst subjects, or effective and ineffective ways of learning.

Other ideas might be setting individual learning goals for the year, term, or unit of study; designing a personal shield or other product about themselves as learners; contributing to a class book, *All About Us*, which rotates from home to home, documenting what they do, who they are with, and so forth; going on a "people hunt," during which they find classmates who match certain descriptions (like "someone who's read all the *Harry Potter* books" or "someone who's visited a science lab"); or undertaking "buddy interviews," in which students find out interesting facts about a classmate and share those with others in the class (Riley, 2000). Smutney et al. (1997) recommended interviewing young children, asking questions like: What are some of the things you do best? What are some things that you like to do? What do you like best in school and why? All of these approaches give "insight into the child's thinking, aspirations, home situation, and sense of self-determination" (Smutney et al., p. 9).

Involving parents is another avenue for developing a profile of giftedness. Smutney et al. (1997) recommended requesting pictures, products, and information about children's strengths, interests, and experiences. This moves beyond simply involving parents in formal identification of giftedness and should be facilitated in every classroom early in the school year.

More formal approaches to understanding interests and learning preferences may also be utilized. For example, George (1997), Renzulli and Smith (1978), and Heacox (1991) have provided learning style inventories. Renzulli (1996) has developed the Interest-A-Lyzer for examining present and potential student interests. Within this group of inventories, Kettle, Renzulli, and Rizza (n.d.) created My Way . . . An Expression Style Instrument, used for helping students and their teachers understand product preferences. Winebrenner (2001) included an interest survey in her book *Teaching Gifted Kids in the Regular Classroom*, Rogers (2002) created both an interest inventory and ways of learning scales for students, and Riley (2000) provided two additional suggestions: All About Me and What If?

Finally, Clark and Callow (1998) reiterated the value of using observation as a technique for better understanding students because it gives a "fuller picture of a child beyond tests and statutory assessment procedures . . . [and] as far as able children are concerned, this fuller picture might ensure that they are not bored or demotivated by what is on offer" (pp. 77–78). Observation provides inside information on what students achieve and how they achieve it. Careful observation gives teachers clues for evaluating and planning—direct feedback on what works and what doesn't. Clark and Callow take observation a step further in suggesting that it be partnered with regular discussions with gifted and talented students. As they stated, "able students are more capable of such discussion, which can shed light on how they learn and how they learn best" (pp. 78–79).

Determining individual differences in learning is the foundation of differentiation for all students. Preassessment of readiness, interests, and learning preferences is a necessary component of differentiation. But, it requires more than just doing it. Action based on preassessment is then required, resulting in appropriate differentiation.

Putting the Theory Into Practice

The strategies for creating qualitatively differentiated opportunities for gifted and talented students in regular classrooms may be facilitated by a single teacher or through a schoolwide approach. Both of these are examined in this section, beginning with the most frequently recommended practices for individual classroom teachers. It should be noted that, while these classroom strategies can be used by individual teachers, they will be enhanced by schoolwide collaboration and organization.

Classroom Strategies

Curriculum Compacting. Almost every text, article, or Web site devoted to strategies for regular classroom practice refers to curriculum compacting, a technique that takes the notion of preassessment up a notch by crediting students for what they already know *and* allowing them opportunities to "buy back" their time in different ways. It involves the following three steps:

1. Define the goals and outcomes of a particular unit or segment of instruction.
2. Determine and document which students have already mastered most or all of a specified set of learning outcomes.
3. Provide replacement strategies for material already mastered through the use of instructional options (Reis & Renzulli, n.d.).

Winebrenner (2001) gave a useful analogy for explaining compacting: Think of a trash or garbage compactor. The information and skills students have demonstrated mastery of is "trash"—it is expendable and can be thrown away without being missed because they already have enough of it. Taking this a bit further, by getting rid of the rubbish, students can "recycle" their time for enriched or accelerated learning. Simply put, curriculum compacting "is the process of identifying learning objectives, pretesting students for prior mastery of these objectives, and eliminating needless teaching or practice if mastery can be documented" (Reis, Burns, & Renzulli, 1992, p. 10).

Implementation of curriculum compacting is eased by the use of The Compactor, which documents a student's areas of strength, mastery, and alternate activities (Renzulli & Smith, 1978). For example, a student may demonstrate strength in the skills of formal letter writing, which is documented through a pretest in which students were asked to write a formal letter. Because this student showed mastery of the task, prior to being taught, he is given accelerated or enriched alternative activities. With careful documentation (evidence of mastery), the elimination of all drill, practice, review, homework, quizzes, worksheets, and activities related to formal letter writing is justified. The student may move ahead to the next objective, or he may venture out into new and different areas in his area of strength and interest. Winebrenner (2001) advised, "Never use the time students buy back from strength areas to remediate learning weaknesses. Always allow students to capitalize on their strengths through activities that extend their exceptional abilities" (p. 33). Remediation of weaknesses and development of new understandings should take place when the whole class or a group of students within the class is working in those areas.

Research conducted by the National Research Center on the Gifted and Talented has shown the effectiveness of curriculum compacting in meeting the needs of gifted students:

1. Ninety-five percent of the teachers in their study successfully identified high-ability students and documented their strengths. For those areas not mastered, 80% of the teachers could document those, list appropriate instructional strategies for students to demonstrate mastery, and determine an appropriate mastery standard.
2. Approximately 40–50% of traditional classroom material could be eliminated for targeted students in one or more of the following content areas: mathematics, language arts, science, and social studies. Mathematics and language arts were most frequently compacted.
3. When teachers eliminated as much as 50% of the regular curriculum for gifted students, the out-of-level postachievement test results in reading, math computation, social studies, and spelling were positively affected (Reis et al., 1993).

Reis and Renzulli (n.d.) described the third step, student buy-backs, as one of the most exciting aspects of teaching. It is in this stage that the many other regular classroom strategies take the front seat. Qualitative differentiation also comes into play, with the content, processes, and products of learning taking off and spinning out in many different directions.

However, the research conducted by Reis et al. (1993) indicated that replacement strategies did not often reflect the types of advanced content that would be appropriate for high-ability students. By implementing the strategies described in this chapter and coupling them with the principles of qualitative differentiation, that drawback can be avoided.

Spin-Outs. The term *spin-out* has different meanings in different contexts. In the United States, it most commonly refers to a car going out of control. In Australia, it is a slang term for something that causes amazement or shock. In the regular classroom context, it refers to independent or small-group study, as either a replacement activity in curriculum compacting or a stand-alone opportunity for learning that allows gifted students to pursue their passions. Heacox (2002) described "spin-offs" as student projects based on a teacher-provided general topic in relation to a specific unit or curricular area. She gave three types of spin-offs—teacher-directed, projects with a required product, and student-directed—the last of which she identified as the most appropriate for gifted learners. Tomlinson (1999) described "orbital studies," which, again, revolve around some facet of the curriculum. And, finally, Smutney et al (1997) referred to "branching" as a means of extending the basic or core curriculum. With each of these three concepts, a connection is made between the gifted and talented students' pursuits and the regular curriculum through independent or small-group investigation.

The term *spin-out* is used in this chapter because gifted and talented students should be able to move beyond the curriculum—out and away from the basics to those areas representative of their individual strengths and interests. Secondly, it is important to remember the innate ability of many gifted and talented students to make seemingly obscure, and certainly abstract, connections among ideas. And, finally, amongst the common characteristics associated with gifted and talented students are their many, sometimes unusual, interests, which by preference would absorb most of their time. If students are only allowed to spin off, branch off, or revolve around a set of central, core objectives, they may become too reigned in or confined in their learning. Gifted and talented students should be given the chance to push those boundaries, following their strengths and interests, as well as those dictated by the curricular goals and objectives.

Independent and small-group study, preferably conceived as a spin-out *and* a spin-off, should allow in-depth investigation of student-selected content, processes, and products. Though they can be structured in different ways, the most important element is that of student choice, particularly in the selection of the topic to be investigated and the final outcome, or product. Students and teachers should collaborate in decision making, negotiate goal setting, and agree to learning and working conditions (Winebrenner, 2001).

The following are step-by-step guidelines for facilitating independent or small-group study:

1. Students begin by selecting a topic. They may already have an idea (or a multitude), or it may be helpful for the teacher to interview the child (Smutney et al., 1997). Interest inventories are also useful in topic selection, as are the other forms of assessment previously discussed.
2. Many students may select a topic that is too broad. They should be given the opportunity to browse the topic by reading, talking to others, searching the Internet, and so on. Winebrenner (2001) and Heacox (2002) have provided topic browsing forms or planners for recording resources and ideas. A time limit of a couple of days or weeks for browsing may also be useful.
3. Once a topic has been narrowed down, a contract or agreement form should be completed by the student. This can include the general and specific topics, key areas of focus, product ideas, materials needed, timeline for completion, and evaluation criteria. See Winebrenner (2001), Heacox (2002), and Smutney et al. (1997) for samples.
4. Projects should be completed during class time. To manage students, Winebrenner (2001) suggested an independent study agreement be signed by the teacher and student. This should highlight student requirements, such as speaking quietly, keeping a daily log of progress, participating in class when asked, and working within the timeframe. Teachers might also consider adding their end of the bargain: being available for weekly check-ups or chats, allowing time each day for the student to work on his or her project, or providing resources.
5. Teachers should also develop student checklists or project planners with due dates for major goals, such as collecting resources, describing their product plans, and sharing products (Heacox, 2002; Winebrenner, 2001).

Additionally, students will need physical space within the classroom to work and store their resources, as well as guidance from the teacher. Regardless of their age, students who are inexperienced in undertaking independent or small-group study will need teachers to devote considerable time and attention as facilitators in the initial stages of the project. Students need explicit directions, whether those are around timetables, classroom rules, or product development. For students who have shown evidence of underachievement, the goals set should be reasonable and closely managed. As Winebrenner (2001) stated, "Students will be more successful . . . if procedures and expectations are clearly explained before they begin their work" (p. 168).

Independent and small-group study can also be facilitated by adapting the guidelines from Chapter 13 in this book. Furthermore, Renzulli's Type III enrichment, described in the schoolwide provisions later in this chapter, provides a nice framework. However it is managed, the bottom line for independent or small-group study is the provision of an opportunity for gifted students to spin out their passions. If teachers actively work to allow gifted students a chance for passionate pursuit, supporting it with high expectations and clear guidance, the result will be just as the Aussies describe: something that causes amazement and shock.

Learning Spots. Places in the classroom for self-directed exploration of differentiated content can take several shapes: learning or challenge centers, learning stations, or browsing areas. In this chapter, all of these are referred to as *learning spots.*

A learning center, which Heacox (2002) called a "challenge center," is an area in the classroom containing a collection of activities and materials aimed at teaching, reinforcing, or extending a skill or concept (Tomlinson, 1999). A learning station is similar, except that students move from task to task simultaneously, with the aim of traveling from station to station within a given time period or based on student needs. While both learning centers and stations involve student activities or tasks, browsing areas are simply collections of resources about a particular topic (Winebrenner, 2001). KIDS KITS (U.S. Department of Education, 1995) are good examples of browsing areas. These kits are based on different topics of student interest and contain books, filmstrips, tapes, models, transparencies, videos, and other resources.

Though they may be content-driven, learning spots also allow opportunities for differentiated process skills and products. Each of these strategies provides students with choice and encourages independent or small-group work (Heacox, 2002). Learning spots are also appropriate for every subject area and age level (Heacox; Tomlinson, 1999). They can be used to extend the curriculum (Heacox) or to delve into topics of student interest outside the curriculum (Tomlinson). Learning spots can be integrated into lessons through planning for all students. For example, Heacox recommended "challenge center days," a regular time slot for students to move through the tasks and activities of their choice. Learning stations are used in a similar manner. Heacox also suggested using learning spots for warm-ups, to arrange flexible student groups, and as cool-downs—extras for those students who finish early.

When making decisions about the focus of learning spots, teachers can rely on their curricular aims and objectives or student interest inventories. By focusing on learning outcomes, teachers can be assured that the time spent in learning spots will result in significant achievement gains (Heacox, 2002). There is, however, motivational value in developing centers based on student interests (Tomlinson, 1999), whether these match the curricular aims and objectives or not. For example, in one classroom, all students were given an interest inventory, and, from those, four major areas of interest shone through: famous African Americans, inventions, the upcoming Presidential election, and explorers. Consequently, these became the focuses of the initial browsing areas, and, because they stemmed from student interests, as opposed to the teacher's, they were well utilized. So, a balance between student-driven and curriculum-driven purposes is most desirable.

Another alternative for deciding the focal point of learning spots is using Gardner's theory of multiple intelligences (Heacox, 2002; Smutney et al., 1997) to creating centers or areas for each of the intelligences. For example, a logical-mathematical spot would include projects with puzzles, graphs, charts, models, experiments, or surveys. A visual-spatial focus would encourage students to paint, draw, design, or just doodle. Writing, storytelling, reading, and language exploration would be encouraged in a verbal-linguistic center. A musical spot would include activities and materials to encourage rhythm and melody. Group activities could be facilitated in an interpersonal center, and, for those who have intrapersonal skills, a quiet place for independent assignments, self-reflection, journal writing, or just time alone can be designed. The naturalist would no doubt enjoy a center that had natural materials like rock collections, plants, animals, and insects that could be sorted, classified, studied, or categorized. Finally, the child who loves to do things would find pleasure in a bodily-kinesthetic area with hands-on manipulatives like puppets, clothes for dressing up, woodworking and mechanical materials, or building blocks. When using a multiple intelligences approach, Winebrenner (2001) suggested focusing on key concepts, but different ways of learning based on student choice. So, while all children may be undertaking study in nutrition, the activities and products related to their learning echo the eight intelligences.

The key to successful learning spots is careful planning and management. The steps teachers should take in creating effective learning spots are:

1. Choose an area of focus.
2. Outline the cognitive and affective goals and objectives by asking, "What should students gain?"
3. Design activities that are differentiated in content, processes, and products, thus reflecting student abilities and interests and ranging from simple to complex, short-term to long-term, structured to open-ended, and concrete to abstract. Bloom's (1956) Taxonomy of Educational Objectives is one framework around which activities can be designed to better ensure this range.
4. Collect resources and materials to enhance activities. Package the resources and activities with a title, instructions, and procedures for recordkeeping and assessment.
5. Give clear directions, both written and oral. Step-by-step instructions should be designed so students can be successful in working independently.
6. Design a system for monitoring student involvement and evaluating their performance. This may take the form of a student work journal, peer or self-evaluation, or a teacher-student contract.

7. Evaluate the overall use and effectiveness, making adjustments to better meet student needs (Follis, 1993; Heacox, 2002; Tomlinson, 1999; Winebrenner, 2001).

Learning spots are invitations for learning. Hence, they should be attractive and eye-catching (Follis, 1993), although they do not have to be elaborate (Winebrenner, 2001). They can be located on bookshelves or in file folders, as display boards or portable packages. Activities, described on task cards, can be coded by colors, symbols, signs, or terms. Finally, learning spots can be teacher-designed, student-made, or commercially packaged.

It is important to remember that, for gifted learners, learning spots should move beyond a cursory exploration of topics and practice of basic skills; they should provide greater breadth and depth on interesting and important topics. To ensure this, teachers should extend and move away from the core curriculum, querying student interests and determining their strengths. Furthermore, learning spots should help promote independent, self-directed learning and allow students to make individual choices and decisions. As Smutney et al. (1997) wrote in relation to learning centers, teachers will "be amazed at the decisions children make about what they want to learn and how they wish to learn it" (p. 37).

Learning Agreements. Another recommended classroom strategy is the use of learning contracts for gifted and talented students (Smutney et al., 1997; Tomlinson, 1999; Winebrenner, 2001). A learning contract is "a negotiated agreement between teacher and student that gives students some freedom in acquiring skills and understandings that a teacher deems important at a given time" (Tomlinson, p. 87). It is a written, signed agreement between a student and teacher that outlines

1. what the student will learn or accomplish;
2. how the student will learn and what materials or resources will be needed;
3. what period of time will be necessary;
4. what the student product or outcome will be;
5. how students will behave as independent learners;
6. how performance will be evaluated; and
7. what the positive and negatives consequences will be should the contract be broken (Smutney et al.; Tomlinson; Winebrenner).

Contracts may be completely open-ended so that students and teachers fill in the blanks (Smutney et al., 1997), or they may be more specific, with optional teacher-designed activities from which students may choose (Winebrenner, 2001). In taking on the latter option, teachers determine the skills, concepts, and understandings needed by students. In this case, a learning contract assumes teacher responsibility for deciding the important goals for learning and is largely teacher-directed (Tomlinson, 1999).

This sort of explicit teacher direction has the potential to conflict with some of the goals of qualitative differentiation (i.e., choice, flexibility, self-selected). Many gifted and talented students bring to the negotiation a unique set of skills and abilities. As recognition of those skills, rather than contracting, perhaps teachers should be agreeing. A contract is defined as a legally binding agreement between two parties; however, the word *agreement* usually refers to a more harmonious understanding or course of action between two parties. If a learning agreement approach is taken, then another dimension should be added: teacher roles and responsibilities. In other words, if the student is expected to complete a particular project in a given timeframe under specified working conditions, then the teacher should also promise time, resources, support, regular meetings, and so on. Figure 1 gives an example of a learning agreement. In the agreement, both parties negotiate the content, processes, and products, with the expectation that collaborative learning will take place.

Learning agreements may be used in conjunction with the strategies previously discussed, namely, to support curriculum compacting or independent studies. Agreements can also be enhanced by using personal agendas, which are personalized lists of tasks to be completed within a given timeframe (Tomlinson, 1999). Essentially, they are planning guides facilitated by teachers with conferences and instructions and initialed by students and teachers as tasks are completed. Because they are personalized, with each student having his or her own agenda, they allow students a bit of freedom alongside the development of good time-management skills. They also enable teachers to keep track of student progress.

Another tool for managing contract work is the establishment of a set of working conditions (Winebrenner, 2001). These are mainly behavior-management techniques that include things like staying on task, using quiet voices, moving on to another activity if stuck, and working autonomously without bragging or disturbing others. Consequences of failure to adhere are given, and, like a contract, both the teacher and student sign in agreement. In the spirit of agreement, teacher obligations should be stated, as well.

Learning agreements have the potential to foster gifted students' self-direction and independence, thus increasing their motivation. However, there is danger in creating one-way agreements that are teacher-driven. Additionally, students must be oriented to the process of contract development and implementation and aided in the development of the skills required for successful independent learning. Teacher support and assistance is especially important when learning agreements are used for content, processes, or products that are new to the students involved. It is possibly for these reasons that Winebrenner (2001) and Tomlinson (1999) recommended more structured learning contracts, whereby students are offered a limited array of options from which to choose.

Student's Name: _____

Teacher's Name: _____

Content (what we want to learn)

Process (how we will learn)

What we will do?

What materials we will need?

How will we work together?
Student will:

Teacher will:

Product (how we will show what we've learned)

This will be completed by _____ (date) and shared with
_____ (audience). It will be evaluated based on these goals:

Student's Signature: _____

Teacher's Signature: _____

Figure 1. Learning agreement

Menus, Choice Boards, or a Game of Tic-Tac-Toe. Just as travellers often take different routes to get to the same destination, students should be given the opportunity to achieve similar goals using differentiated means. This can be facilitated with menus or choice boards, whereby teachers design a range or matrix of possible activities to target students' needs (Heacox, 2002; Smutney et al., 1997; Tomlinson, 1995; Winebrenner, 2001). The activities normally revolve around a particular concept or topic, but are differentiated based primarily on the processes and products. Teachers can construct activities based on student ability or readiness levels (Tomlinson), complexity (Heacox), related topics (Winebrenner), or learning preferences or styles. When providing students with choices, they can also be invited to create their own options. As Heacox stated, "Offering choices is an important way to motivate students and get them interested" (p. 101).

Winebrenner (2001) suggested using Bloom's (1956) Taxonomy in creating menus. Table 2 shows one way teachers can create menus using the taxonomy. Students can select from three main areas: appetizer (knowledge and comprehension), entrées (application and analysis), and desserts (synthesis and evaluation). Just like patrons in a restaurant, there will be those who are starving and need a starter before the main course. Others will go straight for dessert. The point here is that, while many educators recommend that Bloom's Taxonomy be inverted for gifted students, with the main focus on the upper levels, students must have the basic skills of knowledge and comprehension in order to successfully analyze, synthesize, and so on.

The ways students are presented with choices can take several formats. Tomlinson (1999) suggested choice boards, with laminated cards placed in pockets. These may be on a bulletin board, wall hanging, or card file. Another approach is a tic-tac-toe menu (Smutney et al., 1997; Winebrenner, 1992). Students are given nine activity options, choosing a vertical, horizontal, or diagonal strategy for completion. However, this should by no means limit students in their choices (Winebrenner). Teachers will no doubt have other ideas for creative ways of presenting students with options, but the bottom line when using menus or choice boards should always be to find more than one way of getting to the same destination.

Flexible Grouping. Heacox (2002) identified three types of grouping: flexible groups, ability/aptitude groups, and cooperative groups. However, given the plethora of research related to each of these types, for the purposes of this chapter, only flexible grouping will be examined. This is because, in relation to regular classroom practices, students can, and should, be grouped for different purposes based on their strengths, interests, needs, and learning preferences.

Heacox (2002) distinguished flexible grouping from other forms of grouping as having the following hallmarks:

- Responsive to student needs because group composition is determined based on teacher perceptions or evidence of students' learning needs. For

Table 2

Creating a Menu for Bloom's Taxonomy

Courses	Ingredients	Selections
appetizer: Knowledge and Comprehension	Who? What? When? Where? Recalling and understanding information	Worksheet, quiz, poster, diagram, report, summary, response, drawing, outline, conclusion, speech
Entrees: Application and Analysis	How many? Which? What is it? Why? Using old ideas in new ways; understanding the parts of a whole	Model, plan, prediction, demonstration, survey, construction, solution, diagram
Desserts: Synthesis and Evaluation	What would happen if? How can we solve? What do you think? Putting parts together to form a new whole; judging the value	Invention, play, game, ad, critique, review, editorial, recommendation, song, discussion, experiment

gifted and talented students, needs may be translated as strengths, interests, and preferences.

- Fluid membership, with group members constantly changing as tasks are matched to needs. "Mix things up whenever possible to meet specific needs" (p. 89).
- Different activities for different groups.
- Grouped and regrouped as appropriate.
- Occurring as needed.
- Based on individual students.

Flexible grouping is not in conflict with the philosophy of heterogenous grouping (Tomlinson, 1999; Winebrenner, 2001). This is because, amongst gifted students, there is no homogeneity; gifted and talented learners are first and foremost individuals with different ways of thinking, acting, performing, feeling, and creating. So, even when homogeneously grouped—for example, by ability—

there will still be variations. With flexible grouping, gifted students are placed with peers of similar minds for similar purposes with similar outcomes. But, given their individuality, this does not mean gifted and talented students are always with the same peers.

When employing flexible grouping, students work in many patterns: as a whole class; by ability; across abilities based on interests; or by choice, as students self-select their groups. Gifted and talented students may work alone, in pairs, or in groups of several students. Teachers who use flexible grouping must be clear about their instructional goals and objectives and the gifted and talented students in their classrooms. By matching those two elements, teachers are then able to "personalize learning activities according to students needs" (Heacox, 2002, p. 85).

Schoolwide Strategies

The Schoolwide Enrichment Model. This model is designed to provide an organizational plan for talent development, with maximum utilization of both regular classroom teachers and enrichment specialists who deliver a differentiated core curriculum, a myriad of enrichment learning and teaching opportunities, and a continuum of special services aimed at gifted and talented students (see Figure 2).

The goals of this model, intended to meet the needs of gifted and talented students in tandem with developing talent in all students, are outlined by Renzulli and Reis (n.d.) as

- maintaining and expanding a continuum of special services through the provision of challenging programs (both in school and extracurricular) for students with superior performance or the potential for such;
- to saturate the regular classroom with activities that challenge all students and, at the same time, create an enriched, responsive environment for the identification and development of specific strengths and interests; and
- the maintenance of specialist teachers and personnel, as necessitated for effectively carrying out the first two goals.

For the purposes of this chapter, only the second goal will be further discussed.

The Schoolwide Enrichment Model incorporates changes to the regular classroom curriculum in the following ways:

1. differentiation of challenge levels through curriculum compacting (i.e., preassessment of goals and objectives) and content modifications;
2. content intensification through the replacement of already known or mastered skills and knowledge with student-selected, in-depth study; and
3. application of the Enrichment Triad Model through the integration of enriched teaching and learning within the core curriculum.

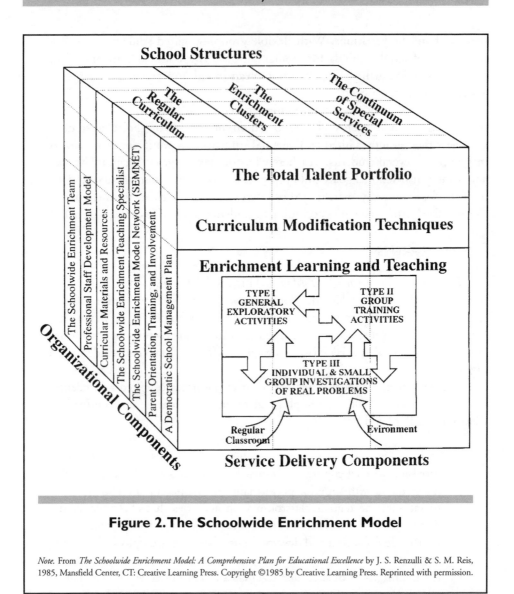

Figure 2. The Schoolwide Enrichment Model

Note. From *The Schoolwide Enrichment Model: A Comprehensive Plan for Educational Excellence* by J. S. Renzulli & S. M. Reis, 1985, Mansfield Center, CT: Creative Learning Press. Copyright ©1985 by Creative Learning Press. Reprinted with permission.

Curriculum compacting and independent study have already been discussed, but a closer examination of the Enrichment Triad Model is needed because it can be adopted in regular classrooms. The model consists of three types of enrichment, each of which is interrelated, as opposed to being sequential. These types of enrichment are reliant on a responsive, flexible environment for success. Type I, general exploratory activities, and Type II, group training activities, may be viewed as catalysts for the development of student skills and interests. Type III enrichment, individual and small-group investigations of real problems, is an outgrowth of first two, reliant on higher ability levels, creativity, and task commitment. Hence, educators have grown to recognize the value of Types I and II for all students, yet the special creativity, ability, and energy required by a smaller set of students (i.e., the gifted and talented) to carry out Type III activities successfully (Davis & Rimm, 2004).

Type I enrichment is designed to expose students to a wide variety of experiences not normally afforded within the scope of the regular curriculum. These experiences include "disciplines, topics, occupations, hobbies, persons, places, and events" (Renzulli & Reis, 1997, p. 137), using many vehicles for introduction, such as speakers, field trips, demonstrations, and performances, and a wide variety of media (both print and electronic). The purpose of such wide exposure is not simply to look at ideas, but to become involved with them (Davis & Rimm, 2004). Thus, another component of Type I is the participation of teachers, parents, and community members in organization, planning, and delivery. Additionally, for Type I enrichment to be relevant, topics are negotiated with students and facilitated for individuals, small groups, or the entire class. Davis and Rimm have offered a plethora of possible topics for enrichment, including everything from robotics, political cartooning, and silk screening, to Shakespeare, journalism, and stamp collecting.

Type II enrichment has a process-orientation, with the intent of enabling students to carry out investigations of real problems by enhancing their skills, abilities, attitudes, and strategic planning. It consists of "methods, materials, and instructional techniques which promote the development of a wide range of thinking and feeling processes" (Renzulli, 1977, p. 24). The overall objective is not to divorce processes of thinking and feeling from advanced content, but to enable students to deal more effectively with it, particularly as they pursue Type III endeavors. Renzulli and Reis (1985) identified four areas of development:

1. creative thinking, problem solving, critical thinking, decision making, and affective processes;
2. learning-how-to-learn skills, such as data collection and analysis;
3. utilization of advanced level reference and resource materials; and
4. written, oral, and visual communication skills. (p. 310)

Again, this type of enrichment is both teacher- and student-driven, some planned and some arising out of student needs and interests. There are indeed skills, attitudes, abilities, and strategies to be developed in all students; however, it is the escalation of these processes that is pivotal to the development of gifted and talented students (Renzulli & Reis).

These skills might be pragmatic and specific to a student's independent project, or they may be less concrete, with the goal, for example, of increasing self-confidence and self-understanding. In other words, the process skills taught are both cognitive and affective, which helps gifted students develop positive self-concepts, positive interpersonal and social skills, and educational and career motivation (Davis & Rimm, 2004).

For gifted and talented students, the pinnacle of Types I and II enrichment is Type III, individual and small-group investigations of real problems. The hope is that students become "interested in pursuing a self-selected area and are willing to commit the time necessary for advanced content acquisition and process training in which they assume the role of first-hand inquirer" (Renzulli & Reis, 1997, p. 138). It is in this arena of enrichment that students begin to research real problems, creating original products and solutions. Students shift from the role of consumers of information to producers of knowledge. This requires teacher facilitation as students actively formulate problems, design methodologies for research, and plan final products for relevant audiences. Clearly, this type of intense focus requires many abilities and qualities inherent in gifted and talented students; but, it also necessitates and enhances the acquisition of advanced content, methodologies, product development, and self-directed learning skills. There are two other aspects critical to this type of enrichment: the emulation of real professional investigators and the consequential free flow effect, as students move in and out of Types I and II on a need-to-know basis while involved in Type III.

Research surrounding the continuing development of the Schoolwide Enrichment Model is generally positive, with gains shown in teacher attitudes, student productivity, and suitability for the identification and servicing of typically underserved students (i.e., underachievers and those with learning disabilities; see the summary of research on this model in Chapter 3). These studies, and others, provide educators with a platform of practical know-how from which the model can be implemented in a wide variety of settings and age groups (Renzulli & Reis, n.d.). While the model generally aligns itself well with differentiated principles and practices, it may be difficult to implement due to the complexity of total school reorganization and the need for specialist teachers and a schoolwide commitment premised on teacher understanding of and interest in gifted and talented students. Yet, few educators could argue with Renzulli's (1998) statement that "Schools are places for developing the broadest and richest experiences imaginable for young people. Special programs can serve as a basis for making all schools into laboratories for talent development" (p. 111).

The Parallel Curriculum Model. A recently introduced model guiding the design of curricula that develop potential and provide challenge for all students, including the gifted and talented, is the Parallel Curriculum Model (Tomlinson, Kaplan, Renzulli, Purcell, Leppien, & Burns, 2002). This multifaceted approach to curriculum design is a publication of the National Association for Gifted Children, and while research regarding its effectiveness is impossible given its infancy, it reflects "the long term knowledge of our field and the contributions of many thinkers" (Tomlinson, 2001a, p. 10). The model is premised on several key ideas regarding curriculum development:

- Appropriate curricula for gifted learners are rooted firmly in "good" curricula for all learners.
- Individual differences in learners blur the lines between high-quality curricula for the gifted and high-quality curricula for everyone.

- A curricular model designed to advance gifted learners should help in the design of curricula for all learners (Tomlinson et al.).

Hence, the Parallel Curriculum Model has as its primary focus the development of effective and excellent curricula for every student, with direction for ascending intellectual demand appropriate for gifted and talented students. In essence, the model is designed to function as a catalyst for identifying potential, as well as enhancing it.

The Parallel Curriculum Model is comprised of four strands, which may operate in isolation of, or in tandem with, one another. The first is the Core Curriculum, which is comprised of the key concepts, principles, information, and skills of a particular discipline. The second parallel is that of the Curriculum of Connections, whereby the elements of the Core Curriculum are applied across and within disciplines, times, cultures, and locations. This parallel is basically an integrated curriculum, taking into account the relationships not only between content areas, but also those that exist in view of the big picture of the world in which we live. The Curriculum of Practice is the third layer and is designed to develop students' understandings by "increasing their skills and confidence as professionals . . . for the purpose of promoting expertise as a practitioner of the discipline" (Tomlinson et al., 2002, p. 29). It is at this level that students emulate the roles, skills, thinking, and actions of archaeologists, journalists, psychologists, and other professionals. The fourth extension of the Core Curriculum is the Curriculum of Identity, whereby students engage in self-reflection using a particular discipline as a lens. Given their content-related understandings, it is within this parallel that they contemplate their relationship with the discipline both now and in the future; the connections with their lives; and their interests, strengths, and needs. The belief here is that "by looking outward to the discipline, students can find a means of looking inward" (Tomlinson et al., p. 37). Finally, in order to meet the needs of individual learners, the parallels can be combined and used "in concert with one another" (Tomlinson, 2001a, p. 10).

This model has been developed with good intentions: the provision of high-quality, highly challenging curricula with flexibility of planning and implementation. It is supported by a comprehensive set of practical guidelines (Tomlinson et al., 2002), as well as the promise of future research and professional development opportunities.

The Multiple Menu Model. Developed by Renzulli, Leppien, and Hays (2000), the Multiple Menu Model is designed as a practical planning tool for regular classroom teachers at all levels who have the desire to design in-depth curricula for gifted and talented students. The emphasis of this model is to balance "authentic content and process, involving students as firsthand enquirers, and exploring the structure and interconnectedness of knowledge" (Renzulli et al., p. 1). Hence, the model is based on several assumptions: Teachers who are inspiring to young people share their passions for particular disciplines of study; authentic learning experiences have, as their foundation, opportunities for students, in both learning processes and products, to act as practicing professionals in the field; and that the purpose in curricula should be to enable students to think, act, and feel as experts in the field.

The model is referred to as a menu, in that it offers teachers many different options in the design of a curriculum that brings together the knowledge of a discipline, both its content and methodologies, with a range of instructional strategies, as shown in Figure 3. The authors refer to this flexibility as resembling a pull-down menu on a computer program or an a la carte menu in a restaurant. The model has a menu for knowledge, another for instructional techniques, and a third for instructional products.

The knowledge menu examines content, with emphasis on the structure, basic principles, and methodologies of a discipline. The purpose here is to help students understand not only the what, who, why, when, where, and how of a discipline, but also its relationship with other disciplines. For example, students might ask questions like "What is psychology?," "What do psychologists study?," "How is psychology similar to sociology or anthropology?," and "What role does psychology play within the social sciences?" It is also within the knowledge menu that students explore the facts, conventions, trends, principles, generalizations, theories, and structures of the discipline. The knowledge menu aims for both depth and breadth of content, with emphasis placed on curricula designed around concepts, as opposed to topics, and the utilization of both general and specific research methodologies.

The instructional techniques menu provides educators with the tools for considering pedagogy, organization, and sequencing of the curriculum. There are four menus provided, all of which lead to the instructional products menu: instructional objectives and student activities, instructional strategies, instructional sequences, and artistic modification. The objectives and activities menu is basically a reworking of Bloom's Taxonomy using the instructional verbiage of assimilation and retention, information analysis, information synthesis and application, and evaluation. So, teachers using this menu for planning might consider student involvement in listening, manipulating, producing, interviewing, judging, and so forth. The instructional strategies suggested in the next menu are a broad means of organizing the delivery of the curriculum and include everything from recitation and drill, to role-play, simulations, mentorships, field trips, debates, and guest speakers. The instructional sequences menu moves teachers through the design of activities to gain student attention and develop their interest, to those that allow for the application of information to novel problems and different topics. Finally, the artistic modification menu personalizes all instruction, suggesting the inclusion of curricular objectives and activities that give students a chance to share their personal experiences, values, beliefs, and enthusiasm for a particular area of study. "There is no limit to the variety of personal touches that can make learning more engaging and relevant to students" (Renzulli et al., 2000, p. 61).

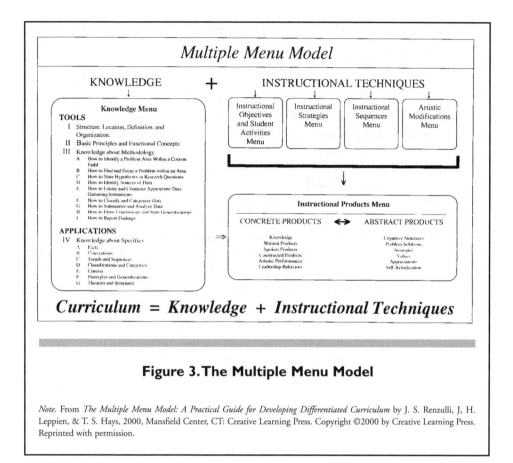

Figure 3. The Multiple Menu Model

Note. From *The Multiple Menu Model: A Practical Guide for Developing Differentiated Curriculum* by J. S. Renzulli, J, H. Leppien, & T. S. Hays, 2000, Mansfield Center, CT: Creative Learning Press. Copyright ©2000 by Creative Learning Press. Reprinted with permission.

The final menu is the instructional products menu, which is divided into concrete and abstract products. The list of concrete products suggested is nearly exhaustive; it includes artistic, performance, spoken, visual, models/constructions, service and leadership, and written products. The intention in this menu is to allow students a wide variety of means to demonstrate their learning, and the authors suggest everything from skits, wood carvings, inventions, and 3-D figures, to radio programs, speeches, comic strips, and marketing plans. Abstract products include both cognitive and affective structures, developing, for example, students' self-esteem, problem-solving strategies, persistence, metacognitive skills, and values.

To utilize this model effectively, curriculum developers must first understand the concepts within each menu and then be able to use the menus to write the curriculum (Renzulli et al., 2000). To assist with this, the developers of the model provide planning guides and templates, along with in-depth descriptions and examples, in their book, *The Multiple Menu Model: A Practical Guide for Developing Differentiated Curriculum* (Renzulli et al.). To date, there is no research indicating the effectiveness of the model; however, its value may lie in its use as a framework for the development of many excellent units of study in schools (J. Renzulli, personal communication, 2002). Finally, the model has been deemed suitable for all learners, with the developers stating that the curriculum must be differentiated in order to accommodate student diversity and respectful learning experiences (Renzulli et al.).

Enrichment Clusters. Imagine a group of students, drawn together by their similar passions and guided by someone equally enthused, yet more experienced, meeting on a regular basis to design a Web page, conduct a survey, explore early life in America, or learn the art of storytelling. What's been imagined is an enrichment cluster, part of the Schoolwide Enrichment Plan, which can be developed and implemented independently.

These are weekly 90-minute blocks of time during which groups of students sharing common interests, but not necessarily of the same age or grade, come together with a facilitator to create a product, produce a performance, or provide a service (Renzulli, Gentry, & Reis, 2003). It is recommended that clusters last 8–10 weeks, with a series occurring in the first part and latter part of the school year, taking a break in the middle. All teachers and students participate, along with community and parent volunteers, to make "use of relevant knowledge and apply thinking skills to common problems" (Renzulli et al., p. 16).

The guidelines for enrichment clusters are outlined by Renzulli et al. (2003), and many of these mirror the sort of differentiation previously discussed:

1. the integration of real content and processes, which results in a product so that "all cluster activity is directed toward . . . production . . . for an authentic audience" (p. 19);
2. the facilitation of student and teacher choice based on preassessment of interest and learning preferences;
3. the creation of cross-age groups based on common interests;
4. the use of "just-in-time" planning and delivery of content, processes, and products;
5. the utilization of authentic methods and advanced content used by professionals;
6. the development of talents through a division of labor that focuses on individual strengths and abilities;
7. the designation of blocks of time for enrichment clusters; and
8. the avoidance of traditional school structures, regulations, and ways of doing things, making clusters as "unschool-like as possible" (p. 30).

Renzulli et al. (2003) provide not only the theoretical rationale for enrichment clusters, but also the strategies for putting the theory into practice. The research supporting enrichment clusters is positive, demonstrating program success, as well as encouraging effects on students and teachers. The most promising research results are those that indicate changes in regular classroom teaching practices, with almost 60% of the teachers involved reporting voluntary changes to content and teaching methods (Renzulli et al.).

Cluster Grouping. Another schoolwide organizational strategy is cluster grouping, "the practice of identifying the top five to eight academically talented (or intellectually gifted) students at a grade level and placing them in the same classroom at that grade level with a teacher best suited and qualified to work with gifted students" (Rogers, 2002, p. 224). The remainder of the teacher's class, like others at that grade level, is heterogeneously grouped. Students are identified for the cluster group based on a combination of local and standardized criteria, with particular emphasis placed on demonstrated abilities in reading, mathematics, or both (Winebrenner, 2001).

Gentry (1999) identified several major benefits of cluster grouping:

- gifted students have regular interaction with intellectual and age peers;
- removing the highest achievers from most classrooms allows other achievers to emerge;
- cluster grouping reduces the range of achievement levels that must be addressed within the classrooms of all teachers; and
- curricular differentiation is more efficient and likely to occur when a group of high-achieving students is placed with a teacher who has expertise, training, and a desire to differentiate the curriculum than when these students are distributed among many teachers.

According to Winebrenner (2001), the only potential drawback to cluster grouping can be parental pressure. However, if clear selection guidelines are in place and communicated, this can be avoided.

Cluster grouping is "a full-time gifted education program that requires only minimal funds to support it" (Winebrenner, 2001, p. 176). The key to implementing cluster grouping successfully is moving beyond simply grouping students to ensuring that a qualitatively differentiated education is delivered; so, this schoolwide strategy must be complimented with the classroom strategies previously discussed. This can happen if professional development for all staff and specific training in gifted education for cluster teachers is provided as part of the schoolwide plan.

A Few Other Strategies. There are several other schoolwide strategies to be briefly considered: cross-grade/age grouping, multiage classrooms, mentorships, and weekly planning.

Cross-grade/age grouping and multiage classrooms are commonly defined as one in the same: grouping students by their achievement in a subject, rather than their age or grade level (Rogers, 2002). However, the two are differentiated here as two schoolwide organizational approaches commonly used in New Zealand that potentially serve gifted students well. Many New Zealand schools organize themselves in syndicates, which are cohorts of classrooms across several grade levels that work together in both planning and delivery of the curricular goals and objectives. For example, a primary school may have a junior syndicate, composed of new entrant (e.g., kindergarten) through year 2 classes; a middle syndicate for years 3 and 4; and an upper syndicate of year 5 and 6 classes. Within each of these syndicates, students are often cross-grouped for at least part of the day, depending on their abilities and needs, and matched to teacher strengths. Multilevel classes, referred to in New Zealand as "composite classes," also exist, which are fulltime arrangements with classes composed of two grade levels. For example, a school may have a year 3–4 class and a year 5–6 one.

Rogers (2002) has reported that the research related to the effectiveness of multilevel classes for gifted and talented students is inconclusive, namely because the reported studies she analyzed did not address gifted students separately and the overall results are contradictory. However, "common sense might suggest that for gifted children, exposure to two years' curriculum for each year in school would be advantageous" (Rogers, p. 181). She further recommended that, in a multilevel class, the gifted child would need to be one of the youngest in the group. Although Rogers' synthesis of research related to cross-grade grouping demonstrates positive academic effects, the social/emotional outcomes have yet to be explored.

Mentorships are a highly recommended practice in gifted education, and they, too, have their place in the regular classroom (Heacox, 2002). Schools can arrange for mentoring opportunities by undertaking a community interest survey and creating a mentor database. For regular classroom teachers, mentors can be invaluable in differentiating content, processes, and products. Their roles can range from advancing students' knowledge and skills, to simply answering questions (Heacox). Additionally, making use of mentors enhances the relationship between schools and the community. Parents, other teachers, retired citizens, and other local community members can step into a classroom, enhancing learning for all students. However, as Rogers (2002) has pointed out, for gifted students a true mentorship—being placed with an expert to develop skills and understandings that cannot be provided in the regular school setting—does not occur unless all other avenues have been exhausted. Chapter 16 gives many details on mentoring and should be referred to for more information.

The final schoolwide approach is related to weekly planning. Lesson plans can be formatted to show exactly how and when gifted students are being challenged though differentiated opportunities. Both short- and long-term plans can be designed to demonstrate evidence of appropriate grouping and differentiation. Heacox (2002) also recommended creating a matrix plan that uses Bloom's Taxonomy coupled with Gardner's multiple intelligences as a framework for designing instructional objectives. In this way, objectives are categorized by their levels of challenge and complexity, as well as different ways of thinking and learning. To create differentiated activities, Heacox (p. 72) offered a simple formula:

Content + Process + Product = Learning Experience

This is supported with the Content Catalysts, Processes, and Product (CCPP) Toolkit, a menu-like approach that encourages teachers to move around a wide array of content, process, and product possibilities. Heacox's book, *Differentiating Instruction in the Regular Classroom* (2002), provides teachers with reproducible planning forms and the CCPP Toolkit, along with many examples of their use. Another planning approach is described in Chapter 7 in this book.

Other Issues in Educating Gifted and Talented Students in the Regular Classroom

As with any educational strategy, every answer leads to another question. This section briefly explores some of the frequently asked questions about teaching gifted students in regular classrooms.

What About Grading?

One of the implications of qualitatively differentiated classrooms is that the playing field begins to level. In other words, as students are better matched to their learning activities and working alongside like-minded peers, those at the top may well find the complexity, challenge, depth, and breadth moves their A's to B's. This can be frustrating, disappointing, and confusing to children and their parents. It can also demotivate high-achieving students who always aim for top marks.

To avoid this situation, the first step is communicating openly with parents and students, explaining the principles and practices of differentiation. The second step is rethinking grading policies and procedures. Firstly, if gifted students are working above and beyond their grade level, they should receive credit and recognition by being awarded the highest possible marks at their grade level (Winebrenner, 2001). Secondly, differentiated products require differentiated assessment, so teachers should use portfolios, rubrics, and other alternative evaluative measures. Finally, teachers may allocate two sets of grades: one for achievement on grade level and a second for achievement above and beyond grade level. Grades may also be given in recognition for effort.

What About Homework?

The same rules of qualitative differentiation apply to homework as to any other learning activity. The purpose in homework should be to reinforce or extend concepts and skills. If gifted students have demonstrated mastery of the basics, then their homework should reflect that. Homework should be just as relevant and meaningful as any other task.

What About Our Gifted Program?

Regular classroom strategies do not replace a school's gifted and talented program; rather, they are just some of the threads that create the tapestry of an appropriate education. In fact, regular classroom practices should compliment any other provisions a school may have for gifted students and vice versa. So, if all teachers are viewed as teachers of the gifted, then all teachers need professional development and support in gifted education, as well as the skills of collaboration and consultation.

A concern frequently raised in the field is that gifted programs are all too often fragmented add-ons to the total school picture. To avoid this, all teachers must be encouraged to differentiate the content, processes, and products of learning for gifted and talented students. In doing so, the traditional role of the gifted education specialist must also change. Rather than pulling out, perhaps it is time gifted educators push in. In schools where regular classroom practices are differentiated, gifted education specialists can serve in different capacities: as mentors, professional development leaders, consulting teachers, or as another teacher in the regular classroom.

What About Parents?

Parents need to be kept informed and abreast of their son or daughter's education, and this can be facilitated through parent evenings, newsletters, and one-on-one conferences. Additionally, parents can play a valuable role in the identification of special abilities, locating resources and materials, and mentoring and facilitating individuals or small groups. As Winebrenner (2001) noted, "Educating gifted students is a responsibility that parents and teachers must share" (p. 201). By forming a partnership with parents of gifted students, any fears teachers may have about pushy, demanding, frustrated parents can be eliminated.

But, Isn't This Elitist?

No! In a system of education that strives for equity and excellence, special provisions for gifted and talented students must be part of those efforts. As Howard Gardner said, "The biggest mistake of past centuries in teaching has been to treat all children as if they are variants of the same individual, and thus to feel justified in teaching them the same subjects in the same ways" (cited in Tomlinson, 1999, p. 9). Approaches that do not recognize individual differences, including those inherent in gifted and talented students, mimic the one-size-fits-all strategy used by clothing manufacturers. As Tomlinson has pointed out, this sort of plan will swallow some learners and pinch others. Qualitative differentiation for gifted and talented students across all provisions and beginning in the regular classroom is one way of moving a step closer to excellence. It is not elitist; it is only fair.

Where Do We Go From Here?

In the gathering, reading, and preparation of materials for writing this chapter, two future directions for gifted and talented education came to the fore: the call for professional development in gifted education at both pre- and in-service levels for all teachers and the need to research the effectiveness of the practices used to teach gifted students in regular classrooms. All teachers require professional development that will assist them in understanding concepts of giftedness and talent, the associated behaviors and characteristics, identification and assessment strategies, qualitatively differentiated classroom-based techniques for working with gifted students, and the ongoing evaluation of effective classroom practice. Specialists in gifted education should take the lead in creating, implementing, and evaluating professional development opportunities.

Many of the strategies recommended for differentiated regular classrooms appear to be sound; however, empirical research supporting the implementation, maintenance, and impact of these strategies is limited. Systematic monitoring and evaluation to study the efficacy of these strategies must occur. Otherwise, "we, as a field, will continue to flounder, being excited by novelty rather than proven effectiveness" (VanTassel-Baska, 1993, p. 69). Research, both quantitative and qualitative, should be undertaken to examine

1. the cognitive and social/emotional effects of these strategies on gifted and talented students and their other classroom peers;
2. the ease and difficulty with which teachers are able to implement and maintain the strategies;
3. the impact of using these techniques on one's teaching and perceptions of giftedness; and
4. parental perceptions, as well as those of their children, of the usefulness, appropriateness, and enjoyment of these strategies.

Conclusion

It is likely that gifted and talented students will continue to spend the majority of their education in mainstreamed, regular classrooms. Therefore, it is vitally important that all teachers are able to recognize and develop these students' special abilities through qualitatively differentiated learning experiences. In 1993, the National Research Center on the Gifted and Talented investigated regular classroom practices (Archambault, Westberg, Brown, Hallmark, Emmons, & Zhang, 1993), and, a decade later, their recommendations remain relevant. These included

1. the continuation of gifted and talented programs in which students have opportunities to interact with like-minded peers and specialists teachers;
2. concentrated efforts to assist teachers in the development of appropriate curricular materials for gifted students, as well as professional development to assist in identification and teaching;
3. more differentiated opportunities within regular classrooms for gifted and talented students; and

4. a redefinition of the role of gifted education specialists that encompasses their need to support regular classroom teachers.

By implementing, maintaining, and evaluating the classroom-based and schoolwide provisions suggested in this chapter, each of these recommendations can be brought to life. When that happens, gifted and talented students will find themselves dining in the educational equivalent of five-star restaurants with a great menu and top chefs.

Discussion Questions and Activities

In the spirit of differentiation, choose the activities and questions that best suit your strengths, interests, abilities, and needs.

- Develop a schoolwide plan for professional development in gifted and talented education, focusing on regular classroom practices. Include a timeline, topics, speakers, and activities.

- Plan a unit of study for a regular classroom. Demonstrate differentiated learning opportunities for gifted and talented students.

- Design a practical resource for regular classroom teachers. This resource may be a Web page, book, set of pamphlets, PowerPoint presentation, or another product of your choice.

- Describe the principles of qualitative differentiation as they apply to regular classroom teaching.

- Observe gifted and talented students in a regular classroom setting. Reflect on their learning opportunities and record your thoughts. Write suggestions for the teacher.

- Formulate a research proposal that focuses on regular classroom practices. Include research questions, a review of the literature, methodology, and ethical considerations.

- Evaluate a classroom-based or schoolwide strategy for gifted and talented students in regular classrooms. Present your findings and recommendations.

- Discuss the strategies for differentiated classrooms, including the barriers to such provisions and ways of addressing them. Brainstorm the many possibilities.

Teacher Resources

Books

Heacox, D. (2002). *Differentiating instruction in the regular classroom*. Minneapolis, MN: Free Spirit.

Renzulli, J. S. (1994). *Schools for talent development: A practical plan for total school improvement*. Mansfield Center, CT: Creative Learning Press.

Renzulli, J. S., Gentry, M., & Reis, S. M. (2003). *Enrichment clusters: A practical plan for real-world, student-driven learning*. Mansfield Center, CT: Creative Learning Press.

Renzulli, J. S., Leppien, J. H., & Hays, T. S. (2000). *The multiple menu model: A practical guide for developing differentiated curriculum*. Mansfield Center, CT: Creative Learning Press.

Renzulli, J. S., & Reis, S. M. (1985). *The schoolwide enrichment model: A comprehensive plan for educational excellence*. Mansfield Center, CT: Creative Learning Press.

Smutney, J. F., Walker, S. Y., & Meckstroth, E. A. (1997). *Teaching young gifted children in the regular classroom*. Minneapolis, MN: Free Spirit.

Tomlinson, C. A. (1999). *The differentiated classroom: Responding to the needs of all learners*. Alexandria, VA: Association for Supervision and Curriculum Development.

Tomlinson, C. A. (2001). *How to differentiate instruction in mixed-ability classrooms* (2nd ed.). Alexandria, VA: Association for Supervision and Curriculum Development.

Tomlinson, C. A., Kaplan, S. N., Renzulli, J. S., Purcell, J., Leppien, J., & Burns, D. (2002). *The parallel curriculum: A design to develop potential and challenge high-ability learners*. Thousand Oaks, CA: Corwin Press.

Winebrenner, S. (2001). *Teaching gifted kids in the regular classroom* (2nd ed.). Minneapolis, MN: Free Spirit.

Web Sites

The Schoolwide Enrichment Model—http://www.gifted.uconn.edu/sempage.html

KIDS KITS—http://www.ed.gov/pubs/EPTW/eptw10/eptw10i.html

Publishers

Thinking Caps for the Gifted
P.O. Box 26239
Phoenix, AZ 85068
(602) 279-0513
Publishes learning centers for gifted students based on Bloom's Taxonomy.

Creative Learning Press
P.O. Box 320
Mansfield Center, CT 06250
http://www.creativelearningpress.com
Publishes materials to support the Enrichment Triad and Schoolwide Enrichment
Models, plus lots more.

Prufrock Press
P.O. Box 8813
Waco, TX 76714-8813
http://www.prufrock.com
Publishes many materials in gifted education.

References

Archambault, F. X., Westberg, K. L., Brown, S. W., Hallmark, B. W., Emmons, C. L., & Zhang, W. (1993). *Regular classroom practices with gifted students: Results of a national survey of classroom teachers.* Storrs: National Research Center on the Gifted and Talented, University of Connecticut.

Bloom, B. (Ed.). (1956). *Taxonomy of educational objectives: The classification of educational goals. Handbook I: Cognitive domain.* New York: Longman Green.

Braggett, E. J. (1994). *Developing programs for gifted students—A total school approach.* Victoria, Australia: Hawker Brownlow.

Clark, C., & Callow, R. (1998). *Educating able children: Resource issues and processes for teachers.* London: Fulton.

Davis, G. A., & Rimm, S. B. (2004). *Education of the gifted and talented* (5th ed.). Boston: Allyn and Bacon.

Delisle, J. (2000). Mom . . . apple pie . . . and differentiation. *Gifted Child Today, 23*(5), 36–37.

Follis, H. D. (1993). A step-by-step plan for developing learning centers. In C. J. Maker (Ed.), *Critical issues in gifted education: Programs for the gifted in regular classrooms* (pp. 296–304). Austin, TX: PRO-ED.

Gentry, M. L. (1999). *Promoting student achievement and exemplary classroom practices through cluster grouping: A research-based alternative to heterogeneous elementary classrooms.* Storrs: National Research Center on the Gifted and Talented, University of Connecticut.

George, D. (1997). *The challenge of the able child* (2nd ed.). London: Fulton.

Heacox, D. (1991). *Up from underachievement.* Victoria, Australia: Hawker Brownlow.

Heacox, D. (2002). *Differentiating instruction in the regular classroom.* Minneapolis, MN: Free Spirit.

Kettle, K. E., Renzulli, J. S., & Rizza, M. G. (n.d.). *Exploring student preferences for product development: My Way . . . An Expression Style Instrument.* Retrieved June 15, 2004, from http://www.sp.uconn.edu/~nrcgt/sem/exprstyl.html

McDaniel, T. R. (2002). Mainstreaming the gifted: Historical perspectives on excellence and equity. *Roeper Review, 24,* 112–115.

Ministry of Education. (2000). *Gifted and talented students: Meeting their needs in New Zealand schools.* Wellington, New Zealand: Learning Media.

Reis, S. M., Burns, D. E., & Renzulli, J. S. (1992). *Curriculum compacting: The complete guide to modifying the regular curriculum for high ability students.* Mansfield Center, CT: Creative Learning Press.

Reis, S. M., & Renzulli, J. S. (n.d.). *Curriculum compacting: A systematic procedure for modifying the curriculum for above average ability students.* Retrieved June 15, 2004, from http://www.sp.uconn.edu/~nrcgt/sem/semart08.html

Reis, S. M., Westberg, K. L., Kulikowich, J., Caillard, F., Hébert, T., Plucker, J., Purcell, J. H., Rogers, J. B., & Smist, J. M. (1993). *Why not let high ability students start school in January? The curriculum compacting study* (Research Monograph 93106). Storrs: National Research Center on the Gifted and Talented, University of Connecticut.

Renzulli, J. S. (1977). *The enrichment triad model: A guide for developing defensible programs for the gifted and talented.* Mansfield Center, CT: Creative Learning Press.

Renzulli, J. S. (1996). *The Interest-A-Lyzer family of instruments: A manual for teachers.* Mansfield Center, CT: Creative Learning Press.

Renzulli, J. S. (1998). A rising tide lifts all ships: Developing the gifts and talents of all students. *Phi Delta Kappan, 80,* 104–111.

Renzulli, J. S. (1999). What is this thing called giftedness, and how do we develop it? A twenty-five year perspective. *Journal for the Education of the Gifted, 23*, 3–54.

Renzulli, J. S., Gentry, M., & Reis, S. M. (2003). *Enrichment clusters: A practical plan for real-world, student-driven learning.* Mansfield Center, CT: Creative Learning Press.

Renzulli, J. S., Leppien, J. H., & Hays, T. S. (2000). *The multiple menu model: A practical guide for developing differentiated curriculum.* Mansfield Center, CT: Creative Learning Press.

Renzulli, J. S., & Reis, S. M. (1985). *The schoolwide enrichment model: A comprehensive plan for educational excellence.* Mansfield Center, CT: Creative Learning Press.

Renzulli, J. S., & Reis, S. M. (1997). The Schoolwide Enrichment Model: New directions for developing high-end learning. In N. Colangelo & G. A. Davis (Eds.), *Handbook of gifted education* (2nd ed., pp. 136–154). Needham Heights, MA: Allyn and Bacon.

Renzulli, J. S., & Reis, S. M. (n.d.). *Research related to the Schoolwide Enrichment Model.* Retrieved June 15, 2004, from http://www.sp.uconn.edu/~nrcgt/sem/rrsem.html

Renzulli, J. S., & Smith, L. H. (1978). *The learning styles inventory: A measure of student preference for instructional strategies.* Mansfield Center, CT: Creative Learning Press.

Riley, T. L. (2000). *Assessing for differentiation: Getting to know students.* Retrieved June 15, 2004, from http://www.tki.org.nz/r/gifted/pedagogy/assess_diff_e.php

Riley, T. L. (in press). Qualitative differentiation for gifted and talented students. In D. McAlpine & R. Moltzen (Eds.), *Gifted and talented: New Zealand perspectives.* Palmerston North, New Zealand: Massey University.

Rogers, K. B. (2002). *Re-forming gifted education: How parents and teachers can match the program to the child.* Dayton, OH: Gifted Potential Press.

Smutney, J. F., Walker, S. Y., & Meckstroth, E. A. (1997). *Teaching young gifted children in the regular classroom.* Minneapolis, MN: Free Spirit.

Tomlinson, C. A. (1995). *How to differentiate instruction in mixed-ability classrooms.* Alexandria, VA: Association for Supervision and Curriculum Development.

Tomlinson, C. A. (1999). *The differentiated classroom: Responding to the needs of all learners.* Alexandria, VA: Association for Supervision and Curriculum Development.

Tomlinson, C. A. (2001a). From the President. *Communiqué, 14*(2), 1, 10.

Tomlinson, C. A. (2001b). *How to differentiate instruction in mixed-ability classrooms* (2nd ed.). Alexandria, VA: Association for Supervision and Curriculum Development.

Tomlinson, C. A., Kaplan, S. N., Renzulli, J. S., Purcell, J., Leppien, J., & Burns, D. (2002). *The parallel curriculum: A design to develop potential and challenge high-ability learners.* Thousand Oaks, CA: Corwin Press.

U.S. Department of Education. (1995). *Kids Interest Discovery Studies KITS (KIDS KITS).* Retrieved June 15, 2004, from http://www.ed.gov/pubs/EPTW/eptw10/eptw10i.html

VanTassel-Baska, J. (1993). A reaction to local program development as a disjointed exercise. In C. J. Maker (Ed.), *Critical issues in gifted education: Programs for the gifted in regular classrooms* (pp. 63–70). Austin, TX: PRO-ED.

Willard-Holt, C. (1994). Strategies for individualizing instruction in regular classrooms. *Roeper Review, 17*, 43–46.

Winebrenner, S. (1992). *Teaching gifted kids in the regular classroom.* Minneapolis, MN: Free Spirit.

Winebrenner, S. (2001). *Teaching gifted kids in the regular classroom* (2nd ed.). Minneapolis, MN: Free Spirit.

Chapter 20

Public Relations and Advocacy for the Gifted

by **Joan D. Lewis** and **Frances A. Karnes**

ou are a 5th-grade teacher of the gifted who wants to acquaint the community with your students' accomplishments. Recently, they participated in a service learning project with the Keep America Beautiful campaign to clean the local river. Your reasons for sharing this information about your students might include the following: (1) they made significant contributions beyond what might be expected for their ages; (2) they developed an extensive knowledge of the environment, local industrial processes, and public relations strategies; (3) you want to see children and youth receive positive recognition; and (4) you want to see gifted students and their instruction featured in the news so people will recognize that there are practical reasons for supporting their education.

Another scenario might be that you are the enrichment specialist in your school, teaching elementary gifted students in resource classes and collaborating with teachers for their cluster groups in the regular classroom. Parents have come to you about extending the gifted program beyond the elementary school level. This has been a concern of yours for some time. You would like for your district to provide a comprehensive array of services for gifted learners at all grade levels. Your reasons might include the following: (1) program options are limited in your district; (2) research supports qualitatively and quantitatively differentiated instruction for gifted learners; (3) gifted students are a heterogeneous group that cannot be served adequately with only one *program option; and (4) atypically gifted students are more likely to receive services with expanded educational options.*

Definition of Terms

The terms *advocacy, lobbying,* and *public relations* are at times used synonymously, yet their meanings differ. Consider the following dictionary definitions (*Merriam-Webster's*, 1993):

advocacy: the act or process of advocating or supporting a cause or proposal.

lobby: to conduct activities aimed at influencing public officials and especially members of a legislative body on legislation. (1) to promote (as a project) or secure the passage of legislation by influencing public officials. (2) to attempt to influence or sway (as a public official) toward a desired action.

public relations: the business of inducing the public to have understanding for and goodwill toward a person, firm, or institution; also the degree of understanding and goodwill achieved.

West (1985) described public relations in education in a comprehensive manner that identifies some of the key concepts that will be employed throughout this chapter:

Educational public relations: a systematically and continuously planned, executed, and evaluated program of interactive communication and human relations that employs paper, electronic, and people media to attain internal, as well as external support for an educational institution. (as cited in Kowalski, 1996, p. 7)

Rationale for Public Relations in Gifted Education

Professionals in gifted education have voiced their concerns regarding the lack of public relations and advocacy for more than a decade. Gifted children and youth are often misunderstood and victims of myths and stereotyping (Karnes & Riley, 1991). Grika (1986) stated that these misconceptions could foster public resistance to funding for gifted education. Dettmer (1991) indicated that advocacy is usually conducted out of crisis, rather than by design, and that public relations have taken a lesser role to other issues in the field. Renzulli (1993) reminded us that researchers are guilty of "preaching" to the converted and more emphasis should be put into writing for professionals in other areas of education. It is not only researchers, but also practitioners in the classrooms who need to write and speak to other publics.

Advocates for gifted learners need to take the same approach as those who fought for the rights of students with disabilities. Supporters of the gifted need to educate school and community personnel about the characteristics and needs of high-ability learners. In addition, they need to provide teachers and their administrators with clear, concise reasons why it is not only appropriate, but equitable to teach all students to the highest level of which they are capable. The issue is frequently seen as a conflict between equity and excellence, yet these two philosophies need not be viewed as mutually exclusive. When all students receive an education that meets their cognitive and affective needs, both equity and excellence will be achieved.

Educators and the communities that support them must remember the diversity of today's classrooms. Students come from families with different socioeconomic, racial, ethnic, language, religious, geographic, moral, health, and experiential backgrounds, and they also have a range of physical and mental abilities. It is no small task for educators to meet the many and differing needs that are found in today's schools. It is critical that advocates for gifted students bear in mind this diversity. Although gifted learners are not the only children with special need, theirs are more likely to be ignored precisely because of this diversity and the prevailing belief that such bright children can "make it on their own" (Clark, 2002).

Historically, educators have made little use of public relations, but in the current era of school reform, greater value is being placed on these skills (Kowalski, 1996). The U.S. Department of Education's 1993 report *National Excellence: A Case for Developing America's Talent* stated that

> to accomplish the goal of identifying and serving students with outstanding talent so that they reach their full potential, we must elicit the help of the entire community. Policymakers, educators, business leaders, civic organizations, and parents can all play important roles in improving education for America's most talented students. . . . Only a challenging educational environment that elevates standards for everyone can create the schools our students need to take their places in tomorrow's world. (p. 14)

Unfortunately, there has been resistance to gifted education (Clark, 2002), perhaps because giftedness is not well understood. It does not help that the popular press prints few articles about gifted learners and their education in newspapers (Lewis & Karnes, 1995; Meadows & Karnes, 1992) or in magazines (Lewis & Karnes, 1996). Thus, parents, teachers, and other professionals in the field need to write articles based on their knowledge and experiences to broaden the general public's understanding of gifted children. It is important for each of us to speak out for the needs of our students and educate ourselves with the necessary skills to employ various public relations strategies when appropriate so we can make the dream of high-quality education a reality.

Targeting Your Audience

The general population is comprised of many subgroups based on interests. When planning public relations, it is important to target the specific population or populations that will benefit the most. The specifics of the message itself and the manner in which it is delivered may vary depending on the interests of these groups, even though the basic message remains the same.

Public relations may be viewed as planned and unplanned. Part of your planning will include identifying your target audiences and devising strategies that will best explain your goal and supporting purposes. Every person working on public relations activities must speak the same message to avoid confusing the audience. This is easier to accomplish when working toward a particular goal. It is, however, highly important the rest of the time, too. Your unplanned interactions with people throughout your school and community also need to perpetuate a central message, otherwise your problems and complaints tend to be what is heard, not the positive aspects of gifted children and their education.

Audiences Internal to the Educational System

Audiences with a background or special interest in education will likely be more informed about general educational issues than individuals whose primary interests may be elsewhere (see Figure 1). However, even within this group, expertise will vary widely. Although they are likely to have in common a strong interest in the education of young people, their beliefs about how children should be taught can be very different. Analyze who is supportive already, which educators have little or no knowledge about gifted education, and finally who may be actively opposed to giving gifted children a different education from other students. Solicit the help of the first group to broaden your base of support.

The second group, those who have little or no knowledge about gifted education, will be the focus of the bulk of your public relations strategies. Individuals who are opposed to gifted education will require special attention. Learning about their concerns and misconceptions can often be a useful tool for designing your message (Yale, 1995). Refrain from directly disagreeing with an opponent since this only calls attention to their views. It is usually more effective to counter the misinformation obliquely. That is, write or speak accurate information about gifted children and their education as your main goal. The errors espoused by your opponents will be countered in the process of disseminating your main message.

When targeting parents or guardians and other family members, keep in mind their concern for providing what they believe is best for their children;

There are a wide variety of people that work within the educational system or are directly accessed through the educational system. The nature of the information you provide to them will be somewhat different than for individuals that are not closely related to the educational system. Check all the following that you wish to impact. Note their probable level of understanding of gifted learners using the following scale: supportive, little or no knowledge, not supportive. Jot down the names of specific individuals who may be particularly accommodating or opposed.

	Supportive	Little/No Knowledge	Not Supportive
_____ School boards	_____	_____	_____
_____ Superintendents	_____	_____	_____
_____ Assistant superintendents	_____	_____	_____
_____ Principals	_____	_____	_____
_____ Assistant principals	_____	_____	_____
_____ Curriculum specialists	_____	_____	_____
_____ Media specialists	_____	_____	_____
_____ Guidance counselors	_____	_____	_____
_____ School psychologists	_____	_____	_____
_____ Special education directors	_____	_____	_____
_____ Coordinators of gifted programs	_____	_____	_____
_____ Teachers—elementary	_____	_____	_____
_____ Teachers—secondary (specific content areas)	_____	_____	_____
_____ Teachers—gifted/talented	_____	_____	_____
_____ Support staff	_____	_____	_____
_____ Students	_____	_____	_____
_____ Parents/guardians	_____	_____	_____
_____ Family members	_____	_____	_____

Figure 1. Audiences internal to the educational system

however, the amount of time and energy they have to contribute may be limited. Remember that family members are both an audience and a potentially powerful force for advocacy. The students themselves are also an audience and can be excellent advocates. Who better to speak to the benefits of quality services than the students themselves? (See the section on involving others for suggestions.) The categories of students and parents include all levels of ability and need, not only those with ties to gifted education. Public relations planners would be wise to take into consideration the needs and feelings of these diverse groups.

The manner in which you approach various groups may need to be different. To parents and guardians, the individual student is paramount. The difficulties of meeting the needs of a heterogeneous population are often not recognized. Most educators, of necessity, tend to focus their primary attention on the majority. Keep in mind that your fellow educators have differing educational and experiential backgrounds, as well as different amounts of exposure to gifted individuals. In addition, they already have enormous responsibilities that require their time and attention. It is not too surprising that research shows that they are inclined, if only by default, to let gifted children learn on their own (Archambault, Westberg, Brown, Hallmark, Zhang, & Emmons, 1993; Westberg, Archambault, Dobyns, & Slavin, 1993). Relative to the needs of the majority and the evident needs of students with disabilities, the needs of gifted learners do not seem very pressing. Sometimes, they may not be noticed at all.

Audiences External to the Educational System

The broadest of all audiences is the general public, which includes both people inside the educational system and those who are not overtly connected to the schools (see Figure 2). Neighbors, friends, and relatives are people you see every day and often do not think of in terms of public relations. Similarly, you may not recognize your informal dealings with various organizations, religious affiliation members, and others within your community who can have a powerful impact on perceptions of gifted children and their education. The general public may also be thought of in terms of people in the arts, business and industry, the media, political organizations, the government, and the many professions. The way your message is packaged and delivered to the arts community may need to be a little different from the way it is presented to businesses or the media.

Public Relations Strategies

A wide variety of strategies is available for bringing your message to the attention of your targeted audience(s). These include nonprint, print, and other media as a means for information dissemination. An extensive shopping list of strategies is provided with a brief description of each in Figures 3, 4, and 5.

Some of these methods are free, while others range in cost. When selecting the strategies, consider the overall cost, the effectiveness for reaching your targeted audience, and the ease of use. You want to be sure to get the most "bang for your bucks," and that does not always equate with free or inexpensive. It is worth the time to consider carefully a suitable mix of strategies. For specific suggestions on writing techniques and media relations, see Alvino (1991), Karnes, Lewis, and Stephens (1999), Pentecost (1997), Steinke and Steinke (1987), and

Members of the general public comprise the broadest possible group. Within this classification are many heterogeneous audiences, each with a range of experience and knowledge of gifted education. Your strategies may need to differ slightly depending on whether you want to focus on certain groups. Check the specific audiences of interest to you, the general public to reach all audiences, or the general public with emphasis on one or two particular groups. Analyze each potential audience as to the amount of support that might be available, noting individuals who may be particularly helpful or antagonistic.

	Supportive	Little/No Knowledge	Not Supportive
___ General public	___	___	___
___ Neighbors	___	___	___
___ Friends	___	___	___
___ Relatives	___	___	___
___ Civic and service organizations	___	___	___
___ Arts	___	___	___
___ Business and industry	___	___	___
___ Media	___	___	___
___ Political and government leaders	___	___	___
___ Professionals	___	___	___
___ Religious affiliation members	___	___	___

Figure 2. Audiences external to the educational system

Wood (1999). An example of an extensive and creative media campaign conducted by a state gifted organization in Wisconsin is described in Grika (1986). Many of her strategies could be used locally by scaling them down in size, even "gift wrapping" the capitol building with ribbon signed by gifted children from all over the state.

Some of your former public relations activities can be recycled (Horowitz, 1996; Yale, 1995), a strategy that is practical for any size public relations campaign. Horowitz (1996) suggested collecting news articles in a file for future use on a bulletin board, in a "brag book," or in media publicity packets. Teachers can use a bulletin board in their classrooms, in the library, or in the entry of the school as a place to display articles and photographs chronicling their participation in various activities (e.g., academic competitions, special programs, community service, student contributions to the newspaper, special events, and

Nonprint media consist of oral communication methods, some with pictures. The potential for reaching your target audience increases when you combine multiple methods. Some of these methods combine well with Other media to enhance their effectiveness. Consider the options provided by the following media. Use them to help you expand your public relations/advocacy plans.

Computer Graphics (amateur, professional, student-generated)
_____ Part of a multimedia presentation
_____ Use on school, program, or district Web page
_____ Other _____

Radio
_____ Community calendar
_____ Editorials
_____ Hard news
_____ Human interest stories

_____ Interviews
_____ Public service announcements
_____ Talk shows

Teleconferencing
_____ Classes
_____ Interviews

_____ Meetings
_____ Staff development

Telephone
_____ Advertised hotlines
_____ Planned networks to spread news rapidly

Telephone answering machine
(publicized number can be available at scheduled times)
_____ Class news
_____ Organization updates

_____ Program updates

Television
_____ Community calendar
_____ Editorials
_____ Hard news
_____ Human interest stories

_____ Interviews
_____ Public service announcements
_____ Talk shows (use national and local experts, gifted students, other individuals/groups)

Video (professional, amateur, or student-made)
_____ Displays (at meetings, malls, fairs, conferences)
_____ News releases for TV
_____ Public interest segments on TV and ETV
_____ QuickTime or streamed video (in Web-based class or staff development, on Web page)
_____ Staff development

Webcam (continually running, activated at set times)
_____ Class activities
_____ Special events

Figure 3. Nonprint media

Print media encompasses all use of print in any form and may be accompanied by pictures or graphics. Some of the following strategies are suitable for small, local advocacy plans, while others are intended for statewide or even national campaigns. Look at the selection and check those that could help you achieve your goal. Keep in mind the audience(s) that you would be targeting and the people who would be responsible. Consult your completed Points of Personal Power and Talent Identifier of Unique Skills to help you. Organize your plans on the Public Relations Annual Plan calendar.

Advertising—donated or paid; display or classified

_____	Journals	_____	Television
_____	Magazines	_____	World Wide Web
_____	Newspapers		

Advertising slug (specialized imprint that accompanies stamp for bulk mailing)

_____	Logo	_____	Slogan (short phrase)

Articles—single or series, electronic or paper

_____	Journals	_____	Newsletters
_____	Listservs (electronic mailing lists)	_____	Newspapers
_____	World Wide Web	_____	Magazines

Bibliographies—electronic or paper (book listings on variety of topics)

_____	General list	_____	Specific list

Billboards (unused space available rent-free for nonprofit groups)

_____	General information	_____	Specific information

Bookmarks

_____ Key information about gifted students, class, program, organization
_____ Logo of program, organization, special project
_____ Slogan

Brochures or flyers

_____ General information about gifted children
_____ Information about organizations (local, state)
_____ Information about program (school, Saturday, summer)
_____ Specific topics

Bumper stickers

_____	Program information	_____	Recognition
_____	Slogan		

Bus placards (side panels donated on space-available basis)

_____	General information	_____	Specific information

Direct mail (packets of selected information mailed to targeted groups)

_____ Specific audience external to school _____
_____ Specific audience internal to school _____

Editorials—guest or invited, electronic or paper

_____	Journals	_____	Magazines
_____	Listservs (electronic mailing lists)	_____	Newspapers
_____	World Wide Web	_____	Newsletters

continued on next page

Figure 4. Print Media

Figure 4 continued from the previous page

Electronic bulletin boards
_____ Newsgroups
_____ Private (you belong to the organization that sponsors it)
_____ Public

Electronic signs (external message boards for short public service information)
_____ Banks   _____ Schools
_____ Businesses   _____ Other

E-mail
_____ Individual and group mailings   _____ Mailing lists (listservs)

Fact sheets—single or series, electronic or paper
_____ Specific audience external to school _____
_____ Specific audience internal to school _____

Handbook—electronic or paper (compiled by local, state, national organizations)
_____ Advocacy methods
_____ Characteristics and needs of gifted students (primarily for parents)
_____ Identification procedures
_____ Instructional strategies

Journals—electronic or paper (professional publications)
_____ State _____
_____ National _____
_____ International _____

Letters to the editor
_____ Educator written   _____ Student written
_____ Parent written

Magazines—general and specific topic publications, electronic or paper
_____ State _____
_____ National _____
_____ International _____
_____ News releases   _____ Calendars of upcoming events
_____ Advertising (paid or donated)   _____ Editorials
_____ Articles (single or feature series)   _____ Letters to the editor

Newsletters—electronic or paper (in-house publications for employees and members)
_____ Businesses _____
_____ Organizations _____
_____ Schools _____

Newspapers—electronic or paper
_____ Advertising   _____ Editorials
      (paid or donated; display or classified) _____ Letters to the editor
_____ Articles (single or feature series)   _____ News releases
_____ Community calendars   _____ Public service announcements

News releases—immediate or continuing news coverage
_____ Brief summary of special events   _____ Opinion pieces
_____ Feature stories   _____ Other items of interest

Novelty items—print with logo or slogan

_____	Buttons	_____	Pens
_____	Dry erase boards	_____	Other school items
_____	Magnets	_____	Post-It notes
_____	Mugs	_____	Hats
_____	Pencils	_____	Visors

Piggy-back mailing (information included in another group's mailing)

_____ Brochure
_____ Fact sheet
_____ Other _____

Position papers (various key topics)

_____ Local _____
_____ State _____
_____ National _____

Postcards

_____	Calendar of special events	_____	Meeting reminder
_____	Invitations	_____	Special messages

Posters—various sizes, colors, messages

_____	In buses	_____	In store windows
_____	In business windows	_____	On school bulletin boards
_____	In libraries		

Rubber stamp (use with bright-colored ink on all outgoing material)

_____	Program logo	_____	Program slogan

Stickers (various sizes and colors)

_____ Program logo
_____ Program slogan
_____ Small stickers (make envelopes and papers stand out)
_____ Large stickers (attract attention on car bumpers)

T-shirts (use or special events, trips, gifts)

_____	Program logo	_____	Program slogan

Thank you letters—sent by individuals or organizations

_____	Continuing support	_____	Favorable vote
_____	Expected favorable vote		

Wire service (forward quality news for broader coverage and listing in news data bases)

_____ Specific article _____
_____ Specific wire service _____

World Wide Web home page (link numerous resources within own site or to other sites, permits access to a wide array of documents, may contain internal search tool)

_____ General articles (single or series)
_____ Specific articles (single or series)
_____ News releases
_____ Advertising
_____ Announcements
_____ Calendars
_____ Link internally
_____ Link externally (articles, ERIC documents, school homepages, organization home pages, search engines)

Other media are a collection of opportunities to call attention to your cause that combine print and nonprint materials in unique ways. Displays are a variation on a sign or billboard. They have the advantage of taking little time to set up and maintain, yet they are seen by many people, often repeatedly. Special events can only be used infrequently; however, they are usually fairly conspicuous when they occur so they gain a lot of attention. Speeches impart useful information and are usually targeted at a particular audience unless transmitted by radio, television, videotape, or webcam. Student performances can be very effective. Students are often their own best advocates.

Displays (instructional materials, student work, scrapbook, competition trophies)
_____ Business and industry lobbies
_____ Conferences
_____ Libraries
_____ School or district office lobby
_____ Store windows

Special events
_____ Booths at conferences or malls
_____ Contests
_____ Conferences
_____ Panel discussions
_____ Proclamations (governor announces state gifted month, mayor names local gifted week)
_____ Ribbon cutting or wrapping
_____ Recognition ceremonies for supporters (with or without a meal; present certificates, gifts, or plaques)
_____ Recognition of student or class contributions to the community
_____ Seminars
_____ Sponsorships
_____ Staff development
_____ Workshops

Speeches—local, state, national, international (present at various conferences, events, and meetings)
_____ Business
_____ Civic
_____ Education
_____ Social groups

Student performances—local, state, national, international (present at various events)
_____ Meetings
_____ Conferences
_____ Fairs
_____ Mall events
_____ Other _____

Figure 5. Other media

newspaper articles about the gifted program). This can be a source of pride for the students and the school, as well. These same types of materials can be kept in a scrapbook or "brag book" and displayed in the school lobby, the library, at meetings such as PTA/PTO, and open houses. These ideas are so commonplace that we tend to overlook their value for building an understanding about your students and your program. Students and their families love to see their names in print, and most teachers collect clippings about their students to tape on the door. Now there is an even greater incentive to "make news" so there is more material for the bulletin board (it needs a catchy name) and the "brag book."

Horowitz (1996) pointed out that another simple, yet effective method for getting extra mileage from earlier news articles is to gather them into media publicity packets and keep multiple copies of the packets in a convenient location. That way, school staff can share them with visitors such as community groups, school board members, business leaders, or legislators when they come to the school, taking advantage of the unexpected opportunity to provide positive information about your students and program. Finally, if several articles were published about your program, such as the Keep America Beautiful example in the first scenario, this shows that the topic is newsworthy. You can use this leverage to bring the news to a local radio, cable, or public access television station for additional coverage.

Basic Planning for Effective Public Relations

Public relations activities need to be approached with careful planning to maximize their effectiveness. Individual strategies in isolation do not work as well as a coordinated plan for the year. If your time and resources are limited, start small with one or two activities. New strategies can be added each year. You can publicize class activities on your own, but it is easier and more efficient to share the load with others. Consider working with colleagues from your school or district, teachers from other districts, and parents of your students. Whether you are working as a member of a small group or for a large organization, it is important to develop a basic plan. It will save more time and energy than it consumes and will enhance your effectiveness. Local parent support groups and state, national, and international gifted organizations need to appoint a standing committee charged with the development of a public relations plan for the organization.

Another important aspect of planning is familiarizing yourself with district policies that regulate publicity. Check with a school official about district guidelines. People in small schools need to follow the chain of administrative command, which usually starts with the principal or superintendent, while large school systems usually have a person designated for public relations. Work closely with this individual to increase the effectiveness of your public relations efforts. Written parental permission is usually needed for using photographs of children and youth. Remember, too, that you are always under obligation to disseminate information in a clear and accurate manner so as not to misrepresent your position.

Be clear about what you want to achieve and why. Before selecting the public relations strategies you will use, it is critical that you are clear about what you want to achieve and why. Is your goal primarily to inform the community of your students' activities and accomplishments, or do you want to make something occur or prevent an action? Write down what you want to do and why in clear, concise language. Note supporting reasons to explain why you are taking this action.

Agree on your goal and develop a goal statement. Everyone working on the public relations (publicity) activities needs to come to an agreement on a specific goal. A goal statement is then developed to help provide direction. Activities that do not effectively further this goal should be carefully reviewed, and decisions should be made on an individual basis.

Know your subject before working to convince others. This basic requirement is so obvious it can be overlooked. All participants in public relations activities should have an adequate knowledge of the needs of gifted children and be able to explain clearly how what you want to accomplish will further the goal of meeting these needs. Preparing a fact sheet for your own use will save time and reduce the chances of someone making a costly error. Confusion or misstatements can hinder the goal. An added bonus of this fact sheet is that it can double as one of your public relations strategies (see Figure 4).

For accurate supporting information, contact the Council for Exceptional Children (CEC), the National Association for Gifted Children (NAGC), and the National Research Center on the Gifted and Talented (NRC/GT; see Teacher Resources). CEC has gathered together numerous digests and fact sheets on a variety of topics (one specific to the gifted and public relations has been developed by Karnes & Lewis, 1997). The question-and-answer service at AskERIC, which is supported by CEC, will provide a quick response via e-mail from their Web page, direct e-mail without using the Web, or the telephone. NAGC has developed a number of position papers that can prove useful when you are gathering background information for your public relations. The 14 divisions of NAGC specializing in critical areas of gifted education can provide more specific supporting facts. Abstracts of recent research reports, as well as other useful materials, are available at the NRC/GT.

Successful advocacy often depends on more than being knowledgeable about gifted education. Advocates also need to be familiar with local and state policies that govern gifted education, the processes whereby these policies were created, and how they can be changed (Robinson & Moon, 2003a, 2003b). Even if your current public relations efforts are focused on educating various constituencies and not on policy change, becoming familiar with relevant policies and the people who have power over them will help you target your efforts and prepare for the future.

Determine your target audience(s). Determining who comprises your primary audience(s) can save time, money, and energy. Your audience will be determined by what you want to accomplish. Ongoing public relations can increase collective understanding of the characteristics and educational needs of gifted learners by targeting the general public or specific individual groups.

Dealing with crisis management or implementing program change is somewhat different. Each requires separate strategies, but they can work in tandem. To meet a crisis or implement changes in policy requires that you identify those who wield the power and their advisors. Target people who can accomplish what you want, rather than the general public. In the first scenario at the beginning of the chapter, you could easily accomplish your goal by targeting the general public. This is an example of ongoing public relations.

The second scenario is more complicated, and both general and specific audiences would need to be targeted. Your main audience to change district policy will be those individuals internal to the school, such as the superintendent, director of gifted programs or special education, curriculum developers, building principals, and teachers (gifted, regular, special education, and special content area; see Figure 1). Target others who are likely to be affected. Disseminating *all* your information to everyone in the community may not be very efficient; however, including the general public when publicizing the unique characteristics and educational needs of gifted students will help raise general awareness in your community for future use. In addition, it can enhance economic development by building partnerships with key members of the business community. A strong educational system is an asset when attempting to attract new business and industry to an area. Targeting the media is usually worthwhile regardless of the intended outcome because the media can help you share your message with a wider audience.

Decide on your basic message. It is necessary to decide on the basic message you want to deliver so that your public relations plan, regardless of size, is focused and free of educational jargon that can be confusing. After that decision is made, all members of the public relations committee need to practice the message so that everyone speaks with the same voice. It is particularly important to be clear about what you want and why. Refer to the reasons and support statement you recorded earlier.

Establish a realistic timeline. A reasonable timeline needs to be developed based on the nature of your plan. Allowing either too little or too much time can lead to failure. Each individual activity should also have a specific time limit. These activities are placed on the calendar in a logical order, and the feasibility of completing them all in the time set aside is determined. The number of activities is then adjusted to make sure the overall time table can be kept. In the community scenario, the timeline would be short, otherwise the news will be old. Fast-breaking stories, such as the Keep America Beautiful community scenario, need to be dealt with in a timely manner. Expanding educational program options for gifted children may need several years, with shorter timelines for the various components necessary for achieving such a broad goal.

Determine evaluation criteria so you will know you have succeeded. Ask yourself what you will need to *see* to know that your public relations strategies have been successful. These criteria will vary depending on your goals. Just writing letters to key people, publishing articles in the newspaper, or talking to school officials does not mean anything was accomplished. These are the means, not the ends you are trying to achieve. In scenario one, a news article with a picture in the local paper and perhaps television coverage may be your criteria. In the second scenario, a preliminary criterion might be the formation of a committee to investigate possible educational options for gifted students. Later criteria might include implementation of a specified number of these options.

Get others involved. Organizations need to appoint a committee to coordinate their public relations activities. Individual teachers and parents who want to contribute to improving the public's view of gifted education should locate at least one or two others with whom they can work. They might even begin a special interest group or work within another organization. Public relations can be carried out by one person, but it is more effective to involve others. Once the nucleus of a committee has completed the basic planning, acquire as many volunteers as possible to broaden your support base and increase good will. Be certain these volunteers are also clear about the goal and the message.

The Message

You have decided on your basic message and selected one or more strategies to disseminate it. Figure 6 lists questions that will help you select one or more topics for articles, speeches, or discussions on radio or television. Your message to the general public in scenario one will include information generated by answering questions 1, 4, 6, and 7. For scenario two, your responses to question 1 will be formatted in a considerably different manner when targeting the general public and school officials. You could also target the latter group with topic 7 and descriptions of exemplary classes and programs from around the country (a variation of topic 5).

Print media will be an important strategy, and there are several formats that can be effective (see Figure 4). Consider reaching out beyond your local newspaper, even for a local program or school issue. Newspapers with regional or state coverage can spread your message and possibly gather support from other com-

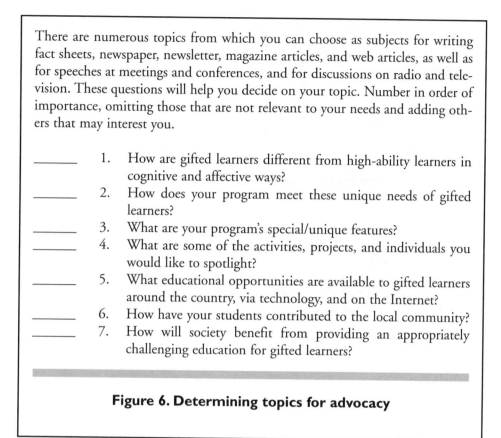

There are numerous topics from which you can choose as subjects for writing fact sheets, newspaper, newsletter, magazine articles, and web articles, as well as for speeches at meetings and conferences, and for discussions on radio and television. These questions will help you decide on your topic. Number in order of importance, omitting those that are not relevant to your needs and adding others that may interest you.

_____ 1. How are gifted learners different from high-ability learners in cognitive and affective ways?

_____ 2. How does your program meet these unique needs of gifted learners?

_____ 3. What are your program's special/unique features?

_____ 4. What are some of the activities, projects, and individuals you would like to spotlight?

_____ 5. What educational opportunities are available to gifted learners around the country, via technology, and on the Internet?

_____ 6. How have your students contributed to the local community?

_____ 7. How will society benefit from providing an appropriately challenging education for gifted learners?

Figure 6. Determining topics for advocacy

munities that are working on similar problems. Newsletters for various community or even state organizations and businesses have broad audiences. You can increase your support base by involving others in reciprocal or collaborative projects. With so many people accessing the Internet, (1) doing mass mailings using e-mail, a local or national listserv, or bulletin board or (2) Δ635creating your own Web page linked to the school or district Web site are additional ways to spread your message and elicit support.

Talent Identification

In the earlier sections of this chapter, we discussed a variety of public relations strategies. Now it is time to identify your Points of Personal Power (see Figure 8). What can you do as an individual to contribute to the development or implementation of a public relations plan? You have far more power than you realize, and you know many others who will help once they know you need them. Our lives are comprised of many overlapping areas of influence. Your friends, colleagues, and acquaintances in each of these areas are not only your audience, but also part of your support. Use Figure 9 to document those many connections.

Information can be disseminated in different formats. Consider the options below and select one or more that will meet your particular needs. You may wish to prioritize them for current and future use.

Format for publication choices

_____ Advertisements
     _____ Paid
     _____ Donated
_____ Article(s)
     _____ Single
     _____ Feature series
_____ Brochures
_____ Editorials
_____ Fact sheets
_____ Letters to the editor
_____ News releases

Many publication sources are available. Consider your target audience(s) and decide on the breadth of your advocacy and/or public relations plans. Select one or more of the following choices for publishing your information.

Publication sources for articles and news

_____ E-mail
_____ Electronic bulletin boards
_____ Letters
     _____ Personal
     _____ Piggy back mailing
_____ Listservs (mailing lists)
_____ Magazines (electronic or paper)
     _____ Local
     _____ State
     _____ National
     _____ Professional
_____ National wire services
_____ Newsletters (electronic or paper)
     _____ Business/industry
     _____ Organization
     _____ School district
_____ Newspapers (electronic or paper)
     _____ Local
     _____ State
     _____ National
_____ Postcards
_____ World Wide Web pages
     _____ District
     _____ Program
     _____ School
     _____ Other _____

Figure 7. Information dissemination

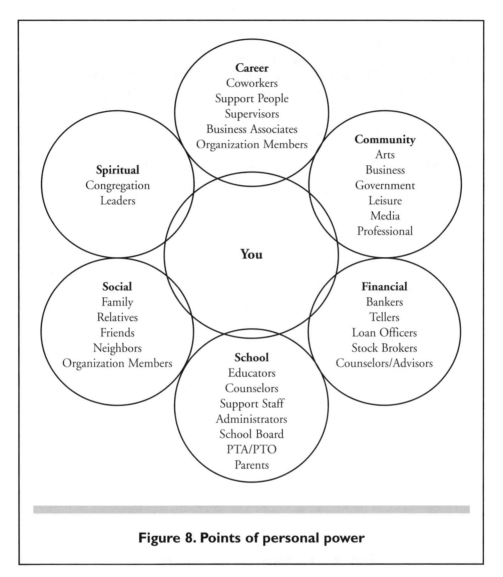

Figure 8. Points of personal power

The purpose of your public relations is to convert members of your audience to supporters. Consider first those people with whom you come in contact because of your career. These include not only coworkers, but also support people, supervisors, business associates, and members of professional organizations to which you belong, to name just a few. For teachers, there will be considerable overlap of career and school. The school sphere includes people internal and external to the school (see Figures 1 and 2).

Who are your contacts when managing your money? Bankers, tellers, and loan officers are a few of the most common. Some people have financial advisors, stock brokers, or investment counselors. You may belong to a club or organization focusing on financial issues.

Socially, there are many possibilities. Family and neighbors are important

Everyone has family, friends, and acquaintances that can help during a public relations campaign. Consider the people with whom you interact in the various spheres of influence and record those names. These are your personal power connections. Make use of them as you plan your public relations.

Career _____

Community _____

     •   Arts _____

     •   Business _____

     •   Governmental _____

     •   Leisure _____

     •   Media _____

     •   Professional _____

Financial _____

School _____

Social _____

Spiritual _____

Figure 9. Personal power connections

contacts. With whom do you spend time? This can be in person, on the phone, or even online. Include acquaintances, as well as your closest friends. You may know them from organizations, leisure activities, or work. Who do you know because of your religious affiliation? This can include spiritual and lay leaders and members of the congregation.

Community is an amorphous whole that can be subdivided into various groups. The arts includes the fine arts of painting and sculpture, photography, dance, theater, places that house the arts, and museums. There are many businesses in any town, such as supermarkets, drug stores, and specialty shops. Include large and small industries in this category, too. Government encompasses local, county, state, and national leaders and their supporters. Leisure can include sports, entertainment, exercise, crafts, reading, and much more. Newspapers, radio, and television comprise the media. And, finally, the category of professionals includes doctors, nurses, dentists, lawyers, architects, and the people who work for them. Using Figure 9 as a guide, note whom you know in each of these areas who might be supportive or have skills that can help you. Remember to gather job and special interest information from the parents of your students. Each of these contacts can be included in a resource file for future use.

The people you know in each of these dimensions are Points of Personal Power for you. Now it is time to begin identifying your own and others' talents (see Figure 10). To produce continuous public relations, gather committee members with creative, developmental (obtaining money), interpersonal, organizational, speaking, and writing skills or those who have connections to people with expertise in these areas. The task can sound daunting until you consider the contacts you and your colleagues and parents can assemble together.

What are your unique talents? Using Figure 10, place your initials beside each of the skills that you consider a strength, adding examples as needed. Do the same for your collaborators, then include names from your resource list to fill holes in critical areas. It is not necessary to have someone for each unique skill, particularly if your present plans are for a small publicity effort. More comprehensive public relations plans will utilize a larger number of talents.

To inform the community of your students' excellent work with the Keep America Beautiful committee (scenario one), you could write a news release for the local newspaper. That is a good beginning, but you need to consider additional options. You, a parent, another adult, or the students themselves could develop a videotape about their work that could be used to raise awareness of community conservation efforts while increasing public understanding of gifted students' capabilities. Depending on the content, the tape could then be used as a community interest feature on television; at meetings of Keep America Beautiful, Rotary, Kiwanis, PTO/PTA, and other organizations; as a display in the mall; as an educational tool to share with other children in the school and district; and as staff development for district teachers. The children could create a before-and-after display at the library or in a store window. Your students could conduct a survey of their classmates and members of the community about environmental issues. They could share their results by writing letters to their legislators, letters to the editor, and a news article for national newspapers. Students could also share what they learned from their projects by making presentations to various organizations, at conferences, and on local radio and television talk shows. Legislators could be invited into the classroom or taken on a tour of the site while the students explain the conservation issues. The media are usually willing to cover the activities of public figures, and, by association, your students and your educational program would receive excellent news coverage. Meanwhile, your students learn useful interpersonal skills.

You and your supporters have many useful skills between you. Write your initials on the line by each area you consider a strength. You may want to use just the main heading, such as "Creative Skills," or you may want to single out a specific subskill, such as "Graphics" or "Advertising." Repeat the process for your supporters or potential supporters. It is not necessary to have all these skills covered, only if they are important to your plan. Actively recruit people to fill critical vacancies.

Creative Skills _____

- Advertising _____

- Displays _____

- Graphics _____

- Slogans _____

- Videos _____

Development Skills _____

- Annual giving _____

- Goods and services _____

- Grant proposals _____

- Scholarships _____

Interpersonal Skills _____

- Build alliances _____

- Facilitate collaboration _____

Organizational Skills _____

- Committees _____

- Governmental _____

- Plan projects _____

- Power brokers _____

- Special events _____

Speaking Skills _____

- Presentations _____

- Radio interviews _____

- Telephone calls _____

- Television interviews_____

Writing Skills _____

- Advertisements _____

- Brochures _____

- Fact sheets _____

- Letters to legislators _____

- Letters to the editor _____

- News articles _____

- Newsletter articles _____

- Surveys _____

Figure 10. Talent identifier of unique skills

Involving Others

Everyday interactions with other teachers can influence their thinking about gifted education, whether you intend that or not. Remaining positive even amid challenges facing you and your students is important. Collaborating with classroom teachers will help dispel notions of elitism and improve education for all students (Hertzog, 1998).

Visitors who have been invited to your classroom and people you meet while on field trips or other school outings are both an audience and potential new advocates for gifted education. The way you and your students present yourselves to the outside world influences the attitudes people form about gifted children and their education. Preparing visitors and people you know you will meet on field trips for the kinds of questions gifted children ask will help them understand your students better and avoid embarrassment. People who are not used to little children asking big questions can come away from such an encounter with negative feelings. However, when they know what to expect, they are more likely to appreciate the children's advanced thinking.

Students can be empowered to advocate for themselves in many ways. Learning appropriate behavior for different social situations is a useful life skill that usually needs to be taught. Children need to learn about the unintended consequences of their actions or words. They can learn how to speak appropriately with school personnel, business leaders, and legislators. Class instruction can include how to write press releases, create videos, develop displays, conduct interviews, and design T-shirts.

Bisland (2003) suggested teaching gifted students oral and written communication and other process skills in the context of a unit on public relations. The students themselves could help develop and implement strategies for publicizing their program, from developing their public relations goals, to evaluating the effectiveness of their plan and its individual strategies. These are authentic learning opportunities that will enhance their adult lives. Examples of possible strategies include participating in and conducting interviews, creating displays of their projects, giving performances of personal or group creations (e.g., songs, plays, poetry), writing press releases, producing a class newsletter, and even creating a scrapbook that can be displayed at meetings and events or in the school's lobby. Another interesting idea for student-led public relations is having gifted students give a tour of the school to business, industry, and community leaders and government representatives. The students would need to be trained to use the appropriate personal and interpersonal skills to be able to highlight key educational opportunities, accomplishments, and perhaps the history of the school ("VIP Tour," 1991, cited in Bisland).

Teachers of the gifted can coordinate with other teachers, parents, and the students when organizing special displays and activities for the school or community. The various holidays provide opportunities for students to display their creativity in the form of plays, music, art, and creative writing. Performances can be given at a PTA/PTO meeting, a civic or business group's meeting, or a locally held convention. Creative writing or artwork can be displayed in the local library or store windows. These public relations activities are much easier to arrange when teachers include others in the arrangements.

When your legislators are in town, invite them to your class to see for themselves what gifted students are learning. This would also be a good opportunity to thank them for past support with a plaque, certificate, or some other memento. Invite the local media to take pictures and write an article for the newspaper, or do the news coverage yourself and give it to the local paper. Invite local artists, business leaders, and professionals to the class to discuss careers or help provide instruction in a content area. Remember, this is a learning experience for the guests, as well as for your students. Parents and teachers coordinating their efforts can make the arrangements more easily and effectively than either working alone.

Yet another way to involve others is to hold a contest to create a slogan for bringing more attention to your particular program or for a full-fledged public relations campaign. The competition could be as small as the gifted classes in your school or expanded to the district, community, state, or even national level, depending on your purpose. Even a small competition within the school can be an event with local celebrities judging the entries (Roberts & Inman, 2003), thus involving people from the community.

Parents have a great deal of power. They can advocate for your students and your program in ways that you as a teacher cannot, such as talking with administrators about specific needs and concerns. Parents can help with publicity by writing news releases and newsletters, the latter of which can be disseminated to all parents, school personnel, community leaders, and legislators. Additional writing projects might include a letter to the editor congratulating the school district on its gifted and talented program and letters to legislators thanking them for their support. Parents can advertise coming events with posters and telephone trees and take photographs and videos for publicity. Use the talent identifier (see Figure 10) to find the unique skills of your students' parents and invite them to help build a strong, positive image for gifted learners.

Staff development targeted to gifted education is needed in every school. Few general educators have sufficient knowledge of gifted students' cognitive and social/emotional characteristics to work with them effectively, and new research on the identification of underserved populations and improved instructional methods is being conducted all the time. When experts in the field are not available to give the training, videotapes can deliver needed information (Karnes & Lewis, 1996; Lewis & Karnes, 1997).

Working within an organization can be a practical method for increasing public awareness about the need for gifted education. Whether you help start a parent/teacher support group or you work with an established organization, you have the resources of many people to help disseminate the message. In either case, a public relations committee needs to be formed that will plan and coordinate all activities. You can be the catalyst that motivates the group to extend its informational reach beyond its current level. Ask to be on the agenda and describe briefly the advantages of planning and working together. If your organization already has an active public relations program, you can suggest some of the strategies provided in this chapter.

An important strategy for any organization, local, state, or national, is getting to know new legislators and other officials by visiting or talking with them on a regular basis (Robinson & Moon, 2003a). The contacts can be invaluable when it comes to advocating for or against specific legislation. Locally, members of parent support organizations (or you as an individual) can begin building relationships with key school board members, district administrators, and school principals in case their help is needed to protect, modify, or expand gifted programming. You may find yourself invited to serve on committees or task forces that help make the decisions.

Use of Organizers

The checklists provided in this chapter will help you organize your thoughts as you make your plans for ongoing public relations and advocacy. Whether you are wanting to share information about gifted students in your class or initiating a large state campaign, using an organizer will improve your efficiency. Use Figures 1 and 2 to identify your audience and Figures 3, 4, and 5 to select strategies that will help you reach your goal. You may discover that you can enhance your chances of success with only a small increase in work if you coordinate several strategies.

Use the worksheets provided in Figures 7 and 8 to expand your base of supporters. They can be disseminated to groups such as those at staff development, educational and community meetings, conferences, and parent meetings to determine the strengths of potential new volunteers. People are often motivated to help with a project or join a committee when they see that their strengths are valued and needed. These people may also know of others who are able and want to help (Figure 7). Small and large organizations can use the Talent Identifier of Unique Skills (Figure 8) to survey their members for strengths and interests. Teachers can use these organizers to collect information from the parents of their students. You will find you have a rich supply of talent among the family members and their friends for class activities, as well as for public relations and advocacy. Both individual teachers and organizations benefit from a group of supporters who can share responsibilities for regular, ongoing public relations.

If one article or activity can increase public awareness of gifted children and their unique needs, how much more effective is a year of coordinated strategies? The annual plan is a way to organize and coordinate your public relations, whether for your classroom; a school or district gifted program; a local, state, national, or international gifted organization; or other supporters of gifted education (see Figure 11). Even if you or your group can only fill in one or two activ-

Month	Objectives	Strategies/Activities	Person Responsible	Date Due	Expected Outcome
Aug.					
Sept.					
Oct.					
Nov.					
Dec.					
Jan.					
Feb.					
Mar.					
Apr.					
May					
Jun.					
Jul.					

Figure 11. Public relations annual plan

ities, it's a beginning. Next year, or even next month, you may realize you can add another component. By keeping track of what you're doing, who's responsible, and how effective your technique is, you will discover you can use your planning time more efficiently. In addition, it will help you be more aware of whom you are reaching and whom you need to target.

Most schools have an open house in the early fall and holiday programs near the end of the year, which provide public relations opportunities. Decide how to make use of them and note them on your calendar. Plan to write about some of your students' special accomplishments and submit them to your local newspaper several times during the year. Educators frequently neglect to follow this simple step, but how else is the community to become aware of what transpires in your classroom? Stories about children and their accomplishments provide a necessary counterbalance to the usual news, reminding us that the next generation is hard at work preparing to become productive citizens and future leaders. For examples of public relations activities aimed at increasing educator and community awareness, see Figure 12.

Organizations might include membership drives, fundraising plans, and conventions or special programs as base activities on their annual plan. Writing news articles, a brochure, a fact sheet, and a Web page and seeing that this information is disseminated appropriately might come next. These are only generic ideas for public relations with no specific plan behind them. To be effective, it is important to coordinate activities around a particular goal. Organizations need to continually build a strong base of support among the general public, the educational community, business and industry leaders, government officials, and the media in order to be prepared to protect or increase services to gifted students when necessary.

Involving Other Constituencies

Reaching out to other constituencies can provide useful collaboration between organizations (Riley & Karnes, 1993a). One method for determining the degree of support for gifted education from the general public is to conduct a public opinion telephone survey. Karnes and Riley (1997) found the response from a representative, statistical sample of residents in a given state was very positive toward the gifted, and results were disseminated to key state representatives and senators to encourage increased state funding.

Teachers and other advocates in gifted education may wish to join together with specific educational groups and associations at local, state, and national levels to determine advocacy and public relations opportunities. One way to achieve this is to assess the needs of the members of a given group or association through a mail survey. Two such studies have been conducted (Riley & Karnes, 1993a; Troxclair & Karnes, 1997), in which professional educational organizations were surveyed to determine such information as the total membership, publications, conferences, and needs of each group pertaining to gifted education (see Figure 13).

Month	Objectives	Strategies/Activities	Person Responsible	Date Due	Expected Outcome
Aug.	Build supportive atmosphere	Welcome letters to students and parents.	Teacher	Week 1 of school	Students/parents feel welcome
Sept.	Parents, educators understand program	Open house, students share selected activities and learning goals. Student-planned/directed as part of student-led PR	Teacher/student leaders (part of student-led PR)	School open house	Parents/educators can explain what students do in G/T
Oct.	Develop rapport with other teachers	Put short fact sheet about G/T; tic-tac-toe activity, simple differentiated lesson, or similar in teacher's mailboxes each week.	Teacher	Mon., weeks 1–4	One or more teacher(s) more understanding; differentiate some lessons, less busy work
Nov.	Increase community awareness of G/T	Students work w/ Salvation Army to gather food, toys for needy as part of service learning unit. Publicize in newspaper, local TV station	Teacher/student leaders (part of student-led PR)	Publicity: Dec. 1 Project end: Dec. 20	Awareness of student contributions to community
Dec.	Increase parent/educator awareness of G/T students	Publish 1st-semester newsletter to parents/district personnel; students write articles on activities, upcoming events, book list	Teacher with HS newspaper sponsor	Wed., week 2	Parents/educators speak positively about program
Jan.	Build understanding and cooperation with gen. ed. teachers	Begin lunch bunch for teachers. Rotate bringing treats and responsibility. Discuss diversity and how to build student success.	School counselor (hide own role to increase success)	Every Friday	
Feb.	Demonstration of talent to local community	Performance of student written, acted, directed play for PTO; publish news article with pictures in local paper	Teacher/student leaders (part of student-led PR)	Monthly meeting	Increased awareness of student talent, G/T program
Mar.	Demonstration of talent to state G/T teachers/educators	Performance of play as lunch entertainment at state gifted convention; article and picture in state newsletter	Teacher and parent volunteer	Annual convention	Statewide recognition through newsletter
Apr.	Build legislator recognition of G/T program	State/local legislators speak to class; students share their learning; newspaper pictures. Follow up with student-written thank you notes.	Teacher/student leaders (part of student-led PR)	Week 3	Legislators can talk knowledgeably about G/T program
May	Increase parent/ educator awareness of G/T students	Publish 2nd-semester newsletter; summarize accomplishments, share summer activity options	Teacher with HS newspaper sponsor	Wed., week 2	Parents/educators speak positively about program
Jun.	Build differentiation skills	Staff development on differentiation for all teachers. State G/T speaker.	Teacher	Immediately after school ends	Teachers create 1 differentiated lesson each, share
Jul.	Build differentiation skills	Work session(s) with willing teachers on differentiation.	Teacher	July 31	Teachers create differentiated lessons, express greater comfort teaching G/T

Figure 12. Sample public relations annual plan

Name of Organization: _____

I. Association Information

Person completing this survey form
Name: _____ Title: _____

Address: _____

_____

Telephone:_____ Approx. no. of members in the association: _____

II. Association Publications

Journal Title: _____ No. Issues per year _____

Newsletter Title: _____ No. Issues per year _____

Approximate no. of articles relating to gifted education in your association's journal
during the past 3 years   _____
newsletter during the past 3 years   _____

Other publications addressing gifted education topics during the past 3 years
(monographs, books, etc.). Give complete reference.

Number: _____

Reference: _____

III. Association Conferences (Please check appropriate responses.)

Approximate number of workshops or presentations devoted to gifted education
at association conferences during the last 3 years
_____ 0   _____ 7–8
_____ 1–3   _____ 9 or more
_____ 4–6

Topics addressed as association conferences during the past 3 years
_____ Characteristics of the gifted
_____ Identifying and screening the gifted
_____ Teaching strategies for the gifted
_____ Parenting the gifted
_____ Issues and trends in gifted education
_____ Curriculum development in gifted education
_____ Organization and administration of gifted education

_____ Legal issues in gifted education
_____ Funding gifted education
_____ The future of gifted education
_____ Gifted/Learning Disabled/ADHD
_____ Others _____

Would your group be interested in including gifted education workshops and presentations as you plan future conference programs?

_____ Yes (If yes, please encircle topics listed on front of sheet in preceding section that would be of primary interest.) List additional topics here:_____

_____ No

Conferences Scheduled

2004   Location: _____

        Dates: _____

2005   Location: _____

        Dates: _____

IV. Association Commitment

Does your association have a position paper that is specific to or includes gifted children?

_____ Yes (If yes, please attach a copy of the statement.)
_____ No

Does your association have an active gifted education committee or special interest group?

_____ Yes (If so, group's name.)

Please rate your Association's interest in or commitment to gifted education on a scale of 1 (low) to 6 (high).

_____ 1 Lowest
_____ 2
_____ 3
_____ 4
_____ 5
_____ 6 Highest

Figure 13. Gifted education survey

Riley and Karnes (1993a) reported the results of a survey to 23 associations in Mississippi, with 15 groups responding for a 48% return rate. There were approximately 370,000 individuals within the 15 associations, with memberships ranging from 125 to 66,000. All of the responding groups published a newsletter, and three produced journals. All had state conferences, with four providing one to three workshops and one offering four to six sessions on the gifted over the prior 3 years. All groups responded positively to a question regarding interest in including sessions and presentations in gifted education at future conferences. The requested topics were characteristics of the gifted, learning-disabled gifted, personal and social problems of the gifted, and science fair projects for the gifted. None of the responding organizations had a position statement or an active committee on the gifted.

Similar information was rendered from the study conducted by Troxclair and Karnes (1997). There were a total of 156,823 members in the responding organizations, with a range of 60 to 66,000 per group. Thirteen of those responding published a journal. Within the prior 3 years, four organizations had published from one to three articles on the gifted. Twenty-six organizations published a newsletter, with three groups having one or two articles pertaining to the gifted. Four groups held one to three sessions with topics pertinent to the gifted, and 18 organizations indicated they would welcome sessions on gifted/learning-disabled/ADHD and teaching strategies for the gifted in specialized programs and in the regular classroom. One organization had a position paper and one had a committee on the gifted.

State organizations should develop both short- and long-range public relations plans. One strategy suggested by Riley and Karnes (1993b) is to establish an advocacy/public relations committee within the state gifted association. The committee would have multiple purposes such as coordinating articles for newsletters and journals to other state professional associations, establishing a speaker's bureau for other groups' conferences, and assisting those groups wanting to establish a committee or write a position paper for the gifted.

State associations have developed a variety of public relations tools for advocacy (Karnes, Lewis, & Pentecost, 1996; see Figure 14), with the most widely used tool being the newsletter, followed by brochures, proclamations by mayors and governors, special events, and student performances. Displays, T-shirts, posters, hotlines, buttons, videos, and bibliography listings were employed by some associations. Media contacts were most often through newspapers—feature articles, editorials, and letters to the editor. Only one third of the state associations employed radio and television for public relations, and less than 12% used paid advertisements. Half of the associations had a public relations committee, but only 14 indicated having planned media campaigns and 24 reported having an annual plan.

These studies were designed to be used as models for other states, but they can be easily adapted for groups at local and national levels to develop appropriate public relations and advocacy strategies. Both of the studies indicated the

Name of Organization: _____

I. Association Information

Person completing this survey form
Name: _____ Title: _____

Address: _____

_____

Telephone: _____ Approx. no. of members in the association: _____

Please respond yes or no to each of the following items if your organization has
employed them for public relations.

II. Association Printed Public Relations Materials

Newsletter   yes _____   no _____

Affiliate Newsletter   yes _____   no _____

Journal/Magazine   yes _____   no _____

III. Specialty Public Relations Strategies

Billboard   yes _____   no _____

Brochure
    About Organization   yes _____   no _____

    Other topic   yes _____   no _____

Bibliographies   yes _____   no _____

Bookmarks   yes _____   no _____

Buttons   yes _____   no _____

continued on next page

Figure 14. Public relations survey

Figure 14 continued from previous page

Displays	yes _____	no _____
Posters	yes _____	no _____
Proclamation from mayor or governor	yes _____	no _____
Special events	yes _____	no _____

    Examples _____

Student performances	yes _____	no _____
T-shirts	yes _____	no _____
Telephone hotline	yes _____	no _____

Video
About organization	yes _____	no _____
Gifted characteristics	yes _____	no _____
Teaching techniques	yes _____	no _____
Other	yes _____	no _____

IV. Media Contacts for Public Relations

Newspapers	yes _____	no _____
Editorials	yes _____	no _____
Feature articles	yes _____	no _____
Letters to the editor	yes _____	no _____
Paid ads—Display	yes _____	no _____
Paid ads—Classified	yes _____	no _____
Television	yes _____	no _____
Radio	yes _____	no _____

Other _____

V. Public Relations

Do you have a public relations committee?   yes _____   no _____

Do you have a planned media campaign?   yes _____   no _____

Do you have an annual public relations plan?   yes _____   no _____

Do you network with other organizations?   yes _____   no _____

Do you contribute to other
organization's newsletters?   yes _____   no _____

Do you provide speakers for other organizations?   yes _____   no _____

Do you have presidents of other organizations
on your advisory board?   yes _____   no _____

VI. Other Public Relations Ideas We Have Found Effective

_____

_____

---

many opportunities for the development of collaboration and partnerships with other professionals. By networking with other organizations, greater results will transpire than are possible when working alone.

Recommendations for reaching out to other constituencies include, but are not limited to, the following suggestions: Encourage gifted teachers and other gifted specialists to publish in the newsletters and journals of organizations outside gifted education, including those of other education and counseling organizations, community organizations, business and industry, and the popular press. They need to submit proposals to conferences and speak at meetings of many different constituencies in order to broaden the audience who hears about the needs of gifted children. Finally, organizations supporting gifted education need to include on their advisory boards key legislators, business leaders, and representatives from other organizations and encourage members of their own organizations to serve on other boards. The contacts gained from working together in this way can have far-reaching effects.

Summary

Public relations is a continuous need in gifted education. Selecting the appropriate target audience(s) for your public relations efforts is an important initial decision. In addition, you need to be sure that all participants understand the basic message and speak with one voice. To make this critical component easier to accomplish, it is recommended that a basic plan be clearly written. A wide variety of public relations strategies are available, and it is crucial to select the appropriate strategies for each target audience. Objective evaluation criteria are needed to determine if your public relations plan has been effective. Joining with other interested individuals and organizations gives you the potential to expand your ability to reach your chosen audiences. The goal of disseminating accurate information about gifted learners and their education is never-ending, yet worthwhile. How else will people outside the classroom learn about how gifted students contribute to their communities or why gifted learners require a differentiated education to help them fulfill their considerable potential? Every person in gifted education needs to make a lifelong commitment to become public relations specialists for gifted children and youth.

Teacher Statement

Being given the position of district coordinator for the high-ability learners (gifted students) in our district, I was faced with many new challenges and concerns. The first obstacles were revising and utilizing our district plan, coordinating a team of educators with whom to collaborate, and beginning a program of public awareness for our new gifted program.

To understand the importance of public relations and to have another look at what steps I might need to take in implementing public awareness, I reviewed material that I had used in college. This chapter was one of my primary sources for help. It explained the need for voicing support and advocacy for the gifted, how to develop an effective plan so you can move in the right direction, the use of a variety of strategies and ideas to present information with a new approach or style, and how to deliver that message to your audience in a clear, complete way.

Overall, what ended up being the most useful information in the chapter was how to broaden the existing support base of my gifted program to include a variety of groups, businesses, and organizations that allow for involvement and awareness. Many public relation activities are listed in the chapter that provide ideas and participation not only for educators, but for parents and community members, as well. My favorite activities were those that allowed for student involvement. Having your students writing press releases and creating public displays not only opens up creative approaches to learning, but allows opportunity for parental involvement, as well.

—Valerie Vincent

Discussion Questions

1. Discuss why it is necessary to formulate a plan of action for your proposed public relations campaign, whether it is a small parent- or teacher-run activity or a statewide campaign developed by the state's gifted association.

2. How would you decide who would make effective members of your planning committee? Consider such variables as committee size, the support you would gain, and the unique skills members might bring.

3. Discuss the pros and cons of the following strategies:
    *   writing a letter to the editor about something that pleases you about the gifted program and a letter expressing your displeasure that the district does not provide a service you want;
    *   writing an article for the local newspaper describing your students' work with Keep America Beautiful (first scenario);
    *   submitting an article to another organization's newsletter;
    *   developing a newsletter for your gifted program;
    *   inviting school board members and legislators to speak to your students; and
    *   developing a fact sheet to distribute to your fellow educators.

4. Discuss how you could use your students to enhance the public's understanding of their gifted education opportunities and benefits. Consider also how your students could learn from these experiences. Could you build some of these opportunities into your curriculum?

5. Explain how you have personal power within your career, financial, school, social, and spiritual contacts.

6. Explain how you have personal power within the following groups from your community: the arts, business and industry, government, leisure, the media, and the various professions.

7. Using the Annual Plan Organizer, develop four activities you could use to let more people know what your students are doing during one school year and support your reasons for selecting each activity.

8. If you were the chairperson of the public relations committee for your state organization, what resources would you select for a yearlong campaign? Are free methods better choices than those for which you must spend some money? Explain your reasoning for your choices.

Teacher Resources

There are few materials focused on developing public relations for special programs. Articles addressing the needs of public relations in gifted education are listed in the references. Listed below are some useful resources.

Books of Public Relations for Schools

Banach, W. J. (2001). *The ABC complete book of school marketing*. Lanham, MD: Scarecrow Press.
Holcomb, J. H. (1992). *Educational marketing: A business approach to school-community relations*. Lanham, MD: University Press of America.
Kinder, J. A. (2000). *A short guide to school public relations* (Fastback #464). Bloomington, IN: Phi Delta Kappa International.
Kowalski, T. J. (1996). *Public relations in educational organizations*. Englewood Cliffs, NJ: Merrill.
Lober, I. M. (1997). *Promoting your school*. Lanham, MD: Scarecrow Press.
Pyle, J. (1994). *Building community support for schools: A step-by-step method to gain support for schools using relationship-building techniques*. Dubuque, IA: Kendall/Hunt.
Warner, C. (2000). *Promoting your school: Going beyond PR* (2nd ed.). Thousand Oaks, CA: Corwin Press.

Handbooks on Legislative Advocacy

Arkansas Association of Gifted Education Administrators. (n.d.). *Legislative handbook: How to communicate with state and national policymakers*. Little Rock: Author.
Bootel, J. A. (1995). *CEC special education advocacy handbook*. Reston, VA: Council for Exceptional Children.
California Association for the Gifted. (1996). *Advocacy in action: An advocacy handbook for gifted and talented education*. Mountain View, CA: Author.
Mitchell, P. B. (Ed.). (1981). *An advocate's guide to building support for gifted and talented education*. Washington, DC: National Association of State Boards of Education.
National Association for Gifted Children. (n.d.). *Advancing gifted and talented education in the Congress: An advocacy guide for parents and teachers*. Washington, DC: Author.

Periodical Issues Focused on Advocacy

Gifted Child Quarterly, Winter 2003
Parenting for High Potential, March 2003

Both of these are publications of the National Association for Gifted Children. For information about how to obtain a copy, go to http://www.nagc.org and click on "Publications."

Addresses

Council for Exceptional Children (CEC)
1110 N. Glebe Road, Ste. 300
Arlington, VA 22201-5704
(703) 620-3660
(703) 264-9494 (fax)
service@cec.sped.org
http://www.cec.sped.org

National Association for Gifted Children (NAGC)
1707 L St., NW, Ste. 550
Washington, DC 20036
(202) 785-4268
(202) 785-4248 (fax)
nagc@nagc.org
http://www.nagc.org

National Research Center on the Gifted and Talented (NRC/GT)
University of Connecticut
2131 Hillside Road, Unit 3007
Storrs, CT 06269-3007
(860) 486-4676
(860) 486-2900 (fax)
http://www.gifted.uconn.edu/nrcgt.html

National School Public Relations Association (NSPRA)
15948 Denwood Road
Rockville, MD 20855
(301) 519-0496
(301) 519-0494 (fax)
nspra@nspra.org
http://www.nspra.org

U.S. Department of Education ED Pubs
P.O. Box 1398
Jessup, MD 20794-1398
(877) 433-7827
(301) 470-1244 (fax)
http://www.edpubs.org/webstore/Content/search.asp

Web Sites

Searchable ERIC Digests—http://ericadr.piccard.csc.com/extra/ericdigests/index

National School Public Relations Association—http://www.nspra.org
Numerous Web sites are available that offer information about college and university classes on public relations, list agencies that provide public relations for businesses and organizations, or list other contacts in this field. These links are targeted primarily at the business community and are usually commercial. This site is an exception; it includes articles and online help for schools, as well as several publications among its resources.

NAGC State Affiliate Association Websites—http://www.nagc.org/state/stateweb sites.htm
This site contains a list of NAGC's state affiliate association Web sites, many of which have information on advocacy and state laws.

The following Web sites provide information on advocacy that is not state-specific:

Mississippi Association for Gifted Children—http://www.msms.k12.ms.us/MAGC/advocacy.htm

Nebraska Association for Gifted—http://www.nebraskagifted.org/advocacy.html

Tennessee Initiative for Gifted Education Reform—http://www.tigernetwork.org

The Gifted Association of Missouri—http://www.mogam.org/www/advocacy.shtml

References

Alvino, J. (1991). Media relations: What every advocate should know about the tricks of the trade. *Gifted Child Quarterly, 35*, 204–209.

Archambault, F. X., Jr., Westberg, K. L., Brown, S. W., Hallmark, B. W., Zhang, W., & Emmons, C. L. (1993). Classroom practices used with gifted third- and fourth-grade students. *Journal for the Education of the Gifted, 16*, 103–119.

Bisland, A. (2003). Student-created public relations for gifted education. *Gifted Child Today, 26*(2), 60–64.

Clark, B. (2002). *Growing up gifted: Developing the potential of children at home and at school* (6th ed.). New York: Merrill.

Dettmer, P. (1991). Gifted program advocacy: Overhauling bandwagons to build support. *Gifted Child Quarterly, 35*, 165–171.

Grika, J. T. (1986). Gifted children—waste not, want not: The how-to's of a statewide g/c/t awareness campaign. *Gifted Child Today, 9*(1), 25–29.

Hertzog, N. B. (1998). The changing role of the gifted education specialist. *Teaching Exceptional Children, 30*(3), 39–43.

Horowitz, S. (1996). What to do after your story gets covered by the media. *Trust for Educational Leadership, 25*(4), 22–23.

Karnes, F. A., & Lewis, J. D. (1996). Staff development through videotapes in gifted education. *Roeper Review, 19*, 106–110.

Karnes, F. A., & Lewis, J. D. (1997, May). *Public relations: A necessary tool for advocacy in gifted education* (ERIC Digest E542).

Karnes, F. A., Lewis, J. D., & Pentecost, C. H. (1996, December). Use of public relations by state associations for the gifted. *NAGC Communique, 9*(2), 4.

Karnes, F. A., Lewis, J. D., & Stephens, K. R. (1999). Parents and teachers working together for advocacy through public relations. *Gifted Child Today, 22*(1), 14–18.

Karnes, F. A., & Riley, T. L. (1991). Public relations strategies for gifted education. *Gifted Child Today, 14*(6), 35–37.

Karnes, F. A., & Riley, T. L. (1997). Determining and analyzing public support for gifted education. *Roeper Review, 19*, 237–239.

Kowalski, T. J. (1996). *Public relations in educational organizations.* Englewood Cliffs, NJ: Merrill.

Lewis, J., & Karnes, F. A. (1995). Examining the media coverage of gifted education. *Gifted Child Today, 18*(6), 28–30, 40.

Lewis, J. D., & Karnes, F. A. (1996). *A portrayal of the gifted in magazines: An initial analysis.* (ERIC Document Reproduction Service No. ED405710)

Lewis, J. D., & Karnes, F. A. (1997). Videotapes in gifted education will enhance staff development. *Special Populations Division Newsletter, 6*(2), 8.

Meadows, S., & Karnes, F. A. (1992). Influencing public opinion of gifted education through the newspaper. *Gifted Child Today, 15*(1), 44–45.

Merriam-Webster's collegiate dictionary (10th ed.). (1993). Springfield, MA: Merriam-Webster.

Pentecost, C. H. (1997). Media relations in gifted education: A teacher's guide. *Gifted Child Today, 20*(5), 32–34, 36–37.

Renzulli, J. S. (1993). Research and you can make a difference. *Journal for the Education of the Gifted, 16*, 97–102.

Riley, T. L., & Karnes, F. A. (1993a). Joining together with other associations: Strategies for cooperation. *Roeper Review, 15*, 250–251.

Riley, T. L., & Karnes, F. A. (1993b). Shaping public policy in gifted education. *Gifted Child Today, 16*(2), 23–25.

Roberts, J., & Inman, T. (2003, March). Building advocacy with a public relations campaign *Parenting for High Potential*, 24–27.

Robinson, A., & Moon, S. M. (2003a, March). Advocating for talented youth: Lessons learned from the national study of local and state advocacy in gifted education. *Parenting for High Potential*, 8-13.

Robinson, A., & Moon, S. M. (2003b). National study of local and state advocacy in gifted education. *Gifted Child Quarterly, 47*, 8–25.

Steinke, G. L., & Steinke, R. J. (1987). *Public relations for special education.* (ERIC Document Reproduction Service No. ED345431)

Troxclair, D., & Karnes, F. A. (1997). Public relations: Advocating for gifted students. *Gifted Child Today, 20*(3), 38–41, 50.

U.S. Department of Education, Office of Educational Research and Improvement (1993). *National excellence: A case for developing America's talent.* Washington, DC: U.S. Government Printing Office.

Westberg, K. L., Archambault, F. X., Jr., Dobyns, S. M., & Slavin, T. J. (1993). An observational study of classroom practices used with third- and fourth-grade students. *Journal for the Education of the Gifted, 16*, 120–146.

Wood, M. E. (1999). *Selling without $$: Grassroots advocates of gifted and talented education meet the media.* (ERIC Document Reproduction Service No. ED440502)

Yale, D. R. (1995). *Publicity and media relations check lists.* Lincolnwood, IL: NTC Business Books.

Chapter 21

Teaching on a Shoestring:

Materials for Teaching Gifted
and Talented Students

by **Tracy L. Riley**

s the new teacher of gifted and talented students, I was certain I would be faced with many challenges, primarily those associated with teaching in a rural school and working with culturally diverse students. What I did not anticipate was the empty classroom I would be allocated—no furniture, no books, not even a chalkboard. I knew I had 34 gifted children, ranging in age from 8 to 17, and I had signed a contract to be their enrichment teacher. What I did not quite know on that hot August day was how I might fulfill those obligations.

So, my search began for materials for teaching. It began on the school grounds, but eventually took me down many other paths. When I left that classroom, I knew my students had been enriched by the many lessons I had taught (and learned). Our bookshelves were bulging in a bright, colorful classroom filled with resources. This chapter gives you the roadmap of my journey in the hopes that you, too, will be able to discover the joys of teaching on a shoestring.

Materials for teaching gifted and talented students come in many shapes and sizes and with a variety of purposes. Yet, while text after text describes the importance of teachers of the gifted having a solid understanding of methods *and* materials for teaching, little has been established to answer the questions teachers might have regarding the selection, acquisition, and utilization of appropriate teaching materials. For example, how and where are materials obtained? And, perhaps more importantly, what constitutes "good" resources for teaching and learning?

This chapter explores the general nature of suitable materials for gifted students and shares criteria for their selection. Following is a discussion of the types of materials and strategies for locating them, and the chapter concludes with the how-to's of obtaining and teaching with free and inexpensive materials.

Differentiated Materials

Gifted and talented students bring to the classroom a unique set of learning characteristics that demand recognition and attention. It is important to recognize that the gifted and talented are first and foremost individuals with unique blends of traits, although common clusters of characteristics related to learning, creative thinking, motivation, social leadership, and self-determination are often associated with giftedness (McAlpine & Reid, 1996). Having a solid understanding of who gifted and talented students are is the foundation of the effective use of any method or material.

Because the learning needs of gifted students differ, sometimes dramatically, from their peers, educators must respond with differentiated instruction. Differentiated instruction requires adjustments or modifications to the content, processes, and products associated with teaching and learning so that they more closely mirror the abilities and interests of individual students. In order to differentiate these three components effectively, the teaching and learning materials must also be taken into consideration, especially in relation to the learning characteristics of gifted and talented students.

Materials should provide advanced content that is interdisciplinary in nature, has variety, is timely, and shows complexity and authenticity (Maker & Nielson, 1995; Renzulli, 1977; VanTassel-Baska, 1997). In addition, the content should be relevant and meaningful, matching the knowledge needed by those professionals who study and work within the disciplines. For example, Tomlinson Kaplan, Renzulli, Purcell, Leppien, and Burns (2002) distinguished between scholars who complete "expert-like" work and practitioners who work at "expert levels," pointing out that gifted and talented students generally require the latter because of its "greater intellectual demand" (p. 31). Thus, expert-level materials should be made available to students and their teachers. Additionally, the content should be examined in light of moral, ethical, cultural, and personal perspectives, and it should be gender-balanced and inclusive.

Differentiated content is a crucial component of qualitatively different programs, which must take into account individual uniqueness. It should be based on students' strengths, interests, qualities, and abilities, as well as their needs. Hence, opportunities should be given for students to make choices and decisions about what they are learning and the materials that support their learning. A gifted and talented student's knowledge may stretch well beyond the textbooks, resources, and other materials appropriate for the majority of students. Following the lead of the student, teachers should select materials that are driven by content that is personally relevant, meaningful, and appropriate.

For gifted and talented students, it is extremely important that process skills not be viewed in isolation of a meaningful, relevant context. The process skills of thinking, communication, research, and personal understanding must always be embedded in differentiated content, and this should be evidenced in teaching materials. Materials that provide opportunities for open-ended, discovery, or problem-based learning should be sought. Given the rate at which gifted and talented students master new information, the pace of delivery must be adjusted to better match their abilities; hence, materials that stifle or restrain a student's rate of learning should be avoided.

The skills of research—library and scientific, basic and advanced—should be taught to gifted students, and these should mirror methodologies in a real or professional sense, giving gifted students the "tools of the trade." For success in meeting their personalized, differentiated learning goals, students also need the skills of organization, time management, planning, decision making, and goal setting. Reflecting on their own thinking through the development of metacognitive skills will assist gifted students in applying their skills to a variety of different contexts. The purpose in developing these skills is to "allow students to do something with what they know" (Tomlinson et al., 2002, p. 10). By selecting materials that have a sense of authenticity, complexity, and challenge, teachers can enhance these important process skills.

Student products, the pinnacle of differentiation, is the outcome of integrating advanced content with appropriate process skills. Fostering independence and accountability should be a goal of differentiation and can be further enhanced through product development (see Chapter 6 in this book). Products have been described by Maker and Nielson (1995) as the tangible or intangible results of learning; they serve as evidence that learning has occurred (Ministry of Education, 2000). Products demonstrate gifted students' transformation of ideas as they challenge what exists with what might be possible. The selection of appropriate materials for teaching gifted and talented students should allow for, and encourage, the products of their learning to expand to a myriad of possibilities.

Before even considering the array of materials suitable for gifted and talented students and their teachers, it is important to reflect on the common characteristics and behaviors associated with giftedness and, consequently, the principles of qualitative differentiation. The strengths, interests, and needs of gifted and talented students provide the platform from which learning experiences are launched, and the materials used can be seen as the rocket boosters of that launch.

Materials and Criteria for their Selection

"A spectrum of resources, materials that support student learning in the teaching and learning activities, can be tapped for instructional purposes by classroom teachers" (Purcell, Burns, Tomlinson, Imbeau, & Martin, 2002, p. 311). These resources may be teacher- or student-developed or published locally, nationally, or internationally. They may be intended for teacher or student use (all students or gifted students) in regular classrooms or specialized programs. In fact, the resources most appropriate for gifted and talented students might not be designed solely for classroom use, although they should match the teaching and learning goals and objectives. The cost of materials will vary, as will their accessibility, effectiveness, and appropriateness.

The array of materials to support the teaching and learning process is shown in Table 1, as adapted from the work of Purcell et al. (2002). Although the most readily used resources are often textbooks, books, and articles, it is argued that qualitatively differentiated teaching and learning experiences designed to meet the needs of gifted students incorporate *all* of these (Purcell et al.). They further argue that realia and primary source documents—and this might include human resources, too—are critical in that they provide "'ceilingless' opportunities to analyze and interpret information" (p. 313).

With so many possibilities, it is important that teachers have a good understanding of how to best select the materials that fill their desk drawers, line their bookshelves, pile up in their resource files, and are bookmarked in their Web browsers. Apart from the general principles previously discussed, Karnes and Collins (1985) have given a range of general, student, and teacher considerations for selecting materials for gifted students, as shown in Figure 1. These criteria are intended as a screening device, not an evaluative instrument, and teachers are urged to use the questions in relation to their own context, keeping the needs of their gifted students at the forefront of any decision making. Hence, the checklist can be modified.

The Curriculum Division of the National Association for Gifted Children (NAGC) has designed a rubric to determine the alignment of curricula with the differentiated learning needs of the gifted (Purcell et al., 2002, pp. 312–313). It was initially developed to support an annual curriculum competition; but, more recently, it has been deemed suitable for evaluating materials. The rubric examines 12 features and quality indicators, which are outlined below:

1. Clarity of Objectives—stated, specific, unambiguous;
2. Nature of Objectives—transferable across disciplines, incorporating concepts, principles, cognitive skills, methodologies, and dispositions;
3. Evaluation—multiple assessment measures, including preassessment;
4. Learning Activities—different types involving constructivist learning, problem solving, cognitive engagement, and/or hands-on learning;
5. Instructional Strategies—different strategies, including inductive teaching, teacher as facilitator, high-level questioning, or teacher as mentor;
6. Student Products and Assignments—open-ended, creative, or real-world products;
7. Resources—varied and including primary source material;

Table 1

The Spectrum of Resources for Teaching Gifted Students

Human Resources	Parents, community members, experts, teachers
Print Items	Textbooks, books, articles
Nonprint Resources	Videos, audio recordings, Internet, pictures, graphs, maps
Recyclable Materials	Throwaways like boxes, paper, wood scraps
Realia	Objects that relate to real-life, like clothing or equipment
Primary Source Documents	Firsthand information, including photos, journals, letters, maps

---

8. Alignment—sequenced with objectives, assessment, introduction, teaching strategies, learning activities, products, and resources;
9. Nature of Differentiation—explicitly described and accommodating to learning needs;
10. Opportunity for Talent Development—chances for talent spotting; individualization; career, leadership, or real-world application; interaction with role models; exploration of advanced content and skills; authentic product development;
11. Evidence of Effectiveness—systematically implemented and evaluated; and
12. Ease of Use—explicit, well sequenced, and easy to follow.

As the authors state, "Instead of relying solely on advertisements, unwarranted publishers' claims, or colleagues' opinions, the use of the rubric during the curricular review or adoption process ensures the systematic analysis and evaluation of the vital facets and components of any set of commercial materials" (Purcell et al., 2002, p. 318). Teachers may decide to adapt both the Karnes and Collins (1985) and NAGC selection criteria by designing their own checklist. But, ultimately, the selection should center around the needs of gifted and talented students so that the materials used in their teaching and learning will begin closing the gap between their abilities and learning experiences.

While these guiding questions and criteria are useful and will potentially lead to more careful selection, teachers of the gifted must remember that, as with any

In order to facilitate the analysis of instructional materials under consideration for use in educational programs for gifted students, a checklist entitled "Criteria for the Selection of Educational Materials for Gifted Students" has been designed. This checklist has three basic components: General Considerations in Materials Selection, Student Considerations in Materials Selection, and Teacher Considerations in Materials Selection. General Considerations are applicable for the selection of all educational materials. Student Considerations pertain specifically to the educational needs of gifted students. This portion of the checklist is designed to be the most helpful in determining whether a material promotes or allows for differentiated educational experiences for gifted students. Teacher Considerations are designed to promote the selection of those materials that will enhance the role of the instructor as a facilitator of the learning process. This checklist is not viewed as all-inclusive. Additional items may be added to meet local considerations.

This checklist is designed not as an evaluation instrument, but rather as a screening device. The number of positive and negative responses should not determine final selection or rejection of a particular material, as no material will contain all facts incorporated into the checklist. The selection of a specific educational material should be based on positive responses to those items that best express student, program, and teacher needs.

Modification of the checklist for the selection of educational materials for gifted students to meet local or individual program needs is encouraged. This checklist should not be perceived as all-inclusive. It is intended to serve as a guide to materials selection, and the questions included are suggested ones for consideration.

In some cases, items that reflect particular program goals may be added. In other cases, educators at the local level may wish to delete certain items and retain those they perceive to be the most important.

Numerical ratings have been intentionally omitted from this checklist. We feel that including a rating scale would usurp professional judgment at the local level. Teachers and administrators of programs for gifted students may wish to devise their own rating system to use with this checklist. When this is done at the local level, materials can then be rated and subsequently selected to fit individual programs and objectives.

Certain cautions are advised in the selection of commercial educational materials for gifted students. Materials marked "enrichment" should be carefully examined to determine the nature of the educational objective. Enrichment activities appropriate to the gifted should extend learning experiences and not reinforce concepts already mastered. Some enrichment materials that are attractively packaged lack depth and challenge.

Materials with specific indicators of age, grade level, or both should be analyzed to determine if their content is appropriate to the development level, abilities, and interests of a gifted student. Using materials designed for particular grade levels at lower grade levels does not, in itself, constitute an appropriate educational program for gifted students. The overuse of games and puzzles in programming for the gifted is discouraged, as well as the sole use of commercial instructional materials. Educational materials should not constitute the total instructional program for gifted students. The manner in which materials are utilized, adapted, and supplemented by teachers determines the direction, focus, and quality of differentiated programs for the gifted. These students should be allowed to assume responsibility for their own learning, including content, learning style, and rate.

General Considerations in Materials Selection	Yes	No
Does the material include general learning objectives?	___	___
Do the learning objectives of the material support the goals of the program?	___	___
Are the concepts presented in the materials valid?	___	___
Does the material have an attractive format and design?	___	___
Are the materials durable?	___	___
Are the materials conveniently packaged?	___	___
Are the materials portable?	___	___
Are the majority of the materials nonconsumable?	___	___
Is the cost of the material commensurate with the use and learning objectives?	___	___
Is the necessary equipment available for the utilization of the material?	___	___
Is the purchase of additional materials necessary?	___	___
Is the suggested grade or age level specified?	___	___
Is the material designed to be used individually?	___	___
Is the material appropriate for group instruction?	___	___
Is an instructional guide provided?	___	___
Are there sufficient numbers of students to utilize the material?	___	___
Are the learning materials presented in sequence?	___	___
Has the material been field tested?	___	___
Do the learning objectives justify the amount of time required for the activity?	___	___
Do the concepts presented in the materials conflict with community standards?	___	___
Are the materials presented in such a way so as to be nondiscriminatory in terms of culture, race, sex, or handicapping condition?	___	___

continued on next page

Figure 1. Criteria for the selection of educational materials for gifted students

Note. Adapted from *Handbook of Instructional Resources and References for Teaching the Gifted* (pp. 15–20), by F. A. Karnes & E. C. Collins, 1985, Newton, MA: Allyn and Bacon. Copyright ©1985 by Allyn and Bacon. Adapted with permission.

Figure 1 continued from previous page

Student Considerations in Materials Selection for Gifted Students	**Yes**	**No**
Are the students' interests reflected in the materials?	____	____
Is the mode of presentation commensurate with the learning style of the student?	____	____
Can the concepts presented be employed by the student in other learning situations?	____	____
Is self-evaluation an integral part of the material?	____	____
Do the materials encourage the student to undertake further study and research in related areas?	____	____
Are appropriate references provided for use by the student?	____	____
Are the processes taught applicable to a variety of learning situations?	____	____
Is the content of the material consistent with the student's developmental level or prior experience or training in this area, rather than grade-level oriented?	____	____
Do students develop products; and if so, are appropriate outlets for students' products suggested?	____	____
Does the material promote development in one or more dimensions of learning appropriate for the gifted?	____	____
A. Does the material foster and enhance the development of oral and written communication skills?	____	____
B. Does the material foster and enhance the development of higher cognitive processes of analysis, synthesis, and evaluation?	____	____
C. Does the material foster and enhance the development in the affective domain, such as understanding ourselves and others?	____	____
D. Does the material foster and enhance the development of logical thinking, such as inductive and deductive reasoning and problem-solving skills?	____	____
E. Does the material foster and enhance the development of critical thinking, such as the judgement and decision-making processes?	____	____
F. Does the material foster and enhance the development of divergent production, such as open-ended responses and self-expression?	____	____
G. Does the material foster and enhance research skills (e.g., library research skills) and knowledge and application of the scientific method of research?	____	____

	Yes	No

H.   Does the material foster and enhance development
in values clarification, such as defining, expressing, and
assuming responsibility for personal values?   _____   _____

I.   Does the material foster and enhance the development
of group dynamics, group interaction processes, and
communication and discussion techniques?   _____   _____

J.   Does the material foster and enhance the development
of creativity, such as fluency, flexibility, originality,
and elaboration?   _____   _____

Teacher Considerations in Materials Selection for Gifted Students

Are specific teaching suggestions provided?   _____   _____
Do materials allow for teacher initiative and adaptation?   _____   _____
Are guidelines given for making some of the necessary materials,
rather than purchasing them?   _____   _____
If specialized training is required for teachers' utilization of materials,
do instructions accompany the material?   _____   _____
Is the amount of required teacher preparation time consistent
with the scope of the learning objectives?   _____   _____
Are appropriate references and resources suggested?   _____   _____
Is the teaching style suggested in the materials parallel
with the instructional style of the teacher?   _____   _____
Are suggestions provided for the elevation of student progress?

good tool, it is the *way* in which the materials are used that determines their effectiveness. The purpose in any material selected for gifted students should be to enhance their differentiated learning experiences, and achieving this requires careful planning, goal setting, organization, and evaluation. As Karnes and Collins (1985) stated,

> Educational materials should not constitute the total instructional program for gifted students. The manner in which materials are utilized, adapted, and supplemented by teachers determines the direction, focus, and quality of differentiated programs for the gifted. These students should be allowed to assume responsibility for their own learning, including content, learning style, and rate. (p. 20)

Thus, after the careful selection of materials, the next step to their effective use relies on the competencies and skills of good teachers of the gifted. Feldhusen (1997) described some of the skills needed by teachers of the gifted, including the ability to facilitate fast-paced instruction, creative and critical thinking skills, appropriate instructional grouping, and curricular differentiation. Purcell et al. (2002) added to this the ability to make adjustments to breadth, level of abstraction, and level of complexity. Other research has indicated that teachers should be able to develop their own materials (Hultgren & Seeley, 1982). Being able to critically evaluate and appropriately select teaching and learning materials is equally important, as long as we remember that their effectiveness will be far greater in the hands of a well-trained and knowledgeable teacher.

Finally, amongst the selection criteria listed by Karnes and Collins (1985) is a crucial one: Is the cost commensurate with the use and learning objectives? This is an important criterion, but a more important reality check for some teachers might be to ask, "Is the cost commensurate to the budget allocated for gifted and talented education?" Those of us in gifted and talented education are all too aware of budgetary constraints and must be careful in spending, being highly selective in what goes in the shopping cart. Gifted programs often suffer from lack of funding or, when funding is available, are the most vulnerable to cutbacks. When funding for gifted programs is not a priority, careful management of each classroom teacher's budget quickly becomes a priority.

The Search for Materials

With the plethora of educational materials available today, any search for materials must begin with a clear sense of purpose. Lewis and Munn (1989) suggested six guiding questions to be asked prior to beginning an investigation of available teaching materials, and these have been elaborated on in relation to gifted and talented students in Table 2.

The purpose in beginning with a clear sense of direction and focus is to ensure that any materials sought and obtained are appropriate to the needs of gifted and talented students, whether they are in a regular classroom environment, mentoring program, accelerated class, or enrichment classroom. This means any time, money, or energy spent in securing materials is worthwhile. Teachers should also remember to use the selection criteria previously outlined *before* obtaining materials, if possible. In the selection of materials, keep these key points in mind:

- how the materials relate to learning goals and objectives;
- practicalities, such as costs and durability;
- suggested uses and potential modifications to content, processes, and products;
- content validity and appropriateness; and
- most importantly, the strengths, needs, and interests of individual gifted and talented students in your classroom.

Table 2

Searching With Purpose

Ask Yourself These Questions	Find the Answers by Considering
What information do I want?	Curriculum goals and objectives, student strengths and interests, program aims
Why do I want it?	An analysis of current resources in relation to needs
When do I need it?	Advanced planning, timelines, calendars
How do I collect it?	Communication, print media, Internet, journals
Where can I find it?	Local, state, national, and international sources for general and gifted education
From whom do I get it?	Educational organizations, business and industry, families, government agencies

Human Resources

Parents, community members, experts, and other teachers can serve as rich resources for teaching gifted and talented students. Renzulli, Gentry, and Reis (2003) suggested the following possible human sources:

1. parents, their friends and coworkers, and the Parent-Teacher Organization;
2. community members, such as retirees and members of religious organizations and service clubs;
3. businesses, through federal and state agencies, partners in education, and colleges and universities; and
4. teachers and staff within your own school and other schools.

They further stated that "Parents and community volunteers may . . . be able to provide resources, materials, and authenticity within a specific profession or topic that can be extremely exciting and motivating to students and adults as well" (Renzulli et al., p. 41). The facilitation of a "people factor" can take different shapes: face-to-face meetings, letter writing, or telecommunications. In other words, the human resources used to enhance gifted programs may be real or virtual. Additionally, the roles played can range from sharing expertise or coaching a Future Problem Solving team, to supplying classroom materials or chaperoning a field trip.

There are many strategies teachers can utilize to locate human resources. Ask other teachers and parents for suggestions through school newsletters, staff meetings, or a flyer on a bulletin board. Contact the local Chamber of Commerce, senior citizens groups, service organizations, and clubs. Take clippings from the local newspaper of human interest and community features and start a file on topic experts. Get to know local businesspeople by contacting their organizations, remembering that many businesses have community outreach programs. A good place to start looking for information is to "let your fingers do the walking"—peruse the yellow pages of your local phone book. Finally, do not forget the teachers within your own school; the history, science, or math teacher may well enjoy spending time working with gifted and talented students. Why not conduct an interest inventory of your fellow teaching colleagues and parents?

In today's technological world, the Internet allows easy access to people with a wide range of expertise outside the local community. For example, there are many "Ask an Expert" Web sites available that allow students to ask questions via e-mail of professionals working in many fields. Some sites also have a set of Frequently Asked Questions and their answers. Telementoring is another technological advance that connects gifted and talented students with online expertise and can be facilitated for individuals or groups of students. See the Teacher Resources at the end of this chapter for recommended sites, or conduct a search using a search engine and the keywords *ask an expert* or *telementoring* for many more possibilities. Students may also try their hand at e-mailing a Web site. For example, a 10-year-old investigating Thomas Edison's life e-mailed the Thomas Edison Birthplace Museum with his questions, and, much to his chagrin and surprise, he received answers from the curator within 24 hours.

In this age of technology, it is important not to overlook other forms of communication. Calling 1-800 numbers, sending a fax, or writing letters can be just as effective. You may obtain the contact information needed from telephone directories, Web directories, magazines, books, and other print media. Or it can be as simple as checking product packaging. For instance, a student interested in chocolate production called Hershey's using the phone number from his candy bar wrapper and was delighted to not only have his questions answered, but also to receive a consumer information pack in the mail.

Most children enjoy sending and receiving "snail mail," and Michael Levine has developed a great resource in *The Kid's Address Book* (2001), which contains more than 2,500 addresses of celebrities, athletes, entertainers, civic organizations, world leaders, and businesses, along with Internet contact information where available. The book is premised on the idea that "Corresponding is an active dialogue between the minds of two people" (p. xii). The purpose in considering human resources, regardless of how their contact with gifted students is facilitated, is to enhance the abilities of gifted students—and to relieve the teacher of having to be the expert in everything.

Print Media

There seems to be a tendency in schools toward the use of print resources, so the possibilities for sourcing books, magazines, newspapers, and so on are endless. There are many publishers of educational materials for gifted and talented students (see the Teacher Resources at the end of this chapter for details.) Additionally, there are many more general education publishers. For gifted and talented students whose interests and strengths are often well beyond the expected, print media of all types should be considered. Magazines, journals, and newspapers offer the latest information and are in many ways of greater value than books that may be out of date before hitting the shelves.

But, before purchasing anything, teachers should play the role of detective and find out as much as possible about the resource. Visit publisher Web sites or order a catalog to view their products. Talk with other teachers who may have used these resources; in fact, ask if they have the resource. Visit Amazon.com (http://www.amazon.com), which features book reviews, links to similar books, and secondhand books. Discuss potential resources with students, asking about their usefulness, appropriateness, and so on. Take advantage of conferences, which often have materials displays where you can browse through the resources and talk with publishing company representatives.

In sourcing print materials without overstretching the budget, begin by checking the local library, your school district's professional library or resource center, and college and university libraries. Visit secondhand bookstores and garage sales. Ask parents, family members, friends, and community members, as well as your gifted and talented students, to check their personal libraries. For example, one family member donated more than 100 copies of *National Geographic* and was delighted not only for my gifted and talented students, but for her tidy attic space. Given the diverse interests of many gifted students and their often insatiable hunger for books and other print resources, their families tend to have well-stocked home libraries.

Another avenue is to ask publishing companies if they have a damaged and defected books program. Harrington and Christensen (1998) reported that some publishers provide book samples free of charge to economically disadvantaged schools. These may be overruns, returns, or slightly damaged and defective copies. Often, publishers are sent desk copies of new materials, and these simply collect dust on office shelves. For example, one publisher sent my class a box of unused resources after receiving our request for donations. In making queries of this nature, it is useful to be specific about the topics, and even titles, of the printed materials being sought.

Investigate the availability of print resources available on the Internet. For example, the Free Books Home Page (http://www.free-books.org) features online e-books for children, including lots of classics like *Black Beauty*, *A Christmas Carol*, and *Jane Eyre*, plus American history realia such as inaugural speeches by famous U.S. Presidents and the U.S. Bill of Rights. Software for both the Microsoft E-Book Reader (http://www.microsoft.com/reader/default.asp) and the Adobe E-Book Reader (http://www.adobe.com/products/acrobat/readstep2.html) is freely available to download, allowing the viewing of e-books on personal computers or palm devices. The University of Virginia's E-Book Library (http://etext.lib.virginia.edu/ebooks/ebooklist.html) provides 1,600 free e-books to view with these readers. The Web also offers many online references at the cost of an Internet connection. Check out Refdesk.com (http://www.refdesk.com), which claims to be the single best source for facts on the Internet. At this site, students can search the Web and access online dictionaries, thesauruses, and encyclopedias. There are also links to worldwide weather, news, facts at a glance, and experts. Another resource is the Digital Reference Library (http://www.xrefer.com), which includes 130 online reference books, including dictionaries of Shakespeare, rhyming, science, the Renaissance, British history, and more. Bookmark Artcyclopedia (http://www.artcyclopedia.com), an extensive Web-based resource for great works of art.

Arts and Letters Daily (http://aldaily.com) is a fabulous Web site for accessing other print resources. The site has links to newspapers and news centers around the world, magazines, columnists, radio news and music, and search engines, plus interesting articles of note. Students can design their own personalized newspaper by visiting CRAYON: Create Your Own Newspaper (http://crayon.net). The system lets users get information on whatever they want—weather, news, sports, even comics—and exclude topics in which they are not interested. LookSmart's FindArticles (http://www.findarticles.com) is a vast archive of published articles you can search for free. Constantly updated, it contains articles dating back to 1998 from more than 300 magazines and journals. And, finally, do not forget that most college and university libraries subscribe to databases that enable access to hundreds of full-text magazines and journals.

Nonprint Resources

Videos, music, pictures, graphs, and maps are just some of the nonprint resources available to teachers and their gifted and talented students. Many of the same search methods previously described can be used to secure nonprint media. For locating videos and compact discs, check the local library's lending program; these are often available at low or no cost. Through their community services, Blockbuster Entertainment offers free rentals of more than 275 videos on everything from fire safety to health and nutrition, plus discounts for classroom teachers on other products. Museums often have lending materials available for the low cost of postage. For example, the National Art Gallery has a free loan program of multimedia on subjects ranging from Impressionism to American Art. The Federal Reserve Bank offers similar services, with videos and films on consumer finance and economics, as well the Federal Reserve System itself. Video Placement Worldwide (http://www.vpw.com) provides information on free educational videos. By visiting their Web site, teachers can find an array of videos, including ones about Lewis Latimer, an often forgotten African American inventor who worked alongside Thomas Edison, as well as women inventors and their inspiration.

Though the music entertainment industry has not made available quite so many freebies, samples are often available, and it is worth contacting music recording companies. For the technologically savvy, the World Wide Web offers an array of musical possibilities. Teachers can search for just the right tune by visiting the WWW Music Database (http://www.roadkill.com/MDB). There are currently more than 21,000 albums and 7,300 artists listed here, and access to the Web sites of distributors for every artist from B.B. King to ZZ Top is available. Links to many online sound bytes can be found at MIDI & Music Technology Resources for Teachers (http://www.isd77.k12.mn.us/resources/staffpages/shirk/midi.html). By following just one link, I had the choice of more than 314 tunes to the fiddle, from Celtic to Mississippi classics. With the right equipment, music can be played from the classroom computer or, with enough smarts, downloaded and saved onto compact disc with a CD burner (just be aware of any copyright laws).

The Internet also allows easy access to free software for students and teachers. Some software is absolutely free and yours to keep, while others offer free trial periods. For example, Sheppard Software offers teachers educational games like Astro-mania and mathematics software like Brainbuilder (see their Web site at http://www.sheppardsoftware.com). For the development of critical thinking skills, mapping software such as ReasonAble! is readily available (teachers can download a trial version by visiting http://www.goreason.com). By visiting Arachnoid.com (http://www.arachnoid.com), teachers can access "careware," including programs for building Web pages, editing and presenting electronic slide shows, and creating graphs. Kids Freeware (http://www.kidsfreeware.com) provides a kid-safe collection of free software with everything from a typing tutor program to a word morph, which allows students to create their own words. The site also includes collection organizers, games, Web page tools, and programs for languages, mathematics, science, reading, and writing.

Many businesses have created educational packages, which include posters, charts, graphs, and maps. Local movie theaters, grocery stores, travel agents, and even bus companies would probably gladly dispose of their extra or dated posters and pictures for classroom use. Most state tourism offices and foreign embassies will happily provide teachers with informational packets that include brochures, historical information, posters, and so on. Automobile associations and other businesses in the travel industry can provide free or inexpensive maps. The children's book *Free Stuff for Kids* (published annually by Free Stuff Editors) features lots of nonprint media—postage stamps, dinosaur paper, animal bank notes from foreign countries, and bookmarks, to name but a few.

On the Internet, there are several image search engines to explore. Students will enjoy The Amazing Picture Machine (http://www.ncrtec.org/picture.htm), which features pictures of aircraft, American cities, animals, dinosaurs, famous people, 20th-century world leaders, and more. Many search engines provide image searches; for example, try your hand at the Google Image Search (http://images.google.com). The National Geographic MapMachine (http://plasma.nationalgeographic.com/mapmachine/index.html) provides access to a variety of maps, including street maps, facts and flags maps, historical maps, and maps of Mars. When using the World Wide Web, these images can be viewed on screen, printed, or saved to the computer, if copyright laws permit.

Recyclable Materials

"One man's trash is another man's treasure," or so the saying goes. "Throwaways" like boxes, paper, wood scraps, plastic bottles, and old magazines are resources teachers can obtain at little or no cost. Rather than discarding these types of materials, teachers can reuse them for art projects, musical instruments, invention fairs, science experiments, technology adventures, wearable arts competitions, and building creations of all types. For more crafty ideas and instructions for using recyclable products, visit Trash to Treasure (http://familycrafts.about.com/cs/fork6/l/bltrashtr.htm), where you will learn how to create a standing picture frame from a CD holder, a turtle from a tuna can, and a didgeridoo from PVC pipe.

A wide range of recyclable materials is shown in Figure 2. No doubt gifted and talented students, especially creative thinkers, will add to this list. Consider natural recyclables, too, like acorns, pine cones, sea shells, coconuts, twigs and branches, and leaves.

There are many ways to obtain recyclable materials. Parents and community members are often happy to get rid of their "trash" and can be requested to do so through school or classroom newsletters, or by running a want ad in the local paper. Garage sales and auctions offer a treasure chest of possibilities. Local businesses can be asked to recycle their office supplies: Paper and envelopes often end up in the waste bucket, but are still great for kids' draft copies, plans, and ideas for their projects. Ask if the students can place a recycling box near the photocopy machine of local businesses to be collected on a regular basis. Also, remember that, by making donations of old equipment, computers, printers, or office furniture, many businesses can get tax breaks. As you involve the community, do not forget save-the-label programs, whereby schools can gain funding for materials and supplies by collecting labels, bottle tops, and box lids from consumer products. For example, in the Campbell's Labels for Education program, schools can collect labels and exchange them for free educational merchandise, including computers, sports equipment, and musical instruments. For information, see their Web site at http://www.labelsforeducation.com.

Many cities have recycling centers, and some have developed recycling arts centers where recyclable goods can be bought at very low prices. Surplus materials suppliers salvage high-quality industrial materials, and it is worthwhile investigating these in local areas. Creative Educational Surplus is one such company,

Bags	Coffee Filters	Plastic jugs
Beans	Cotton Balls	Plates
Bottle caps	Cupcake Liners	Popsicle sticks
Bottles	Drinking Straws	PVC pipe
Buttons	Egg Cartons	Puzzle pieces
Boxes	Film Containers	Rope
Buckets	Gloves	Socks
Cans	Greeting Cards	Sorting trays
Cardboard	Hangers	Strawberry baskets
Carpet scraps	Jars	String
Catalogs	Lids	Styrofoam trays
CDs	Magazines	Tackle boxes
CD cases	Milk cartons	Toothpicks
Cloth	Newspapers	Wallpaper
Clothespins	Packing peanuts	Wood scraps

Figure 2. Recyclable materials

which began "when a group of educators were frustrated that they were unable to obtain suitable materials to match their needs and pocketbooks" (Harrington & Christensen, 1998, p. 126). Request their quarterly publication, which contains many items at reasonable prices: latex gloves, trays, masking tape, sandpaper, pizza wheels, and nets, to name but a few (the address is in the Teacher Resources section of this chapter).

Finally, gifted and talented students can be involved in the search for recyclable materials. Given their predisposition toward real issues, leadership qualities and abilities, and interests in social concerns, many students will enjoy being involved in recycling. Why not investigate recycling as a topic of study? Start with *Sir Johnny's Recycling Adventure* (Paulson & Hutto, 1999), a book that combines an entertaining and informative story with a compendium of highly useful tips about recycling matters. Create a recycling club. Students can create a school-based recycling program in classrooms, the teacher's lounge, school office, or school cafeteria. Teachers and students could start a worm composting program (a guide is available from http://www.stopwaste.org/wormcomp.html), and the compost could be used for school gardens or sold for a small profit. A good place to start looking for ideas on how recycling can be explored in classrooms is Kids Recycle! (http://www.kidsrecycle.org).

Realia and Primary Source Documents

Firsthand information and objects that relate to real life are rich resources for teaching and learning, yet they are often overlooked. Resources include, but are not limited to, food, period clothing, pictures and photographs, catalogs, letters and diaries, primary source accounts, postcards, and toys. Primary source materials include speeches, testimonials, and interviews; newspaper articles; news film or video; autobiographies; statistics and raw data sets; original scientific research; legislative hearings and bills; pictures and maps; poetry, drama, novels, music, and art; and artifacts, such as jewelry, tombstones, or fossils. By using a range of authentic materials, gifted and talented students learn through stimulating all their senses.

To resource these materials, teachers can use other means previously discussed: family and community members, auctions and garage sales, secondhand shops, and other educators. Additionally, many libraries and materials centers, particularly for teacher education, have collections of realia and primary source documents. Some museums have classroom lending programs for their collections, or they will visit the school and bring realia directly into the classroom. The county courthouse and local historical society may also be able to assist, particularly in sourcing primary documents. Antique dealers, theater groups, and collectors' clubs are often more than willing to work with students. Finally, contact local senior citizens associations, whose members are living history themselves and who probably have attics, closets, scrapbooks, and chests full of realia.

With the Internet, teachers have access to virtual realia—digitized objects and items. An amazing amount of primary source documents is now available via the Internet. As one site states in its introduction, "Don't depend on someone else's interpretation of a document. Read it yourself and draw your own conclusions. Listen to speeches and hear for yourself who said what." One of the first places to look for primary sources is the Web site of the U.S. National Archives and Records Administration (http://www.archives.gov). Also, visit The Library of Congress American Memory Historical Collections (http://memory.loc.gov). At Archiving Early America (http://earlyamerica.com), students will discover a wealth of resources from 18th-century America, including original newspapers, maps, and writings. The Internet History Sourcebooks (http://www.fordham.edu/halsell) provide access to primary sources in ancient, medieval, and modern history, plus African, East Asian, global, Indian, Islamic, Jewish, scientific, and women's history. Venture into the science history link to read the telegram announcing the Wright Brothers' first successful flight; full-text originals by scientists like Darwin, Pasteur, and Freud; or a Byzantine mathematics textbook. A list of primary source materials, which includes historical recipes of different cultures, eyewitness accounts of historic events, and even spy letters of the American Revolution, is located at http://www.kn.pacbell.com/wired/fil/pages/listdocumentpa.html#cat1.

There are two alternative and exciting ways to collect realia and primary source materials: the Artifact Box Exchange and Travel Buddies. Both of these programs match classrooms around the world with other classrooms. Classes taking part in The Artifact Box Exchange (http://www.artifactbox.com) collect realia from their local community, which their buddy class uses along with clues to figure out their location. For example, students from the Mississippi Delta might send a cotton boll, a Muppet character, and a blues CD in hopes that their buddy class would discover that the Delta is a region where cotton is king and the birthplace of Jim Henson and many great blues musicians. Younger children, especially, will enjoy Travel Buddies (http://rite.ed.qut.edu.au/oz-teachernet/projects/travel-buddies), a Web-based program in which each class sends a stuffed animal on an adventure to another location and follows the journey using e-mail. Their Web site describes the program, and though realia and primary source documents are not explicitly included, the potential is there.

Finally, as teachers and their students collect items of realia, they can work as a school and community to develop Kids Interest Discovery Studies (KIDS) KITS (http://www.ed.gov/pubs/EPTW/eptw10/eptw10i.html). These kits are developed based on different topics of student interests and contain books, filmstrips, tapes, models, transparencies, and other resources. Students can also develop more realia and primary source documents through activities like recording oral histories, taking photographs of local and historic sites, or visiting records archives, and those items can be added to the kit.

Free and Inexpensive Materials

Multiply the wide range of teaching materials recommended in gifted and talented education by the diverse strengths and interests of just a single classroom of gifted and talented students, and it does not take a mathematician or a financial advisor to come to the conclusion that a resource-rich environment is needed. For many teachers, especially those with financial constraints, matching students with the right stuff can sometimes become problematic. Free and inexpensive materials are a practical, user-friendly, and readily available solution.

Free and inexpensive materials are seldom designed solely for gifted and talented students; however, given the diverse range of content and types of materials, many are appropriate. The subject matter of many free and inexpensive materials moves beyond the typical academic curricular areas to topics like careers, travel, multicultural education, and women's roles in history. Given the diversity of content-related topics, many of the materials integrate math, science, language arts, technology, social studies, health and physical education, and the arts.

The types of free and inexpensive resources available to educators and their students include

- teachers' guides and lesson plans;
- reference/informational materials;
- printed resources for students (i.e., books, magazines, pamphlets);
- how-to guides/instructions;
- films, videos, audiotapes, CDs, and software;
- teaching aids like posters, maps, and manipulatives;

- interactive and informational online resources;
- consumable materials like arts and crafts supplies; and
- fun surprises for kids like stickers, toys, stamps, and games.

Why Teachers Should Take Advantage of Free and Inexpensive Materials

Many free (or almost free) materials, when carefully selected, mirror the defining characteristics of appropriate learning experiences for gifted and talented students, as outlined below:

- *Advanced content.* Though the level of complexity will vary, many free and inexpensive materials do not have an age or grade specification. And, even if they do, teachers are certainly not required to match the age or grade level of the resource with their students.
- *Interdisciplinary nature.* Many free and inexpensive materials focus on topics that weave various subjects into a tapestry, rather than isolate them as separate threads.
- *Variety.* The content, processes, and products associated with free and inexpensive materials are diverse. Also, as outlined previously, there is a wide variety of different types of materials.
- *Timeliness.* The content in many of the materials is relevant and current, especially in the materials produced by business and industry. When using Web-based resources, many "hot topics" are thoroughly covered and constantly updated with the latest information and ideas.
- *Complexity.* Often, the vocabulary, issues, and activities are not superficial, but are of a complex nature suitable for gifted students.
- *Authenticity.* Many of the resources are relevant in today's world and to the strengths and interests of gifted and talented students.

With free and inexpensive materials, the sheer range of content, mixed with the variety of process skills utilized to develop unique products, is a free ticket for classroom teachers to create a learning environment that focuses on the special interests, qualities, and abilities of individual gifted and talented students. There is more room for choice, autonomy, flexibility, depth, and breadth in learning environments that are well heeled in resources.

Fortunately, many teachers are well aware of the need for a wide variety of teaching and learning materials; however, as Vest (1991) reported, purchasing items remains the most common means of obtaining classroom resources, while donation is the least common. As Harrington and Christensen (1998) pointed out, "In the face of the basic material shortfalls prevalent in the national education system, teachers often find themselves spending personal funds to enhance their classrooms and curricula" (p. ix.). A marketing study conducted in the United States in 2002 (Market Data Retrieval) reported that the average out-of-pocket spending of classroom teachers was $400 per annum, compared with average classroom budgets of less than $250 per year. Given the vulnerability of gifted and talented education, alongside the need for a variety of resources, the out-of-pocket dollar figure would probably rise and the annual budget decline. These sorts of figures are surprising given the availability and abundance of free and inexpensive materials. So, rather than paying with personal funds, holding bake sales, or selling raffle tickets, teachers should investigate the avenues of free and inexpensive teaching materials.

Facing the challenges of gifted and talented students, a differentiated educational program, and limited funding *can* be rewarding. As Cruickshank (1990) stated,

> The public is particularly laudatory of teachers who, without benefit of special resources, overcome seemingly extraordinary obstacles to help their pupils succeed, thus demonstrating that other teachers could make a difference, too, if they tried harder or were more creative. (p. 16)

The positive outcomes of seeking and using free and inexpensive materials are great in terms of both the resources themselves and the recognition (Vest, 1991). Remember, this recognition extends beyond the classroom teacher: The availability and use of free and inexpensive materials is a two-way street. There are rewards for the businesses, government agencies, community members, and others involved as they invest their resources wisely. As one executive said, "What a joy it is to take a seed of an idea and watch it grow, further a concept and make it a reality, and experience rewards of helping others as we build multiple assets of our business" (Harrington & Christensen, 1998, p. ix). Teachers, students, and the wider community all reap the rewards of free and inexpensive resources.

Buyer Beware

The arguments for using free and inexpensive materials are only convincing if the materials are carefully selected and appropriately used. Apart from the previously discussed criteria for materials selection, there are further considerations for free and inexpensive materials:

- The materials should be used in tandem with other learning tools. As a stand-alone resource, some low-cost items may not be adequate for meeting learning goals and objectives.
- The reliability and authenticity of the content information should be carefully scrutinized (particularly on the Internet). The accuracy, completeness, and objectivity are also important. Remember, some commercial products are designed more for consumer persuasion than consumer education.
- The materials should be carefully checked for bias and stereotyping, particularly in relation to culture and gender. When using primary source documents, especially related to history, be aware that there may be a mismatch between yesterday's and today's language, thinking, and

behavior; raw, unedited sources could offend some students. This can be mostly defused by ensuring that students use the sources within a particular context of learning, rather than in isolation.

- The content and reading level of materials need to be carefully scrutinized, ensuring that both will match the interests and strengths of gifted and talented students. Many educational freebies, like lesson plans or units of study, are designed for regular classrooms. However, with some modifications and when used above grade level, they may be perfectly suitable for gifted and talented students.
- Many of the Internet-based sites require not only good computer skills, but also up-to-date operating equipment and software. When using the Internet, time is another important factor to consider.
- The actual cost involved may exceed expectations. While some materials appear to be free, there are often additional or hidden costs, such as shipping and handling, Internet costs, or supplementary materials associated with their use.

With careful selection and planning alongside good teaching, teachers of gifted and talented students can create resource-wealthy learning environments without breaking the bank. The advantages of using free and inexpensive materials can far outweigh the potential negative spin-offs.

The Search for Free and Inexpensive Materials

Apart from the previously discussed ways of finding free and inexpensive teaching materials, there are several good guides for teachers and students. The most comprehensive and up-to-date educators' books for locating free materials are published by Educators Progress Service. This company annually produces educators' guides of printed materials, videotapes and films, computer resources, and mixed media resources by grade level and curricular areas (see the Teacher Resource section at the end if this chapter for contact details and their latest titles). You can get a free sample via e-mail (and within minutes) by visiting their Website at http://www.freeteachingaids.com. The sample gives an indication of the quality of their resources, plus bonuses not listed in the guides.

Barry Harrington and Beth Christensen have written a neat resource book called *Unbelievably Good Deals That You Absolutely Can't Get Unless You're a Teacher* (1998). In its second edition, the book features materials and ideas for rewards and resources, reading and book materials, technology, global awareness, teacher education and professional development, and all the major curricular areas, including writing, social studies, math, arts, science, health, and the environment. The book also includes suggestions for using materials in the classroom and networking within individual communities.

The Teacher's Sourcebook of Free (and Inexpensive) Materials (Benson, 1998) is an incredible list of addresses of more than 200 organizations that offer a variety of products. The book covers all the major curricular areas, but also includes the contact information (physical addresses and Web sites) for the tourism offices of the United States, Canada, and some foreign countries. As Benson noted, tourism offices will send you free brochures with historical information, posters, and other educational materials. For example, in New Zealand, one group of students recently used these types of resources to plan a trip for which they had to decide where to go and why, how they would travel, their budget, and itinerary.

Freebies Magazine is published five times a year, plus you can access their free e-mail newsletter and up-to-date freebies for everything from books to jewelry by visiting its Web site (http://www.freebies.com). The magazine has been in publication since 1977, but, as one teacher discovered, its content varies little from the content on its Web site (apart from subscription costs). This site has only a few Web-based links, but it features mail-order items such as the free books *America's Heroes and You* and *The Wonder of Crystals*. Because this magazine is intended for a wider public audience than just educators, it highlights many other "surprises in the mailbox" like pins, stickers, suncatchers, and grab bag offers.

The World Wide Web is home to many free and inexpensive resources. Several comprehensive and regularly updated sites are featured below, but teachers can find more by using a search engine and key words like *free*, *inexpensive*, and *low-cost classroom or teaching materials*. Given the sheer amount of information available on the Internet, to avoid being inundated, educational terms (e.g., *teachers*, *lesson plans*, etc.) are a necessity for conducting a fruitful search.

The online resource Education World features two articles, "Fabulous Freebies: Free Materials for Teachers!" (http://www.education-world.com/a_curr/curr110.shtml) and "MORE Fabulous Freebies: Free Materials for Teachers" (http://www.education-world.com/a_curr/curr109.shtml), that give an overview and contact information about several interesting resources from corporate and government sponsors: Dole Food Company, the American Kennel Club, the Federal Reserve Bank, the Environmental Protection Agency, and the Thomas Edison Fund. Links to shareware resources, which enable teachers to download software for a limited time and at no cost or obligation, are also given. As the editors warn, Internet stories have longer shelf lives than free and inexpensive materials; but, while some of the resources listed may no longer be available, most of the sponsors still offer materials for students and their teachers, and these can be explored by visiting their Web sites.

Starters and Strategies (http://www.teachingonline.org) is a New Zealand-based site featuring teacher links and an online magazine. Although designed for the New Zealand teaching audience, the magazine and Web site feature many ideas relevant to teachers everywhere. For example, a recent edition of the magazine featured space-age technology developments in Antarctica, with a Web site and activities sponsored by the International Antarctic Center. It also has links to ThinkQuest (http://www.thinkquest.org), a Web site made for kids by kids from around the world. As the Web site states, "young people work together in teams, use the Internet to research a topic in science, mathematics, literature, the social sciences, or the arts, and publish their research as an educational web site for peers and classrooms around the world."

Reach Every Child (http://www.reacheverychild.com) is a Web site designed by a teacher with more than 5,000 free and inexpensive resources he's collected and used in his classroom over the years. It covers major subject areas and is changed on a regular basis to reflect current events and the calendar. There is also information on classroom support materials for teachers, including lesson plans, tips for new teachers, and awards and scholarships. This site has some interesting sidetracks: business associations, career information, computer hardware and software, and sports.

Tools for Teachers (http://www.suelebeau.com/freetools.htm) is a fantastic resource with free online tools like a crossword puzzle builder, timeline generator, language translator, and puzzle-making center that are great for student product development. There are also links to organizational templates for the classroom, places to post homework, Web page builders, bookmarks, and free e-mail accounts. Unlike the other sites, this one focuses more on the processes and products for teaching and learning, as opposed to the content.

Finally, there are a few guides for children on the lookout for freebies. The most popular is probably *Free Stuff for Kids*, annually published by Meadowbrook Press. In its 25th edition, the book provides students with instructions for ordering materials, plus photographs and descriptions for each item. It has sections for sports, hobbies and activities, toys, stickers and tattoos, school supplies, animals, world history and culture, awareness and self-esteem, and science and the Internet. Canceled foreign stamps, an off-center coin from the U.S. Mint, an exotic tree frog puzzle, and personalized book labels are amongst the many things students can receive in the mail.

For product development, *Free Stuff for Crafty Kids on the Internet* (Heim & Hansen, 1999) is a must-have compendium of ideas. The book not only has information about Web sites that offer free advice, tutorials, and how-to's for everything from cartooning to soap and candle making, but also gives extensive directions and advice for students on using the Web. The editors have also created guides for sewing, quilting, and stitching that, while intended for adults, certainly have valuable information for kids interested in arts and crafts.

Tips for Teachers and Their Students

In acquiring and using teaching materials, especially given the vast amount available, resource management is essential. Renzulli and Reis (1985) recommended the creation of a resource file. Whether it is computer-based, an index file, or a filing cabinet, it should contain the information illustrated in Figure 3. Resource files can be located in individual classrooms, but a schoolwide resource file would serve a much wider audience of students and teachers. In addition to organized files, schools

Theme/topic: _____   Content areas: _____

Age/Grade level: _____   Resource type: _____

Name/Title of resource: _____

Contact Information

Address: _____

Phone/Fax/E-Mail: _____

Web address: _____

Cost: _____

Notes:

Overall Rating: *Poor*   1   2   3   4   5   *Excellent*

Figure 3. Sample resource file card

may establish a centralized storage area of resources with a system for borrowing. For Web-based resources, sites can be organized as bookmarks within a favorites folder, which allows quick access to the most frequently visited Internet sites. Finally, teachers may work with students to organize kids' stuff in similar ways.

When ordering free or inexpensive items, there are tricks of the trade that will ensure success. The following, for both teachers and students, have been adapted from *Freebies for Teachers* (n.d.):

1. To ensure satisfaction, carefully follow instructions that appear with items.
2. For mail orders, legibly print or type orders, preferably on school letterhead.
3. Specifically state quantities, preferences, titles, and other choices if you are given options. Vest (1991) suggested that teachers initially request only one copy of an item of interest in order to check for suitability.

4. Include your name and address with every order.
5. Suppliers may require a long, self-addressed, stamped envelope (LSASE). This is a #10 business-sized (4-1/8" x 9-1/2") envelope with your name, address, and zip code printed on the front center and first-class postage affixed. Mail it folded inside another envelope addressed to the supplier.
6. Remember, *P&H* means "postage and handling." This can be a hidden cost.
7. Where indicated, send a check or money order, not cash, in the amount specified, payable to the offer supplier.
8. Allow up to 6 weeks for your order to arrive. If you do not receive it in that time, write to the supplier with full details of your order. If you still do not receive your order or a resolution to your problem, write to the source where the information originated so they can update their files.

Free Stuff for Kids (Free Stuff Editors, 2002) includes a checklist for students that can be very useful in ensuring successful returns. It includes all of the above checkpoints, plus tips like double-checking the address and including a postage stamp. Teachers may create their own checklists, if students are involved in the quest for materials.

In the request for materials, it is important to be specific with details, particularly if you want a particular resource. However, there may be times when teachers and students are investigating a topic or searching for materials for which they are unaware of specific resources. In that case, a more general request should be made, as seen in the sample letter in Figure 4. As shown, it is still important to be specific about the age level of students, topics of interest, and return address. For students who are involved in requesting free and inexpensive items, it may be useful to create a series of form letters they can adapt. It is also important to thank those who contribute items. In my experience, a thank-you note from two 12-year-old students resulted in a second donation of books for our classroom.

A Sampling of Free (or Almost Free) Ideas

With so many possibilities for teaching materials, differentiated educational programs for gifted and talented students can be greatly enhanced. In fact, the most difficult task for teachers may be deciding just what to use, when to use it, and how to find time to make the most of all the resources available. As an example, Figure 5 shows a list of free and inexpensive materials teachers can use in a study of *exploration*. The resources used in this study are further described below, and contact information for each one is provided in the Teacher Resource section at the end of the chapter.

- The Inventive Thinking Curriculum Project is produced by the U.S. Patent and Trademark Office. The project has been designed to assist

SCHOOL LETTERHEAD
NAME, ADDRESS, PHONE, FAX, E-MAIL

Dear Colleague,

I am seeking materials for my 5th-grade gifted and talented class, which will soon be studying a unit on space exploration. If you have any complimentary materials available, please forward them to the address below:

Your School
Street
City, State, Zip Code

Thank you in advance for your generous contribution in enriching the lives of my young students.

Sincerely,
Teacher of the Gifted

Figure 4. Sample letter of request

students in developing and applying their creative and critical thinking skills through innovation or invention. The teacher's guide features more than a dozen activities. Also included is a primer for understanding patents, trademarks, and copyrights and copies of primary source documents from the Patent and Trademark Office.

- Too Much Too Little is a program of the Federal Reserve Bank that includes a video program and student comic book. Combining U.S. history, social studies, and economics, the program traces the history of the Federal Reserve Bank by taking a trip back in time. This is just one of the many aspects of the Federal Reserve Bank that students can explore.
- The National Gallery of Art offers students a chance to visually survey the art of the Age of Exploration with Circa 1492: Art in the Age of Exploration. In their loan program, teachers can borrow 20 slides, 15 study prints, and a booklet of activities that represent the artistic achievements from Europe, Asia, and the Americas at the end of the 15th century. This is only one of the many resources available from the Gallery.
- A Virtual Journey Into the Universe is just one of hundreds of ThinkQuests students can explore. It is an information-rich, interactive educational tour of the solar system, covering a range of topics from planets and their moons to theories and phenomena. While learning

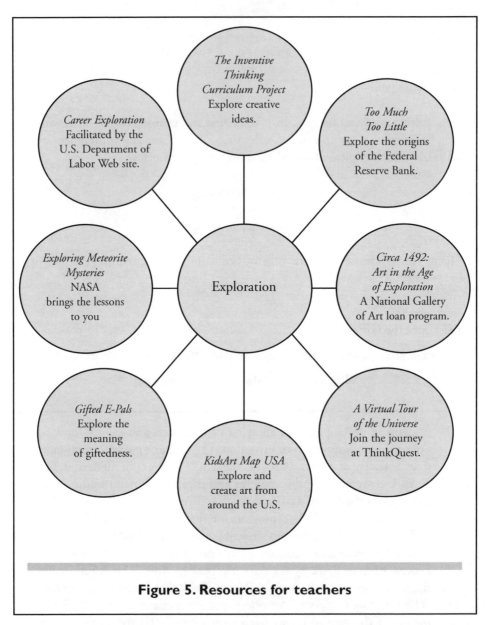

Figure 5. Resources for teachers

about theories and laws, students can see the action of planetary orbits from many views. They can select a planet, see the facts, and interact with the movies showing each planet's features.

- Students can also explore and experiment with art from around the United States with KidsArtMap USA. The map links geographic regions to their native art. For example, an exploration of the Pacific Northwest leads to instructions for a native mask; the New England states, a weather vane; or the Deep South, instructions for a watercolor painting of the Blue Ridge Mountains.

- The National Foundation for Gifted and Creative Children offers a private, protected pen pal and e-mail list for gifted children that includes students' Web pages. This is a good forum for discussing issues related to giftedness and could be supplemented with in-class discussions relying on materials like *The Gifted Kids' Survival Guide* (Galbraith, 1999).
- Among the many, many resources produced by the National Aeronautics and Space Administration, one is a slide show called "Exploring Meteorite Mysteries." The program highlights many of the meteorites collected and studied by NASA scientists, as well as the classification and formation of meteorites.
- Finally, students can explore their career options by visiting the Department of Labor Web site. The link "Jobs for Kids Who Like . . ." allows students to venture into careers for each school-based subject area. For example, by exploring mathematics, there is career information for engineering, accounting, mechanics, architecture, and computer science. Information is provided about what people in each career do, jobs, salaries, employment forecasts, and career study/preparation. Links are also provided to professional organizations for each career.

These examples are by no means exhaustive. They merely give an indication of a few of the teaching resources available at little or no cost. Figure 6 gives an example of how students can use free and inexpensive resources using Winebrenner's (2001) student choice menu. Like a game of tic-tac-toe, students can choose any three activities vertically, horizontally, or diagonally.

Tying It All Together

The learning, creative, motivational, and leadership qualities and abilities of gifted and talented students necessitate the provision of qualitatively differentiated educational opportunities. Differentiating the content, processes, and products of teaching and learning in response to individual gifted and talented students is enhanced by the integration of an array of materials. Print, nonprint, and human resources, in combination with recyclable materials, realia, and primary source documents, when carefully selected and placed in the hands of a well-informed teacher can add richness, depth, breadth, and excitement to learning. Using materials for teaching the gifted and talented requires forethought, planning, and careful evaluation—whether these are high- or low-cost.

There are many free and inexpensive materials available for teachers and their students that provide the authenticity, complexity, and relevance gifted and talented students seek. With careful searching, teachers can access everything from lesson plans, to teaching aids, to videos, to consumables. Remember, "enriching your classroom and curriculum need not be expensive" (Osborn, 1993, p. 7). Many materials and resources are available at little or no cost—just for the ask-

Explore a State Write to the state tourism office or visit their Web site to create a travel brochure for the state.	**Explore Exploration** Using refdesk.com find out all you can about the word *exploration*: What does it mean? What are its translations, synonyms, or rhyming words?	**Explore a Place** Take a virtual tour of the White House, Mars, or the human body by visiting the bookmarked exploration sites. Write a review of the site you visit.
Explore the Famous Investigate the life of a famous woman by visiting the National Women's History Web site. Imagine you are her and write a diary entry.	**Explore Your Own Idea** Find out about anything you'd like to know about exploration. You decide the content, process, and product. See me for a contract.	**Explore a Book** Read an e-book by or about an explorer or one that involves an exploration. Create a review, diorama, bookmark, or any other product for keen readers.
Explore a Topic Venture on a Web quest with 2 or 3 friends. Follow the instructions and explore a topic: animals, people, places, you name it.	**Explore Art** Take a tour of the National Gallery of Art. In the role of an art critic, choose an artist or style of art and write a critique.	**Explore an Explorer** Using the *Kids' Address Book* or an ask-an-expert Web site, get in touch with an explorer. Ask them five interesting questions about their explorations.

Figure 6. Student choice menu for exploration

ing. On a shoestring, teachers can bring the world right into their own classrooms, opening doors for gifted and talented students and making learning more exciting than ever.

Teacher Statements

This chapter will inspire educators to seize the moment, to cast a wide net, and to think flexibly when finding resources to meet the special learning needs of their gifted and talented students. Teaching on a shoestring challenges and explodes that most enduring myth of gifted education: that the special learning needs of gifted and talented are so resource-hungry that they become an all-too-quickly accepted barrier to effective provision. The focus of resource provision for gifted and talented students has often been solely on the string. I am confident that this chapter will become a much sought-after reference, a well-thumbed resource for practicing teachers who will be able to meet the needs of their gifted and talented students on a shoestring, with a shoestring, and without any form of string at all.

—Pam Hook

I am particularly impressed with the wide range of resource ideas offered in this chapter. It will serve not only as a source of new ideas, but also as a memory prompt for those teachers who have previously used suggested resources to good effect, but have forgotten about them. Additionally, it will serve the purpose of a brainstorm starter, providing an opportunity for teachers themselves to expand their resource repertoire considerably.

—Anne Sturgess

Discussion Questions and Activities

1. Discuss the principles of qualitative differentiation of content, processes, and products for gifted and talented students. Based on these principles, what are the implications for teachers in the selection of materials for teaching and learning?

2. Create a checklist for teachers to assist in the selection of materials for teaching gifted and talented students. Keep in mind the criteria discussed in this chapter. Use the checklist to screen up to 10 Web-based resources for gifted and talented students, their teachers, or both.

3. Discuss the spectrum of resources for teaching gifted and talented students, brainstorming how teachers might access and utilize a wide array of teaching and learning materials.

4. Compile a resource file, including those at little or no cost, for a conceptual theme or topic for elementary, middle, or secondary school students.

5. Create a Web-based resource for teachers and students. Select a conceptual theme or topic for a specific age level and include links for teachers and students.

Teacher Resources

Publishers in Gifted and Talented Education

Alternative Learning Publications (ALPS)
P.O. 1654
Greeley, CO 80632
http://www.alpspublishing.com

Creative Learning Press
P.O. Box 320
Mansfield Center, CT 06250
http://www.creativelearningpress.com

Engine-Uity, Ltd.
P.O. Box 9610
Phoenix, AZ 85068-9610
http://www.engine-uity.com

Free Spirit
217 Fifth Ave. N, Ste. 200
Minneapolis, MN 55401-1299
http://www.freespirit.com

Great Potential Press
P.O. Box 5057
Scottsdale, AZ 85261
http://www.giftedbooks.com

Interact
P.O. Box 900
Fort Atkinson, WI 53538
http://www.interact-simulations.com

National Association for Gifted Children (NAGC)
1707 L St., NW, Ste. 550
Washington, DC 20036
http://www.nagc.org/Publications/index.html

Prufrock Press
P.O. Box 8813
Waco, TX 76714-8813
http://www.prufrock.com

Zephyr Press
814 N. Franklin St.
Chicago, IL 60610
http://www.zephyrpress.com

Teacher and Student Guides to Free and Inexpensive Materials

Teacher's Guides to Free Materials series published by
Educators Progress Service
214 Center St.
Randolph, WI 53956
http://freeteachingaids.com

> *Elementary Teachers Guide to Free Curriculum Materials*
> *Middle School Teachers Guide to Free Curriculum Materials*
> *Secondary Teachers Guide to Free Curriculum Materials*
> *Educators Guide to Free Videotapes–Elementary/Middle School Edition*
> *Educators Guide to Free Videotapes–Secondary Edition*
> *Educators Guide to Free Films, Filmstrips, and Slides*
> *Educators Guide to Free Internet Resources–Elementary/Middle School Edition*
> *Educators Guide to Free Internet Resources–Secondary Edition*
> *Educators Guide to Free Science Materials*
> *Educators Guide to Free Social Studies Materials*
> *Educators Guide to Free Guidance Materials*
> *Educators Guide to Free Family and Consumer Education Materials*
> *Educators Guide to Free Health, Physical Education and Recreation Materials*
> *Educators Guide to Free Multicultural Materials*

Benson, L. L. (1998). *The teacher's sourcebook of free (and inexpensive) materials*. Grand Rapids, MI: Instructional Fair.
Free Stuff Editors. (2002). *Free stuff for kids*. New York: Meadowbrook Press.
Harrington, B., & Christensen, B. (1998). *Unbelievably good deals that you absolutely can't get unless you're a teacher* (2nd ed.). Chicago: Contemporary Books.
Heim, J., & Hansen, G. (1999). *Free stuff for crafty kids on the internet*. Lafayette, CA: C&T.
Levine, M. (2001). *The kids' address book*. New York: Perigree.

Magazines

Freebies Magazine
P.O. Box 21957
Santa Barbara, CA 93121
http://www.freebies.com

Starters & Strategies
P.O. Box 229
Tuarangi, New Zealand
http://www.teachingonline.org

Surplus Companies

Creative Educational Surplus
1000 Apollo Road
Eagan, MN 55121-2240
(651) 452-5788

Organizations Sponsoring Free and Inexpensive Materials

American Bar Association
321 N. Clark St.
Chicago, IL 60610
http://www.abanet.org/publiced/k12_tools.html
Many no- or low-cost teaching guides, including the book *Putting on Mock Trials*.
Contact your state association for other law-related materials.

American Forest and Paper Association
1111 Nineteenth St., NW, Ste. 800
Washington, DC 20036
http://www.afandpa.org
Visit their Web site for downloadable brochures and pamphlets, plus instructions
on how to make your own paper. Other free materials include a Youth Action Kit.

American Society for Microbiology
1752 N St., NW
Washington, DC 20036
http://www.asm.org
Curricular materials, science mentor database, visual resources, and career information available at little or no cost.

Department of Education Resources
National Gallery of Art
2000B S. Club Dr.
Landover, MD 20785
http://www.nga.gov/education/education.htm
See the kids page for activities and virtual tours. On the educators page, there is
information on their free loan program of multimedia ranging from
Impressionism to American Art and online resources for teaching Matisse,
Picasso, Van Gogh, and others.

The Department of the Treasury
Bureau of Engraving and Printing
15th and Pennsylvania Ave., NW
Washington, DC 20226
http://www.ustreas.gov/education/index.html
Lots of materials online, including a virtual tour of the Treasury and fact sheets.
Plus, if you visit http://www.ustreas.gov/kids, you'll discover other links for kids
to government Web sites, including the White House and U.S. Mint.

Federal Reserve Bank of New York
33 Liberty St.
New York, NY 10045
http://www.ny.frb.org
Just one of the 13 Federal Reserve Banks offering free and inexpensive educational
materials: student programs, instructional guides, online publications, videos.

National Women's History Project
3343 Industrial Dr., Ste. 4
Santa Rosa, CA 95403
http://www.nwhp.org
Inexpensive teaching resources, plus online biographies and a teachers' lounge
with links and activity ideas.

Smithsonian Institution for Education and Museum Studies
P.O. Box 37012
A&I 1163, MRC 402
Washington, DC 20013-7012
http://www.smithsonianeducation.org/educators
Most teaching resources are accessible online. Contains numerous amazing
online resources, particularly in art and design, science and technology and his-
tory and culture.

U.S. Census Bureau
Public Information Office
4700 SIlver Hill Road
Washington, DC 20233-0001
http://www.census.gov/dmd/www/teachers.html
Teaching materials on how to teach statistics using the U.S. census, with lots of
information available online at their Web site.

U.S. Chess Federation
3068 US Route 9W, Ste. 100
New Windsor, NY 12553
http://www.uschess.org

Teachers and students can access *A Guide to Scholastic Chess* and a beginner's page with everything from basic rules to how to establish your own chess club.

U.S. Department of Energy
1000 Independence Ave., SW
Washington, DC 20585
http://www.energy.gov
Links to an interactive periodic table, Ask a Scientist, or Kidszone, where you can play a game of element hangman. Some published materials are also available.

U.S. Department of Labor
Frances Perkins Bldg.
200 Constitution Ave., NW
Washington, DC 20210
http://www.dol.gov/asp/fibre/main.htm
Many educational resources, including information on the history of the Labor Department and loads of career information.

General Web Sites

Fabulous Freebies: Free Materials for Teachers!—http://www.education-world.com/a_curr/curr110.shtml

MORE Fabulous Freebies: Free Materials for Teachers—http://www.education-world.com/a_curr/curr109.shtml

Free Things for Educators—http://www.freethings4educators.com

Reach Every Child—http://www.reacheverychild.com

Free Tools for Teachers—http://www.suelebeau.com/freetools.htm

Ask-an-Expert Web Sites

Ask an Expert Sources—http://www.cln.org/int_expert.html
The sites on this page are links to experts in K–12 curricular-related topics. Nicely organized index of sites where you can ask an expert.
Pitsco's Ask an Expert!—http://www.askanexpert.com
The kid-friendly expert site links to hundreds of experts in science, technology, career, and other categories who will answer questions for free.

Scientific American: Ask the Experts—http://www.sciam.com/askexpert_directory.cfm
From astronomers to zoologists, this site has it all for the scientifically able.

Telementoring Web Sites

IBM Mentorplace—http://www.mentorplace.org
Through this corporate volunteer program, IBM employees provide students with academic assistance and career counseling.

Intercultural E-Mail Classroom Connections—http://www.iecc.org
IECC is a free service to help teachers link with partners in other cultures and countries for e-mail, classroom pen-pal, and other project exchanges.

International Telementor Program—http://www.telementor.org
The International Telementor Program provides academic mentoring support from professionals of ITP-sponsor companies. All student-mentor communication is project-focused and facilitated by a teacher or parent.

Other Web Sites

Adobe E-Book Reader—http://www.adobe.com/acrobat/readstep2.html
Freely available to download, this software allows the viewing of e-books on personal computers or palm devices.

The Amazing Picture Machine—http://www.ncrtec.org/picture.htm
This Web site features images of aircraft, American cities, animals, dinosaurs, famous people, 20th-century world leaders, and more.

Amazon.com—http://www.amazon.com
Features book reviews, links to similar books, and secondhand books.

Arachnoid.com—http://www.arachnoid.com
Teachers can access "careware," including programs for building Web pages, editing and presenting electronic slide shows, and creating graphs.

Archiving Early America—http://earlyamerica.com
Features primary source documents from early America.

Artcyclopedia—http://www.artcyclopedia.com
A great Web-based resource "where the world finds great art."

Artifact Box Exchange—http://www.artifactbox.com
Information and registration available here for this program.

Arts and Letters Daily—http://aldaily.com
The site has links to newspapers and news centers around the world, magazines, columnists, radio news and music, and search engines, plus interesting articles.

Campbell's Labels for Education—http://www.labelsforeducation.com
Schools can collect labels and exchange them for free educational merchandise, including computers, sports equipment, and musical instruments.

CRAYON: Create Your Own Newspaper—http://crayon.net
The system lets users get information on whatever they want—weather, news, sports, even comics—and exclude topics in which they're not interested.

Digital Reference Library—http://www.xrefer.com
This site contains 130 online reference books, including dictionaries of Shakespeare, rhyming, science, the Renaissance, British history, and more.

LookSmart's FindArticles.com—http://www.findarticles.com
A vast archive, constantly updated, of articles dating back to 1998 from more than 300 magazines and journals.

FirstGov—http://www.firstgov.gov
Links to all government departments and agencies, many of which have resources for educators or students available online. See the FirstGov for Kids link, which includes a "Web Treasure Hunt" with links to sites on career development, math and science, government, arts, recreation, and more.

1000+ Free Books, MP3 Books—http://www.free-books.org
Online e-books for children, including lots of classics such as *Black Beauty*, *A Christmas Carol*, and *Jane Eyre*, as well as lots of American history realia such as inaugural speeches by famous U.S. Presidents and the U.S. Bill of Rights.

Google Image Search—http://images.google.com
Conduct an image search using key words.

Human Genome Project—http://www.ornl.gov/TechResources/Human_Genome/education/education.html
Loads of downloadable curricular materials related to genetics, with links to many other sites.

Internet History Sourcebooks—http://www.fordham.edu/halsell
Provides access to primary sources in ancient, medieval and modern history, plus African, East Asian, global, Indian, Islamic, Jewish, scientific, and women's history.

KidsArt—http://www.kidsart.com
There are many activities under "Quick Art," and the KidsArt MapUSA connects geographic regions of the country to an art project you can make, with a complete materials list, illustrations, and instructions. There are also links to online museums for kids and a KidsArt gallery featuring artwork and stories of how they were created.

Kids Freeware—http://www.kidsfreeware.com
A kid-safe collection of free software.

Kids Interest Discover Studies KITS (KIDS KITS)—http://www.ed.gov/pubs/
EPTW/eptw10/eptw10i.html
Information and registration available here for this program.

Kids Recycle!—http://www.kidsrecycle.org
A good place to start looking for ideas on exploring recycling in classrooms.

The Library of Congress American Memory Historical Collections—http://memory.
loc.gov
A gateway to rich primary source materials relating to the history and culture of
the United States. The site offers more than 7 million digital items from more
than 100 historical collections.

Microsoft E-Book Reader—http://www.microsoft.com/reader/default.asp
Freely available to download, this software allows the viewing of e-books on personal computers or palm devices.

MIDI and Music Technology Resources for Teachers—http://www.isd77.k12.mn.us/
resources/staffpages/shirk/midi.html
Links to many online sound bytes.

NASA Quest—http://quest.arc.nasa.gov/index.html
Offers a full suite of online resources, including profiles of NASA experts,
monthly live interaction with NASA experts, audio and video programs, and lesson plans and student activities.

National Budget Simulator—http://www.nathannewman.org/nbs
This simulation asks students to adjust spending and tax expenditures in the
budget proposed by the White House in order to achieve either a balanced
budget or any other target deficit.

*National Foundation for Gifted and Creative Children Pen Pal and E-Mailing
Lists*—http://www.nfgcc.org/gkids.htm
A private, protected pen pal and e-mailing list for gifted children.

National Geographic MapMachine—http://plasma.nationalgeographic.com/map-
machine/index.html
Provides access to a variety of maps, including street maps, facts and flags maps,
historical maps, and maps of Mars.

Official State Websites—http://www.state.[state abbreviation].us
To link to all official state websites, enter the two-letter state abbreviation in the address above. For example, Mississippi's site is http://www.state.ms.us.

Primary Source Materials—http://www.kn.pacbell.com/wired/fil/pages/listdocumentpa.html#cat1
An "Internet hotlist" of links to primary source materials.

ReasonAble!—http://www.goreason.com
Download a trial version of their mapping software.

Refdesk.com—http://www.refdesk.com
This site allows access to online dictionaries, thesauruses, and encyclopedias, as well as worldwide weather, news, facts at a glance, and experts.

Sheppard Software—http://www.sheppardsoftware.com/teachers.htm
Free educational software for teachers.

ThinkQuest Internet Challenge Library—http://www.thinkquest.org/library/index.html
Take students on a virtual tour of the universe or have a close-up look at the seven wonders of the world in 3-D by visiting this library of more than 5,000 sites built by kids for kids as part of ThinkQuest Internet Challenges.

Trash to Treasure—http://familycrafts.about.com/cs/fork6/l/bltrashtr.htm
For crafty ideas and instructions for using recyclable products.

Travel Buddies—http://rite.ed.qut.edu.au/oz-teachernet/projects/travel-buddies
Information and registration available here for this program.

University of Virginia's E-Book Library—http://etext.lib.virginia.edu/ebooks/ebooklist.html
Provides 1,600 free e-books to view with these readers.

U.S. Fish and Wildlife Service—http://educators.fws.gov
Includes online videos, pictures, and maps for conservation education, plus curricular resources, community service projects, FAQs, and links to other Web resources.

U.S. National Archives and Records Administration—http://www.archives.gov
Primary source documents without the field trip.

U.S. Patent and Trademark Office—http://www.uspto.gov/kids
Download The Inventive Thinking Curriculum Project, plus follow links to other great information for students and teachers.

Video Placement Worldwide—http://www.vpw.com
This site provides information on free educational videos.

Virtual School for the Gifted—http://www.vsg.edu.au
This is an Australian-based online community where like minds can meet regardless of age, gender, or geography, offering enrichment courses across all curricular areas.

Worm Composting—http://www.stopwaste.org/wormcomp.html
A guide for starting a worm composting program

WWW Music Database—http://topquark.roadkill.com/MDB
There are currently more than 23,000 albums and 8,800 artists listed here, and access to Web sites and distributors for each one.

References

Benson, L. L. (1998). *The teacher's sourcebook of free (and inexpensive) materials*. Grand Rapids, MI: Instructional Fair.

Cruickshank, D. R. (1990). *Research that informs teachers and teacher educators*. Bloomington, IN: Phi Delta Kappa.

Feldhusen, J. F. (1997). Educating teachers for work with talented youth. In N. Colangelo & G. A. Davis (Eds.), *Handbook of gifted education* (2nd ed., pp. 547–552). Needham Heights, MA: Allyn and Bacon.

Freebies for teachers. (n.d.). Retrieved June 20, 2004, from http://www.freebies.com/teacher.html

Free Stuff Editors. (2002). *Free stuff for kids*. New York: Meadowbrook Press.

Galbraith, J. (1999). *The gifted kids' survival guide* (Rev. ed.). Minneapolis, MN: Free Spirit.

Harrington, B., & Christensen, B. (1998). *Unbelievably good deals that you absolutely can't get unless you're a teacher* (2nd ed.). Chicago: Contemporary Books.

Heim, J., & Hansen, G. (1999). *Free stuff for crafty kids on the Internet*. Lafayette, CA: C&T.

Hultgren, H. W., & Seeley, K. R. (1982). *Training teachers of the gifted: A research monograph on teacher competencies*. Denver: University of Denver School of Education.

Karnes, F. A., & Collins, E. C. (1985). *Handbook of instructional resources and references for teaching the gifted*. Boston: Allyn and Bacon.

Levine, M. (2001). *The kids' address book*. New York: Perigree.

Lewis, I., & Munn, P. (1989). *So you want to research! A guide for teachers on how to formulate research questions*. Edinburgh, Scotland: Scottish Council for Research in Education.

Maker, C. J., & Nielson, A .B. (1995). *Teaching models in education of the gifted* (2nd ed.). Austin, TX: PRO-ED.

Market Data Retrieval. (2002). *Teachers' direct buying power approaches $2 billion*. Retrieved March 1, 2003, from http://www.schooldata.com/pr30.html

McAlpine, D., & Reid, N. (1996). *Teacher observation scales for identifying children with special abilities*. Wellington: New Zealand Council for Educational Research.

Ministry of Education. (2000). *Gifted and talented students: Meeting their needs in New Zealand schools*. Wellington, New Zealand: Learning Media.

Osborn, S. (1993). *Free and almost free things for teachers*. New York: Perigree.

Paulson, R. P., & Hutto, J. (1999). *Sir Johnny's recycling adventure*. Sparta, NJ: Crestmont.

Purcell, J. H., Burns, D. E., Tomlinson, C. A., Imbeau, M. B., & Martin, J. L. (2002). Bridging the gap: A tool and technique to analyze and evaluate gifted education curricular units. *Gifted Child Quarterly, 46*, 306–321.

Renzulli, J. S. (1977). *The enrichment triad model: A guide for developing defensible programs for the gifted and talented*. Mansfield Center, CT: Creative Learning Press.

Renzulli, J. S., Gentry, M., & Reis, S. M. (2003). *Enrichment clusters: A practical plan for real-world, student-driven learning*. Mansfield Center, CT: Creative Learning Press.

Renzulli, J. S., & Reis, S. M. (1985). *The schoolwide enrichment model: A comprehensive plan for educational excellence*. Mansfield Center, CT: Creative Learning Press.

Tomlinson, C. A., Kaplan, S. N., Renzulli, J. S., Purcell, J., Leppien, J., & Burns, D. (2002). *The parallel curriculum: A design to develop potential and challenge high-ability learners*. Thousand Oaks, CA: Corwin Press.

VanTassel-Baska, J. (1997). What matters in curriculum for gifted learners: Reflections on theory, research, and practice. In N. Colangelo & G. A. Davis (Eds.), *Handbook of gifted education* (2nd ed., pp. 126–135). Needham Heights, MA: Allyn and Bacon.

Vest, B. J. (1991). *Free classroom resources: Conducting a successful search.* (ERIC Document Reproduction Services No. ED438985)

Winebrenner, S. (2001). *Teaching gifted kids in the regular classroom* (2nd ed.). Minneapolis, MN: Free Spirit.

Chapter 22

Getting What You Need:

Locating and Obtaining Money and Other Resources

by **Kristen R. Stephens** and **Frances A. Karnes**

 teacher of the gifted in a rural school district has worked diligently for several years to receive more than $600,000 in grants. A staff development day for teachers of the gifted at a local university offered her an overview of researching funding sources and procedures for writing grant proposals. With a 1-hour seminar as her introduction to the fund-development processes, she successfully perfected her skills and now makes presentations on the topic to groups of teachers.

With the limited amount of money available in school districts for classroom materials and projects, finding external funding opportunities has become necessary for many teachers of the gifted. This chapter provides an overview of the types of funding agencies that exist and how to locate them, as well as how to develop an idea and write a grant proposal. Information on other sources of funding is also given, as well as procedures for determining policies at the district level.

Status of Federal Funding For Gifted Education

At present, the only federal legislation that exclusively designates funds for gifted and talented education is the Jacob K. Javits Gifted and Talented Students Education Act (1990). This act directs the Secretary of Education to make grants and contracts for programs and projects to meet the educational needs of gifted and talented students. For the fiscal year of 2003, Congress allocated $11.25 million for the Javits program. These funds will support

- the National Research Center on the Gifted and Talented;
- demonstration grants, awarded on a competitive basis, to examine ways to identify and serve underserved gifted students; and
- statewide grants, awarded on a competitive basis, to support programs and services.

Since gifted students are offered limited protection under both federal and state laws and are not covered under the Individuals With Disabilities Education Act (IDEA, 1990), many supporters of gifted education are advocating that new legislation is essential to meet these students' unique educational needs. At the time of this writing, a gifted education state formula grant legislation has been introduced in Congress by Senator Charles Grassley (Iowa) and Representative Elton Gallegly (CA-24). The bills S. 501 (2003) and H.R. 1191 (2003) would distribute grants based on a state's student population to each state education agency. States would then provide grants to local school districts on a competitive basis to support

- professional development;
- innovative programs and services, including service learning;
- making materials and services available through state regional educational service centers, institutions of higher learning, or other entities;
- challenging, high-level coursework that utilizes emerging technologies, including distance learning, for individual students or groups of students; and
- direct educational services and materials, including strategies designed to address the educational needs of gifted students such as curriculum compacting, acceleration, independent study, and dual enrollment.

States have flexibility under this proposed legislation in how they will allocate the funds, although they must match 10% of the federal funds, either in cash or in kind, for the benefit of gifted and talented students. In addition, the grant money must supplement, not supplant, funds currently being spent. Each state would receive funding, with the smallest states receiving .5% of the total funds available (visit http://www.nagc.org/Policy/allotments.htm to see an estimate of what each state would receive if Congress were to provide $50 million for this program). The bills also allow state education agencies to use some of the funds to disseminate general program information, provide support for parent education, establish a state advisory board, monitor program evaluation, and provide technical assistance. S. 501/H.R. 1191 would supercede the competitive state grants program in the Javits Act, which allocates approximately $3.75 million for five state grants, so a greater impact would be achieved. To download a copy of S.501 or H.R. 1191, go to http://thomas.loc.gov and insert S.501 into the box labeled "Bill Number."

Another source of federal dollars that can be used for gifted programs is 1988 Title VI–The Innovative Education Program Strategies Program found in the reauthorized Elementary and Secondary Education Act of 1965. Local Education Agencies (LEA's) can apply for this funding directly through their state's department of education. Programs should focus on high standards for all students, professional experiences that better prepare teachers to teach to high standards, flexibility to stimulate local initiatives coupled with responsibility for results, and the promotion of partnerships among families, communities, and schools. Contact the Title VI representative from your state department of education for additional information.

Types of Funding

There are essentially two types of funding: public and private. Some projects will be appropriate for both types of funding, while others may be best suited for one or the other. Private sources often will not support projects for which there are already substantial amounts of public funding available, such as in the area of children with disabilities. Furthermore, the purpose of public funds is set by legislation, whereas private funds focus on emerging needs and issues pertaining to special interest populations. It should be noted that funding within the school district and at the state department of education should also be explored. Some states have monies for instructional aids, technological equipment, and other materials.

There are several other differences between public and private funding sources. For example, public funding sources generally have the most money to award and are more likely to pay all project costs. In contrast, private funders may be more restrictive in what expenses are covered, and, with the exception of the major foundations, most offer smaller amounts of money. The proposal format is another area in which the two funding types differ. Public sources use prescribed formats for proposals, which can be lengthy and complex, whereas proposals for private sources are often less formal.

Public funding can be located through federal, state, and local agencies. Some examples of federal agencies include the U.S. Department of Education, The National Institutes of Health, and The National Science Foundation. State and local agencies may be more geographic in scope, limiting their funds to specific regions in which they are involved.

Private funding sources include foundations, corporations, and professional and trade associations. Examples of foundations are The Carnegie Foundation, The Kellogg Foundation, and the Spencer Foundation. Corporations that provide grant monies include AT&T, Toyota, and Whirlpool. Some examples of associations providing grant monies are The American Association of University Women (AAUW), The National Education Association (NEA), and The Council for Exceptional Children (CEC).

Once the project idea has been determined, the search for the funding source that best fits the need can begin. The funding agency's priorities must match project goals. The size of the awards offered, geographic focus, eligibility requirements, restrictions, and deadlines for submitting a proposal will all need to be considered. Thorough research into these key areas can assist the grant-searching process.

Developing an Idea

Developing and refining a project idea should be the first step in the grant-searching process. Taking the initial time to outline ideas and goals can assist in locating the most relevant funding source. Keep in mind that goals and priorities must match those of the selected funding agency.

The first step in cultivating an idea is assessing needs. What areas in the classroom, school, or community need to be initiated, need improvement, or need to be adequately addressed? A needs statement can give purpose to the project and will inform a potential funder of the importance of the proposed project. It is also necessary at this point to research any previous work that has been undertaken in the needs area to establish that the problem exists statewide and nationally. The further one can broaden the potential scope and impact of the idea, the more likely funding is assured. Also, the more innovative the idea, the better the chances of finding support for the project (see Figure 1).

After the area of need has been identified, compile a list of goals, objectives, and activities for the proposed project; this is the plan of action. It will help identify the population the project intends to address, the staffing areas that will be needed, and the time frame in which one will be operating. Ask colleagues for advice and assistance in the development of this phase of the plan. In some schools, teams of teachers work on schoolwide projects.

Determining a working budget will also be beneficial at this point. Since many funding sources have limited funds, establishing whether one needs $100,000 or $1,000 to execute a proposed project will have a substantial impact on identifying a funding source. In developing a budget, be sure to consider all expenses related to equipment and supplies, personnel, facilities, travel, communications, general operating expenses, and overhead, which includes light, heat, and so forth. There may be individuals within a school's finance department or development office who can be of assistance when determining budget expenses. Having a preestablished budget figure will assist in eliminating many funding agencies, making the information sifting easier.

Locating a Funding Source

Once the need has been identified, a plan of action has been created to address the need, and a general idea of the amount of money being requested has

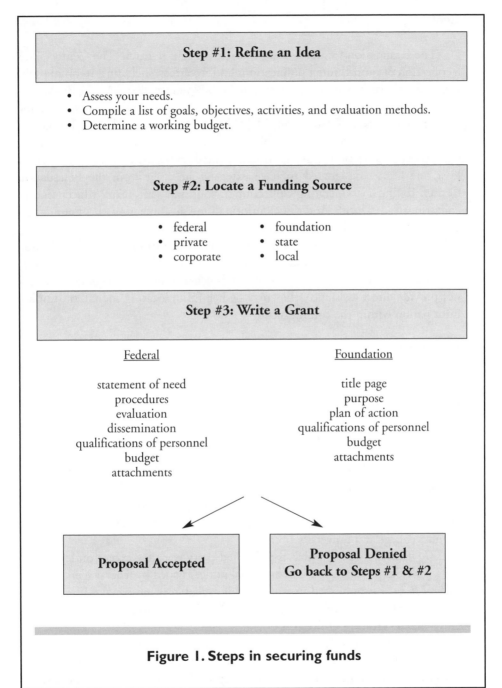

Step #1: Refine an Idea

- Assess your needs.
- Compile a list of goals, objectives, activities, and evaluation methods.
- Determine a working budget.

Step #2: Locate a Funding Source

- federal
- private
- corporate
- foundation
- state
- local

Step #3: Write a Grant

Federal

statement of need
procedures
evaluation
dissemination
qualifications of personnel
budget
attachments

Foundation

title page
purpose
plan of action
qualifications of personnel
budget
attachments

Proposal Accepted

**Proposal Denied
Go back to Steps #1 & #2**

Figure I. Steps in securing funds

been determined, it is time to research potential funders. Several resources can assist during this endeavor: databases, libraries, and publications. Thorough research to locate a funding source whose priorities match project goals can be a challenging, yet potentially rewarding experience.

Centers

The Foundation Center is a good place to begin research. The Center offers a collection of fund-finding publications and resources, including an online subscription service that lists approximately 70,000 grantmakers. A CD-ROM version of this database is also available for purchase, or it can be accessed at the Center's Libraries in Washington, DC, New York, Atlanta, Cleveland, and San Francisco. To accommodate people who do not live near these locations, Cooperating Collections exist across the United States. In each state, there is at least one library designated to have extensive holdings from the Foundation Center. To find a Cooperating Collection in your state visit, http://fdncenter.org/collections/index.html. Additional information on contacting the Foundation Center about its work is found at the end of this chapter.

If one lives near a college or university, many institutions of higher learning have an Office of Research and Sponsored Programs. These offices assist university faculty in developing proposals and finding grant sources. Although they may not provide direct assistance, they may be helpful in locating sources of funding information within the community.

Publications

The Catalog of Federal Domestic Assistance (CFDA) describes all the federal government's programs that give money. This source is published annually by the Office of Management and Budget (OMB), and it is available at major libraries. The most current information relating to eligibility, application and award processes, addresses, and contacts are given.

The Chronicle of Philanthropy is a newspaper that includes articles on fundraising and philanthropy. Lists of recent grants and profiles of foundations and corporations are also given. The newspaper is published biweekly and is available through The Chronicle of Higher Education, Inc. It can be found online and in most college and university libraries.

The Federal Register, which is published every weekday except on legal holidays, provides public regulations and legal notices issued by federal agencies. *The Federal Register* is published in paper and is available at most major libraries. An online database of *The Federal Register* is also available through the U.S. Government Printing Office (GPO).

The Congressional Record is a daily record of the activities within the U.S. Congress; it includes information on bills that are introduced and debated. Because legislation is directly tied to funding availability for many programs, it is essential to stay abreast of the latest information from Washington. Copies of *The Congressional Record* can be found at most libraries.

Grants for K–12 Biweekly provides up-to-date listings of available grants, foundations, school programs, and business partnerships from across the country. It also includes important deadlines from *The Federal Register*, online resource listings, and regional grants updates, plus an inside track on the U.S. Department of Education.

SchoolGrants Newsletter is published bimonthly and provides practical grant-writing tips, online grant-writing resources, upcoming deadlines, grant opportunities for K–12 schools and teachers, and more.

Information on how to contact or subscribe to the above publications is listed at the conclusion of this chapter. The above list is by no means comprehensive. Check local or college and university libraries for additional sources.

Analyzing Sources

Once information has been assessed on funding agencies, there are several things to identify:

- *What are the priorities of the agency, and do they match the proposed goals and objectives?* For example, the agency may focus its efforts in urban areas, but the proposed project may be in a rural area.
- *What are past projects that this agency has funded?* Request an annual report from the funding agency and look at what projects are currently being funded or have been funded in the past. Patterns may be present. For example, even though a foundation may say it funds projects nationally, 80% of the projects funded in the past may be located in the same state or geographic region.
- *What are the limitations and restrictions?* Many agencies do not fund individuals, for-profit organizations, or political or religious associations. There may also be geographic restrictions. For example, many corporations and companies may restrict giving to areas in which there is a company presence. Also, there may be restrictions on how the money can be used. Equipment, salaries, and overhead may not be covered.
- *Is a letter of inquiry required?* Many agencies—foundations in particular—want a brief letter explaining the organization, the goals and objectives of the project, and the proposed budget prior to submitting a formal proposal. If the proposed idea matches the agency's priorities, a more detailed proposal will be requested.
- *Are there necessary application forms?* Many agencies have standard application and cover forms that will need to be requested. Some agencies have these available for downloading from their Web sites. Check to make sure that all the proposal guidelines are addressed so the agency is provided with all the information requested.
- *What is the deadline?* Most deadlines follow an annual pattern, meaning they are on the same date from year to year; however, since government programs depend on legislation for funding, many programs may be

changed or cut. Furthermore, some government programs do not award grants annually. Many foundations accept applications at any time with no established deadlines. Board members may meet periodically throughout the year to review proposals.

- *What is the average grant size?* It is important to find out what the average award is for each agency. For example, a specified project may need approximately $100,000 of support, but a particular agency may only make an award of up to $5,000. Find an agency that can financially support the proposed idea.
- *What is the length of support?* Many federal grants will support projects for approximately 3 years. Continued support may be available if the project proves to have made an impact. Furthermore, many agencies want to know in the proposal how the program will be supported once funding is terminated. The potential sustainability of the program is paramount to funding agencies when making the decision to provide financial support to a project.

By addressing these questions and thoroughly researching potential agencies, a lot of time can be saved and frustration avoided. Nothing can be more disappointing than spending long hours developing a proposal and sending it to the wrong agency based on an overlooked detail. Research the funding agency inside and out. If there are legitimate questions, contact the agency or foundation before writing the proposal.

Major Components of a Grant Proposal

The major components and guidelines of a grant proposal differ slightly according to each funding agency. When applying to foundations and corporations, the following components are usually requested: title page, purpose, approach, qualifications, budget, and attachments. In addition to those components, state and federal agencies usually require information on the statement of need, procedures, evaluation, and dissemination.

Foundations and Corporations

The *title page* of a proposal to a foundation or corporation should have the title of the project; legal name of the submitting agency; address, name, and phone number of the contact person; a short summary; amount of money requested; signatures of approval; and other assurances, such as a nondiscrimination clause.

The *purpose* section should set forth the goals and objectives; description of those to be served, including geographic location and number; needs and significance of the project; and relevance to the donor's purposes.

The *approach* or the *plan of action* contains specific outcomes, staff responsibilities and training, and the evaluation design. Project dissemination activities are usually described, as well. Donor recognition should be mentioned.

The *qualifications* of the key project staff should be given along with names of any consultants and all cooperating agencies. If special facilities, equipment, and so forth are needed and available, mention them to demonstrate capability of conducting the project.

A detailed *budget* is usually required, and all items essential to the project must be included. Asking for additional funds after the project has been approved is typically denied. Components of the budget may include, but are not limited to, personnel, travel, supplies and materials, data processing, printing/postage, facilities, equipment (if allowable), and indirect costs. It is important to list indirect costs such as office space, lights, heat, equipment usage, and the like. Other items to be included would be monies from other agencies, often referred to as matching funds, if any; a description of how the project will be supported after the requested funding period expires; and plans for additional fundraising, if appropriate. Consult the financial officer of your district or institution about matching funds and indirect costs.

The *attachments* requested from the potential donor may include the names of the members of the board of directors and their affiliations; a copy of the IRS determination; the organization's last annual report; information describing the organization; and letters of support.

Always be thorough in reviewing the requirements of the foundation or corporation because more or less information may be necessary. Only submit what has been requested, as these two groups are usually not interested in lengthy proposals.

State and Federal Agencies

The proposals forwarded to state and federal agencies usually require more detail and specificity. Components, again, differ somewhat from those required by foundations and corporations, and only those necessary components will be reviewed.

Following the title page, the abstract of approximately 200–500 words, the purpose, and the proposal to a state or federal agency should emphasize the *statement of need*. In this section, a thorough description should be given of the problem that is to be addressed and reasons why it is important. The emphasis should be on significance, timelines, and broad application of the solution. Recent local, state, and national statistics about the problem should set forth the need in a clear and concise manner.

The *procedure* section varies somewhat as to a research- or nonresearch-based project. In the latter, a general description should be offered, followed by details on the method, the participants, organization, and timelines. In the former, the data instruments should be described, as well as how the information is to be collected, analyzed, and reported.

The *evaluation* section of the grant proposal should include evidence that the purposes of the project have been accomplished. Information should include data collection, analysis, and evaluation; selection or development of instruments to be utilized; and the reporting procedures.

In the *dissemination* portion of the proposal, specifics should be given on how the findings or products of the project will be distributed (newspaper releases, presentations at conferences, journal articles, etc.). Reporting procedures to the funding agency, if and when required, should also be described.

Although the *qualifications* component has been briefly described in the above section on corporations and foundations, a few other points need to be considered when submitting to state and federal agencies. Résumés, along with a listing of publications, should be included for the key personnel and consultants. The amount of time each of the key personnel will give to the project and his or her responsibilities is usually required. A staff-loading chart, which depicts who will be responsible for selected activities, is often necessary.

A detailed budget with indirect costs and any matching funds is critical. Again, be sure to consult with the financial officer or grant writer in your district or institution.

Sources of Funding in Your Community

There are many other sources of funding available in addition to foundations, corporations, and state/federal agencies. Sources of private-sector funding include denominational groups; neighborhood and fraternal charities; retail merchants; volunteer and business/professional associations; United Way; Chamber of Commerce; small and large businesses; local franchises of regional, state, and national companies; postsecondary institutions including community colleges and 4-year colleges and universities; civic groups; and arts councils. Local philanthropists, celebrities, professional athletes, and agency directors may have discretionary funds. Some local private funding sources may have guidelines for requesting monies, so call or write to determine the procedure for requesting support. A 1-page summary with the purpose, goals, activities, and budget may be all that is necessary. Making an appointment with the person to discuss the request is sometimes the best procedure, while some associations or people prefer to receive the information via mail or e-mail.

At the local level, people funding requests may wish to be personally involved in the funded program, or they may wish to remain anonymous. Ask for preferences so as not to cause any embarrassment.

Creative Fundraising

For years, schools have developed fundraising strategies for various projects. Walsh (1990) suggested the following activities:

- *Balloon Blast-Off.* Students, teachers, parents, and community members sponsor, for a specific fee, a balloon with their name, address, and phone number attached. The person with the balloon traveling the farthest receives a prize.
- *Auctions.* These are great events. With items donated, the profits can be substantial.
- *Breakfast, Lunch, or Dinner With a Special Person.* Everyone likes to have a meal with a celebrity such as a famous athlete, TV personality, or local celebrity.

Palent (1985) advocated the following fundraising activities: a marathon (running, walking, biking, etc.), a sale of goods (antique, baked goods, etc.), and a sale of services (babysitting, car wash, house cleaning, yard work). Swan (1990) suggested contests (fishing, golf, tractor pulls, etc.) and sales of items (candy, cards, light bulbs, etc.) and services (handyman, house sitting, window washing, lawn care, etc.).

Additional ideas include a Quarter Rally, where double-stick tape is placed from one end of the mall to another and shoppers are asked to put down a quarter in support of the cause; a wish list that can be published in a local newspaper or sent to area businesses, organizations, or past donors; advertising by asking a local supermarket to print a message on its shopping bags for a month (this is not a direct fundraising activity, but it does generate a lot of publicity); and Rock-a-Thons, where supporters get pledges to rock in rocking chairs for a day (ARCH, 1992).

Gensheimer (1993) directed ideas on fundraising to both teachers and parents. Ideas included a used goods sale, clothesline sales, knowledge-a-thon, and a school carnival. Two unique ideas were a birthday party and a penny war. The former can be held for local children at a school with a fee charged to cover all expenses. The latter idea is based on the fact that people don't like to carry extra pennies with them. Students decorate coffee cans and place them at various local locations for the public to dispose of extra pennies.

The Ultimate Guide to Getting Money for Your Classroom and School (Karnes & Stephens, 2003) offers more than a hundred ideas for creative fundraising activities. When planning for activities, Karnes and Stephens suggested keeping the following steps:

- *Get permission.* Determine the local school board policies and local, state, and federal laws and regulations regarding fundraising. Many schools do not allow students to conduct door-to-door sales and require parental permission for students to participate. Legal matters such as tort liability, taxes, insurance needs, and so forth should also be explored.
- *Form a committee and name a chairperson.* It takes many hardworking individuals to conduct a successful fundraiser. Committees should meet regularly and evaluate progress toward established goals.

- *Set goals.* It is important to have a clear purpose for the fundraiser and clearly communicate why the money is needed, how much is needed, and who will benefit from the monies raised.
- *Select an idea that will work.* Determine what has been successful in the past, is most feasible, and will be most likely to generate the amount needed.
- *Determine time and place.* Find out when other events in the community are scheduled and avoid planning additional events around the same dates. Keep in mind that some events may be better suited for certain times of years (e.g., flower sales at Valentine's or Mother's Day).
- *Make a plan.* The fundraising committee should develop a plan that details the materials and number of volunteers needed. It is also helpful to begin designating tasks, developing a master schedule of important dates and deadlines, and establishing rules and procedures that should be followed by all those involved. Ideas for promotional materials, kick-off activities, and volunteer appreciation should also be considered in the planning phase.
- *Recruit and organize volunteers.* Volunteers are vital to the success of any fundraiser. Recruit individuals who have the skills to perform the tasks associated with their specific responsibility and who have a sincere interest in the project. Make certain that all volunteers are communicating the same message to potential donors regarding the purpose of the money and who will benefit from the collected revenue.
- *Target potential donors and sponsors.* The key to successful fundraising is participation. Determine which individuals within the community would be most interested in contributing to the particular cause. For example, a retired librarian might be especially interested in a fundraiser for new books for the media center.
- *Promote the event.* Publicize the fundraiser with banners, bulletin boards, flyers, radio announcements, newsletters, newspaper stories, and the local media. Don't forget to include marketing expenses in your budget.
- *Wrap things up.* A comprehensive evaluation should be conducted at the conclusion of the event. Consideration should be given to areas that may need improvement next time, as well as providing some sort of recognition to those individuals who donated their time to help meet the project's goals.

Old Strategies/New Practices

Over the last decade, public elementary and secondary school districts and programs have successfully employed fundraising strategies that had previously been associated primarily with postsecondary institutions: annual giving, endowments, commemorative planned giving, and unrestricted and restricted gifts. Local, state, and national associations are also engaging in fund development.

Annual giving is usually conducted through a wide spectrum of groups. The most obvious are students, their families, and alumni. Others to be included within the school would be the board members, teachers, administrators, and staff. In the community, those targeted for annual giving should include vendors, service groups, professional organizations, small businesses, local corporations, foundations, and the general public. Giving may be requested through personal visits, telephone calls, and letters. Gifts may be monetary (cash, checks, money orders, and charges to approved credit cards) and nonmonetary (bonds and securities, goods and services, real estate and personal property, royalties, copyrights and trademark rights, and insurance policies stating the school district or program as a beneficiary). Wereley (1992) suggested writing a clever "want ad" for a community partner. Publish the ad in the local newspaper or create a flyer to distribute to area businesses and organizations.

Commemorative gifts are becoming more popular within education. The gift is given "in memory of" or "in honor of" either a deceased or living person, and it may be restricted or unrestricted. A donor may wish to leave, either through a will or another instrument, an insurance policy for general or specific purposes. Large amounts of money may be given for endowments with the interest spent as designated by the donor (Karnes, Stephens, & Samel, 1999).

Personal property that can be donated include art, equipment, and cars. Examples of real property include a residence, business, building, or undeveloped land. Real and personal properties must be assessed by a certified professional appraiser, and they are only helpful to districts if they can be used or sold. School districts engaged in fund development should have board-approved policies written within state and federal guidelines under the advisement of a tax attorney. They should also have developed policies on strategies to be used, such as methods of acknowledgment/recognition and confidentiality.

Conclusion

With the limited amount of money allotted to gifted education, it is imperative that teachers and administrators become knowledgeable in grant writing and in locating additional sources of funding. Through careful research and innovation, an idea can be turned into a reality with the discovery and acquisition of a funding source. Although the process requires a lot of work, the rewards will be well worth the efforts.

Teacher Statement

Innovative teachers know that tight budgets lead to little or no funding for their gifted classroom students, and because of this fact, grant writing has become a necessity, not an option. The advice given in this chapter is dead-on. We can either gripe about not having materials to offer unique units of study or we can do something about it. Teachers must seize the opportunity to learn how to write successful grants. Find a professional development seminar and attend with the positive attitude that you *can* do this. Look for these opportunities at universities or contact your state department of education. The time, effort, and money (if you have to pay) are well worth the results.

Learn to persevere! Rejection should be taken in stride. Just because your grant was not funded by one source doesn't mean it isn't a good project. Learn to match your grant idea with the grant source's "pet" projects. Some prefer fine art projects, while others want science or math. Be sure to read and follow the grant directions and find out what areas get preference in funding by the source. Following the directions carefully is crucial; they will eliminate your grant if it is two words over the limit—that is one less grant for them to read and indicates a willingness on your part to play loose with the rules.

Now, to get started: Think about that unit of study that needs something extra. Be innovative—you have to set your grant apart from all of the other grant applicants. Offer some sort of culminating activity that includes publicity for the grant. Grant sources like to see involvement by parents and the community, and it never hurts to give them credit in the media and in your final products. I have actually sent videotapes of the activities to the grant providers with my final report.

Don't give up on having the classroom of your dreams. Read this chapter again and get started.

—Lia Landrum

Discussion Questions

1. Make a list of five items that your school or classroom needs. Where might you start looking for necessary funding in order to meet each of the listed needs?

2. Determine what your school or district's policy is in regards to fundraising. Are there necessary signatures and approvals? How much planning time is needed to obtain these approvals? Create a timeline detailing the steps that need to be taken to secure necessary funding.

3. Discuss the pros and cons of securing funds from a federal agency, private foundation, and a corporate agency.

4. You have just been asked to chair a committee at your school to write a grant for money for new materials for the enrichment classroom. What individuals within and outside of the school will you recruit to participate in the committee's activities? Develop an agenda for the committee's first meeting.

5. Navigate the Department of Education's Web site at http://www.ed.gov. What are this agency's priorities? How have these priorities changed over the years? What legislation influences these priorities? Make some predictions about forthcoming priorities.

6. Who are the major stakeholders within your community in regards to gifted and talented education? What methods would be most advantageous in informing these individuals about your school or district's needs?

Teacher Resources

Publications

Bauer, D. G. (1996). *Educator's Internet funding guide: Classroom Connect's reference guide to technology funding*. Lancaster, PA: Wentworth Worldwide Media.

Brewer, E. W., Achilles, C. M., & Fuhriman, F. R. (1995). *Finding funding: Grantwriting and project management from start to finish*. Thousand Oaks, CA: Corwin Press.

Gensheimer, C. F. (1993). *Raising funds for your child's school*. New York: Walker.

Graham, C. (1993). *Keep the money coming: A step-by-step strategic guide to annual fundraising*. Sarasota, FL: Pineapple Press.

Hall, M. (1988). *Getting funded: A complete guide to proposal writing*. (3rd ed.). Portland, OR: Continuing Education.

Ferguson, J. (1997). *Grants for schools: How to find and win funds for K–12 programs*. New York: Soho Press.

Orlich, D. C. (1996). *Designing successful grant proposals*. Alexandria, VA: Association for Supervision and Curriculum Development.

Ross, D. M. (1990). *Fund raising for youth: Hundreds of wonderful ways of raising funds for youth organizations*. Colorado Springs, CO: Meriwether.

Ruskin, K. B., & Achilles, C. M. (1995). *Grantwriting, fund raising, and partnerships: Strategies that work*. Thousand Oaks, CA: Corwin Press.

Addresses

AT&T Telecommunications
32 Sixth Ave.
New York, NY 10013
http://www.ATT.com

American Association of University Women
1111 16th St. NW
Washington, DC 20036
http://www.aauw.org

The Catalog of Federal Domestic Assistance
General Services Administration
1800 F St. NW
Washington, DC 20405
(202) 708-5126
http://www.gsa.gov/fdac/default.htm

The Carnegie Corporation of New York
437 Madison Ave.
New York, NY 10022
http:www.carnegie.org

The Chronicle of Philanthropy
1255 23rd St. NW
Washington, DC 20037
http://www.philanthropy.com

Commerce Business Daily
Government Printing Office
732 N. Capitol St. NW
Washington, DC 20401
(888) 293-6498
http://cbdnet.access.gpo.gov

Congressional Record
Government Printing Office
Mail Stop: SDE
732 N. Capitol St. NW
Washington, DC 20401
(202) 512-1800
http://www.gpoaccess.gov/crecord

Council for Exceptional Children
1110 N. Glebe Road, Ste. 300
Reston, VA 22201
http://www.cec.sped.org

Education Funding News
4301 North Fairfax Dr., Ste. 875
Arlington, VA 22203
(703) 528-1082

The Federal Register
Government Printing Office
732 N. Capitol St. NW
Washington, DC 20401
(202) 512-1800
http://www.access.gpo.gov/fr

Javits Gifted and Talented Students Education Program
Office of Elementary and Secondary Education
400 Maryland Ave. SW
Washington, DC 20202-6200
http://www.ed.gov/programs/javits

W. K. Kellogg Foundation
1 Michigan Ave. E
Battle Creek, MI 49017
http://www.WKKF.org

The National Education Association
1201 16th St. NW
Washington, DC 20036-3290
http://www.nea.org

The National Endowment for the Arts
Public Information Office
1100 Pennsylvania Ave. NW
Washington, DC 20506
(202) 682-5400
http://arts.endow.gov

The National Endowment for the Humanities
1100 Pennsylvania Ave. NW
Washington, DC 20506
(800) 634-1121
http://www.neh.gov

The National Institutes of Health
900 Rockville Pike
Bethesda, MD 20892
http://www.nih.gov

The National Science Foundation
4201 Wilson Blvd.
Arlington, VA 22230
(703) 292-51111
http://www.nsf.gov

The Spencer Foundation
875 N. Michigan Ave., Ste. 3930
Chicago, IL 60611-1803
http://www.spencer.org

Toyota Motor Sales USA
P.O. Box 2991
Torrance, CA 90509
http://www.toyota.com

Whirlpool Corporation
200 M-63 N
Benton Harbor, MI 49022–0692
http://www.whirlpool.com

Web Sites

The Foundation Center—http://www.fdncenter.org
Provides links to and information on nearly 100 private foundations, 54 corporate grant makers, and 18 grant-making charities.

LEGO Education: Finding and Applying for a Grant—http://www.legoeducation.com/grants.asp
A wide array of links to funding agencies and other resources helpful to educators as they pursue the grant writing endeavor.

U.S. Department of Education—http://www.ed.gov
Includes information on the Secretary of Education's initiatives, agency publications, legislation, press releases, programs with application procedures, and agency personnel with contact information.

References

ARCH. (1992). *Creative fund-raising activities*. Chapel Hill, NC: ARCH National Resources Center for Crisis Nurseries and Respite Care Services.

Elementary and Secondary Education Act of 1965, 20 U.S.C. §36 (1988).

Gifted and Talented Students Education Act of 2003, S. 501, 108 Cong. (2003).

Gifted and Talented Students Education Act of 2003, H. R. 1101, 108 Cong. (2003).

Jacob K. Javits Gifted and Talented Students Education Act, H.R. 637, 106 Cong. (1990).

Individuals With Disabilities Education Act, 20 U.S.C. §1401 et seq. (1990).

Gensheimer, C. F. (1993). *Raising funds for your child's school*. New York: Walker.

Karnes, F. A., & Stephens, K. R. (2003). *The ultimate guide to getting money for your classroom and school*. Waco, TX: Prufrock Press.

Karnes, F. A., Stephens, K. R., & Samel, B. (1999). Fund development in gifted education: An untapped resource. *Gifted Child Today, 22*(5), 30–33, 52.

Palent, S. A. (1985). *Fund raising for park, recreation, and conservation agencies*. Washington, DC: National Park Service.

Swan, J. (1990). *Fund raising for the small public library*. New York: Neal-Schuman.

Title VI of the Elementary and Secondary Education Act of 1965, 20 U.S.C. §7311 et seq. (1965).

Walsh, E. (1990). Fund raising made easy. *Parks and Recreation, 25*(10), 60–63, 78.

Wereley, J. (1992). Developing and maintaining a school partnership. In C. S. Hyman (Ed.), *The school-community cookbook: Recipes for successful projects in the schools: A "how-to" manual for teachers, parents, and community* (pp. 88–93). Baltimore, MD: Jewish Community Federation of Baltimore, Children of Harvey and Lyn Meyerhoff Philanthropic Fund, Fund for Educational Excellence.

About the Authors

Editors

Frances A. Karnes is professor of curriculum, instruction, and special education at The University of Southern Mississippi and director of the Frances A. Karnes Center for Gifted Studies. She is widely known for her research, writing, innovative program developments, and service activities in gifted education and leadership training. She is author or coauthor of more than 200 articles and coauthor of 25 books on gifted education and related areas. She is the former president of The Association for the Gifted and is the founder and first president of the Mississippi Association for Gifted Children, and she has served on the board of the National Association for Gifted Children. Honors include a Faculty Research Award, granted by the University of Southern Mississippi Alumni Association; an honorary doctor of education degree from her alma mater Quincy University; and an award presented by the Mississippi Legislature for outstanding contributions to academic excellence in higher education. She has received the Power of One Award bestowed by the governor of Mississippi and recently was named one of 50 female business leaders by the *Mississippi Business Journal*.

Suzanne M. Bean is director of the Center for Creative Learning, director of graduate studies, and professor of education at Mississippi University for Women (MUW). For the past 20 years, she has served in the field of gifted studies as a teacher of gifted students, director of the Mississippi Governor's School, and founder and director of various other programs for gifted students and their teachers and parents. She is currently serving as coordinator of gifted youth programs and graduate programs in education at MUW. Dr. Bean has coauthored five books for young adults and has had numerous publications in professional journals. She serves on the editorial review board for *Gifted Child Quarterly*, the *Journal of Secondary Gifted Education*, and *Roeper Review*. She has been president of the Mississippi Association for Gifted Children and is now serving as a delegate to the executive board of the National Conference on Governor's Schools and chairperson for the advisory board for the Mississippi Association for Gifted Children. She serves on numerous institutional committees and is a member of the statewide Mississippi Educational Research Group.

Contributors

Elissa F. Brown is the director of the Center for Gifted Education at the College of William and Mary, where she also teaches graduate courses in gifted education. Elissa received her Ph.D in educational planning, policy, and leadership with an emphasis in gifted education from the College of William and Mary. Prior to her work with the Center for Gifted Education, she was director of the Chesapeake Bay Governor's School for Marine and Environmental Science. She has also been a gifted program coordinator, and she has more than 11 years of teaching experience in a multitude of educational settings. Elissa is the current past-president of the Virginia Association for the Gifted and was appointed to serve on the State Advisory Committee for the Gifted. She has coordinated state and national gifted conferences and presents widely on a variety of topics in gifted education.

Carolyn M. Callahan, professor and department chair at the Curry School of Education at the University of Virginia, is currently director of the University of Virginia site of the National Research Center on the Gifted and Talented. She has written more than 150 articles and 35 book chapters. She has done research across a broad range of topics in gifted education, including the identification of gifted students, the evaluation of gifted programs, the development of performance assessments, issues facing gifted females, and gifted program options. She is a past-president of The Association for the Gifted and the National Association for Gifted Children. She also sits on the editorial boards of *Gifted Child Quarterly*, the *Journal for the Education of the Gifted*, and *Roeper Review*.

Mary Ruth Coleman is director of Project ACCESS (Achievement in Content and Curriculum for Every Student's Success), funded by the Office for Special Education, and Project U-STARS~PLUS (Using Science, Talents, and Abilities to Recognize Students~Promoting Learning for Underrepresented Students), a Javits-funded project. She is a senior scientist at the Frank Porter Graham Child Development Institute at the University of North Carolina at Chapel Hill and clinical associate professor in the School of Education. She serves on the review boards of several journals and has put together two special issues of the *Journal for the Education of the Gifted* (one on gifted girls and women and one on underserved gifted). She has also guest edited a special issue of the *Journal of Secondary Gifted Education* on gifted students with learning disabilities. Dr. Coleman serves on the board of directors for the Council for Exceptional Children and is serving in her third term on the board of the National Association for Gifted Children (NAGC).

Bonnie Cramond is associate professor of gifted and creative education in the Department of Educational Psychology and Instructional Technology at the University of Georgia. She is also the director of The Torrance Center for Creativity and Talent Development and is a Torrance Research Fellow. In addition, she is a member of the board of directors of the National Association for

Gifted Children (NAGC) and is on the NAGC President's Education Commission. She is the editor of the Journal of Secondary Gifted Education, is on the editorial advisory board for the Journal of Creative Behavior and the Korean Journal of Thinking and Problem Solving, and works with several other journals. She's had experience teaching and parenting gifted and creative children; has published papers, chapters, and a book on giftedness and creativity; and has presented at local, national, and international conferences. Currently, she teaches graduate-level courses in giftedness and creativity and directs activities at the Torrance Center. Her research interests are in creativity assessment and the nurturance of creative abilities.

Shelagh A. Gallagher is associate professor in the Department of Special Education and Child Development at the University of North Carolina at Charlotte. In this position, she is integrally involved in coordinating the doctoral, M.Ed., and licensure programs in education for the gifted. She also directs Project Insights, a Javits grant implementing a new model middle school program for gifted disadvantaged students. Dr. Gallagher was also director for Project P-BLISS (Problem-Based Learning in the Social Sciences) and project manager of the Science Grant at the College of William and Mary, where she oversaw the development of seven PBL science units. She first learned about PBL while at the IMSA, where she was a part of the Science, Society, and the Future project. Dr. Gallagher has served on the board of directors of the National Association for Gifted Children and the North Carolina Association for the Gifted and Talented, and she is coauthor of Teaching the Gifted Child.

Krystal K. Goree is director of clinical practice and teaches classes in gifted and talented education at Baylor University. She has worked in the field of gifted education for more than 15 years in the roles of parent, teacher, consultant, presenter, and program administrator. She currently serves on several state committees and provides consultation and program evaluation for school districts. In addition to presenting at state and national conferences, she has authored or coauthored several articles and book chapters. She is past-president of the Texas Association for the Gifted and Talented and serves as senior editor of *Gifted Child Today*.

Barbara G. Hunt is professor of elementary education and gifted studies at Mississippi University for Women, where she holds the Ruth Robinson Smith Chair in the Division of Education & Human Sciences. She taught gifted 6th graders for 12 years in Houston, TX. She continues to do workshops and conference presentations at state and national levels. In 2004, she was invited to Dallas to present a keynote for the Gifted Students Institute Distinguished Lecture Series. Her area of expertise and interest is in meeting the social/emotional needs of gifted children. She teaches a graduate class on counseling the gifted child. She has been the director of a summer camp for 8 years that meets the needs of local gifted children, grades K–6. She has served in various roles as an officer and on committees in the Mississippi Association for Gifted Children and has studied gifted programs in England and the Netherlands.

Susan K. Johnsen is a professor in the Department of Educational Psychology at Baylor University. She directs and teaches courses in the area of gifted education at the undergraduate and graduate levels. She is the editor of *Gifted Child Today* and serves on the editorial boards of *Gifted Child Quarterly* and the *Journal of Secondary Gifted Education*. She is the coauthor of the Independent Study Program and three tests that are used in identifying gifted students: Test of Mathematical Abilities for Gifted Students (TOMAGS), Test of Nonverbal Intelligence (TONI-3), and the Screening Assessment for Gifted Students (SAGES-2). She has published numerous articles and is a frequent presenter at state, national, and international conferences. She is past-president of the Texas Association for the Gifted and Talented and serves on the board of The Association for the Gifted.

Sandra N. Kaplan is clinical professor of teaching and learning at the University of Southern California. She has served as president of the California Association for the Gifted and the National Association for the Gifted and is currently an executive board member of the World Council for the Gifted. Sandra has received awards of service and recognition from the California Association for the Gifted and the National Association for the Gifted. She has served as a consultant and speaker for both foreign and state departments of education, school districts, and universities. Her interest and expertise are in the areas of curriculum and instruction.

Joan D. Lewis is associate professor of teacher education at the University of Nebraska at Kearney, where she is the director of gifted education for all of the University of Nebraska system and chair of graduate programs for the Teacher Education Department. She has published widely and speaks frequently at local, state, national, and international conferences about the affective needs of gifted learners, gifted girls, nonverbal assessments, public relations and advocacy in gifted education, rural gifted, using Internet resources and technology in gifted education, and university-level instruction. Since moving to Nebraska, Dr. Lewis has added rural concerns to her long-standing interest in multicultural issues. Developing programs across the state that identify and serve gifted learners from all ethnic and socioeconomic groups at appropriate challenge levels has become her highest priority. She has chaired the University of Nebraska Gifted Plan Committee, which continues to coordinate the dissemination of teacher education classes in gifted education across all UN campuses, and she works with the Nebraska Association for Gifted to support teachers of gifted learners across the state.

D. Betsy McCoach is assistant professor in residence at the University of Connecticut, where she teaches courses in research design and statistics. She combined doctoral work in school psychology, gifted and talented education, and educational research and statistics. She has worked with Mentor Connection, a University of Connecticut summer program for high school students, and is also active in the American Education Research Association and the National Association for Gifted Children. Her research interests include the underachievement of gifted students, ability grouping, measuring ability and achievement, and instrument design.

Barbara Moore is coordinator of undergraduate programs in teacher education and assistant professor of education at Mississippi University for Women. A former high school English teacher and coordinator of programs for gifted students, she received her Ph.D. from the University of Virginia, where she focused on curriculum and academic underachievement among gifted high school students. Currently, she is a program reviewer for the Association for Childhood Education International and a book reviewer for *Childhood Education*.

Stephanie A. Nugent is assistant professor of secondary education at the University of Arizona South. She has authored or coauthored several journal articles and presented at state, regional, national, and international conferences on various topics related to gifted education. With more than 10 years of experience teaching in junior high and high school classrooms, her research interests include moral development, integrating the affective domain in secondary curricula, effective technology-integration strategies, and developing teacher leaders. Dr. Nugent earned her Ph.D. in curriculum, instruction, and special education with an emphasis in gifted studies at The University of Southern Mississippi.

Sandra Parks has served as a curriculum and staff-development consultant on teaching thinking since 1978. Since 1983, she has presented professional development institutes for the Association for Supervision and Curriculum Development and at national and regional conferences. She conducted research on teaching critical thinking at the Indiana State University Laboratory School and was founding president of the Indiana Association for the Gifted. She taught gifted education courses at the University of North Florida and the University of Miami. Sandra Parks currently serves as the facilitator of the Teaching Thinking network of the Association for Supervision and Curriculum Development.

Sally M. Reis is professor and the head of the Educational Psychology Department in the Neag School of Education at the University of Connecticut, where she also serves as principal investigator of the National Research Center on the Gifted and Talented. She has also been a classroom teacher in public education, as well as an administrator. She has authored or coauthored more than 130 articles, 11 books, 40 book chapters, and numerous monographs and technical reports and worked in a research team that has generated more than $35 million in grants in the last 15 years. Her research interests are related to talent development in all children, as well as special populations of gifted and talented students. She is also interested in extensions of the Schoolwide Enrichment Model for gifted students and as a way to identify talent and potential in students who have not been previously identified as gifted.

Tracy L. Riley is a senior lecturer in gifted education in the Department of Learning and Teaching at Massey University in New Zealand. Tracy teaches undergraduate and postgraduate courses in gifted education and presents and publishes both nationally and internationally. She is especially passionate about the development, implementation and maintenance of differentiated educational experiences for gifted and talented students within their school environment.

Julia Link Roberts is the Mahurin Professor of Gifted Studies at Western Kentucky University, where she teaches graduate courses in gifted education. She initiated and directs The Center for Gifted Studies, which provides services to gifted students, parents, and educators. In 1998, she was named Distinguished Professor at Western Kentucky University. In 2001, she received the first National Association for Gifted Children David W. Belin Award. Dr. Roberts currently serves on the boards of NAGC, the Kentucky Association for Gifted Education, the Kentucky Advisory Council for Gifted and Talented Education, and *Gifted Child Today*.

Richard A. Roberts is professor of teacher education in the Department of Curriculum and Instruction at Western Kentucky University, where he teaches graduate courses in curriculum and teaching strategies. Dr. Roberts has been a developer of the Kentucky Teacher Internship Program, and he directs the internship program at Western Kentucky University. He has been actively involved in providing various types of support for programs for children and young people, educators, and parents that are offered by The Center for Gifted Studies.

Robert W. Seney is professor in gifted studies at Mississippi University for Women, coordinator of graduate programs in education, and director of the Mississippi Governor's School. He is active in the World Council for Gifted Children, the National Association for Gifted Children, the Mississippi Association for Gifted Children, and the Texas Association for Gifted Children. He is a regular presenter at their annual conferences and has served in leadership positions in each of these organizations. He is a member of the NAGC board of directors and served on the first editorial advisory board of NAGC's *Parenting for High Potential*. He is also a contributing editor of *Roeper Review*. Before university service, he served as coordinator of gifted programs for Spring Branch Independent School District in Houston, TX, and as a teacher of the gifted. His current interests and areas of study are leadership in gifted girls, creativity, young adult and children's literature, and curriculum design.

Del Siegle is an associate professor in gifted and talented education at the University of Connecticut, where he coordinates the Three Summers master's degree and online graduate classes program. He is also cochair of the National Association for Gifted Children's Education Commission, which created and coordinates mentoring experiences for NAGC members. He serves on the board of directors of NAGC and The Association for the Gifted. His research interests include student motivation, teacher biases in identifying gifted students, and teaching with technology.

Dorothy Sisk holds an endowed chair in education of the gifted at Lamar University in Beaumont, TX, where she directs the C. W. Conn Gifted Child Center. Currently, she is the principal investigator of a Jacob K. Javits grant working with middle and high school teachers to increase the achievement of underrepresented students in Beaumont Independent School District. Dr. Sisk authored the book *Creative Teaching of the Gifted* and coauthored *Intuition: An Inner Way of Knowing, Leadership: Making Things Happen, Growing Person, The Futures Primer, Teaching Gifted Children in the Regular Classroom*, and *Spiritual Intelligence: Developing Higher Consciousness*.

Melissa A. Small is a doctoral candidate in educational psychology at the University of Connecticut with areas of concentration in gifted and talented education and evaluation and measurement. She is also a staff member at the Neag Center for Gifted Education and Talent Development. Her areas of research interest include mathematically talented students and gifted females' career development. She frequently works with school districts to provide in-service training in the Schoolwide Enrichment Model, curriculum compacting, and differentiation. She is a former Future Problem Solving Program coach and has evaluated for Michigan, Maine, and Connecticut FPSP competitions. Prior to her work in gifted education, she taught secondary mathematics.

Kristen R. Stephens is coordinator of educational outreach for Duke University's Talent Identification Program (TIP) and adjunct assistant professor for programs in education at Duke University. She also serves as editor-in-chief of the *Duke Gifted Letter*. She received her Ph.D. in special education with an emphasis in gifted education at The University of Southern Mississippi. She has presented at local, state, national, and international conferences; published numerous journal articles pertaining to gifted child education; and is the coauthor of several books.

Joyce VanTassel-Baska is the Jody and Layton Smith Professor of Education and executive director of the Center for Gifted Education at the College of William and Mary, where she has developed a graduate program and a research and development center in gifted education. Dr. VanTassel-Baska has published widely, including 15 books and more than 275 refereed journal articles, book chapters, and scholarly reports. She also serves as the editor of *Gifted and Talented*

International. Dr. VanTassel-Baska has received numerous awards for her work, including the National Association for Gifted Children's Early Leader Award in 1986, the State Council of Higher Education in Virginia Outstanding Faculty Award in 1993, the Phi Beta Kappa faculty award in 1995, and the NAGC Distinguished Scholar Award in 1997. She was selected as a Fulbright Scholar to New Zealand in 2000 and a visiting scholar to Cambridge University in England in 1993. Her major research interests are on the talent-development process and effective curricular interventions with the gifted.

Index

academic planning (see assessment)
acceleration, 42, 55, 75, 80–81, 85, 91–92,
    217, 234, 474, 564, 582, 702
Advanced Placement, 55, 75, 77, 80–81,
    85, 91, 98, 237, 258, 486
advocacy, 80, 430, 615–617, 619, 621–625,
    627–629, 631–633, 635, 637, 639–643,
    645–647, 649–654
    definition of, 616
affective domain, 221, 409, 413, 415–418,
    420, 426, 428–429, 664
    issues in, 417–418
    reasons schools neglect, 416–417
affective education, 409, 411, 413,
    415–419, 421, 423, 425, 427–429, 431,
    433, 435
affective instructional strategies, 420–426
    definition of, 416
Affective Taxonomy, 413–415
analogical thinking, 323, 344
analysis tasks, 249, 273, 278
apprenticeship, 126, 298
Ask an Expert, 162, 482, 514, 539, 668,
    693
assessment
    academic planning, 44–45

authentic assessment, 47, 67, 229,
    369, 371, 374
content assessment, 217
    IEPs, 47–49
outcome assessment, 212–213
portfolio, 4, 47, 50, 66, 68, 154, 271,
    275, 534
process assessment, 217–218
product assessment, 167, 218, 396
Responsive Learning Environment
    Checklist, 40–41, 65
self–evaluation, 39, 41, 50, 65, 152,
    166, 214, 230, 450, 581, 591, 664
student questionnaire, 50, 53, 425
Attention–Deficit Hyperactivity Disorder,
    22, 25, 317, 646
Attribute listing, 326–327, 343, 382
    analogy chains, 326–327
audiences
    external to educational system, 620
    internal to education system, 618–620
    targeting, 618–620
    authentic audience, 163, 389, 604
Autonomous Learner Model, 83, 134, 146,
    214, 223, 321, 359, 380, 383, 386, 401,
    507

BaFá BaFá (see simulation games)
Barnga (see simulation games)
bibliotherapy, 58, 412, 421–423, 426, 431, 458
Bloom's taxonomy, 116, 134–135, 146–147, 190, 205, 392, 454, 595–596, 602, 606, 611
brainstorming, 139, 157, 322–323, 331, 333, 360–361, 388, 390, 393, 688

career awareness, 474, 476, 495, 503
character education, 423, 426, 432–433
checklists, 8, 17, 50, 230, 396, 404, 446, 450, 584, 589, 640, 682
cinematherapy, 421, 426, 432
classroom management (see environment)
cluster grouping, 127, 605
cognitive abilities, 57, 249–250, 260, 275
cognitive objectives, 259
cognitive stimulation programs, 258
Compactor, 49, 587
competitions, 166, 237, 338–340, 344, 347, 460, 490, 621, 672
concept map, 269–270, 277
constructivism, 138
content
    complex, 184, 187, 192, 194–196
    core, 111, 113, 115, 127, 179, 184, 187, 189, 191–192, 194–195, 205, 276, 290, 532
content transfer, 259
continuous progress, 179–180, 182, 188, 193, 195, 205–206, 495
contracts, 50, 60, 362, 384–385, 532, 592–593, 701
convergent thinking, 85–86, 137, 331, 333, 380
cooperative learning, 223–224, 263, 463, 519–525, 527, 529, 531, 533–535, 537–539, 568–569
    elements of, 522–525
    models of, 520–521
    strategies for, 525-527
    role of teacher in, 534
    use with gifted students, 521–522
counseling needs, 41, 56–58
    asynchronous development, 42, 57, 65, 411, 417, 422
    emotional depth, 9, 19, 57, 412
    noncounselor educators, 58
    strategies for preventive counseling, 58

creative problem solving, 44, 59, 76, 85, 137, 148, 152, 156, 174, 305, 330–331, 333–334, 340, 342, 345, 359, 401, 564
creativity, 5–11, 13–15, 19, 24, 69, 76, 82, 134, 143, 148, 152, 175, 225, 313–321, 325, 328, 330, 334–336, 338–340, 343–344, 346, 348, 358, 369, 380, 382, 411–412, 425, 430, 445, 447–451, 478, 480, 552, 560, 562, 564–565, 598, 638, 665
    adaptive, 316, 412
    blocks to, 334–338
    expressive, 315–316
critical thinking, 30, 56, 76, 89–91, 111, 137–138, 140, 145–146, 148, 152, 215–216, 218–219, 234, 249–265, 267–269, 271–273, 275–282, 296, 300, 321, 403, 406, 444, 463, 523–524, 550, 565, 599, 664, 666, 671, 683
cultural diversity, 18, 126, 523, 552
curriculum
    concept–centered, 294
    development of, 38, 66–67, 75–76, 90, 99, 110–111, 114, 188, 218, 235–236, 293, 306–308, 600, 611, 644, 716
    models, 75–79, 81, 83–85, 87, 89, 91–95, 97, 99, 134, 214, 242, 321
curriculum compacting, 68, 82–83, 388, 586–588, 593, 597–598, 702

data analysis, 237, 240
data collection, 237–238, 240, 333, 354, 364, 529–530, 599, 710
data retrieval chart, 266
differentiation, 56, 76, 91, 107–108, 112, 115–116, 130, 146, 179, 181–182, 190, 192–194, 196, 216, 235–236, 239, 523, 526, 578–583, 586, 588, 593, 597, 604–608, 610, 643, 659, 661, 666, 688
    qualitative, 578, 580–582, 588, 593, 607–608, 610, 659, 688
discipline, 61–62
    preventive, 61
    supportive, 61
    corrective, 61–62
divergent thinking, 59, 331, 342, 426, 463

dual enrollment, 55, 702

early college entrance, 55
Effective Independent Learner Model, 134
Encounter lesson, 325–326
enrichment, 7, 14, 30, 42, 55, 76, 79, 81–83, 85, 92, 96, 100, 134, 214–215, 217–218, 223, 226, 228, 236, 260, 263, 321, 358, 362–363, 370, 374, 380–383, 386–387, 402, 404, 453, 463, 474, 486, 491, 495, 497, 507, 579, 582, 589, 597–600, 604, 611–615, 657, 662, 666, 698, 715
Enrichment Triad Model, 81–82, 215, 218, 223, 236, 358, 380–381, 491, 597–598
environment
    classroom management, 59–62, 65, 236
    modification of, 38–39
    needs of, 39
    nonthreatening, 54, 420, 465, 556
    optimal learning, 40, 42–43, 65, 534
    physical, 40–41
    Responsive Learning, 39–41, 60, 65
    social/emotional, 42–43
Exemplars, 161
expert, 30, 113, 161–162, 167, 219, 228, 286–288, 338, 395, 398, 475, 482, 495–497, 514, 526, 539, 606, 658, 668–669, 693
expertise, 64, 81, 88, 213, 230, 237, 256, 286, 288–289, 338, 361, 398, 476, 478, 480, 484–485, 488, 496–499, 509, 581, 601, 605, 618, 635, 668

flow, 61, 141, 154, 232, 297, 300, 320–321, 394, 403, 476, 497, 505, 600
followship, 445, 461
funding, 89–90, 231, 265, 431, 486, 579, 616, 642, 645, 666, 672, 677, 701–710, 713–717, 719
    locating a funding source, 704–705
    private, 703, 710
    public, 703
    sources in your community, 710
fundraising, 642, 706, 709–712, 715–716
Future Problem Solving, 339, 345, 347, 361, 668

gifted education
    federal funding for, 701–703
gifted students
    characteristics of, 3, 6–
    cognitive and affective characteristics of, 8–11
    gifted disadvantaged, 6, 17–18, 87, 297, 309
    gifted females, 17, 20–21, 43, 479
    social/emotional characteristics of, 11–13
    with disabilities, 3, 21–27
giftedness
    ambivalence about, 43
    definition of, 43, 107, 235, 416
    federal definition of, 439
    inner locus of control, 9, 54, 419
    self–acceptance, 43
    self–evaluation, 39, 41, 50, 65, 152, 166, 214, 230, 450, 581, 591, 664
grant proposal, 701, 708–710
    components of, 708–710
graphic organizers, 262–263, 266, 269, 271, 273, 275
grouping, 38, 41–42, 62–63, 67–68, 77, 90, 92, 107, 127, 519, 525, 535, 595–597, 605–606, 666
    cluster grouping, 127, 605
    flexible grouping, 41, 62, 595–597
    heterogeneous grouping, 62, 525
    homogeneous grouping, 62

habits of mind, 223, 292, 300
High School Personality Questionnaire (HSPQ), 444, 446, 448, 450
human resources, 142, 660–661, 667–668, 685
humor, 9, 11–12, 15, 22, 56, 61, 322, 336, 342, 412, 419, 501, 567

I/DEPPE/I Model, 156
ideation, 317, 322–323, 344
illumination, 320
Imaginative Harmonizers of People, 444
incubation, 164, 320–321, 340–341, 343–344
Incubation Model, 321, 340–341, 343
independent study, 30, 55, 60, 82–83, 85, 92, 122, 136, 141, 260, 262, 359, 379–383, 385–389, 391–405, 475, 495, 507–509, 589, 598, 702

definition of, 380
evaluation of, 395–396
models of, 380–386
steps in, 389–296
Individuals With Disabilities Education
Act (IDEA), 702
inferential reasoning processes, 250
Infotactics (see simulation games)
infusion lessons, 263
Integrated Curriculum Model, 90, 96, 99
International Baccalaureate (IB), 45, 69,
75, 77, 237

Jacob K. Javits Gifted and Talented
Students Education Act, 701–702

Kaplan Grid, 85, 91, 99
KWL chart, 158
Land of the Sphinx and Land of the
Rainbow (see simulation games)
lateral thinking, 328, 344

leadership
current research on, 444–445
definition of, 440–441
giftedness and, 445–446
identifying, 446–452
potential, 439–441, 443, 445–447,
449–453, 455, 457, 459–461,
463–465
skills, 43, 137, 256, 345, 439–440,
446, 448, 452, 454, 457, 463–466,
550–551, 578
theories of, 441–442
learning ceiling, 179, 181, 183–185, 187,
189, 191, 193, 195–197, 199, 201,
203, 205–207
learning center, 154, 401, 590
learning disabilities, 21–24, 26, 83, 152,
370, 372, 600
learning-disabled gifted, 258–259, 370,
646
learning issues board, 292, 294, 296, 301
learning styles, 8, 30, 39, 42, 44–46, 64,
67–68, 152, 155, 264, 374, 379, 455,
496, 498, 507, 520, 535, 579
cognitive, 45
creative or divergent thinkers, 46
visual–spatial learner, 46
lobby, 616, 626–627, 638
definition of, 616

Maker Matrix, 86–87, 91
mentee
benefits to, 474, 476
selection of, 494–500
training of, 505
mentor
benefits to, 477–478
selection of, 488–494
training of, 484, 486–487, 502–505
mentorship
definition of, 475–476
effectiveness of, 417
evaluation of, 505–507
for underserved populations, 479–481
telementoring, 482–
metacognition, 258–259, 262, 273, 292,
298
metaphorical thinking, 318, 410
mixed-ability class, 362
moral development, 413–414
Kohlberg's six stages of moral development, 413–414
morphological analysis, 326, 328–329,
382
morphological synthesis, 326
multiple intelligences, 5, 50, 84, 86, 368,
415, 591, 606
Multiple Menu Model, 358, 601, 603,
611
Multiple Talent Approach, 134
multipotentiality, 421, 474
My Way . . . An Expression Style
Inventory, 155, 498
Myers-Briggs Type Indicator, 46, 68, 444,
451, 498

national standards, 78, 90, 182, 187–188,
207–208, 216–217, 375
National Oracy Project, 141
Nonprint resources, 661, 670

Odyssey of the Mind, 339–340, 347
organizational skills, 24, 134, 152, 158,
636
outcomes
affective outcomes, 221, 234, 243
group outcomes, 223–225
individual outcomes, 223–225
psychomotor outcomes, 223
overexcitabilities, 410, 412, 426, 428

Parallel Curriculum Model, 87–88, 600–601

Parlé (see simulation games)

perfectionism, 9, 19, 23–24, 411, 417, 419, 421

portfolios, 30, 44, 47, 50, 171, 584, 607

postassessment, 182, 184, 188–189, 193, 453

preassessment, 182, 184, 188–189, 193–194, 196, 206, 212–213, 238, 584, 586, 597, 604, 660

print media, 623, 630, 667–669

Problem–Based Learning, 262, 264, 285, 287, 289, 291, 293–295, 297, 299, 301, 303, 305–309, 371, 525–526, 533, 537, 581, 659

problem solving, 13, 18, 43–44, 59, 76, 85–86, 92, 137, 148, 152, 156, 174, 180, 190, 195, 215, 239, 250–251, 256, 259, 285, 287–288, 290–292, 297–298, 300, 305, 307, 316, 324, 326, 330–331, 333–334, 336, 338–340, 342–345, 347–348, 357, 359, 361, 371, 401, 419, 429–430, 432, 444, 446, 450, 452–453, 463, 519, 524, 527, 533, 549, 552, 564, 599, 660, 668

    expert problem solver, 286, 288

    ill–structured problems, 289–290

process modifications

    higher levels of thinking, 135, 581

    open-endedness, 135, 342

    discovery learning, 135–136, 138, 549

    evidence of reasoning, 135–136

    freedom of choice, 135–136

    group interaction, 135–136, 552, 665

    pacing, 126, 135, 137, 239, 319, 394

    variety of processes, 135, 137, 564

process skills, 64, 67, 76, 90, 133–135, 137, 139–141, 143, 145–147, 152, 169, 175, 190–191, 195–196, 218–219, 234, 288, 371, 429, 502, 590, 599, 638, 659, 676

Process Skills Rating Scales–Revised, 139, 140–141, 147, 191, 218, 234

product development, 151–159, 161, 163–165, 167–175, 177, 207, 394, 589, 600, 659, 661, 680

project–based learning, 371

psychological safety, 318–319

psychometric properties, 453

public relations, 166, 170, 425, 615–623, 625, 627–635, 637–643, 645–654

    definition of, 616

    planning for, 627–630

    rational for, 616–618

    strategies, 620–627

pull–out, 55, 127, 243, 279, 299, 301, 486, 525

Purdue Pyramid, 381, 383

Purdue Secondary Model for Gifted and Talented Youth, 85, 100

Purdue Three–Stage Enrichment Model for Elementary Gifted Learners, 85, 100

Quality Circles, 330, 333

realia, 660–661, 670, 673–675, 685, 695

reasoning, 11, 22, 79, 135–136, 140, 142, 145, 234, 249–251, 259, 266, 275, 282, 286–288, 292, 296–297, 302, 410, 413, 544, 651, 664

reflection, 50, 157, 163–165, 170, 181, 287, 290–291, 298, 300, 319, 335, 344, 412, 420, 461, 477, 563

Reporter Project, 544–545

research process, 157–158, 354–355, 358–360, 372, 380, 404

    steps in, 360–369

    student as researcher, 356

research readiness, 158

resource room, 55, 256, 390, 578

rewards, 14, 123, 319, 321, 440, 442, 463, 498, 520–521, 527, 529, 547, 550, 677–678, 713

risk taking, 14, 19, 41, 43–44, 46, 152, 155, 317, 416, 420, 464, 565

role-playing, 43–44, 58, 333–334, 366, 452, 458, 502, 543–546, 554, 560, 563

Rubistar, 168

rubrics, 50, 167–169, 175, 219, 221, 228, 230, 271, 275, 279, 369, 396, 607

scaffolding, 260

SCAMPER, 44, 323, 382

Schoolwide Enrichment Model, 7, 14, 81–82, 96, 134, 214, 218, 226, 228, 321, 387, 404, 507, 579, 597–598, 600, 611

scoring guide, 189

self-concept, 5, 28, 39, 50, 67, 85, 223,
    234, 410, 414, 416–419, 430, 440,
    450, 476
self–directed learner, 134, 289, 291
sequentially developed cognitive instruc-
    tion, 258
service learning, 166, 423, 425–426,
    433–434, 465, 533, 615, 643, 702
simulation, 58, 153–154, 528–529,
    543–572, 696
        advantages and disadvantages of,
            565
        background and definitions,
            543–547
        benefits of, 550–553, 563
        comparison with other teaching
            methods, 563–564
        design of, 558–561
        effectiveness with gifted students,
            547–549
        elements of, 556–557
        how to use effectively, 557–558
simulation games,
    BaFá BaFá, 546, 553, 556, 562, 572
    Barnga, 546, 553, 556, 572
    Infotactics, 546, 554, 559
    Land of the Sphinx and Land of the
        Rainbow, 546, 554, 556–557, 562,
        564, 567
    Parlé, 546, 550, 555–556, 558, 562,
        566–567
    Star Power, 546
    Tag Game, 546, 555–556, 563
Six Thinking Hats, 137, 330
sociodrama, 334
sociometric devices, 446
speaking skills, 143, 165, 637
staff development, 89, 91, 127, 236, 263,
    278, 430, 433, 622, 626, 635,
    639–640, 643, 701
stakeholder, 236, 289, 291–292, 298, 303
Stanley Model of Talent Identification
    and Development, 79
Star Power (see simulation games)
stimulation, 44, 62, 258–259, 319–321,
    344, 498
Strength–A–Lyzer, 48
Structure of Intellect Model, 99
Student Product Assessment Form, 167,
    396
Study of Mathematically Precocious

Youth (SMPY), 80, 485
surveys, 237–238, 354, 360, 364, 366,
    393, 591, 637
Synectics, 44, 273, 324, 382

Tag Game (see simulation games)
Talent Identification Program, 80
talent development, 81, 84, 498–499,
    509, 597, 600, 661
talent identification, 79–80, 631
Talents Unlimited, 88–89, 91, 100, 134
teachers of the gifted, 43, 50, 54, 56, 58,
    63, 110, 113, 124, 128, 146, 242,
    250, 263–264, 278, 296, 302, 354,
    356, 420, 423, 454, 473, 546, 608,
    638, 657, 661, 665, 701
        characteristics of, 54–56
        role of, 56–57
teaching materials, 344, 433, 657, 659,
    666, 675, 677–680, 682, 692
telementoring (see mentorship)
thinking skills
    analytical, 249, 280
    creative, 141, 205
    critical, 30, 138, 216, 218, 249–251,
        253, 255, 257, 259–261, 263, 265,
        267, 269, 271, 273, 275, 277–281,
        296, 403, 565, 666, 671, 683
transformation, 152, 157, 162–165, 175,
    239, 300, 309, 411, 659
Triarchic Componential Model, 89
Type I Enrichment, 82, 358, 380, 599
Type II Enrichment, 82, 358, 402, 599
Type III Enrichment, 82, 358, 589, 598

underachievement, 26–27, 82, 589
visualization, 318, 325, 338, 342, 344,
    412

warm–up, 321–322, 334, 344, 346